From Continuity to Contiguity

STANFORD STUDIES IN JEWISH HISTORY AND CULTURE

EDITED BY *Aron Rodrigue and Steven J. Zipperstein*

From Continuity to Contiguity

*Toward a New Jewish
Literary Thinking*

Dan Miron

STANFORD UNIVERSITY PRESS

STANFORD, CALIFORNIA

Stanford University Press
Stanford, California

©2010 by the Board of Trustees of the Leland Stanford Junior
University. All rights reserved.

This book has been published with the assistance of the
Taube Center for Jewish Studies at Stanford University.

This book has been published with the assistance of the Institute
for Israel and Jewish Studies, Columbia University.

Printed in the United States of America on acid-free, archival-
quality paper

Library of Congress Cataloging-in-Publication Data

Miron, Dan.
  From continuity to contiguity : toward a new Jewish literary
thinking / Dan Miron.
      p. cm.
  Includes bibliographical references and index.
  ISBN 978-0-8047-6200-7 (cloth : alk. paper)
  1. Jewish literature—19th century—History and criticism.
  2. Jewish literature—20th century—History and criticism.
  3. Hebrew literature, Modern—History and criticism.
  4. Yiddish literature—History and criticism. I. Title.
  PN842.M57 2010
  809'.88924—dc22

                              2009038331

Typeset by Bruce Lundquist in 10.5/14 Galliard

"You were interrupted a while ago: do you still know what you were going to say?"—If I do know now and say it—does that mean that I had already thought it before, only not said it? [—] When I continue the interrupted sentence [—] was only one continuation possible in these circumstances? Of course not!

—Ludwig Wittgenstein, *Philosophical Investigations*, 633–634

Contents

Abramovitsh and His Mendele Between Hebrew and Yiddish

Acknowledgments

This book being the result of a lifetime of studying, thinking, teaching, discussing, and writing about Jewish literatures in modern times, I would like to mention here the names of teachers, mentors, colleagues, friends, writers, and some of my many erstwhile students (now esteemed younger colleagues) with whom I engaged throughout the years in an on-again, off-again dialogue focusing on the issues that form the core of my present argument. This dialogue—sometimes cordial and harmonious, but often enough polemic, and in some cases downright stormy—was, in all its moods and tonalities, tremendously edifying and challenging. There were many with whom I could not agree—among them teachers and colleagues of immaculate intellectual integrity and of great probity (such as my mentor Dov Sadan), and who were and still are my guides. From them I learned more than from those whose views and methodologies were closer to mine. I owe them an everlasting debt.

Among my teachers in Israel and the United States, I would like to mention here Dov Sadan, Shimon Halkin, Gershom Scholem, Ya'akov Katz, Chaim Shirman, Leah Goldberg, Khone Shmeruk, Moshe Frank, Alexander Aronson, Max and Uriel Weinreich, James L. Clifford—all of them of blessed memory; and, to separate the living from the departed—my teachers and dear friends Shmuel Verses, the éminence grise of modern Hebrew literary studies, and the Shakespearean scholar Ruth Nevo.

Writers who took interest in issues that are deliberated here and were willing to articulate their "take" on some of them in long conversations I had with them in different periods of my life were: Sh. Y. Agnon,

Uri Tsvi Greenberg, Avraham Shlonsky, Nathan Alterman, Yokheved Bat-Miriam, Yonatan Rattosh, Avot Yeshurun, Abba Kovner, Avraham Regelson, Gavriel Preil, Ya'akov Glatshteyn, Irving Howe, S. Yizhar, Ya'akov Shabtai, Yehuda Amichai, Avraham Sutskever—all of them of blessed memory; and, to separate the living from the departed: Chaim Gouri and A. B. Yehoshua.

Colleagues and contemporaries who were part of my professional life (many of them dear friends as well): Gershon Shaked, Ezra Fleischer, Dan Pagis, Yosef Even, Isadore Twersky—of blessed memory; and, to separate the living from the departed, Benjamin Harshav, Marvin Herzog, Adi Tsemakh, Menakhem Brinker, Sidra Dekoven-Ezrakhi, Ruth R. Wisse, Tsipora Kagan, Aminadav Dikman.

My erstwhile students, now my colleagues: Uzi Shavit, Nurit Govrin, Alan Mintz, David Roskies, Yael Feldman, Avraham Balaban, Avi Matalon, Marc Caplan, Beatrice (Brukhe) Caplan, Hannan Hever, Yigal Schwartz, Gidon Nevo, Uri S. Cohen, Mikhal Dekel, Dror Burshteyn, Mikhal Arbel, Hamutal Bar-Yosef, Shakhar Bram, Anita Norich, Mikhhail Krutikov, Jan Schwarz, Delphine Bechtel, and last but not least, the late Yehudit Bar-El, a great loss to modern Hebrew literary studies.

I also want to mention with love some of my dear friends (in the 1960s and 1970s) at the Max Weinreich Center of the YIVO Institute of Jewish Research, who helped me to see the Jewish literary complex through Yiddish eyes, as well as the Hebrew ones I brought with me: Alexander (Oleg) and Rachel (Shoshka) Erlich, Khana Friszdorf, Shlomo Nobel, and Dina Abramowitz—a candle to the memory of these wonderful people. I want to thank here the Taube Center for Jewish Studies at Stanford University, and the Yosef Yerushalmi Institute for Israel and Jewish Studies at Columbia University for supporting the publication of this book with their assistance.

The book is based on an embryonic short essay, which was written and published in Hebrew, and then translated into German and published by the Simon Dubnow Institut in Leipzig. I owe much to my meticulous and demanding Israeli editor, Ilana Hammerman, and to Am Oved publishing house in Tel Aviv, as well as to my German translator and editors Liliane Granierer, Monika Heinker, Nicolas Berg, and to Dan Diner who wrote the introduction to the German edition. Out of these short Hebrew and German versions, a different and a much more extensive text evolved, grew, and branched out—in English, seeking new readers in a country that is not my native land, but in which I have been living and teaching for many years; a country on whose soil and in whose academies the interest in the questions this book ponders has been kept alive perhaps more than anywhere else.

D. M.

COLUMBIA UNIVERSITY,
NEW YORK CITY, FEBRUARY 2010

Note on Transliteration

Transliteration into English in the field of Hebrew Studies (and to a lesser extent in that of its Yiddish counterpart) is an author's despair. No matter how ardent his wish to systematize transliteration and to cling to a strictly phonetic rendering of words, names and titles, his best intentions would be undermined by current non-phonetic, quite arbitrary but prevalent and familiar transliterations, which, presumably, the reader has come to expect. It took the courage and determination of some editors of scholarly publications in the field of Slavic Studies to superimpose (with partial success) upon the reader "oddities" such as Dostoevskii (instead of Dostoyevsky) or Mendeleev (instead of Mendeleyev). But one still looks in vain for a publisher who would allow the replacement of Sholem (or Sholom) Aleichem by Sholem aleykhem, Isaac Bashevis Singer by Yitskhok Bashevis Zinger and Amichai and Zach by Amikhay and Zakh. The sources of the current mess are too many and too historically complicated to be followed here. Among other things, we still encounter—in the transliteration of Yiddish words and of Jewish names—the totally anachronistic tendency toward gentrification through Germanization (hence the Feurbergs, Frischmanns, and Vogels who are still to be found in many publications). In Hebrew a purist adherence not to sound but to grammar is responsible for monstrosities such as Hanukkah and Shabbath.

In its journey, my work has encountered and incorporated many of the spelling variations and transliterating systems innate to such a study. I was unable to reduce the transliteration confusion to a reasonable order, and more often than I like to admit accepted compromises, which like all compromises would not satisfy anybody, myself included.

Nevertheless I went as far as I could in the direction of a truly phonetic rendering. I used the English combination "kh" for both the Hebrew *khaf* and *khet*, according to the current Israeli pronunciation, and the combination "ts" for the letter *tsadi*. However, for names of well-known people I followed the spelling by which they are most familiar to readers of English or the spelling they themselves used in his or her own English publications. For example, instead of Khayim I used Chaim; rather than Perets, I used Peretz. Occasionally, I followed the spelling in the *Encyclopedia Judaica*. In the notes the spelling follows the work cited. I made some effort at consistency, but have not restricted myself to one system of transliteration.

D. M.

From Continuity to Contiguity

One   Prologue: Old Questions;
Do They Deserve New Answers?

What is this thing called (since the 1860s) *hasifrut ha'ivrit hakhadasha* (the new Hebrew literature)? In what does its "newness" subsist? How does this newness indicate a break from an "old" Hebrew literature? In what did the passage from that "old" literature to the "new" one differ from the normal evolving of other literatures through changes of style, poetics, philosophical underpinnings, and socio-historical circumstances? What justifies the sweeping separation of the new Hebrew literature from the presumably old one, drawing between the two a historical demarcation line that is so much bolder than the lines separating the Italian literary baroque from Italian neoclassicism or English medieval literature from its Renaissance continuation; and that, in spite of the fact that the advent of the new Hebrew literature never involved a linguistic shift as sharp and far reaching as the one that separates Chaucer from Spenser?! And when and where did the new Hebrew literature begin—in the last two decades of the eighteenth century, in Germany, as part of the so-called Enlightenment revolution, as the majority of scholars maintain, or half a century earlier, when Hebrew writing in Italy and Holland assumed some of the stylistic and generic characteristics of European neoclassicism, as other scholars and Chaim Nachman Bialik, the greatest modern Hebrew poet, believed; or in the sixteenth century, when Hebrew poetry written in Italy gradually distanced itself from its medieval origins and absorbed the spirit of the Italian Renaissance, as one single scholar (Eisig Silberschlag)[1] insisted? And what about the old literature with which the new one presumably broke; was there ever such a thing? Was there a unified and continuous premodern or medieval Hebrew literature, or what the historical record

3

really shows is that there were quite a few old Hebrew literatures (in themselves forming a part of the larger complex of Jewish literatures), each with its separate traditions, themes, ideational presuppositions, and poetics; and that some of them, for instance, the medieval Spanish (actually, Andalusian) Hebrew poetry, in both its main genres, the sacred and the secular, has in reality been continued—in North Africa, Iraq, and other centers in the Middle East—alongside, and totally independently, of the contemporary new literature, well into the twentieth century? For how can we subsume under the single roof of an old Hebrew literature completely divergent entities such as: the vast domains of the rabbinical legal discourse; a tradition of philosophical-rationalist writing informed by the medieval legacy of Aristotelianism; an aggregate of commentary on the sacrosanct texts, which was split in two and ran in opposite directions; a quasi-philological one, which strove to discover the "simple" meaning of the holy text within its specific context, and a homiletic-midrashic one, which deconstructing the text, tearing parts of it from their respective contexts and conflating them with other parts with which they ostensibly had no real connection, elicited from them the exegete's own ethical and theological cogitation; a liturgical tradition of a poetry written with the purpose of supplementing the synagogue ritual—periphrastic, allusive, astoundingly innovative in its style, and yet surprisingly continuous in its forms and prosody, and in its abiding by a separate taxonomy of generic traditions, all its own, which it did not share with the other poetry written in Hebrew at the same time: a poetry based on Arabic models, with meters, forms, and genres borrowed from these models; a poetry that could be hedonistic, sensual, celebrating the pleasures of wine and sex (both heterosexual and homosexual), of manicured gardens, music, fragrances, and the sweet flow of the seasons within the sheltered courtly world of the rich and pampered, and at the same time—metaphysical, spiritual, philosophical, somberly pondering the realities of death and decomposition, the awesome dimensions of the universe, the ultimate reality of an unseen God, the inability to grasp the various aspects of His being, and the yearning for His proximity, for an intimate contact with Him; a moralistic narrative literature of didactic and edifying parables, legends, and hagiography (stories about the lives, deeds, and sayings of holy and wise people); counterbalanced by collections of witty and comic tales, written in flowery rhyming prose, misogynist in its tendency, sexist, replete with salacious double entendres, and offering a view of human behavior as lowly and debased, conditioned by greed, lust, egotism, and inherent obtuseness; a mystical tradition replete with Neoplatonic myths and metaphors, dramatizing the history of the universe as having undergone a primal metaphysical big bang, a catastrophe that destroyed the conduits through which the divine overflow could reach the lowly world of matter through the ten spheres of God's immanence. Did all these belong within one old literature? If it was religious faith that cemented all the different old Jewish literatures in one monolithic continuity, and the new Hebrew literature resulted from a crisis of faith and from secularism in the theological rather than socio-cultural sense of the term (the loss of "the primal certainty that all the phenomena of life are played against the background holiness by which their value is measured," Baruch Kurzweil),[2] then the beginning of that new literature must be moved to the last decades of the nineteenth century.

During the first half of that century, Hebrew literature did not report any significant crisis of faith, and its creators would have violently objected to their description as secularists who lost their faith in a personal God and a divine providence. On the contrary, they regarded themselves as the true defenders of "pure" religion, based on faith in God's revelation to Moses and the prophets, as well as on the assumption that in post-biblical time, "the windows of heaven were shut off" (Y. Erter),[3] and that therefore the law, as well as a reasonable interpretation of God's will based on contemplation of the cosmos and of history, had to replace epiphany as the basis of faith. The very diluted deism of these writers hardly went beyond the boundaries of the traditional Maimonidean Jewish medieval rationalism.

Besides, we never hear of the emergence of the far more radical deism of Voltaire as having caused a schism in the history of French literature, tearing it from its historical moorings and resulting in the creation of a new French literature in which Voltaire and Diderot belonged but from which Racine and Pascal were excluded. For that matter, no one would dream of pointing to the advent of atheism as the spiritual event that presumably ruptured English literature into two separate historical entities, the old and the new English literatures. Clearly, the crisis of faith, which emerged as an experiential focal point in Hebrew writing of the end of the nineteenth century, by no means cut off the various historical continuities that unified, in spite of all ideological and artistic shifts, the Hebrew literature of the Enlightenment and the nationalist era.

Thus, it is possible that at least the new Hebrew literature was not completely cut off from certain, distinct parts of its so-called old predecessor (actually, predecessors). Probably there was no one old Hebrew literature anyway. Perhaps the new one, while being truly and totally divorced from some of the older literatures, was not as dramatically different from others, such as the previously mentioned medieval Hebrew-Andalusian poetry that focused on the vicissitudes of the human condition, or the delectable love poetry written in Italy during the Renaissance and the Baroque by a host of elegant Hebrew sonneteers? Perhaps the new literature formed mere new links or chapters within the chain or narrative, which connected it with much or some of what had preceded it.

Moreover, was the literature marked as new the only new Hebrew literature? What, for instance, was its position vis à vis the literature of the Hasidic movement, which chronologically was coterminous with it, indeed, running alongside it throughout the span of the last two hundred and fifty years? At first regarded by the new literature as its mortal enemy, which it set out to uproot and destroy, this other new literature eventually was looked upon by its rival as a source of inspiration and models that it sometimes tried to emulate. By the same token, what was the position of the new Hebrew literature vis à vis the equally new Yiddish one, which was born together with its Hebrew counterpart in the Germany of the waning eighteenth century (if, indeed, these were the date and place of the birth of both literatures), as much a part of the Jewish "Enlightenment Revolution" as the other one; and then, in the first half of the nineteenth century, moved together with it to eastern Europe? Are these twin literatures, one written in a spoken vernacular of Germanic origin and the other in the somewhat Europeanized language of the Bible, just two branches of one (*eyntsike*) modern Jewish literature, as a well-known bilingual

Yiddish-Hebrew critic (Baal-makhshoves, Isidor Elyashiv, 1918) put it?[4] Or were the two literatures, in spite of whatever they had in common at one time or another, two separate literary entities, not only differentiated by language but also by ideological underpinnings, different brands of cultural and linguistic dynamism, and separate artistic trajectories, as both ardent Hebraists (such as the Zionist philosopher Achad ha'am) and determined Yiddishists (Chaim Zhitlovsky, Nathan Birnboym et al.) insisted? And what was the connection between the new Yiddish literature and its own old predecessors? Was it in any significant way a continuation of a literary Yiddish tradition started in northern Italy, Switzerland, and south Germany about half a millennium before its modern follower? This was a literature of collections of didactic fables and *Gesta*; translations and adaptations of the Pentateuch and the narrative sections of the Bible, written as epics in the characteristic stanza and meter of the German *Niebelungen Lied*, or as a simplified version of the Pentateuch embroidered with midrashic glosses for the benefit of women who could not understand the weekly portion of the Torah when read in Hebrew in the synagogue every Sabbath morning. It also included a semi-secular literature of entertaining and adventurous romances of love, intrigue, chivalrous valor, and princes and princesses fleeing cruel usurpers and then regaining their legitimate birthrights as spouses and rulers. In addition, it was comprised of sequels of religious poems, often written by learned and pious women, through which Jewish women could communicate with God, unburden in His presence individual and collective tales of woe, bring to Him their requests, and participate in occasions of national mourning.

Or maybe the canonic new Yiddish literature (although it would not be granted even the rudiments of a canonic stature before the 1880s) was somehow continuing the sub-canonic semi-anonymous homiletic chapbooks (short pietistic novellas wrapped with moralistic warnings and ethical guidance), which some of the new writers imitated either for the purposes of parody and satire or with the wish of smuggling in this manner some maskilic good sense into the minds of unsuspecting, naive readers (most of whom were women)? Or was the new Yiddish poetry a continuation of the anonymous eastern European Yiddish

Folklied, or of the witty and sometimes quite biting rhyming harangues
of traditional wedding jesters? Was the new canonical Yiddish literature
essentially secular and anti-traditional, as the Soviet Yiddish critics insisted; or was it, while attempting to replace religion, also informed and
enlivened by it, as the American Yiddish critic Baruch Rivkin believed.
And what was its position vis à vis its own, Yiddish, Hasidic "sister,"
which at the beginning it wished to obliterate (indeed, there are reasons to believe that its very existence was allowed or suffered by exponents of the Jewish enlightenment, most of whom loathed Yiddish and
could not wait for the day of its replacement by Russian or German, for
the sole reason of it being an effective weapon against Hasidism and
its popular Yiddish literature), but eventually it tried to emulate—of
course, smoothing its rough edges, gentrifying, and aestheticizing it?

Then, how did both the new Hebrew and Yiddish literatures position themselves within the larger Jewish literary complex? Jewish writers wrote "Jewish" texts (whatever the definition of this Jewishness)
also in non-Jewish languages. Did a specific and definable brand of
Jewish writing exist outside the boundaries of Jewish languages (not
only Hebrew and Yiddish, but also Judesmo, better known as Ladino,
the Jewish vernacular of Jews of Hispanic origin; Jewish Persian, Jewish Arabic, etc.)? If it did, how could it be detected and differentiated
from the general non-Jewish literary context. Clearly the mere Jewish
extraction of the author was not enough of a defining shibboleth, for
there were many writers, born as Jews, who were quite indifferent to
their ethnic background, saw themselves and were seen by many others
as participants in an altogether non-Jewish literary endeavor (for instance, that of Russian modernism, which was greatly enhanced by
the contributions of Jewish participants such as Boris Pasternak and
Osip Mandelshtam, who, as writers, were not a bit more Jewish than
their Christian contemporaries and artistic allies). By the same token,
the treatment of Jewish themes in itself had nothing quintessentially
Jewish about it. Biblical themes were, of course, the legacy of all Christian literatures; even interest shown in relatively late Jewish figures and
issues was no proof of the existence of that evanescent and indefin-
able thing sometimes referred to as Jewish "essence" or "condiment,"
which, Achad ha'am said, added a special tanginess to the Russian or

German writing of Jews, even when they did not intend or wished it to be there.[5] But of what did this essence consist? It was supposed to be a salient characteristic of the writing (not only on Jewish themes) of Heinrich Heine; but how exactly was Heine's historical novella of the tribulation of Jews in fourteenth-century Germany, "Der Rabbi von Bacherach," different, as a "Jewish" text, from the historical drama featuring the sixteenth-century thinker "Uriel Acosta," (published only a few years after Heine's tale), in which a non-Jew, the rebellious exponent of "Jung Deutschland," Karl Gutzkow, used the parable of the Jewish apostate, whose biblical criticism lead to his excommunication by the rabbis of Amsterdam, to enhance his contemporary struggle as a German against clericalism and autocratic regimes? And in what inhered the difference between Gutzkow's drama and the Jew Berthold Auerbach's novel about the life, persecution, and eventual triumph of Baruch Spinoza, which treated the same theme? Or was Marcel Proust's portrayal of an assimilated Jew (Swann), who negotiated a precarious social role in the milieu of the French aristocracy, where he belonged but also did not altogether belong, more Jewish (because of the author's emotional ties with his Jewish mother) than James Joyce's portrayal of an assimilated lower-middle-class Jew (Bloom), whose Catholic wife replaced him in her bed with gentile, uncircumcised lovers? Was Franz Kafka a "Jewish" writer, in spite of the fact that he almost never mentioned in his stories and novels the word Jew and never as much as hinted (in his literary works, to be differentiated from his letters and diaries) at the specific kind of alienation the portrayal of which became known as Kafkaesque, as being in any way rooted in the Jewish experience? If he was quintessentially "Jewish," as Max Brod, Martin Buber, Franz Rosenzweig, Gershom Scholem, and many others insisted, in what did Kafkaesque Jewishness inhere? Was Scholem justified in maintaining that the parable "Before the Law," and the lengthy interpretative controversy that followed it (in the cathedral chapter of *The Trial*), was the epitome of Talmudic cogitation, in which the light of the Talmudic mind was brilliantly broken into its componential bright colors, and that *The Trial* as a whole was a sequel to the book of Job, the only text, Scholem maintained, with which the novel could be meaningfully and productively compared?[6] Or was Franz Rosenzweig right when he said that Kafka related to God as only the authors of the biblical books did?[7] Or maybe Jewish literature written in non-Jewish languages had to be narrowly defined (as it was by Dov Sadan) as only that literature written by Jews for Jewish consumption; a definition that rendered this literature almost devoid of substance because the writers to whom it could be applied were solely those highly forgettable epigones who, for a short while, served conservative Jewish communities in Germany and to some extent also in Russia, and who adopted the language of their respective host societies but did not yet achieve the level of acculturation that would have allowed them to participate in these societies' cultural and literary dialogues. If this is what this literature is about—a tasteless fodder for a community in transition to temporarily feed on— perhaps it cannot be of interest to the literary scholar and critic, and only the cultural historian can elicit from it some significant insight.

These, as well as many similar questions, were asked, answered, and debated by a host of critics, thinkers, and literary scholars throughout the first half of the twentieth century. They were regarded then as burning questions, the immediate relevance of which was not to be questioned, and since the answers to them were not only different, but also mutually exclusive of each other, they triggered heated polemics. However, in the second half of the century, these questions were marginalized and soon enough all but forgotten. Almost no Hebrew or Yiddish literary scholar regarded them as deserving of further elaboration; even with the few scholars (mainly living and working out of Israel) who still raised them, their temperature plummeted. They were not seen anymore as vital and worth quarreling over.

That process of marginalization started during the 1950s. When in 1959 the critic Kurzweil published his essays focusing on these questions in a volume with the provocative title *Our New Literature—Continuation or Revolution?*, most members of the then young Israeli intelligentsia already regarded the topics of this volume as passé, irrelevant, unexciting. Among other things, they were rubbed the wrong way by the sheer word *sifrutenu* (our literature), a substantive in the possessive case, regarding it as old fashioned and somewhat ridiculous. Such endearing references to Hebrew literature as "ours" had abounded in Hebrew writing of the first half of the century, when titles like *Sifrutenu hayafa* (*Our Belles-Lettres*), *Shiratenu hatse'ira* (*Our Young Poetry*, the title of Bialik's trail-blazing essay of 1907), *Meshorerenu* (*Our Poet*), and so on could be met everywhere. Dov Sadan's famous essay, in which this highly original critic and scholar articulated his unique take on the above-mentioned questions, was called: "Al sifrutenu—masat mavo" ("On Our Literature—An Introductory Essay").[8] Suddenly such titles, which had clearly conveyed a sense of intimacy, of belonging, and of being directly impacted by the literature, its goals, achievements, and failures, seemed inappropriately coy and parochial. The particularistic focusing on "our" literature was replaced by an interest in literature per se. The major literary-scholarly periodical of the era carried the title *Hasifrut*, literature with the definite article, that is, literature per se. The fact that most of the interpretative and theoretical articles published in this periodical either focused on modern Hebrew texts, such as poems by Bialik and Shaul Tchernikhovsky or on the prose fiction of Shalom Ya'akov Abramovitsh, or illustrated the rhetorical or structural concepts they discussed with examples culled from canonical Hebrew texts of the twentieth century, did not mitigate this radical shift from what was ours to what presumably belonged within the universal domain of general literature. On the contrary, it rather emphasized the shift; for the scholars, who now referred to those classical texts, regarded and presented them as illustrative of the sheer literary components of literary texts. Most (although not all) of them were essentially uninterested in the historical uniqueness of the new Hebrew literature—a literature that was written out of a national territory and in a language that was still unspoken; in fact, a language that only a short while ago had been yanked out of its historical matrix of sacrosanct texts and was still highly charged, underneath its secularized surface, with dangerously high theurgist voltage (as Gershom Scholem described it in a famous open letter to the philosopher Franz Rosenzweig[9]) emanating from the millennia-long association and friction of the language with the anagogic and the theological, and ready to explode in the faces of those who naively employed it for the purposes of mundane communication. Where angels should have feared to tread, they rushed into the rather idiosyncratic and somewhat skewed space of this literature, looking there for examples for the many kinds of metonymies, synecdoches, and their figurative impact, the various brands of allusions, "interlaced speech" (the enriching of a third-person narration by unmarked quotations from, or paraphrases of, the described protagonist's interior monologue), and such poetic or rhetorical devices.

The illustrations for all of these had to be culled from modern Hebrew texts since, paradoxically, most of these students of the literary phenomenon in its universal quintessence, as well as all of the readers of their studies, had a very limited access to literatures other than Hebrew. Unlike the predecessors they rejected, who spoke and wrote three or four languages and read four or five literatures in the original, they, being the products of the monolinguist, Zionist, Hebrew education in Palestine and Israel, could not gauge the literary depth of a text in any language but Hebrew. Thus Hebrew literature had to be used by them as "the literature." This led, of course, to the quick decline of interest in whatever was historically unique and non-normative about Hebrew literature as they read and understood it. They came up with, for example, general theories of translation that they based on translations into Hebrew—mainly from Russian and German—without taking into account the unusual and strange aspects of these translations, which, well into the 1920s, had been targeted at a reading public who either had already read the translated texts or could have read them in their original versions—the translations were informed by a poetics of translation that deviated in essential ways from those of contemporary normative translation into English or French as an equivalent in a different language of an original text targeted at readers for whom that original text was inaccessible.

The question we want to explore here is whether the issues that occupied Hebrew and Yiddish literary scholars before the Israeli era deserve to be salvaged from oblivion and rendered once again an integral part of the Hebrew and Jewish theoretical literary agenda of the twenty-first century. Were not those who "forgot" these issues and made others forget them justified? Had not the focusing on the issues pertaining to the unique Jewish literary condition resulted in deflecting attention and analytical acumen from the literary phenomenon in and of itself, replacing the attempt to understand what was literature by partisan quarrels over a tangle of meta-literary concerns, which actually belonged within the domain of cultural, ideological, and political struggles that have lost their relevance once the Jewish state had been established? Was it not the right thing to do, to sweep clear the space of literary-theoretical thinking, relegating the cumbersome baggage of bygone generations to the junk attic and using whatever remained alive of Hebrew literature for the purposes of illustrating universal literary phenomena?

It seems to me, that the answer to these questions must be a negative one, or it has to be, that as much as the shift under discussion here was necessary (and, indeed, inevitable) when it occurred, it should not anymore condition our perspectives and guide our current literary theoretical thinking that must be performed, under altogether different circumstances. The shift *was* necessary, and indeed inevitable, not only because contemporary Hebrew literary scholarship had to shore up its antiquated theoretical presuppositions with the formalist-structuralist methodologies then (the 1950s) dominating Western culture studies in general and linguistic and literary studies in particular, but also, and perhaps more importantly, because it directly resulted from the new cultural horizon opened up by the establishment of the State of Israel and that astounding historical novelty: Jewish political independence within a Jewish nation-state after eighteen centuries of extra-territorial collective Jewish existence as minorities within more or less hostile host societies. This novelty thoroughly reconditioned and changed the sense of Jewish collective existence. It seemed to have terminated what was constantly referred to as the abnormalities of this existence and launch a period of purported normalcy in modern Jewish history, with the Jewish people, at least in its quintessential part that gathered in Israel, becoming like "all the nations" (no matter how many times David Ben Gurion reiterated his mantra of "Light unto the nations"). Thus, normalcy was presumably restored not only to Jewish political and social history but also to Jewish cultural life. Hebrew became a natural language, spoken and written by those who absorbed it in infancy as their mother tongue. Israeli literature was written in it as a matter of course, and not because the writer was a Zionist and chose to resort to Hebrew rather than to Yiddish or to one of the European languages he mastered.

By the same token, the readers of Israeli literature, themselves products of the circumstances that now controlled its production, regarded it not as a brand, one of many, of a historically unique mode of Jewish writing, but rather as literature with the definite article. At the most, they tended to organize their understanding of Jewish and Israeli literatures in universally applicable systems or poly-systems. Their literature was to them a metonymy, that representative part of general or world literature with which they happened to be familiar; rather as French people conceptualized literature through the formidable metonymy of their national literature. It was not anymore a metaphor representing the specific Jewish cultural condition with its strange twists and turns, which in modern times had split it into a plethora of hybridist Jewish modern cultures.

Thus the new Israeli intelligentsia, inclined to accept the criterion of normalcy as obligatory in cultural matters, as well as in political and social ones, celebrated its normal Israeli literature, many of whose spokesmen (such as the novelist A. B. Yehoshua) proselytized (and still proselytize) the virtues of normalcy. The formalist-structuralist approach to Israeli literature, and through it to world literature, was therefore, a clear expression, on the abstract-conceptual level, of the common cultural consensus of nascent Israel as experienced and articulated by young Israelis, the so-called "state generation," unburdened of the ballast of the pre-state Zionist past. As a matter of fact, it was the most sophisticated and best articulation of this consensus; and for this reason it enjoyed a popularity that academic scholarly disciplines rarely enjoy. It was, in this respect, not dissimilar to the discipline of archaeology, in most modern cultures a rather arcane field of study, reserved for its professional acolytes, but in Israel of the 1950s and 1960s—a national craze, which attracted and entertained the general public, and that, for the same reasons that rendered, for a time, the niceties of figurative language and the nuances of point of view in narrative, exciting more than they are usually believed to be. Whereas archaeology demonstrated the normalcy of rootedness in place of territoriality, the new literary discourse insisted on the normalcy of cultural space, that is, being on equal footing, on a par, so to speak, in the world of the spirit (why Agnon could be studied by the same methods applicable to Henry James, and the poetry of the national poet Bialik was a fertile field for the study of the use of the metonymy in poetry or of poetic closure). How could exilic issues, such as Jewish multilingual-

ism with its frustrating splintering of Jewish literature into Jewish literatures, and, for that matter, all other "abnormalities" fostered by the exilic
condition, compete as an area of academic and non-academic interest
with the new exciting topics? What's more, all those Jewish issues reeked
of the all too familiar sour smells of ideological polemics and pathos,
which the young Israeli intelligentsia of the time regarded as downright
disgusting. Was it now to contaminate its enjoyment of, and interest in
literature with leftover ideological conflicts?! No, it could safely relegate
them to the quotation marks that now, with the Zionist project having
achieved its highest goal, have robbed the concept of Zionism itself of its
erstwhile respectability.

This was a liberation of sorts; however, the liberation has proven premature, or rather, unwarranted. The Israeli etatism of the Ben Gurion
era was dispelled by a series of events and developments that undermined it throughout the 1960s and led to its final collapse in the 1970s.
The latter came in the wake of the 1973 War and the subsequent political
mahapakh (reversal) of 1977, when Labor Zionism, which had dominated Israel and the pre-Israeli *yishuv* (the Jewish contingent in Palestine) for forty-four years (since the death blow it had dealt in 1933 to its
only rival, Vladimir Jabotinsky's Revisionist Zionists) was defeated and
humiliated by a new generation of Israeli voters. More important than
the events in the early 1960s, which directly led to David Ben Gurion's
fall from power, was the Eichmann trial of 1961, which undermined the
official Zionist understanding of the Holocaust and of its own role as
the Jewish answer to the destruction of European Jewry. Riveted by
survivors' accounts of the events that had taken place during World
War II (which were heard in the courtroom in Jerusalem), many Israelis
understood for the first time that the chasm between themselves, as
those who had left Europe "in time," and those who "went like sheep
to slaughter" was imaginary and that Zionism was the answer to Hitler
only due to the two hundred miles that separated Rommel's African
army from Mandatory Palestine, which the British were about to abandon, were it not for Montgomery's victory at El-Alamain. The complex
reality of the position of the Jewish European communities, living in
the midst of inimical host societies and facing the sophisticated and fully
industrialized state-run German annihilation machine was understood

now as it had never been before—even by the survivors themselves. The latter, quite suddenly, regained their voice and their memories that had been silenced in the heady atmosphere of the Ben Gurionist era, and whoever was not altogether brainwashed could see how trivial had been the official "counterbalancing" of the "shame" of the annihilated millions by emphasizing the heroism of the few ghetto rebels. Clearly the Holocaust was the defining historical event in recent Jewish history, and much of what directly and indirectly conditioned the behavior of the Israeli polity was prescribed by its impact as much as by that of Zionist ideals and socio-economic achievements. Psychologically, as well as socially and economically, Israel was what it was because of the Holocaust and its aftermath, as much as it was impacted and guided by any other factor. Israeli society and Israeli culture were thus sucked back, at least to a certain extent, into a pre-state exilic reality. Whereas the official Israeli ethos persisted in presenting statehood and military prowess as the diametrical opposite of Jewish exilic vulnerability, much of what Israel did as a state and as a military power was dictated by lurking Holocaust memories and fears. The myth of Israeli normalcy crumbled together with the illusion of its cultural unity based on the assumption that mere statehood conferred identity. Thus, by the mid-1960s, the presumably unifying etatist ethos of the 1950s waxed moribund, leaving behind it an ideological vacuum that was quickly filled—after the overwhelming Israeli victory in the Six-Day War of 1967—by a pseudo-messianic surge of territorial aspirations. Israeli society was now split into irreconcilable splinters—political, social, ethnic, and religious. Culturally, Israel was thrown into a *Kulturkampf*, and yet Israeli intellectuals were largely unable to develop concepts and methodological stratagems that would have helped them to both understand the dynamics of the cultural situation and attempt to negotiate compromises between its various binary oppositions. Cultural or artistic developments that pretended to be representative of some common Israeliness (such as Naomi Shemer's popular ballads or a good part of the canonized Israeli prose fiction) progressively waxed either specious and inauthentic or hopelessly anachronistic, but Israeli official intellectual discourse was tardy in conceptualizing a situation in which what was unabashedly partisan and partial was truly expressive of the cultural reality.

The contribution made by structuralism as a scholarly methodology and a Weltanschauung to this myopia was considerable. In its insistent search for universal rules based on ubiquitously present infrastructures or "deep structures," its tendency to reduce all multifariousness to neat "systems," and in its attitude of indifference to, if not rejection of, "surface" variations, differences embedded in the uniqueness of historical situations, as well as to all other forms of irreducible cultural heterogeneity and alterity, it equipped Israeli intellectuals with tools they really had no use for. While Israeli imagined commonality (beyond the very real fear of Israel's enemies) was being quickly dismantled, an eminent Israeli sociologist grappled with a theorem that would identify the components (and their structural interrelatedness) of a concept of Jewish civilization that would be applicable to all three millennia of Jewish history[10]—that at the time when outside of Israel, the concept of a unified Jewish culture or civilization was being discredited by historians and sociologists and replaced not only by the plural Jewish cultures, but also by cultures of the Jews that eliminated the essentialist adjective "Jewish," and preferred the historical and existential reference to Jews, or to specific Jewish groups that lived in different times and places and evolved different cultural articulations of their sense of collectivity.[11] Structuralist methodologies, being most effectively and elaborately practiced in Israel by literary academicians, the Israeli academic study of literature functioned as one of the main barriers to the introduction of post-structuralism into the Israeli intellectual discourse—a development that took place only in the 1990s, about thirty years after post-structuralism had changed the intellectual climate in France, Germany, England, and the United States. Thus, the universal tendency in Israeli literary studies, the wish to break out of the narrow confines of all those Jewish concerns and turn attention to "the literature," produced a paradoxical effect. As much as it was motivated by the familiar Israeli yearning for joining "the big world," it actually distanced Israeli intellectual discourse from contemporary Europe and America, where attention was consistently drawn toward difference, hybridity, the divergent and disorderly, the unsystematic, which refuses to be neatly ordered in the framework of a structuralist theorem.

It is because of this that the old and disqualified literary discourse, which had focused on the idiosyncratic and the specific in Jewish cultural history (or rather histories) should be granted a fresh examination. While the exponents of this discourse knew well enough that the literary text consisted of universally present literary components, they did not focus on the abstraction of literature per se, with the definite article, as a worthwhile topic of study. For them, this abstraction first had to be refracted through the prism of a concrete and specific historical and cultural reality even before its universal components could be identified and defined. Being Jewish scholars imbued with the ethos of Jewish nationalism, they chose the Jewish literary complex as their prism; and since that complex was characterized by a complexity reflective of Jewish historical realities, they suspected general *Literaturwissenschaft* of being unable to accommodate the uniqueness of the phenomena they were interested in. Bialik went as far as warning his reader "not to forget to forget" all general literary-critical "rules" when trying to grasp the essence of a quintessentially "Jewish" writing such as that of Abramovitsh.[12] In any case, those who had evolved the pre-Israeli literary-critical discourse chose to ponder this complexity and pose questions that it gave rise to. In these questions, if not in the answers they provided, some members of the superseded "old" old guard emerge now as more relevant and up-to-date than some of the members of the "new" old guard, who had deposed and replaced them. I am not suggesting that we either can or should wish to return to the old and long defunct intimate literary republic of *sifrutenu* and *shiratenu hatse'ira* that was the product of irreproducible circumstances. But I do suggest that we should take seriously the literary concerns that motivated the best citizens of that republic: seriously enough to be re-examined in the light of current circumstances. Perhaps it would not be altogether detrimental to absorb some of the "abnormality" of Hebrew and Yiddish literary thinking of the era before the elimination of European Jewry and the establishment of the State of Israel; an abnormality which, reflecting far from a normal national condition (no matter how such a conditioned is defined), nevertheless had been more authentic and real than the purported normalcy that replaced it. The latter, as the social and cultural history of Israel has shown, can be both bogus and dull. Perhaps a grain of the salt of the abnormality of the pre-Israeli condition would add some sorely missed tanginess to a discourse that has waxed insipid. As some contemporary thinkers teach us, you cannot have a three-dimensional view of the norm unless you step out of it and watch it from the vantage point of the other.

The following chapters survey some of the issues we mentioned earlier and ponder their ramifications. They add up to a scholarly essay rather than a formal scholarly study; an essay which is written in the very tradition it reflects upon, that of Dov Sadan, Shmuel Niger, Chaim Nachman Shapira, Kurzweil, and Shimon Halkin, although it would reject most of the conclusions these brilliant scholars and critics had reached. As such, it cannot be burdened with the full apparatus of academic discourse (long quotations, meticulous historical contextualizations, etc.) that in this case would have quadrupled the sheer volume of a text that wishes to remain unencumbered, focusing on argument rather than offering solid proof, offering an ongoing narrative rather than being historically descriptive, being argumentative and conceptual rather than mimetic.

For the last forty-plus years, since the so-called Tel Aviv structuralist school of poetics became the dominant force in the academic study and teaching of Hebrew literature, we have grown used to the notion that until that development took place, the study of Hebrew literature had been devoid of a theoretical component. Biblical literature presumably was studied mainly either using the tools of Semitic philology or those of ancient Middle East historiography and archaeology, but rarely with tools targeted at gauging its aesthetic depth or understanding the significance of the formal and stylistic devices its creators employed and the way these devices impacted their reader or audience. Medieval Hebrew poetry, we thought, also was studied by philologists and historians, as well as through the traditional (based on Arabic models) assumptions regarding its prosody, forms, and genres, without adding to the probing of this historical poetics, the insights offered by current twentieth-century understanding of form, and its aesthetic functioning in the literary text. As for the so-called new Hebrew literature, the one created since the waning of the eighteenth century, its study was left either in the hands of "impressionistic" critics or in those of historians of modern Jewish ideologies and cultural-political movements, such as the haskala (the Jewish enlightenment) or Zionism. The former based their conclusions on vague impressions and gut feelings, the aesthetic ramifications of which were never rigorously examined; whereas the latter, mired in ancillary bio-bibliographical research, were actually summarizing the ideational contents of literary texts that were used as documents illustrating aspects of a modern Jewish history of ideas—viewed through Zionist eyes. They had never studied either the intrinsic dy-

20

namics of literary history (i.e., its evolvement as an artistic tradition energized and propelled by the dialectics of aesthetic perception) or the aesthetic organization of the individual literary text, for their work had not been based on a methodology that could offer ways and means of systematically conducting such a study. In short, the study of Hebrew literature as a whole had no literary theoretical framework or basis for its operations.

This rather patronizing view, while based on a justified critique of some parts of the scholarly and critical tradition that had accumulated around the study of the new Hebrew and Yiddish literatures throughout the first half of the twentieth century, was blind to other parts or aspects of the same tradition, and, on the whole, was not corroborated by the documentable facts when viewed through the proper historical perspective. The new Jewish literatures were studied—since the emergence in the 1890s and the first decade of the twentieth century of a literary scholarship in this field—within the frameworks of contemporary literary-theoretical assumptions. If we tend to dismiss these assumptions as irrelevant or non-theoretical, we should remind ourselves that the concept "theory" itself constantly fluctuates and changes and that our own theoretical presuppositions would certainly be similarly dismissed by future generations. Therefore, it behooves us as historians to subsume all organized and causally interrelated thoughts about the nature of literature, its aesthetic functioning, and its historical development under an evolving concept of theory, whether we agree or disagree with any of its changing formulations. Thus, the theoretical study of the Jewish literatures was not born in Tel Aviv or Jerusalem in the 1960s but rather in Warsaw, Berlin, Paris, and even in New York or at Harvard University (where the first formal history of the new Yiddish literature was written in the late 1890s by the Slavicist Leo Wiener,[1] the father of Norbert who was to establish the science of cybernetics).

In its infancy, the theoretical framework of the study of the new Hebrew and Yiddish literatures was thoroughly conditioned by late nineteenth-century positivist *Literaturwissenschaft* as it was conducted in Germany, France, and Russia. It predicated the existence of direct causal ties between the literary text and the biography of the writer, the influences of other literary texts, and of course, the historical, political,

cultural, and literary backgrounds (or "moments") against which the
text was written. Therefore, to understand the text, one had to study
its origins or roots in these respective backgrounds. Whereas the biography of the writer, the study of which was conducted mainly on
the basis of documents (diaries, letters, unpublished drafts of the literary text, and all other relevant archival materials), presumably offered
insights into the personal and unique aspects of the writer's work,
those of its place and role within a large historical and cultural arena
were highlighted by studying the ways in which the historical situation made its contribution to their formation. Thus in the 1890s, the
letters of the chief Hebrew writers of the nineteenth century (the novelists Avraham Mapu and Peretz Smolenskin and the poet Yehuda Leyb
Gordon) were collected and first, biographically-oriented monographs
of them were written—two of them by the then popular literary critic
Reuven Braynin.[2] Of the three formal histories of the new Jewish literatures, two were based on dissertations written at the Sorbonne (Nahum
Slouschz's *The Renaissance of Hebrew Literature*, 1903,[3] and Meir Pines's
History of the Literature in "Judeo-German" [i.e., Yiddish], 1911[4]), and
were, as a matter of course, based on the positivistic models then dominating French academic literary studies in their understanding of literary developments as triggered mainly by extrinsic historical and cultural
circumstances. In the case of Slouschz, who was to evolve as a scholar
deeply interested in ancient Semitic Mediterranean cultures (which he
viewed as essentially Hebraic), his early study of the new Hebrew literature already contained a "racial"-Semitic component; this, however,
was also prescribed by many late nineteenth-century positivist theories
of culture and literature and in France primarily on the concept of literary history as formulated by Hippolite Taine. Other scholars studied
the development of Hebrew literature in monographs focusing on particular genres, where the concept of development was based on positivist principles, such as Israel Davidson's history of Jewish and Hebrew
parody (1907).[5]

The legacy of positivism lingered throughout the 1920s and 1930s
but was definitely challenged by the exponents of the more up-to-
date methodologies then employed in contemporary culture studies.
Thus, Yosef Klausner, the well-known critic, historian, and editor of the

prestigious literary monthly *Hashilo'akh*, when invited in 1925 to teach modern Hebrew literature at the just-launched Hebrew University of Jerusalem, chose to conduct his teaching and research following the methodologies of *Literaturwissenschaft* as he absorbed them in the 1890s when he studied German literature at the University of Heidelberg and attended the lectures of the then famous scholar Kuno Fischer. That is, he studied in detail the biographies of the writers and the cultural history of their times and arranged the information he culled within a rather simplistic literary map of neoclassical, romantic, and realist periods, with the periodization being dictated by extrinsic historical-cultural developments, which presumably triggered changes in style and Weltanschauung. His monumental *History of the New Hebrew Literature*,[6] the six volumes of which appeared between 1930 and 1950, is a prime example of the lingering of late nineteenth-century theoretical presuppositions in twentieth-century Hebrew literary scholarship. Similarly, at the Vilnius YIVO (acronym of Yidisher visnshaftlekher institut—the Jewish Scientific Institute), which like the Hebrew University of Jerusalem, was established in 1925 but as the Yiddishist "answer" to the establishment in Jerusalem of the Zionist-Hebraist academic center, positivist philology and historiography (focusing on the Yiddish language and on east European Jewish social history) dominated the intellectual atmosphere with literary studies trailing behind in the form of bio-bibliographical projects (Zalman Reyzen's *Lexicon of Yiddish Literature, Journalism and Philology*),[7] the publication of academic editions of classical texts (Max Weinreich's edition of the collected works of the early nineteenth-century playwright and poet Shlomo Etinger, 1925),[8] and the study of the historical and biographical backgrounds of Yiddish texts from different periods (cf. Max Weinreich's, *Rungs—Four Studies in Yiddish Philology and Literary History*, 1923, and *History-in-Vignettes of Yiddish Literature*, 1928).[9]

However, the nationalist positivism, in both its Jerusalemite and Vilnius brands, met strong methodological opposition. Klausner's approach to modern Hebrew literature was squarely confronted by many, among whom nobody was more prominent than the veteran critic and scholar Fishl Lakhover and the Hebrew Lithuanian scholar Ch. N. Shapira. Lakhover was a disciple of both David Frishman (the most prominent Hebrew critic of the turn of the nineteenth century and the beginning of the twentieth century and the chief advocate for aestheticism and lyricism as the desiderata of the new Hebrew literature) and Micha Yosef Berditchevsky (a Nietzschean philosopher and writer of prose fiction and the most audacious defender in Hebrew literature at the same time of individualism, anti-traditionalism, and the acting out of vital instinctual urges). As such, he set out to write a history of modern Hebrew literature in which aesthetic continuities and disruptions and artistic, rather than ideational, achievements were emphasized.[10] Ch. N. Shapira received his education (philosophy and Semitic philology) in Vienna and was an avid follower of German intellectual life and literary scholarship of the period of the Weimar republic. Upon being appointed a professor of Semitic languages and Hebrew literature at the University of Kaunas (1931), he started writing his own, highly original anti-Klausnerian history of the new Hebrew literature, of which only the first magisterial volume, published on the eve of World War II, survived.[11] The other already written parts perished together with the author and the rest of the Kaunas Jewish community. On the one hand, Ch. N. Shapira brought to bear on his topic the lessons of cultural scholars and philosophers such as Wilhelm Dilthey (particularly his concept of *Erlebnis* [intensified, epiphanous experience] as the source of poetry), Oskar Walzel, whose book on form and content in the literary text was used at the time as a textbook in some German universities and high schools, and the art historian Heinrich Woelflin (whose innovative understanding of classicism and the baroque, Ch. N. Shapira whole heartedly adopted, applying it to late eighteenth-century and early nineteenth-century Hebrew texts). On the other hand, Shapira fully internalized the innovative approach of Gershom Scholem to the history and phenomenology of Jewish religion and mysticism,[12] using it as a basis for his own non-positivist understanding of modern Jewish cultural history as propelled by both intrinsic semi-unconscious "terrestrial" (libidinal) elements and extrinsic influences such as that of the German *Aufklärung* (rationalism). Based on these principles, which brought Shapira very close to the then most advanced intellectual and academic circles in Germany, he dismissed Klausner's historical approach, undermined his periodization table, and exhibited an altogether different method of text analysis. Other scholars, not necessarily theoretically inclined, such as Israel Zinberg in Leningrad and Meir Waxman[13] in Chicago, challenged not only Klausner's but also all other attempts at writing a history of Jewish literature within the framework of one linguistic tradition, Hebrew or Yiddish, by offering wide-ranging surveys that purported to cover all the ideological and linguistic brands of Jewish literature, or as Zinberg more carefully put it, the literature written by Jews (see his particularly careful phrasing of the title of his multi-volume history: *literatur bay yidn* rather than *yidishe literatur*[14]). Thus these scholars indicated (without conceptualizing their argument) that the Jewish literary complex should be studied from a holistic vantage point.

As for the Vilnius Yiddishists, they too were challenged and attacked from various vantage points. Some of their American counterparts went beyond their positivistic historical-causal thinking by studying the evolving of the new Yiddish literature within the context of the history of ideas, projecting a view of this literature as energized and propelled forward by a dialectic relationship between two essential ideas, played one against the other, but also merging into a constructive synthesis. Such a Hegelian argument informed, for instance, Baruch Rivkin's theoretical book *Basic Drives in American Yiddish Literature*.[15] For others, the historical positivism of the YIVO scholars was marred by their nationalist-idealist Yiddishism, whereas what was needed was the application of the scientific methodology of Marxist materialism. The fiercest attack came from the Yiddish academic establishment in the Soviet Union, which flourished in the 1920s, then gradually petered out in the Stalinist 1930s, in special academies that were established in the centers of the two Soviet republics (Byelorussia and the Ukraine), where Yiddish culture and language were acknowledged by the authorities as the legitimate cultural heritage of part of the population, which could be put to "progressive" use if studied and proliferated by scholars who were ideologically and methodologically "mature," namely, scholars who based their work on the proper Soviet-Marxist-Leninist principles of cultural theory and practice. These scholars, among them intellectual luminaries such as Meir Viner and Max Erik, attacked the nationalist study of Yiddish literature that failed to understand culture and literature as "superstructures" informed by class struggle and basic developments and changes in society's material base, and exhibited a positivist-Marxist approach of their own in the analysis of nineteenth-century classical texts such as those of Yisroel Aksenfeld, Abramovitsh, Sholem Aleichem, and many others. Both scholars had to base their Marxist critiques on severe self-criticism, since both had launched their careers as critics and literary historians during the 1920s, before they emigrated to the Soviet Union, and their early work had not been conducted along Marxist lines but rather was informed by nationalist-modernist concerns. Viner had undergone a nationalist-spiritualist-Buberian phase, which had found its expression in his interest in Hebrew medieval poetry (as a co-editor, together with the scholar Chaim Brody of the *Anthologia Hebraica*, 1922) and in his earlier (1920) *Der Lyrik der Kabbalah*, whereas Erik, won over by expressionism and formalism, had made a name for himself with his formalistic studies of Yitzhak Leib Peretz's symbolist verse-dramas, *The Golden Chain* and *At Night in the Old Market Place*,[16] and particularly with his monographs on the pre-modern Yiddish literature and novel of the Middle Ages and the Renaissance.[17] However, converted to Marxism, these scholars put their wide erudition, philosophical training, and European cultural flair at the service of a learned Marxist critique of nationalist Jewish scholarship. Both focused on the analysis of bourgeois, nineteenth-century Yiddish culture and literature, emphasizing their class-consciousness and revolutionary, anti-traditionalist implications. Viner and Erik conducted ongoing scholarly battles with Yiddishist scholarly ideology (as implicit not only in literary scholarship, but also, for instance, in folkloristics and ethnography), branding Yiddishist-nationalist scholarship as proto-Fascist. At the same time, the former fended off "vulgar" and simplistic applications of Marxism (by Yiddish critics in the Soviet Union) to cultural and literary issues.[18] Like many other Marxists, Viner and Erik (particularly the former) were very much theoretically inclined and often exhibited brilliant analytical acumen. In the late 1930s, as cultural scholarship became progressively more risky and prescriptive in the Soviet Union (with the "right" attitudes and terminology changing every few years even as the history of the Bolshevik party changed from one edition of the Soviet Encyclopedia to the next), these and other scholars limited themselves to the publication of excellent academic editions of the works of "democratic" or "progressive" nineteenth-century writers, even as some of the beleaguered Russian formalist critics did at the time. Erik, exiled to a Siberian concentration camp, perished (1937) in the Stalinist purges of the late 1930s.

Marxist methodologies invaded the study of Hebrew literature in Palestine in the 1930s and 1940s as the members of the Marxist-Zionist groups (*Hashomer hatsa'ir* and the leftist segment of the historical *Akhdut ha'avoda*) came of age intellectually. Arriving in Israel as young pioneers in the 1920s, these intellectuals (such as Menachem Dorman and David Kena'ani) took their time before rushing into print, but once they got going they quickly became influential, particularly among the committed youth who were exposed to Marxist education in various youth movements, in particular *Hashomer hatsa'ir*, with its inherent penchant for intellectualism, which rendered it the greenhouse where a large group of young writers were planted and allowed to flourish. The fact that these critics and scholars, all committed Party members, as well as members of kibbutzim, had no academic affiliations did not diminish their appeal as far as the young intelligentsia of the time was concerned. On the contrary, it lent their intellectual activity the credibility bestowed by political activism and daily realization of communist principles. The change during World War II in the initially negative Zionist public assessment of the Soviet Union and of communism (because of their opposition to Zionism, the suppression of Hebrew culture in the Soviet Union, etc.), with the Red Army now perceived as the savior of eastern European Jews and the Soviet Union as the staunchest enemy of Nazism, helped in legitimizing Marxism as an intellectual discipline and a political orientation. By the time Israel was established and fought its war of independence, a large part—perhaps the major part—of the young Israeli intelligentsia accepted Marxism as a dominant intellectual system that offered convincing explanations of historical developments, including those of cultural and literary history, and put in the hands of critics and literary scholars sharp and precise tools vouchsafing the scientific rigor of their approach to literary analysis. Acquaintance with translations from the "approved" Marxist writings of Georg Lukacs, such as his essays on realism and his monograph on the historical novel (but not his early, brilliant, pre-Marxist *Philosophy of the Novel*) was now

de rigueur in progressive intellectual circles. At the same time, sociological literary criticism of a non-Marxist nature was also written by Hebrew scholars and of a very high level—as witnessed, for instance, by
Tsvi Vislavsky's Weberian analyses of matters pertaining to language, literary genres (see his essay on the novel versus the short story[19]), and individual texts (such as his brilliant essay on Bialik's "Hamatmid," ["The
Talmud Student"]).[20]

Somewhat less fortunate was the fate of psychoanalysis as an influence and a guide in contemporary Hebrew literary studies. It made its
appearance as an intellectual vector in the early 1930s when it was brilliantly introduced to Hebrew criticism by the most subtle and sophisticated literary critic then active, Dov Sadan (called then Dov or Berl
Shtok). Sadan was deeply influenced by and fully conversant in current
Freudian culture analysis. In a series of studies of the works of several
Hebrew writers, particularly Yosef Chaim Brenner and Bialik, which he
wrote in the 1930s (some of which are still unsurpassed in subtlety and
originality), he offered not only the expected Freudian insights into the
biographical narrative and the personality structure, which shed light
on the works of these respective writers, but also altogether unexpected
insights into such matters as the inner rhyming or the meaning of repetitive phrases in Bialik's poems, as well as the symbolic functioning
of the main Bialikian leitmotifs and primal visionary sights. Sadan conceptualized the psychic development of the creative personality in a way
that allowed him to present Bialik as an essentially "blocked" poet[21] and
Tchernikhovsky as a poet who functioned on two separate developmental levels with no significant connections between them.[22] Sadan was
the most prominent but not the only critic who at the time based his
insights on the psychoanalytic theory of art as sublimating inner conflicts. However, for reasons too complicated to dwell upon here, the
growing appeal of psychoanalysis, which triggered in 1930 the publication in Hebrew translation of Freud's *Die Traumdeutung* (with a special
introduction for the Hebrew reader written by the author), the first
major modern European theoretical opus to be translated into Hebrew
(the next one would be *Das Kapital*, translated in the 1940s), was halted
and diminished by the tragic events of the 1940s. Even Sadan, never reneging on his psychoanalytic convictions, saw fit to somewhat conceal

them, refraining from psychoanalytic nomenclature and replacing it by idiosyncratic codes that were not deciphered by the average reader. As a matter of fact, it was in Marxist criticism (such as in David Kena'ani's essays and monographs, particularly his monograph on Uri Tsvi Greenberg[23]) that the influence of Marxist Freudians such as Otto Fenichel and Erich Fromm, was, by the end of the 1940s and the beginning of the 1950s, still unabashedly acknowledged.

In the 1940s, the influence of literary formalism, particularly as it was practiced in Germany and Switzerland in the form of *explication des textes* (close reading, mainly of poetry) slowly found its way into the teaching and analyzing of Hebrew literary texts. For reasons that will be commented on later in this chapter, its chief carriers were the *Yekes* (German Jews), who had arrived in the country and found their place in the Hebrew educational system of the 1930s. Chief among them was the German-Hebrew poet Arye Ludwig Strauss, who did not publish much, but exercised a formidable influence through his seminars and, eventually, lectures on European writers at the Hebrew University. His meticulous close readings of Psalms, texts from the high-holiday prayers, and of some modern Hebrew poems set a model of sensitive formalistic interpretation.[24] Even the already mentioned Kurzweil, although his cultural agenda was totally different from that of the formalists, for awhile taught the Hebrew reader of the 1940s, who followed his interpretative essays on Agnon's modernistic stories as they were published at the time, to carefully focus on a given literary text, pay attention to its details and their structural arrangement, and perceive the commensurability of its form, style, and contents.[25] Later on, in the 1950s, younger critics, most of them born or raised in Israel with English as their second language, brought to the analysis of Hebrew literary texts the methods developed in the 1930s and 1940s by the British and American "new critics," such as I. A. Richards, William Empson, Cleanth Brooks, W. K. Wimsatt, and Monroe Beardsley. For a while, close readings as practiced by these critics became their *formme maitresse*, the chief critical genre these critics practiced.

Thus, clearly the record must be set straight. It was not that theory was not present before the emergence of the Tel Aviv structuralist school; it was continuously present, only its was not, with few exceptions, the formalist-structuralist theory this school swore by. True, the literary scholars and critics of the first half of the twentieth century were not in the habit of flaunting theoretical formulations. They resorted only occasionally to extensive disquisitions on abstract conceptual themes, but of course, they did resort to such topics. See, for example, Yehezkel Kaufman's magisterial philosophical-socio-cultural opus *Exile and Alienation* (1929–1930), in which he integrated extensive comments on Hebrew writing in the nineteenth and early twentieth centuries into his radical Zionist theory of Jewish culture under exilic conditions[26] or Shlomo Zemach's comprehensive philosophical monographs on major issues of aesthetics, such as the essence of the beautiful and of the comic;[27] and most of them were not inclined to practice formalistic analysis. But that was not because Hebrew and Yiddish critics and scholars of the period were either rejecting theory as such or unable to rise to the intellectual level that theory demanded as was sometimes intimated. The latter accusation was blatantly wrong, for in their erudition, mastery of several languages, exposure to and absorption of European culture, keen interest in four or five European literatures, and acquaintance with their socio-cultural backgrounds, the critics and scholars of the first half of the twentieth century had an enormous advantage over their Israeli detractors. As for sheer intellectual acumen and experience in conceptual thinking, scholars such as Sadan, Fishl Lakhover, Ch. N. Shapira, Kaufman, Vislavsky, Halkin, Viner, Yekhezkel Dobrushin, Erik, and Nachum Baruch Minkov, as well as critics such as Brenner, S. Zemach, Ya'akov Rabinovitsh, Rachel Katzenelson-Shazar, Ya'akov Fichman, Ya'akov Glatshteyn, Avraham Epshteyn, Avraham Kariv, Leah Goldberg, Shlomo Grodzensky, Moshe Litvakov, Yekhiel Yeshaya Trunk, and Yehoshua Rapoport—to mention only a few—would hardly need to tip their hats to any scholar or critic working in the second half of the century. No, their relative abstaining from overtly theoretical discourse had nothing to do with any dearth in talent, intellect, education, and erudition, not to speak of stylistic and expositional felicity, in which many of them could put to shame almost all those who came after them with the exception of a very few; for there can be little doubt that in whatever concerns the quality of the writing, its fluency and expressive power, there has been a general lowering of standards, which explains why much of the literary scholarship and criticism of the later part of the twentieth century, be it as important and interesting content-wise as it may, is so much less readable than what preceded it.

The abstinence from conceptualism and overt theoretical considerations was the direct result of the historical-cultural situation or situations in which the Jewish literatures had been created before the onset of World War II and the subsequent rise of the State of Israel. These situations were so drastically altered after the war, the Holocaust, and the establishing of the Jewish polity that most of us today can hardly conjure a vague mental image of their erstwhile reality. We have to exert ourselves, making a deliberate effort of the historical imagination to remind ourselves of how and what they were. For the purpose of doing that, it may be helpful to enumerate—not necessarily in the order of importance—four major factors, which having been very influential at the time, were eventually erased or submerged in the depth of the historical record by later developments and thus, pushed out of the space that is immediately visible to us.

First, as already noted, all or most of the Jewish scholars and critics of the first half of the twentieth century were raised in Europe in more than one language. Many of them received a university education in one of Europe's centers of knowledge: St. Petersburg, Berlin, Marburg, Heidelberg, Paris, Zurich, Bern, Lausanne. They spoke, read, and often also wrote in four languages or more (mainly Russian and German—in addition to, of course, Hebrew and Yiddish; scholars and critics raised in the United States also absorbed, in most cases, at least one additional European language to complement their English, and often they spoke Russian with members of the older generation of immigrants) and were steeped in the literatures written in those languages. With some of them, the ties with those languages and literatures was deep and emotionally charged, albeit more often than not also problematic. In any case, they faced no linguistic or mental barrier when they came to read literary studies written in the languages they mastered and on texts they knew well—both contemporary studies and those written in the past. Bialik read and was greatly impressed by the highly original investigations of poetic language written in the nineteenth century by A. A. Potbnja, the forgotten Russian theorist who was rescued from oblivion by the Russian symbolists,[28] as much as he read the theoretical writings of the symbolists themselves such as those of Andre Bely. Frishman read French and German symbolist and Nietzschean literary-theoretical writings. Berditchevsky was fully conversant in German aesthetics and critical literature. S. Zemach attended Henri Bergson's public lectures and steeped himself in current French, German, and Russian aesthetic and literary lore. Viner absorbed in the 1920s all modernist theoretical trends then current in Vienna, Berlin, and Zurich, and later delved into Marxist theory in both German and Russian. Others did not lag far behind. This fact in itself created a situation that made the developing of theoretical arguments in either Hebrew or Yiddish—with both languages still not ready for highly conceptualized literary discourse—quite unnecessary. The small community of Jewish scholars and literary critics had free access to such discourse in its original versions. Whereas the above mentioned periodical *Hasifrut* published translations and summaries of articles written fifty years earlier by Viktor Shklovsky and V. Vinogradov, the community of scholars and intellectuals active in the 1920s read the self-same articles as they appeared in the Leningrad periodicals of the Russian formalists. What to Israeli readers of the 1970s was excitingly new, was for those earlier intellectuals just one of the many contemporary voices that they heard, took into account, but did not feel the necessity to be guided by or bring to readers whom they knew were hardly open to this kind of literary analysis and theorizing.

Secondly, and more importantly, the scholarly study and critical evaluation of the Jewish literatures formed an integral part of the revolutionary projects that informed and shaped the literatures themselves. Since the literatures were to shoulder a burden no lighter than the replacing of the traditional Jewish cultural ethos, the one created and promulgated by the rabbinical-halakhic leadership or by the Hasidic establishment, with a new humanist ethos, their critics and scholars were self-evidently expected to do their share; and it was a formidable one, for the humanistic significance of the literary texts had to be elicited from them, separated from its imaginative aesthetic reifications, and articulated for the benefit of the readers in formulations the latter could easily grasp. To the same extent, the historical revolutionary significance of the relatively short "new" literary traditions (mostly perceived as having been spawned at the turn of the eighteenth century) had to be highlighted and summarized by the literary historians. This was essential if the literatures were to be used (as they were expected to be) for the purpose of educating generations of new cadres. This pertained to Yiddishist or socialist non-Zionist and anti-Zionist literary critics every bit as much as it was the assumed duty of Hebraic-Zionist ones. We should not understand this sense of mission that informed much of what was written on the Jewish literatures as necessarily resulting in propagandist flatness and the compromising of the critic's or the scholar's intellectual independence and integrity. Such was not the case at all. Whoever believes it to have been (as some so-called post-Zionists scholars seem to do), thinks in terms of historical models that are hardly relevant, such as those of literary criticism and scholarship evolving under totalitarian regimes rather than in the context of a genuine, non-coercive cultural revolution. The critics remained loyal to their aesthetic impressions and insights (some, like Frishman, professed their total subservience to purely aesthetic criteria); the literary scholars were bound by the historical facts as they understood them, as well as by what they believed to be the proper methodological principles by which the facts could be arranged and made sense of. Nevertheless, the previously mentioned sense of mission was pervasive and unavoidable. Even Frishman, the aesthete par excellence, as much as he felt free to judge the poems of Bialik as his aesthetics prescribed, and therefore—to the chagrin of other, more "nationalistic" critics—had to question the understanding of Bialik's leading literary and cultural role as that of the national poet, and to reject his prophetic effusions as undermining his genuine talent, which was that of a modern master of the lyrical—even he justified his adulation of lyricism in terms dictated by a sense of a national mission: only lyrical writing (the lyrical poem in particular), with its direct emotional impact, he maintained, would "revive" the "heart" of young Jews, wake them up to self awareness, and sublimate their raw emotions. As such, it would do its full share in the enhancing of the national so-called renaissance.[29] The same pertains—about two decades later—to the poet David Fogel, presumably a non-Zionist, individualistic poet who never allowed the Jewish collective themes to obfuscate his universalistic vision. However, Fogel offered in his novel *Conjugal Life* (1929–1930) the most ferocious anatomy of the failure of the assimilated Jewish intellectual (whose assimilatory cravings were exposed as emanating from dormant homosexuality) and justified his "lean" Hebrew and the poetics based on a minimalist approach to the linguistic medium as commensurate with Hebrew having become the spoken language of the new Jewish contingent in Palestine.[30] Thus the Hebrew and Yiddish critical projects, as a whole, were conceived of in terms of a national spiritual mission.

Naturally, a literary scholarship and a critical corpus that were forged in the smithy of modern Jewish nationalism and fraught with ideas and terms forming a part of the nationalist baggage, had to focus on national issues and essences as reflected in literary configurations rather than on the formal and structural aspects of the literary text. They had to ask questions pertaining to content and ideology rather than to form and artistic devices, such as: what was the writer's view of the national condition or situation; how did he or she understand the crises inherent in this situation; how did his or her characters and plot (in prose fiction) or the rhetoric and themes (in poetry) reflect this understanding; what were the writer's future perspectives, solutions, or premonitions, and so on? Many critics thought in terms of *basifrut uvakhayim*, (in literature and life, a combination they borrowed from Russian literary and cultural discourse), terms that indicated their interest in the relationships between literature and its socio-cultural background. The previously mentioned Frishman bestowed the highest praise on Abramovitsh's narrative art by telling how he read the author's novels while traveling in a train throughout the Jewish pale of settlement in the Czarist empire and, as he raised his eyes from the page and looked through the window, was unable to perceive a difference between real life and its fictional recreation, or by stating that if Jewish life in eastern Europe would somehow be erased and lost (an unintended dark prophecy), it would be possible to reconstruct it in all its details with the help of Abramovitsh's novels and short stories.[31] In a literary ambience in which the boundaries separating fact from fiction or emotion from its organized poetic articulation were all but erased, no aesthetics and poetics that predicated the autonomy of the literary artifact could gain popularity and become a widely used currency. The autonomous status of the work of art could not be respected when art was expected to directly bear on the burning issues of life.

Thus, although many of the critics and scholars were acquainted with formalism (or what was sometimes called in Poland "Pure Form") and its understanding of literary development as achieved through defamiliarization and renewal of perception, which, in themselves, were achieved through the employment of defamiliarizing structural and stylistic devices, very few of them could and wanted to follow its analytical procedures. Some did—for a while. Thus Erik, as already mentioned, launched his career as a critic with an extended formalist analysis of Peretz's symbolist dramas. M. Mezheritsky attempted a combination of Marxist and formalist analytical procedures in his essay on Abramovitsh's *Fishke the Lame* as a picaresque novel (1927).[32] However, these exceptions highlighted the strength of the norm. The critics would or could not abide by their early formalist preferences. The trajectory of Erik, which carried him first to positivist-nationalist projects such as his histories of the old Yiddish literature (1928) or the old Yiddish novella (1926), then toward a total identification with Marxism and the social-economic understanding of the literary phenomenon (for which he earned during the Stalinist purges of the late 1930s the wages of exile and ignominious death in the Gulag), is indicative in this respect.

Significantly, when the influence of formalism and its Anglo-American version, new criticism, made inroads in the late 1940s and then, with ever stronger impact, in the 1950s, into the teaching and the critical interpretation of Hebrew literature, it was a development the significance of which was not limited to the intellectual, aesthetic, and educational domains. Rather, it was a development with far-reaching social and political ramifications. Certainly opting for close reading of literary texts and for focusing on their formal arrangements went hand in hand with distancing oneself from the thermal center of the Zionist endeavor, with a cool attitude toward the nationalist ethos, an indifference that often bespoke rejection, if not downright disgust. Thus Strauss, the founding father of Israeli critical close reading, a member of the inner circle of Martin Buber's followers (he was the philosopher's son-in-law), who sought his Jewish identity in a Buberian neo-religiosity, was also affiliated with *Brit shalom*, a group of intellectuals and academicians who propagated the establishment of a binational Jewish-Arab state in Palestine and opposed the unilateral decision to declare the existence of a Jewish nation-state as a fait accompli and face an all-out military showdown with the Arab world (its leader, Judah Loeb Magnes, went to Washington in the winter of 1948, when the war in Palestine was already revving up toward its most bloody phase of the spring and early summer of that year, in a last minute attempt to avert the "catastrophe" of D. Ben Gurion's declaration of May 14th by the prospect of American disfavor and a refusal to grant the new state its recognition). Strauss, like Buber, was deeply critical of the war and of the exiling of 600,000 Arab inhabitants of Palestine and gave poignant expression to his opposition and moral outrage in the poems he wrote at the time.[33] Kurzweil was a disciple of the Frankfurt new orthodoxy as it was updated and interpreted by its twentieth-century ideologue Isaac Breuer, an anti-Zionist, who regarded modern Jewish secularism as a fatal breach in the continuity of Jewish culture. He too viewed the militarization of Zionism and the etatist cult that flourished in the new Jewish state with suspicion and foreboding.

As for the young critics of the 1950s, for instance, the poet Nathan Zach, who at this early phase of his career was known primarily as a literary critic, they were perhaps the first articulators of what might be called the post-Zionist mood. It has often been remarked that Zach's harsh critique of Nathan Alterman's "mechanical" rhythms and decorative imagery was more than anything a socio-political critique disguised as a prosodic and formal analysis; a critique targeted at the core of inhumanity and indifference to the travails of the individual and the society in their mundane, day-to-day existence, which the poet-critic ascribed to D. Ben Gurion's "visionary" etatism, and which, he believed, were reflected in the aesthetics of Alterman's poetry. Zach's alternative tradition, his critical project of reshuffling the Hebrew poetic canon and moving to its center erstwhile presumably marginal figures such as Fogel, Avraham Ben-Yitskhak, Gabriel Preil, and others,[34] was aimed at turning the attention of readers away from the paragons of Zionist poetry to poets who, whether they adhered or did not adhere to Zionism as private citizens, refrained in their poetry from absorbing the Zionist pathos and dwelling on Zionist themes. Where his

choice of a candidate for the alternative poetic tradition did not altogether dovetail with a presumed indifference to Zionist emphases, as
in the case of Ya'akov Shteynberg (a member of the second aliya and
a writer who was close to *Hapo'el hatsa'ir*, the non-Marxist Socialist-
Zionist party), Zach simply "de-Zionized" him as he did by selectively
anthologizing Shteynberg's poetic corpus, removing from it all Zionist "excesses," and then, basing his critical argument on the selection
he himself had fashioned, pointed to Shteynberg's austere individualism as the gist of his work and his legacy.[35] Where this could not be
done, as in the case of Greenberg, Zach made a point of relating only
to the universalistic, understated, and dispirited segments in the poets'
corpus, such as Greenberg's sequel "Anacreon on the Pole of Sorrow,"
while disregarding all the rest.[36] Other critics and scholars indicated,
each in his own manner, similar—or what could be seen as similar—
preferences. Thus, for instance, my own decision as a budding scholar
in the 1950s and 1960s to study Hebrew literature within the context
of a more comprehensive Jewish non-Hebraic literary complex, and
to invest in Yiddish literature scholarly efforts that were as intensive
and demanding as those expected from whomever aspired to achieve a
level of scholarly expertise in the field of Hebrew literary studies, could
be—and was—interpreted as non-Zionist if not anti-Zionist. Thus, a
cultural-political message could be codified in close readings of some
of the psalms, of poems written by the great medieval masters, of
poems written by Bialik and Tchernikhovsky, or of prose-fiction texts
by Abramovitsh, Gnessin, Brenner, and Agnon.

Thirdly, during the period here under discussion, Jewish literatures
were created against the backdrop of fierce ideological struggles and
in the atmosphere of clashes and acrimonious polemics. There was no
real choice of remaining neutral, of not taking sides, because omis-
sions or no reaction were almost as politically indicative as were commitments and declared partisanships. Whoever was about to launch a
career as a Jewish writer was immediately faced by a series of choices
he or she had to make, with each of the choices made pitting him or
her against those who rejected it or preferred another one to it. First
and foremost one had to opt for a specific linguistic matrix. The choice
here, whether made after conscious deliberation or intuitively based

on preferences not brought to a conceptual level and thus remaining largely inarticulate, had momentous implications; for the choice of language amounted to a choice of a cultural Jewish future. By making this choice, a writer intentionally or unwittingly expressed faith in a specific brand of a Jewish cultural future: it was to be a Hebraic (and therefore, necessarily, Zionist) future in which a new Jewish national culture would be based on the millennia-long Hebraic tradition going all the way back to the Bible; or it would be a Yiddish-speaking (and therefore, necessarily, exilic or territorialist, i.e., either guided by the belief that Jewish cultural autonomy could be maintained within non-Jewish states and host-societies, or by the belief that an independent Jewish community, forming the majority within its own state or within an autonomous region, was indispensable for the preservation of Jewish national life and culture; only it could not be located in Palestine and wax Hebraic), modern, secular culture based on the collective memory, folklore, and social history of eastern European Ashkenazic Jews; or it would be a culture developed in a non-Jewish language, such as Russian, German, and later on, English, and whether anti-Zionist, non-Zionist, or even Zionist (for the founding fathers of political Zionism projected an independent Jewish community living in its own *Judenstadt*, but conversing and evolving its culture in a modern European language, preferably, German), it was based on the reality of Jewish cultural merging with non-Jewish modern, industrialized societies such as those that flourished in Western Europe or North America; or it based itself on what was seen as a fertile Jewish/non-Jewish cultural symbiosis, such as the one envisioned by some German-Jewish, anti-nationalist, and anti-Zionist philosophers and writers (the formidable example of the neo-Kantian philosopher Herman Cohen comes to mind) or by Jewish-Russian intellectuals such as Mikhail O. Gershonzon.

After the linguistic choice was made, the writer had to prepare himself or herself for the charges and ridicule he would have to fend off. If the choice was Hebrew, he or she would have to face the charges that he or she chose to write in a dead language, inaccessible to most living Jews, indifferent to the fate of the masses, unable, because of its stiffness, bookishness, and antiquity, to articulate the current Jewish condition, and, on top of all that, objectively reactionary because of its historical association with the clerical past, with religion, liturgy, the synagogue, the middle ages. If the choice had been Yiddish, he or she would be told that he or she chose to write in a language with no significant literary tradition, a provincial vernacular severed from the cultural past and therefore unable to project the cultural future; a language that is already being undermined and obliterated by a progressively accelerating process of acculturation, which eventually would render inevitable its total replacement by the non-Jewish language of a given host society—German, French, Russian, English; for this had been the fate of all Jewish jargons, shed, sloughed off, and forgotten when cultural circumstances changed, whereas Hebrew, the true national language, was kept alive, albeit unspoken. If the choice fell on a non-Jewish language, he or she would be told that he or she opted to use a language that was not rooted in the national essence, and that therefore could touch only the surface of a Jewish theme, never evoking the subtle nuances and associations that only the memory inherent in a national language could conjure; moreover, his or her linguistic choice, whether he or she willed it or not, smacking of assimilation and objectively weakening the national spirit, would at the same time never result in a genuine and fruitful cultural symbiosis and thus allot them a niche in the cultural tradition of the host society they wished to join. This criticism would be proliferated not only by Zionists, Hebraists, and Yiddishists, but also by some of the very same Jewish writers who chose to write–or regarded themselves as unable not to write–in a non-Jewish language. Thus Franz Kafka, as we shall see, told his fellow German-Jewish writers that their attempt at severing themselves from their Jewishness and immersing themselves in Germanity was futile and doomed to failure.[37]

True, in the 1890s and the first decade of the twentieth century, it seemed for a short while, that making the choice between Hebrew and Yiddish was not obligatory. And that one could be creative in both languages, as the literary practices of some of the literary luminaries of the day, particularly Sh. Y. Abramovitsh and Y. L. Peretz, seemed to prove. This important episode, which gave rise to a theory predicating the continuity and unity of a single bilingual Hebrew-Yiddish literature, is discussed later in this volume. However, when World War I broke out, and actually already before then, it became obvious that the bilingual option was imaginary and that erstwhile bilingual writers could no longer evade the linguistic choice that had been inherent in their work even before they acted on it. Thus Sholem Asch, Hersh Dovid Nomberg, Avraham Reysen, and other writers, who had made bilingual debuts at the beginning of the twentieth century, became one hundred percent Yiddishists. Others, like Ya'akov Shteynberg or Aharon Reuveni and later Greenberg, all of them upcoming Yiddish or Hebrew-Yiddish young writers, left their Yiddish past behind them once they made aliya and became committed Hebraists. There were some exceptional cases, such as that of Zalman Shneur, who was a Hebrew poet and a Yiddish writer of prose fiction, but such cases became progressively marginal and indicative of a certain block or schism in the development of the "schizoid" writer's literary personality. In the case of Shneur, it probably had to do with the poet's failure to find a place for himself in Palestine of the 1920s, as well as perhaps his resentment of the far from triumphant reception given to him after Bialik and Tchernikhovsky became the crowned heirs-apparent of the new Hebrew-speaking community there. Thus, in the second half of the 1920s, he shifted his creative energy, pushing Hebrew poetry to the backburner and focusing on Yiddish prose fiction, becoming one of the most popular Yiddish novelists of the inter-bellum period. Even Shneur's lingering bilingualism, therefore, illustrated the petering out of the bilingual option. Essentially all writers had to make a choice, which was interpreted as a vote of confidence, whether they meant or did not mean it as such. When Judd (Yehuda Leyb) Teller, the bright hope of modernist Yiddish-American poetry in the 1930s, for example, switched over in the 1940s to writing in English, the switch was justifiably interpreted (and bitterly commented upon) as indicative of the young writer's loss of faith in the survival of Yiddish in America.

Once a linguistic choice had been made, the prospective Jewish writer encountered a new series of options that demanded commitments and taking sides. During the inter-bellum decades he or she could not, for instance, just choose to write in Yiddish. He or she had also to opt for a certain understanding of the *meaning* of Yiddish writing, and the option preferred inevitably impacted the writing and its reception. For what *was* Yiddish? Was it a national (if not *the* national) Jewish language and the proper vehicle for the flourishing of a modern Jewish national culture, as the Yiddishist activists who convened in August 1908 in Czernowicz, Bukovina, declared it to be? Or was it the language of the oppressed Jewish proletariat, as well as other exploited and marginalized minorities (like women)—vis-à-vis the non-Jewish languages spoken by the assimilated Jewish plutocracy, the rabbinical Hebrew through which the clerical establishment (historically the ally of the plutocracy) conducted its halakhic business, or the modern, quasi-secularized Hebrew favored by the chauvinistic lower-middle class? As a national language, Yiddish should prompt its writers to articulate the entire historical, national Jewish experience (seen, of course, from a modern humanist-nationalist vantage point), root themselves in the Bible and the other sacrosanct, ancient texts, as Peretz, the Yiddishists' mentor,[38] demanded, re-translate and adapt these ancient and medieval texts into modern Yiddish (as did the poet "Yeho'ash" [Shlomo Blumgarten] in his translation of the Bible,[39] the journalist and scholar Simcha B. Petrushka in his translation of the Mishna,[40] or the poet Y. Y. Shvarts [Israel Jacob Schwartz] in his translations from medieval and modern classical Hebrew poetry),[41] and present the nation, in spite of all inner differences and conflicts, as a living historical organism, as for instance, did Asch in his metaphorical prose-poem *Dos shtetl* (The Hamlet, 1904). As a language of an oppressed class, its writers should expose the vacuity of the myth of Jewish historical unity, as did Itshe Mayer Vaysenberg in his superb metonymic-synecdochal novella *A Shtetl* (*A Hamlet*, 1905), a fierce rebuttal of Asch's harmonistic vision, search the old traditions for the democratic and rebellious elements inherent in them, the only ones worthy of preservation, enhance class consciousness and class struggle, and so on. Whoever chose the first definition had to bond with the Yiddishists, whether in Poland and other eastern European countries or in the Americas; whereas the choice of the other inevitably allied the chooser with the radical Jewish left, and after 1917, the Jewish communist groups taking their cue from Moscow, that were at the time very noisy and active in western countries, and particularly in North America.

Having made this second choice, the contemporary Yiddish writer and literary critic often faced yet another one. The Yiddish establishment in the Soviet Union, for example, was, at least for a certain time, split between Marxists-fundamentalists, so to speak, who accused their rivals of revisionism (in the sense this term was used in socialist circles) and lingering nationalist sympathies, and more seasoned and nuanced Marxists, who retorted by accusing their accusers with "vulgar," unsophisticated, and non-dialectical Marxism. The first group believed in a revolutionary Yiddish literature that cut itself loose of the irredeemable clerical and bourgeois pasts, both tarnished by reactionary trends to the point that any contact with them was contaminating.[42] The second group quoted comments made by Marx and Engels on quintessential bourgeois writers such as Balzac, who, in spite of their reactionary attitudes, pointed in their realistic portrayal of bourgeois society to the inevitability of the future victory of socialism. They demanded a sophisticated approach to the cultural and literary past, which would differentiate between its reactionary components and the ones that, under the historical circumstances of the period, could be regarded as democratic or progressive.[43] The critics and scholars in this second group paid much attention to the masters of bourgeois Yiddish literature of the nineteenth century. Both groups acrimoniously attacked the nationalist Yiddish literature produced in Poland and America and particularly the non-communist Yiddish literary scholarship, which as mentioned previously, they labeled fascist.[44]

Those who joined the Hebrew camp had to make choices of their own. As mentioned previously, their choice necessarily involved some form of cultural Zionism. If a genuine differentiation between Hebraism and Zionism still had been possible at the advent of the Zionist movement during the last two decades of the nineteenth century—when quite a few Hebrew or Hebrew-Yiddish writers, such as Abramovitsh and Peretz did not commit themselves to Zionism and were critical of it—the differentiation disappeared together with the era that came to an end with the start of World War I. Before the war, a central literary figure such as the previously mentioned critic Frishman could, with some effort, propagate a Hebraic national renaissance, the fate of which was presumably independent of the fortunes of Zionism as a political movement. After the war and the Balfour declaration of 1917, such a separation became untenable. Even those few Hebrew writers who evinced an attitude of relative indifference to Zionism's political struggles and goals could not withhold recognition from and deference to the reality of a Hebrew-speaking community in Zionist Palestine as the custodian of Hebraic culture and the natural audience the Hebrew writer, wherever one chose to live and whatever one's stylistic tonality or the objects of one's mimetic art were. The previously mentioned example of Fogel, a non-Zionist (having emigrated to Palestine in 1928, he quickly left it to those who were willing to suffer the heat of the *hamsin* and the bites of mosquitoes and resumed his clochard-like existence in Paris), who nevertheless defended his stylistic choices with Zionist arguments, speaks for itself. The American-Hebrew poet Preil, although he rarely treated Zionist themes in his poems and shied away from all forms of pathos, progressively injected into the language of his poetry the prosaic quality of spoken Palestinian Hebrew, as well as its musical inflections. In this way, he made his commitment to the Zionist project apparent in a manner that was by far subtler and at the same time more substantial than that of some of his overtly American Zionistic colleagues. In this way, he also vouchsafed the readability of his poetry in the Israel of the second half of the twentieth century. By and large all Hebrew writers who lived out of Palestine during the interbellum period, and so much more so after World War II and the founding of the State of Israel, acknowledged the cultural supremacy of the Palestinian-Israeli center, not only by absorbing much of its ethos but mainly through streamlining their Hebrew in accordance with the Israeli spoken idiom, dropping their use of the Ashkenazic Hebrew that had been used by their predecessors (as well as by themselves in earlier phases of their literary activity) and adopting the Israeli Sephardic accentuation and pronunciation, a shift that triggered nothing less than a musical revolution in Hebrew verse.[45]

Having said that, one must add, that in the inter-bellum period, Zionism itself became an arena, where fierce ideological and political struggles took place. Even at the beginning of the twentieth century, right after the emergence of Theodore Herzl's World Zionist Organization in 1897, Zionism was polarized by conflicting trends and definitions of purpose, as prove the struggles between political Zionism (Herzl, Max Nordau, Berditchevsky, to the limited extent that this writer can be deemed a Zionist, and most western European Zionists), cultural or spiritual Zionism (Achad ha'am, Buber, Chaim Weizmann), religious Zionism (Yitskhak Ya'akov [Isaac Jacob] Raynes, Samuel Mohliver, Yechiel Michael Pines), socialist Zionism (Nachman Syrkin, Ber Borokhov, D. Ben Gurion, Berl Katzenelson), and "cosmic" Zionism (the philosopher Aaron David Gordon and his followers). Nevertheless, some kind of Zionist literary consensus (like the one personified by Bialik) was still maintainable. After the war, as the Zionist dream was being gradually reified in mandatory Palestine, this consensus was shattered, as Bialik himself learned to his chagrin in 1931 when his cultural leadership was resoundingly challenged by both the Palestinian modernist literary rebels, headed by Eliezer Shteynman and Avraham Shlonsky, and by the Zionists revisionists headed by Jabotinsky, Bialik's erstwhile admirer and brilliant translator into Russian. Each of these Zionisms had literary and stylistic proclivities of its own. Thus, the so-called general Zionism, more or less the heir of Herzl's political Zionism and now, in a more pragmatic version, led politically by Chaim Weizmann, based its cultural model on the poetry of Bialik and the literary conventions of the poet's Odessa entourage (for which Bialik received permission from Stalin in 1921 to leave the Soviet Union and emigrate to Palestine, through the intercession of Maxim Gorky). The literature and style that were associated with this group were guided by the pre-war achievements of writers who were now old or middle-aged. They represented the old guard, what the rebels sardonically referred to as "Odessa depalestina" (the Palestinian Odessa) — romantic in its poetry, realistic in its prose fiction, thematically concerned with what had been *there* rather than with what was evolving *here*, stylistically keeping to the synthesis achieved by Abramovitsh and Bialik—the dexterous mingling of biblical, Mishnaic, Talmudic, and Midrashic vocabulary and syntactical structures, and thus available only to whomever had had a yeshiva education, that is, neither to women, who now made their voices heard, particularly in Hebrew poetry, nor to members of the young generation who had gone through modern Hebrew education, whether in Palestine or still in eastern Europe. Jabotinsky's Zionist Revisionists, who because of their rejection of Zionist evolutionism and demand for the establishment of a Jewish state in all of by now partitioned Palestine regarded themselves as the "true" heirs of Herzl, favored an altogether different literary and stylistic approach. Their leader, himself a brilliant Russian writer with no Jewish education at all, opted for everything that was new, non-exilic, and action-oriented. He was one of the most articulate and influential defenders of the proposition that the Palestinian Sephardic accentuation and pronunciation of Hebrew, with its virile emphasis on the ultimate syllable in the word, would replace the softer and more feminine Ashkenazic counterpart, with its emphasis on the penultimate syllable and its tendency to replace some vowels by diphthongs. The latter sounded too close to Yiddish, which Jabotinsky loathed, as he confessed in his autobiography.[46] In his Hebrew prose and extraordinary translations of romantic and symbolist American and European poetry, he rejected all intertextuality that smacked of yeshiva erudition and favored a modern, transparent, relatively simple, and direct style—a parallel on the stylistic level to his political demand for action, military organization, and a policy of pressure and blunt demands to the British government and its Palestinian emissaries to live up to the promises of the Balfour declaration and the language and spirit of the mandate Britain was granted by the League of Nations to rule and administer Palestine in a way that would enhance the building of the "national home" there for Jews. Jabotinsky's disciples, among them some budding writers, were inspired by the leader's lean, muscular, and disciplined style. However, when Greenberg joined the revisionists in 1930, he brought with him to the political party, whose literary spokesman he became, an altogether different stylistic and literary flavor, that of the stormy expressionism that had engulfed Yiddish and Hebrew poetry in the wake of World War I and the civil wars it triggered—a style characterized by unbridled pathos, Whitmanesque loquacity, the abrogation of traditional aesthetic strictures, free rhythms, and mixed metaphors. Although Greenberg himself, now writing political poetry, reined himself in stylistically for the purpose of being fully communicative and immediately effective,[47] his stormy presence changed the tonality of the revisionist discourse, particularly of those in the movement who now deviated from Jabotinsky's nationalist liberalism and absorbed some tenets of the fascism of the 1930s.

Also, Greenberg, in contradistinction to Jabotinsky, was steeped in Yiddish and Jewish religious lore, emotionally still part of both the Polish Yiddish-speaking shtetl and the groups of pioneers in the kibbutzim of the Jezrael valley who were socialists and stalwart supporters of leftist Labor Zionism. A part of the young adherents of the revisionist movement, particularly the part that eventually organized itself around the anti-British underground militia known as *Lekhi*, or—to the British— as the Stern Gang, became his followers, and the revisionists started to speak in two distinct and different voices.

As for Labor Zionism, it too spoke in more than one literary voice. With most of its cultural agencies presided over by its mentor and ideologue Berl Katzenelson, its literary politics were basically conservative. Whereas Katzenelson, the chief exponent of the mentality of the second aliya, was able to appreciate the revolutionary modernism of Greenberg (who had been affiliated with Labor Zionism before his switch to the radical right wing), he was committed to an egalitarian culture accessible to the workers and expressive of their concerns and thus unreceptive to modernist experimentalism, Hermetism, and individualism. Unlike A. D. Gordon, who had thought that literature in Palestine should be written by manual workers as an extension of their physical and mental encounter with the elements, Katzenelson accepted a literature written by sophisticated professional writers, provided it was spiritually attuned to and politically aligned with the workers. In addition, Katzenelson believed in Jewish continuity and favored writers whose poetic or narrative world was recognizably Jewish, such as Agnon. These were the principles that guided the cultural politics of *Davar*, the official Labor Zionist newspaper (whose editor Katzenelson was), and its influential literary supplement (edited by Katzenelson's trusted literary critic and activist Dov Shtok, later Sadan), as well as the publishing houses Katzenelson founded and controlled. Among other things, these policies prescribed total rejection of the modernist, neo-symbolist style promulgated by Shlonsky (an erstwhile protégé) and his disciples, Goldberg and Alterman, which Katzenelson branded as elitist, faddish, uncommunicative, focused on avant-garde Paris rather than on the Zionist project in Palestine, disconnected from the Jewish ambience, past and present, and fashionably despondent, where optimism

curbed by realism was what an upcoming community of pioneers and
workers needed. This rejection proved to be Katzenelson's big cultural-
political miscalculation.

However, his powerful presence was not the only influential one
in the cultural domain of Labor Zionism. In many of the agricultural
settlements, a somewhat different cultural approach was adopted consisting of a much less sophisticated understanding of cultural egalitarianism. Here a demand arose for a simple and immediately consumable
literary fare with an all but exclusive emphasis on the experiences of
agricultural labor and salubrious exposure to nature. The model upon
which this brand of Labor Zionist literature based itself was the poetry
of Rachel Bluvstein, the popular poetess from Kinneret, who died of
tuberculosis in 1931. A sophisticated disciple of the Russian Acmeists,
such as Anna Akhmatova, Bluvstein (herself Katzenelson's darling and
the literary mascot of *Davar*) made full use of the politics of simplicity, emotional straightforwardness, and figurative minimalism, while
writing poems that looked much simpler than they really were.[48] Her
self-appointed disciples took her at face value and produced a literature
(mainly poetry) that was stylistically and formally old fashioned and
thematically quite limited.

In contradistinction, the radical leftist *Hashomer hatsa'ir*, a movement
with a penchant for intellectualism and modernity (to its Marxist orientation, it added an alliance with psychoanalysis, which influenced the
educational system developed in its kibbutzim), evolved cultural politics that were diametrically opposed to those of the other segments of
Labor Zionism. After some years of indistinct literary production that
was not much different from that of the other collectivist agricultural
settlements, it bonded, in a surprising turnover, with the neo-symbolist
modernists. Much to the chagrin of some of its ideologues (including
Avraham Ya'ari, its political mentor), it gave Shlonsky (whom a few
years earlier its spokesmen had branded as an uprooted nihilist) the keys
to its literary fiefdom basing itself on the model of the historical align-
ments between socialist movements and the exponents of experimental
modernism (such as the Bolshevik-Mayakovsky connection). Of course,
the modernists themselves (Shlonsky, Goldberg, Raphael Eliaz et al.)
were ready at this juncture (against the darkening backdrop of a Europe

sliding into fascism, an impending world war, and the existential threat to the survival of Europe's Jews) to abandon their erstwhile individualism and commit themselves to socialism and its concept of progressive culture. Whereas the movement of the modernists toward such a commitment formed part of the general sea change then re-shaping the landscape of western art and literature (e.g., the leftist-modernist connection in the United States of the depression era or the bonding of eminent surrealists like Louis Aragon and Paul Eluard and of cubists such as Pablo Picasso with the French Communist Party), the similar development in Zionist Palestine had surprising results. It was the single most successful cultural-political move the radical Zionist left had ever made. Under the guidance of Shlonsky, the best literary educator, editor, and translator of the period, *Hashomer hatsa'ir* and its publications became the seminary where an almost entire new literary generation, the so-called *Palmakh* generation (called after the elite commando unit of the *Hagana*, the official paramilitary organization of the Zionist contingent in Palestine) sprouted. Robbing the cultural initiative from almost all other contemporary movements, *Hashomer hatsa'ir*, until then a rather marginal entity, now "owned" —for more than a decade— the better part of the young, mostly Israeli-born, intelligentsia, a fact that had far-reaching political implications, as D. Ben Gurion, a sworn rival, was quick to detect and do everything in his power to stymie and deflect. It rendered the neo-symbolist style of Shlonsky and Alterman, with its emphasis on striking, non-referential figurative language, strictly monitored (through meter, rhyming, and controlled euphony) musical apparatus, and symbolist essentialism, the mainstream style of Hebrew and Israeli poetry until its rejection in the late 1950s by a new generation of Israeli poets and critics, members of the so-called State Generation.

There were other, smaller, enclaves in the Zionist-cultural map, such as that of *Hamizrakhi*, the religious Zionists, who of course favored a culture and a literature close to the religious tradition, the context of the *piyut* (the liturgical poem written for synagogal use), and the mentality of the Midrashic sources. Whereas their literary aspirations were best represented by the extraordinary (albeit often of an uneven artistic level) ecstatic religious expressionism of Yosef Zvi Rimon, a marginal poet of considerable interest, the contemporary prose fiction they allowed into their separate educational system consisted mainly of the pseudo-pietistic, quasi-legendary stories of Agnon, simplistically taken at face value. At the opposite edge of the cultural map were the Young Hebrews, or the Canaanites, as Shlonsky pejoratively labeled them, headed by the magnificent symbolist poet Yonatan Rattosh, originally a radical revisionist who belonged to the proto-fascist group in Jabotinsky's movement, who had also absorbed the artistic influence of Shlonsky and the French symbolists, and produced the most successful collection of hermetic symbolist poems ever written in Hebrew, *Khupa shekhora* (*Black Canopy*, 1941). His hauntingly suggestive musicality, neologistic, presumably pre-biblical Hebrew, as well as the symbolic world he created, where archetypes from the ancient Canaanite pantheon conveyed the tragic existentialism of the modern rebel, committed to *action directe*, life and death by the sword, and burgeoning sexuality, went together with a radical ideology, which was at the same time anti-British and anti-Zionist. Rattosh predicated the birth of a new Hebrew nation in Palestine, cut off from its Jewish and Zionist roots and bound on uniting the Israeli-born Jews (the first new Hebrews) together with the other Semites of the fertile crescent within a new Semitic national movement with a Hebraic culture of its own, based on that of the ancient pre-monotheist western Semitic civilization. After chasing European colonialism out of the Middle East, as well as Judaism and pan-Islamism, this movement would establish a new Hebrew empire stretching throughout the space separating the Euphrates from the Nile. With no political influence whatever, the group nevertheless had a considerable cultural and literary impact, and Rattosh's thesis, differentiating between Zionist literature (which he labeled "Jewish Literature in the Hebrew Language") and a genuine new Hebrew national literature[49] seemed for a while acceptable to part of the young Israeli intelligentsia.

Thus Hebraism was as much (if not more) splintered and internally contentious than Yiddishism. It lived and evolved in a combustible atmosphere of polemics and ideological-literary bickering. This was also the atmosphere in which literary criticism and scholarship evolved (which, again, does not mean that critics and scholars directly followed party lines; the impact of the ideological strife was, in the cases of the subtler critics and better scholars, tangential, indirect, but for this very reason also more osmotic or pervasive). In this atmosphere, critics and scholars were called upon not only to offer well-argued and illustrated diagnoses of literature as they believed it to be or to have been in the past. They also had to formulate prognoses, draw future perspectives, direct, guide, warn, pontificate. Whereas they were not expected to do that in the jargon and tone of the propagandist (this does not take into account critics who did evoke such jargon and tone, being, in fact, the cultural commissars of political parties; there were quite a few of these), and scholars were certainly expected to abide by scholarly methodologies, they could not but participate in the heated cultural dialogue. It was not by accident that at least two of the most prominent Hebrew literary scholars of the time were openly identified with political parties: Klausner with the Zionist revisionists and Sadan with official Labor Zionism. Yiddishist scholars (even out of the Soviet Union, where political commitment was inevitable) were more often than not associated with political groups (such as the Bund in Poland and America; Trunk was a party member, and M. Weinreich was a fellow traveler). This led to the fact, that almost all contemporary scholars and literary critics also developed sideline activities as journalists or what was then called publicists (i.e., commentators on current events and topics of public interest), and with some of the most prominent among them, such as Sadan, Rabinovitsh, S. Zemach, Kaufmann, Niger, Weinreich, Rivkin, Litvakov, and many others, the weight of their *publitsistika* within their respective overall intellectual projects by far exceeds what it is nowadays believed to be).

In our time, there is no need to insist on the acknowledgement of the all but self-evident fact, that all cultural and literary studies are in one way or another permeated by ideological undercurrents. We also know for a fact that the more theoretical a study is, the more ideology-oriented it must be. Nevertheless, we should not lose sight of the difference between such an inevitable orientation and the openly declared ideologism of the nature we have described. With the study of culture and literature being so inherently fraught with fierce ideological and political tensions, quantity (the measure of ideological involvement) becomes quality. We can hardly expect to encounter, in situations such as the ones in which Jewish literary studies of the period under discussion were conducted, a scholarly discourse sequestered in its academic enclave, protected from the concerns of "the madding crowd" by high fences of professional jargon and a high level of abstraction, conceptualization, and attention to minute technical considerations of which is bound to render it inaccessible to the wide reading public. Of course, the work of the Tel Aviv structuralists was as ideology-oriented as that of earlier literary scholars (its ideological ramifications, I trust, have been sufficiently clarified); however, its ideological orientation found expression in a way that was altogether different from the one those earlier scholars had taken—by far more indirect, round about, and hidden behind masks of purported objectivity. We must remind ourselves that the wearing of such masks was impossible or unacceptable in the first half of the twentieth century, when even the most learned and technical discourse, supposedly targeted at a limited community of professionals, almost never lost sight of the larger reading public, which expected from the scholar not only knowledge, but guidance as well.

Hence the fourth factor, that of the reading public and of the scholar's or critic's dialogue with it. It was in many ways a peculiar reading public; an essentially Ashkenazic and eastern European one, it was modeled after the Russian intelligentsia and thus largely unlike historical Western reading publics; that is, it was a much less stratified reading public than that which can be broken into the habitual categories: readers who read (mostly popular fiction) for entertainment and diversion; readers who read serious, canonical fiction and poetry for the purpose of emotional engagement and intellectual stimulation; readers who read (popular histories, biographies, etc.) for information and orientation; the fewer, more intellectual readers, who were interested in and able to read highly ideational, conceptualized, and scholarly non-fiction, and so on. Of course, the reading public we discuss here consisted of readers of all the aforementioned kinds, but the boundaries among these separate strata of the reading public were blurred. The same reader could be a rather naive reader of canonical fiction and at the same time be interested in philosophy, which if he could not read in its original articulations would be looking for relatively popular and more communicative summaries of the arcane philosophical arguments. For example, he would not be able to follow Nietzsche's arguments as they were developed in the philosopher's aphoristic works, but he would avidly read Georg Brandes's popular presentation of Nietzsche's ideas, or he would at least read a newspaper article on Georg Brandes's monograph. We are talking about readers who were in most cases autodidacts, with no university or even high school systematic education, and yet they were thirsty for knowledge, which they expected literature, in the broad sense of the term (including non-fiction and even journalism), to supply; and, as said before, they expected from their literature much more than knowledge and emotional sublimation. Only in the Russia of the nineteenth century could a novel appear under the title *What's to Be Done?* (by the literary critic and publicist Nikolay Chernyshevsky from which readers expected and received straightforward directives to be followed in their social, intellectual, and emotional life). By the same token, Hebrew literature written in Russia at the turn of the century could reach a defining moment with the publication (in 1898) of a novella written by the young writer Mordecai Ze'ev Feierberg, whose title *Le'an?* (wither; where to?) related not only to the perplexity and confusion of its troubled protagonist, but also, directly to those of the troubled readers.

This was then a reading public who looked up to literature (including fiction and poetry), expecting it to tell it what to do and where to go; and if the message of imaginative literature was not direct and clear enough, this reading public turned to its literary critics and scholars and expected them to tell them in so many words what this message, hidden behind the symbolic and mythical screens in poems such as Bialik's "Dead of the Desert" or "The Scroll of Fire," or underneath the mimetic surface of a novel by Abramovitsh or a short story by Berditchevsky, was. The critic's article that purported to elucidate this message would be read with almost the same interest that the original imaginative text had given rise to and sometimes trigger gut reactions that were even stronger than those that had followed the reading of the more ambivalent and multilayered original texts. Certainly the Russian critics of the nineteenth century caused as much excitement and controversy as any of the literary giants they discussed. The same held true for Hebrew critics and essayists, such as Achad ha'am, Berditchevsky, Frishman, and Brenner, whose pronouncements were as eagerly expected as were Bialik's poems and Brenner's novels. The reading public we are talking about amounted in many ways to a writer's dream and a critic's paradise. Never was literary criticism less sequestered and less limited in its appeal than in Russia of the nineteenth century and the Jewish-Russian literary republics of the first half of the twentieth century.

However, this popularity and sense of immediate relevance had a flip side and exacted a price: the price of an inherent tendency to simplify and popularize. Critics attempted to close the gap between writing and colloquy. Following in the wake of the nineteenth-century subgenre of the critical causerie (chat), best exemplified by Saint Beuve's well-known Monday's literary chats (*causeries de lundi*), which earned for the French critic such appellations as "the prince of critics" or "Uncle Beuve." Hebrew and particularly Yiddish critics waxed intimate and chatty with their readers. Frishman, as mentioned previously, wrote some of his most incisive criticism in the form of faux-personal letters to a woman friend or as feuilletons. Yiddish critics threw precise, conceptual language to the winds and adopted a *zaftik* (juicy), idiomatic, colloquial discourse that sat better in the mouths of a Mendele Moykher Seforim or a Sholem Aleichem, the classic loquacious personae of nineteenth-century fiction, than on the tip of the pens of critics who insisted on writing their articles in the form of *shmusen iber bikher* (chats about books).[50] The scholar, too, had to accommodate a reading public devoid of intellectual preparation; a public that had to be led by the hand, talked down to in abecedarian terms. In Hebrew, an existing tradition of conceptual discourse mitigated this drawback, but there, too, it often flattened and simplified both critical and scholarly writing about literature. Paradoxically, the only place where this happened to a much lesser degree was the Soviet Union, where the need to talk to the masses was part of the state's religion. There, more than anywhere else, critics and literary scholars allowed themselves the use of the Marxist jargon, which was essentially the jargon of mid-nineteenth-century German post-Hegelian philosophy. Perhaps resorting to this jargon was a vital precaution in the Soviet Union, for there one had to incessantly flaunt one's ideological credentials, to parade one's loyalty to the up-to-the-last-minute reformulation of the party's official version of correct Marxist argumentation.

In any case, the intensive relationship between the literary commentator and the reading public of the period was, to a very large extent, responsible for the relative paucity or dilution of the conceptual component in contemporary meta-literary discourse. Characteristically, where the relationship between critic/scholar and a wide reading public was less intensive, the rudiments of such a discourse emerged. For instance, Ch. N. Shapira, relatively closeted in his academic position as a teacher of a small and select group of young intellectuals (the Kaunas Hebraic group that included members such as Goldberg, Shimon Gans, Daniel Ben Nachum, and E. D. Shapir), could develop in his *History of Modern Hebrew Literature* a discourse by far more abstract and scholarly than the ones employed in Warsaw and Israel by the authors of similar histories such as Klausner, Lakhover, and Aharon Orinovsky or, indeed, by himself in the articles he published in various literary journals. The style of Shapira's historical book would have been quite unacceptable on Mount Scopus in Jerusalem and would have probably triggered there hilarious parodies and any number of witticisms.

Nevertheless, and in spite of everything said thus far, the critics and literary scholars of the first half of the twentieth century did not altogether refrain from evolving a certain kind of a literary-theoretical discourse with a style of its own. They turned away from one kind of such discourse only to focus on another, which bore more directly on concerns and issues that were of paramount significance in their eyes. The discourse they distanced themselves from was the one they all absorbed in high school or as externs preparing themselves for the baccalaureate exams. It was the discourse of official *Slovesnost* or *Literaturwissenschaft*, which purported to answer questions such as: What is literature? What are the definitions of its various genres? What is a metaphor? In what subsists the differences between classicism, romanticism, realism, and so on. Not that the evolving of such a discourse was not attempted in Hebrew during the nineteenth century. Hebrew manuals of rhetoric and neoclassical poetics, themselves based on a long tradition of such manuals going all the way back to medieval treatises on grammar, poetics, and rhetoric, such as Moshe Ibn Ezra's disquisition known as *Shirat yisra'el* (*The Poetry of Israel*—the original Arabic title was different; the book was written in the last decade before the author's death in 1135), were written (Shlomo Levisohn's *Melitsat yeshurun*, [Hebrew poetic decorum], 1816) in the first and the beginning of the second halves of the nineteenth century, using the Bible as the text on the basis of which taxonomies of the literary genres or the tropes of figurative language could be developed and illustrated. Poets attempted in lengthy introductions to their collections to define the nature of poetry and its relations with and differences from other forms of verbal communication (see, e.g., Naphtali Herts Vayzel's introduction to his didactic epic, deducing moral lessons from the life story of Moses [1789], where the grammarian-poet unfolded a theory concerning the divine origin of poetry and its ubiquity as a sign of the divine spark to be found in all humans including savages such as the Australian aborigines of which Vayzel learned from Captain Cooke's reports of his various voyages).[51] Similar remarks on the essence of poetry and the characteristic of poetic language were smuggled into commentaries on various biblical texts, particularly those culled from Psalms. This kind of discourse, however, quickly petered out when Hebrew professional literary criticism appeared in the 1860s. In 1859, the poet Y. L. Gordon still introduced his collection of rhyming parables à la La Fontaine with a long disquisition on the genre and its history since antiquity.[52] When Avraham Ya'akov Paperna, one of the founding fathers of professional Hebrew criticism, wanted to criticize a new allegorical drama by the poet Adam hakohen Lebenzon, he saw fit to base his critique on a book length disquisition about *The Drama in General and the Hebrew Drama in Particular* (1868),[53] and he also intended to write a monograph on the novel as a basis for a critique of current Hebrew novels such a Abramovitsh's *The Fathers and the Sons*.[54] However, at this point, this kind of neoclassical prescriptive poetics suffered a drastic devaluation in a manner reminiscent of the rejection of neoclassic poetics by the European romantics. In 1872, Abramovitsh poked fun at it in his novel of ideas *Di klyatshe* (*The Nag*), where he satirically described the torture undergone by a Jewish extern as he prepared himself for the examination in *Slovesnost*. More than thirty years later Bialik, in an essay on Abramovitsh's narrative art, made the sarcastic comment that has already been mentioned, namely, the reader should "not to forget to forget the science of literature" when he tried to read and understand an Abramovitsh text, for the author was presumably a unique, idiosyncratic, and inimitable original Jewish artist to whom the rules of literary theory did not apply. Thus the rejection of theory was justified not only by the tenets of romanticism but also by the demands of nationalism.

In any case, the official theoretical discourse here under discussion was rejected toward the end of the nineteenth century or rather relegated to the various school textbooks such as S. L. Gordon's *Theory of Literature*[55] or the many compendia of selected literary texts (the so-called *khristomatyes*), the publications of which the growing popularity of Hebrew schools at the beginning of the twentieth century justified financially. Since most of these, like their Russian counterparts, were divided into generic rather than thematic segments, each segment would be introduced by a short definition and description of the genre it represented. But such disquisitions were now the proper domain of teachers rather than of serious critics and were supposed to form part of a youngster's basic education rather than a topic for scholarly contemplation. The latter turned to altogether other matters, assuming the acquaintance of the readers with the basic taxonomies and run-of-the-mill terminology. Thus, literary scholars gradually evolved what we shall refer to as a theory of Jewish (or Hebrew) literature, which to them as nationalists and as intellectuals informed by the romantic belief in the superior importance of the unique, the historically, and in the case of individual writers, biographically specific, seemed the right theoretical path to follow. We shall now survey the development of this theory not in the framework of a scholarly, historical monograph (which would demand the writing of a history in several volumes) but rather for the purpose of asking whether this theory, obsolete as its intellectual underpinnings are now, has something to offer us nowadays in our attempt to re-think the problematic of the Jewish literary complex. For such a purpose, a bird's-eye view may, perhaps, suffice.

The cornerstones of the meta-literary tradition we have in mind were
laid as early as the last decades of the eighteenth century; and this, indeed, is one of the reasons for seeing the "new" Hebrew literature as
a whole emerging at that time. In dividing any historical continuum
into segments, that is, in superimposing upon it the arbitrary concept
of periodization, one should always inquire whether contemporaries,
the people who actually were present when a new period presumably
commenced, knew or felt, no matter how vaguely, that something new
was taking form, and that in some important way, they were being cut
off from their traditional moorings. Only such evidence can give the
historian the assurance that his segmented chronological scheme, whatever the principles or arguments it is based on, is not altogether his
own anachronistic superimposition. Thus, perhaps the notion that a
new kind of literature was emerging should be corroborated by some
such evidence—the evidence left by writers who lived and worked at
the time and thought they were doing or witnessing something significantly new. In the records of Hebrew literature of the period, now
referred to as early new times rather than late middle ages (the appellation used by older historians) in Jewish history, we can hardly find such
clear evidence before the 1780s. A group of Hebrew intellectuals, most
of them members of Moses Mendelssohn's circle and participants in his
Jewish cultural projects, organized and decided to publish a Hebrew
literary periodical, the first of its kind, by the name of *Hame'asef*. It was
not only new ideas and concepts that guided them, but also their wish
to establish a new venue of communication, a literary arena that had
not existed before that conveyed their sense of doing something quite

unprecedented; for in literary history, the means of communication are as important as its contents, and the creation of a new public space goes hand in hand with the proliferation of ideas that are regarded as new.

They regarded the public that they confronted as potentially new because it lived in a new time: the European host societies in whose midst these intended readers lived were undergoing a far-reaching permutation or, at least, what the group of writers and intellectuals gathered around *Hame'asef* understood as such a permutation. Basing their assessments on the *Toleranzedikt* (Edict of Tolerance) announced by the Habsburg emperor Josef II (1781), into which they read much more than it actually said, they foresaw Jewish societies, at least in western Europe, shedding their medieval identity as a cast (defined by its religion) within a polity subsisting of many casts, which the central authorities controlled and adjudicated collectively, and assuming the identity predicated by citizenry in a modern state, namely, a state that established a direct legal relationship with its inhabitants as individuals. Such a change, even before it could reach its fully fledged form of total legal emancipation, presented European Jewry with tremendous new opportunities and challenges, which necessitated the establishment of a new intellectual leadership; for the traditional Jewish leadership, consisting of the rabbis usually allied with an old-fashioned local Jewish plutocracy (the *parnasim*), possessed neither the information nor the mentality necessary for negotiating the perplexities and possibilities of the new Jewish condition. This called for people who had been exposed to the influence of the Enlightenment and for their involvement in a new institution, which had to be a literary one. Since Jews had no rulers and could not form parliaments of their own, it would be through the collective efforts of these writers and commentators that various approaches to and comments and ideas about the issues upon which the welfare of the Jews now depended would be processed and clarified. The new Hebrew literature was to become such an institution, a Jewish literary parliament, a self-appointed custodian of the national welfare, so to speak.

That was the essence of what was new about this literature. It was to promulgate the ideas of humanism throughout European Jewry, to encourage rationalist (but by no means anti-religious, let alone atheistic) thinking, to militate for changes in the structure and contents of Jewish education (so that it exposed the child not only to the study of the Jewish law but also to such disciplines as history, geography, the sciences, and the study of non-Jewish languages) and, of course, develop new sensibilities through emotive writing and educate aesthetically through belles-lettres based on current European models and focusing on human experience and emotions. However, in none of these, taken separately or even collectively, subsisted the fundamental innovation the new literature saw itself as offering. That fundamental innovation inhered in the self-definition of the literature as a guiding institution that was now to replace the rabbinical establishment in everything that did not directly and strictly pertain to its field of expertise and responsibility, that of the religious law, which was, of course, to be adhered to. Belles letters based on Arabic and then European models and focusing on human affairs and emotions (such as love, suffering, intellectual curiosity, fear of mortality, etc.) had been written in Hebrew in Spain, Provence, Italy, and other Mediterranean countries throughout the high middle ages and the Renaissance and flourished in Italy and Holland in the eras of the Baroque and Neoclassicism. Rationalism (curbed by the faith in divine revelation as witnessed by the Bible, which most of the exponents of the Enlightenment never questioned) had formed a central philosophical current in medieval and renaissance Jewish intellectual discourse. Humanism had not been unknown to Jewish thinking and writing of the sixteenth and seventeenth century. What was really new was the institutional role ascribed now to Hebrew literature, its function as "The Watchman unto the House of Israel" (to quote the title of Yitskhak Erter's seminal series of satires, written during the 1820s and 1830s; the title was based, of course, on Ezekiel 3:17, highlighting the author's idea, that the new writers amounted to latter-day prophets, although their arguments were based on reason and morality and not on revelation, which had become inaccessible after biblical times).[1]

What the new writers had to do in their role as watchmen was much more than survey the national scene, criticize, offer suggestions for improvement, and so on, or proliferate up-to-date information about topics traditional Jewish education evaded or sublimate emotions through the power of poetic language (which, as mentioned before, they believed to be propelled by a divine spark).[2] They had to do all that, but within a context of a national dialogue based on a new understanding of the Bible and a new definition of the Hebrew language as contained in and exemplified by the Bible. The biblicism of the new literature, which for over a century dominated much of its thematic contents and even more of its stylistic stratagems, was based on much more than the sheer sanctity of the Bible and its presumed aesthetic perfection. First and foremost, it was based on the understanding of the Bible as the only genuine Jewish national literature—literature created under circumstances of freedom such as that for which Jews now could aspire. Hebrew—"pure," biblical Hebrew—was "the last remnant" or vestige of ancient Hebrew freedom, as well as of an ancient Hebrew literature. The poet Adam hakohen Lebenzon wrote (in the 1830s):

> I was thinking of all the glories we lost:
> The land, independence, the pomp of kingship,
> The temple and its servants, our shepherds ...
> In my despondency I sought some comfort:
> Has any vestige of our freedom survived?
> I found our language. It is still ours;
> The hands of strangers have not touched it.
> It escaped into the holy books and was rescued.[3]

Consequently, one of the foremost challenges facing the new Hebrew writer was to revive biblical Hebrew. If Vayzel was the first "new" Hebrew poet, as the editors of *Hame'asef* indicated in a open letter to him,[4] it was not only because of the high poetic merit the signatories of the letter ascribed to his work but mainly because in their estimation, he was the first to attempt such a linguistic revival. The new literature started with him, they said, because he was presumably the first to pluck the lyre left by the ancient Hebrew poets hanging on the willow trees of the rivers of Babylon and play a melody on it that resounded with the full sweetness and resonance of biblical Hebrew poetry. Hence the new literature involved the secularization of Hebrew and of the Bible not only in the sense of removing them from the enclave of synagogal ritual and religious study and projecting them into modern reality as living forces, but also, and more importantly, in the sense of understanding them as realizable national assets that could be invested in new national projects.

The secularization of Hebrew, of which much has been said, inhered primarily not in the application of the language to mundane contemporary realities (first as a written and then as a spoken language), but in its redefinition as a usable national tool. This was what the new literature was about and as such, its newness had to do with being reconnected with the Bible and its world (as a world defined by a national history, as much as it was defined by a religious one) rather than by being cut off from a more recent old literature; for at its inception the exponents of the new literature did not present it as directly oppositional to what had preceded it. That was why in their meta-literary writing, while it insisted on newness and rebirth, the binary opposition of new versus old did not loom large. Indeed, it was rarely mentioned.

This changed in the second half of the nineteenth century, particularly as the genre of professional and practical literary criticism was forged in Hebrew in the 1860s. Again, the sense that something new was happening was felt and articulated by contemporaries; however, this time it was articulated through a sense of sharp differentiation — of the new being decisively cut off from the old. The founding father of Hebrew literary criticism, Avraham Uri Kovner, sharply divided (in two articles containing the blueprints for a first history of the new Hebrew literature, 1865) the continuum of Hebrew literature not only into an indefinite old segment and a new one, starting in the second half of the eighteenth century, but also internally into well-differentiated segments, with the new or last one radically different from the former: that former, the "Mendelssohn Era," ending more or less in the 1840s, and the "Era of the Newest Literature," starting in the 1850s with the publication of the first Hebrew novels (the first one, Mapu's *Love of Zion*, was published in 1853), and the establishment, after the demise of Nicholas I and his restrictive regime (in 1856), of the Hebrew weeklies (such as *Hamelits*), which were about to play a decisive role in the development of Hebrew literature and of Jewish public life in Czarist Russia for many decades.[5] Whereas the Mendelssohn Era had cut itself off from the old rabbinical literature by replacing legalistic quibbling, as well as superstition, with rational-causal discourse and an appeal to the aesthetic sensibility, the Era of the Newest Literature was heralded by the rearrangement of literary expression so as to create a direct correspondence, whether mimetic or discursive, between its form and contents and social reality. The rationalism, humanism, and aestheticism (expressed through biblicism) of the former era had been only the necessary preconditions for the direct literature-reality nexus initiated by the latter; for only through such a nexus could the literature properly play its role as "a watchman unto the house of Israel" within a real public space rather than in a vacuum.

Kovner was referring to an accumulation of new factors, which in fact dramatically changed the status of the new literature in the 1850s and 1860s. Whereas two of the major genres of earlier Hebrew belles lettres, the neoclassical didactic epic and the allegorical drama, were petering out, they were replaced by two new genres, the novel and the romantic narrative poem (called in Hebrew, as in Russian, *po'ema*), the former, whether historical or contemporary, allowing for direct mimetic engagement with social reality, while the latter replacing the distant, didactic epic speaker, with a new and emotionally liberated one, who viscerally reacted to and commented on the dramatic events fitted into the relatively short and often chronologically discontinuous narrative span of the *po'ema*. In addition, the old forms of literary criticism (rhetorical manuals, commentaries on biblical passages) were replaced with practical criticism written in the form of articles analyzing and evaluating (often very harshly) texts by contemporary authors on the basis of their social contents and aesthetic and ethical merits. That this innovation was directly based on the models of contemporary Russian literary criticism—from Vissarion Belinsky to Dmitry Pisarev and Chernyshevsky, as all historians of Hebrew criticism noted and demonstrated[6]—should be mentioned here, not for the purpose of historical precision as much as for enabling us to understand the kind of public space Hebrew literature was creating for itself at this juncture in the new Hebrew weeklies that Kovner mentioned (which replaced almanacs and sluggish, infrequently published periodicals) and with the help of a growing reading public (mainly attracted through the popularity of the new novels, both original and adapted). The emergence of this larger reading public rendered possible the continued publication of the weeklies, as well as the emergence of the rudiments of a publishing industry. It was the eastern European, and more particularly, the Russian brand, of literary public space, that was—now and for the next sixty or seventy years—adopted by Hebrew literature and made to inform and guide its activities. As mentioned in an earlier chapter, this public space was considerably different from those of contemporary western literatures in its blurring of the demarcation lines separating literary entertainment from a literary discourse that engaged a responsive intelligentsia in its search for authentic individual and social life. This kind of discourse now quickly evolved in the new Hebrew weeklies, where the genre already referred to as *publitsistika* enjoyed an unprecedented florescence.[7] The best writers of the period, such as Y. L. Gordon, Smolenskin, Abramovitsh, and more than all others, Moshe Leib Lilienblum,[8] the chief practitioner of the genre at the time, invested tremendous energies not only in writing poems (as Gordon did) or novels (Smolenskin, Abramovitsh), but also, and as insistently, in writing articles and monographs, sometimes of book-length dimension, on burning social and cultural matters, which the authors endeavored to illuminate both historically and topically. Literary criticism and thinking actually merged now with this upsurge of *publitsistika*, which, to a large extent, explains the form and tonality they were to evolve during the next half a century. Thus literary issues, often with theoretical ramifications, were now debated as matters pertaining to life itself, and under a new literary charter defined in terms of the intense relationship between writers and readers in both directions: the writers focusing on the realities of the readers' social and individual existence, and the readers revving up their response to the writing directed at them, accepting its self-appointed role as a guide of *The Perplexed in the Paths of Life*, to use the title of Smolenskin's chief novel (1868–1869).

Indeed, one of the first new foci of literary thinking to emerge now was the issue of the novel as a genre, namely, the intellectual and social value of presenting mundane reality through mimetic description, in prose, and within the framework of the romance-like plot (the love of young people and their ability or inability to assert it through a conjugal union), which, at the time, was inseparably identified with the very concept of the roman (novel). Once again, literary historians should pay close attention to the ideas and concepts prevalent among the writers whose place in history they try to determine. It was only during the 1850s and 1860s that Hebrew writers became aware of and started commenting on the emergence of Hebrew novel writing; or, to use the sarcastic but quaint expression one of the objectors to such writing coined, it was only then that "henetsu haromanim" ("the novels budded"; a wordplay on "henetsu harimonim" from Solomon's Song 6:11: "I went down into the garden of nuts to see the fruits of the valley, and to see whether the vine flourished, and the pomegranates budded.").[9] This should discount in advance and put to rest all attempts to somehow push the presumed emergence of the genre back in time and endow the Hebrew novel with the prestige of an older and better-established tradition (as witnessed by the rather futile attempts to crown Yosef Perl's epistolary parody-satire *The Revealer of Secrets* [1819] with the crown of "the first Hebrew novel"[10]). It should rather call our attention to the pronounced belatedness of the Hebrew novel, which must be understood within the wide context of novel writing as a philosophical and social fiat. Such a fiat could not be acceded to by Hebrew writers before the 1850s because Hebrew literature had not been ready not only for a fictional but direct mimesis of society, but also, and mainly, for the intensified interest in the erotic as expressive of quintessential humanity. It was this connection between social mimesis and erotic expressionism that triggered now one of the first truly significant polemics in the history of Hebrew meta-literary thinking. Strangely enough in the eyes of the modern observer, the novel, which in all European literatures had assumed by the mid-century the status of a literary *formme maîtresse* (this was the heyday of Balzac, Dickens, Thackeray, Turgenev, and young Tolstoy and Dostoevsky), had been shunned by Hebrew writers (but not by Yiddish ones) until the 1850s. When it finally made its appearance in 1853 with A. Mapu's *Love of Zion*, its validity as a literary genre was heatedly debated by the Hebrew "conservative" *maskilim*, who suspected its philosophical validity as fiction (i.e., as telling an untruth) and recoiled with horror from its inherent interest in the erotic life of its protagonists. At the same time, the "radicals" (Mapu, Kovner, Abramovitsh) maintained that the novel was the foremost literary vehicle for exploring social and psychological reality and that eroticism, being a major biological and emotional factor in human life, had to be understood and artistically presented. Of course, the debate, which went on for a decade, ended with the total victory of the radicals.[11] However, the polemics illustrated what now became the central issue of Hebrew literary thinking: the issue of the truth and its appropriate presentation. The questions heatedly debated were whether fiction could convey the truth, and whether the truth literature conveyed should encompass such areas as human sexuality, as well as the array of human instincts and physical functions. These led to the questioning of the very concept of literature as a presentation of life. What was it? What were its aims?[12] What was the reason for its being written in Hebrew, a language that was both unspoken and inaccessible to most contemporary Jews? As such, could it reflect the social or psychological truth? If this was doubtful, what would be its future? Could it indeed count on having a future, or it was toiling in a vacuum and bound to peter out as the process of Jewish acculturation accelerated? Thus, the "romanen (novels)-polemic" evolved as the first truly significant indication of Hebrew literature having achieved the modicum of self awareness that rendered meta-literary thinking not only possible but indeed essential.

This self questioning was carried on by the new critics (Kovner, Paperna, Abramovitsh, Y. Y. Lerner) but not only by them. Practitioners of all the new genres contributed to it. Whereas the new critics started stormy critical debates that electrified the sluggish literary scene, the novelists carried on this debate by filling their fictions with literary and critical discussions of all kinds. In the 1850s, Mapu maintained that Hebrew literature needed novels that would attract a wide reading public, impacting audiences who were not yet ready for conceptual discourse and negotiating for them a concept of truth—historical, philosophical, and existential. At the same time, it sorely needed literary criticism, which would challenge novelists and poets and differentiate between their productions according to artistic merit and intellectual seriousness.[13] In his novels, Mapu investigated the difference between the categories of the sublime and the beautiful as applied to the mimetic descriptions of human events and the vicissitudes of human affairs (particularly love affairs). Arriving at the conclusion (in *Love of Zion*) that it was the latter category that best fit the description of private lives, whereas the former one suited extraordinary historical events (particularly as described in the author's second historical novel, *The Guilt of*

Samaria), and found its pure articulation in prophecy, which, to some extent, put it beyond the domain of modern fiction. Smolenskin dedicated a good part of his early novel *The Hypocrite's Joy* to a detailed critical discussion contrasting Goethe's *Faust* with Shakespeare's *Hamlet*. Abramovitsh, as mentioned before, discussed in his *The Nag* (already written in Yiddish) the issues of the cogency of literary theory and the relevance of myth and symbols as conduits of literary truth. The novelist R. A. Broydes made the burgeoning literary scene of the 1860s and early 1870s the background for his major novel, *The Religious Law and Life* (1877), whose protagonist's character and life story were modeled after those of Lilienblum, the foremost Hebrew "publicist" of the day. Everywhere, including in its poetry, as written by Y. L. Gordon and his followers, the literature of the time exhibited the keen self-awareness that renders meta-literary thinking necessary; however, it also entwined literary thinking with social and cultural commentary. It was in this seminal period that the merger of literary criticism with moral and social commentary, which the critics and theorists of the second half of the twentieth century would dissolve, was cemented.

In this atmosphere, the consensus upon which the earlier concept of literary criticism (mainly rhetorical and stylistic) was based could not be upheld. Ideas about the "drama in general" or what were the staple characteristics of poetic language were fine, but they hardly attracted the interest that was drawn to deliberations of a new kind. A fault line emerged that started to split the syntheses the exponents of the earlier Enlightenment had forged. Thus, quite suddenly the question emerged whether the new Hebrew literature added a new dimension to the Jewish literary tradition or absolutely parceled its continuity in separate bundles, the old one containing the Bible itself. As we noted, earlier writers had evaded this question. Now the radicals, such as Kovner, demanded an acknowledgement of the total unrelatedness of current writing to the preceding one. Mendelssohn and his followers had cut the ties connecting the literature of his time from the Talmudic tradition. Likewise, present day novelists and poets like Mapu and Gordon cut the ties connecting current realistic writing with the idealistic perception of reality that had informed the earlier literature, replacing it by focusing on matter, economics, and biology as the principles that explained both individual (erotic) and social (economic) behavior, and shedding light on the flow of history as basically material and socio-biological processes, the substitution of the "fathers" by the "sons." Whereas until now, all exponents of the Jewish enlightenment had conceived of change and progress as totally dependent on education, and therefore invested their best efforts in devising a new Jewish educational agenda, now at least some of the new writers, such as Abramovitsh, were searching for other, more systemic or structural concepts of societal and cultural change, and, without reneging on educational ideals, projected progress as emanating from economic factors and changes in the class structure of Jewish society. All these indications of rupture and discontinuity drew sharp responses from the conservatives, such as the poet Avrom Ber Gottlober and the activist, editor, and historian (of the Jewish community of Vilnius) Sh. Y. Fin, the former attacking the notion that Mendelssohn's brand of Enlightenment based on *Vernunft* (reason) and belief in the sanctity of the Torah was outdated,[14] and the latter, systematic advocate of compromise between tradition and modernity, suggesting (in his extensive review of the poems of Adam Hakohen, himself at this point a bastion of conservatism and the speaker of the old guard in Hebrew literature) that the new literature had been tied to preceding literary developments, such as the neoclassic, early eighteenth-century poetry and poetic dramas of Moshe Hayyim Luzzatto (who also had been a cabbalist and the author of a popular religious ethic manual).[15]

The issue of stylistic biblicism also gave rise to debates. Whereas nobody yet questioned the supremacy of the biblical stylistic models, critics and writers heatedly debated their proper use. Much of the negative practical criticism written at the time had to do with what was now pejoratively referred to as *melitsa*, by which the critics meant a verbose, elaborate, and decorative style that purported to compensate with floridity for the paucity of contents. The old Hebrew term *melitsa*, had until now been used approvingly or neutrally as indicating poetic language, the heightened and adorned language fit for verse. Often, as in Levisohn's ode "Hamelitsa medaberet" ("Poetic Decorum Speaks"), the concept became all but identical with that of poetry itself. But now, starting in the 1850s and 1860s, it was used as a damning label for a certain kind of florid, redundant, and imprecise style that consisted of mosaics of quotations from the Bible. Thus the notion, still a common-place, that the new Hebrew writing should be cast in the "pure" language of the Bible, became qualified and more nuanced, since writers had to differentiate between a "good" or legitimate biblicism and a bad one, which obfuscated meaning, burying the plain sense of a statement under decorative biblical leftovers. At the same time, the emergence of the novel with rudiments of mimetic realism and the need for the creation of a spoken dialogue gave rise to the question whether biblical style in and of itself could support prose fiction. Even Mapu, perhaps the greatest practitioner of the neo-biblical style, who used the mosaic formula with surprising dexterity and inventiveness, owned that in his novel *The Hypocrite*, a large-scale attempt at unfolding a panorama of contemporary eastern European Jewish life, he also had to resort to Aramaic, gentle Hebrew's "maiden" and follower, to render the dialogues of Lithuanian rabbinical scholars credible and fluent.[16] Abramovitsh, focusing in his first Hebrew novel, *Learn to Do Good*, on Hasidic family life in a Ukrainian provincial town, studded his dialogues with literal Hebrew translations of Yiddish idioms.

He was also one of the first (together with some other pioneers, such as the lexicographer Y. M. Lifshits) to ponder the possibility of making systematic literary use of Yiddish. In the first half of the nineteenth century, Yiddish was anathema to almost all writers of the Jewish enlightenment (with very few exceptions, such as Y. Sh. Bik). In their attempt to stymie the spreading influence of Hasidism and its mystical and hagiographic literature, a large part of which became widely popular in its Yiddish versions, some Hebrew writers in Galicia and the Ukraine resorted to Yiddish as a weapon that in the heat of battle must be used, but characteristically they were either not allowed (by the respective Austrian or Czarist censors), or they did not want to publish their works, which they circulated in handwritten copies. The first writer of the Enlightenment who capitalized on the potential existence of a relatively large Yiddish reading public was E. M. Dik, who in the 1840s and 1850s published scores of novellas cast in the form and style of the religious Yiddish chapbook, into which he smuggled a modicum of mild and diluted maskilic precepts. However, it was Abramovitsh, and later also the satirist Y. Y. Linetski, who understood that with the appearance of the first Yiddish weekly *Kol mevaser* (a Yiddish supplement added to the weekly issue of *Hamelits*), a new Yiddish public space was created in which a new kind of Yiddish writing could flourish. Still bound by the purely utilitarian justification of writing in Yiddish, they nevertheless also gauged the artistic potential of addressing a relatively unsophisticated audience to whom the concepts of the Enlightenment were still alien and that therefore should be approached through a mediating narrator and commentator, a Janus-faced folksy raconteur, who was at one and the same time part of the traditional Jewish society and its "enlightened" critic. Thus, in 1864 the famous "Mendele the Book Peddler" ironic persona came into being, and the foundation for modern, artistic Yiddish fiction was laid.

All these could not have happened without a sturdy meta-literary discourse being developed—a polemic and often acerbic discourse, but vital and indispensable, and its presence became the very essence of the literature's newness. This in itself should alert us to the possibility that the habitual inclusion by historians of the developments discussed here under the general umbrella of one protracted Enlightenment era that supposedly stretched throughout an entire century, from the 1780s to the 1880s, is historically wrong. Nor does the dividing of this era into various sub-periods (such as those of neoclassicism, romanticism, and realism) offer the necessary correction; for in addition to the substantive errors it involves (the writers of the 1850s and 1860s were not realists in the current sense of the term, and romanticism did not truly emerge in both Hebrew and Yiddish literatures before the 1890s), it hardly did justice to the radicalism and innovative characteristics of these decades, which were every bit as important as those of the 1880s. It is a skewed Zionist reading of nineteenth-century Jewish literature that led scholars to point to the advent of an organized Zionist movement in the wake of the pogroms of 1881–1882 as the event that launched a new period, when even the nationalist idea was mulled over by Hebrew and Yiddish writers during the 1860s and 1870s in the novels and essays of Smolenskin and Abramovitsh, as well as in the narrative poems of Y. L. Gordon and in this poet's and Lilienblum's articles.

Nevertheless, during the 1880s and the 1890s, with the emergence of Zionism (and other Jewish nationalist movements) and the mood of *teshuva* (repentance and return), which characterized some of the radical *maskilim* who now, having undergone a conversion, re-emerged as radical nationalists, the meta-literary dialogue changed considerably. The chief question now asked was what was the essence of Jewish nationhood, and, by inference, what was the national character of Jewish literatures. Lilienblum, now an ardent Zionist, pondered these questions and faced some of their complexity. On the one hand, he maintained, the entire project of the so-called new Hebrew literature was nationalist from its very inception. In his article "The First Nationalists in the Former Century,"[17] he predicated a decisive difference between the Mendelssohnian enlightenment, which by its total reduction of Judaism to religion, devoid of the nationalist component, led to assimilation and conversion, and the Enlightenment of the founding fathers of the new literature (the group that had established *Hame'asef* and their followers), who by sticking to Hebrew and redefining it as a national language opted for a modern Jewish culture that was essentially nationalist. This amounted to an extraordinarily significant insight, which the historians of Hebrew literature have yet to follow to its far reaching ramifications. On the other hand, however, in his practical criticism, such as in his attack on the poetry of Y. L. Gordon (charging it with indifference to the national interest as viewed through a narrow Zionist perspective),[18] Lilienblum lowered the level of the new nationalist literary thinking to simplistic chauvinism. Actually, these two levels of discourse were mutually contradictory. If the Hebrew enlightenment had been, from its very beginnings, a nationalist brand of Enlightenment—an Enlightenment that insisted on the modernization of Jewish life and the absorption by Jews of the universalistic ideals of humanism without breaking the particularistic mold of a national culture, then Y. L. Gordon certainly was the preeminent nationalist in nineteenth-century Hebrew literature, when in narrative poems such as "In the Lions' Teeth," "In the Depth of the Seas" (both published in 1868) and "Zedekiah in Captivity" (1879), he brilliantly conflated the pathos of historical Jewish suffering, the outrage of the persecution, and the tragic pattern of downfall and exile, and an incisive humanistic critique of Jewish other-worldly historical conduct. Here was the prime example of the Hebrew poet as "the watchman unto the house of Israel," as well as the first example of what Brenner would later label "self-evaluation" or national self-criticism, which represented, arguably, the highest forms of nationalist sensibility. The dichotomies and inner contradictions in Lilienblum's nationalist literary thinking were indicative of the intellectual immaturity of the early Hebrew nationalism and of its habitual sliding during the 1880s into short-sighted nationalist sentimentalism—the same sentimentalism that severely limited the achievements of contemporary, pre-Bialikian Zionist poetry. A similar ideational rawness can be detected in writings and arguments of other critics and thinkers of the time, such as Mordekhai Ben Hillel Hakohen, Y. H. Ravnitzky, Epshteyn, M. L. Levinsky, and Nakhum Sokolov. The latter, a master of the causerie-like feuilleton and the editor of the weekly *Hatsefira*, which in 1887 became the chief Hebrew daily, albeit unusually well-informed and a graceful stylist, exhibited this rawness in a popular book on anti-Semitism[19]—chock full of historical information but devoid of historical insight, thus establishing the model for the habitual Zionist tendency of finding anti-Semitism everywhere and of minimizing the differences between different kinds of anti-Semitisms, sprouting under different historical circumstances and propelled by different motives and causes. In the aesthetic domain, the same immaturity characterized the discussions focusing on the question whether there was a "special" or a "unique" kind of Jewish beauty (cf. Sokolov's essay "Jewish Grace").[20] The discussions, carried on throughout the 1890s, bearing particularly on the evaluation of the narrative art of Abramovitsh, who was now raised to the status of the chief Hebrew classical writer of prose fiction, lead to theoretical blind alleys such as Bialik's already mentioned refusal to acknowledge the applicability of the methodologies of literary analysis to Abramovitsh's works, as well as to the unwillingness of other critics to see the European connections and parallels of modern Hebrew writing that emanated from a chauvinistic "Judaization" of its aesthetics. This tendency marred even the thinking of the most perspicacious of Hebrew critics of the time, Frishman, whose analysis of the art of Abramovitsh's prose fiction[21] nevertheless offers an example of a narrow and simplistic nationalist reading of the complex texts.

In the 1890s the meteoric rise of the Zionist philosopher Achad ha'am changed the discourse we are following. Achad ha'am was the first culture hero (soon to be joined by Abramovitsh and the young poet Bialik) of the so-called Hebrew Renaissance of the two decades preceding World War I. Materially and socially this renaissance was supported by the astounding growth of the Hebrew reading public in the 1880s. The impact of widespread pogroms, restrictive and reactionary attitudes on the part of the authorities (in the wake of the assassination of Alexander II in 1881), the rise of both official and popular anti-Semitism, and, perhaps most importantly, the economic deterioration of the Jewish lower-middle class as the Czarist empire entered its period of high capitalist entrepreneurship, "modernized" and politicized the traditional Jewish middle class, ripening it for the absorption of the new nationalist mood. The members of this class now started to ponder the chances of emigration to the West versus those of establishing Jewish colonies in Palestine. They developed an interest in the economic developments that undermined their existence as the local mediators between a rustic population and provincial commerce, in international politics, in the colonialist projects of the major European powers (particularly those that involved the Middle East), in the social and economic circumstances under which Jews lived in far-off parts of the world, and so on. This interest, in its turn, justified the existence of a Hebrew daily press. Since all members of the traditional Jewish middle class had a traditional Jewish education and therefore read Hebrew, Hebrew literature (in the widest sense of the term, including Hebrew journalism, which was at the time very literary) became their chief source of information, as well as the guide that helped them in the forming of ideas, concepts, and plans. This enabled modern Hebrew writing for the first time in its history to address a truly national reading public that numbered in the hundreds of thousands (whereas the reading public of the Hebrew enlightenment until the 1860s could be measured a few thousand), which rendered possible the rise of a burgeoning Hebrew publishing industry. In this sense, as Sokolov would later reminisce, the new Hebrew literature as a public institution, was born in the 1880s.[22]

This solid socio-economic basis was used for the purposes of reforming and modernizing Hebrew writing in general and its meta-literary discourse in particular, and Achad ha'am, whose articles and philosophical essays (which started to appear in 1889) overwhelmed and delighted contemporary readers with their ideational depth and maturity, their expositional clarity and stylistic grace, precision, and soberness, was the first to convey the sense that Hebrew non-fictional writing was experiencing a quantum leap into modernity. He set out to redefine Jewish nationhood, as well as its literary implications. Since nationhood was, by his assessment, about to replace religion as the defining component in the makeup of Judaism, it had to be both thought-through and asserted in reality in new ways. Thoroughly secularizing the basic concepts of the Bible, Achad ha'am defined the essence of Judaism, its Hegelian *Geist*, as prophetic morality, presenting the prophet as an uncompromising moralist who followed the fiats of the "the God in his heart" (i.e., his conscience) rather than conveyed those of a transcendental God.[23] To assert their character in the historical arena, Jews had to re-gather in their biblical homeland, where they would form a just society and as such play their role in history. This, of course, entailed huge practical difficulties, and therefore, what needed to happen first, long before the eventual establishment in Palestine of a Jewish state, was the forming there of a spiritual center, consisting of an elite community, which would pave the way for the future ideal society, and at the same time help unify the Jewish people, modernity having effected it primarily in the form of cultural fragmentation (rather than assimilation), since Jews, while remaining members of their national group, became increasingly acculturated into culturally divergent host societies. Hebrew was the only language that could hold Jews all over the world culturally unified, since it was the only language that tied the Jewish present (and future) with the Jewish past, and as such formed the DNA of the national heredity throughout the ages.[24] This was why the new Hebrew literature was of such momentous importance, and why no Jewish writing, in whatever Jewish or non-Jewish language other than Hebrew can aspire to impact the national culture unless it is cast into a Hebrew version that the readers regard as an original text. The current florescence of Yiddish and its literature, Achad ha'am pontificated, was ephemeral (Yiddish being bound to disappear in the process of modernization and acculturation of Jews within their respective host societies) and added little to the treasure of Jewish national lore accumulating throughout the millennia. Only Hebrew literature would survive as the Jewish national literature.[25] But the renewal of Hebrew literature, a momentous project, had commenced with a false start. The new Hebrew writers of the Enlightenment had channeled their efforts in the wrong direction and therefore, by and large, had failed in evoking the true potential of the literary renewal they had initiated. Attempting to achieve their goal of modernizing the Jewish spirit mainly through belles lettres, written in the "sublime" language of the Bible, they had misfired both as the creators of a truly artistic literature and as educators of the people. Their failure resulted from a misunderstanding of poetic language and the way it functioned; for poetic or emotive language could do its job of heightening and sublimating emotions only when it functioned within a connotative framework, when it activated not only the dictionary meanings of the words but also a plethora of idiosyncratic associations and suggestions to which the words in their specific combinations within the literary text gave rise. Since such connotation was possible only when a language, by being spoken and put to actual daily use, tied words with the non-verbal physical and mental aspects of existence, current Hebrew literature could not aspire to extraordinary aesthetic achievements and had to turn from a connotative to a denotative use of the language, namely, from poetry (in the sense of the German *Dichtung*, which includes emotive prose) to clear and precise cogitation.[26] A genuinely aesthetic Hebrew literature would emerge in the Palestinian spiritual center, where Hebrew will be the spoken idiom. For the time being, Hebrew literature had to align itself to the philosophical tradition best represented by the personality and work of Maimonides, whom Achad ha'am regarded as the ultimate Jewish rationalist, as well as the ideal Jewish writer under exilic conditions.[27] Thus, the new literature, while being new (i.e., conveying a view of reality that was modern and scientific), was not to be cut off from its pre-modern predecessors, who had attempted an understanding of reality and of the role of the Jewish people in history according to the intellectual and scientific concepts of their time, such as Yehuda Halevi in his philosophical opus *Hakuzari*, and particularly Maimonides in his *Guide to the Perplexed*. It was not accidental that one of the few worthwhile books written during the Enlightenment era was, according to Achad ha'am, Nachman Krochmal's *Guide to the Perplexed in Time*, which was directly connected with the tradition Achad ha'am espoused.[28] In 1896 when he founded the prestigious literary monthly *Hashilo'akh*, Achad ha'am made this line of reasoning the basis for its editorial policy, which he proclaimed in a programmatic article,[29] triggering a heated polemic that did not subside for a long time.[30]

We shall return to this polemic, but not before we turn our eyes back to the 1880s and early 1890s to glance at contemporary developments from the vantage point of Yiddish writing. As a matter of fact, the 1880s were the decade in which Yiddish literature as a cultural institution was born. Before then, the basic assumption that writing in Yiddish somehow accumulated to something like a recognizable literary entity had been altogether nonexistent. Whereas such writing was practiced for propaganda purposes by some of the exponents of the Enlightenment, and justified as the lesser of two evils, and as unavoidable under the circumstances of a fierce battle over the hearts of the Jewish masses, it was not viewed as an activity that might have a value beyond its immediate usefulness. For one thing, it was not expected to survive a certain period—hopefully a short one—during which education and modernization, preferably prescribed by the authorities, would render the language expendable and replace it by the official language of the state, Russian or German. Aksenfeld, the first Yiddish novelist, and one of the only two writers in the first half of the nineteenth century whose only language of literary production was Yiddish (the second one was the poet and playwright Etinger; all other Yiddish writers were bilingual, in most cases—Hebraists), prophesized in his only surviving novel, *The Headband*, that with the help of an imperial ukase, Yiddish would become obsolete within fifty years at the most.[31] Then there was the assumption (absurd from the linguistic point of view) that Yiddish was not a real language and certainly was not capable of being used for aesthetic and literary purposes. It was an inferior , broken-German jargon with no grammar, no orthography, and no established correct (i.e., literary) or generally used dialect.[32] Thus, informed by the eighteenth-century demand for "correct," direct, transparent, and controlled relationship between "words" and "things," that is, between language and both objects and concepts, the detractors of Yiddish branded it as inherently unable to correctly convey informational, intellectual, and ethical messages. Those who had to use it were called upon to do whatever they could to tame, as far as it was possible, its wildness and superimpose upon it a modicum of linguistic regularity. They therefore Germanized their orthography and often took great pains to also Germanize its vocabulary and grammar, producing stilted texts written in an artificial style and failing to tap the expressive idiomatic resources the language held for those who knew how to upgrade it without tearing it from its colloquial roots (such as Abramovitsh and Linetski). Overall, resorting to Yiddish involved a pervasive sense of shame, which resulted in an almost universal use of pen names, as well as in anonymous publication. Among the many different uses of folksy personae, such as "Mendele the Book Peddler," not the least was their service as covers for writers (like Abramovitsh) who had the reputation of a Hebraist to maintain. This shame sometimes contained a sexist component, Yiddish being supposedly the language of uneducated women and thus, a "feminine" language, devoid of the assertive virility inherent in grammatical norms. Those who wrote Yiddish were seen not only as ministering to ignorant women (Jewish men were supposed to know Hebrew—a myth that was not borne out by cultural reality; only a thorough and prolonged traditional Jewish education, which the lower classes never got, could result in the mastering of Hebrew; which, of course, discounted the entire working class), but also as indulging in an extra-marital affair. More often than historians of Yiddish literature cared to acknowledge, the literary use of Yiddish was associated—on the metaphorical level—with illicit sexuality. Abramovitsh, writing in the late 1880s about his decision in 1864 to publish a story he had written in Yiddish compared his nightly sojourns with "the Jewish woman" (i.e., Yiddish) to clandestine cohabitation with a concubine.[33]

Now, in the 1880s, the same nationalist mood of "repentance," which changed the ambience of Hebrew literature, made some writers and intellectuals change their attitude toward Yiddish, the language of the masses. Proud Hebraists who had written in Yiddish in the past, now unabashedly acknowledged this activity. Lilienblum wrote a Zionist play in Yiddish (*Zrubavel*); Peretz, until then known only as the author of Hebrew poems and tales, started writing the Yiddish short stories and narrative poems that would soon (in the early 1890s) catapult him to the status of a Yiddish cultural and literary hero. Members of the Russian Jewish intelligentsia, now swept by the nationalist mood, assumed the *narodnik* (populist) attitude of many Russian intellectuals and either started writing also in Yiddish (as did the poet Shimon Frug) or paid attention to Yiddish writing in the articles they published in their Jewish-Russian periodicals (such as the historian Shimon Dubnov who now followed the development of Yiddish writers in his role of a literary critic under the pseudonym "Criticus"). Above all else, Yiddish writers themselves began regarding their activity as adding up to some entity of national value. Suddenly the term "jargon literature" appeared, with popular Yiddish writers using it as means of gaining prestige for their underrated productions. Ya'akov Dinezon, the author of the popular tearjerker novel, *The Black Young Fellow*, wrote a pioneering article, defending Yiddish as a language that could support a serious literature.[34] Eliezer Shulman, a Hebrew novelist and translator, launched the study of the history of Yiddish literature from its inception in the Middle Ages, reassuring his readers that the rise of a new Yiddish literature would not pull the rug from underneath its older and more respectable Hebrew sister.[35] An interest arose in the yet unpublished Yiddish writings of the *maskilim* of the late eighteenth and early nineteenth centuries, most of whom had been known, if at all, only as Hebraists, such as Mendl Lefin-Satanover, Yitskhak Ber Levinson (known by his acronym RIVAL and by appellation, "the Mendelssohn of the Hebrew Haskala in the Ukraine"), the Hebrew poet Gottlober, and others.

The most important and influential figure among those now attempting to gentrify Yiddish and gain recognition for its literature was young Sholem Aleichem. As his pen name indicated, he was the heir to the masters of the "personae" period of the 1860s and 1870s, Abramovitsh (*Mendele*) and Linetski (*Eli kotsin hatskhakueli*). A Hebraist and a semi-Russianized intellectual, his intention was to become either a Hebrew or a Russian writer or both (he would try both options with scant success). He bumped into Yiddish, as he said, by sheer accident, an issue of the St. Petersburg Yiddish weekly *Dos folksblat* (*The People's Sheet*) having fallen into his hands and convinced him that the language he spoke could also be used for literary purposes. Sending to the self-same weekly a series of risqué satires (he was then a government-appointed rabbi of a Jewish community whose notables he ridiculed) under the funny pen name that meant something like "how d'you do," he was greeted by an overwhelming popular acclaim, that prescribed the keeping of the pen name, and, its evolvement into a lively, loquacious literary persona that would merge with his personality and permeate his very being as a writer. More importantly, Yiddish writing, first induced by popularity, soon became for him a spiritual quest and, as he said, a "*meshugas*" (craziness).[36] The language, its rhythms and inflexions, captivated him, allowing him to tap its resources and activate its dormant energies as nobody had done before or would do since. At the same time, he also felt that Yiddish writing had to be upgraded into respectability and rendered *Salonfähig*; so, in addition to writing six novels within less than a decade, many satires and short stories, poems in verse and in prose, and feuilletons, he became active as a literary critic and ideologue, attempting to launch a meta-literary Yiddish discourse. In this role, his vantage point was the concept of realism. Himself an admirer of the great Russian realists, Gogol, Turgenev, Shchedrin, and Tolstoy, he believed Yiddish literature, emanating from the people and activating their language, should be loyal to the realities of their social life. In other words, it had to be mimetic and descriptive and focus on the characteristic and habitual rather than on the extraordinary or the fantastic. With this criterion in hand, he set out to create for Yiddish literature a classical tradition of social realism. In a series of critical articles, he created the public images of old timers such as Linetski, Dik, and Avraham Goldenfaden (a poet, playwright, and the founding father of the Yiddish professional theater in the 1870s) as mimetic artists loyal to the realities of Jewish traditional life. The crown he reserved for Abramovitsh, who at the age of fifty was dubbed by him "the grandfather" of Yiddish literature, a hoary and strict artist-mage who taught impatient youngsters (like himself) the secrets of slow and ardent grappling toward artistic perfection (by which he meant consummate mimetic descriptionism).[37] At the same time, Sholem Aleichem waged a fierce critical battle against the producers of "trash," popular romances with melodramatic, improbable plots. In secret he also learned some of the tricks the more dexterous among them (particularly the prolific Nahum Meir Shaykevitsh) employed, for he wanted not only to chase them out of the Yiddish literary arena but also become the heir to their popularity. His most theoretical contribution to the nascent Yiddish meta-literary discourse was the concept of "the Jewish novel," which presumably was different from the novel at large because within the context of traditional Jewish life, the erotic core of novelistic plots had to be shrunk to a bare minimum, because it had to remain loyal to Jewish social reality, in which romance played a marginal role and also, so as not to compromise the purity of the archetypal Jewish daughter.[38] In fact, this theory, for all its "realistic" reasoning, was informed by the prevalent chauvinistic-sentimentalist mood of the 1880s, which has already been referred to. Its idea, or rather ideal, of the immaculate "Jewish daughter," who would rather die than compromise her Jewish-feminine virtue, was as mawkish as any of the ideas about a unique and special Jewish beauty and a unique and special Jewish literature to which the norms of universal literary taste could not be applied. The "Jewish novel" theory, as well as the novels it informed, exposed the author's conservatism and Victorianism and explained why his early work did contain at best the palest of promises of the artistic splendor of the mature work that he would create, outgrowing his role as a literary ideologue and mentor, as well as some of his petit bourgeois sensibilities and inhibitions. Essentially, young Sholem Aleichem, as the foremost Yiddish literary "thinker" of the 1880s, evinced a rawness or immaturity similar to (albeit not altogether identical with) that of the Hebrew nationalists of the day, whose sentimentalist Zionism he shared. His congenital sense of humor could not yet counterbalance this sentimentalism (which asserted itself in a series of idealizations: of Jewish women, of music, of sheer emotionalism), certainly not in his articles and the more serious and ambitious prose fiction he wrote. Essentially, the common denominator that resulted in the similarity between his literary thinking and that of the contemporary Hebrew sentimentalists, the exponents of the so-called *khibat tsiyon* Hebrew writing (to some of whom he was also close socially) was that of the simplistic understanding of the uniqueness of the Jewish character and condition.

Since Sholem Aleichem could not supply the ideological basis that nascent Yiddish literature needed as it approached, throughout the 1890s, its own moment of renaissance, he had to be dethroned as its mentor.

His place was summarily occupied by his rival, the writer who would soon become the standard bearer of that renaissance, Peretz. Peretz was a bilingual Hebrew-Yiddish writer but as a literary *raisoneur*, he appealed primarily to the new Yiddish intelligentsia, whereas the Hebrew literary "republic" appreciated him only as a raconteur, the author of psychological and pseudo-folktale-like fiction, and a master of the short story. His rejection as a literary mentor by the Hebraists resulted not only, and perhaps even not mainly, from his skeptical attitude toward Zionism (there were at the time other prominent Hebrew writers, such as Abramovitsh and Frishman, whose reaction to Zionism was as reserved and critical, which did not diminish their prominence as cultural leaders), but mainly because the concept that dominated his nationalist and literary thinking was the romantic concept of peoplehood, "the folk," the living, organic community, which was the custodian of a civilization, a way of life, a perception of reality, a mindset, a system of manners, customs and mores; which in contradistinction to all abstractions that endeavored to define the supra-historical essence of Judaism (as was borne out by his disrespect for Achad ha'am's nationalist philosophy). Peretz's nationalism was "folkist" and people-oriented. The meaning of the concept of folk, as he understood it, was somewhat different from that of its twin and rival, the nation. Whereas the latter inevitably contained a political element (a nation perforce was an entity with political history and prospects), the former was essentially civilizational and apolitical. Peretz was uninterested in and unimpressed by the Zionist yearning for a nation-state, a *Judestadt*. He believed all states were coercive and culturally reductive[39] and identified the folk as the only genuine source of national creativity. It harbored "a mass of life force, a trove of energy," he wrote in an early article (1891); it was "an eternal flower." But the flower, under circumstances that were not conducive to growth and blossoming, could wilt and be covered with dust and mud if left unattended; and those whose duty was to attend to it were the intellectuals who managed to keep intact their ties with the folk and remain rooted in its civilizational base.[40] Their role was that of bold innovators within the context of an unbroken continuity. They had to redefine the essence of the specific civilization of which the folk was the historical carrier; retell the quintessential myths of the folk, project its values in new and updated symbols, guide the folk in its attempts to adapt to modern conditions and mentality while remaining itself, loyal to its basic civilizational ethos and mission; awaken it to the challenges of modernity, as well as to those of meeting them without self-effacement; inculcate self awareness, a sense of purpose, a perspective of goals and the steps that had to be taken for these goals to be realized. In short, the intellectuals were both to learn from the folk and teach it, educate themselves by delving into its cultural depths and thus become educators. If they could live up to both these tasks, they would be in a position to liberate the folk by activating its own hidden resources of dormant energy. This was what the Hasidic movement had done in its days of glory, the second half of the eighteenth century; and this was what a modern humanistic, but also quintessentially Jewish, literature had to do in the present. The folk sorely needed the ministrations of such a literature since for over a century with, on the one hand, the moral and the intellectual deterioration of the Hasidic movement (its lore and legacy had to be rescued by modern Jewish intellectuals and writers, such as Peretz himself) and on the other hand, the alienation from and rejection of the folk by the exponents of the Enlightenment; the people, bereft of an authentic intellectual leadership, were left to shift for themselves. As long as the modernists remained uprooted and disdainful, they would not be able to participate in a genuine national renewal. Only a rapprochement between them and the folk would trigger an upsurge of a new national vitality, and such a rapprochement had to include a rehabilitation and modernization of the folk's erstwhile disdained language, Yiddish; for only within the arena of a renewed Yiddish discourse could the folk be approached and grappled with. Hence, the supreme importance of a new Yiddish literature, which was or should have been this very arena. This literature must be at one and the same time informed by both the tenets of modernism and the traditional ethos of the folk. It should be able to listen to and reinterpret the legends of the folk, reaching beyond and beneath their surface of superstition and supernatural nonsense, and delving right into their ethical and imaginative core. Thus, Peretz laid out the foundations for a literary project, which he himself endeavored to realize throughout his literary career, and that would guide scores of twentieth-century writers, both Yiddish and Hebrew ones, including great masters such as Agnon and Der Nister (Pinkhas Kahanovitsh).

Clearly all these appealed primarily to the new Yiddish intelligentsia. While many Hebraists learned from Peretz's art, almost none could internalize the ideological gist of his project. This progressively prodded him in the direction of Yiddishism, although for a long time he insisted on maintaining his position as a bilingual writer and as a major writer of Hebrew prose fiction. The showdown that forced his hand took place in 1908, in the Czernowitz conference, where he emerged as the authority behind the Yiddishist agenda as defined by the conferees. With Yiddish proclaimed a national language, its literature—a national Jewish literature—and the ideal of a Jewish state rejected, Peretz's ties with his Hebraist friends, such as Bialik (whom he revered, the admiration being reciprocated), all but snapped. At the same time, his longstanding ties with Yiddishist and anti-Zionists political movements such as the Marxist Bund and the Folkist party in Poland tightened. Peretz became the intellectual leader of Yiddishism, and his role in the Yiddish renaissance was equivalent to those of Achad ha'am and Bialik put together in its Hebrew counterpart. Although he kept demanding from Yiddish literature adherence to the Hebrew sources of Jewish culture, particularly the Bible, in which, he insisted, Yiddish writers had to strike deep roots,[41] his cultural and literary program went past and beyond Hebraism. He even pleaded with Bialik to stop praying in a sequestered minyan (quorum) and join "the large synagogue of the people," that is, to switch from Hebrew to Yiddish.[42]

Yiddishism had other guides and torchbearers, such as Nathan Birnbaum (who was known by his pseudonym Mathias Akher) and Chaim Zhitlovsky, both among the organizers of the Czernowitz Conference and influential presences in it. Birnbaum, a Viennese-Galician Jew, came to Yiddishism from Zionism, an ideology he had upheld and militated for in the Austro-Hungarian domain since the early 1880s, fifteen years before the appearance of Theodore Herzl, when he, Birnbaum, had invented the very term "Zionismus." He enthusiastically joined Herzl's movement in 1897, but then his prolonged and convoluted intellectual and ideological peregrination started. First, he joined the opposition to Herzl within the World Zionist organization, preferring the spiritual or cultural Zionism of Achad ha'am's disciples to the official political Zionism of the leader and his close allies. Then, with Herzl's death after the contentious Uganda congress of 1904, Birnbaum altogether cut off his connection with Zionism and Hebraism, replacing them with political and cultural work aimed at protecting and enhancing Jewish rights in the Diaspora and at supporting and energizing a modern nationalist but non-Zionist Jewish culture rooted in Yiddish and the folk traditions. It was at this stage of his development that he conceived of the need for a festive public occurrence, in which the already won achievements of Yiddish and its literature would be celebrated and the future trajectory of the language and its culture planned and proclaimed. Thus, he was the initiator of the plan that eventually led to the Czernowitz Conference. But this was not the final phase in his restless quest. In the second decade of the century, he became progressively enamored of and committed to Yiddish as the language of a traditional, pre-modern, religious Jewish community rather than that of a secular humanistic Jewish culture. Thus, Birnbaum broke his ties with Yiddishism even as he had cut himself free of his early Zionist moorings. Eventually, he joined the Jewish neo-orthodoxy, which commenced after World War I to organize itself politically, socially, and culturally in an attempt to confront both Zionism and secular Yiddishism as inauthentic Jewish responses to modernity. The Uganda controversy and the subsequent crisis in the Zionist movement gave birth to the territorialist ideology and organization, which projected an independent Yiddish speaking Jewish state away from Palestine, allowing many erstwhile Zionists to join the Yiddishist camp. These included not only people like Birnbaum who had never been vitally connected with Hebrew and its modern culture, but also deeply rooted Hebrew-Yiddish writers such as Hillel Zeitlin, the ecstatic poet-philosopher, who endeavored to develop his Hasidic legacy within the context of a twentieth-century religious-existentialist philosophy. Thus, this bosom friend of Brenner and Gnessin and an intimate member of their so-called Homel (or Gomel) center of rebellious Hebraism, triggered the ire of Bialik who exposed his "villainous" conduct in his pseudo-prophetic poem "A Speech" (1904). Territorialism would remain for a long time an active ideological current in Yiddishist circles and among Yiddish writers—among the latter some of the leaders of the ultra-modernist trends in Yiddish inter-bellum literature, such as the poet Aaron Glants-Leyeles, one of the co-founders and the chief literary ideologue of the *In zikh* literary group or school in the United States. With its promise of a realistic political solution for the conundrum of keeping Yiddish and modern Yiddish culture alive independently of the accelerated acculturation processes that pulled the rug from underneath them not only in the Americas but also in eastern Europe, territorialism could not but appeal to Yiddishists and Yiddish writers of the time.

Unlike the Zionist Birnbaum and the Hebraist Zeitlin, Zhitlovsky, a signatory of the invitation to the Czernowitz Conference, came to Yiddishism from the radical Russian socialist underground movement. From his early youth in the 1880s, he invested himself in an unceasing effort not only to enhance the projects of both the socialist revolution and the Jewish nationalist autonomy, but also to negotiate a truce between the two on the ideological and organizational levels. He believed genuine socialism did not contradict the nationalist spirit as long as the latter remained progressive and non-chauvinistic. At the same time, he thought the concept of Jewish nationalism had to be redefined within a socialist-materialist context. Expressing his views as early as 1887 in his *Thoughts on the Fate of Judaism* (1887), he drew to himself the fire of both Zionists (who dubbed him: the "Jewish Anti-Semite") and the exponents of other Jewish nationalist ideologies such as Shimon Dubnov, with whom he was to cross swords more than once during his long career, ridiculing "Mr. Dubnov's spiritual Nationalism." Zhitlovsky was both one of the founding fathers, as well as a spokesman and a representative of the Russian Social Revolutionary party and of socialist Jewish groups that joined the Bund as soon as it was founded in 1898. His attitude toward Zionism was not thoroughly consequential. Essentially he was an anti-Zionist who insisted on the unbridgeable difference between Zionism and socialism and demanded a clear-cut choice. Nevertheless, he attended the first Zionist Congress (suggesting that the organization established there would include non-Zionist Jewish nationalist groups and ideologies) and in the wake of the Balfour declaration, he also joined for a short while the *Po'aley tsiyon* party, which had been founded by Marxist Zionists such as Borokhov and counted among its members D. Ben Gurion and Yitskhak Ben Tsvi (the latter, the second president of the State of Israel). He became then the butt of a joke about the *melamed* (teacher) who once drove to a fair without anything to sell and no money to make a purchase and when asked for the purpose of his coming, he answered: "So as to catch a ride back."[43] Whatever his political maneuvering, Zhitlovsky always was and remained to the very last the staunchest supporter of Yiddish and a modern Yiddish progressive culture, predicating an inseparable unity between Jewish nationalism and Yiddishism (see his *Jewish People and the Yiddish Language* of 1904). He asserted his commitment to Yiddish culture and literature through establishing, editing, and tirelessly participating in numerous Yiddish periodicals, among them the well known *Dos naye lebn*.

Nobody offered the Yiddishist cultural agenda better support in the form of a broad historical context than the already mentioned Russian Jewish historian Dubnov. Dubnov himself was not a Yiddishist in the strict sense of the term. A member of the Odessa circle of Hebrew writers (which included Achad ha'am, Abramovitsh, Bialik, et al.), he admired their achievements and kept alive his ties with some of them. He had nothing but praise for the florescence of Hebrew literature and was also supportive (as well as critical) of the Zionist settlement project in Palestine. Nevertheless, his historiosophy, as well as its political application (the founding of the Folkist party in eastern Europe), offered Yiddishism a much sought-after ideological and organizational base. Having distinguished himself during the 1880s and 1890s as the pioneer historian who brought eastern European Jewry and the Hasidic movement into the domain of scholarly historiography, he set out in the first decade of the twentieth century to compile the first comprehensive history of the Jewish people written from a nationalist vantage point—a sequel and an antithesis to Heinrich Graetz's masterful *History of the Jews*, which had unfolded the same vast canvas as seen through the lens of the Enlightenment and of the German-Jewish *Wissenschaft des Judenthums*. Dubnov's multi-volume opus, long before its last parts were completed and published, became the chief historical text of the Jewish national renaissance, allotting to him his place as one of the intellectual leaders of that renaissance. In the process of planning and writing this magnum opus, the author, pondering the over-all patterns of Jewish history, came up with a theory that was immediately put to use as the ideological basis of a new nationalist movement called autonomism, the principles of which were spelled out in 1907 in a book with the title *Letters on the Old and the New Judaism*. Dubnov was a European (and particularly Russian) liberal and a Jewish nationalist. Unlike his nemesis, Zhitlovsky, who, as a socialist and Marxist, foresaw the inevitable dismantling of bourgeois society, he believed in its ability to overcome its structural dichotomies and evolve along liberal lines. Within such liberal societies, Jewish cultural autonomy would have to withstand a severe test, for liberalism, secularization, and enhanced individual freedom would inevitably accelerate Jewish acculturation and assimilation. Whereas a similar prognosis led Dubnov's friend and ideological rival Achad ha'am to Zionism as the only means that would vouchsafe the survival of the Jewish civilization, Dubnov held an altogether different view of the Jewish cultural future. As positive as his attitude was with regard to the establishment of an elite modern Jewish community in Palestine (Achad ha'am's panacea), he did not agree with the Zionist philosopher's interpretation of Jewish history. Zionism, he opined, was not only unable to offer real solutions to the political, social, and economic problems contemporary Jews faced (with this Achad ha'am would have definitely agreed), but it also could not in itself alleviate the cultural distress of most modern Jews. There was no way a large chunk of a people, rapidly approximating in size a dozen million and living mostly in relatively modernized and industrialized parts of the world, could or would squeeze itself into a tiny desert country devoid of the rudiments of a modern economy. By the same token, the sheer existence in Palestine of an elite, Hebrew speaking community of pioneers, as desirable as it was, could not solve, for the acculturated Jew who lived in a modern country and, at least to some extent, participated in its culture, his problem of retaining his Jewish identity. Nor could Hebrew alone, being a language known to a minority of Jews, be expected to address the cultural concerns of all and sundry. Whereas Zionism could furnish a select minority with an answer to their political and cultural difficulties, the people at large needed other answers. Fortunately, such answers were forthcoming, for Jewish history itself had fashioned the mental, social, and cultural apparatus that had consistently, throughout the two millennia of the exilic period, supplied them. Thus, the inevitable failure of maximalist Zionist and Hebraist aspirations would not necessarily mark the impending demise of the Jewish civilization in the modern world. The unique quality of the Jews as a nation and as the carriers of a civilization asserted itself primarily in the fact that when their ancient commonwealth had been destroyed by the Romans, they did not suffer a national death as did many of the other contemporary ethnic groups whose independent existence was terminated. Rather, they invented a new kind of national existence, which was extra-territorial and multilinguistic and depended on the retaining of a communal and cultural autonomy within non-Jewish host societies. True, Jewish exilic existence faced severe historical crises and was from time to time economically and existentially threatened, even destroyed. However, Jews learned how to come to grips with such dangers not through reestablishing their political independence, which, as the fate of their ancient commonwealth proved, did not necessarily promise either economic flourishing or security. Instead, they learned to put to use their well-honed instinct for extra-territorial survival by removing themselves in large masses from places where their existence became too difficult or directly threatened, to other places, where circumstances were more conducive to their success and the maintenance of their autonomy. Thus, Jews moved from Spain to various Mediterranean countries, from German-speaking principalities into the Slavic space, and from there, to the industrialized West in general and to North America in particular.

Thus exterritoriality, cultural autonomy, and massive emigration in times of crises have become since the second century C.E. the staple characteristics of the national Jewish existential modality, and there was no way in which the majority of Jews could be pushed back into territoriality and monolingualism. The Jews had developed a multilingual culture when they still had their state in the era of the second commonwealth, and they were going to evolve such culture or cultures as long as they existed. The survival of the Jewish civilization did not depend on either the existence of a Jewish nation-state or on that of a monolingual culture. Rather, it depended on the ability of Jews, under changing historical circumstances, to retain their cultural autonomy, and the means for doing that had to be constantly adapted to new conditions. What could function well for a time—like the autonomous organization of the entire eastern European Jewish community under the tutelage of a common rabbinical leadership in the Polish kingdom of the sixteenth and seventeenth centuries—became dysfunctional in the eighteenth century, as the Polish state fell apart and had to be replaced, as it was, by the Hasidic movement. The classical autonomous formation of the partly self-governing Jewish *kehila kedosha* (holy congregation), a virtual tiny state within a state, the foundations of which had been laid already in the era of the second commonwealth, failed to withstand the challenges of modern times and became obsolete. Now new political and social mechanisms of Jewish autonomy had to be devised; and with secularism undermining religious authority and the modern state basing governance on the direct legal relationship between the state and the individual rather than the group or the cast, these mechanisms would have to be voluntary and guided primarily by a cultural sense of belonging within a national net of various brands of modern Judaism. Hence the momentous importance of a set of modern Jewish cultures that could appeal to and unify as many individual Jews as was possible and vouchsafe their sense of national identity. Literature serving in modern times as a central arena in which the sense of national ethical identity was negotiated by means that were both imaginative and emotive and discursive and rational, the importance of the role played by Jewish literatures, particularly those written in the Jewish national languages, could not be overstated. Bilingualism being the norm rather than the exception in the development of Jewish culture since the era of the second commonwealth, there was no need to either pit one language and its literature against the others, or even choose between them. Hebrew and Yiddish literatures could coexist and each assert its particular strength. Hebrew literature could aspire to prophetic heights, enlivening and intensifying the people's ties with the origins of their civilization, the Bible, the Mishna, and medieval Hebrew poetry of the Spanish era. Yiddish literature could develop an intimate dialogue with the largest and most vibrant segment of the Jewish people—Ashkenazic, Yiddish-speaking Jews in eastern Europe and the centers of immigration in the West. It could articulate their concerns, delve into their collective welter of cultural associations, present their specific way of life, become their artistic voice, and thus empower them and guide them in their difficult journey toward modernity. What was necessary, therefore, was the harnessing of the tools of social and cultural engineering to the project of keeping the Jewish languages and literatures alive.

Having said that, an objective survey of Dubnov's cultural trajectory since the 1880s would have to face up to the fact that his commitment to Yiddish had been both deeper and more consistent than his Hebraic inclinations, as witnessed by his activity as a literary critic (under the aforementioned pen name Criticus) and the essays collected in his book *From Jargon to Yiddish* (1929). The very title of that book clearly underlined the particular importance the author ascribed to the metamorphosis it pointed to: a despised vernacular morphing into a national language of Jews. Perhaps Dubnov's preference had to do with the relative weakness of Yiddish and its literature when he had started his own career as a historian and a Jewish public figure in the 1880s, and his fond memories of the support he had offered both in his periodical *Voskhod*. The fact that his autonomism was rejected by most Hebraists and adopted as the official ideology of a Yiddishist political party (the Folkists) also inevitably deepened an already existent bias. In his later years, the historian became increasingly involved with the enhancement of Jewish studies as they were practiced by the Yiddishist scholars of the Vilnius YIVO, where he was looked up to as the éminence grise of the institution and of Jewish scholarship. In contradistinction, his relationships with the Zionist historians of the Hebrew University of Jerusalem were not cordial. The very fact that he, the dean of modern Jewish nationalist historiography, was never invited to teach at the Jerusalemite institution spoke for itself.

Four

The Jewish Literary Renaissance
at the Turn of the Nineteenth and the
Beginning of the Twentieth Centuries

Turning from the field of Yiddish back to the Hebraic one, we must pick up our survey where we left it—Achad ha'am's dominance during the 1890s and the challenges it faced in the last three years of that decade and much more so during the first decade of the twentieth century. Whereas the clarity and strict causal progression of his arguments seemed overwhelmingly convincing to many, nevertheless, something in them was felt to be wrong. Even Bialik, who regarded himself the philosopher's disciple and based quite a few of his poems on insights garnered from Achad ha'am's essays, could not but intuit the existence of a serious error. At the beginning he was so deeply convinced by the philosopher's explanation of the poverty and irrelevance of current Hebrew belles lettres that when Achad ha'am invited him in 1896 to become a contributor to his new monthly, *Hashilo'akh*, he refused. He wrote a letter to his mentor in which he not only vilified contemporary Hebrew poetry—including his own—but actually suggested that the periodical, "from which we can expect so much," should give up Hebrew poetry altogether as hopelessly inadequate and limit its belles lettres section to prose fiction such as that of Abramovitsh.[1] Nevertheless, Bialik not only became a frequent contributor to the periodical, but by the poems he published there (and elsewhere), he clearly disproved Achad ha'am main literary thesis that a poetry not written in a spoken language could not aspire to use language connotatively and imaginatively and thus be truly suggestive, replete with semantic overtones, and possess a far-reaching emotive impact. It can be stated clearly and simply: Bialik absorbed Achad ha'am's influence and regarded himself his loyal acolyte to the extent that he would be blamed by Peretz for having presumably inhibited himself as a poet, not allowing his poetic talent the free range it deserved because he let himself be caught by "the spider web" of Achad ha'amism.[2] This assessment would be later reinforced by Dov Sadan.[3] However, it was Bialik, more than anybody else, who supplied with his poetry the living proof that undermined the very foundations of the philosopher's theory of Hebrew literature and rendered it irrelevant. Of course, he did not do it all by himself. The poetry written by his contemporary, Tchernikhovsky, as well as by a host of their younger followers deepened Bialik's unique poetics by endowing it a full orchestral resonance. However, it was primarily the success of Bialik's poetic revolution that belied Achad ha'am's Zionist prognosis that only the existence of a Hebrew-speaking community in Palestine would levitate Hebrew poetry to the level of connotative and imaginative effectiveness. Bialik and his followers managed to achieve that very goal out of Palestine and in a language that was still unspoken but rather acquired by learning. The proof of this was so incontrovertible that Bialik, commenting in 1907 on the first poetry collections of some young Hebrew poets, all of them under his direct influence, could celebrate this triumph in a metaphorical conclusion: "Our old tree, which flourishes intermittently, once in a blue moon, suddenly decided to cover itself again, at its dotage, with white flowers. . . ."[4] What went wrong then in the logic of Achad ha'am's argument? His concept of poetic language was wrong. Indeed, poetic language depended on connotation and suggestiveness, and thus a language retained in books and writing only, no matter how rich its written legacy, would fail poetry, unless its bookish life involved a lively and unceasing reformulation and reconnecting of its separate components in new ways; for language, to be alive, needed constant "kneading"; "the richest language, if its capital does not change hands, is being removed and replaced, squeezed and rummaged, improved and perfected every hour and every minute" quickly deteriorates and degenerates, said Bialik.[5] When spoken, a language undergoes such a process all but automatically. But the language of the book could also be kept alive if its frozen constructions are being constantly deconstructed and its components reunited in an authentic need to express new emotions and ideas; and this was exactly what the poet and his contemporaries did. Steeped in the textual sources, he nevertheless refrained from mere replication of their cadences, which he exposed to a tremendous emotive pressure, thus constantly dissolving them and formulating new cadences, changing in the process the entire climate of modern Hebrew culture and subtly but unmistakably pointing to the inadequacy of Achad ha'am's reductive literary theorem. Achad ha'am, therefore, hardly could go on functioning as the chief philosopher of the Hebrew renaissance once Bialik was in full command of his poetic voice. He had to relinquish the editing of *Hashilo'akh*, since the chief Hebrew literary periodical of the day could not afford anymore the exclusion of the new poetry, which blatantly undermined the cultural politics of its editor. Soon, he also was to leave both Russia and the Hebrew literary scene and remove himself to England where he wrote infrequently and focused on issues other than the literary ones that had occupied him in the 1890s. By 1903–1904, his tenure as a literary mentor was over. To a very large extent it was taken over by a younger philosopher, who was also a stormy publicist and a writer of short stories and novellas, Berditchevsky.

An erstwhile yeshiva student, in the 1890s Berditchevsky went to German and Swiss universities where he immersed himself in idealist and post-idealist German philosophy. As the title of his dissertation— "The Relationship between the Aesthetic and the Ethical"—indicated, he went, as a philosopher, beyond Kantianism (since Kant demanded strict separation of the ethical from the aesthetic). In fact, he was informed by Schopenhauer's theory of the will and deeply influenced by Nietzsche's existentialism. The lore of the latter in particular was at the root of his incisive critique of Jewish historical life, culture, and literature. The Jews, bound by a strict spiritualist and communal set of norms, diminished themselves as individuals and repressed their earthly and instinctual needs. Berditchevsky called for the total freeing of the Jewish individual from communal strictures, for total intellectual freedom, and for the Jews as people and as a people to assert their physicality, will to power, and national egotism. Early on he took umbrage with Achad ha'am's nationalist philosophy in general and his reductive literary agenda in particular. As the latter was summed up in the programmatic article that launched the first issue of *Hashilo'akh*, Berditchevsky immediately attacked it. The notion that Hebrew literature should focus on discursive non-fiction at the expense of its emotive and imaginative parts was to him a prescription for a literary schizophrenia, which he labeled *hakera shebalev*, (the tear in the heart). Literature gave expression to the entire personality, or it was not expressive at all and because the main goal of modern Hebrew writing should have been to explore the interiority of the Jewish individual, thaw its frozen instinctual and emotional areas, enlarge and set them in motion, and, above all else, map them and make the reader aware of the entire gamut of his subjectivity, Hebrew literature had to enlarge the scope of its emotive part and enrich its contents rather than abrogate and neglect it, as Achad ha'am demanded. Only by doing this would it make the contribution to the national awakening a literature could make.[6] When Achad ha'am retorted that perhaps that was what the literature should do or what his opponent wanted it to do, but the question was whether it could do it, and one should never lose sight of the gap between the will and the ability to fulfill its wishes.[7] Berditchevsky's answer was that in matters pertaining to the spirit, such quantifications of will versus ability were irrelevant. What mattered here was the authenticity of the need and the intensity of the will to satisfy it. If the need and the will were real, the battle over the realization of the desired change was half won. By and large, the reality of the painful experience of paucity and deficit was the source of a possible plenitude, since pain, when authentically experienced, could be as spiritually bountiful as comfort. The sine qua non condition for the creation of a worthwhile literature was the authenticity of the experience and that of its articulation, not the contents of the experience as such. In fact, almost every achievement in the new Hebrew literature that was of enduring value expressed a sense of missing, of craving for what was not yet available, rather than a sense of having, of satisfaction, and satiety.[8] That was inevitable, since contemporary Jewish life was one of unceasing mental and physical hunger. What Hebrew writers needed to do was to articulate this Jewish hunger—a hunger for love, wealth, and the satisfaction of one's instinctual urges (for Jews were human beings—flesh, blood, and nerves—and not disembodied brains) for them to render an inestimable service and live up to their national mission.

As for Achad ha'am's contention that no connotative, that is, genuinely poetic, articulation could be expected from a language that was not spoken but only read and written, here too the philosopher was in error. Berditchevsky, basing himself on Bialik's insights in his essay "Khevley lashon" ("Language Birth Pangs"), enlarged and further theorized their message. Poetic language was that language in which the verbal formulation of an idea or an articulation of an emotion involved the entire interiority of the writer. What mattered was not whether the vocabulary or the syntax were based on the spoken language or on the literary tradition, but whether the unique personality and experience of the writer "rearranged" the linguistic elements it borrowed or left them unchanged. If no metamorphosis had taken place, literary language fell dead from the writers' pen, whether it imitated spoken dialogue or quoted literary sources; for the genuine writer never took language as a ready-made commodity. Rather, he "created" it or participated in its creation. The Jewish people being, at least for the time being, "bookish,"—thinking and perceiving reality through texts—a genuine Hebrew literature would inevitably also be bookish and intertextual, or it would forfeit its authenticity. But that, as the language of Bialik's poetry and of Abramovitsh's prose proved, did not imply tone deafness or the lack of connotation and suggestion.[9] Achad ha'am was also wrong in his critique of the Hebrew literature of the Enlightenment and its use of biblical Hebrew. Whatever its enduring aesthetic value, this literature had done the right thing; for the choice of style was the choice of message, the two being indivisible in literature. In Hebrew, the Bible and its style, having been created by a free, independent, and "normal" community, stood for freedom, individualism, heroism, power, assertion of will; whereas later strata of the language and particularly its conflation with Aramaic, stood for religious submission, weakness, collectivity. The former was the language of the Hebrews; the latter— that of the Jews, and the duality of Hebrews versus Jews amounted to no less than the difference between two separate nations. The founding fathers of the new literature, rebelling against the rabbinical tradition they challenged, could not adopt any style other than that of the Bible. Their choice was motivated not only by aesthetic preferences. Consciously and unconsciously it was a political and a philosophical choice, and as such it also was the right choice.[10] Indeed, Berditchevsky himself, as a writer of prose fiction, chose not to follow the lead of Abramovitsh, who had wrought the "synthetic" style that synthesized the various historical strata of Hebrew, but rather to develop a neo-biblical dialect of his own; and his choice, as much as it had to do with what he wanted to narrate and with the fictional world he created, was in essence ideological and philosophical along the lines drawn out in his defense of the literature of the Enlightenment; for in a large part of his prose fiction, he focused on themes and characters that illustrated a repressed but still active Jewish "earthiness" and instinctuality, asserting themselves through acting out of unconscious instinctual drives.

Furthermore, since the Hebrews and the Jews were two different nations, bilingualism and diglossias in Jewish literatures were inevitable,[11] and indeed, such diglossias—the Hebrew/Aramaic and currently the Hebrew/Yiddish ones—were not only to be expected but also welcomed as an authentic expression of the complex linguistic patterns that the actual Jewish historical experience gave rise to. Here, as everywhere else, the actuality of real experience and its authentic articulation outweighed any abstraction. Whereas Achad ha'am's concept of a supra-historical collective Jewish historical psyche in which Hebrew was the only linguistic link between past and future was such an abstraction, the fact that Ashkenazic Jews spoke and wrote Yiddish for an entire millennium rendered such abstraction irrelevant. What if Yiddish as a language was based on some dialects of old German? Jews throughout the ages "rearranged" these dialects, amalgamated them with "loshen-koydesh" (Hebrew + Aramaic) and other (Latin and mainly Slavic) components, and by using the amalgam while evolving their specific Ashkenazic civilization, totally "Judaized" it, and a Yiddish literature was more than legitimate as a Jewish literature, as long as Yiddish was not bastardized by gentrification through re-Germanization.[12]

Berditchevsky adored Sholem Aleichem and thought he did for the Yiddish language what Rashi (Rabbi Shlomo Yitskhaki, the great medieval exegete, whose commentaries on the Bible and the Talmud assumed for hundreds of years the status of the classic and official Jewish commentaries) did for Hebrew. Berditchevsky was, indeed, the first intellectual who gauged the depth of the Yiddish master's work and pointed to the brilliance of his achievement.[13] He himself wrote stories and articles in idiomatic Yiddish as much as he wrote a considerable part of his output (stories, articles, but particularly scholarly works) in German. Indeed, guided by his existentialist aesthetics and stylistics, multilingualism—inevitable in Jewish writing under existing circumstances—was perfectly acceptable to him, as long as the multilingual reality in Jewish cultural life persisted, and as long as the multilingual Jewish writer did not try to do in one language what he could or should do in another, and, in particular, did not write one text in two languages as so many Jewish writers did at the time. Since verbal articulation formed the immediate and inseparable extension of the contents of what was being said, and style and message were indivisibly enmeshed in a genuine literary text, the idea that one original text could be written twice in two different languages, rather than be merely recast as the pale semblance translation could offer, amounted to a logical impossibility and to an aesthetic fallacy.[14] What's more, each language had a distinct historical "personality," which could or could not accommodate the specific message the writer wanted to convey. A message that could be decoded with equal success in two different languages, must have been flawed at its very inception by imprecision and lack of semantic specificity. Thus Berditchevsky, while approving of Jewish literary multilingualism, totally rejected the concept of a supra-linguistic single and continuous Jewish literature. Linguistic difference was mental difference, psychic difference, and as such, a literary barrier that could not be erased. Jewish literary multilingualism predicated the existence of many different Jewish literatures, or, as we label it later—of Jewish multi- or bi-literaturalism.

Clearly, it was Berditchevsky as a thinker who supplied the Hebrew renaissance with its broadest and most sophisticated rationale. It was not in vain that the best among the young Hebrew writers who made their debuts before World War I, such as Brenner and Gnessin, regarded themselves as his disciples and in Palestine, Labor Zionist pioneers regarded him as their ideologue, as much if not more than they saw themselves as following in the wake of those who devised theoretical stratagems for conflating Zionism with socialism (such as Syrkin and Borokhov). Young David Ben Gurion, upon arriving in Palestine and immediately Hebraizing his name (originally David Green), went so far as adapting

Berditchevsky's Hebrew pen name Micah Yosef Bin Gorion. True, some of the writer's critical campaigns, which he conducted with vehemence and bitterness, were of no avail whatever. For instance, his demand from Yiddish writers to remain loyal to an ideal of "pure," colloquial, idiomatic Yiddish, unadulterated by modernisms and by vocabulary and syntax smacking of the influence of other languages (mainly German), went unheeded, and, in reality, could not have been followed if Yiddish literature was not to remain stuck in a quasi-folkloristic phase. His attacks on Peretz, to whom he pointed as the main culprit in this respect, were not perceived as worthy of refutation. By the same token, his crusade against parallel bilingualism, namely, the writing of one text in two languages, which Abramovitsh had set up as a normative model, was paid little if any attention to even by his loyal followers. Since the reasons for this are commented on elsewhere in this volume,[15] it will suffice here to note, that in both cases, Berditchevsky actually undermined his own aesthetic existentialism by vestiges of romantic essentialism and forgot that reality, of culture and literature included, was always stronger than abstraction; for what was the ideal of pure Yiddish if not a romantic and essentialist abstraction, which a living literature, propelled by its needs and goals, was bound to disregard? The objections to parallel bilingualism, as much as they rested on solid theoretical arguments (within the limitations of Berditchevsky's romantic philosophy of language), indicated a total misunderstanding of the cultural situation in which this kind of bilingualism was not only legitimate but actually inevitable. In both literary campaigns, Berditchevsky fell victim to the weaknesses of which he had justifiably accused Achad ha'am: clinging to abstract and pure essences, falling into the trap of setting the rules, being restrictive, pontificating, and expecting of objectively unstoppable developments to somehow fall in line and correct themselves. This probably was the reason why Berdichevsky's influence could never cross the border separating Hebrew literature from its Yiddish counterpart. He had little to offer that contemporary Yiddish writers could use, whereas his contribution to contemporary Hebrew literature, particularly his theoretical debunking of Achad-ha'amism, was formidable.

Of course he was not alone in advancing a nurturing theoretical rationale around which young Hebrew writers could rally. Others helped

in liberating Hebrew literature from reductionism and self-abnegation.
Frishman had a sizeable share in the systematic inculcation of the notion that the direction Hebrew literature must follow was that of deepening its emotive contents and sharpening its aesthetic sensibilities. In
contradistinction to the cerebralism and discursive and argumentative
clarity recommended by Achad ha'am, he tirelessly insisted on lyricism
as the chief contribution the new literature could make to the national
reawakening. The critic Reuven Braynin focused on the need to enrich
and expand the mimetic scope of Hebrew fiction and narrative poetry,
bringing it closer to the psychological and social realism and naturalism of contemporary European literatures. Klausner, both as a critic
and as the editor of *Hashilo'akh* (he replaced Achad ha'am when the
latter terminated his tenure in 1902), although he regarded himself and
was seen as Achad ha'am's disciple, openly supported rebels, poets of
burgeoning eroticism, and "anti-Judaic" attitudes such as the "hellenic"
Tchernikhovsky, and later the "decadent" Shneur, both informed by
Nietzschean tenets. As soon as he assumed the role of the editor, the
tonality and cultural priorities of *Hashilo'akh* changed dramatically, to
the extent that the miffed founder and former editor of the periodical
could not but regard what he had expected to be a discrete change of
the guard to have resulted in the sensational triumph of his opponents
(implemented by his so-called disciple) and the demise of the periodical as he had created it.[16] Actually, the sweeping changes implemented
by Klausner, the fact that the periodical now serialized Brenner's first
novels, and systematically published poetry written by members of the
young generation saved *Hashilo'akh* from irrelevance and upheld its status as the hegemonic Hebrew literary monthly until the breaking out
of World War I. The fact that in 1904 Bialik became for a few years the
co-editor, responsible for its belletristic section, added, of course, to
its literary eminence. These were the years in which being published
in *Hashilo'akh* amounted to all but a consensual acknowledgement of a
young writer's right to be counted among the established citizens of the
Hebrew literary republic.

These were also the years, as noted before, in which the scholarly interest in both the new Hebrew and the new Yiddish literatures emerged.
Just to remind ourselves, the first book-length monographs on the his-

tories of the new Hebrew and Yiddish literatures (by Wiener, Slouschz, Meir Pines) appeared between 1899 and 1911. Critics such as Braynin, Klausner, and M. M. Faytelzon, and historians like Shimon Dubnov, Shaul Ginsburg, and Zinberg wrote essays and monographs that already projected literary topics into historical perspectives and treated them in scholarly terms. Ginsburg together with the ethnographer P. Marek published (in 1899) a comprehensive collection of Yiddish folksongs, arranged and transliterated according to current standards of scholarly folkloristics. Peretz himself started writing a monograph entitled "Jewish Life According to the Jewish Folksong." Articles on Jewish literatures and Jewish writers were commissioned by the editors of Russian and German encyclopedias. Yiddish and Hebrew stories were being systematically translated into Russian and German and then into French and English as well. The Yiddish poetry of Morris Rosenfeld, translated into English by Wiener and then (from the English) into half a dozen European languages, acquired for a time something like an international reputation. The arrival of Sholem Aleichem (the "Jewish Mark Twain") in New York in 1906 was sensationally celebrated by the American English press. All these were the results, or the fringe benefits, so to speak, of the Jewish literary renaissance achieving a national and international presence, which was not devoid of political implications. It was not accidental that the defense of Slouschz's dissertation at the Sorbonne was attended by no less a personality than Max Nordau, then regarded not only as a brilliant European iconoclast-commentator on matters of culture and literature, but also as the chief western Zionist intellectual and a political leader second only to Theodore Herzl in the hierarchy of the World Zionist Organization. The flowering of Hebrew and Yiddish literatures was effectively used as a political weapon by Herzl's Zionist opposition, the so-called democratic fraction, headed by Weizmann, Martin Buber, and Berthold Feiwel, in their attack on Herzl's total investment of Zionist initiatives in the domain of international politics rather than in educational and cultural activities. This was also a way of pointing to the leader's patronizing attitude toward eastern European Zionists. Weizmann and Buber were as much as saying that while Herzl was completely immersed in barren meetings and discussions with the Turkish Sultan, the German Kaiser, the Pope, and other dignitaries, leading Zionism toward an impasse, national culture was being revived by *Ostjuden*, with Hebrew and Yiddish writers of eastern Europe doing the real work Zionism was supposed to do.[17] Upon the publication of Herzl's Zionist utopian novel *Altneuland* in 1902, it was scathingly critiqued by Achad ha'am (for its all but total disregard for Jewish culture and the Hebrew language as indispensable for the realization of the Zionist dream).[18] The Viennese leaders, to their chagrin, learned that the strictures of a mere Hebraist who lived in Odessa, published in this antiquated language, could cause real political damage, diminishing the stature of the leader and raising serious questions with regard to his understanding of and respect for Jewish cultural concerns. Max Nordau was called to the rescue; however, his vitriolic response to Achad ha'am did not cut much ice. Jewish literatures and Hebrew and Yiddish writers suddenly emerged as powerful presences, which even official Zionism had to take into account. More than incorporated in the literary texts themselves, the presence of the renaissance manifested itself in the public perception of its reality and vitality. The intellectual formulations, which had a share in the engendering of this consciousness, were responsible for this important development as much as the actual achievements of poets and writers of prose fiction; for the meta-literary discourse, the evolvement of which we follow here, did not take place in a vacuum. It was created within a densely populated public space, which it impacted as much as it was impacted by it. Within this space, which kept steadily growing, its aesthetic and literary ramifications immediately intertwined with social and political ones.

During the decade preceding World War I, the glitter gradually peeled off the Hebrew renaissance. After the Uganda crisis and the death of Herzl (1904), the Zionist movement split (a sizable segment of it, headed by the English Jewish novelist Israel Zangwill, having deduced from the failure of Herzl's diplomatic efforts that the ideal of establishing the Jewish state in Palestine was politically unrealizable, and that therefore the Jewish state should be established elsewhere, in a place of lesser interest to the monotheistic religions and to the colonialist powers, seceded from it and established the Jewish Territorialist Organization), was mired in mutual mistrust (the eastern Europeans in it never forgot the Uganda plan Herzl had superimposed upon them), and generally slinked into stagnation. Although significant Zionist activities were still taking place in Palestine (this was the heyday of the second aliya) and in Russia (the Helsinki conference of Russian Zionist groups in 1905 and the important plan of harnessing Zionism to the struggle for Jewish rights in the Diaspora while keeping on the struggle over Palestine), Zionism as a movement and an ideology was entering a decade of doldrums, out of which only the Balfour Declaration and the occupation of Palestine by the British army in 1917 would stir it into renewed vitality. Hebrew and its literature were in the same boat. The Jewish youth of eastern Europe, their main reservoir of activists and readers, neglected it, joining first (before the failed 1905 Russian Revolution) the illegal Russian revolutionary groups and then, in the wake of the widespread pogroms, triggered by the failed revolution, either the Jewish nationalist Yiddishist groups (such as the Bund), or were swept by the strong current of hedonism, sexual freedom, and egotistic individualism that inundated the Russian intelligentsia of these "Sanin" years (called after the protagonist of Artsibashev's eponymous novel, a vulgarized Nietzschean superman or man-of-nature who promulgated and practiced the ideals of free and immediate instinctual self gratification).

The crisis came to a head in the years 1906–1907, when the publication of Hebrew periodicals and books ground to a halt because of the disinterest of readers. Even the publication of *Hashilo'akh* was temporarily suspended as the number of subscribers fell beneath the one thousand minimum. Hebrew activists were dumbfounded. M. Ernprayz, an erstwhile follower of both Berditchevsky and Herzl, announced that Hebrew literature and culture had suffered a stroke. It awoke one day to find itself devoid of its voice and doomed to dumbness.[19] The truth was that many had seen the crisis coming. Bialik had warned against it in dark prophetic poems as early as 1904 and in 1905; he dramatized it in his richly symbolic prose-poem "The Scroll of Fire." At the same time, the situation was hardly as desperate as the alarmists believed. From 1908 to 1910, a process of recovery allowed the eastern European-based Hebrew renaissance to regain some of its earlier energies and resume many of its projects and habitual activities, all the time

demanding support (which never materialized) from the enfeebled Zionist organization—until the outbreak of World War I dealt it the blow
from which it could not recover.

The literary ideologues of this late phase of the Hebrew renaissance
were not Achad ha'am or Berditchevsky, both writers having sequestered themselves far away from the literary arena they had once dominated. Achad ha'am, his stream of publications steadily petering out,
lived in London, taking care of the business of the Wissotsky Tea Company, while Berditchevsky, regarding his literary mission as having been
exhausted and undermined, secluded himself in Germany, where he invested his energies in scholarly work, which was to be written mainly
in German. Their places in the literary republic were taken now by their
respective disciples, Bialik and Brenner, both being, of course, literary
giants and independent intellectuals to whom the concept of disciple-
ship hardly clung.

As a poet Bialik had reached the zenith of his power and productivity around 1905–1906. The poems he would write afterward would be
every bit as brilliant as the earlier ones, but they would become progressively rarer and informed by a dark mood of despair and a sense of
isolation. Already, at the end of "The Scroll of Fire," the poet as much as
announced the end of his mission as a public figure, a latter-day Jewish
prophet, and dubbed the poetry he could still write as *shirat hayakhid*,
the poetry of the sequestered individual. In the prophetic poems he
wrote in 1906, in the wake of and as a response to the 1905 pogroms,
he actually sealed his public poetry. In the next few years he would invest the better part of his creative energies in the completion of *Sefer
ha'aggada*, the magnificent comprehensive anthology of Talmudic and
Midrashic tales and sayings he co-authored with Ravnitsky, endowing
the vast amount of material collected there with continuity, structure,
and intellectual coherence it never had had, as well as brilliantly translating it from Aramaic into Mishnaic Hebrew. In spite of this magisterial
anthology immediately becoming a best seller that also was universally
acknowledged as one of the monumental achievements of the Hebrew
renaissance, Bialik's silence as a poet weighed heavily on the minds and
hearts of Hebraists everywhere as a possible indication that their renaissance was on its last legs. Nevertheless, Bialik's influence as the leader

of Hebrew culture and literature was at this point (and well until after the War) enormous. As such, his complex and not necessarily altogether coherent literary ideology calls for a close examination.

In 1907, triumphantly summing up the achievements of the young generation of Hebrew poets, mostly his disciples (in response to the appearance of the first collections of poems by Ya'akov Kahan, Shteynberg, and Shneur—the latter his favorite), Bialik went as far away as he would ever go from the reductionist and self-effacing legacy of Achad ha'am. Not only was he celebrating the burgeoning creativity of Hebrew poets since his own and Tchernikhovsky's appearance, in spite of Achad ha'am's gloomy prophecies, (which Bialik gently ridiculed by ironically regretting the unreasonable insistence of the exponents of those marginal categories in Hebrew culture, emotion, and beauty, whom the philosopher had relegated to their proper place in the house of literature, "the corner between the door and the doorpost," on drawing attention to themselves[20]); he also seemed to bestow his unhesitating approval upon the direction Hebrew poetry seemed to have taken: distancing itself from "the national poetry" of collective woe and complaint and progressively waxing more individualistic and universalistic in its attempt to encompass and contain the "big" existential dichotomies of life and death, pain and pleasure, sensuality and spirituality, "God and Satan."[21] Here he stood right where Berditchevsky and Frishman had stood. Somewhat bewildered—how could all this suddenly come into being?—and also with a hint of a doubt about what the future held ("What are these? Autumn flowers or spring buds? Would the flowers yield fruits—or the first storm would carry them like chaff?"), for Bialik was far from unconditionally trusting the "Hebrew heart," which might or might not have been really primed for the absorption of "beauty" as one of its self-evident and enduring functions.[22] Nevertheless, he conferred his unstinted (perhaps exaggerated) blessing on those he regarded as the harbingers of the new craving for beauty.

But this upbeat mood and universalistic perspective were not to become his firm point of departure. As he submerged himself in his own poetic crisis, as well as in his work on *Sefer ha'aggada*, he increasingly viewed modern Hebrew culture and literature (even like the Zionist project itself, the chances of which he at this point had all but lost hope) as weak, disoriented, and in need of a thorough change of strategy. The meticulous anthologizing of the Talmudic and Midrashic tales made him feel that the support modern secular Hebrew culture needed might be found in a gigantic project of collecting and anthologizing, along the lines he and Ravnitsky had devised, of the entire corpus of past Jewish writing in all genres, in all places, in all periods. In his secret heart, he harbored grave doubts with regard to the chances and relevance of such a project even if undertaken by some institutional authority in possession of the resources and organizational tools needed for such a project to be realized. In a poignant elegy he wrote after having completed *Sefer ha'aggada,* he frankly admitted that the ancient texts, which had meant so much to him in his young days as a Talmudic scholar, lost all meaning and relevance. He vehemently turned to the densely printed pages of the ancient texts: "To me your lines are necklaces of black pearls, whose string broke. Your pages are bereaved, and every single letter stands alone, orphaned." Nevertheless, publicly Bialik stood fast by his program of *kinus* (ingathering) or the historical consolidation of *hasefer ha'ivri* (the Hebrew book), and in late summer of 1913, he unfolded its blueprints in a keynote speech held at the Conference of Hebrew Language and Culture—the Hebraic answer to the Yiddishist Czernowitz Conference of 1908—which took place in conjunction with the eleventh Zionist congress then convening in Vienna.[23]

This was his recipe for modern Hebrew culture and literature. They were to become the custodians of the entire Jewish literary past and as such, overcome the chasm opened by the Enlightenment between the old and the new. Rather than opting for the continuity and presumed unity of modern Jewish cultures and literatures (written in Hebrew, Yiddish, Russian, and other languages), Bialik projected a postmodern Hebrew continuity, linking the present with the many different Jewish cultural pasts. Modern Hebrew writing needed tradition to strike its roots into; of course, a living tradition that constantly would be rearranged and reinterpreted. In fact, Bialik's concept of *hasefer ha'ivri* (the Hebrew book) was not much different from T. S. Eliot's concept of "Tradition" as the fertile ground from which the authentic "individual talent" sprouted. Bialik expected the World Zionist Organization to shoulder the organizational and financial responsibility for his over-reaching program, which, of course, it never dreamt of doing. In his famous "Halakha ve'aggada" essay, written in the midst of the War,[24] he came full circle to his earliest Achad-ha'amist attitudes and ideas, belittling belles lettres and the free play of the imagination (*aggada*), and demanding a return to the somber and stark discipline of prescribed actions and a daily behavioral regime (*halakha*). Presenting these two not only as two potential literatures but also as two oppositional mental attitudes and ways of life, the greatest Jewish poet of his time clearly preferred the anti-imaginative and anti-emotive option.

This went together with a growing disbelief on his part in the expressive potential of language per se and subsequently in the relevance of poetry. In "Giluy vekhisuy balashon" ("Revealment and Concealment in Language"),[25] his most important essay on matters pertaining to poetry and language, which was written and published together with "Halakha ve'aggada," Bialik projected poetic language, and, by inference, poetry itself, as an extremely brittle and barely reliable vehicle. The essay, as already mentioned, was influenced by the ideas of Potbnja, the forgotten nineteenth-century Russian philosopher, linguist, and literary historian, whose reputation was revived in the first decade of the twentieth century by the Russian symbolists, such as Bely, who adopted his notion of language as having originated as a welter of images rather than a semantic system of communication. Bialik also accepted this theory of the origin of language, or rather of words, which presumably had been originally created not for the purpose of communication but rather as ecstatic and frightened responses on the part of primitive man to the overwhelming sights and sounds of the cosmos. Language as a communicative system of mere signs evolved as its primeval expressionistic origins degenerated: words lost, through their constant usage within mundane contexts, their immediate pictorial and emotive contents. In this Bialik came very close to the symbolists, and particularly to Bely. However, whereas the symbolists deduced from these presuppositions their call for poetic language to regain its pre-communicative status as sheer magic, and the notion that the poet could and should renounce sheer communicability and become the shaman of modern times, a master of the dormant oneiric and theurgic powers of language, Bialik based on it a tragic view of language in general and of poetic language in particular as man's feeble attempt to overcome the initial horror and awe of existence. The language of daily communication, as well as that of prose did it by hiding the realities of existence underneath a solid stratum of hackneyed signs, sucked dry of their emotive contents by constant use; the poet, in contradistinction, was trying to regain some contacts with this content, and he did it by hammering at the solid sub-stratum, breaking through it, or opening in it "windows" to the reality of chaos. Thus the writer of prose could be compared to a person who walked on the solid layer of ice that covered a river in winter, not even thinking of the dark currents underneath; whereas the poet was like a person who crossed the river in the spring, when the ice thaws, and one had to jump from one moving floe to the other, always aware of the sweeping currents and in danger of being swallowed by them.[26] Poetry was then not only in danger of its project (that of recharging language with its original magic) being momentarily undermined and disman-tled, but also tragic for its project even when successful, was that it was bound to end in an encounter with chaos or with what Bialik called *blima*, nothingness, sheer emptiness. Thus the poet ended his essay pre-ferring to poetry other, pre-linguistic, forms of human self-expression. Besides the "language of words," he said, God created also "wordless languages" such as music, crying, and laughing, which "start where the words peter out," and open up instead of covering, directly connecting us with the "abyss," and, in fact, surging up from the abyss and being part of its magma-like contents. All these went together with the poet's growing frustration with words and language and his yearning for si-lence to which he gave clear expression in the few poems he still wrote at the time. In one of these, he compared his words with a flock of white doves he had sent out of their dovecot in the morning only to get them back in the evening as dirty and noisy ravens, "a hideous scream in their throat and carrion meat in their beaks."[27] In another, the great elegy "One by one, by nobody seen," he projected not only the current cessation of dialogue between himself and the world, but also his inner-most wish to regain, let it be for only one minute before his death, the original wordless wonder of the infant as he woke up to the world of sights and sounds—in fact, a pre-linguistic and pre-communicative in-fantile paradise regained (a world that was "a garden closed and sealed, sawn with riddles and wonders, unsullied by a hand's touch, and unsullied by words of mouth").[28] Yet another poem was written as an ode to the silent ones, those who lived without words. They were the greatest artists, the true high priests of beauty, the poet said, for they never felt the need to externalize their aesthetic experiences in the form of art—visual, verbal, or musical—but knew how to protect them fresh and undiminished and thus, rescued them from the inevitable vulgarization that artistic externalization involved, hiding their treasures in the innermost chambers of their hearts.[29]

Bialik was inching toward the apostasy of denuding literature from all values and relevance. At the same time, however, he was pondering Hebrew literature, of which he himself personified the cusp or cutting edge and its historical progression. More and more he came to doubt the conventional historical narrative that he himself had upheld in his earlier 1907 pronouncement: the new Hebrew poetry was started by the German founding fathers of the Hebrew enlightenment, rhymesters who swathed it with their tepid and nondescript effusions. Then it kept crawling throughout its undignified apprenticeship until it was espoused by a heavy-handed but "virile" and "potent" master, Y. L. Gordon, who fertilized and impregnated it only to ensure the further growth and strengthening of the delicate issue in the hands of current masters, Bialik himself, Tchernikhovsky, and their disciples. Now Bialik doubted the developmental causality such narratives were based on. What seemed to him particularly doubtful was the developmental linkage tying himself and his contemporaries to their maskilic predecessors. As much as he could not deny the direct connection between his own early poetry and that of Gordon (whom in his youth he had admired although he found he was unable to follow the older master's lead successfully), he now refused to see in it his only link with the poetic tradition. Thus, he invented a new theory of the history of Hebrew poetry, indeed, of the history of poetry in general, which he spelled out in a series of lectures held in Odessa a short time before the outbreak of the War in 1914:[30] Hebrew poetry—poetry in general—evolved simultaneously on two different, and basically disconnected or independent levels, the surface level, that of the habitual, chronological-causal ordering of literary events, and the subterranean one, where poetry like an undercurrent, surged upwards from time to time, and like an artesian well sent its water into the heights; then it regressed into its underground channel where its onward journey was resumed until the next outburst. Whereas the developmental parentage of mediocre poets (in the new Hebrew poetry, all Bialik's predecessors, Gordon included) could be accounted for by events that took place at the surface level, that of exceptional poets (i.e., Bialik himself) was better indicated when traced at the subterranean level. Thus, of course, Bialik's poetry could be causally tied to that of Gordon; however, his real progenitors had lived and worked hundreds of years earlier. The closest (in time) of them was the early eighteenth-century, visionary poet Moshe Luzzatto; but far beyond him loomed the glimmering figures of the Spanish era in the eleventh and twelfth centuries: Yehuda Halevi and Shlomo Ibn Gabirol (the latter, a poet-philosopher who wrote the most personal and affect-full Hebrew poems of the Middle Ages, was Bialik's idol, to the collecting and editing of whose poetry he would dedicate years of hard scholarly work; the former, a philosopher-poet and an unparalleled Hebrew virtuoso came to be seen as the quintessential national Jewish poet, the author of "Zion, don't you enquire?" that Bialik had adapted, together with some of Halevi's best sea-voyage poems into Yiddish, thus starting the project of translating into Yiddish the work of the medieval Hebrew masters, to be continued by Shvarts and others); and beyond them—far against the edge of the historical horizon—the biblical poets and prophets themselves.

As we already noted, the notion that Luzzatto and his Italian and Dutch eighteenth-century followers (such as the playwright-poet David Franco-Mendes), rather than Vayzel and his German Hebrew followers, were the initiators of the new Hebrew poetic tradition that had been floating around for quite some time. Conservative or "moderate" *maskilim* (such as Fin) sometimes suggested it, wishing to shift the starting point of the new literature from the *Aufklärung* revolution to pre-Enlightenment precedents and thus endow it with a pedigree of historical continuity. At the beginning of the twentieth century, in the heyday of Jewish nationalism, critics and scholars, such as Slouschz (in his above mentioned pioneering history of the new Hebrew literature, entitled in its English translation *The Renaissance of Hebrew Literature*), believed the aesthetics and poetics of the new poetry had coalesced in the work of this pre-Enlightenment master, and thus the all too tight knot, tying the new poetry with the universalism of the Enlightenment (now rejected in the name of nationalist loyalties) could be somewhat loosened. As for the cabbalist context of Luzzatto's lifework and his ties with post-Sabbatean mystical messianism, which until now had deterred many from bestowing the literary primogeniture upon a person who had so clearly belonged in the pre-modern era in the history of Jewish culture, they too, and not only his aesthetic and stylistic innovations, encouraged now those who regarded Zionism as a latter-day version of historical Jewish messianism, to assign to Luzzatto the throne of the founding father of the new literature. Thus, the cultural polemicist Shaul Israel Ish-Hurwits, in an essay deploring the suppression in both the rabbinical tradition and that of modern Jewish culture of the mystical and messianic legacy of the seventeenth-century Messiah of Izmir, concluded his argument by pointing to the "positive" developments triggered by Sabbateanism in spite of its historical failure and its consequent vulgarization and deterioration by the Frankists, and the chief among these was the pioneering role presumably played by Luzzatto as the renovator of Hebrew culture and literature. The lingering "subconscious" influence of the Sabbatean movement, Ish-Hurwits argued, encouraged "renewal, the love of beauty and the splendor of nature, the unfettering of the heart's emotions, the revival of the Hebrew language as necessary for the redemption of the Hebrew spirit." It guided Luzzatto, prodded him to do his work, both as a poet and as a mystic, on a grand scale, to "renew and bring back to life the Hebrew language so that it could become once again what it once had been—the language of a living nation residing in its own territory, the language of an independent people who created vital values as independent people did." Thus, this poet-Messiah "became the founding father of the entire new Hebrew literature."[31] Bialik's adoption of Luzzatto as the initiator of the new literature was based on a more subtle argumentation. It was based, on the one hand, on Luzzatto's replacing of the Arabic quantitive meter of medieval Hebrew poetry with a syllabic and much more relaxed one, and particularly of his rejecting of "Mosaic" biblicism (i.e., a poetic Hebrew based on quotations from the Bible) and devising a "natural" or non-referential biblical style, which, informed and defined by the grammar and vocabulary of biblical Hebrew as it was, nevertheless refrained from direct quotations and thus allowed for a free and direct poetic expression. On the other hand, Bialik refrained from simplistically identifying with Luzzatto's mysticism but saw in it a genuine "outburst" of the subterranean Hebrew poetic spirit. As such, it could belong content-wise to the old, and yet prefigure, or be a precursor, of the new. With Bialik throwing his formidable weight in support of the Luzzatto thesis, it gained in importance and found new followers to the extent that it drove the historians of the new literature into half a century of deliberations and polemics, rendering the issue of Luzzatto's belonging or non-belonging within the new literature a lacmus paper of sorts, by which the ideological underpinnings of the respective scholar or an author's ideological bias could be told; which is why we shall have to come back to it later in our survey. We should, however, try here to understand the special stake Bialik had in this issue. As much as he both reiterated and prefigured the arguments with which historians had (and would in the future) buttress the Luzzatto thesis (mainly Luzzatto's neoclassical prosody and stylistics and his adulation of *mekhkar*, the inquisitive and critical mind), the poet's commitment to it was of an order different from theirs. What Bialik was essentially interested in was the complementing of the normative positivist-causal understanding of the genesis of important poetic phenomena with a parallel "tectonic" understanding of such geneses. To him, Luzzatto was not only a precursor of literary modernism but primarily an example of how the underground shifts in the development of culture and literature occurred. Once the worldly Spanish poetry of the Hebrew middle ages dwindled and presumably disappeared (that was the accepted notion that more recent research has rendered questionable), it was "swallowed" into the underground current of the Jewish poetic tradition, which channeled it for more than three hundred years into the mystical-cabbalist reservoir. For the time being, because of severe cultural and political circumstances, only there could Jewish mythopoetic cogitation evolve. Then the crisis of Sabbateanism in the seventeenth century, which stirred the intellectual Jewish world to its very depths, triggered the underground tectonic shift, which freed a potent but until then pent-up poetic stream, and thus the revolution-ary poetry of Luzzatto was released. This notion could be used both as a basis for a historical description and as a parable, for Bialik regarded his own poetry as having been the result of a similar tectonic shift (trig-gered by the advent of Jewish nationalism), which released the pent-up mythopoeia from under the heavy, gray slabs of the Hebrew poetry of the Enlightenment. The question of whether this fascinating theory has been corroborated or disproved by what we now know about either the development of the Jewish mystical tradition or that of Hebrew renaissance and baroque literature is beside the point here. What we need to take note of is the poet's extraordinarily subtle perception of what substituted both revolution and continuity in literature in general and in Jewish literature in particular. Looked at through the perspective of Bialik's dialectics, the more revolutionary a literary event was, the more it indicated the persistence of literary continuity. Thus, Luzzatto's poetry, by being presumably totally new, was also the continuation of the poetry of the medieval masters, which had completed its historical detour through the mystical tradition. What Bialik was grappling with was a theorem that collapsed the binary opposition of revolution versus continuity. To him, the opposition informing Kurzweil's title: *Our New Literature—a Continuation or Revolution?* would have seemed as ad-vancing the quintessentially wrong question, the right answer to which should have been: our new literature—continuation *and* revolution; or even: our new literature—revolution and *therefore* also continuation.

At a later stage, Bialik came up with yet another explanation of the dynamics of poetic development. This time he was looking for an un-derstanding of the modernist revolution in the Hebrew poetry of the 1920s, which brought to an end the quarter-of-a-century dominance of his poetics as adopted, adapted, and further developed by his disci-ples.[32] The poet now searched for a model that could explain how such upheavals occurred, and he replaced the subterranean or tectonic met-aphor by an astral one, that of the "pleiade" (the concept was clearly based on the model of the French seventeenth-century poetic pleiade headed by Ronsard), the system of stars orbiting around a sun. This metaphor, he opined, best explained what "periods" in the history of poetry really were. A poetic period existed, and was not just a concept superimposed by historians, when a strong enough poet exerted an influence (like astral attraction) over other poets in a manner that gave rise to the creation of a style, a certain tonality, a particular way of putting words together, which in spite of inevitable differences and nuances due to the individual inclinations of the various participants, functioned as a common denominator. Of course, this tonality was the one dictated by the "sun" or the central poet (that Bialik was referring to himself goes without saying). But then, every period also exhibited at least one notable exception; a poet or a poetic development, which as much as it shared the common tonality also and distinctly introduced alien sounds, harboring a subdued dissonance. Like a small but rain-promising cloud, this exceptional poetic development hung close to the horizon of a sun-drenched sky, but the storm-to-come was already contained in it. This had been the role of Afansy Fet in Pushkin's *pléiade*, and this, Bialik believed, was the role played by Shteynberg in his own period (the poet was talking unabashedly about *tekufati*— "my period"). Once again, it is not important whether Bialik's argument carries scholarly conviction, or whether it could truly take one anywhere beyond the brilliant metaphor itself. What is of importance is the lesson this metaphor teaches once again with regard to a poet's understanding of both revolution and continuity. Here, too, Bialik tried to yoke the two together and harness both to the carriage of the same dialectical approach to literature: revolution inheres in continuity; one period contains its rival; one system of poetics harbors its future replacement. With Bialik being the uncontested central figure in the new Hebrew literature, this view of his of the dynamics of literary change is perforce indicative of trends and currents that ran very close to the ideational core of this literature.

Nevertheless, as influential and authoritative as Bialik was, Brenner, a rival mentor, challenged him at every point. Brenner was an innovative novelist (whom Bialik had welcomed and published in *Hashilo'akh* during the years he edited its belletristic segment), but even more than that, he was an existentialist thinker, a fiery publicist and literary critic, a fierce critic of historical Jewish life and mores, a tireless literary activist who constantly wrote, edited, lectured, established new literary periodicals, and translated throughout his truncated literary career (he was

assassinated near Jaffa by Arab rioters in May 1921). In these roles, he
often won Bialik's disapproval, for the poet was miffed by both his vehemence and by what he regarded as Brenner's "shoddy style," by which
he referred not only to the writer's unadorned and stark means of self-
expression, but also to what he, Bialik, regarded as his presumed refusal
to pay closer attention to composition and focus on narrative and description rather than on argument and discursive analysis. Of course,
the stark and monochromatic articulation, the "disheveled" composition, and the penchant for "excessive" discussion and conceptual ideation were intentional on the part of Brenner and very carefully crafted.
Whereas this was to be discovered by literary critics at a later time and
during Brenner's life, many readers shared Bialik's view of him as an
uneven and careless artist, Brenner nevertheless managed to assume at
the time a literary status second only to that of Bialik. Readers, particularly the Zionist pioneers in Palestine, regarded him as a moral mentor,
a relentless seeker of the truth, and a writer who had freed himself from
all decorative accoutrements for the purpose of starkly articulating the
truth as he saw it. Thus Brenner's literary thinking, even before his emigration in 1909 to Palestine, became as influential as anybody's in the
Hebrew literary republic.

Brenner, on his part, admired Bialik's poetry but disagreed with both
his cultural-literary agenda and with his conduct in his role of the leader
of Hebrew literature. When crisis hit the Hebrew literary project in
Russia, Brenner, then in London (fleeing the Czarist authorities since
he had deserted the Russian imperial army at the time of the Russo-
Japanese war), started, with no financial resources at all, a monthly of
his own (*Hame'orer*), which purported to rescue Hebrew literature
from its paralysis. Heroically, he kept it alive for two years, with himself doing the work of the typesetter, the printer, the editor, the sec-
retarial organizer, the bursar, and the dispatcher of the slim issues as
they appeared, never being sure whether the next issue would also see
the light. Eventually, due to the Hebrew periodicals in eastern Europe,
including *Hashilo'akh*, being shut down one after the other, *Hame'orer*
served as the only active Hebrew literary periodical of any significance.
Soon enough, however, it transpired that what Brenner offered was not
only a venue of publication when all other such venues were blocked.

He also developed a new style of editing, of evolving a dialogue with writers and readers, of relating to both literary and non-literary issues. Out of the narrow window of Brenner's Whitechapel garret went the pretended objectivity and heavy respectability of *Hashilo'akh*, its bourgeois *Salon fähigkeit*. Brenner, as a commentator and an editor, gave short shrift to the pretentious, pseudo-scholarly style of articles published in the prestigious monthly, the glossy finish of its poems and stories, the latter often achieved through Bialik's (in his role as the editor) systematic retouching or rewriting. Instead, the hot and short breath of Brenner could be directly felt as one leafed through the slim issues of the partisan periodical. The editor, directly and excitedly conversed with the readers, imparting the atmosphere of a last ditch struggle for survival, defining his publication as the "Masada" of contemporary Hebrew literature. Most of the articles (a sizeable number penned by the editor) dealt with the issues at hand, whether literary or social, directly, energetically, emotionally, and pointedly, with no words minced. Some of them, like Brenner's reaction to the issue of Jewish self-defense in the wake of the 1905 pogroms (written in the form of a son's monologue, where he attempts to convince his worried mother, who would rather have him safe at home, why, in spite of his congenital "Jewish" cowardice, he had no choice but join the fighters), became classics, an integral part of Zionist education. The stories and poems the editor elicited from the young writers he respected (and with whom he evolved a friendly, one may even say, brotherly, correspondence) did not exhibit perfection or even full maturity. What Brenner was looking for was the throbbing nerve, the awakening need for articulation, rather than a finished, well-rounded product. Thus he offered publication outlets and otherwise encouraged beginners who, having been rejected by Bialik and the literary establishment, were nevertheless to become important writers (such as Ya'akov Lerner, Agnon, L. Orloff-Arieli, Aharon Re'uveni, and many others). In short, Brenner created in *Hame'orer* and the publications he later initiated in Galicia and Palestine, the alternative Hebrew periodical of the era, its anti-*Hashilo'akh*. In this he not only articulated the sensibilities of a new generation, but also, and more importantly, pointed to the reality of the impending decline and fall of the Hebraic centers in eastern Europe, the eventual depletion of Hebrew literary creativity there, and the rise of alternative centers, particularly in Palestine, but also in other places to which eastern European Jews emigrated such as England and North America. Brenner saw this as a development that was much more portentous than the sheer geographical shift of the center of literary activity it involved; for the shift in space had to be followed by a change of tonality and social orientation. The era of a Hebrew renaissance based on the nationalistic sympathies of a more or less secure middle class was drawing to an end. Therefore, an attempt to address the same middle class in Jaffa and Jerusalem (such as was done by the novelist Sh. Ben-Tsiyon in his Palestinian pseudo-*Hashilo'akh*, *Ha'omer*) were doomed to failure. Now Hebrew literature would be written by immigrants or pioneers addressing an audience that consists of poor immigrants and pioneers and whose mood and concerns were utterly different from those of the habitual Odessa-Warsaw readers of Abramovitsh's novels and Bialik's poems (both writers having been given their full credit by Brenner in his role as a literary critic); and it was Brenner, rather than Bialik or any of his disciples, who could best articulate these new sensibilities. That was why as soon as he arrived in Palestine—without being a committed Zionist, for he had faith in neither the Herzlian vision of a prosperous Jewish European polity in the Middle East nor in Achad ha'am's vision of a "spiritual center," where an elite community dedicated to Jewish studies and to the moral legacy of the biblical prophets would bring the light to the fragmented Jewish nation and to humanity at large—he became the literary and moral mentor of the second aliya. As a matter of fact, Brenner was preparing Hebrew culture and literature for their next phase, that which would emerge after World War I, with the final collapse of the eastern European Hebraic renaissance and the commencement of a new era when the tenets of Hebraic culture would have to be reified, as much as the Hebrew language itself would be reborn as a spoken vernacular. There is little doubt, that had his life not been cut short at the age of forty and at the zenith of his intellectual forces, he would have been one of the leaders, if not the leader, of Hebrew culture in mandatory Palestine.

Himself a product of the Hebrew renaissance, Brenner disagreed with many of its entrenched cultural assumptions and presuppositions. For one thing, he had little respect for the cultural Jewish past, much less respect and use than those his erstwhile mentor, Berditchevsky, had for it. Berditchevsky rebelled against the tradition, but experienced his rift with it as tragic, a veritable bleeding gash. His work was informed by a schizophrenic duality that expressed itself in what he called "the pain of Jewish history." Brenner had been, like Berditchevsky, a yeshiva student, and his thorough Talmudic education left an indelible imprint on his Hebrew style, which was by far less purist than that of the older writer. However, he did not share the latter's "historic pain." If at all, his was a historic outrage; for he saw nothing elevated or inspiring in exilic Jewish history and was not even particularly impressed with pre-exilic, ancient biblical Hebraism. He scandalized the Hebraic (and Jewish) intelligentsia by saying that it was time for the "hypnosis" of the Bible to be dispelled and by referring to the New Testament as if it formed a legitimate part of the Bible.[33] He clearly did not ascribe much intellectual worth to either the Talmud or the Midrash. Bialik's program of *kinus*, most probably struck him as bogus, for what the contemporary Hebrew reader needed to be exposed to were the contemporary existential truths, as well as the works of Dostoevsky, Schopenhauer, Nietzsche, Ibsen, Hauptmann, and Oscar Wilde (he was the first to publish a translation from the latter's works, the symbolist drama *Salome*, in *Hame'orer*), rather than to new anthologies of Jewish midrash or medieval ethical treatises.

The Hebrew literature that he regarded as relevant had started with the Enlightenment, which, he used to say, was the old and decrepit, but still the only "mother" of the modern Hebrew project, as well as of anything that was valuable in modern Jewish culture. He refused to be "ashamed" of it. The legacy of the Enlightenment was to him particularly pertinent wherever its exponents outgrew the critique of Jews as insufficiently Europeanized to become equal citizens of their countries (which were far from willing to confer equality on their Jewish subjects, whether Europeanized or not) and developed what he called "self evaluation"—the ability to delve into the depths of Jewish historical and contemporary existence and measure it by the strict criteria of radical humanism. At a time when the reputation of Y. L. Gordon reached a low ebb, he wrote a glowing evaluation of his achievement, which is still the most insightful piece of literary criticism dedicated to the greatest Hebrew poet of the nineteenth century.[34] In a magisterial essay on Abramovitsh,[35] a current culture hero, he totally disregarded the critical clichés of the period, which added up to a cult of the author as a supreme "artist," a master of mimetic description, the "painter of the convocation of Israel," and the quintessential and inimitable original "Jewish" writer—all these superlatives, deeply imbued with the colors of sentimental chauvinism. To him, the purpose of all these was to directly and indirectly deflect attention from the master's incisive critique of Jewish life and mores, from his often savagely indignant satire. Whereas these have been apologetically ascribed by Frishman to Abramovitsh's maskilic beginnings, Brenner's analysis was based on the assumption that it was exactly through this critique and satire that the author had outgrown his naive beginnings and established a vital modern literary tradition, the staple characteristic of which was daring, unsentimental, demystifying national "self evaluation."

In that sense Brenner regarded himself as the current exponent of this maskilic tradition. Far from sharing with the literature of the Enlightenment its intellectual underpinnings—rationalism, faith in progress, in the unlimited improvability of the human condition through education and rationalization of individual and collective behavior (he was, philosophically, a pessimist existentialist who regarded suffering and internal conflicts as the inalterable characteristics of the human condition)—he nevertheless upheld its belief in the tangential proximity of art and life. His keen interest in European "decadence" and current "Silver Age" Russian symbolist writing notwithstanding, he believed in "realist symbolism" (i.e., the ability of a truly realist representation of a person, an event, a landscape to represent and subsume a larger and more comprehensive truth) and in the need of literature to directly involve itself in the existential issues the writer and his readers were facing. Thus, he judged literature (as the best literary critic of the time) by its moral message as much as by its artistic level, and allowed himself, as a writer of prose fiction, to be at one and the same time almost directly autobiographical, the writer of personal-confessional fictions, and an indefatigable commentator, essayist, moral educator, and psychological interpreter—which led many of the critics of the time to regard him as a moralist and therefore a compromised artist.

The worst literary sin to him was deviousness, the lack of intellectual integrity, rather than the lack of artistic mastery. Thus, he scathingly criticized what he labeled "the Palestinian genre," the prose fiction written in Palestine by those who ascribed to the sheer presence of Jews in their ancient homeland a redemptive quality that asserted itself in their presentation of reality through the haze of idealization, no matter how slight and diaphanous. He himself did not regard the Jewish contingent in Palestine, its modern secular-Zionist part included, as in any way different from any other aggregate of Jewish immigrants anywhere else in the world (North America, London's Whitechapel, Argentina, South Africa) with the exception of those few among its members who were seriously trying to break away from the essential characteristic of Jewish exilic life, which was the holding on to an intermediary role, that of the commercial or intellectual mediator between those who did the "primary work of life" (i.e., satisfied the basic human needs) and those who consumed the products of the former's hard labor. Nothing was going to change in the Jewish condition before sufficient number of Jews made the excruciatingly difficult shift from mediation to manual labor, and to the extent that this happened in Palestine and was historically possible only there, "this was our only genuine revolution";[36] this, in spite of the fact that Brenner never idealized manual labor and never regarded it, as did A. D. Gordon, the philosopher of the second aliya, as the Jewish people's sole chance to revive their "cosmic" being, which had been truncated and shriveled by the exilic condition having removed them from a direct encounter with the elements and the universe. Brenner admired Gordon's integrity and fortitude (the latter, arriving in Palestine at an advanced age, insisted on living only on what he could earn by manual labor, and persisted in this to the end of his life) and fictionalized him as one of the main protagonists of a comprehensive Palestinian novel, but he disagreed with him on most intellectual issues. As much as he disparaged all the delusions about the Jews somehow becoming "a light unto the nations"—for him being another regular nation that produced its bread rather than bought it from others was quite enough—he also would not buy into the mystification of labor and its cultivation as a "religion." Rejecting all cults and religions, Brenner, a staunch atheist, was the great demystifier in modern Hebrew culture and literature, the sworn enemy of all mystagogues, and his literary thinking, which was a direct extension of his moralist secularism, bore witness to this.

With diametrically opposed literary ideologues such as Bialik, Brenner, and Frishman, the literary era under consideration here had to be fraught with dichotomies, conflicts, and disputations, and these directly informed its meta-literary thinking. At least three major polemics electrified the literary atmosphere during the years preceding World War I. Two of these pitted Frishman against Bialik and positioned the two as the representatives of two conflicting attitudes with regard to the directions in which the Hebrew renaissance should evolve, but also involved many others, who in one way or another sided with either of the main contenders. The first polemic, already briefly referred to, broke out when Frishman, in 1909, audaciously attacked Bialik's prophetic poems written between 1902 and 1906; audaciously—because in the meantime these poems had been elevated to a status of secular sanctity and pointed to not only as proof of Bialik's supreme ability to fulfill his mission as the Jewish national poet, but also of his ability to revive the ancient biblical genre of the prophetic "burden" and thus link modern Hebrew poetry with its biblical antecedents. A veritable cult had been established around these poems, and it was exactly this cult that the critic wished to undermine and dismantle. Frishman sarcastically dismissed the notion that the poems formed an authentic continuation of the prophecies of Isaiah and Ezekiel. Biblical prophecy, he maintained, had emerged from a mental world so alien to ours that it could not, in any real way, be revived and continued. As a "natural outburst" gushing from the welter of fervent religious ideas and beliefs of a primitive civilization, it was forceful but devoid of the artistic sophistication and self-awareness that were the soul of modern culture and literature. Thus Bialik, who more than all other Hebrew writers, managed to instill into his poetry the conscious subjectivity and the sophisticated relativity of the modern mind, reneged on his own cultural mission when he created in his prophetic poems artistic (i.e., artificial) imitations of a discourse a true modernist should have shunned. He should have stuck to his calling, which was the exploration through mature and self-conscious emotionality and virtuoso-like technique the psychological nuances of the modern Jew's sensibilities and the full realization of his lyrical and musical talent, rather than lead Hebrew poetry into the blind alley of recidivist and imitative pathos.[37]

Frishman was immediately accused (by Klausner) of formalistic aestheticism and fashionable *Schöngeisterei*. Admitting that biblical prophecy was a part of a civilization very different from ours, Klausner insisted on the possibility of the historical gap being bridged by inspired modernists who maintained a spiritual tie with ancient texts. After all, biblical prophecy formed the basis of modern Hebrew creativity, that of the writer who was, like Ezekiel, "a watchman unto the house of Israel"; and what was at stake was not the chances of an actual rebirth of biblical prophecy, but rather the modern writer's ability to levitate himself to the height from which the Jewish condition in its entirety could be viewed and a genuine national castigation and consolation could emanate. True, such levitation, as the one achieved by Bialik, did indicate the existence of a certain continuity within the Hebrew tradition; a continuity Frishman could not appreciate and fathom because of his facile skepticism and aesthetic recoiling from pathos even where it was fully justified, and, indeed, necessary.[38]

With these first volleys shot by such heavy critical artillery, the warfare commenced. Although the majority of readers and critics stuck by their faith in the legitimacy of Bialik's prophetism, Frishman's skepticism also found followers (such as the poet and critic Y. L. Baruch).[39] The ongoing debate, lasting for almost half a decade, amounted to one of the seminal clashes of ideas and tastes in the development of modern Hebrew literary culture. Substantively, Frishman's argument was flawed. The critic neglected to notice that the poet was continuing not only the Bible but a thriving modern romantic genre of pseudo-prophetism (which influenced not only Russian and English romantics and American transcendentalists but also the existentialist Nietzsche, whose pseudo-prophetic masterpiece, *Also Sprach Zarathustra*, Frishman himself had just beautifully translated into biblical Hebrew); a genre which was being currently modernized by the symbolists and about to be further developed by expressionists, futurists, and imazhinists. He also neglected to realize that Bialik's prophet was Achad ha'am's secularized one and that therefore, an evocation of the prophetic voice on his part was more anti-biblical and revolutionary than it was "pro-biblical" and traditional; for as much as Nietzsche resorted to Luther's version of the Mountain sermon, only to announce from the heights of Zarathustra's mountain God's demise and disappearance, Bialik's prophets, even his God, whom he made the speaker of his prophetic response to the Kishenev pogrom, announced God's bankruptcy, as well as the irrelevance of the Jewish supreme religious gesture of *kidush hashem* (the sanctification of the Name through the readiness to die or even murder one's family and oneself rather than renege on Him and convert).[40] Putting all these, as well as other objections aside, Frishman nevertheless did articulate the concerns of a certain kind of Jewish modernity (such as that of Fogel or Yehuda Amichai) and pit it against another brand of that modernity (that of Bialik and Greenberg, for instance). As a matter of fact, his polemic rather dovetailed with a current poetic mood of poets and readers, who toward the end of the first decade of the twentieth century grew tired of a poetry of sweeping pathos and larger-than-life romantic gestures, and were ready for a decade of intentionally small-scale impressionist lyricism. In the 1920s this mood will change, and Frishman's strictures would sound unwarranted. With the emergence of the Israeli poetry of the 1950s, Frishman's arguments would also re-emerge as cogent as they had been in 1909.

The second polemic erupted in the summer of 1913 from the podium of the already mentioned Conference of Hebrew Language and Culture that took place in Vienna as a side show of the eleventh Zionist congress. This last public celebration of the Hebrew renaissance, with the skies about to fall and crush it within less than a year, was arranged with the purpose of having Hebraists take stock of their achievements and failures, delineate the future perspectives of the Hebraic project, and last but not least, present the congress with suggestions and plans, and demand from it organizational and financial support for the struggling Hebrew project. The congress was also to be made aware of the need for a Hebrew-speaking theater, for the purpose of which Nahum Zemach, who within a few years would establish in revolutionary Moscow, under the auspices of Sergey Stanislavsky and his Moscow art theater, the experimental Hebrew speaking studio *Habima*, affiliated with this theater, brought to Vienna a semi-professional Hebrew-speaking show (which the delegates to the

congress crassly and blatantly failed to attend). The main drama in the
conference, however, took place in its second day, when following Bialik's already mentioned keynote speech of the preceding evening (the
one unfolding the poet's *kinus* program), Frishman gave a talk that
was immediately understood as a resounding rebuttal. Whereas Bialik demanded that the Zionist movement shoulder the burden of his
gigantic project of anthologizing the entire historical Jewish textual
legacy, Frishman insisted that the only useful thing the Zionists (he
himself was not one of them) could do was to support and encourage new Hebrew belletristic creativity in the present and the future.
What Hebrew culture needed were not historical anthologies, no
matter how well arranged and creatively edited, but rather new and
better novels, plays, short stories, and above all else, lyrical poetry.
No superimposed order was called for but rather freedom of expression, movement in various and even contradictory directions, better-
honed artistic sensibilities; and, for an enhancing of the chances of
such freedom and mobility, more and wider publication venues were
necessary—supported but unsupervised publishing houses, literary
periodicals, and so on. Of course, the Zionists had no intention of
following either Bialik's or Frishman's recommendations (although
the eleventh congress was not deaf to the voices of Hebraic cultural
renaissance; for instance, at its center loomed large Weizmann's report
of the purchase of a sizable lot on top of Mount Scopus near Jerusalem for the purpose of building there a Hebrew university in which
all the branches of science, that of Jewish studies included, would be
explored and taught in Hebrew and from a Hebraic-nationalist vantage point). However, the clash between the poet and the critic was
seen as sensational and was commented on by the press, including the
non-Hebrew one. The two contenders exchanged bitter altercations,[41]
each insisting on being misunderstood and on his respective recommendation not excluding that of his rival. The truth of the matter,
however, was that Bialik and Frishman did articulate two oppositional
views of both the shortcomings of current Hebrew culture and literature (Bialik: roots struck not deep enough in the tradition; Frishman:
insufficient innovation and openness to new and wider artistic vistas)
and the direction they should follow in the future. Again, the two at-

titudes would re-emerge in many variations in mandatory Palestine, inter-bellum Poland, Lithuania, and the United States, and, of course, in Israel, in the second half of the twentieth century.

The third polemic, albeit of a seemingly technical nature, was, as a matter of fact, of the highest substantive and theoretical importance. It had been brewing for almost two decades because in the late 1880s and the early 1890s, the syllabic meters of the poetry of the Enlightenment were replaced by tonal-syllabic ones, namely, by the meters practiced by most nineteenth-century European poets, and particularly by Russian ones (according to which every verse within a poem should include not only a fixed number of syllables, but also a fixed number of accentuations, appearing regularly in the same places along the entire poem). It is hard to overstate the impact this prosodic shift had. One can safely say, that without it, the poetry of the Hebrew renaissance would not have been what it was and would hardly acquire the influence it exerted. One of the first things readers and commentators noticed upon the publication of Bialik's first poem, "To the Bird," was the mellifluous musicality the young poet endowed it with by dexterously employing in it the tonal-syllabic meter. In contents and figurative language, the poem was hardly innovative; but the music sounded fresh and compelling. And, indeed, without Bialik (and Tchernikhovsky) fully controlling the musical nuances and felicities of the tonal-syllabic meters, their poetry would have hardly possessed its emotive and suggestive magic, for the new music incorporated the very soul of the new subjectivity these poets wanted to foster. At that point, however, those knowledgeable (like Bialik) became aware of the fact that the Ashkenazic pronunciation and accentuation they followed (with its accentuation of the penultimate syllable in every multi-syllabic word) was "incorrect," as the musical annotation of the Bible (the so-called *te'amim*) suggested. The Sephardic pronunciation, with its accentuation of the ultimate syllable of most words, was by far closer to the ancient norm. Voices from Palestine and its modern Jewish contingent (particularly that of Eliezer Ben Yehuda, the lexicographer, Zionist activist, and the fanatic cultural leader who insisted on the revival of Hebrew as the only spoken language of modern Jews in the land of Israel, but also from other scholars, teachers, and culture activists) called for the immediate adoption of the Sephardic

pronunciation and accentuation by contemporary Hebrew writers and
Hebrew speakers. Some (like the scholar and educator David Yellin)
suggested various "compromises" between the two systems. Among
the poets who emigrated to Palestine, there were those (such as Sh. L.
Gordon, a pre-Bialikian author of narrative poems) who started scanning the new poems they wrote there in accordance with the Sephardic
norms, publishing their poems with indications of the metrically correct
places of accentuation. Bialik worried about this from a very early stage
in his career,[42] foreseeing a time when spoken Hebrew would shift from
the Ashkenazic to the Sephardic modality, and then, since poems gov-
erned by the tonal-syllabic meter totally depended for their musical and
emotional effect on regularity of accentuation (similarly the rhyming
and the euphony in the poem depended on both the accentuation and
the pronunciation), their poetic impact would be greatly diminished
if not altogether obliterated. Forgetting this problem for a while, he
wrote around 1900, within the Ashkenazic prosodic and euphonic matrix, the most musical Hebrew lyrics ever written; but then, the problem re-emerged in his thinking, particularly since with the second aliya
the number and cultural importance of the readers in Palestine who already spoke Hebrew the Sephardic way increased. He sought a solution
for the prosodic conundrum in what he believed was the original meter
of biblical poetry, an accentual meter focused on a fixed number of ac-
cents in each verse with no attention paid to the regular appearance of
the stress in the same places along each verse, and the replacement of
rhyme and stanza with parallelism. With no need for an exact repetition of the accentuation pattern, and with no rhyming, he believed his
poems (particularly the prophetic ones) would not be devastated by the
metrical shift he assumed was inevitable.[43] However, as the Hebrew renaissance celebrated its triumphs, with scores of new poets using more
or less effectively the tonal-syllabic format, the problem was pushed to
the backburner for about a decade. It nevertheless reared its head in the
years before World War I, with the literary center in Palestine growing
in size and importance, and the question whether Hebrew poetry could
go on being written in the modality, which was alien to the one used
by Hebrew speakers there, triggered a heated and lengthy debate. It
should be remembered that many of the Zionist pioneers came to Pales-

tine with no or very scanty Hebrew, and the Hebrew they learned there was already informed by the Sephardic regulations. As some of them, like the future poet and writer of short stories Tsvi Shats, resorted to the poetry of Zionist luminaries such as Bialik and Tchernikhovsky, they bitterly complained of the wooden taste of the poetry they wished to fully experience musically (as most readers of Russian poetry, they could not acknowledge poetic musicality that was not regulated by tonal-syllabic meter and its concomitant full and rich rhyming).

Of course, the debate had political and social implications, as well as poetic and aesthetic ones. What was at stake was the cultural authority of those, who, by emigrating to Palestine and teaching themselves to speak Hebrew there, became the "true" Zionists. One of those pioneers, Shats, would contend, right after the War, that Hebrew "classical" poetry (i.e., Bialik, Tchernikhovsky, and their followers) was "in exile," and indifferent to the needs of "the workers" in Palestine, which meant that the Ashkenazic modality was not only anti-Zionist but also anti-socialist and non-egalitarian.[44] Tchernikhovsky was the poet who more than any other felt threatened. In a seminal article he published in 1912, he clearly explained what the poetic ramifications of a shift to the Sephardic modality would be and what a devastating impact on the poetry of the Hebrew renaissance it would have.[45] He rejected the notion that Palestinian speakers of Hebrew, due to sheer location, should be allowed to have the final word in such matters, which had far-reaching aesthetic consequences. Rather, these matters should be decided by writers and poets, and the majority of these were using the Ashkenazic modality. This modality should be adhered to not only for the purpose of saving from a musical catastrophe the already written poetry, like his own, but also because of its superiority as far as its musical potential was concerned—Sephardic Hebrew, sounding monotonous and hammer-like due to the sharp accentuation of the last syllables and devoid of softness and nuance due to the paucity of diphthongs. Tchernikhovsky concluded his essay with an emotional appeal to his readers: he would rather have them not read his poems at all then read them musically castrated.

The pro and con responses to his article kept appearing for a full year. Then the debate would intermittently come alive until the outbreak of the War, and the shutting off of most Hebrew European periodicals put a temporary stop to it. It would be taken up and renewed after the War, particularly by Jabotinsky, who became the most ardent believer in the superiority and the inevitable victory of the "correct" (that is, Sephardic) pronunciation and accentuation. Jabotinsky would also be the best practitioner of the Sephardic modality, and in his brilliant translations (from Dante, Poe, Rostand, Fitzgerald, and others) would practically prove that, when handled by a virtuoso, the musical potential of that modality was inexhaustible. In spite of these poetic triumphs and the substantive arguments Jabotinsky developed, with him the matter was essentially political in the widest sense of the term. Ashkenazic Hebrew was exilic and close to Yiddish; Sephardic Hebrew was Palestinian, and as far as the Ashkenazic speaker was concerned, new, fresh, unburdened by cultural atavism. In addition, the sharp accentuation of the ultimate syllables sounded like it meant action, decisiveness, prowess, virility.[46] Jabotinsky, however, was not alone in this preference.[47] One of the first things Ben Gurion taught himself when he arrived in Palestine in 1904, already a Hebrew speaker and writer, was to accentuate the ultimate syllable of Hebrew words so forcefully, that from that point on, his words sounded like a series of shouts. Listening to him from afar one heard almost only the stridently accentuated ultimate syllables. When two arch-rivals such as Jabotinsky and Ben Gurion agreed, history had no choice but to be on their side. Tchernikhovsky and his fellow poets stood no chance.

In the meantime, in the Yiddish domain, somewhat less agitated spirits seemed to reign. Having celebrated its victory in the Czernowitz Conference of 1908, the Yiddishist option seemed now eminently accessible and inviting, and scores of young writers, among them great talents such as Bergelson, Der Nister, Yosef Opatoshu, H. Leyvik, and M. L. Halpern, flocked to it without qualms, since the struggle with the radical Hebraists à la Achad ha'am seemed to have been won or become irrelevant. Indeed, the dimmer the star of Hebraism waxed in the last years of its renaissance, the brighter the Yiddishist one shone. Yiddish literature was winning something of an international acclaim (as with the resounding success Sholem Aleichem's works had when a comprehensive selected edition of them appeared in Russian translation and the sensational success of Sholem Asch's melodramas on the stages of Berlin). The vitality of this literature was such that no reasonable reader and critic, whatever his or her ideological bias, could question its legitimacy as at least one of the major conduits for current Jewish self-articulation. Some Russian Jewish commentators who continued to justify this legitimacy were clearly anachronistic and actually made fun of by "genuine" Yiddishists.

This friction between Yiddishists and their Russian-writing supporters indicated, however, that not everything was quiet and upbeat on the Yiddish front; for those supporters, as we shall see, went on offering the, by now, unnecessary support mainly because they were about to militate for the legitimacy of their own Russian writing as a Jewish writing, thus raising the notion of the possible legitimacy of Jewish writing in all non-Jewish languages practiced by Jews, to which most Yiddishists, let alone Hebraists, were adamantly opposed.

The Yiddish literary republic was at this juncture presided over by its chief spokesman and strategist, Peretz. However, under Peretz's broad and enveloping overcoat, some inner conflicts started to evolve. Chief among them concerned the issue of the bond that tied Yiddish literature to the folk and to Yiddish as a folk language. To some, this tie seemed self-evident; to others, it seemed too tight and limiting. With the justification of Yiddish writing by its accessibility to the masses now less necessary, some Yiddish modernists felt that it was high time for their literature to also sport some modernistic elitism and even hermetism. While Peretz went on demanding from Yiddish writers deeper involvement with the Jewish national traditions (as in his 1910 article "What Our Literature Lacks"), some trail-blazing modernists were intentionally pulling in the opposite direction, wishing primarily to free Yiddish writing from its traditional folksy and colloquial tonality. Young Yiddish critics and culture-activists, such as Shmuel Niger and A. Vayter made a point of translating into Yiddish some of the most radically "decadent" or modernist works of current Russian prose fiction, with the message that as much as they did not necessarily favor this kind of literature, Yiddish was now perfectly able to accommodate it, and Yiddish writers were welcome to explore poetic combinations, topics, characters, and narrative situations that were as far removed from the world and the language of the shtetl as anyone could imagine. Bergelson, the great new writer of prose fiction, to some, the all but official heir of Abramovitsh, Sholem Aleichem, and Peretz (others preferred Asch), made a point not only of distancing himself thematically from his predecessors, but actually of radically breaking away from the common denominator they all shared: conversationalism, the fluency of spoken language. Systematically preferring third person omniscient narration to the monologue form, he also invented syntactically difficult, protracted periods complex enough to render quick, recitation-like reading impossible. The syntax, parallel to that of contemporary modernist and elitist Russian writing, was as much as making a statement: Yiddish writing outgrew colloquialism. Instead of imitating fluent and garrulous speakers, it was now creating its own educated and thoughtful artistic voice and with it, its educated and thoughtful artistically-minded readers.

In America, a similar development was taking place as the Yiddish literary scene was being washed clean of the vestiges of socialist and anarchist "shop literature" (i.e., a propagandist literature agitating against the exploitation of the poor immigrants in the damp sweatshops of lower Manhattan) by a group of young impressionists and symbolists who called themselves *Di yunge* (the young ones). Presumably, these writers were waging war against a literature of sheer propaganda and rhyming slogans, but actually their critique went far beyond this. What they really wanted was to replace a literature of colloquial narration and mimetic description of Jewish life by a literature of atmospheric moods (*shtimungen*), suggestive evocations, individualistic sensibilities. Their poets, led by ideologues such as Reuven Ayzland and by poets such as the meticulous Mani Leyb and the more ironic and playful Zishe Landoy, invested their energies in inventing a Yiddish that was fluent and "natural" and yet completely "purified" of colloquialism and folk-like inflections; their writers of prose fiction split in two groups, that of the "pure" symbolists (headed by David Ignatov), rejecting the powerful mimetic and psychological realism of Opatoshu, who headed the rival one. If all these growing conflicts did not altogether undermine the impression of a relative Yiddishist unity, it was only because of the royal presence of Peretz, whose home in Warsaw became the high tribunal of

Yiddish writing, a veritable literary court. Fortunately, Peretz himself was a writer who worked not only with many genres (novellas, short stories, lyrical and narrative poetry, parables, poems in prose, prose and verse dramas, essays, journalism) and with a very broad thematic palette, but also with various poetic modalities (realism, symbolism, impressionism, even expressionism, as the analysis of his verse plays has shown[48]). Thus the desires and needs of every taste and trend could be satisfied by some segment of his large output. However, the tensions behind or underneath the throne were growing. When Peretz died in 1915, Yiddishists were in a state of shock. Not only was their cultural project too young to have lost its mentor; but also with him, they felt, their ties as modernists with the Jewish past and the Jewish folk were endangered, and thus Yiddishism could lose its, until then, common denominator. "What were you to us?" the poet Halpern, one of the most prominent among the *Yunge*, asked in his famous elegy, referring to the dead Peretz as "the dust of our pride." His answer was:

> A last charred log at night
> Smoldering in the steppe in a gypsy tribe's camp;
> A ship's sail struggling with the wind and sea;
> The last tree in an enchanted mazy wood
> Where lightning cut down at the roots
> Of giants, thousands of years old.[49]

Had Peretz survived the War, one presumes, his kingdom would have exploded in his face as the Hebraic kingdom did in that of Bialik. His death, however, clearly signaled the end of the pre-War Yiddish renaissance, or rather of that phase in the development of Yiddish literature in which its polarizing tensions and its rivalry with the Hebrew one were still relatively contained.

In 1910, however, the Yiddishists found themselves embroiled in a battle they perhaps had not expected. As noted before, their cause had been belatedly espoused by Jewish Russian activists who regurgitated the old verbiage about the legitimacy of Yiddish literature due to its accessibility to the masses, and so on. If this rubbed Yiddish critics the wrong way (and also tickled their sense of humor), it was not only because such arguments belonged in yesterday's struggles, and also sounded patronizing (when coming from Russian-writing publicists, representing the dominant, major culture, and now recommending the efforts of their humble brethren, who ministered to the uneducated hoi polloi), but mainly because it also was exactly what the Yiddish "moderns" did not want to hear; they would rather be acknowledged as modernists and artistic contemporaries than as writers ministering to an underdeveloped readership. Singing the praises of the *mame-loshn*, the Yiddish critics maintained, these Russian Jewish writers, who probably still spoke or understood Yiddish, were being downright hypocritical. If Yiddish literature was so necessary and had such a positive impact, why did they not join its ranks? Niger, the up-and-coming Yiddish critic, attacked them—in good Russian—labeling them "reverse Marranos." Whereas the historical Marranos, coerced by sanctions and the tribunal of the Inquisition, pretended to be good Christians, when, in their hearts, they abided by Judaism, the reverse Marranos made a fuss about their Jewish sympathies, but were, in their hearts, sheer gentiles or assimilationists, without any real tie to genuine *yidishkeyt*. Their Jewish nationalism was a mere show devoid of substance. A stormy polemic ensued.[50] The Russian Jewish intellectuals were up in arms: they did not write in Russian because of any cultural snobbism, but rather because they had been raised and educated in this language, and it was their only and natural venue for self-expression. If their roots in "Jewishness" were weak, they at least wished to strengthen them, whereas the Yiddishists, protecting *yidishkeyt* as if it were their own little turf, were arrogant, opinionated, and blinded by ideological slogans. Chief among these combatants were the Jewish Russian writer and revolutionary activist S. An-sky (S. Z. Rapoport). Affiliated with the Russian underground socialist-revolutionary faction, he was also a writer of prose fiction, a Jewish ethnographer and chronicler, and the author of the world-famous balladic drama *Between Two Worlds*, popularly known as *The Dybbuk*. An-sky's retort was insightful and honest: all Jewish modernists were to some extent "reverse Marranos," whose wish to be identified as Jews by far exceeded their authentic "Jewishness." Thus the sheer wish to come closer to Judaism should not be pooh-poohed, for it was the best modern Jews could genuinely come up with. Then, going beyond the boundaries of the "reversed Marranos" polemic, An-sky opened an altogether new can of theoretical and ideological worms. Since the reality of Jewish cultural life was what it was, that is, many Jews were conducting their cultural affairs in non-Jewish languages, such as Russian and German, why limit the space of Jewish literature to Hebrew and Yiddish writing only? One should rather develop a concept of trilingual or even multilingual Jewish literature, written in the various national Jewish languages and in non-Jewish ones as well, when the latter were employed by Jews informed by Jewish interests and concerns.

The Yiddishists were horrified. Having just won their Jewish literary legitimacy alongside the Hebraists, were they now to share it with those who write in non-Jewish dominant languages such as Russian and German?! Would that not drive talented writers to dedicate themselves to writing in languages that had great literary traditions, were highly developed, and commanded the attention of a reading public that was by far larger and better educated than the one they addressed?! Basing themselves on the old romantic notion concerning the intimate and irreplaceable tie connecting organic peoplehood with a national language (the same theory quoted earlier by the Hebraists), they cried foul. Resorting to non-Jewish languages could lead only to assimilation—the habitual and by now threadbare accusation. Not surprisingly, perhaps, Bialik, whose relationships with Yiddishists, including his erstwhile friend Peretz, became very strained after the Czernowitz Conference, joined them in rejecting the concept of a Jewish literature written in a non-Jewish language. Differentiating the Arabic Jewish literature of the Middle Ages (Halevi, Maimonides, Yona Ibn Janakh, et al.) from the German and Russian Jewish writers of the Enlightenment and modern eras, he accused the modernists of being apologetic and seeking favor with the non-Jewish reader. The medievalists sought to serve the needs of their people and resorted to Arabic only where there was no Hebrew vocabulary for the philosophical or grammatical-rhetorical treatises they wanted to write; whereas the moderns used foreign languages to advance the unrealizable agenda of emancipation and always wrote as if the non-Jewish reader was peeping behind their back. The only exception to this he knew was the ardently nationalistic Russian Jewish writer M. Y. Ben ami (Rabinovitsh).[51] Bialik's argument was not very persuasive. Evading the full significance of the medievalist's resort to Arabic, his sweeping accusation of all modern Jewish writers of apologetically currying favor with an imagined non-Jewish readership was in many cases unjustified and could easily be proven wrong. He did not bother to show how the work of Ben ami escaped this demeaning attitude and was essentially different from that of other Russian Jewish nationalists. His critique hardly dovetailed with either his own attachment, as a beginner, to the Russian-Jewish poetry of Frug (which had strongly influenced his own early poems, as well as the Hebrew poetry of the time as a whole) or with his admiration in his later years for a Russian-Jewish novel such as Jabotinsky's *Samson the Hermit*, which, he said, successfully performed the feat of creating a modern Jewish myth.[52] Bialik also evaded the simple truth to which An-sky (whose *Between Two Worlds* he would translate from Russian into Hebrew, for the play to be staged, with resounding international acclaim, by the *Habima* group) had pointed—that most Jewish writers who resorted to non-Jewish languages did that because they could not write in any language other than the German or Russian that was their mother tongue and the only language in which they could achieve cultural creativity; nor were Hebrew and even Yiddish accessible to the larger part of the reading public they targeted.

Such rejections coming from threatened Hebraists and Yiddishists could not, however, obfuscate the cogency of the questions An-sky asked. These questions, once clearly articulated, simply would not go away. As much as it was heartily disliked by Zionists and Yiddishists alike, the option of Jewish literatures being written in German, Russian, French, and English loomed large and larger as Jewish acculturation within non-Jewish societies progressively became the essential reality of Jewish cultural life in the twentieth century. Although some Jewish writers writing in non-Jewish languages (most notable among them, Franz Kafka) would fully and clearly articulate what they believed to be their awkward, or in fact "impossible" linguistic situation,[53] the reality of such writing was potent enough to silence all qualms, even as Kafka's unpublished texts were too potent and commanding to be destroyed according to his wishes. After the Holocaust and the tragic disappearance of the Yiddish reading public, the very existence of a Jewish literary culture outside Israel depended on the tenability of that option. In other words, the possibility of writing Jewish literary texts in non-Jewish languages offered and still offers the only chance for the survival of the Jewish literary polyphony that had begun more than two millennia earlier, in the days of the second Commonwealth. The historical facts and circumstances swept aside the objections and vindicated An-sky's contentions, which, by the way, were not exclusively his, since other prominent nationalist thinkers and ideologues, such as Berditchevsky, formed similar concepts of multilingual Jewish literary creativity. Jews did use (and are still using) non-Jewish languages for negotiating, whether in imaginative or discursive writing, their Jewish identity, and this writing of theirs could not and would not be pushed out of the boundaries of Jewish literature or literatures, even where this writing was and is accepted as an integral part of the major national literatures written in the respective non-Jewish languages. Even then such writing had often to assume the position of minority-discourse, as Delueze and Guattari have shown in their essay on Kafka. And as often, not far beyond this marginalization lurked a subtle rejection. Were Jewish writers who negotiated their Jewishness in non-Jewish languages really "accepted" and gathered into the lap of the national literatures of their respective host societies? (This question was articulated at the beginning of the twentieth century with total clarity by Kornei Chukovsky).[54] Was not Heine labeled by his anti-Semitic detractors the representative of "Young Judea" rather than of *Jung Deutschland*? Were not Jews allowed to both participate in a non-Jewish literature and yet also contribute to a Jewish one? All these questions hovered in the air as the Hebrew-Yiddish renaissance was about to end. They would re-emerge in the inter-bellum period and then assume critical importance in the era following the Holocaust and the birth of Israel.

Five The Inter-Bellum Decades: Hebrew

The war years brought the roof in the house of the Hebrew-Yiddish renaissance crashing down on the heads of those in it. Peretz, Sholem Aleichem, and Abramovitsh died in 1915, 1916, and 1917, respectively. Bialik experienced his last outburst of intense poetic creativity from 1915 to 1916. During the last two decades of his life—he died in 1934—he would add little of significance (with the exception of the four chapters of an autobiographical epic cycle he published between 1928 and 1934) to his already crystallized and finalized poetic corpus. Almost all the European and Palestinian Hebrew and Yiddish literary periodicals either temporarily shut down or folded completely. When literary life resumed in 1918–1919 both literatures were not what they had been. Hebrew literature was by far more impacted than its Yiddish counterpart. The reason was that its readers were concentrated in places that were distant from its centers of production (the editorial offices of periodicals and newspapers, the main publishing houses, the printers' shops). Whereas most of the production work took place in Warsaw, and to a much lesser extent also in Odessa, the Hebrew reading public resided in Lithuania, Byelorussia, the northwestern Ukraine, Palestine, and the United States. After Warsaw was occupied by the Germans, who also quickly penetrated the southern Ukraine, and eventually occupied Odessa as well, the connecting lines that had tied production to readers broke one after another. The fronts tore the "Hebrew space" of eastern Europe to pieces and rendered communication within it impossible. This space was never to be truly stitched together, since the war would be followed by civil wars and pogroms of unprecedented magnitude; then, the victorious Bolshevik regime, which would take charge of the erstwhile Czarist Empire, would gradually—always prodded by the viscerally anti-Zionist and anti-Hebraic Jewish "section" of the Bolshevik party (the so-called *Yevsektsya*)—eliminate all public Hebrew activities in the Soviet Union.

Yiddish literature was somewhat less impacted, since its readers, whether in Poland, Galicia, or the Ukraine, lived closer to its centers of production, and its organizational and financial basis was less dependent on long-distance communication and transportation. Yet, the war wreaked havoc on it, too. Many Yiddish writers who lived in the West (such as Sholem Aleichem, who due to his delicate health lived in Italy, Switzerland, and Germany), were cut off from their venues of publication and sources of income. Both the war and the civil struggles it triggered cut its centers from each other (thus, for instance, Galicia and its cultural Jewish center Lemberg [Lviv], first occupied by the Russian imperial army, then "liberated" by the Austro-Hungarian army, was totally cut off from both Warsaw and Odessa). Quite a few young writers, both Hebrew and Yiddish, were drafted, sent to various fronts, and, if not killed in battle, deserted, hid themselves, froze in Siberian prison camps, or were detained in Austrian and German camps designed for subjects of enemy countries (most of them had Russian passports).

All this notwithstanding, the meta-literary discourse we have been following did not altogether evaporate. On the contrary, it seemed as if the devastating dislocations and the horrendous scenes of battles, pogroms, and homelessness that many writers were exposed to, sharpened rather than dulled the edge of both old and new literary debates; and as soon as an opportunity made it possible, these debates found vigorous expression, no matter how irregular and discontinuous. One such opportunity presented itself after the March revolution of 1917, when a sudden blast of freedom hit the war-torn Russian expanses. Immediately, Hebraists—who were also energized by the Balfour Declaration, the formation by Jabotinsky and Yosef Trumpeldor of the "Jewish Legion" and its participation as part of the British army in the battles that "liberated" Palestine—became hectically active. Bialik published a comprehensive one-time literary almanac that contained, among many other things, all the new poems he wrote during the war years, as well as his two most important meta-literary essays "Halakha ve'agada," and

"Giluy vekhisuy balashon." In Moscow (the Pravoslav capital, in which until now almost no Hebraic activities had been permitted), a new Hebrew daily appeared; *Habima*, a Hebrew-speaking theatrical troupe, was established as one of the experimental studios of the Moscow Art Theatre. A rich Jewish merchant who was also an ardent Hebraist, A. Y. Shtibel,[1] laid the foundations of a large-scale publishing house of a kind unknown until then in the history of Hebrew publishing. Guided by Frishman, it launched a grandiose project of not only housing under its roof the best Hebrew contemporaries (among them: Berditchevsky, Brenner, Agnon, Tchernikhovsky, Shteynberg, Fichman), but also, and perhaps primarily, of translating into Hebrew the best in world literature, from Homer to Tolstoy, from Anacreon to Heine and Lermontov to Rabindranath Tagore, and from Dickens to Flaubert, Anatol France, and Romaine Rolland. In addition, it also published a Hebrew literary quarterly of mammoth dimensions, *Hatekufa* (*The Epoch*), which was supposed to be open to all trends and currents, old and new, in Hebrew writing. It brought back to Hebrew writing old-timers such as Berditchevsky, but also serialized a long novel by the arch-modernist Eliezer Shteynman; it published poems by Tchernikhovsky and the members of the Bialikian *pléiade* but also created a sensation by publishing for the first time the work of young Hebrew poetesses, among them Elisheva Zhirkova, a Russian poetess, who converted—not to Judaism but to Hebraism. All this was overwhelming and, of course, short lived. Within a short time the October revolution would render this frenetic Hebraic awakening in Russia obsolete. Shtibel's publishing house and *Hatekufa* would be moved to Warsaw; most established Hebrew writers and educators would leave the Soviet Union—on their way to Palestine or Warsaw or Berlin of the Weimar Republic. *Habima*, protected for some years by many Russian luminaries such as Gorky and Stanislavsky, would struggle against the growing pressure of the Yevsektsya, which adamantly demanded the abolition of the state-financed "clericalist-Zionist" theatrical group, and then leave revolutionary Russia, its artistic cradle.

Clearly, the foundation and apparatus of the pre-war Hebrew renaissance were shattered. Its territorial base, as well as its readers were torn in two parts, the one that stayed within the new boundaries of the

Soviet state and the one contained within the new eastern European republics and constitutional monarchies engendered by the Versailles peace treaty. The latter part was then further splintered into the separate locales and groups residing in those new nation-states that had risen from the ruins of the Habsburg and part of the Czarist empires. Most of these states were chauvinistic and adamant in their wish to superimpose a dominant nationalist culture and language on all ethnic minorities through cultural and economic "Polonization," "Rumanization," and so on. This, in spite of the considerable autonomy theoretically granted to these minorities by the international agreements to which the respective new states had to agree for their legitimacy to be internationally recognized. Their independence based on the principle of national self-determination, first espoused by Lenin and then copied by Woodrow Wilson into his famous blueprints for a stable universal peace, these states nevertheless loathed that principle when it empowered their own ethnic minorities. Before the ink dried, the documents guaranteeing ethnic cultural autonomy were being circumvented and reneged on. Hebrew culture activists, while using the official policy of cultural self-determination for developing a net of Hebrew educational institutions throughout Poland, Rumania, and the Baltic republics, immediately realized they were facing an uphill battle that would become progressively harder. The Hebrew renaissance, which had been economically and socially dependent on the continuity and essential unity of the eastern European Jewish space, could not survive these new conditions. In the Soviet Union, it was now regarded as an ideological enemy to be repressed and obliterated. In other countries, its resources, support systems, and audiences were depleted, curtailed, and fractured. If nevertheless the Hebraic project would not be altogether moribund in eastern Europe, it would be mainly because of the excellence of the Hebrew schools there and the ever-tightening ties with mandatory Palestine, where the new Hebrew center was evolving at an accelerated pace.

This connection with Palestine and its new Hebrew institutions (publishing houses, literary periodicals, newspapers, and schools producing a new generation of Hebrew readers, teaching all disciplines and topics in Hebrew and using Hebrew textbooks for all disciplines rather than solely for the Hebrew and Judaic ones) would not, however, become firm and dependable before the second half of the 1920s; and for the time being, the Hebraic project was in a state of flux and disorientation—its fate, unpredictable. New centers, like so many flashes in a pan, kindled sudden and short-lived fires in places where Hebrew possessed no local, social, and financial anchorage. Outwardly reminiscent of the hectic Hebraic activities and high hopes in Kerensky's Moscow of 1917, these ephemeral bursts of activity were essentially different. Whereas the short-lived era of Hebrew florescence in Moscow could have been continued, were it not for the change of the regime (Moscow being now the capital of the state, it could have become the center of Hebrew activity in the Soviet Union, were such an activity to be permitted), no such continuity could be expected in Berlin of the Weimar years, where some splendid Hebrew publication activities, funded from abroad, flourished for a while under the circumstances of the great inflation of 1923. Paris could count among its hordes of artistic and intellectual expatriates also a small group of Hebrew and Yiddish writers, but no continuous publication activity could be expected to evolve there, and Hebrew Parisians, such as Shneur, Haim Hazaz, and Fogel, were either living on honoraria arriving from abroad or reduced to the status of semi-clochards. London, now a center of Zionist activities (in the wake of the Balfour Declaration and in preparation for the mandate over Palestine being trusted with the British government by the League of Nations) had its own little group of Hebraists, who had no ties with and received little support from established English Jewry, its Zionist contingent included. Vienna, in spite of its historical connections with Galician Jewry and the throngs of eastern European refugees who had arrived there during the war, also had no Hebraic *Hintergrund* of its own, now that it was politically severed from the erstwhile eastern parts of the lost empire. Thus, Hebrew activity in all these places was temporary and erratic. Only the Hebrew center in the United States (particularly in New York) and, of course, the one in Palestine had some stable communities to which they ministered. Both centers, established more or less at the same time (the 1890s and the first decade of the twentieth century) as extensions of the eastern European hub, had developed styles and modi vivendi of their own, the former catering to readers of Hebrew among those involved in Jewish education and to some extent also synagogue services in America; the latter, targeting besides Palestinian Hebrew educators and Zionist functionaries, also the five or six thousand Labor Zionists, the pioneers of the second aliya, who started newspapers and periodicals of their own. The Palestinian center had been devastated by the war, and all but dismantled as the retreating Ottoman army desperately tried to stop the advancing British forces. However, it was being quickly put together and enlarged now that the third aliya was bringing to the country tens of thousands of young, educated Jews. However, its reorganization, as noted before, would take a few years, not only because it would have to start almost from scratch, but also because the influx of the new arrivals would necessitate a shift in its premises and priorities. Carried by the winds of war, pogroms, civil struggles, and the October Revolution, as well as the modernist revolution in European philosophy and arts, these new members of the Palestinian center would bring to it concepts and temperaments very unlike those of their predecessors. Thus, it was usually only in the distant American center (and to a much lesser extent the Warsaw-Polish one) that the ambience and tonality of the pre-war Hebraism was continued and allowed to evolve rather than be abruptly interrupted and challenged. In all other centers, where the Hebrew pre-war establishment imploded or was destroyed, the atmosphere of the first post-war years would be conducive to revolutionary innovations and revisionist reversals, including innovations and reversals in the meta-literary discourse. It was as if the splintering of the Odessa-Warsaw axis, on which the steady mobility of the Hebrew chariot had depended, triggered many erratic short-range sprints, that would be streamlined into some kind of orderly mobility only as the third decade of the century wore on and mainly in Palestine.

In 1918 in war-ravaged Vienna, before the rumble of cannonade was silenced, G. Shofman, the master of the Hebrew short story, and the essayist Tsvi Dizendruk, began publishing the slim brochures of a new Hebrew monthly, *Gevulot* (*Borders*), which featured for the first time poems by Fogel (mostly written when the poet, as a Russian subject, was incarcerated in Austrian detainee camps), as well as some of the Hebrew war poems written by Greenberg when he served as a soldier at the Serbian front. Clearly, here one heard perhaps for the first time the voices of Hebrew expressionism, which resonated with Dizendruk's short essays about language. *Gevulot* did not survive its first year of publication but was followed by other short-lived periodicals or one-time miscellanies of Hebrew belles lettres and essays by various writers, most of them modernist and expressionist in orientation, such as *Kolot* (*Voices*) in Warsaw, *Rimon* (*Pomegranate*) in Berlin, *Peret* (*A Seed* or *A Grape*) in Vienna. Even in far-away Moscow and Leningrad, beyond the now sealed border of the Soviet Union, young Hebrew "Octoberists" (Hebrew writers who believed in the possibility of developing in Communist Russia a new Hebrew writing, informed by the ideals of the October Bolshevik Revolution) were striving to find a venue for the publication of their work—poetry stamped by the imprint of Esenin's imazhinism and Mayakovsky's "constructive" futurism, and prose influenced by the satirical style of Ilf and Petrov or by the expressionist short stories of Isaac Babel. (Babel was in touch with the members of this group and allowed the publication of some of his short stories in their forthcoming almanac in a Hebrew translation that he, a *kheder* graduate, supervised.) After untold struggles, they managed in 1926 to obtain permission to publish their first and only miscellany *Bereshit* (Genesis), the last Hebrew publication to be granted an official Soviet permit, which had to be printed in Germany because Russian printing houses with Hebrew letters, all controlled by the *Yevsektsya*, refused to print it.

Perhaps the most interesting among these sporadic publications was *Eretz* (*Land*, the Zionist overtones of the title were unmistakable), published on the worst kind of blotchy wartime paper in Odessa in 1919, in the midst of a savage civil war ravaging the Ukraine, and ongoing pogroms in which close to one hundred thousand Jews were murdered, maimed, or raped. It was put together not by an organized group but rather by a random collection of young writers: some of them (like the poet Y. Karni) residents of Odessa; but most of the others, writers whom the vicissitudes of the troubled era brought there for a short time, such as the poet Avigdor Hame'iri, an officer in the Austro-Hungarian army who was on his way from the Siberian camp of war prisoners where he had spent two horrendous years; the critic S. Zemach, a pioneer of the second aliya who had studied agronomy in France, and when caught there by the war, managed to join his wife's family in the Ukraine; or Shteynman, the perennial maverick, who had spent most of the war years in Warsaw as Frishman's personal secretary, then joined the editorial board of *Hatekufa* in Moscow, declared himself after the October Revolution "a Hebrew Communist," then fled to Odessa, from which he was to return to Warsaw (where he would found and edit *Kolot*), and so on. An oppositionist in principle, and always the carrier of the banner of the new, Shteynman now energized this motley company (some of the members of which, like Zemach, would soon develop visceral animosity toward him) in its attempt to declare a Hebrew literary revolution in Odessa, the capital of the more conservative and classical contingent in the pre-war Hebrew establishment, the citadel of Abramovitsh, Achad ha'am, and Bialik.

Eretz, like the other post-war publications, contained more or less new or modernistic poems, short stories, and essays. However, unlike other contemporary literary collections, it was arranged in a peculiar order, which highlighted its rebellious character. The various stories, cycles of poems, and articles were separated from each other by special ornamental pages, in which one of the writers-editors sang, in a highly poetic and metaphorical style, the praises of a certain writer from the past or the present. Thus, the young editors were pointing to what for them was the "living" tradition in modern Hebrew writing. The list started with Mapu, the mid-nineteenth-century author of the famous biblical romances *The Love of Zion* and *The Guilt of Samaria;* it included Berditchevsky and Frishman and idolized Gnessin (this was the beginning of the Gnessin cult, which would be upheld and further developed throughout the 1920s and 1930s by the various groups of the modernistic Hebrew avant-garde). Conspicuously missing in the list was Abramovitsh who until now had been almost consensually regarded as the founding father or the creator of artistic Hebrew prose fiction. This lacuna was more than explained in the chief (and the only outstanding) piece of literary criticism that the publication featured, a ferocious critical attack—written with sparkling élan and clarity by S. Zemach—on the "Mendelean" narrative manner. Disdainfully dismissing the accepted notion that this manner represented a uniquely Jewish way of narrating—by pointing to the similarity between it and the European picaresque novels of the seventeenth and eighteenth centuries, the critic accused Abramovitsh of seeing only the tattered outer social-ethnic surface of Jewish existence, without ever delving into its emotional and intellectual depths. What Abramovitsh offered was superficial and lowly realism, and wherever he influenced other writers, such as Sholem Aleichem or Bialik (in his prose fiction), the results were vulgarity and shallowness. This was the essential statement, which clarified the intent of the publication as a whole: the living, modern Hebrew tradition was lyrical rather than epic, expressionist rather than mimetic, imaginative rather than realist, poetic rather than prosaic. It started with Mapu, rather than with Abramovitsh, because the former had presumably given free range to his colorful "oriental" imagination. Until now marginalized as a naive *romancier*, the author of idyllic or blood-curdling melodramatic novels of villainy pitted against pure love, he was now nominated the founding father of the new canon. That canon culminated in the scant (in quantity) but superb (in quality) legacy of Gnessin (who had died in 1913 at the age of thirty-three) because at the time he was regarded (quite wrongly) as the Hebrew master who had merged prose with poetry and created a new, modernist kind of lyrical-psychological narrative art (Frishman had said, after Gnessin's premature death, that all his four major novellas amounted to chapters in one poetic cycle.[2] Gnessin actually was primarily a meticulous and brilliant master of prose (as a poet he never transcended mediocrity), who introduced to Hebrew fiction something similar to a stream of consciousness technique (pre-dating both James Joyce and Virginia Woolf), which he had partly learned from the Russian symbolists. Whereas most of the poems and stories published in *Eretz* were not particularly memorable, as a meta-literary statement this assemblage was quite coherent and of considerable significance.

Of course, the dynamics of the new meta-literary discourse were to be negotiated primarily in Palestine, with the American Hebrew center lagging behind, in spite of the fact, that among the American Hebraists a rather large group of critics and poet-critics, such as M. Ribolov, Epshteyn, Shimon Ginzburg, Shimon Halkin, Avraham Regelson, Ayzik Zilbershlag, Yeshayahu Rabinovitsh, and many others, some of them people of erudition, intellectual acumen, and elegant style, rendered non-fictional essayistic writing in general and literary criticism in particular, a genre second in importance only to poetry in American Hebrew writing. In no other Hebrew center throughout the inter-bellum period was this genre as prominent and dominant as it was in the United States. This group, evinced conservative attitudes, and therefore, in the stormy atmosphere of the 1920s, had little influence beyond the boundaries of their own narrow enclave. Their relative conservatism was rooted in the social base of American Hebrew literature. Catering mostly to educators and cultural functionaries and supported by the same Jewish American middle class that maintained the system of Hebrew schools (after-hours and Sunday classes, which added some Hebrew component to the education dispensed by the American public school system), their social and financial underpinnings were different from those of the pre-war Odessa-Warsaw writers only to the extent that in an immigrant society that swore by the slogans of the melting-pot ideology and whose highest dream was that of sloughing off, as soon as was possible, its immigrants' "greenness," and pursuing acculturation and upward financial mobility, the status of the Hebrew teacher and writer was by far lower than it had been in pre-war eastern Europe and his or her essential experience was one of marginality and expendability. Thus most American Hebrew writers were unable and unwilling to challenge the tenets of bourgeois respectability. They rather strove to acquire as much such respectability as they could lay their hands on through academic or pseudo-academic seriousness and through maintaining a conservative poetics informed by romantic ideals and those of American Victorianism and nineteenth-century transcendentalism. Unlike American Yiddish writing, which was rooted in the immigrant experience of the hardship and exploitation of the working class and focused for better or worse on the actual existence of proletariatized shtetl Jews in the industrialized metropolis, the Hebraists, until the appearance of avowedly urban and modernist poets such as Preil in the 1930s and M. Ts. Halevi in the 1940s, evoked scenes and figures from a rural New England-like America that was not theirs. Their pessimistic and low-spirited sense of cultural marginality and bleak future perspectives they conveyed through epic poems focusing on the tragic experience of the American Indians and the hardships of the American blacks (G. Preil would include in a poem dedicated to one of these epic bards, the poet and philosopher Yisrael Efrat, the insightful remark: "What was written about Indians, for instance, / Now almost amounts to a historical finding. Wearied and suspicious / I my-self am an Indian wondering in a darkening mirror."[3]). Almost none of them (before the above-mentioned Preil and Halevi, to whom one may add Barukh Katsenelson, in his poetic apprenticeship a practitioner of Fogel's low-keyed expressionism) crossed, ideationally or stylistically, the threshold of modernism—again, in contradistinction to their Yid-dish counterparts, who in the 1920s quickly and avidly absorbed the influences of Anglo-American modernism and became, together with the contemporary *khaliyastre* ("gang") of Warsaw-centered expression-ists and futurists, the leaders of the modernist school in Yiddish writ-ing. The American Hebrew center was the only one in the inter-bellum period where the Bialik-Tchernikhovsky poetics was further developed, instead of being challenged and dethroned, which did not imply that its best members (poets such as Halkin, and particularly the unique and idiosyncratic Regelson) were not innovative and original. Even as they carried on the Bialik tradition, they thoroughly changed it, for instance, by intensifying, rather than diluting, the literary and bookish quality of the style they employed—to the point that it assumed a tor-tuous baroque density that suited their "metaphysical" tendencies and charged their poems with a combustible emotional-intellectual high voltage but was totally alien to the relaxed, transparent, and harmoni-ous flow of Bialik's characteristic style. Informed by romantic metaphys-ics and transcendentalism, the American Hebrew poets also added to the Bialik-Tchernikhovsky poetic formula a heavy dose of philosophical cogitation, which they needed to defend against both the old-fashioned ideals of sentimental emotionalism and the new fangled modernist (ex-pressionist) emphasis on the externalization of raw emotion.

Thus their meta-literary thinking, best represented by a series of bril-liant essays Halkin wrote in the 1920s, was essentially defensive and apologetic. It had to explain and justify their anachronistic "American-ism," which modernists-Hebraists in Europe and Palestine found old-fashioned, nineteenth-century Hiawatha-like, and unappealing. Turning to Hebrew American poetry (and to a lesser extent prose-fiction, al-together an underdeveloped genre), those European and Palestinian Hebraists wished to catch through it the echoes of American Whit-manesque egalitarianism, the rhythms of conveyer-belt industrialism, and the symphonic cacophony of the modern metropolis. Instead they found in it lakes, mountains, pantheistic musings, and rural idylls, in which Tchernikhovsky's old shtetl Jewesses and rustic gentile crones were replaced by New England Puritan spinsters.[4] Halkin had to fend off their criticism, explaining how the American Hebraist needed all these to assert his poetic individuality, and why he could not satisfy the "Americanist" expectations of those who did not share the American experience of the marginalized custodian of the Hebraic legacy in the land of Columbus.[5] To the same extent, he had to justify the cerebralism of the Hebrew American writer, who, in his isolated position, could not but process feelings through conceptualized cogitation. To buttress his argument and legitimize poetic cerebralism, Halkin referred to the poetry of Shneur, where discursive deliberation played an important role.[6] This in itself was a tactically "wrong" move, since almost none of the members of the Bialikian *pléiade* was being at this juncture as drastically demoted as Shneur. In fact, Hebrew America was Shneur's last bastion, where his erstwhile renown as a Hebrew poet, vouched for by Bialik himself, was kept almost intact, but in both eastern Europe, and particularly in Palestine, his reputation dwindled. Once the presumed exponent of urbanism and modernity in Hebrew poetry, he was now judged by the modernists to be passé, since his urbanism was informed by the turn of the nineteenth-century concepts of progress and technical audacity, whereas the "correct" urbanism of the post-war era was desperate, nihilistic, and chaotic—the failed urbanism of Oswald Spengler's *Decline of the West*. Thus the American Hebraic meta-literary discourse formed a sequestered, conservative enclave in the new literary dialogue now evolving in Europe and mostly in mandatory Palestine.

In Palestine, the official literary ethos in the first half of the 1920s was an upbeat one of literary truce (between the old and the new guards) and joint effort. The great literary center in eastern Europe was in shambles, and a difficult transition of the literary hub from Odessa and Warsaw to Palestine was underway. This situation called for young and old, classical, and modernist writers to work together rather than engage in literary feuds and polemics. Thus, new literary periodicals, established in the early 1920s, such as *Ma'abarot* (here in the sense of fording, crossing a body of water) and *Hedim* (*Echoes*), proclaimed a policy of coexistence

and openness. Edited respectively by Fichman, a member of the Bialikian *pléiade*, and, conjointly, by A. Barash and Ya'akov Rabinovitsh,
both seasoned writers of the second aliya, these periodicals announced
and practiced inclusion. *Hedim* in particular went out of its way to attract and publish the modernists (both Hebrew ones and Europeans
whose work was translated here into Hebrew for the first time). In fact,
the editors were so committed to their promise of conveying to their
readers the echoes of different tunes and rhythms that they invited the
young poet Shlonsky, a pioneer working in the collective agricultural
settlement Ein Harod and a proverbial modernist, to join them, and
bring to the editing of the periodical the sensibilities and élan of the
third aliya, the new kibbutzim in the valley of Jezrael, and the modernist Russian poetry, particularly that of Sergey Esenin, who at that point
could have been said to be Shlonsky's poetic mentor.

   Hedim, both the periodical and the publishing house affiliated with
it, was, indeed, to play a very important role in the advent of Palestinian Hebrew modernism. However, the hope for literary harmony and
cooperation expressed by its editors was unrealistic, and, as the 1920s
wore on, progressively untenable, which might have been one of the
reasons for the editors' decision in 1928 to terminate the publication of
their periodical. The polemics, which would undermine the illusion
of peaceful coexistence and eventually precipitate the Palestinian literary
republic into a state of a literary civil war, were started, in fact, on the
pages of *Hedim* itself—by Shlonsky and others. As soon as he arrived
in Tel Aviv and at the *Hedim* editorial office—a room in Barash's bourgeois apartment there—Shlonsky published a translation of Esenin's "A
Hooligan's Confession"[7] and a series of short and pointed articles, intentionally written in an associative, non-discursive, free style, by which
he differentiated between the two forces that vied with each other for
dominance in the development of culture and literature: the force of
those who demarcate boundaries and erect fences (*godrim*), and those
who barge on, break through (*portsim*), and demolish the impediments
that threaten to stop them.[8] It was clear, of course, in which of the two
groups the young poet was positioning himself.

   Under the cultural circumstances of the period, the fence builders
were, among others, the exponents of the spirit of the second aliya,

who systematically demanded, from writers, as well as from Zionist politicians, slow and patient progression, diminished expectations, small steps, unpretentious but authentic achievements, and a clear-eyed assessment of realities and a tenacious but unhurried effort to change them. This rubbed the young *portsim* the wrong way. Pioneers of the third aliya, with the blasts of the Bolshevik October blowing in their sails, they wanted to throw patience and evolutionism to the winds. Shlonsky had already had an opportunity to lock horns with one of the most revered representatives of the second aliya, the philosopher A. D. Gordon, now terminally sick. In 1921, as part of the ongoing efforts to reorganize and enhance the literary activity in Palestine, the Organization of Hebrew Writers in Eretz Yisra'el was founded—in the spirit of the cooperative movement, which would exert a far-reaching influence over Zionist activities, particularly those of Labor Zionism, in mandatory Palestine. The moribund philosopher, already canonized and semi-beatific, when invited to give the keynote speech in the new organization's statutory meeting, told his listeners that there was no need for a writer's professional union, or, for that matter, for professional writers. Whereas making a profession out of writing and art was questionable under all circumstances, perhaps it was acceptable in "normal" societies, where a majority of the population busied itself with basic productive labor. In Zionist Palestine, where the children of Jewish merchants, clerks, and Talmud students were attempting to change the Jewish character, and mentality wielding the pen as a professional tool was not only practically impossible, but also morally unacceptable, since professional literary activity would deflect the writer away from the only modus vivendi that rendered one's presence in the country significant and redemptive: manual labor. Thus, writers in Palestine should be manual laborers, who in their free time articulated in writing their experience of physical and spiritual encounter with the elements. The literature they should produce was to be "a literature of labor," that is, a direct extension of manual labor.[9] Many, including Labor Zionist activists and leaders such as Berl Katzenelson, disagreed with Gordon's extremely restrictive definition of the concept of "literature of labor." However, no one expected a twenty-one-year old boy with a flowing artistic *chevalure* to openly and forcefully defy the hallowed old man, demanding from him, without mincing words, a recognition of literary work as legitimate a form of labor as any, and dismissing the notion that literature could or should be created by weekend amateurs, who sought in writing mere self-expression. Writers, Shlonsky insisted, should be professionals, and the more professional they were, the better. The encounter between the veteran laborer-philosopher and the insolent youngster, who at the time had barely published a dozen poems, was symbolic of a generational and cultural collision that would imbue the literary and artistic life in mandatory Palestine with the colors of war.

This collision occurred in the form of a series of encounters that gradually added up to a fault line splitting the contemporary literary landscape in two parts. It was not a straight fault line, and the division of the landscape it entailed was not always continuous and clear cut. Rather the fault line consisted of numerous foci of turbulence, indicated by interjecting, juxtaposed, and parallel cracks. Those who placed themselves on one side of the line when focusing on a specific issue, sometimes found themselves on the other side when a different issue presented itself. Nevertheless, the division was always present, and its presence progressively generated more friction, which, in its turn, raised the temperature of the literary and cultural debate, until it reached the point of boiling around 1931. When viewed from a sufficient distance, the fault line could be seen as evolving around four or five foci, which, in themselves, were made of clumps of smaller points of friction. One of these major foci can be defined by the opposition contraction/expansion. Whereas nobody denied the need for Hebrew literature to grow, expand, and measure itself by the new and larger dimensions of the Hebrew project in Palestine, where Hebrew was becoming a spoken language, the matter of size and contour line was hotly debated. The modernists generally favored open-endedness, large dimensions, poli-centrism, fuzzy contour lines. Basing themselves on current European post-symbolist literary practices, they devised new genres that were characterized by formal open-endedness. Particularly prominent in the mid-1920s was the kind of poem, which the scholar Uzi Shavit, following the lead of Shlonsky, then one of the chief practitioners of this genre, described as "the wild song" (Shlonsky had written: "If the world is a drunkard and a vagabond, / I am its wild song").[10] It was a relatively long poem, not unified by a continuous narrative plot nor by a single situational framework or clearly articulated single topic or idea. It was written mostly in free verse, in long paragraphs rather than traditional stanzas, free of rhyming and also supposedly of metrical order, although in actuality, the verses were mostly metrical, and only their length (which with some poets, particularly Greenberg, reached mammoth proportions) would constantly change. With poetic modalities—lyrical, descriptive, discursive—freely alternating, pathos was usually present throughout the poem, which was conveying a mood of emotional turbulence, whether chaotic or ecstatic, and which was presented as emanating from a reality experienced as apocalyptic (dystopian or utopian). Figurative language was also allowed to break free of the bonds of commensurability between subject (or tenor) and vehicle, wax "non-referential," project an intensified mood rather than point to a pictorial or situational semblance. Content-wise, the poem, while being intensely personal and sometimes also daringly confessional, was always concerned with the big supra-personal issues: the falling apart (à la Spengler) of Western civilization, the destruction of the Jewish people by wars and pogroms, the redemptive drama of Zionism, particularly as it was played by the young pioneers who became the bricklayers of the new Palestine or the tillers of the fields of the Jezrael valley. Not all the modernist poets shared all the characteristics of this popular poetic modality. Some, like the poetess Bluvstein, rejected the genre altogether. She wrote short, stanzaic, rhyming, metrical, and very personal poems, the modernity of which was conveyed through their all but colloquial style, based on the spoken Palestinian Hebrew, their stark, unadorned candor, direct, poignant, albeit also contained and carefully husbanded, emotionality, and their references to the poetess's experience as a pioneer and an agricultural laborer. Others, adopted some of the model's characteristics while rejecting others. Thus the poetess Esther Raab systematically resorted to free verse in her excited, energetic, and often emotionally explosive expressionistic poems, but at the same time she recoiled from length, verbosity, discursiveness, changes of mood and topic, and adhered to mono-centric structures and tonalities. Most notably, Fogel, adopted free verse in a fashion that was by far more methodical than that of most others (in most of his poems, he genuinely refrained not only from rhyming and metrical scanning but also from repetitive rhythmical patterns, allowing the syntax of each sentence to engender its own unique rhythm and form a separate non-stanzaic unit in the structure of the poem).[11] At the same time, however, he eschewed high pathos, length, and poly-centricity—writing short, succinct poems, relatively simple in style, that conveyed clearly differentiated moods and focused on personal experience (although the poet, in his habitual somber mood, would often refer to common humanity subjected to the strictures of the human condition, which he pessimistically viewed as allotting all human beings the same reduced, even stunted measure of vitality, thus rendering them more similar to each other than they were aware of).

All these differences notwithstanding, the tendency to unfetter poetry was common, and its best meta-literary advocate, the most radical of modernists, Greenberg, waged a continuous campaign against the norm of condensation or minimalism, to which he ironically referred by the cabbalist concept of *tsimtsum* (reduction, contraction; according to the Zoharic cabbala, God, whose being filled the universe to the brim, reduced or contracted it to make room for the world He meant to create. This myth was used by those who favored brevity and condensation in poetry as a parable that tied creativity to brevity) and presented it as indicative of an obsolete mentality and aesthetics.[12] Expansion and freedom rather than reduction, restrictions, and reining oneself in were to him quintessentially modern and contemporary, being predicated by both aspects of modernity: the mental conversion triggered by man's conquering of nature through modern technology (here the poet evoked the arguments similar to those of the Italian futurists)[13] and the destruction of all boundaries and restrictive norms of behavior caused by the dismantling of Western civilization through global war and perpetual revolution. In Palestine, expansion and the abolition of restrictions were mandated by the rhythm and goals of "The Hebrew Revolution," which aimed at nothing less than creating a large and strong "Jewish kingdom" in which the majority of Jews would find refuge before Christian Europe, now wild with political chaos and moral decrepitude, would murder them.[14] Here, *tsimtsum* meant not only reductive aesthetics but also national weakness and defeatism. As much as

Zionism, now being reified, had to "think big" and act assertively and quickly, so Hebrew writing had to recalibrate its forms and perception, overcoming all fears of the monumental and even of the hyperbolic. By the same token, the legacy of the cultural literary past had to be reexamined, and the tradition should be overhauled and rearranged according to a new set of priorities. Biblical prophecy (to which Greenberg occasionally referred as "modernistic," dubbing Ezekiel "a Dadaist"), the cabbala (rather than Maimonidean rationalism), the emotionally turbulent poetry of Ibn Gabirol, the revolutionary messianism of Shlomo Molkho and Shabbetai Zvi, the pantheistic philosophy of Spinoza (rather than the deism of the Enlightenment), the ecstatic mysticism of the Hasidic movement, the corrosive irony of Heine, the prophetic poems of Bialik, and the unbridled despair and honesty of Brenner should become the main building stones of the living tradition, as much as the horror tales of Edgar Allen Poe and the gushing democratic poetry of Walt Whitman, on the one hand, and the existentialist philosophy of Nietzsche, particularly in his *Will to Power*, on the other hand, should become the main non-Jewish sources of influence.[15]

In prose fiction, a considerably less developed genre at this point, also a tendency to expand can be detected. Whereas modernists (such as Shteynman, Hurwitz, N. Bistritsky, Fogel, and primarily Agnon and Hazaz) attempted—grappling in different directions and on very different levels of artistic self-awareness and sophistication—the writing of experimental novels, other writers were now practicing more and more the genre of the novel in its various traditional sub-categories, steadily advancing toward larger and more extensive forms—trilogies, sagas, and *roman-fleuves*. The shift pointing in this direction became obvious right after the war with the publication of Berditchevsky's *Miriam* and Brenner's *Breakdown and Bereavement*, a short time before the two writers' deaths in 1921. This was an obvious departure from the literary generic hierarchy of the pre-war Hebrew renaissance, in which the short story or the long short story (or novella) featured as the chief form of prose fiction to which the best writers of the era (such as Peretz, Feierberg, Ben-Tsiyon, Nomberg, Shofman, Gnessin, Berkovits, Agnon, but also poets such as Bialik, Shteynberg, Shneur, and many others) continuously contributed. With the exception of Brenner (who besides his novels, or what he regarded as anti-novels, also wrote short stories and novellas, in which, perhaps, he achieved greater artistic perfection), those who practiced novel-writing were relatively marginal as far as the current canon went. With Chekov and the new Scandinavian masters as their prime models, writers sought perfection in relative brevity, using the short-story format or that of the lyrical novella for making condensed and suggestive statements, while assuming that readers with more popular expectations would satisfy their needs by reading novels in either Russian or Yiddish. Now the trend was veering toward epic plots and wide panoramic backgrounds—a fact that at least partly could be explained by the emergence in Palestine of a new, Hebrew-speaking, reading public to whom all foreign languages (Yiddish included) were inaccessible (this also made sense of the sudden inundation of the Hebrew book market by multivolume translated novels: Tolstoy, Dostoevsky, Dickens, Victor Hugo, Balzac, Flaubert, Pierre Lotti, Galsworthy, Rolland, Thomas Mann, Jakob Wasserman, Franz Werfel, etc.).

Here the historical and ideological justification was surprisingly supplied by Y. Rabinovitsh, who had been numbered among the fence builders rather than the expansionists.[16] Primarily a Zionist publicist and a literary critic of the second aliya, he also wrote short stories and novellas and was now about to try his hand at novel-writing. Rabinovitsh explained and justified the shift not only in sociological terms (the new reading public and its needs), but also in ideological and aesthetic ones. As long as Zionism was a mere dream, with no concrete reality to support it, Hebrew writers of fiction had to focus on the archetype of the "uprooted" Jewish intellectual, whose life subsisted of cogitation and discussions, and therefore could not successfully follow in the wake of the great realist novelists. However, with Zionism being reified, becoming part of the "real" active life of many people who, having experienced war and revolution, sought real solutions for their plight by emigrating to Palestine, a significant and extensively plotted narrative was within one's artistic reach. In a way, the sheer eventfulness and "density" of the era, replete with huge upheavals and life-changing metamorphoses, demanded the enlargement of the fictional format. Also, now Zionism could supply the writer with a perspective that ren-

dered possible an inclusive narrative synthesis. It resembled in this respect the Hebrew enlightenment, which, peaking ideologically and also
regarding itself, in the 1860s and 1870s, as having reached the verge of
reification and becoming a way of life, gave birth to the nineteenth-century Hebrew novel in the works of Mapu (whom Rabinovitsh admired
and would try to imitate in his historical novel *When Nations Collapse*),
Smolenskin, Abramovitsh, and Broydes. Rabinovitsh certainly was one
of the more thoughtful Zionist literary critics of the era.

The ones who offered a different view of the cultural and literary
situation were usually conservative, albeit not necessarily old, writers
and critics. They demanded a poetry, which, whether emotive and expressive or mimetic and descriptive, was devoid of opacity and pathetic
bavardage, talking straightforwardly, and preferably in a condensed
manner, to the sensibilities of the "normal" reader. They strongly condemned non-referential figurative language as so much hot air intended
to turn the heads and blind the eyes of naive readers. Their most articulate spokesman, S. Zemach (yes, the same Zemach who in 1919 had
"dethroned" Abramovitsh and dismissed the so-called Mendele manner or style) explained that a metaphor, when non-referential, namely,
when it contains a vehicle but is devoid of a real tenor, was not only
formless (for the form of a legitimate metaphor depended on the presence of both factors: the subject of the comparison [the tenor] and the
comparison itself [the vehicle]), but also open to endless manipulation
with no basis in reality.[17] Since it could not be fully articulated or completed, it was subject to a continuous whipping as a messy figurative
cream, with one arbitrary comparison being engendered by another in
an endless progression. Zemach opposed this as a form of prevarica-
tion intended to aggrandize and inflate experience by adding dimensions it did not possess. Thus modernist figurative language, whether
"imazhinist" in its aesthetic presuppositions (i.e., studded with unrelated and often bizarre but pictorially striking images that, accumulating one on top of another, were supposed to engender the emotional
energy and revved-up velocity of the poem) or futurist (i.e., collapsing
the causal logic of the poetic statement upon itself) or expressionist
(i.e., directly externalizing primal, raw emotions with no mimetic reference to a perceived reality) was essentially a means of illegitimately

occupying a space that was much larger than the one the reported experience deserved, or of crashing the reader's consciousness under a big, but hollow, poetic object.

The best, most sophisticated, and suggestive presentation of the case against literary expansionism was put together in the 1920s by the poet Ya'akov Shteynberg, perhaps the most talented and thoughtful member of the Bialikian poetic *pléiade*, who was also, and as importantly, by far the most brilliant Hebrew essayist of the era. Shteynberg attacked the popular "wild song" subgenre, branding it as immature, verbose, self-pitying, full of emotional and ideational hype, replete with exaggerated emotions, reflecting the self rather than the objective reality of its proclaimed topic, such as the heroic labor of the members of the new kibbutzim in Jezrael.[18] "Of all the many actual experiences of the workers," he said, "not one was truly portrayed, although quite a few of them resembled heroic exploits, or at least, self-evidently amounted to real actions." Genuine achievement in the life of both the individual and the collective depended on the establishing of a new ratio between words and deeds, with the reality of the latter curtailing the effervescence of the former. Thus, the new Zionist literature had to focus on deeds, on fate, on real life in the world, rather than on affect and solipsism. By pulling in the opposite direction, the young modernists were actually betraying the essential Zionist tenet of replacing traditional Jewish excitability and wordiness by actions. Shteynberg's poetics were based on a new definition of the concept of *alila* (which means, among other things, both plot and great deeds; *shir alila* being an epic poem, particularly of the heroic kind; *ba'alil* means in reality, clearly perceived through deeds and events rather than verbal reporting). To Shteynberg, this concept pointed to the central paradox of literature as art and a form of perception: being the verbal art par excellence, it achieved its goal only when words were transcended by the events or deeds or the human fate they projected. The events could, of course, be emotional, mental, or intellectual, but they had to rise above their verbal articulation and be clearly perceived by the reader as events (rather than as self-expression). Thus the tighter or more economic ratio between words and events or deeds, the denser their mixture, the more memorable and significant the literary statement. The Bible

supplied the best examples of verbal expression being morphed into
"pure" plots, or what Shteynberg sometimes referred to as "limpid" or
"pellucid" plots or "innocent" and "complete" plots (in Hebrew both
innocence and completeness or wholesomeness are indicated by the
same word, *tom*), each distinct, clearly differentiated from the others,
and self-contained. This, however, happened most often not in books
of the prophets but rather in the historical-narrative books: Judges,
Samuel, and Kings, which the poet regarded as "sublime," and the
highest point ever reached in Hebrew writing—whatever came after
that was of a lesser stature.[19] This perfect ratio between words (as few
as was possible) and deeds, authentic human gestures and actions, un-
disguised and carried to their logical conclusions, emanated, the poet
believed, from both the environment of the Judean hills—where the
strong, perpendicular rays of the sun and the arid and transparent air
rendered all forms distinct, solid, with clearly etched contours—and
the Hebrew language itself. Lapidary and economical, with syntax immeasurably simpler and more direct than that of Indo-European languages, Hebrew supported most of its semantic weight by its complex
system of the verb, which was mainly targeted at describing actions
and deeds, rather than moods. It rejected miasmatic word combinations and was extremely sparing with adjectives and adverbs. When it
needed adjectival qualification, it resorted to its extremely tight forms
of the construct state, where two substantives yoked together in an
intense semantic drama of qualification through subjugation, retained
their noun-like solidity even as one of them assumed the role of an adjective.[20] Thus, Hebrew was the language of the ideal *alila*.

   All these considerations amounted to a firm belief in brevity and
formal clarity and self-sufficiency. In communication, what was of
paramount importance was not fluency and streamlined continuity
but rather the potent sentence, subsuming all others. In poetry, it was
the tightly and elegantly crafted single verse rather than the totality
of the poem; since it was the verse rather than the poem as a whole
that contained the kernel of the deep wisdom one can sometimes take
from a reading of a poetic text, this wisdom always being processed
through the formal arrangement of the verse, independently of its extrinsic, supra-poetic depth or originality. In a good poem, every line

could and should be able to fend for itself, impact the reader as a complete mental event, contain a plot of itself, which was that of a parable, for proper figurative language, never really able to altogether collapse the fence separating tenor from vehicle, was telling figurative stories about how, or in what respect, one thing resembled another.[21] Thus, non-referential and mixed metaphors amounted to stories without continuity and conclusions, and therefore, to stories that had never been told, for only continuity leading to a closure, the arrival at the end of an event, endowed a story with the firm contour without which it would not possess the dimensions of a plot.

The history of Hebrew and Jewish writing recorded the ups and downs of the national spirit in direct relation to the ability of Jewish writers, more or less, to articulate their feelings and thoughts through authentic plots. Certain parts of the Bible (including sections of biblical poetry where the verse lines were tightly, all but epigrammatically arranged) formed the zenith in the historical curvature of this record. The Mishna, with its crystal-clear and well-ordered formulations, occupied a lower, but still very high point. The Talmud was an abyss into which the Jewish mind plummeted. Unbearably wordy and long-winded and endlessly deliberative and contentious, it was a spiritual *monstrum*, and the scanty gold dust of the aggada could hardly conceal its inherent disfiguration and vacuity.[22] In the Middle Ages, Hebrew writing regained some of its potency not only in many memorable verses coined by the master poets of the Spanish period but also in the striking Ashkenazi accounts, from the Jewish viewpoint, of the crusades, as well as in some of the learned disquisitions such as Moshe Ibn Ezra's treatise on Hebrew poetics, a thoroughly secular book, which suggested that poetry was to be preferred to prophecy due to its human originality (the prophets had been only the carriers of God's word).[23] In the Italian Hebrew renaissance, it was the compact sonnet that saved Hebrew writing from triviality and obscurantism. The new Hebrew literature of the Enlightenment and the national revival achieved moments of greatness in some of its poems, where language was transmuted into mental action, as in Y. L. Gordon's "In the Lion's Teeth," or transcended verbiage in tightly plotted lines such as those of Bialik in his short poems—not in his grandiose and wordy "Scroll of Fire" but rather in economical, succinct poems such as "Thou, Seer, Go, Flee," where every verse conveyed a potent truth through its perfect verbal arrangement and equilibrium. As for the current modernistic poetry, it was, as said before, noisy, vacuous, and thoroughly non-poetic. It also undermined Zionism whose goal was bracing of the Jewish vitiated soul submerged in words, polemics, sarcasm, hair splitting quibbling, and sharp-wittedness. Jewish writing in foreign languages (such as that of the German Jewish writers) spread the malaise of Jewish inaction and weakened the "tonus" of the literatures in which Jews now participated.[24] The new Jew needed to learn to speak less, to refrain from exhausting his inner resources by masturbatory self-expression. He needed to redeem himself—through silence wherever possible and preferring deeds to words—from his self destructive Talmudic legacy. Thus Shteynberg offered a coherent neoclassical (or "Parnassian," as it sometimes seems) poetics, which also amounted to a somber national self-criticism as incisive as that of Brenner. Fraught, as Brenner's critique had been, with some Jewish self-hatred, and also contiguous at some points with contemporary far right-wing cultural rationale, it was nevertheless a carefully thought-through Zionist poetics, and the very opposite of the other radical Zionist poetics, that of Greenberg. Indeed, it is more than probable that Greenberg's "Klapey tish'im vetish'a" was written as an answer to Shteynberg's "Hashura" (the [poetic] line) and "Al shirat ha'avoda" (on the poetry of labor). As much as Shteynberg acknowledged Greenberg as the best among the modernists, finding in his poems "a great agitation of the soul,"[25] Greenberg could not but acknowledge Shteynberg as a formidable adversary, the most authentic Hebrew classicist. Historically, Greenberg's argument was more persuasive and time-appropriate than that of his rival. Shteynberg's Hebraic neoclassicism was totally out of synch with contemporary trends and atmosphere, which explains why his own poetry and short stories written in the 1920s and 1930s, and in which he realized his full creative potential, did not elicit at the time much of a response and had to wait for a belated recognition from some of the exponents of Israeli criticism, who, unfortunately, failed to understand their ideological underpinnings and their full national import.[26] Nevertheless, some of Shteynberg's essays in *ars poetica*, particularly his "The Poetic Line," remain of the very best examples of the meta-poetic writing in the Hebrew language.

A second focal point in the division of contemporary Hebrew meta-literary thinking evolved around the issue of the "right" relationship between literature and the "time," namely, the social and political reality. Here the chief players, most of whom we have already met, were grouped along lines that were somewhat different from those separating expansionists from the adherents of contraction and brevity. The old-timers based themselves in this respect on the precedents of the pre-war Hebrew renaissance: Bialik's and Tchernikhovsky's public or national poetry, particularly the former's prophetic poems, and Abramovitsh's satirical panoramic view of nineteenth-century, traditional Jewish society. Both models allowed for a well-controlled relationship between art and life: a relationship that was more limited and regulative than it seemed. Bialik's and Tchernikhovsky's public poetry never truly crossed the border separating public from political poetry. Whereas this public poetry usually expressed the consensual view of the community at which it was targeted, that of the Hebraic-Zionist contingent, political poetry would have had to focus on the divisions and tensions within the targeted community and attempt to persuade readers to support one of the contending factions. Bialik almost never did that. He attacked targets that were extrinsic to the Zionist circumference: the indifference of cynical Jews to the convening the first Zionist congress; the unwillingness or inability of traditional Jewry to adapt itself to modernity as the Zionists understood it; the pitiful weakness of the victims of pogroms who should have forcefully resisted the hooligans, defended the dignity of their women, and their own human dignity. The only occasion that triggered a bitter attack on his part aimed at a group within the Zionists' camp was that of the Uganda crisis, and even then he refrained from attacking Herzl and his fellow political Zionists who superimposed the Uganda proposition upon the agenda of the World Zionist Organization and forced its adoption. Rather, he attacked those who, in the wake of the crisis, were clearly on their way out of the Zionist camp and into that of the Organization of Jewish Territorialists. His prophetic poems, as bitter in their tonality and ominous in their messages, actually remained above the political fracas within Zionism, and therefore consensual, as far as the community that read the poems was concerned. This did not undermine the poem's integrity because

Zionism was still a dream, a hope, and as such amenable to consensual treatment that emphasized its common denominators. The exponents of the traditional poetics expected from the young poets to respond to the realities and hopes of Zionism now being reified in Palestine, but not to cross them into the domain of Zionist politics, where poets, presumably, should fear to tread.

As for prose fiction, its response to public concerns was deemed to be even more problematic than that of poetry. Abramovitsh's satirical stories dealt mainly with traditional Jewish society, although some of them did focus on the helplessness and disorientation of the pre-Herzlian eastern European Zionist groups. Thus his satire was generally (but not exclusively) aimed beyond the community of his readers. Focusing largely on traditional Jewish life, it could also be conflated with a meticulous artistic rendering of the image of the shtetl civilization; a civilization that had crystallized during four or five centuries, and as much as it had clearly become dysfunctional, still presented a milieu with distinct and indelible characteristics, calling for the pen or the brush (Abramovitsh was often referred to as a painter) of the seasoned mimetic and epic artist. As we saw, most readers (with some notable exceptions, such as Brenner) focused on Abramovitsh's descriptive art rather than on his satirical message. Thus, satire was supposed to go as far as it could, as long as it remained within the charmed circle of artistic descriptionism. There was, of course, also the model of Brenner's narrative art, revolutionary and utterly innovative in its day. Brenner discarded mimetic depiction, which was essentially incompatible with the ambience he wanted to invoke—that of "uprooted" young intellectuals, torn by inner conflicts, or that of immigrants and exiles roaming within a totally alien reality without purpose or social role. He replaced it by burdening his stories with confessional outbursts, cogitations of people who were not far from a mental collapse, debates, heated exchanges of ideas, and, often enough, journalism of the most riveting and provocative kind. Thus Brenner had collapsed the partition separating artistic narrative from the burning issues of the day. But Brenner's artistic model had been largely discounted. Paradoxically, as much as he was allotted the status of a Zionist saint in the wake of his assassination in 1921, and as much as his ideas were supposed to inform and guide the thinking of Labor Zionists, his narrative art was frowned upon. He was supposedly a bad stylist and even worse builder of plots and erecter of narrative structures (as Bialik had complained). Quite misunderstood, his most brilliant experimental novel, *From Here and From There* (1911), where the continuity of time and space was shattered in an attempt to convey the chaotic nature of existence, was pointed to as an example of how a serious writer could be derailed by ardently wishing to directly touch upon national public reality at its immediate political and existential surface, without a shred of artistic distance, and as a consequence be reduced to a mere publicist.

Thus the pre-war models, recommended or condemned by traditional literary thinkers, could hardly serve the writers of the inter-bellum period. In the 1920s, the Bialikian prophetic model was evoked by poets time and again both within and outside of the public-Zionist context.[27] However, soon enough, not later than the beginning of the severe crisis of 1925–1926, which temporarily paralyzed the Zionist project in Palestine, there was no way of evading the severe limitations of the Bialikian prophetic model under current circumstances. Zionism being reified, its crises assumed an existential character they had never had before. In the second half of the 1920s, the Zionist contingent in Palestine was shaken to its foundations. Disenchanted pioneers left the country, and Jewish emigration into Palestine, which crested in 1924, bringing tens of thousands of members of the Jewish middle class who believed mandatory Palestine offered better life than anti-Semitic Poland, stopped altogether. There was an epidemic of suicides, idealists who could not master the energy to overcome the crushing disappointment, taking their own lives. Unemployed construction workers and their families in the cities were struck by malnutrition, epidemics, and downright hunger, which rendered them easy prey to the propaganda of the anti-Zionist Palestinian Communist party. A group of third aliya pioneers, now turned communists, left for the Soviet Union, attempting to create in the Crimea *kolkhozes,* what were actually Hebrew-speaking kibbutzim. The agricultural settlements were collapsing financially, their members subsisting on bread and tea. The Zionist project, it seemed, was on its last legs, and the reassurances from leaders who maintained that the crisis was temporary and of a technical-financial nature sounded hollow.

Poets like L. Almi and Gabriel Talpir wrote poems of protest against the Zionist bourgeoisie, which was, presumably, indifferent to the plight of the workers. Even "Mr. Bialik" was ridiculed (by Talpir, in his poem "Hunger") as a well-off bourgeois who did not even deign to meet with the hungry workers who clustered in front of his beautiful new house in Tel Aviv, expecting the great poet to sympathize with their plight and perhaps strengthen them with a word of consolation.[28]

Many writers were themselves on the verge of hunger and home-lessness. Greenberg, "divorcing his muse" (i.e., putting a temporary stop to the writing of poetry), invested his energies in writing a se-ries of reportages, as vibrant as they were tragic that vividly conveyed this atmosphere of despair, desolation, and bitter disenchantment for *Davar*, the workers' daily. He refused to accept the conventional expla-nation of the crisis as having been triggered by economic factors; to him the crisis was that of Zionism itself as an ideology and a political movement. In a revolutionary era, social and national movements had to sweepingly move forward or they would be defeated. The timid, evolutionary policies of the leadership of the World Zionist Organiza-tion, headed by Weizmann, exposed its weaknesses to its enemies, and, even more importantly, bitterly disappointed the Jewish masses who wanted to see it succeeding and offering them a realistic alternative to their progressively more threatened existence in Europe. Having lost faith in the Zionist leader Weizmann, they withdrew their support, po-litical and financial; hence the economic crisis, a mere symptom rather than the chief cause of the current situation. Even the British govern-ment, the concerns and wishes of which the Weizmann leadership was so eager to accommodate, was disappointed with Zionism, which it had once believed could prove a valuable political ally. Weakened and servile, the Zionist leadership now pushed the imperial power into the arms of the Arab nationalist movement, the enemy of Zionism. The "Hebrew Revolution" was therefore on the brink of disaster. Under-mined by the political and financial impotence of its leaders, it would also be attacked militarily by Palestinian Arabs who would know how to utilize its weakness and the government's pro-Arab inclination. It could be saved only by a revolutionary change of leadership, even if this could be achieved only in undemocratic ways. Greenberg expected his leaders, namely, those of radical Labor Zionism: D. Ben Gurion and Berl Katzenelson, to initiate the move that would terminate Weizmannism and replace it by Lenin-like leadership and policies. Resuming his activity as a poet (in 1928), he therefore moved from the position of a public poet to that of the political poet. Even before this development, he had been accused of mixing poetry and politics, by which his detractors meant that he "lowered" his public poetry to the journalistic level of dealing with mundane topics and issues, which poetry was supposed to eschew. Referring to the Brenner precedent and positioning himself as Brenner's heir, he then responded to their challenge by declaring: "I shall make this non-poetic word—politics—sing."[29] Now, however, he moved beyond this promise, recalibrated his poetic tools (through a drastic simplification of forms and style) and viciously attacked the Zionist establishment by demonizing its representatives and calling for their immediate dismissal. He also published at this point his brilliant manifesto-essay "Against Ninety-Nine," which redefined the goals and methods of Hebrew modernism. It not only justified the debunking of Hebrew classicism and romanticism, presenting them as expressive of mental attitudes and formal and aesthetic preferences that twentieth-century realities had rendered obsolete, but also demanded the unhesitating harnessing of Hebrew literature to the wagon of the "Hebrew revolution." Expounding the concepts of poetic expansion, of free rhythms, and of style and form that conveyed the essence of the mental revolution caused by modern technology and social fermentation, he also prescribed the politization of Hebrew literature, now being created under revolutionary circumstances, which necessitated the activation of the political potential of the written word. Politization was certainly the direction in which he himself as a poet moved.[30]

When he realized that the leaders of Labor Zionism refused to participate in the putsch he had recommended, he parted ways with them, turned against them, and gravitated toward their rivals, Jabotinsky's Zionist revisionists, whom he officially joined in 1930. He became an all-out political poet and a spokesman of the Zionist radical right wing. His warning (of 1928) concerning the impending Arab military attack was vindicated by the wide-spread Arab riots (actually, a rather well-planned military offensive) of summer 1929, and this elevated him to the position of a politically committed prophet, which he upheld throughout the 1930s (and beyond) in a fashion totally different from that of Bialik's precedent. Bialik himself learned the hard way that circumstances did not allow anymore for the poet-prophet's enjoying a consensual status. When in 1931, in the wake of the seventeenth Zionist Congress, where Weizmann, under attack from all directions, but particularly from that of the revisionists, had to resign, he published a new bitterly exhortative public poem.[31] He found himself attacked and denigrated by both Jabotinsky, who labeled him a "has been poet,"[32] and by Shlonsky, who exposed him as no poet at all but rather a publicist who wrote an article in stilted, old-fashioned verse lines.[33] Thus political poetry exacted a stiff price, and by choosing to practice it, the poet rendered himself political fair game. Nevertheless this was the direction in which some of the modernists of the 1920s now moved, with Greenberg, as a right winger, at their head, and Alexander Pen, the proto-Communist (he would later become the official poetic spokesman of the Israeli Communist party), following.

However, the other modernists, with Shlonsky at their head, moved, for a full decade—the 1930s—in the opposite direction. Replacing the "wild" poem as his major genre, by the cycle of polished, virtuously rhyming, rigorously metrical, pedantically stanzaic, and thematically focused short poems, Shlonsky moved, poetically, from his earlier post-symbolism to his mature neo-symbolism. In the process, he gave up on the relatively unrestricted free verse in favor of a controlling and unifying *melos* (informed by orderly, metrically-based rhythms and surprisingly rich euphony), as much as he gave up on the open-ended flow of images in favor of the controlling symbol and the discursive evocation of its psychological and metaphysical ramifications. As a matter of fact, now he rejected his earlier expansionist poetics, adopting one that was closer to Shteynberg's Parnassian adulation of the polished, syntactically and euphonically equilibrated, semi-autonomous single line than he would have liked to believe (Shteynberg being a sworn literary enemy). He renounced now the proximity and mutual interpenetration of art and socio-political life, which, he believed, lead Hebrew poetry to what he labeled "articleism" (i.e., the reduction of the poem to the level of a journalistic article), or "Yalagism"; this appellation being based on the acronym by which the nineteenth-century poet Y. L. Gordon was referred to. Thus he totally rejected both the ideologically-engaged poetry of the Hebrew enlightenment and the public poetry of Bialik and his disciples. (In 1930 the centennial anniversary of Gordon was celebrated by the veterans of the pre-war renaissance, as well as by Greenberg, who, as a poet engaged in ideological warfare, saluted the courageous and seasoned poetic-warrior of the former century. Shlonsky used the opportunity to militate against a regressive sliding back to the maskilic format.) Poetry was supposed to avoid the surface and explore the depths of the human condition (often understood in Freudian terms), and therefore poets had to be "divers" rather than surfers. The literary group or school Shlonsky founded together with the ubiquitous E. Shteynman attracted the best young poets of the day—Nathan Alterman, Goldberg, and at a somewhat later stage also the brilliant Rattosh (who, having started his career as a rather strident political poet of the far-far right, proto-fascist wing of Jabotinsky's Revisionist party, transcended this early phase, becoming the most hermetic and magical of the Hebrew neo-symbolists). Alterman took the poetic tenets of Shlonsky a few steps further. While he partly disagreed with the master's denouncement of Bialik's public poetry and of public poetry in general,[34] he firmly believed that poetry, at least major poetry, functioned through suggestion and sensuous impact rather than through ideas and references to extrinsic, non-poetic reality,[35] and the poems he wrote were therefore, by far, less ideational and discursive than those of Shlonsky. At the same time, however, Alterman evinced the most lively and intelligent interest in current public affairs and was constantly prodded by an inherent need to respond and react to them in verse. He thus faced a poetic conundrum that he early on overcame by sharply dividing his poetic writing into canonical and non-canonical segments. Whereas the canonical poems he collected in his brilliant, epoch-making collection *Stars Outside* (1938) touched upon social issues (such as the alienation characteristic of current urban existence, the decline of Western civilization, the rise of fascism, the Zionist endeavor in Palestine) through the most tangential, symbolic correlatives demanding a total separation of the autobiographical person from the alien and independent persona of the poetic speaker,[36] the non-canonical poems he wrote on a weekly

basis for more than three decades offered the most engaging and perceptive Zionist poetic commentary on the big and small affairs of the
day during the years of World War II, the Holocaust, the anti-British
struggle in Palestine, the 1948 War of Independence, and the early days
of Israeli independence. Although it was through this non-canonical
part of his work that Alterman eventually assumed the role of a national
spokesman, exerting an unprecedented political influence, the division
that allowed him to uphold the autonomy of his canonical poems (a
division he finally obliterated in the 1950s) was essential to the creation
of the best and most enduring parts in his oeuvre, and rendered him
the culture-hero of the young pre-Israeli literary intelligentsia, which
sought in poetry not the immediate and familiar but rather the magical
and epiphanous.

Thus Hebrew modernism, as represented by the two figures that
loomed largest on its horizon, Greenberg and Alterman, developed in
opposite directions and evolved contradictory meta-literary discourses.
Quite surprisingly, both directions found expression in and were fully
illustrated by the work of the contemporary master of Hebrew prose
fiction, Agnon, which also was split into two different (albeit intimately
and intricately interrelated) segments: a realistic-panoramic one, which,
in a series of novels and novellas, offered an epic view of the evolvement of eastern European Jewish society from the beginning of the
nineteenth century to the Zionist present, and a lyrical-experimental
one, subsisting of a series of symbolist-legendary tales that eventually
morphed into expressionistic nightmare-like short stories (often with
allegorical subplots), where the writer explored the personal unresolved
inner conflicts, which he believed, Jewish modernity inevitably gave rise
to. Whereas the former won for the author his classical status, the latter puzzled readers and critics and triggered the emergence of a special
Agnon criticism of interpretative decipherment. When the two trends
met, or rather collided, in the author's masterpiece, the novel *Yesteryear*
(1945–1946), they presented readers with riddles that until now have
not been fully solved and laid to rest.

This duality sheds light on the final focal point we must dwell on.
From the beginning of the twentieth century, but much more so since
the advent of the third aliya in 1919, the question hovering over the

Zionist cultural project in Palestine was how and in what ways the new culture would or should be different from its mother, the modern Hebraic-exilic one. One of the earliest and more naive answers given to that question was that the new culture should be more "oriental," that is, closer to that of the inhabitants of Palestine, the Arabs and particularly the Bedouins, whose way of life supposedly preserved that of the biblical patriarchs. This elicited the objections of those who believed that the modern Zionist entity in Palestine should bring Europe to the Middle East rather then turn its back on Europe and become Middle Eastern, namely, Levantine. The debate was, of course, pregnant with political ramifications. The leaders of Labor Zionism, such as Ben Gurion and Borokhov, started by opting for the fraternization with the Palestinian peasant (to whom, they maintained, Jews were racially close since the peasantry of Palestine must have subsisted of the progeny of the ancient Israelites who had never left the country when the ruling classes were exiled by the Romans). This was their way of evading the conflict between the principle of class struggle, by which they swore as socialists, and that of a national revival, which entailed the purchase of arable land then cultivated by Palestinian land tenants, their removal from the land and rejection as agricultural day workers so as to enable the pioneers to settle down and change their lives through manual labor. Some Hebrew writers, romantically or realistically, advised the lowering of fences between Jews and Arabs, seeking mutual understanding and exploring ways of cooperation.[37] Others (most notably, Brenner) saw no chance for such a rapprochement. Herzl and young Jabotinsky were adamant pro-Europeanists and frankly could not see how Zionism could surmount difficulties without aligning itself with European colonialism. Herzl (but not Jabotinsky) naively predicted harmony and peaceful cooperation between Jews and Palestinian Arabs, once the latter made peace with the Jewish-Zionist hegemony, realizing how much it improved their social, hygienic, and economic circumstances and elevated their cultural level in comparison with the other Arabic ethnic groups of the region. In the meantime a pervasive trend of "Arabization" influenced such groups as *Hashomer* (the first paramilitary Jewish organization in Palestine that defended Jewish settlements from robbers and rioters), as well as some artists and writers. In the 1920s, with the Balfour Declaration (which the Palestinian leadership vehemently rejected); the clash in the Upper Galilee (1919) between Jews and Syrian nationalists, which ended in the desertion of the farm of Tel Hai and the killing of its leader, the Zionist hero Trumpeldor; and the first politically motivated Arab attacks on the Jewish populations of ethnically hybrid towns such as Jerusalem and Jaffa (1920–1921) as background, the question reformulated itself: should the culture of the Jewish "national home," promised by Balfour and internationally ratified by the League of Nations, be occidental or oriental or Jewishly oriented (i.e., form a more or less direct continuation of modern eastern European Jewish culture). Whereas the Hebraic character of the new culture was generally agreed upon, the definition of Hebraism was hotly debated. Should it entail a total rejection of everything exilic (including, of course, Yiddish, as well as the suppression of the Ashkenazic pronunciation and accentuation and the resolute and final adoption of the Sephardic ones) as many—for instance, Jabotinsky, but also Shlonsky and his group—believed, or should it make use of the rich legacy of eastern European Jewish culture, as Bialik, Greenberg, and Berl Katzenelson believed? Should the new music be based on the eastern European Jewish folk and Hasidic song (cf. Yoel Engel, S. Rozovsky, et al.), or should it absorb the trills and free rhythmical patterns of the Arabic *maqamat* (Karni, Y. Gorokhov-Admon), or perhaps it should be based on Yemenite cantorial sources, which presumably had remained through the millennia close to the ancient psalmody of the Jerusalemite temple (A. Z. Idelsohn)?[38] Should the Hebrew theater go on playing An-sky's *The Dybbuk* (which, in its superb expressionistic staging by the Armenian-Russian *regisseur* Y. Vakhtangov, won for the *Habima* group throughout the 1920s the admiration of the most sophisticated international audiences), or should one explore the possibilities of a biblical, Bedouin-like expressionism as M. Halevi, Vakhtangov's disciple, did in his theatrical adaptation of the story of Jacob and Rachel?

This entailed an ongoing struggle that involved writers, painters, architects, theater people, and meta-cultural thinkers. Orientalism, partly continuing its earlier fin de siècle namesake, which had influenced prewar Hebrew culture both in and out of Palestine, and in part deviating from it, seeking to borrow from the orient not the former *Jugendstil* curves, cuteness, and gentle eroticism, but rather the ferocity and imagined freedom of a desert civilization (of course, both understandings of the "spirit of the Orient" were thoroughly European and very far from either comprehending or following authentic oriental cultural patterns) became influential in Palestine, triggering a meta-literary debate (the poet Karni representing the pro-oriental approach, and the critic Y. Rabinovitsh representing the pro-occidental one[39]). The battle, however, was all but decided by the massive Arab attack on the Jews of Palestine in 1929. This brought about the realization, on the part of the majority of the Jewish Palestinian contingent, of the inevitability of a violent collision of Zionism and the Palestinian national movement.[40] Culturally, this meant an acceptance of conflict-oriented ethos and the all but total occidentalization of the arts and of architecture. The impact of this, to be soon reinforced by the so-called Arab Rebellion of 1936–1939, became progressively more pervasive throughout the 1930s. The arrival of the refugees from Nazi Germany, many of them belonging in their country of origin to the cultural elite, tremendously helped in the Europeanization of Zionist Palestine, which partly explains the eventual victory of modernists such as Agnon or the Shlonsky group. With Jewish Palestine becoming as much a part of western Europe, the German expressionist background of Agnon's non-realistic stories (which were eventually labeled, quite wrongly, Kafkaesque), and the Russian-French symbolist connection informing the poetics of Shlonsky, Alterman, and Rattosh, rendered these writers the representatives of the world-at-large. Agnon was, of course, steeped in Judaic lore and in possession of the keenest Jewish sensibilities, which one did not associate with the work of the neo-symbolist poets. However, with the prospect of a second world war and the premonitions of a Jewish catastrophe in Europe becoming ever so ominous as the 1930s drew toward their end, the entire Palestinian cultural project (with the exception of its "Canaanite" segment) was undergoing a process of re-Judaization, or of seeking a better synthesis between Zionism and Judaism; a process, which, of course, became more pronounced in the 1940s.

In 1939, with a world war "hanging in the air" and then breaking out in the fall, the modernists of the Shlonsky-Alterman school hotly debated the appropriate role literature in general and poetry in particular could play vis à vis the atrocities of fascism and the horrors of war. Shlonsky emphatically denied the possibility of the existence of such a role. Poetry, he opined, could not but be silent in the face of national-ist hysteria and the excesses of war propaganda. Quoting the Midrashic story about God's angry rejection of the angels who sang His praises while the Egyptian army and its horses and charioteers were drowning in the Red Sea (in the biblical story in chapters 14 and 15 of Exodus): "The creations of my hands are drowning in the sea and you come to me singing?!" he demanded poetic silence, as long as people were being killed on the battlefields.[41] By and large he abided by his own dictum, refraining for a long time from publishing new poems, let alone from writing and publishing war poems (with one exception—an ode to the struggle and victory of the people of Stalingrad).[42] In his "Ballad about Death with a Smile on His Lips," he satirized the role played by the poet who became a propagandist of war and heroic death.[43] He responded to the war mainly through translations of European war poems, many of them of a pacifist bent, which he eventually collected (together with some Hebrew war poems) in a special anthology. Goldberg, Shlonsky's loyal disciple, wrote in the first days of the war (the beginning of September 1939) a programmatic article, in which she proclaimed that she would not write "war poems" and would go on writing about love and nature. In time of war, she said, the poet was the one who was not al-lowed to forget life's real values, which had nothing to do with either the politics or the devastating reality of war. Thus, he was not only allowed but actually forced to go on writing love and nature, "for even in time of war the value of love outweighs that of murder."[44] Alterman pointed in the opposite direction. In a rebuttal of Goldberg's article, he insisted on just wars and the heroism of those who struggled against mortal enemies being genuine life values, and thus war poems, as long as they were authentic and good poetry were as legitimate as any other kind of poems.[45] Essentially, Alterman was defending here a position he had articulated about six months earlier in a major political-literary manifesto, "A World and Its Antithesis," in which he bitterly critiqued Western democracies, as well as socialists and communists for not re-sponding on the spiritual and conceptual level to the evil fascination of fascism; for fascism and Nazism impacted people "spiritually." The poets of the socialist revolution promised bread, work, material goods. "The murderous Nazi poets talk not about bread and butter, but of national honor . . . and the glory of the Reich." The fascist regimes in Germany and Italy were more *spiritual* than one could imagine; and it was this spiritualism that represented the most inhumane aspect of them. Thus literature and poetry could not afford to become silent in the face of this assault on the spirit of humanity. They had to raise themselves and prepare for a spiritual combat. "For the safety of humanity, for the sake of its very existence, one had to evoke, strengthen, and shed light on humanity's instinct of self preservation, on the natural instinct of antagonism to its mortal enemies." The impending war was nothing less than "one of nature's most ancient and tremendous struggles: a struggle between two species for world-wide dominance."[46] The debate[47] clearly pointed to the widening political and poetic gap between the dominant figures among the Palestinian neo-symbolists, with Alterman assuming the role that would eventually render him the consensual speaker of democratic Zionism. As early as 1939, he made national existential struggle for survival, which he regarded as part and parcel of the universal struggle against tyranny and totalitarianism, the focus of sequels of poems such as "The Joy of the Poor" (1940) and the "Poems of the Egyptian Plagues" (started in 1939). At that point the dimensions of the attack on European Jewry by the Nazis were yet unknown and unimaginable. Of course, as the reality of the Holocaust dawned on the Jewish Palestinian community (in 1943), the position proffered by Shlonsky and Goldberg became untenable. It was the direction Alterman pointed to which Hebrew literature as a whole turned, with Alterman as its leader.

A similar development, starting earlier and in a much more pronounced form, would soften and in many cases altogether erase the sharp contours of Yiddish modernism, particularly those of American Yiddish modernism, which the Hitlerite fire would melt, as if modernism itself was a crime perpetrated by writers and poets against the persecuted Jewish people; an act of self-alienation that had to be confessed, genuinely repented, and expiated by a return to traditional poetic attitudes and forms.

Six

The Inter-Bellum Decades: Yiddish;
Issues of Cultural Continuity in
Revolutionary Times

During the inter-bellum period, meta-literary thinking and writing
evolved in Yiddish along lines that were essentially dissimilar, but, at
the same time, also strangely parallel to their Hebrew counterparts.
Whereas much in both the Hebrew and Yiddish renaissances seemed
at first sight similar or at least contiguous (in spite of the basic and inherent differences between the two literatures, which could be detected
even then), the downfall in the 1920s of the pre-war, precarious, nationalist consensus, symbolized by the bilingualism of major Hebrew-
Yiddish writers such as Abramovitsh and Peretz, set both Hebrew and
Yiddish literature free, each to follow its own trajectory. The difference
made itself felt immediately in the modernistic outburst or surge, which
in both literatures occurred in the wake of World War I and the civil
struggles that followed it. In Yiddish, this surge was by far more sweeping and immediately influential since it was articulated mainly in a new
kind of poetry, and pre-war European Yiddish poetry had not achieved
anything resembling the crystallization that romantic and symbolist Hebrew poetry had achieved in the era of Bialik, Tchernikhovsky, and their
disciples. In America, the upsurge of modernism met with a somewhat
stronger opposition since there a school of poets who had espoused impressionistic and symbolist poetics (*Di Yunge*) managed to gain dominance during the second decade of the century and thus, was able to
better fend off the new post-symbolist poetics of the *In-zikh* group and
sustain literary warfare throughout the inter-bellum period. However,
there, too, the clash between the traditionalists and the modernists was
by far less dramatic than its counterpart in Hebraic Palestine. Yiddish
poetry lacked the strong neoclassical and romantic traditions for the

modernist revolution to measure itself against; there was no Yiddish Bialik for the modernists to cut their teeth on; or rather, the Yiddish Bialik, namely, Peretz, had asserted his dominance mainly through prose fiction and not through his lyrical poetry. Indeed, the full strength of both Yiddish classicism and romanticism inhered in its prose fiction, and therefore the modernist revolution in Yiddish prose fiction would be furtive, discontinuous, and largely unsuccessful. With the exception of a few outstanding experimental novels and novellas (such as Ignatov's symbolist novel *In the Crucible* [1920], Der Nister's complex symbolist novellas of the 1920s, Moshe Kulbak's brilliant expressionist short novels *Messiah of the Tribe of Ephrayim* [1924] and *Monday* [1926] followed by I. B. Singer's expressionist novel *Satan in Goray* [1935] and the fantastic short stories that were written in its wake, and, perhaps, more than all others, Glatshteyn's two stream-of-consciousness *Yash* novels [1938, 1940]), Yiddish prose fiction throughout the twentieth century was dominated by pre-modernistic trends, mostly realism, sometimes softened by romantic idealization (Asch), or hardened by a modicum of naturalism (Vaysenberg, O. Varshavsky, B. Demblin), or nuanced and rendered more subtle by well contained impressionist sensibilities (Bergelson, L. Shapiro, Opatoshu). The Hebrew contemporary literary scene, both in eastern Europe and in Palestine, presented a different situation. Hebrew poets had to challenge the authority and question the achievements of a poetic establishment headed by the great poets of the pre-war period, and therefore theirs was an uphill struggle. In contradistinction, modernist Hebrew prose fiction, lacking a strong realist tradition, could base itself on the models of its pre-war trailblazers, Brenner and Gnessin, and evolve throughout the first half of the twentieth century, as it did in the work of the chief Hebrew masters, Agnon, Hazaz, and S. Yizhar, while a strong realist prose fiction was also systematically developed, sometimes with the help of the modernists themselves (thus Agnon's novel *A Simple Story* [1935] would elevate Hebrew psychological realism to Flaubertian heights).

This difference, particularly the difference between the opposition the modernist poets met, resulted in different kinds and levels of metaliterary thinking. One only has to compare the manifestos and polemic articles written by Greenberg during the years in which he functioned as one of the chief spokesmen of stormy Yiddish modernism with those he wrote as a trailblazer of the Hebrew Palestinian modernism to assess these differences. Vociferous as the meta-literary discourse of the European Yiddish modernists was (that of Greenberg himself, as well as of his fellow members of the various poetic "gangs"), there was nothing in it that could compare in its breadth and depth with Greenberg's Hebrew "Against Ninety-Nine," "The Added Elements and Changed Concepts in Man's Self-Knowledge," or "In the Outmost Simplicity."[1] By the same token, there was no articulation in Yiddish of a classicist position that resembled in originality and coherence Shteynberg's essays; and the achievements of both theorists were interdependent. Greenberg had to soar much higher than he used to because he faced a Shteynberg he had to surmount. European Yiddish modernist manifestos rarely transcended the declarative, verbose, and less than insightful definition of their poetic message as expressive of the current post-war human condition that was grotesque and monstrous. In its poetry, such as in Peretz Markish's superb "The Pile" (1921) or in Greenberg's extensive and often subtle anatomy of the modernist malaise, "Mephisto" (1920), European Yiddish expressionism reified and articulated its message and method in a manner that was not only more poignant and expressive but also more thoughtful and clearly argued than the many declarations, proclamations, and programmatic articles that filled its literary periodicals such as *Khalyastre* and *Albatros*.

In North America, the situation was somewhat different for the reasons already mentioned. Whereas American Hebraists remained, as we have seen, throughout the inter-bellum decades under the spell of the pre-war Bialikian poetics, young Yiddish poets raised the banner of American urban modernism. In their encounter with their predecessors, "The Young Ones," who had controlled the American-Yiddish poetic scene since the demise of the earlier school of socialist-anarchist poet-propagandists, these new young rebels were driven to come up with sober and clearly argued articulations of their post-symbolist emphases and preferences. With most of them college graduates and exposed to modernist American and British writing and literary criticism, they were better equipped than either their American predecessors or their European contemporaries to evolve a meta-literary discourse. In the first anthology of poetry, *In zikh* (*Within Oneself*), written by members of their new, modernist group, the programmatic essay "Introspectivism" (penned by the three editors: A. Glants-Leyeles, Glatshteyn, and B. Minkov)[2] was more interesting and promising than almost all the poems the collection contained. Later on, as some of the members of the group (particularly Glatshteyn, the foremost Yiddish American modernist) produced subtle, multi-faceted poetry informed by a strong intellectualism, the theoretical and critical interests of the modernists matured together with their poetry, and their periodical, *In zikh*, became the chief arena for modernist Yiddish theorizing about the various aspects of poetry, particularly those of poetic musicality and style within the format of free verse. The chief contributor to these deliberations was Glants-Leyeles (Glatshteyn would emerge as the best Yiddish American literary critic in the 1940s).

The so-called Inzikhists presented a model of a Yiddish literature (particularly poetry; their concept of prose fiction, albeit experimented with already in the 1920s, actually crystallized only during the 1930s together with the appearance of Glatshteyn's two novels *When Yash Traveled* and *When Yash Arrived*) that was totally secular, non-nationalistic, based on the urban experiences of the intellectually self-conscious individual, and free in its choice of themes and topics of any limitations prescribed by a conventional understanding of either the "poetic" or "Jewishness" and in its style and structure of strictures imposed by a traditional (metrical and rhyming) format of versification. Thematically, it could explore all cognitive processes, as long as they were filtered through the writer's idiosyncratic consciousness. Structurally, it could eschew all unities (such as the unity of *shtimung* [mood]) and progress by leaps and bounds, as long as it remained tied to the writer's associative cogitation; and stylistically, it was to be bound only by the free rhythmical fluctuations of an authentic interior monologue. In more than one way, the literary ideals of the Inzikhists were close enough to those of current English and American stream-of-consciousness writing. These ideals pitted them not only against the symbolists of *Di Yunge*, but also against the European expressionists and futurists. They rejected the poetic essentialism of the former that was predicated on the organization of the poem around a single mood and within the format of enriched and regular-ized euphony. At the same time, they also rejected the expressionists' understanding of a poem as the intense externalization of raw and primary emotions and the futurists' undermining of the logic of language and communication through neologisms and blatantly non-referential metaphors. Interested in ideas and discursive arguments, which, they believed, were as legitimate in poetry as anything else, they strove for a poetic tonality that approximated that of intelligent, free conversation somewhat heightened by poetic musicality, free and non-repetitive, but strongly felt. At the same time, they (particularly Glants-Leyeles) also experimented with traditional, formally restrictive poetic subgenres, such as the sonnet, terza rima, and villanelle, as long as they helped in enhancing poetic intellectualism and ideation. This helped them in reassessing earlier poets, such as Yeho'ash (Shlomo Blumgarten), who had by then been dismissed as a loquacious romantic. The rejection of Yeho'ash, they insisted, had been caused by his being a thinking poet, a poet of ideas, rather than a poet of "moods," impressions, and suggestions.[3] Glatshteyn would even dare to rethink the merits and limitations of the poetry of Morris Rosenfeld, the "king" of the socialist-anarchist poets, whom *Di Yunge* had attacked and dethroned as a sheer propagandist.[4] The Inzikhists decided that Jewishness in poetry should not be defined by theme or ideological preference but rather by tonality or even by the sheer fact that the poem was written in Yiddish. By this they meant not only the sheer usage of Yiddish as a linguistic tool, but also the adherence to the conversational ambience of the language, which had, of course, to be updated, modernized, and individualized, so as to truly reflect the consciousness of a modern individual rather than a tribal legacy. Having said that, one can nevertheless point to the realignment of at least some of the Inzikhists with the tradition of a Yiddish literature based on colloquialism and performative expressivity. This clearly distanced them from the Yiddish impressionists and symbolists, who by and large (with some notable exceptions) preferred a language divorced from the patterns and fluctuations of speech. Thus Glatshteyn, in both his poetry and prose fiction, would be closer to Sholem Aleichem and Peretz than to impressionist and symbolist writers of prose fiction such as Bergelson and Ignatov. By the same token, he could be fully appreciative of the wild late poetry of the single member of *Di Yunge*, the poet M. L. Halpern, who, as he matured, transcended musicality and *shtimung*, and replaced them by a singular style of corrosive, intentionally coarse, and seemingly uncontrolled poetic harangues.

Thus, Yiddish poetic modernism evolved two distinct schools, the European-expressionist one and the American-introspectivist one. Both argued the issues of expansion versus contraction, formal and thematic diffusion versus formal and thematic focusing, and so on, which, as we have seen, were at the center of the polemics engaged by the Hebrew modernists. However, they did it in meta-literary frameworks that were based on very different presuppositions, and therefore lead the exponents of the two schools to very different theoretical conclusions and practical results. Hebrew-Palestinian modernism was by far closer to that of the Warsaw expressionists than to that of the New York introspectivists. Indeed, a poet of genius such as Glatshteyn would have probably wilted in the Palestinian-Hebraist environment, being damned by both classicists and modernists due to his cerebralism, irony, dismissal of ideological fiats, and sheer urbanity and informal elegance. Nothing resembling his kind of modernism would project itself into Hebrew writing before the appearance of Preil in the late 1930s; in fact, Glatshteyn and his magic would not be accessible to Hebrew readers before well into the Israeli era, when he would be successfully introduced by culture agents such as Benjamin Harshav and myself to a generation ready to absorb his impact, because it had been reared on the poetry of Amichai and Zach.

By the mid 1920s, however, the skies of Yiddish modernism gradually became overcast. The issue, which from now on would cast an ever-lengthening shadow was that of the survival of Yiddish and of Yiddish literature. In the Americas, all Yiddish writers were immigrants (although those who had arrived before puberty were regarded as natives). Yiddish writing was kept alive and growing by a constant influx of Yiddish-speaking and -writing young newcomers with literary aspirations. When massive emigration to the United States was severely curtailed in 1924, an ominous process was set in motion. Still, a Yiddish-speaking and -reading population, and a relatively large one at that, was present, but it would inevitably grow older, with insufficient new recruits. Even more ominously, as far as the modernists were concerned, its literary taste and expectations would become progressively more conservative and less sophisticated as quick acculturation and Americanization would result in the disappearance of a young and well-educated Yiddish readership. A young generation of Jewish college graduates, avidly interested in ideas, literature, art, ideologies, and international politics, would turn its back on the provincial world of their ancestors and relinquish Yiddish, which they spoke at home; read T. S. Eliot instead of Glants-Leyeles, Joyce and Faulkner instead of Opatoshu and B. Glazman, and Edmund Wilson and Allen Tate instead of Niger and Rivkin. The modernists knew that their rope was getting shorter by the day. Later in the 1930s, Glants-Leyeles would sum up the situation succinctly in an ominous formula-like sentence: those who could understand the Yiddish modernists had stopped reading Yiddish, while those who still read Yiddish would not understand the modernists.[5] With most American Yiddish writers financially dependent on weekly publication in dailies that catered to popular taste, this situation could not but have dire results. Thus Yiddish prose fiction as written or published in the United States became progressively more conservative and less innovative, if not necessarily less vivid and colorful than it used to be, and attempts at writing experimental, modernist novels became fewer and unsystematic. The field of prose fiction was dominated by conservative, mimetic, essentially nineteenth-century novelists such as Asch, Israel Joshua Singer (an erstwhile expressionist experimentalist who had adopted a strictly mimetic, naturalist manner), and Shneur, in his sprawling epic cycles about turn-of-the-nineteenth-century Jewish life in Byelorussia and his multivolume historical novel about Jewish life in the Napoleonic era. Glatshteyn's previously mentioned Yash novels, an inspiring exception to the rule, could not be serialized in a daily newspaper. Also, the space for modernist poetry became progressively narrower. Some younger poets decided to switch from Yiddish to English. A prominent case was that of Y. L. Teller, a brilliant imagist, a poet whose work crackled with both intellectual acuity and sensuous directness, and probably the most talented native (he had arrived in the United States as an eight-year-old) to have joined the older American immigrant-poets. In the late 1920s, when still a *wunderkind*, he joined the Inzikhist group;

but by the early 1940s, he gave up on Yiddish writing and switched to English (in which he emerged as a lively journalist, although he also attempted to write modernist prose fiction), eventually explaining the shift by pointing, in English, to the provincialism of Yiddish literature and to its loss of direction within the American-Jewish cultural domain.[6] Preil, Teller's protégé and another fledgling Inzikhist, gradually shifted the focus of his poetry from Yiddish to Hebrew. American Yiddish poetry, while still being produced by its older masters, progressively ran out of fresh blood.

In eastern Europe, the situation, although superficially very different (with the resources of Yiddish-speaking readers and intelligentsia still abundant), was also worsening due to the corrosive processes of acculturation and assimilation (the two should not be identified with each other; they lead in different directions). In the 1930s, the importance of Warsaw, once the capital of Yiddish writing (with Peretz as its royalty), was on the wane. Still the center of the Yiddish press and publishing industry, with a large community of writers and journalists who congregated in its famous Yiddish literary club at 13 Tlomecka, it nevertheless failed to rear new outstanding Yiddish talents. Those made their appearance more or less far from the capital, whether in Lodz, an industrial city with no deeply rooted Yiddish cultural tradition, but because of its ethnically mixed population and proximity to the German-speaking West, not as deeply impacted by the process of Polonization, or in the Lithuanian city of Vilnius, where the presence (since 1925) of the YIVO Institute of Jewish Research, the deep Hebraic roots of many of its Yiddish intellectuals (proficiency in Hebrew being the characteristic legacy of traditional Lithuanian Jewry), and the proximity of Soviet Byelorussia lent Yiddish writing a special character and tonality. Thus Lodz produced, in addition to some of the best Yiddish literary cabarets, also some distinguished poets and writers of prose fiction, most notably the brilliant Yisrael Rabon; whereas Vilnius, while educating the best Yiddish linguists and historians, gave rise to a group of new and innovative poets such as Kulbak, Leyzer Volf, Chaim Grade, S. Kotsherginsky, and Avraham Sutskever—all to be known as the members of the *Yung vilne* cenacle. Still the processes that gradually blighted the center were also threatening the temporarily livelier periphery.

These developments led to important changes in meta-literary Yiddish thinking. Essentially, the pre-war Yiddishist rationale, as it was summed up at the 1908 Czernowitz Conference and in the theoretical thinking of Peretz, had to be replaced or, at least, considerably modified. The assumption, that Yiddish being the language of the folk could become the vehicle for a modern, humanist Jewish culture that would retain its autonomous existence without a territorial basis, both in eastern Europe and in the centers of Jewish immigration in the West, was clearly undermined by unstoppable historical processes. As much as Yiddishists clung to it, attempting to shore it up by chains of schools with Yiddish as the language of instruction, political parties, and youth organizations, their upbeat verbiage of self-encouragement sounded more and more like whistling in the dark.

Nowhere was this whistling in the dark so clearly heard as in Rivkin's book-length essay *Grunt-tendentsn fun der yidisher literatur in Amerike*, written during the last years of World War II, which were also the last years of the author's life (Rivkin died in 1945). In this, the most comprehensive and ambitious attempt of American Yiddishism at theorizing the development of the new Yiddish literature and offering it a future-oriented perspective, all the tragic dichotomies and inconsistencies, inherent in the cultural situation in which the Yiddishist project was mired, found blatant, albeit unintentional and seemingly unconscious, expression. Rivkin described modern Yiddish literature as propelled by two binary, but not necessarily mutually exclusive, "drives." The first, the *groys takhlesdiker tendents* (the drive of serious purposefulness), had been established in the nineteenth and the early twentieth centuries by the founding fathers of the new literature, Abramovitsh, Sholem Aleichem, and Peretz. They defined the role of this literature as a secular replacement of religion, a purposeful and high-minded moral guide of the Jewish masses on their way toward modernity. The second was a *kemoy teritoryele-literatur tendents* (pseudo-territorial-literature drive). What the author meant by this was the drive toward literary artistic autonomy based on the (false) assumption that Yiddish literature, catering to stable Yiddish-speaking contingents, amounted to a "normal" literature—and in this sense also a "territorial" one—a literature in possession of territorial bases whether in eastern Europe or in North

America. As such, it could and should have inspired to artistic perfection rather than to moral and political authority. This drive was initiated by the *Yunge* group in the United States around 1910 and then was also enhanced in eastern Europe by the Kiev *Eygens* group (including Bergelson, Der Nister, David Hofshteyn et al.) and others. There was also a third, intermediary "drive," which Rivkin dubbed *yerushe fervandlung* (legacy-metamorphosis), which was marked by a specific application of the legacy of serious moralistic purposefulness bequeathed by the founding fathers along new socialist lines; however, only the first two "drives" represented the basic forces that conditioned and guided the development of Yiddish literature. Now (the early 1940s, the years of the Holocaust, of the unspeakable dimensions of which Rivkin was not yet fully aware when writing his book) this development faced an impasse. Whereas until then the two drives had seemed to lead Yiddish literature onto "a broad highway," now they "left it hanging in the air" since the "faux-territorial illusion had lost its support in a reading public, which was falling apart."[7] How could the literature be shorn up? By undergoing a process of reassuming "serious purposefulness," a process that presumably would "call back to it its old reading public and attract a new one." But how could such a resumption of the moral exhortative tone attract a new reading public? Rivkin's answer to this question was fraught with inconsistencies and undermined by logical short circuits. Since the American Jew would presumably take seriously a literature that would help him face the questions pertaining to his very Jewishness, in what it subsisted and how it was to be maintained, Yiddish literature would regain his loyalty if it assumed the role of a guide in this matter. But why should the American Jew seek spiritual help in a literature written in Yiddish and not in the English he spoke and read? This question simply did not occur to Rivkin, or if it did, he decidedly repressed it—this, in spite of the fact that when he wrote his book, a Jewish American literature in English had already existed for more than twenty years (Abe Cahan, Mary Antin, Emma Lazarus, Mike Gold, Henry Roth, Charles Reznikoff, Ludwig Lewisohn, Howard Fast, Delmore Schwartz et al.). Furthermore, to render Yiddish literature ready to answer the questions Rivkin's imagined American Jewish reader might ask, it had, Rivkin insisted, to realign itself with the religion it once had presumed to replace. But how could it do that without reneging on its inherent modernist post-traditional positions and forfeiting its intellectual integrity? Particularly when at the same time, as Rivkin also insisted, it had to drop all its past ideological and literary negative attitudes toward Soviet Yiddish literature, informed by communism and atheism, and join hands with it! Rivkin had been characterized throughout his career as a critic and a culture activist by inconsistencies and idiosyncratic leaps and turnabouts. Essentially an anarchist, he nevertheless joined the Marxist and anti-Zionist Bund. Once settled in New York (1911), however, he committed himself not only to the advancing of the agenda of Jewish schools with Yiddish as the language of instruction, but also to assisting the Zionist pioneers in Palestine. Eventually he was drawn to the Marxist-Zionist *Poaley tsyion*, while still publishing his work in anarchist periodicals. Soon this committed atheist delved into spiritualism and "new messianism," exhibiting a growing attachment to religion and evolving a paradoxical faith that he called "a Religion for non-believers."[8] Whereas all these had marked until now the unpredictable and somewhat erratic career of a person of much brilliance and fertile ideas (some of Rivkin's practical criticism, particularly of American Yiddish poetry, was of considerable interest and insight) but devoid of intellectual discipline, the lack of such discipline in his literary theorizing had now an objective significance, since it emanated from the objective reality of Yiddishism in its dotage. It was not incidental that his *Grunt-tendentsn* was warmly received by Yiddishist critics who, swept by its upbeat albeit unsubstantiated faith in the future of modern Yiddish culture and literature, failed to focus on the pitfalls strewn along its argument.

Such self-delusions were common enough but in spite of all wishful thinking, there was hardly a way of avoiding the realization that acculturation everywhere undermined Yiddish as the language of a modern secular culture. With this as a given, what were the available options? Birnbaum, one of the chief Yiddishist ideologues and organizers of the Czernowitz Conference, reneged on modern Yiddishism, joined the orthodoxy and evolved a personal brand of a Yiddishist orthodoxy. Only a return to religion, he assumed, could vouchsafe the survival of Judaism as an autonomous civilization, and with it, also the survival of Yiddish. Perhaps this was the direction to which Peretz himself had pointed in the conclusion of his symbolist verse-drama "At Night in the Market Place." The gist of this symbolic drama inhered in a blasphemous wedding jester's attempt at shaking moribund Jewry into a godless "renaissance" (symbolized by the Jewish dead leaving their graves and expressing through a wild dance their yearning for the full instinctual and emotional life they had never enjoyed). The jester clearly represented Jewish modernism and its exponents: secular Hebrew and Yiddish literatures announcing a Jewish earthly "renaissance." But Peretz brought the drama to its conclusion with the dismal failure of that renaissance. Now the jester, crestfallen and wounded, calls for a reversal. "*In shul arayn*" (back to the synagogue) is his last exhortation and the final sentence in the text.[9] It triggered, of course, a stormy debate, for this was hardly an option acceptable to most modernists.[10] As unacceptable to Yiddishists was the switching to the creation of a new Jewish culture in a non-Jewish language, such as the switch made by Teller, and, to some extent also by I. B. Singer, who, with his novels and short stories in English translations accepted (in the late 1940s and early 1950s) as American masterpieces, went on writing them in Yiddish, serializing them for decades in the *Forverts* (the chief American Yiddish newspaper), but targeting them primarily at the general American public and regarding their English translations as their final and canonical versions, to be adhered to by all translators into other languages (including Hebrew). This, of course, went against the grain of the Yiddishist ethos and caused much anger and perplexity, which Cynthia Ozick, in a famous novella, interpreted as originating in mere "envy."[11] However, it is doubtful that this explanation truly gauged the depth of the Yiddishists' perplexity. Whereas I. B. Singer's commercial and critical success certainly elicited envy (and not only from Yiddish writers), the opposition to Singer emanated from deeper frustrations. When Judd L. Teller, by no means a successful and widely recognized writer, in his already mentioned English article of 1954, not only delineated the inevitable demise of Yiddish in America but also contended that Jewish writing in English was neither assimilatory nor necessarily uprooted due to linguistic alienation, he caused an outburst of anger (particularly from his erstwhile mentor as a Yiddish poet, Glatshteyn), which was short-lived in comparison with the I. B. Singer polemic only because Teller was not important enough, and also, because in the 1960s, he would undergo a *teshuva* (repentance) of sorts, resuming his writing of Yiddish poems and their publication in periodicals such as *Di goldene keyt*. The real issue was not one of individual success or failure but rather that of collective survival. I. B. Singer's literary politics had caused deep resentment even before his success as a translated writer because they were totally anti-Yiddishist. Already in his first novel, *Satan in Goray*, written in Poland and published there (1935), Singer had attacked Jewish "messianic" modernism, represented symbolically by a Sabbatean demagogue, as "false," vulgar, and morally irresponsible, undermining the only infrastructure that could hold together Jewish existence, that of the old, rabbinical rule, the dominance of the halakha. The Satan who bedeviled the stricken community of seventeenth-century Goray represented a contemporary amalgam of Jewish communists, Yiddishists, and Zionists of the 1930s, all those who promised their coreligionists a godless redemption of one kind or another. During World War II, I. B. Singer wrote articles in which he denied the relevance of Yiddish writing when it was divorced from the old, eastern European milieu. The language was inextricably intertwined with the old-style, God-fearing Ashkenazic European civilization. In this, of course, he pulled the rug from underneath the entire modern Yiddish and particularly the Yiddish-American literary project (that of the Inzikhists more than any other), contending that Yiddish wine was unable to travel and retain its bouquet when transported from continent to continent, from era to era, and from one cultural context to another.[12] This sounded like knelling the burial bell over the corpse of Yiddish literature, not only in Europe, where Yiddish-speaking Jews were being systematically murdered, but also in America and the Soviet Union, as well as Hebraic Israel. Right after the war, Singer projected the fantastic and grotesque reality of Yiddish writing through his monologues—recited by neglected and dejected demons who were still residing in the attics of empty Jewish houses in a de-Judaized Poland, having nothing else to do after one hundred and fifty years of alluring innocent Jews to partake of the imaginary delicacies of European humanism now that the carriers of this humanism had eradicated all Jews and thus left them, the demons, unemployed and unemployable, for seducing Jews was the only thing they knew how to do. These poor devils, living on dust and dried feces of mice, more than once presented themselves as the promulgators of the secular, new Yiddish literature of the Enlightenment and the nationalist eras.[13] At the same time, I. B. Singer was enjoying a growing international reputation as a major Jewish writer in English. All of these pointed in one direction—that of the self-liquidation of Yiddish literature.

Another option was that which never was, but still could be, called the Zionization or the territorialization of Yiddish writing. Yiddish, it seemed, could not survive in the modern world without a territorial basis and the support of a state. Thus the goal should have been to find or establish a state or an autonomous territory in which Yiddish would be supported and maintained. The Zionist Hebraic project seemed to have supplied a model and a challenge. Clearly, Hebrew was losing its footing almost everywhere even before the establishment of a sizeable Zionist contingent in Palestine; and now, with such a contingent established (during the 1920s and 1930s), and Hebrew, quite surprisingly (its adherents would say: miraculously), revived as a spoken language, these developments were energizing the entire modern Hebraic endeavor in Europe and elsewhere. The lesson of this revival could not be evaded: it was through re-territorialization and the support of a state-like structure (like the Zionist "state in perspective," or the Zionist shadow government in Palestine of the 1920s and 1930s) that Hebrew culture and the entire modern Hebrew project were saved. Thus in the 1920s and even more so in the 1930s, territorialism won the hearts of many Yiddishists including, as already mentioned, Yiddish modernist leaders. Before then it had attracted only a few Yiddish intellectuals. Most of Yiddish writers and culture activists wanted to live and work in the midst of Yiddish-speaking populations wherever such populations existed: in eastern Europe and the Americas. However, with their basis of operation constantly being eroded, these writers had to re-think their positions. Now Zionism without Zion and Hebrew seemed to offer a theoretical solution for the Yiddishists' conundrum. However, territorialism offered no more than a theory, a dream. Its leaders, such as the politician-writer Noah Steinberg, now pinning their hopes on the good will of governments such as that of Australia, found their political project at the preliminary stage where Theodore Herzl's plans had seemed to founder more than thirty years earlier. As much as Herzl had been knocking at the doors of the Turkish Porte, the Pope, and Kaiser Wilhelm with scant, if any, success, playing the role of the political beggar, the leaders of Yiddishist territorialism were undergoing a similar humiliation in an international world struck and frozen by the depression of 1929 and hardly amenable to plans of massive immigration. In the meantime the Jewish situation in Germany, anti-Semitic Poland, and the other new eastern European republics, which was quickly deteriorating, demanded quicker solutions.

In contradistinction, the Soviet Union seemed to offer a concrete and immediately available solution. In two of the Soviet republics where large parts of Soviet Jewry still resided, the Ukraine and Byelorussia, Yiddish was acknowledged as one of the official state languages; and according to the Soviet policy of supporting the cultural and linguistic legacies of all ethnic groups (provided, of course, they were reorganized within the framework of the official Marxist-Communist state "religion"), it was taught in schools, researched in official academies, spoken on the stages of state-supported theaters, and used in an array of publications—literary, scholarly, political, and educational. Yiddish writers, as long as they were deemed ideologically kosher, were the recipients of the recognition of the state (which included financial support), and their productions were published by state-controlled publishing institutions. In addition, the Soviet Union, in its struggle against Zionism and its wish to offset Zionist achievements in Palestine, launched projects such as the massive relocation of Jewish populations to new Yiddish-speaking collective agricultural settlements in the southern Ukraine and declared one of its far-off eastern Asian republics, Birobidzhan, a Jewish, Yiddish-speaking one. Hence the pilgrimage throughout the second half of the 1920s and the beginning of the 1930s to the Soviet Union of some of the best Yiddish writers and intellectuals, such as Markish, Der Nister, N. Shtif (the scholar who had evolved the concept of a Jewish academic research institution and wrote the blueprints that were adopted as the official program of the Vilnius YIVO), Viner, Erik, Kulbak, Bergelson, and many others. Their arrival in Moscow, Minsk, Kharkov, and Kiev rendered the Soviet branch of modern Yiddish literature as strong and as fruit-bearing as its Polish and American counterparts, and they adapted themselves as best they could to the obligatory ideological "line," but their motivation was not, in essence, informed by radical socialism as much as by their Zionist Yiddishism, that is, by their search for a state-supported Yiddish culture. Bergelson, one of the leaders of this pilgrimage (but, significantly, one of the last to settle in the Soviet Union), spelled out this rationale in his famous essay "Three Centers,"[14] where he compared the three hubs of contemporary Yiddish culture—New York, Poland, and the Soviet Union—and examined their respective chances of survival. His conclusion was that only the Soviet center could, in the long run, survive and flourish; a conclusion not that different from the one ardent Zionists such as Greenberg arrived at when they decided to "tear themselves" from the language of their heart, Yiddish; emigrate to Palestine; and resort to "the language of their race," Hebrew; on Hebrew soil—the only place where the language would fully come alive and be transformed like the re-incorporated and revived scattered dry bones in Ezekiel's vision (chap. 37).[15]

The Zionization of Yiddish literature continued after the Holocaust and the establishment of the State of Israel by a group of Yiddish writers who tied their fate as writers to that of the Hebrew-speaking state, expecting it to support their efforts, which it halfheartedly did, channeling its support through the powerful *Histadrut* (labor union), then one of the strongest arms of the ruling Labor Zionist Party of the Workers of Eretz Yisra'el (*MAPAI*). A Yiddish three-quarterly, *Di goldene keyt* (the golden chain) was started by the *Histadrut* in 1948 and consistently supported by it for half a century during which, in the hands of its brilliant editor, the virtuoso Yiddish poet Sutskever, it became the most important Yiddish literary periodical after the Holocaust, rallying around it worldwide Yiddish literary activity. This, however, was to remain an isolated show of support and never a part of a thought-through cultural agenda. In the 1950s a group of young Yiddish writers organized itself under the leadership of Sutskever, evolving a rationale of a renewed Yiddish creativity within the framework of a Jewish politically independent community. The group called itself *Yung yisro'el* (Young Israel), wishing, perhaps, to evoke the memory of *Yung vilne*, the last active and upcoming group of Yiddish writers in pre-Holocaust Poland, to which Sutskever had belonged. However, the all-but-total marginalization of Yiddish, its culture and literature in Israel, less intentional than the result of indifference (in spite of all the official lip service) and the sheer cultural dynamics of the young state, did not allow for the development of an authentic Yiddish writing with an Israeli identity, and the group, after a few years of existence and some joint publications, dispersed. It exerted, however, some subtle and indirect influence on the new Israeli Hebrew poetry of the 1950s and 1960s through the mediation of Binyamin Hrushovsky (currently, Benjamin Harshav), then a young Yiddish modernist poet (and a member of the group) and an upcoming Hebrew literary theorist, who as a co-founder and mentor of a group of young Israeli Hebrew poets (known by the title of its publication as the *Likrat* group), instilled into the group's official poetics and polemics some of the ambience and concepts of Yiddish modernism, particularly that of the Introspectivist (*In zikh*) American school. By and large, however, the dream of a Yiddish revival supported by the Jewish state was not realized. Unlike the commitment to Yiddish as the language of the Jewish masses in the Soviet Union before the destruction of its Yiddish elite by Stalin during the last years of his dictatorial rule, there was never a genuine official Israeli intention to resuscitate Yiddish. When Glatshteyn, the greatest Yiddish poet of the era, was invited, during a visit in Israel, to an audience with D. Ben Gurion, the father of the state offered him the help of the state in case he decided to make aliya, brush up his Hebrew, and switch from the Jewish exilic language to that of the reinstated Jewish homeland. The poet justifiably regarded this ludicrous episode as one of the most offensive encounters to which he had been subjected throughout his literary career.

It would be, however, of the greatest interest to the historian of modern Jewish culture to compare Hebrew-Palestinian and Yiddish-Soviet cultures and literatures within the decade and a half before the tragic fate the latter was to suffer during the Stalinist purges. Of course, the objective circumstances were quite different, these circumstances not being subsumed by the very different political realities of the communist state versus those of mandatory Palestine. In the Soviet Union, Yiddish culture was, in spite of its vigor and productivity, marginal.

It developed against the backdrop of a major culture, which attracted the Russian Jewish youth even as American culture attracted the Jewish younger generation in the United States. Its chances of long-term survival, even when supported by the state (and without taking into account the devastating impact of Stalinism), were murky. In Palestine, modern Hebrew culture, for the first time in its history of a century and a half, was not in a position of a minority culture, and its chances of survival were those of the Zionist project as a whole—in spite of great difficulties and severe struggles, rather good. Nevertheless, the two cultures were, in certain respects, uncannily similar, much more than the communities that upheld them—viscerally inimical to and rejective of each other—knew or wanted to know. In both places, new and revolutionary Jewish cultures based on well-controlled educational systems were supposed to evolve. In both cases, these cultures were to be informed and guided by a dominant ideology: Zionism versus communism. To be sure, adherence to ideology could not be in Palestine as obligatory and forcefully superimposed as it was in the Soviet Union (not that there were not some, most notably Greenberg, who wished it to be so; Greenberg openly propagated "spiritual dictatorship"). The Zionist establishment possessed neither the legal tools nor the moral will to harshly dictate ideological loyalty, but it certainly found more subtle and indirect ways of encouraging it. Both cultures were supposed to assume the role of a model for other Jewish cultural centers. The Hebrew-Palestinian culture regarded itself, and to some extent also objectively functioned, as the model for modern Hebrew culture centers in Europe and America. As mentioned previously, eventually even its Sephardic pronunciation and accentuation were accepted as normative by most Hebrew speakers and writers throughout the world. The Yiddish-Soviet establishment regarded itself as "hegemonic" and encouraged its exponents to assert a cultural supremacy throughout the Yiddish cultural and political domains. Both Hebraist Palestine and Yiddish Moscow functioned as Meccas for Jewish writers and public figures who visited and were inspired by what they saw and were told. In both cultures, the issue of what in Soviet Russia was called *yerushe* (legacy, inheritance), and what we may call selective or critical continuity, loomed large and triggered polemics.[16] There were, both in Palestine and in the Soviet Union, revolutionary cadres who altogether rejected Jewish cultural continuity. In Palestine of the 1920s, these were the members of the "legion of defenders of the Hebrew language" and those who rejected whatever smacked of exilic Judaism (they put, for instance, the most successful Jewish drama of the era, An-sky's *Between Two Worlds*, better known as *The Dybbuk*, on public "trial," which was concluded with the condemnation of its staging by Hebrew-speaking theatrical groups).[17] In the 1930s, this trend gradually evolved from staunch Hebraism and visceral anti-exile sentiments to the Canaanism, which declared the Hebrew-speaking contingent in Palestine a new Hebrew nation, cut off from its Jewish communal origins. In the Soviet Union of the late 1920s and early 1930s, the already mentioned call for a cultural "Revision" (the title of a book of literary polemics by the playwright and critic A. Vevyorka, 1931) entailed a condemnation of the Yiddish establishment's acceptance of Yiddish nineteenth-century bourgeois literature and a demand for a literature rooted in uncontaminated proletarian experience. However, in both Palestine and the Soviet Union, the demand for discontinuity and a new beginning from scratch (the Palestinian Canaanites were calling for a "beginning from *alef*," *alef* being the first letter in the Hebrew alphabet and the title of their periodical) was marginalized, and the norm of selective continuity became all but consensual. The question was what kind of continuity would be acceptable under revolutionary circumstances, and what should be the method of selection that would vouchsafe ideological integrity. In other words: what parts of the cultural past could be absorbed by the new Jewish cultures without diluting their respective revolutionary characters, and in what context or light these parts should be presented.

Essentially, the issue of selective continuity had been at the root of the modern Jewish literatures from their inception and was the inevitable result of their particular kind of newness. In general, cultural continuity becomes an issue in situations of drastic changes. Cultures that are developing and, as a matter of course, changing, under evolutionary circumstances are, by far, less concerned with the issue of cultural continuity than those that face revolutionary changes. Often they are only dimly aware of the very concept of continuity, or they couch it in terms that are indicative of their understanding of it as a given, a stable reality, fraught with neither the anxiety nor the exhilaration of crisis. However, the concept assumes particular urgency and drama in situations in which revolutionary developments are seen as threatening or promising the breaking of one's ties with the "origins," whatever those may be; and such, for sure, was the cultural upheaval that gave rise to the new Jewish literatures and informed them throughout their existence. They purported to be new and exultingly advertised their newness; but they also purported to be Jewish, which meant that ties with the past, or at least with parts of it, could not be relinquished. The new literatures were out to create a Jewish cultural alter ego; but they were emphasizing not only the alterity, the otherness, but also the ego, the continuity of the national self; as A. D. Gordon criticized Brenner, when the writer, in his call for an honest (and therefore devastatingly negative) Jewish "self-evaluation," went, according to the philosopher, too far in his rejection of historical Jewish life and culture. Self-evaluation, Gordon reminded Brenner, subsisted not only of evaluation and criticism, whatever their criteria, but also of a solid and continuous self as an entity that could be evaluated and critiqued.[18]

Thus discontinuity was never a real option. Likewise, the assumption that sheer linguistic continuity could suffice (i.e., that a sufficient tie with the cultural past could be secured by the use of one of the national languages), was disproved time and again, as the fate of the Inzikhist project (which based its modernist ethos on such an assumption) showed; for language always transcended sheer communication or personal self-expression; particularly when it was like the Hebrew language, inherently intertextual,[19] and charged with theological tension, which no secularization could eradicate.[20] But even Yiddish could never be completely disassociated from the communal cultural past of Ashkenazic Jewry, for it was replete with the mental vocabulary of its traditional civilization. By resorting to a language, a writer came in touch with what went far beyond sheer linguistic signification and had, in one way or another, exposed himself to a complex of style, idioms, narratives, myths, and Weltanschauung that belonged in a world that was not his anymore. The question, therefore, was, as said before, not *whether* some ties with the past should be maintained, but rather *what* were these ties to be or how the parts of the cultural past one chose to connect with were to be differentiated from the other parts. In nothing did the new literatures convey their sense of troubled awareness of their newness more than in this need to choose and justify the selection, its choice of a past or pasts. At the same time, however, the literatures also asserted their newness through this freedom of choice; for unlike those who had to accept the tradition as a monolith, the new writers could deconstruct it, activate the prerogative of being in possession of an independent discretion through adopting and rejecting parts of that tradition, through reinterpreting those parts which were adopted and adding to them past incidents or personages, which the tradition itself, due to its own biases and preferences, had rejected or marginalized, and through re-anthologizing the past, as Bialik and Ravnitsky did in their *Book of the Aggada* and Berditchevsky did in his Hebrew and German counter-anthologies.[21]

The early exponents of the Hebrew enlightenment, as we have seen, defined continuity in terms of reversion, going back to the pristine sources, namely, to the Bible. This they did, not only for the purpose of equipping themselves with what they regarded as proper style and aesthetic poise, but also for that of sending a moral message. Their neo-biblicism carved for them their niche as watchmen unto the house of Israel, the new national prophets in the age of humanism; for the Bible, unlike the later halakhic literature, offered two different, albeit mutually complementary, ways of connecting man with God: the law and the ritual, but also prophecy. Whereas the former were institutional (priestly) and dominated by codices and technical manuals, the latter was personal, poetic, and emotional; and the new writers certainly wanted to see themselves as the latter-day prophets vis à vis the rabbis, the priests of the exilic era. They left their neo-biblicism with both its functions, the aesthetic and the ethical ones, as their legacy for the new Hebrew literature throughout its historical passage from eighteenth-century rationalism to twentieth-century Zionism. As a stylistic model and a multi-tiered decorum, it largely dominated the literature throughout the nineteenth century with a few exceptions. A system of stylistic options rather than a unified style, it imbued almost all genres with its colors. In poetry, its period of dominance stretched well into the

Bialikian era and beyond. In prose fiction, it was tempered and dexterously conflated with post-biblical components in the 1870s and 1880s,
first, on a smaller scale, by Y. L. Gordon, and then, on a much larger
one, by Abramovitsh as he reverted in 1886 to the writing of Hebrew
prose fiction (which he had launched in the 1860s before switching to
Yiddish). In non-fiction, it set the general tone (albeit with quite a few
interesting exceptions) until it was consigned to the past in the 1890s
by Achad ha'am. Nevertheless it retained in the twentieth century its
acolytes, such as Frishman, Berditchevsky, even Shteynberg. Its long
period of dominance was often regretted and blamed for many of the
shortcomings of nineteenth-century Hebrew writing, but it was essential and therefore historically justified; for it was through the Bible that
the new writers defined not only their Jewish legitimacy, but also their
Jewish modernity. The Bible was to them a political, aesthetic, and stylistic guide to a Jewish civilization that was both pre-exilic and potentially post-exilic. That was the reason why the Hebrew novel had to be
born as a continuation of biblical narrative—not only because Mapu
lacked stylistic tools other than those supplied by the Bible, as was often
said, but because he wished to project into the new literature intense
erotic love and a vision of a free Jewish society in which erotic love
could find its legitimate expression; and that was why Zionism could
find its quintessential poetic articulation in Bialik's "imitations" of biblical prophecy.

     This neo-biblicism was somewhat strengthened by the advent of
Zionism, based on the assumption that a Hebrew culture to be created
in Israel under the circumstances of political independence or autonomy
and the replacement of a Jewish city life of commerce and brokerage by a
reunion with nature and agricultural life of a community of yeomen and
farmers, will have to revive biblical attitudes and gestures; for had not
the Bible been created by an independent and agricultural Jewish society
and against the backdrop of the landscape where now "all Jewish hopes"
(as in the widely sung Zionist lyric "There, in the Land Beloved by the
Fathers"—words penned by the educator Y. Dushman—proclaimed)
were to be realized?! Thus Palestinian Hebrew literature at its inception
(the last two decades of the nineteenth century) was pseudo-biblical to
its core and consciously evaded the allure of the new post-biblical or

"synthetic" narrative formula created by Gordon and Abramovitsh and developed into a normative *nusakh* (manner, style). Men and women of the first aliya wrote stories that in one way or another intended to evoke the atmosphere of biblical narrative. Even the tales of the Talmud and the Midrash were adapted (by Ze'ev Yavets and later by Israel B. Levner) in biblical Hebrew rather than in the historically more appropriate Mishnaic Hebrew, into which Bialik and Ravnitsky were to retranslate them; and under the hands of talented adapters, such as Yavets, acquired some of the lapidary quality, as well as the succinctness, straightforwardness, and freedom from homiletic burden that characterized biblical narration. Bialik himself would follow in Yavets's wake, when in the later part of his career, he would rewrite and expand the Midrashic tales about King David and King Solomon. Even some writers of the second aliya would try to retain this Palestinian neo-biblicism. Thus, Ben-Tsiyon, a very loyal disciple of Abramovitsh and a conscious developer of his manner in the stories he had written until he made aliya in 1905, switched (quite disastrously from the artistic point of view) to the biblical format, after he settled in Palestine. Young Agnon, arriving in Palestine in 1907, experimented (although not exclusively) with this format as a vehicle for modernist (impressionist and symbolist) narration, ironically—because of its semblance of naiveté—refracting his essentially tragic view of the artist (as unable to fully "live") and the interrelationships between men and women through a "simple," transparent, and quasi-legendary stylistic prism.

However, neo-biblicism, although never to be altogether given up as having exhausted its usefulness, could not remain for long the only anchor of cultural and linguistic continuity. It had to be enriched by and, to some extent, hidden underneath other cultural and stylistic pasts. This was so, not only because the language of the Bible proved quite unfit for the purposes of detailed mimetic description of contemporary Jewish life, but also, and more importantly, because the concept of Jewish modernity was being redefined. The concept of modernity created by the early Hebrew *maskilim* could be "biblical," because they understood modernity as an entity different and separate from rabbinic Judaism. Their neo-biblicism was motivated directly by their rejection of the rabbinical context as the one that could direct the Jewish people in the labyrinth of modernity. But this rejection could not be systematically maintained. When Mapu maintained in 1857 that he had to conflate biblical Hebrew with Aramaic in his novel *The Hypocrite*, this was not just a matter of a search for sheer mimetic credibility and the fashioning of a convincing dialogue between contemporary Talmudic scholars. It went together with a far reaching, if slow and gradual, re-examination and re-assessment of post-biblical Jewish life and culture. The German Jewish *Wissenschaft des Judenthums*, whose impact on modern Hebrew literature has yet to be fully gauged and understood, explored medieval Jewish literature and homily as legitimate and even exemplary products of an authentic Jewish culture. Hebrew scholars, working within the context of the Jewish enlightenment, such as Krochmal, Shlomo Yehuda Rapoport (SHIR), Shmuel David Luzzatto (SHADAL), M. A. Shatskes, and I. H. Weiss, among others, tried to curb the sharp anti-Talmudic critique of some of their contemporaries (such as Y. H. Shor). Krochmal included a very perceptive chapter on the Talmudic and Midrashic aggada in his *Guide to the Perplexed in Time*. In a series of brilliant monographs, Rapoport laid the foundations of the modern scholarly study of the halakhic tradition and the *piyut* of the early Middle Ages and urged his readers to treat the aggada not uncritically but respectfully, seeking in it not the supernatural husk but rather the kernel of moral truth (he, by the way, was also the scholar who made the famous distinction between Hebrew religious poetry written during the Middle Ages by Sephardic and Ashkenazic poets: the former excelled in expressing the individual and charting his way to God, whereas the latter gave voice to the Jewish collective, its tribulations, and faith; less convincing was his ascribing of both strengths to Vayzel's epic on the life of Moses).[22] Shatskes tried to "save" the Talmudic and Midrashic aggada from rejection, as fostering supernatural beliefs and irrational thinking, by an allegorical interpretation of the aggadic tales (a technique he learned from Maimonides's allegorizing of the anthropomorphic sections in the tales of the Pentateuch) while the vastly erudite I. H. Weiss summed up in his magnum opus, *Dor dor vedorshav* (vol. 1 published in 1871), the history of the halakhic tradition as a legal system and a civilizational code.

As importantly, major Hebrew writers started to question the immediate accessibility to the modern Hebrew narrator and commentator of the straightforward and superbly economical biblical narrative or apodictic gesture. Rather, they felt that the Bible had to be reached in a roundabout manner in the form of quotations and references already absorbed into a later tradition of exegesis and deconstructive interpretation. The Hebrew writer, particularly of prose fiction, had to adopt this scholastic approach if he were to create a modern Hebrew causerie, commentary, or discursive narration, which he had to have for the purpose of dealing intelligently with the complex issues to which Jewish life in modern times gave rise. For these issues to be dealt with in a sufficiently nuanced and essentially ironic manner, the writer of prose had to assume the role of a later-day Talmudic or Midrashic commentator (whereas the poet could retain the more elevated posture of the psalmist or the prophet), and this was what Gordon and particularly Abramovitsh did in the prose fiction, as well as the non-fiction they produced in the 1870s and 1880s. This approach to telling and commenting through referentiality and complex intertextuality, and not the sheer synthesis of early and later layers of the language for the purposes of richer and more detailed mimesis, was the core of the Abramovitsh manner. Those, like Berditchevsky, who believed that Jewish life, like all life, in spite of the heavy bookish legacy it was burdened with, was primarily about action and emotional and libidinal outbursts, rejected this manner and abided by the biblical syntax with its overwhelming dependence on the complex Hebrew verb system, which is the heart and lifeblood of classical, that is, biblical Hebrew. Berditchevsky systematically resorted to classical Hebrew syntax because with its heavy dependence on the verb, it enhanced the articulation of his Nietzschean insistence on mobility as the prime principle of existence. Those who, like Abramovitsh and later Agnon and Hazaz, believed that the Jewish mental apparatus had been irretrievably changed by the halakhic tradition and that it now absorbed reality through the prisms of texts and analytic discourse, accepted Mishnaic Hebrew and Talmudic Aramaic as the linguistic models that best served their artistic purposes. Bialik said more than once that the format of the aggada rather than that of biblical poetry was most accessible to the contemporary Jewish imagination.[23] Hence his huge investment in the aggadic literature and its re-injection into modern Hebrew culture.

But Bialik also invested himself in other literary linkages with the past. To him, the foremost Hebrew poets were the medieval Ibn Gabirol (on the editing and interpreting of whose collected poems he worked for many years) and Yehuda Halevi, and he believed that modern Hebrew poetry was rooted, through the mediation of M. Luzzatto in their lyricism. Achad ha'am saw the new literature primarily as a modernized and secularized extension of Jewish medieval rationalism—Maimonides, Levi Ben Gershom, Yosef Albo. The project these scholars and philosophers had undertaken—the reinterpretation of Judaism in terms of and in agreement with the science and philosophy of their time—was, for various reasons, discontinued in the early Jewish modern times, which therefore had been characterized by the stultification and intellectual stunting of Judaism, and had to be re-assumed by the exponents of the Hebrew enlightenment. The latter, having failed to play their role as the modernizers of Jewish scholarly and scientific thinking, produced only two worthwhile Hebrew works, Krochmal's *Guide to the Perplexed in Time* and Weiss's *Dor dor vedorshav*.[24] It was then his, Achad ha'am's, mission to re-direct Hebrew literature to its legitimate course, that of rationalist Jewish cogitation. Berditchevsky, Achad ha'am's rival and critic, identified with those parts of the textual past that retained the echoes of that "other" Judaism: the earthly, political, and physically heroic one. He was one of the first modern writers who focused on the last episode in the history of the Jews' rebellion against the Romans, the heroic defense of the fort of Massada near the Dead Sea and the eventual collective suicide of the defenders so as not to fall into the hands of the victorious legionnaires. Preserved only in Josephus Flavius's historical record, this episode of ancient Jewish stoicism and absolute dedication to political and personal freedom was not mentioned at all by the Talmudic and Midrashic traditions, which totally rejected such ethos as pagan and took umbrage with the entire project of the political activists of the Second Commonwealth era, the so-called *kana'im* (zealots), which brought about the destruction of Jerusalem and its temple. Now Berditchevsky started the elevation of the Massada narrative to the status of one of the formative myths of Zionism (soon to be elaborated on by scores of poets, thinkers, educators, and Zionist politicians).[25] He said its description by Josephus formed one of the two most sub-

lime chapters in Jewish literature, the other one being the story of King
Saul's suicide (in 1 Samuel, chapter 31) by falling on his sword, lest the
victorious Philistines catch and abuse him.[26] Also from the Midrash
and the Jewish medieval novella, Berditchevsky culled those passages
in which he found a reflection or an echo of ancient Jewish individualism and assertive corporality. Tchernikhovsky was one of the first new
writers who shifted the emphasis in the narrative of Hanukkah from the
miracle of the single jar of pure oil, overlooked and therefore not desecrated by the pagan priests who had converted the Jerusalemite temple
into a temple of Zeus, to the heroism and travails of the Maccabees.[27]
Thus, the trend was initiated, which within a few years catapulted Hanukkah from a minor semi-holiday (which did not involve the cessation of mundane activities) to the status of the chief Zionist holiday, for
which countless poems, plays, and stories were to be written and new
rituals invented (in America, of course, Hanukkah became the Jewish
Christmas). Tchernikhovsky also pioneered a revaluation of the *biryonim* (ruffians, hooligans), as the rabbinical tradition dubbed those who
insisted on rebelling against the Roman occupation during the last, hectic decades of the Second Commonwealth.[28] A younger poet, Kahan,
took up and developed this revaluation in a stormy hymn, the ringing
refrain of which ("In blood and fire Judea fell, / In blood and fire Judea
shall rise")[29] would be used by Jabotinsky's youth movement, *Beitar*,
and eventually the anti-British military *Irgun* that Jabotinsky's revisionist Zionists spawned, as their credo. Greenberg would totally identify
with the *biryonim* and the *sikarikim* (the anti-Roman "terrorists" who
hid a short sword under their garments and used it quickly and lethally
on their rivals, whether Roman or Jewish), comparing them not only
with the anti-British underground militias but also with himself as literary rebel and "terrorist." Tchernikhovsky, together with others (most
notably the scholar Slouschz) went further back in time and asserted
the ancient Semitic origins of the Hebrews, which presented a past that
had to be evoked and reinstated, and the exemplary model of the great
Carthaginian military strategist, Hannibal (a sonnet celebrating him
was written in 1921), which the new Hebrew revolution must emulate.[30]
Slouschz supported this assertion by translating into quasi-biblical Hebrew *Salammbô*, Flaubert's historical novel of the Carthaginian-Roman

Wars. (The translation was published in 1922, the translator making a point of transliterating the Phoenician name of the female protagonist not with a *samekh* but rather with the left *shin*, so as to emphasize the proximity of this ancient name to Hebrew names featuring the word "shalom," such as Shlomo or Shelemyahu.) Of course, all these were to be later picked up by the ideologues of the "Canaanites" A. Gurevitsh-Khoron and Rattosh, an identification with real and imagined Semitic origin being their brand of "continuity."

But not only vestiges of ancient Jewish heroism and physical prowess were evoked by the new writers. The recent exilic Jewish past also supplied them with grist for the continuity mill. Peretz, Berditchevsky, Yehuda Shteynberg, and Agnon, linked their work, each in his own manner, with the didactic folkloristic chapbook and with the Hasidic novella. Buber reinforced this trend in his German compendia of Hasidic hagiography and lore, which changed the climate of Jewish-German discourse. Writers with a particularly emphasized Zionist orientation, such as A. A. Kabbak, Hazaz, and Greenberg revived the Jewish eschatological tradition as it had evolved from biblical days through the New Testament and the midrashim of redemption up to the messianism of the Cabbalists, the Sabbateans, and the Hasidim. Hazaz based his "Yemenite" novels, *Thou That Dwellest in the Gardens* (1945) and *Ya'ish* (1947–1950), on these sources, as well as on the Enochian tradition of Hellenistic times and the early mystical "literature of Palaces" and reproduced the imaginary travels of the visionary through the seven heavens, their resplendent palaces and throngs of differently shaped angels. Greenberg regarded himself as the modern Molkho, the messianic prophet of the sixteenth century, a Marrano who re-converted to Judaism and was burnt at the stake by the Inquisition, rewrote Molkho's vision on the dead sea (in his political prophetic poem "The Vision of One of the Legion"),[31] and told how as an Austrian soldier in the Balkan, he went all the way to the distant Albanian village of Dulcina where the body of the converted Shabbetai Tsvi had been interred in a Muslim cemetery, there to salute the failed Jewish Messiah who, presumably, had attempted to re-establish the independent Jewish kingdom.[32]

Even the most despised chapter in the history of Hebrew poetry, that of the *piyut* (the liturgical poem meant to complement and expand the synagogue ritual), found in the twentieth century in the heyday of Hebrew modernism, its admirers and followers. Because of its complex periphrastic poetics and audacious linguistic innovations (with the use of neologisms as the rule rather than the exception in its stylistic system), the *piyut* had been seen by the Hebrew neoclassicists of the eighteenth and the nineteenth centuries as having vitiated the Hebrew language, destroyed its elegant equilibrium, and heaped upon it inane verbiage. Y. L. Gordon and even Bialik expressed their scorn for it, and the word *paytan* (an author of *piyutim*) became a pejorative reference to a mere scribbler of nonsensical verse. However, in the 1920s and 1930s, together with the rise of scholarly interest in and serious study of the *piyut* (pioneered by M. Zulai), poets such as Karni, Shlonsky, Rimon, and the exquisite, but relatively unknown Mordechai Georgo Langer (a Prague intellectual and an acquaintance of Franz Kafka who had undergone a phase of re-orthodoxization and spent a year in the Hasidic court of the Rabbi of Belz) found new use for the neglected forms and the despised linguistic permutations of the *paytanim*. They also reinterpreted the word *paytan* as poet, in general, a term to be used when the reference to a poet was celebratory and within a context emphasizing his professionalism and his being in full control of his poetic tools. Shlonsky went so far as declaring himself (in the ears of the Parisian prostitutes of his *Stones of Void*) as "[a] strange Hebrew paytan from the Land of Canaan."[33] Shlonsky's poetic disciple, the magical Rattosh, basing himself on the Ugaritic texts discovered during the inter-bellum period at the northern Syrian seashore, reinvented a pre-biblical Semitic-Hebraic dialect, which was as pseudo-archaic as it was superbly modernistic.

Yiddish writers charted their own sojourns into a Yiddish past,[34] historical or imaginary. They were exponents of a new literature that was aware of its newness and proud of it, and yet they also had qualms about being, as Peretz put it in 1910, a literature "with only one tombstone" in its cemetery (that of Dik who had died in 1893) and a corpus that could find its place in one bookcase.[35] Abramovitsh firmly believed nothing of merit had been written in Yiddish before he published his early Yiddish works in the 1860s. "The language was then an empty vessel containing nothing worthwhile, only prattle," he wrote.[36] This severe judgment presumably applied even to the best work of Dik, who had started his career as a popular Yiddish writer almost two decades before Abramovitsh. However, even before Abramovitsh pronounced his verdict (in 1889), his disciple Sholem Aleichem had already included Dik in his "great tradition" of "our best folk-writers."[37] In the two volumes of his almanac *Yidishe folksbiblyotek*, he made an effort to go further beyond Dik and publish Yiddish texts written by earlier *maskilim*, such as Levinson (RIVAL). In the early twentieth century, Peretz and his disciples went further back to the Yiddish didactic chapbook, the format of which had been resorted to in the nineteenth century primarily within the context of parody, for the purpose of denigrating through pastiche its ambience of a naive amalgam of didacticism, faith, and superstition. Writers of the turn of the nineteenth century, the pre–World-War, and of the inter-bellum periods, however, such as Peretz, Der Nister, and Ignatov (the latter two—declared symbolists) found in it a source of inspiration and a welter of poetic intuitions that they aestheticized and modernized. I. B. Singer was to continue this tradition as part of his elevation of intentional "foolishness" (in the sense of innocence, naiveté, like that of "Gimpel the Fool"—very much in the spirit of Rabbi Nachman of Bratslav's famous fable "A Tale of a Sophisticated and a Naive Person") to the position of the only authentic and nondestructive attitude toward life, as well as the source of true narration. The Yiddish American novelist Opatoshu, who had written, among other works, historical novels about the relatively recent Polish-Jewish past (the best known among them was *In Polish Forests*, 1918), was so eager to delve deeper into the relatively unknown older Yiddish literary past, that almost as soon as Erik's already mentioned studies of the Yiddish literature of the late Middle Ages and the Renaissance appeared in 1926 and 1928, he put the scholar's hypotheses to imaginative use. Erik, in his attempt to understand the modus vivendi of old Yiddish narrative poetry came up with a hypothesis about the existence of a Yiddish wandering actor-reciter, a Jewish medieval rhapsodist-bohemian, who wandered from one community to the other, lived in taverns, and, when allowed, on occasions such as weddings and other festivities, entertained the sedate members of the community and their womenfolk with his performance, which could at time wax off-color. This hypothesis (already suggested in 1889 by Eliezer Shulman, the first historian of old Yiddish literature, and, of course, based on what was known about German minnesingers [troubadours] of the period), often referred to as "the Spielmann theory," was eventually refuted and discounted. However, it stays fully alive in Opatoshu's exquisite historical novella "A Day in Regensburg" (1933), where the sixteenth-century German Jewish communal leader Yosl of Rossheim arrives in Regensburg presumably to take part in a wedding festivity of some important local family, and in reality to discuss grave matters that threaten the future of the Jews of the Germanic fiefdoms, and, if possible, be granted an audience by the German emperor of the Holy Roman Empire. The imagined, but very lively and colorful, historical background was rendered here as supremely vivacious and three-dimensional. Also, old western Yiddish, which eastern Europe had long lost touch with, but which at this juncture was intensely studied by a group of young and energetic scholars who established the discipline of scholarly Yiddish linguistics, was cleverly used in a dialogue, which was sufficiently understandable, and yet struck the readers as Shakespearean English would have struck twentieth-century theater audiences. All in all, Opatoshu fully succeeded in this, perhaps his most accomplished historical fiction, in creating a figure, realistic and at the same time symbolic, of the Yiddish poet, marginalized by a society that thoroughly enjoyed his witty and pointed verses, but at the same time regarded them as frivolous and worthless; a society, which itself lived under the constant cloud of upheaval, exiling, persecution, and emigration.

Both Opatoshu and Y. Y. Trunk wrote novellas and short stories with the figure of the sixteenth-century writer Eliyahu Levita (also known as Elya Bokher or Bakhur) as their protagonist. Levita was a north Italian Hebrew grammarian-lexicographer, who also wrote Yiddish poetry and romances. Among other works, he adapted into western Yiddish the Italian chivalrous romance *Bovo of Altona* (1541), a story about a Hamlet-like prince, who had been dispossessed of his kingdom by his uncle but eventually regained both the throne and the pleasures of making love to Druzina, his faithful and patient inamorata. This romance, eventually adapted into eastern European Yiddish and known as *Bove mayse* (the tale of Bove; the Italian name could be easily confused with *Bobe*, grandma) was as popular with the uneducated populace as it was despised by the elite, and its title, *Bove mayse*, became an idiomatic expression standing for a fantastic but vapid yarn, what in Shakespeare's England was referred to as "a winter's tale." Now, in the 1930s, it was Levita's romance that was celebrated as an early Yiddish masterpiece. It was retranslated (by Trunk, among others), studied by linguists and literary historians, and its author was hailed as one of the founding fathers of Yiddish poetry. Young Sutskever, the unparalleled virtuoso among modern Yiddish poets, experimented, guided by the famous Yiddish linguist Weinreich, with the writing of poetry in medieval or renaissance western Yiddish. Yiddish novelists explored the distant past of Ashkenazic Jewry and its Hebrew-Yiddish diglossia. In America, Ignatov hankered back to medieval Prague. In the Soviet Union, the critic and scholar Viner wrote historical novels about class struggle within the Jewish communities of Krakau and Venice of the late Renaissance or early new times. Some writers (such as Asch in his *Sanctification of the Name* and young I. B. Singer in his early novel *Satan in Goray*) explored the seventeenth-century crisis triggered by the onslaught on the Jewish community of the Polish kingdom by Khmelnitsky's rebellious Cossacks, the upsurge of Sabbateanism, and then the eighteenth-century apostasy of Jakob Frank. In *Satan in Goray*, by the way, the naive Yiddish chapbook was fully brought to life at the conclusion of the novel, where the story of the possessed heroine, which up to this point had been told as a study in sexual hysteria, was retold in a religious, folksy manner, as a traditional story of a *dybbuk*: the penetration of an alien soul unto the body of a person. Many writers turned to the beginnings of the Hasidic movement in the eighteenth and early nineteenth centuries (as, for instance, in Asch's famous *Psalms Reciter*), Shneur fictionalized the advent of the *Chabad* brand of Hasidism and the conflict between its founder, Rabbi Shneur Zalman, and the Ga'on Eliyahu of Vilnius, the leader of the Lithuanian rabbinical establishment that opposed Hasidism and did everything in its power to forefend against it being implanted in its own backyard, the Byelorussian north. Thus Yiddish writers of the inter-bellum period were hard at work, crafting a historical-literary past that was as much imbued with the tonality of Yiddish speech and writing as they possibly could make it within the limitations of historical verisimilitude. This buttressed their own sense of Jewish continuity. This trend was picked up and carried further even after the Holocaust, when I. B. Singer, for one, projected this total disruption of Jewish life into the historical past of Polish Jewry, as he did in his late historical novels, most notably in *The Slave* (1962).

Seven   Vertical and Horizontal Continuities and Discontinuities

The issue of continuity versus revolutionary innovation dominated much of both the Hebrew and Yiddish meta-literary thinking as it evolved by literary scholars and historians between the end of World War I and the first years of Israeli independence. Even when not directly discussed, these issues forced themselves upon the contemporary literary-scholarly discourse. Where they did not feature overtly, they lurked covertly; and even when they seemed to disappear altogether, they only sank toward the rock bottom of the discourse, influencing from there the patterning and streamlining of its surface level. They bore upon space and time, divergent historical situations and geographical centers, ethnic identities, languages, both Jewish and non-Jewish, contradictory ideologies, social tensions, personal rivalries. The opposition of religion versus secularism was, of course, very central to the evolving discourse. However, by no means was that discourse subsumed by it, as some think. Not only did the meta-literary dialogue go far beyond this particular opposition; but also, importantly, the tendency to focus on it often obfuscated much of what this dialogue was about and resulted in myopia; particularly when both the terms "religion" and "secularism" were left conceptually undefined and historically non-reified (as they often were), which sent the discussion here under consideration into an intellectual blind alley. Similarly the concepts of bilingualism and multilingualism, when referred to without close historical scrutiny, more often than not muddled waters that could have retained clarity. It was not before Uriel Weinreich published his pioneering *Languages in Contact* (1953) that the dimensions of Jewish diglossias were clearly perceived.

This meta-literary thinking, with its ups and downs, breakthroughs and stumbling, can be said to have gravitated to and organized itself along two axes, a vertical and a horizontal one. Those with a proclivity for thinking vertically (which is the more conventional form of historical thinking along the time axis) were intrigued by the questions of whether and how the literature retained a unifying common denominator as it evolved throughout the epochs and eras predicated upon one or another paradigm of periodization. They were mostly, albeit by no means exclusively, Hebrew scholars who studied the development (another concept of questionable usefulness) of Hebrew literature. They asked themselves whether a causal line of continuity that linked the old with the new, and then also the old-new and the new-new could be discerned; and their questions were applied not only to the tension between the so-called old Hebrew literature and the new one, but, eventually, also to a possible discontinuity, which might have snapped the links connecting the new literature with its Israeli extension, or to put it in Rattosh's terms, between the new Jewish literature written in Hebrew and the nascent Hebrew literature created by the new Hebrews, native speakers on native ground.[1]

Those whose thinking gravitated toward the horizontal axis, mostly, albeit not exclusively, non-Hebraic scholars, with Yiddishists at their head, tended to think in spatial terms and look for patterns of significant simultaneity in Jewish writing. The questions that bothered them were first and foremost whether the complex of Jewish multilinguistic writing (particularly in the modern era) could be reduced through some common denominator (such as inherent bilingualism or inherent intertextualism) to an all-inclusive Jewish literature, or, to use Sadan's favorite, *sifrut yisra'el* (the literature of the Jewish nation). These scholars and thinkers concerned themselves primarily with the possible continuity or integrity of an overall Jewish literature as written in different languages; but the linguistic barriers were not the only ones they attempted to surmount. Thus, for instance, they wished to lower, as much as was possible, the fences separating Hasidic literature (written in both Yiddish and Hebrew) from the literature of the Enlightenment (also written in both languages, as well as in non-Jewish ones), Jewish mystical from Jewish rationalist writing, and so on. Some applied the concept of literary simultaneity to issues of aesthetics and poetics. Thus, for instance, Ch. N. Shapira, and subsequently, Halkin, liberated the historiography of Hebrew literature of the Enlightenment from its conventional and arbitrary division into three periods: neoclassical, romantic, and realist ones, showing that this literature was almost from its inception and throughout its existence informed simultaneously by neoclassicist, sentimentalist, and actualist (the term was coined by Halkin)[2] trends, with romantic and realist tendencies (in the aesthetic sense of the terms) barely, and, if at all, intermittently and unsystematically reflected in it until the flourishing of both toward the end of the nineteenth century, already in the so-called nationalist era. More recently, spatial rather vertical thinking has been characteristic of those who checked, within Hebrew literature, the fault lines separating majority and minority discourses, issues of canonicity and marginality due to ethnic or gender differentiations,[3] as well as those who studied the effects of literary liminality, such as the liminality of Hebrew writing outside the boundaries of the "Zionist narrative."[4] There were even those who pondered the possibility of interrelating, within supra-national, extended spatial concepts such as Israeliness or Mediterraneanism, writing by members of different national groups, such as Jews and Arabs in Israel, or Jews of North African and southern European backgrounds who worked, presumably, within a regional frame of reference (the names most often mentioned in this connection were those of writers such as Albert Cohen, Edmond Jabès, Primo Levi, Albert Memmi). Having said all that, it should nevertheless be stated that the major issue the spatialists were negotiating, particularly in the period under discussion, was that of the existence or non-existence of a unified or semi-unified multilingual Jewish literature, and it is obvious why the horizontal axis loomed large in the thinking of Yiddishists, as well as in the minds of those who wrote in non-Jewish languages but regarded themselves as Jewish writers. The former had to negotiate their position vis à vis the Hebrew literary tradition. Their "angst" was one of historical illegitimacy or secondariness, whereas the latter had to prove that literary Jewishness was possible and even inevitable also outside of the net of Jewish languages.

The scholar who more than anybody attempted to conflate the two axes was Sadan, whose vast scholarly project was divided (albeit unequally) between the canonical new Hebrew and Yiddish literatures, and at the same time also between canonical literatures and their sub-canonical extensions, such as writing that belonged in the space between literature and folklore, historiography and linguistics. Sadan made formidable contributions to the study of the canonical centers of both the Hebrew and Yiddish literatures of the last two centuries (focusing on major writers such as Bialik, Brenner, Agnon, Sholem Aleichem, Manger, Sutskever) and that of an array of Jewish-Ashkenazic "peripheries" and was perhaps the first to show that the boundaries between centers and peripheries, as much as they had to be kept in mind, were perhaps not as firmly and sharply etched as we used to think. He also showed by meticulous thematic and linguistic analyses how the work of truly great writers (such as Bialik and Agnon) collapsed these boundaries at their less obvious levels, such as those of inner rhyming, of motif patterning, and of repetition and variation,[5] while at the more overt levels, they clearly and forcefully articulated the concerns and themes of the canonical mainstream. It is because of these invaluable contributions that whoever wishes to study the Jewish literary complex always must go back to Sadan, in spite of the fact that his theory of *sifrut yisra'el*, as we shall see, is perhaps less conducive to new thinking about that literary complex than is generally assumed.

In its vertical version, the problem of continuity was squarely if somewhat simplistically stated by Kurzweil in his previously mentioned book: *Our New Literature: A Continuation or a Revolution?* The question thus stated did not allow for the possibility of the new literature amounting to both a continuation *and* a revolution. Actually, the question could be asked—and was asked—not only with regard to the new Hebrew literature. It was applicable to all brands of Jewish literature whether or not created within the framework of one language. It is questionable whether the Hebrew of the Mishna and the Hebrew of the Bible are or are not two totally different languages. To judge by their respective vocabularies and syntactical formations, the two are as divergent, if not more, than current English and Chaucerian Middle English. However, even if we regard the two as belonging within a single, multi-tiered linguistic system, the question whether the Mishna was—vis à vis the Bible—a continuation or a revolution can be legitimately asked, as can and should be asked other pertinent questions such as: Does the general term "Hebrew poetry" convey any real content? Is there a single and continuous Hebrew poetry if the term must cover a continuum starting with the "Song of Deborah" (Judges 5) and David's lament for Saul and Jonathan (2 Samuel 1:17–27); continuing through biblical prophecy and psalmody, and uniting them with the ecstatic poetry of the Dead Sea sects of the time of Jesus, with the visions of the Sibyls; covering the Palestinian *piyut* of Yanai and Hakiliri, the war poetry of Shmu'el Hanagid, the philosophical ode *Keter malkhut* (crown of kingship) of Ibn Gabirol, the courtly love and wine poetry of M. Ibn Ezra, the sonnets of Manuello Romano and Ya'akov Frances, the verse dramas of Moshe Luzzatto, the triumphant hymns of Eliyahu Chalfan-Halevi(to *pax Napoleonica*) and of S. Levisohn (to poetic diction), the heavy neoclassical odes and elegies of Adam hakohen, the agnostic historical poems of Gordon, and finally reaching to Bialik, Tchernikhovsky, and their younger contemporaries, then to Greenberg, Shlonsky, and Alterman, Gilboa, Amichai, and Zach. If a supra-historical concept of a continuous Hebrew poetry could be formed, then it would have to be very different from seemingly parallel concepts such as French poetry or English poetry, for in the latter, as much as in most poetic traditions created since the Middle Ages in the European vernaculars, a kind of continuity can be traced for which we would look in vain in the annals of Hebrew poetry. The fact that in most brands of poetry written in Hebrew throughout the ages, different modalities of relatedness to the Bible can be pointed to, does not in and of itself amount to a sufficient unifying factor; for if it does, then all Christian literatures, which are informed by a more or less emphasized biblical intertextuality and thus share this common denominator, should somehow belong within a non-existent Judaeo-Christian literature as much as within a Greco-Christian literature. But do they? Does Joyce's *Ulysses* belong within a Greek literary tradition? For that matter, do the poetic works of Cavafy and Seferis and the prose fiction of Kazantzakis, written in modern Greek, belong within a continuous Greek literature that includes Homer, Pindar, and the poets of the Greek anthology?

Obviously, Hebrew poetry, Hebrew literature as a whole, and Jewish literature as an evolving complex are full of disruptions; of new

beginnings almost from scratch; of disparate and unrelated continu-
ations—such as the continuation up to the twentieth century of the
medieval Hebrew Andalusian poetry far from the European centers
(in North Africa, Iraq, Asia minor and elsewhere), where it was supposed to have reached its demise in the fifteenth century; of traditions
that were hardly aware of each other. If they exhibited any kind of
interrelatedness that could be meaningfully referred to as continuity,
it was almost always a continuity that went together with revolutions,
and, at the same time, with secondary evolutionary progresses or developments within the different segments of the complex. Thus there
was something unfocussed and misleading in the very question "our
new literature—continuity or revolution?" However, this fuzziness of
a question, which seemed so sharp and pointed, tells the story that
we try to trace; for as much as it is a story of ideas, concepts, and insights, it is a story expressive of pent-up emotions, of barely defined
wishes and needs, whose pressure sometimes did result in conceptual
fuzziness and a false sense of clarity, where the scholar or critic was not
even fully aware of how unclear and unyielding to conventional taxonomies the matters at hand actually were. Thus, for instance, Kurzweil
was constantly driven by a tragic sense of loss—the loss of an imagined or historically mythologized, primal Jewish unity and harmony
under the aegis of normative-halakhic Judaism. When scholars such
as Scholem clearly showed that such harmonious unity was a mere figment of the unhistorical imagination, the temperamental literary critic
almost jumped out of his skin.[6] By the same token, he rejected with
seemingly uncalled for vehemence any notion that the new Hebrew
literature, at least until the last decades of the nineteenth century, was
by no means atheistic or anti-religious, or that it was triggered not
only by the exposure to eighteenth-century European rationalism,
but also by intrinsic Jewish impulses and urges emanating from the
growing tensions within "traditional" Jewry in the seventeenth and
eighteenth centuries (a notion suggested by Scholem and expanded by
Ch. N. Shapira).[7] Kurzweil was far from conducting a sedate scholarly
debate. He was rather acting out, through historical generalizations,
conflicts and internal dichotomies in himself, as well as in the hearts
and minds of many Jewish modernists, which is why his writing was

informed by a mesmerizing energy and why it should still interest us even though it was based on neither a sufficiently large basis of substantiated historical facts nor on the appropriate concepts that should have helped the critic in intellectually processing such facts. Hence his erroneous understanding of the new Jewish secularism as a crisis of faith, the loss of personal contact with the transcendental, rather than as a gradual absorption on the part of a growing number of Jews of the social, political, economic, and cultural tenets of eighteenth-century modernism, with its subsequent re-focusing of Jewish thinking on the social and political welfare of the Jewish collective, the human physical, emotional, and intellectual needs of the Jewish individual, and the improvement of the lot of both the people and its individual members through modernist-rationalist methods of reorganization, or social and educational engineering; all these together with a rejection of religious bigotry and fanaticism, but definitely without directly or indirectly questioning the validity of revelatory religion as such, and the applicability of the Jewish halakhic norm to those aspects of life to which it was legitimately applicable. Thus, with Kurzweil, as with many others, the issue of literary continuity assumed a poignant existential quality. It involved, more than anything else, the critic's own psychic continuity as a modern Jew. The real questions the critic was attempting to answer while donning the garb of the literary historian were not genuinely historical questions. Rather they were those of a tortured poet-philosopher: who am I as a modern Jew? Am I forever cut off from authentic Judaism (whatever that meant)? Am I contributing to a new Jewish culture or merely participating in the death throes of *the* one and only legitimate Jewish culture, which was the one informed by and based on the rabbinical halakha?

It was this existential fervor that endowed the question whether M. Luzzatto rather than Vayzel was the founding father of the new literature with the importance that it assumed throughout the first half of the twentieth century, and, which it almost suddenly, but totally, lost with the onset of its second, "Israeli" half. Whereas outwardly this seems an arcane issue of little interest to anybody but historians who ascribe exaggerated importance to their schemes of periodization—the super-impositions of beginnings and ends upon a historical continuum—it nevertheless touched, almost from the start, a raw nerve. Luzzatto was certainly a much more intriguing and attractive figure than Vayzel, the sedate and bookish grammarian and exegete, who in his old age also wrote his long-winded (and today unreadable) didactic epic that presented Moses as a moral paragon. In contradistinction, Luzzatto, an early eighteenth-century poet, rhetorician, mystic, and moralist, had been that much intellectually sexier, for everything about him was dashing, colorful, and dramatic. The author of exemplary Hebrew allegorical dramas in which a delicate equilibrium between nature and civilization, faith and reason, emotionalism and contemplation, seclusion and social participation was elegantly negotiated in the spirit of neoclassicism, he was also, and, as far as he himself was concerned, primarily, a Cabbalist, a person to whom a heavenly "speaker" dictated hidden mystical truths and perhaps, a messiah in his own right. The powerful rabbis of the Jewish congregation of Venice (he himself was a Paduan) regarded him with suspicion as a cryptic Sabbatean and forced him to leave his homeland. On his way to Holland, the leaders of the Jewish community of Frankfurt detained him, confiscated his manuscripts, and gave them a formal burial in the local Jewish cemetery. Once in Holland he behaved more carefully, wrote his best-known verse drama, *Praise to the Righteous*, and his ethical manual, *The Path of the Righteous*, the latter becoming one of the most popular Jewish homiletic treatises. He died at the age of thirty-nine in Palestine to which he had emigrated a few years earlier, expecting to be granted there new mystical revelations and perhaps be able to rise to the messianic stature he believed he had possessed.

We have already seen how Hebrew literary thinking at the beginning of the twentieth century, the era of Bialik and of scholars such as Slouschz and Ish-Hurwits, was attracted to Luzzatto and insisted on his primogeniture as the founding father of the new Hebrew poetry. Bialik, as we have noted, would have loved to trace his poetic pedigree to "The Youth from Padua"[8] rather than to the oldish, "watery," and "lukewarm" Vayzel,[9] let alone the non-Hebraic and non-nationalist Mendelssohn. Unlike Lilienblum and Berditchevsky, he and many others failed to fully understand the historical importance and the essentially nationalist significance of the literary project Vayzel and his followers, the members of the *Me'asef* circle, set in motion. Now, in the 1930s and 1940s, the Luzzatto controversy was revived. Outwardly, this resulted from the fact that in these two decades, the attempt at producing detailed and comprehensive histories of the new Hebrew literature, both academic and scholarly ones and also ones more popular and targeted at secondary school students, was in full swing—both in Palestine and in eastern Europe. At least four such histories were written almost simultaneously (by Lakhover, Klausner, Ch. N. Shapira, and A. Orinovsky; significantly, in the six decades that have elapsed since the foundation of the State of Israel only one more general history was produced in Hebrew, by Klausner's disciple A. Sha'anan; other literary histories, such as those of G. Shaked and H. Barzel, were limited to a specific genre, a significant and telling development). The writing of these histories seems to render the revival of the polemic around the issue of the beginning of the new literature inevitable. Thus Lakhover, under the direct influence of Bialik, regarded the transition from the old to the new in Hebrew literature as being neither sharp nor quick. A full century of interim or early new developments had preceded the emergence of the new writing in Germany under the aegis of the *Aufklärung*. A pre-Enlightenment new Hebrew literature flourished within the traditional Jewish communities of northern Italy and Holland, its newness inhering in a new concept of poetic style and the absorption of humanism renaissance-style, as well as the prosody, forms, and motifs of contemporary European (mainly Italian) literatures of the Baroque and the early Neoclassical eras. This position, stated in 1928 in the first volume of Lakhover's *History of the New Hebrew Literature*,[10] was immediately challenged by Klausner (1930), who insisted on the essential "secular" and rationalist character of the new literature, which could not have informed the work of a Cabbalist and a writer of a traditional ethical manual. The new literature emerged as a result of the "falling of the walls of the ghetto" and with Jewish exposure to the Enlightenment and therefore had to be started in Germany and with Mendelssohn, Vayzel, and the members of the *Hame'asef* circle.[11] Shapira, although he totally disagreed with Klausner's understanding of the literature of the Hebrew enlightenment, concurred with him in the matter of its inception and began his history in Germany of the last decades of the eighteenth century.[12] Orinovsky, in his essentially derivative book, reverted to Lakhover's position without further arguing its validity and investing effort in offsetting Klausner's and Ch. N. Shapira's objections.

All these could look like the habitual scholarly game of contesting each other's schemes and theorems; and it certainly was that, too, but at the same time it amounted to much more than that; for such games, as much as they are often vociferously and vehemently played within the academic enclave, rarely spill over into the general intellectual and literary scenes, which in this case the Luzzatto controversy certainly did. Intellectuals and writers felt that what was at stake was the very issue of Jewish modernity, now checked against the backdrop of the actual implementation of the Zionist revolution. The question was whether this modernity was essentially messianic and informed by deep, not necessarily fully conscious undercurrents of Jewish nationalist fervor originating in the messianic idea as embedded in religion in general and in Jewish mysticism in particular, or whether it was essentially modernistic, rationalist, and informed by the ideals of European humanism. Lakhover's position, as much as it was that of a careful and well-balanced scholar, was also that of the disciple of Berditchevsky and his Nietzschean critique of Jewish history. It was his Berditchevskian legacy, as well as his serious and continuous pondering of the emotional origins of Bialik's poetry that prodded him in his search for the emotive-aesthetic drive rather than the ideational one in the development of Hebrew literature. Klausner, in spite of his political right-wing tendencies and his scholarly interest in religion (particularly early Christianity), had been and remained an avowed disciple of Achad ha'am, carrying on his preference of rationalism, belief in the supreme importance of concepts and ideas, and characteristic, late nineteenth-century anthropological view of religion as a form of human consciousness whose role in the drama of human moral progress had reached its end. Thus the scholarly polemic they started immediately ignited a non-scholarly conflagration.

Those who now took up the pro-Luzzatto banner were the modernists in their ongoing battle with the literary establishment, particularly Shlonsky, Shteynman, and the group of writers who huddled around them under the wings of their combative literary weekly *Ketuvim*. Shlonsky compared himself to Luzzatto, identifying with the eighteenth-century poet and Cabbalist as a persecuted mystic and a stylistic innovator. He projected himself as living, like Luzzatto, in "Messianic twilight," and like him, in expectation of a miraculous revelation.[13] The figure of Luzzatto was useful to Shlonsky as, in the late 1920s and early 1930s, he shifted the thematic focus of his poetry from the post-World War I apocalypse of a foundering European society and its antithesis—the exciting reality of the Zionist project of a reunion with nature and instinctual drives as it was realized by the pioneers working in the kibbutzim of the Jezrael valley—to a universalistic (Freudian) view of modern man as the victim of the widening gap between his instinctual core and the cold rationalism and crass materialism of modern society. Shteynman dedicated to the Luzzatto polemic one of the first public lectures delivered at the new literary club, *Amoda'im* (divers) that he and Shlonsky founded, his lecture also appeared as a publication of the club in a separate brochure, under the title *Time as Winnower*. The proclaimed purpose of *Amoda'im* was the search for the inner undercurrents hidden underneath the surface of social and cultural life (hence the club's name).[14] Here Shteynman attacked Klausner and his literary history on various accounts. For one thing, he rejected the scholar's positivistic view of literary history, which should have been pondered and described not as a presumably reconstructed chain of cause and effect, but rather as an intellectual landscape shaped by the formative process of time and the enduring principles it exhibited in spite of the inevitable changes time necessitated. Looked at through such a perspective, neither Vayzel nor the haskala literature as a whole were of real significance (in the 1940s Shteynman was to undergo a "conversion" in this respect and become one of the few admirers of *maskilim* such as Erter and Mapu).[15] In contradistinction, time as a winnower and selector revealed not only the undiminished greatness of Luzzatto, but also his enduring relevance, as the work of the Hebrew modernists clearly manifested. Then, Klausner had arrived at the exclusion of Luzzatto from the new Hebrew literature not only as an old-fashioned historian, but also as the representative of the current Hebraic establishment, which opposed the modernist movement and its quest for psychological and metaphysical depth. The shallow moralism and didacticism of Vayzel suited the historian's cultural positions and attitudes and thus needed to be combated not only as the passé literary products they were but also as an articulation of the regrettable attitudes of a currently active cultural front and as such, they had to be vigorously repulsed.

Interestingly, Kurzweil's diametrically opposed view, to revert back to the domain of literary scholarship, was also rooted in a doctrinal rejection of positivism as a historical methodology. The critic's ongoing battle with contemporary Hebrew literary scholarship and criticism was intellectually buttressed by his rejection, on the one hand, of "fleeting" critical impressionism, to which he often referred as "feuilletonism," and, on the other hand, of the historical positivism of the literary historians. He vowed he would never write a history of the new Hebrew literature since presumably the genre itself was untenable within the methodological context of up-to-date literary studies. Nevertheless, the history of the literature engaged him as a thinker and a polemicist, not as causally interrelated textual events but as the manifestation of underlying unifying "ideas." And the idea that unified the new Hebrew literature was that of the disappearance of the transcendental significance of Jewish individual and collective existence; hence, the centrality of the crisis of faith as the signature motif or syndrome of the literature as a whole, never mind the historical details that confirmed or did not confirm this ideational principle. Luzzatto had to be excluded because his work and personality contradicted this idea. Vayzel and the exponents of the German Jewish enlightenment had to be included, not because they appealed to the critic (far from it), but because their literary activity, he deemed, confirmed the aforementioned idea. Thus Kurzweil regarded the Luzzatto issue as directly bearing on his major thesis of Jewish modernism as the revolutionary cutting off of Judaism from its moorings.

Eventually, it was new scholarship that more or less brought the Luzzatto controversy to its end. Lakhover immersed himself during the last decade of his life (he died in 1948) in the study of the Zoharic Cabbala (as he worked together with the young scholar Y. Tishbi, one of Scholem's most innovative and prolific disciples, on the preparation of a comprehensive anthology of passages from the Zohar, arranged by topic and doctrine, so as to form a coherent and clearly structured philosophical and mystical argument; a project comparable to that of Bialik and Ravnitsky's rearrangement of the Talmudic and Midrashic aggada). Delving into the ideational depths and mythical universe of *The Book of Splendor*, he could not but realize how deeply entrenched was M. Luzzatto's entire life work in the world of mysticism according to the Zohar. The elegant verse dramas, which the *maskilim* had emulated, were nothing if not Cabbalist parables replete with mystical references and hints. The allegorical personification *mekhkar* (systematic study, science), as much as it seemed to embody eighteenth-century rationalism, also stood for mystical contemplation, the analytical detection through the screen of surface phenomena of hidden religious truths. Thus Lakhover himself, in his late scholarly publications,[16] somewhat reversed his former position, predicating the existence of a literary interim space between the old and the new in Jewish intellectual history, as well as in Hebrew literary history, with Luzzatto ensconced in the middle of that space. This reversion was reinforced by the gradual publication of Luzzatto's non-fictional works from the surviving manuscripts. Whereas the plays, and particularly *Praise to the Righteous*, were republished more than once during the Enlightenment era (a scholarly edition by Shimon Ginzburg appeared in 1927), and the ethical manual *Path of the Righteous* was being reissued constantly in numerous editions, the publication of Luzzatto's other surviving works did not begin before the 1940s—the publication in 1945 of his poems (edited by Shimon Ginzburg and B. Klar) and that of his numerous Cabbalist treatises only in the late 1950s. As the extent and the contents of Luzzatto's Cabbalist project became better known, the view of him as primarily grounded in the pre-modern mystical tradition became inescapable. Tishbi, who contributed much to a fuller understanding of Luzzatto's work and personality and thus was one of the chief promulgators of this view, also discovered a new batch of Luzzatto's poems, containing avowedly mystical messianic visions, and those taught us to better read the well-known poems and plays, in which such visions were camouflaged by neoclassical guises. Also, and concurrently, literary scholarship discovered or highlighted other historical facts that changed the view of Luzzatto's role in Hebrew literary history. Until the second half of the twentieth century, the history of Hebrew writing in general, and of Hebrew poetry in particular, in Italy of the Renaissance and the Baroque was unknown to most readers (including Bialik, who was avidly interested in it). It was pioneering publications such as Chaim Shirman's exemplary anthology, *Hebrew Poetry in Italy* (1934), and of the sixteenth-century (and first, or all but the first) Hebrew drama, *A Comedy of Marriage*, by the Jewish Mantuan actor and leader of a theatrical troupe Yehuda (Leone) Sommo (1946), as well his scholarly papers, which called attention to the existence of an extensive and a strong corpus of Hebrew-Italian renaissance literature, and of a tradition that did not peter out in the eighteenth century, when it was continued both in Italy and in Holland (by quite a few poets and playwrights, such as David Franco Mendes and the other members of his "Seekers of the Muse" circle), or merged with the Hebrew writing of the German enlightenment, but rather ran parallel to it but did not forfeit its idiosyncrasy and unique tonality even in the nineteenth century when it asserted itself in the works of prose writers such as Shmu'el Romanelli and poets such as Ephraim Luzzatto, S. D. Luzzatto, and Rachel Morpurgo. Shirman insisted that Luzzatto's plays, original and outstanding as they were, were written within the context of an ongoing Italian-Hebrew theatrical project, which consisted not only of dramatic texts but also of a theatrical performative tradition.[17] Started in the sixteenth century, this project was continued in the seventeenth century by writers such as Moshe Zakut, Yosef Penso, and the brothers Frances (Ya'akov and Immanuel), and thus was enhanced rather than initiated by Luzzatto at the beginning of the eighteenth century.[18] Other scholars displayed the richness of the Italian Hebrew lyrical poetry of the Renaissance and the Baroque, particularly of the Hebrew sonnet, publishing newly discovered texts of both known and anonymous poets. The scholarly publication of the delectable sonnets of Y. Frances (by P. Nave, in 1969) caused something of a sensation since it revealed an erstwhile marginal figure as a major exponent of the Hebrew baroque. Further publications by various scholars elevated the Italian-Hebrew poetry of the Renaissance and the Baroque to a level of one of the most important historical units in the chain of Hebrew poetry in Europe.[19] All these drove home the realization that M. Luzzatto, as one of the true masters of this tradition, was nevertheless an integral part of it, and it was this Italian-Hebraic renaissance context in which his work really made full historical sense. His legacy influenced the poetry of the Hebrew enlightenment but was not part of it. Thus the controversy about his inclusion in or exclusion from the new Hebrew literature was misguided, and, with our current knowledge of the facts, untenable. This new knowledge, of course, prescribes a new historical description and understanding of Hebrew poetry since the Middle Ages as consisting of more than one tradition, that of the Enlightenment and its continuation in the nationalist and the Israeli eras. There were, as mentioned before, also the Italian-Dutch tradition and the Andalusian one carried on by Hebrew poets in Morocco, Egypt, Turkey, and Iraq. Some of these traditions impacted each other, as all three Luzzatti influenced in various way the development of Hebrew poetry in Germany and eastern Europe; but this mutuality hardly obliterated the differences between the traditions as autonomous literary trends, each propelled by its own inherent poetics and ideational core. A truly balanced view of this multifarious scene would have perhaps hindered the late T. Carmi, who was so impressed with the richness of the Italian-Hebrew renaissance literature that in his anthology, *The Penguin Book of Hebrew Verse* (1981), where he justifiably dedicated to it a large section of his selection, he intentionally bypassed the Hebrew poetry of the haskala altogether, refraining from representing it by whatever scanty selections from the works of its masters, Y. L. Gordon and M. Y. Lebenzon, and thus "realizing" Bialik's dream of being directly connected to Luzzatto and forgetting about the Vayzel-Adam hakohen-Gordon link. Like many such realizations of wishful theoretical fantasies, this lead to a travesty, and not only because the unquestionable greatness of Gordon was denied, but also because the anthology unwittingly cut Bialik and Tchernikhovsky from their true historical context, for these poets certainly took off where Gordon and Lebenzon had left. At the same time, Carmi's paradigm predicated the existence of an imaginary century-long interregnum in the development of the new Hebrew poetry. Actually, the anthology merely represented the flipside of the monolinear understanding of the new poetry as solely the product of *Aufklärung* modernism, whereas the true lesson recent scholarship should have taught us was one of multi-linearity, of Hebrew literatures in all post-biblical times consisting of many, both intertwined and mutually unrelated, traditions and trends.

By the same token, recent scholarship in many disciplines of Jewish studies should have set us free from the secularism-religion binary opposition. The relationships between the Jewish enlightenment and the rabbinic tradition (at least as they were seen from the perspective of the Enlightenment), we know now, were, until well into the second half of the nineteenth century, seldom (if at all) formulated as an either/ or proposition. More often the followers of the Enlightenment understood them as based on the advice of Ecclesiastes (7:18): "Thou shouldest take hold of this; yea, also from this withdraw not thine hand." The borderlines were fuzzy and constantly crossed back and forth. The literature of the Enlightenment was new not because it reneged on faith but because it sought to cut to size the expanse of the rabbinical dominance by limiting it to those areas where the halakhic norm was directly applicable and leaving all the rest (such as education, emotional sublimation, aesthetic pleasure, the practicalities of economic and social life, etc.) to the guidance of the new humanists as self-appointed "watchmen unto the house of Israel." As for religious faith per se, the Hebrew enlightenment of the eighteenth and much of the nineteenth centuries regarded itself its defender. It firmly opposed and rejected what it saw as religious nihilism, atheism, and sheer moral licentiousness, to the extent that those made inroads into contemporary Jewish life, and it often pointed to these as the flipside and the inevitable result of bigotry, fanaticism, and brutal coercion (this was one of the basic ideas Mapu conveyed both through his historical novels and through his contemporary one); whereas the Enlightenment and its literature purported to foster faith through philosophical guidance and proper educational persuasion. Thus, the exclusion of Luzzatto should have nothing to do with his being "religious," but rather with the fact that he worked and thought outside of the modern "watchman unto the house of Israel" format, which was "secular" only in the sense that it was intended to complement religion and be applied to those areas of life to which religious law was not relevant. Luzzatto with or without his mystical baggage was a Hebrew European writer and humanist of the early neoclassical era, as much as Vayzel was a Hebrew European writer, a humanist and a neoclassicist, of the era in which neoclassicism was already being challenged by the advent of the stormy trends of "the age of sensibility." The fundamental difference between the two, however, did not inhere in the different sources and thrust of either their humanism or religion (both were devoutly religious), but rather in the fact that they belonged in two different literary traditions with different literary rationales and raisons d'être, namely: the Italian-Hebrew renaissance tradition, which never dreamt of predicating the replacing of rabbinical authority with that of literature, and the German-Hebrew enlightenment tradition, which was launched in 1782 with Vayzel's call for leaving only half of Jewish education ("Godly disciplines") in the hands of the rabbis and entrusting the other half ("human disciplines") in the hands of modern educators and trained professionals.[20]

Before we take final leave of the Luzzatto controversy, we should pay some further attention to Ch. N. Shapira's take on it. As mentioned before, Shapira concurred with Klausner's exclusion of Luzzatto. However, because his general line of reasoning was essentially different from that of the older scholar, his decision could be reversed, as it actually was by Halkin, who in more than one way was Shapira's continuer (perhaps the fact that both scholars developed their ideas far from the Palestinian center was significant in this connection). Shapira struck a path of his own in his understanding of Jewish modernity as it asserted itself in the new Hebrew literature. This modernity, he believed, resulted from the confluence of the impact of European humanism with intrinsic Jewish "earthly" urges, which had found expression in mystical messianism, but also contradicted it, since it pitted it against the modern "earthiness" or what Shapira dubbed "the terrestrial principle." As much as libidinal and antinomian, even anarchist, elements played their roles in Jewish messianic mysticism (Shapira, as previously noted, was a follower of Scholem), they were sublimated by it up to the very heights of "supirality" (other-worldliness). It was only when they were, at least partly, set free of their "supiral" context by humanism that they could truly form the basis of a new Jewish culture. The eighteenth-century Frankists, with their interpretation of Sabbatean messianism in terms of a search for political (even military) power and doctrine of self-liberation through orgiastic sexuality, perhaps formed a connective link with the haskala, as Scholem hypothesized in his "Virtue through Sin," as well as his other studies of Frankism.[21] Since with Luzzatto the supiral drive was paramount, he could not be considered as part of the new Hebrew literature. It is important to remember Shapira's "terrestrial-supiral" doctrine as we approach the examination of Hebrew meta-literary thinking of the

1940s and 1950s, in which Halkin, Shapira's follower, played an important role. It should also be noted here that Scholem's hypothesis, which informed the thinking of both Shapira and Halkin, was subjected, closer to our time, to a meticulous textual-historical verification by Shmu'el Verses, who carefully traced all the references to Sabbateanism and Frankism in the literature of the haskala, many of them unnoticed before, and concluded that the Hebrew enlightenment systematically and totally rejected the ideas and legacy of those mystical movements, and that there was no textual evidence that corroborated a presumed existence of a Sabbatean-Frankist-haskala connection.[22]

Whereas the concerns of most Hebrew literary theorists of the decades before and after the establishment of Israel were mostly "vertical"—pertaining to continuity in time—those of Yiddish literary scholars of the same time were both vertical and "horizontal," that is, pertaining to continuity in historical and geographical space. The Hebraists measured the past and the present, trying to negotiate some compromise between them that would vouchsafe the Jewishness of the cultural future of a politically independent Hebrew community; or, like Kurzweil, they despaired of ever finding such a compromise and therefore regarded the historical continuity of Judaism as irreparably and tragically broken. These were also the concerns of many Hebrew writers, such as Agnon, who in his magisterial *Guest for the Night* (1938) conveyed an ambivalent message consisting, on the one hand, of a full understanding of the impossibility of rebuilding the pre-modern Jewish culture of faith and scholasticism in its original format (as the protagonist of his novel, experiencing a mid-life crisis while visiting his Polish hometown, tried to do), but, on the other hand, also entertaining messianic hopes of seeing the old Polish study house being somehow transplanted to Jerusalem, where it would find its new Zionist format, thus allowing for a reconciliation between secular Zionism and the religious tradition.[23]

Yiddishists made efforts of their own to produce a Yiddish cultural continuity, the longer and more comprehensive the better. First they tried to stretch as much as was possible the history of the new Yiddish literature, push back its beginnings as far as they could. Gone was the erstwhile prevalent notion of Abramovitsh as the founding father, or, as Sholem Aleichem had put it, the "grandfather," of this literature. Even

Dik was stripped of the panoply of the "first." If Abramovitsh was to retain his position as the grandfather, then he had to be surrounded by great-grandfathers and great-grand uncles, who lived and wrote (also or only) in Yiddish fifty years earlier, in the final decades of the eighteenth century and during the first half of the nineteenth: M. Lefin, Y. Aykhel, A. H. Volfszon, Etinger, Bik, Levinson (RIVAL), Perl, Aksenfeld et al. Most of these had been primarily Hebrew writers, but the playwright and poet Etinger and the prolific novelist and playwright Aksenfeld had resorted only to Yiddish and were, indeed, the two first "one hundred percent" new Yiddish writers. The Vilnius journalist, scholar, and lexicographer Zalman Reizen put together a comprehensive anthology of this early, pre-Mendelean new Yiddish literature of the enlightenment, a textbook that ended rather than started with Abramovitsh.[24] He published (from a manuscript) Aykhel's delightful comedy *Reb Hanokh oder Vas Tut Man Damit*, written in the 1790s, and brilliantly juxtaposing languages—spoken East-Prussian German dialect, educated *Hochdeutsch,* Kantian philosophical jargon, émigrés' French, old western Yiddish, eastern European Yiddish—in an attempt to show how the presence of the eastern European Jewish religious educator (a veritable Tartuffe) wreaked havoc in the home of a respectable Jewish-German burger.[25] The linguist M. Weinreich, emerging then as the *spiritus movens* of the YIVO Institute in Vilnius, published a critical edition of the collected works of Etinger, the author of the spirited comedy *Serkele*, which had inspired Goldfaden while still in his apprenticeship as a poet and playwright. Weinreich also showed a special interest in Dik, whom he regarded as the initiator of a special Yiddish Vilnius literary tradition and as the literary personality who seemed to have bridged the gap between enlightenment and sheer traditional Jewish-"Lithuanian" rationalism, common sense, and practical ethics. This interest was fully shared by Niger, who dedicated dozens of studies (including publications of yet unpublished manuscripts) to this immensely prolific and very popular author of mild satirical short stories, as well as naive-sensational novellas, in which melodrama was couched in simple moralizing. Thus, he invested in this "forefather" of rather limited artistic merit a lifelong scholarly effort, which was to be surpassed only by the critic's huge investment in the study of Peretz's literary beginnings. Dik, as indicated before, lured Yiddishist scholars by a veiled promise of showing them the way to bridging the gap between modernity and traditionalism. This rendered him less than popular in the Soviet Union, where the Yiddishists' yearning for toppling the fence separating the modernists from the "folk" was disdainfully spurned. However, there, too, Yiddish scholars dug as deep as they could into the origins of Yiddish enlightenment literature, publishing excellent editions of Aksenfeld's surviving works (Aksenfeld was a natural raconteur and ethnographer, as well as an ardent anti-Hasidic satirist, who, as mentioned previously, wrote only in Yiddish; of his large output only four dramas and one short novel survived)[26] and of other texts of the early Yiddish enlightenment, as well as serious and edifying literary-historical studies of the period. Then Yiddish scholarship went beyond the boundaries of the enlightenment either into the domain of the Yiddish folktale and folksong or into the older Yiddish literature of the late Jewish Middle Ages and the Renaissance. Erik's pioneering studies of the old Yiddish literature in general and the old Yiddish novel and novella have already been mentioned. Almost at the same time as Erik's comprehensive history of the old literature, M. Weinreich's book *Bilder geshikhte fun der yidisher literatur* (history in vignettes of the Yiddish literature, 1928) appeared, like Reizen's anthology ending (rather than starting) with Abramovitsh, but unlike it, beginning not in the late eighteenth century but three hundred years earlier. Weinreich, intentionally, did not draw any clearly demarcated borderline between the old and the new Yiddish literatures. In his famous *History of the Yiddish Language*,[27] on which he worked throughout the better part of his scholarly career, the unbroken continuity of the Ashkenazic Jewish culture as illustrated by the development of the Yiddish language formed a leitmotif, which, like a strong undercurrent, informed the linguistic and socio-linguistic analysis.

However, it was mainly among Yiddish critics and scholars that the search for a horizontal continuity was pursued. Here reigned excitement and worries other than those which bestirred the search for a unified vertical length. Horizontal literary continuity, whether in the present or the past, was understood here not only as legitimizing Yiddish writing as an integral part of a Jewish national literature, but also as promising it a permanent and prominent presence in the Jewish cultural consciousness, rather like that of the writing in Jewish-Aramaic that had achieved such a presence through the canonical Aramaic translation of the Pentateuch, the Talmud, the midrashim, and the mystical literature based on the Zohar. Characteristically, these concerns became ever more pronounced when the glow of the national renaissances, both the Hebrew and the Yiddish ones, dimmed as World War I drew toward its bloody conclusion. It was then that the need for clear-cut affirmations of Hebrew-Yiddish continuity was most sorely felt. During the pre-war renaissance era, this need had not been that urgent. On the one hand, the presence of dozens of bilingual Hebrew-Yiddish writers, among them culture heroes such as Abramovitsh and Peretz, rendered this continuity presumably self-evident, while, on the other hand, the liberating sense of self-sufficiency informing contemporary Yiddish writing, the one that had found expression in the Czernowitz Conference, released an energy, a flamboyance, which, for a time, seemed to have totally erased that sense of inferiority that had plagued Yiddish writers of the nineteenth century in their self-estimation vis à vis the writing in Hebrew or in Russian. Now, in the wake of the war and with the future (physical, economic, and cultural) of eastern European Jewry unclear, some Yiddishist literary ideologues wished to emphasize the linkage between Yiddish and Hebrew—exactly because this linkage, formerly taken for granted, now seemed uncertain. It was in the last two years of the war that Isidor Elyashiv, known by his pen name as *Baal-makhshoves* (the thinker), published his series of articles headed by the programmatic declaration of the essential unity of Yiddish and Hebrew literatures, "Two Languages: One Literature."[28] Elyashiv—himself a bilingual Yiddish-Hebrew critic and essayist, during the first decade of the century, the heyday of the nationalist era—played the role of the chief Yiddish literary critic, a confidant of Peretz, the first to treat Sholem Aleichem's masterpieces with the respect and serious attention they deserved,[29] and a person whose word, almost like that of Peretz himself, could make or break the career of a young writer. At the same time, he published much also in Hebrew, was deeply interested in Bialik (about whom he wrote an important essay),[30] and perceptively discussed issues pertinent to the writing of the young Hebrew fiction writers of the time such as Brenner, Shofman, and Gnessin.[31] (The fact that his Hebrew work has never been collected, and thus forgotten, tells more about

the contentious Hebrew-Yiddish cultural politics of the inter-bellum period than about its merit as literary criticism. Since he had been *the* Yiddish critic, Hebraists recoiled from him.) Elyashiv was therefore a worthy
exponent of the Hebrew-Yiddish proximity during the pre-war period.
Thus the question begs itself of why did he not make his *Tsvey shprakhen:
eyn-eyntsike literatur* in real time, when it seemed self-evidently true; why
did he wait until the writers who best illustrated his hypothesis, Abramovitsh and Peretz, were dead, and he himself was definitely past his prime
and clearly not attuned to the new sensibilities of young Yiddish writers,
which pointed in a direction very different from that followed before the
war? The answer to this question cannot be but: exactly because! Exactly
because the hypothesis was no more self-evidently true, and because the
critic, to reassert his role as a major shaper of opinions, had to cling to an
idealized and largely imagined past when Peretz and Bialik had seemed
to function as the leaders of one integral culture (which they never really
did). With the civil wars in Russia and Galicia devastating Jewish life in
eastern Europe and the Balfour declaration of 1917 turning many eyes
in the direction of Zionism, Palestine, and a nascent Hebrew-speaking
community in this outpost of Jewish hopes, which might become in the
near future a flourishing Jewish center, doubts and dark premonitions
had to be repressed by overconfident declarations.

Similarly, Niger, the Yiddish critic who more or less inherited the
role that had been that of Elyashiv, and during the inter-bellum period
functioned as the Yiddish shaper of consensual literary judgment and
evaluation outside of the Soviet Union, came up with his declaration,
in a little book called *Di tsveyshprakhikeyt fun undezer literatur* (the bilingualism of our literature),[32] in 1941, when the future of Yiddish and
its literature looked murkier than ever. Once again one may ask, why
did the popular critic wait so long with his essay, which he published
two years into World War II, with eastern European, Yiddish-speaking
Jewry already fed into the killing machine that would soon decimate it
and Yiddish speaking and reading in North America in a quick decline?
The answer is clearly that the declaration was a direct response on the
part of Niger as a prominent Yiddishist culture activist to a situation
that seemed to threaten Yiddish creativity and rob it of its future perspectives. Now he was ready to join forces with the American Hebraists,

themselves a threatened culture reserve, but nevertheless a possible link with the burgeoning Hebrew-speaking community of Palestine. (Niger was then one of the initiators of the project *Akhisefer*, the purpose of which was to enhance the acquaintance of Hebrew and Yiddish readers with the literatures of each other, make them aware of the issues confronting Hebrew and Yiddish linguists, and encourage translations from Yiddish poetry to Hebrew and vice versa as means of bringing the two literatures closer to each other and each of them closer to the readers of the other. The project, having engendered some publications,[33] failed to take off.)

Whereas Elyashiv had based his declaration on the recent past—the pre-war bilingualism of many Yiddish and even more Hebrew writers, Niger, understandably could not rely on the evocation of this past, which in the early 1940s was already distant, albeit not forgotten. Instead he offered a wide historical panorama against which the drama of Jewish bilingualism—not multilingualism—had been played throughout the millennia. Already in the era of the second commonwealth, Hebrew functioned as the holy tongue of the Bible, the ritual, and the codification of the halakha. Along with it existed the spoken language, Aramaic, which was a Jewish language, unlike the Greek to which the contemporary assimilationists (then called Hellenizers) resorted. In it, both the halakha and the aggada of the Talmud and the midrashim were created. Since then the dualism of a holy tongue and a spoken language, in which a sizeable portion of the national literature was created, became normative and highly functional. The diglossic nature of Jewish culture both preserved its core and allowed it to branch out and further develop. Whereas the holding on to the holy tongue vouchsafed the live contact with the sacrosanct sources and also allowed for the development of a contemporary high literary culture (like that of Spanish Hebrew poetry), the constant resort to Jewish languages other than Hebrew preserved the ties connecting the culture with the people, as well as with non-Jewish cultures (as was the case in the Arabic-speaking countries) at one and the same time. In modern times, the diglossia Hebrew-Yiddish was responsible for the immense vitality of Ashkenazic Jewish civilization both before and after the advent of the Enlightenment. Diglossia, was, therefore, the norm, not the exception, in Jewish cultural history. Those who wished to see it disappear, like the fanatic Hebraists in Palestine and the enemies of Hebrew in the Soviet Union, were undermining the very basis of Jewish culture. In their misguided pursuance of a monolinguistic "normalcy," they were actually reneging on what was normal in the Jewish sense of the term, for bilingualism was the quintessential characteristic of Jewish cultural existence.

Sadan, an ardent Zionist and the most subtle and erudite of Hebrew literary critics of the 1930s and the 1940s, summed up his horizontal theory of *sifrut yisra'el* (the literature of the Jewish people) right after World War II, the Holocaust, and the War of Israeli Independence. His seminal essay *Al sifrutenu* (about our literature) was published a short time after the victorious conclusion of the latter.[34] Again, this date of publication is highly significant. Although the ideas and concepts that the essay spelled out had been circulating in Sadan's theoretical thinking for quite some time, the fact that their crystallization occurred in the second half of the 1940s speaks for itself. It should be seen within the wider context of cultural life of the Palestinian-Zionist contingent during and immediately after World War II.

In spite of the very real danger of Palestine being stormed and conquered in 1942 by the German North African Corps (a disaster that was avoided in the nick of time due to the British victory at the battle of El Alamein and that would have otherwise led to the liquidation of the entire Jewish population of Palestine and the demise of the Zionist project), the Jewish *yishuv* (the Palestinian-Jewish population in general and its Zionist-modernist segment in particular), serving as the base of a large multinational British army and as a supplier of various services, enjoyed throughout the war economic prosperity, as well as physical security. The latter rested on a firm British decision, taken in the years that had immediately preceded the outbreak of the war, to crush the so-called Arab Rebellion of 1936–1939, which in the face of an impending war had been deemed insufferable. Thus for five full years, no anti-Jewish riots, or indeed, unrest of any kind, were allowed (the situation was different in other Middle Eastern countries, where pro-Nazi elements tried to seize power), and in the heart of the international maelstrom, Palestine remained singularly quiet. Of course, everybody knew that this strange moment of equilibrium was brittle and bound to disintegrate as soon as the war was over, and both Jewish and Arab underground militias prepared themselves for an impending showdown. However, for the time being, stability reigned. In the history of the Jewish *yishuv,* these were the years in which the first generation of Palestinian-born youngsters, the Hebrew-speaking children of the pioneers and immigrants of the 1920s and the products of the Zionist educational system that had been created in Palestine already at the beginning of the twentieth century, came of age and started to take its place in all walks of life. It supplied the various paramilitary underground groups—the all but official *Hagana* (defense) organization, as well as the "secessionist" right wing *Irgun* and *Lekhi* (the "Stern Gang," as the British dubbed it)—with its soldiers and young commanders. It joined the British Army in large numbers to fight Hitler and his allies, and toward the end of the war was allowed to form a separate Jewish brigade within that army that laid the foundation for the semi-professional Jewish army about to fight and win the War of Independence. It produced an array of young intellectuals, writers, artists, theater people, and budding scientists who would form the Israeli intellectual and artistic elite in the 1950s and 1960s. All these developments infused the Jews of Palestine with a sense of energy, self reliance, and perhaps an exaggerated notion of their collective strength. They certainly endowed them with a sense of purpose and idealism, as well as with a robust Hebraic cultural self-confidence.

The war cut off Palestine's connections with the outside world and particularly with Europe, which was where most Palestinian Jews came from and where the large reservoir of the Jewish people as a whole and of the Zionist movement in particular was still located. The news about the fate of this large reservoir and of how these millions of Jews first were being summarily machine-gunned by special military formations and then systematically worked to death in work camps and industrially gassed and burnt to cinder in death camps reached Jewish Palestine slowly and at the beginning were received with some incredulity. The full awareness of Hitler's declared intention to use a war situation to completely annihilate European Jewry being actually carried out did not dawn before 1943, which, of course, caused an unprecedented turmoil and outrage. The reaction to the ongoing Holocaust was, however, complex and multifaceted. On the one hand, most Ashkenazic Jews in

Palestine, as well as part of the Sephardic population (for instance, Jews who had emigrated to Palestine from Greek and other Balkan countries) had relatives—often parents and siblings—who were now being murdered, and a deep sense of having deserted dear and loved ones, with the concomitant inevitable guilt feelings of the survivor swept Jewish Palestine into a state of mourning and terrible frustration. On the other hand, the Holocaust presented Zionism with a conundrum that at the time it was not able to deal with. It "vindicated" its catastrophic prognoses (for whatever reason, the fact that the fate of Zionist Palestine could have been identical with that of the Jews of Warsaw and Vilnius, were it not for the excellence of the British intelligence and the dedication and sacrifice of General Montgomery's army, was somehow swept under the rug). Had it not warned—since the days of Herzl and Nordau—European Jews of lethal anti-Semitism? And then how was its ethos of activism and self-defense to be squared with the facts that millions of Jews were, presumably being led "like sheep to the slaughter?" The sporadic and very small-scale military actions of resistance on the part of Jewish partisans and ghetto fighters (particularly the famous rebellion of the Warsaw Ghetto in 1944) were, of course, avidly latched onto, blown out of proportion vis à vis the unspeakably immense dimensions of the genocide, and the official propaganda yoked together the concepts of *shoa* (holocaust) and *gevura* (heroism), as if the annihilation of six million people could be mentally counterbalanced by the admirable but ineffectual actions of a few thousand. Palestinian Jews were not yet fully registering the trauma, which would eventually become one of the most important psychic factors in Israeli mental life and collective behavior. Not before the Eichmann trial of 1961 would the real internalization of the devastating impact of the Holocaust start.

In the meantime, of course, that impact, as partly internalized and registered as it was, influenced cultural life, was articulated in the literature of the 1940s (as in Greenberg's extensive cycle of laments and prophecies that was collected in 1951 in the poet's best known and most widely read book, *Streets of the River*), and also in the meta-literary thinking of those hectic years. Here, too, the responses elicited by the ambivalent situation—the coming of age and purported robustness of the Zionist contingent in Palestine versus the destruction of European

Jewry—were mixed. On the one hand, the war years with the relative solitude of the *yishuv*, being cut off from the wider Jewish context, gave rise to a Hebraic-Palestinian illusion of identity, that could be, overtly or covertly, either "anti-" or at least "non-Jewish." This imagined identity fed on the accentuated Hebraism and anti-exilic sentiments that had been floating in the air since the 1920s, but it was during the first half of the 1940s, with the seclusion prescribed by the war and the florescence of the first generation of Palestinian-born intellectuals, that it reached its short-lived heyday. It found its radical articulation in the ideology and cultural propaganda of the Young Hebrews (Rattosh's Canaanites), which for a while appealed to youngsters who were eager to see themselves as the first sons of a free and courageous non-Judaic Hebrew nation, and even organized themselves as an anti-British underground movement until they realized that their leaders, while playing the games of conspiration and adopting the slogans of anti-colonialism, left the real anti-British activity to the Jewishly committed *Irgun* and the Stern Gang. The fact that European Jews were being slaughtered without organized resistance seemed to them (unaware as they were of the real conditions under which Jews in Nazified Europe lived, acted, and perished) to demarcate a clear line of difference between themselves and "those Jews," and their leader, Rattosh, shamelessly and unforgivably, called upon them not to be "impressed" even with "the rabbit's heroism" of the Warsaw ghetto fighters.[35] The literary ideology based upon this inverted fascism called for a final self-distancing on the part of a new and authentic Hebrew literature, expressive of the consciousness and concerns of a new Hebrew nation, from its Jewish origins, even when those were Hebraic and particularly when they were informed by Zionist hopes. Writers such as Bialik, Agnon, Greenberg, and Alterman, no matter how artistically meritorious their work was, were Jewish writers who used the Hebrew language, but could not relate to the experience of the young Hebrews, and when they attempted to do that, even to merely portray the Palestinian landscape, they inevitably projected their alienation and the fact that they viewed reality through the eyes of the immigrant.[36] What was necessary was the strengthening of the consciousness of national and mental alterity among the young intellectuals and writers, such as the highly talented, sabra (Palestinian-born) fiction writer Yizhar Smilansky (pen name: S. Yizhar), whose unrivalled intimacy with the Palestinian ambience was still somewhat marred or clouded by vestiges of Zionist ideals.[37]

The overwhelming majority of the young Palestinian intelligentsia, however, did not buy into this. Some of its best representatives, such as the young poet Chaim Gouri, as tempted by the Canaanite vision as they were,[38] firmly rejected it. Having met Holocaust survivors as soldiers of the Jewish brigade or as emissaries of the *Hagana*, these sabras were overwhelmed by this encounter to the point of becoming for life the custodians, among the Israeli intelligentsia, of the "Jewish connection" and of the Holocaust memory.[39] Nevertheless, as a sentiment more than an ideology, Rattosh's Canaanism temporarily spoke to some barely articulated anti-Jewish mood or feeling, which was prevalent enough among those who had grown up in inter-bellum Palestine and educated in the spirit of radical Hebraism. It was this shadow of anti-Jewishness, the proportions and significance of which were perhaps blown out of proportion, which explained much of what had taken place in Hebrew meta-literary thinking of the 1940s and the early 1950s: Avraham Kariv's call for a literary revision, "repentance," and self-castigation; Kurzweil's vehement sounding of the burial knell over the presumed corpse of the authentic Jewish civilization; and, above all else, Sadan's complex and dialectical vision of a Jewish literary and cultural "recapitulation."

Kariv, known by his original name Krivorutshka as a Hebrew poet in the Soviet Union, managed to reach Palestine in 1934 and settled there as an editor, translator, and primarily a critic and a reviewer for the literary supplement of *Davar* (edited by Sadan). Aesthetically on the conservative side, he nevertheless wrote perceptively and elegantly even on the achievements of contemporary Hebrew modernism. His review of Alterman's epoch-making *Stars Outside* (1938), albeit on the whole unfavorable, offered insights that Alterman's fans should have followed and made use of.[40] As the terrible news from Europe arrived, he started to reexamine some of the chief classics of the Hebrew re-naissance and found them tarnished by Jewish self-hatred and self-alienation. His vantage point was an analysis of Abramovitsh's "world," which, he declared, was informed by the debasement of the traditional Jew and of traditional Jewish society, and also deficient, in the mimetic and artistic senses, in its representation of whatever was meaningful in Jewish traditional social and spiritual life.[41] This was not altogether new (Kariv's main findings had already been pointed to by S. Zemach[42] and Y. Lubetsky),[43] but it was very much part of the post-Holocaust *Zeitgeist*. In America Glatshteyn arrived at similar conclusions in his analysis of Abramovitsh's *Fishke the Lame* (1946).[44] However, unlike Glatshteyn, Kariv did not stop at cutting to size the stature of Abramovitsh's, in essence, maskilic, well-honed satires, which as a matter of course, offered negative archetypes rather than the comprehensive anthropological vista of eastern European Jewish life, as the conventional wisdom (of Frishman and many others) had suggested. He believed now that the Hebrew literature of both the Enlightenment and the nationalist eras suffered from a veritable infection of epidemic proportions of Jewish *Selbsthass* and undertook to expose the contamination wherever it could be found. Thus he proceeded from one writer to another—always important and influential ones—and checked the measure of their loyalty, or rather disloyalty, to the Jewish people: Abramovitsh was followed by Frishman, then by Brenner, then by Tchernikhovsky.[45] Kariv's criticism was flawed because it was informed by an unhistorical idealization of an imagined Jewish past, a characteristic modern Jewish version of the romantic fantasy about the existence of a harmonious and intimate *Gemeinschaft* (community) of origin,[46] which the modernists had not only neglected but also vilified. It was also flawed because the critic never really tried to understand the inherent significance of each writer's world and then explain why, within this world, the anti-Jewish element or rather Jewish self-criticism, was necessary. His approach was rather that of the prosecutor who gathers every snippet of incriminating evidence and intentionally suppresses its context. As much as his outrage and exasperation were sincere and poignant, they lacked intellectual probity. Kariv never truly asked himself why the literature he examined exhibited the negativity he regretted and how this negativity emanated from a sense of impending crisis. Nor did he posit to himself the simple question whether revolutionary movements such as the Jewish enlightenment and Zionism, whose goal was to bring about fundamental changes in the national way of life, could avoid such negativity. Did the Enlightenment and Zionism amount to historical "mistakes," as contemporary Jewish Orthodoxy maintained? Kariv lacked the courage of his convictions and would never allow himself to arrive at such a conclusion. Was the modern Hebrew project misguided from its inception? For the "traditional Jew," whose spokesman Kariv presumed to be, had no use for it; it never became part of his value system, and the fact that a Zionist critic with the flowery Hebrew of a Lithuanian *maskil* was now advocating for him was not devoid of unintentional irony. Kariv was altogether unequipped, intellectually or emotionally, to tackle such questions and become aware of the subtle inconsistencies that undermined his own position.

Kurzweil, who had studied *Germanistik* and written a dissertation on the second part of Goethe's *Faust*, but was also, as a scion of a rabbinical family, a student at the yeshiva of Rabbi Sh. Breuer, the leader of the Frankfurt neo-orthodoxy that had been founded in the nineteenth century by Shimshon Raphael Hirsch, arrived in Palestine in 1939. Unfamiliar at this point with modern Hebrew literature, he discovered Agnon, particularly the master's most recent work, such as the novel *A Guest for the Night* and the puzzling, dream-like stories of *Sefer hama'asim* (wrongly translated as *The Book of Deeds*, whereas the true meaning, in this context, of the word *ma'ase*, is simply a story). He read these complex and multifaceted texts through the eyes of a shrewd and perceptive neophyte, who was also trained in textual analysis and thus, succeeded in defamiliarizing them and pointing to their unperceived or insufficiently perceived aspects. That was how he started (in 1942) his career as an important critic, and in many ways, this would be his truly great contribution to Hebrew criticism.[47] Kurzweil attached himself to Agnon with a deep sense of identification with the master because he found in his tales and novels what he believed to be the artistic presentation of the intellectual conflicts that had afflicted his own tormented soul. This lent his interpretations the particular acuity that is arrived at when a sharp intellect is driven by a strong emotional tide; however, at the same time, this inevitably limited the scope of the interpretations, rendering them partial and biased. Agnon, in the eyes of Kurzweil, was the foremost articulator of the malaise of the modern Jewish intellectual who, when still a child or a teenager, had dwelt in the paradise of the totally harmonious and coherent civilization of the religious-rabbinical Jewish tradition, but then, like Adam in the story in Genesis, ate the forbidden fruit of knowledge, and was chased forever out of the charmed garden and into the desolation of modern alienation and existential dread. In fact, this narrative was one of the many Jewish narratives Agnon's works told, and therefore, Kurzweil's reading of it as it featured in the novelist's works was often cogent and sometimes eye-opening. However, the critic's monism undermined him; for the master consistently told other narratives, as well as anti-narratives (the protagonists' experiences, growing up within the traditional Jewish matrix were negative and stunting, and their breaking away from it—liberating), which the critic failed to see and appreciate. Thus, Kurzweil never really understood the lethal irony with which Agnon portrayed traditional Jewish society in allegedly sweet and laudatory "idylls," or his indirect manner of pointing at the yawning gap between the reality of this society's mores and manners and its purported ideal of seeing the world through the lens of the sacrosanct texts and acting in it as if this view of it was the only one possible. Where this irony informed the entire fabric of a comprehensive presentation of the "ideal" civilization, as for instance, in the parodist and incredibly complex and ambivalent pastiche-novel *The Bridal Canopy*, the critic's interpretation was blatantly wrong and imperceptive. Kurzweil also never understood Agnon's ardent Zionism, which informed his career from his aliya as a mere nineteen-year-old (1907) to his becoming, sixty years later, the first signatory of the proclamation of "Greater Israel," which demanded the retaining in Jewish hands of the vast areas occupied by the Israel Defense Forces (IDF) in the Six-Day War of 1967. For Agnon regarded exilic Judaism, even in the golden age preceding the Enlightenment, as totally dependent for the maintenance of its vitality not only on the halakhic norm, which had supervised and organized its daily existence, but also, and as importantly, on the messianic principle, which had charted its future perspectives. As soon as the faith in the tenability of this principle dried up, losing its emotional fervor, Judaism waxed moribund; and that had happened long before the loss of its "paradisiacal" innocence. In modern times, Zionism was the only form of a tenable Jewish messianism, and therefore, even the most learned and saintly rabbi, if an anti-Zionist (as most rabbis of the era were), was nothing but the precursor of the demise of Judaism (as the figure of the rabbi in Agnon's *A Guest for the Night* was presented). True, Zionism itself was "schizophrenic" and tragic, and, in the natural order of things, was also bound to fail, because it had been torn off of the roots of halakhic Judaism. Only if the two could be conflated and synthesized could Judaism be saved. Kurzweil consistently saw only one side of this equation. Nevertheless, as long as he limited his comments to writers who in one way or another shared in his narrative (such as, besides Agnon, Bialik, Feierberg, Greenberg, and to some extent, even Tchernikhovsky), he was walking on firm ground. The ground became by far less solid, and, indeed, often quite treacherous, as soon as he started superimposing this narrative on the new literature as a whole, and on Israeli literature in particular.

The new Hebrew literature, presumably from its very inception in the last decades of the eighteenth century, was, according to the critic, not just secularist (in the sense that it demanded from Judaism more attention to and consideration for the earthly needs and concerns of the Jewish individual and collective) but also inherently and dramatically atheistic, even when the writers themselves were naively unaware of their apostasy. The main story it told, and in which it reached its highest moments of self realization and artistic achievement, was the story of the crisis of faith, the loss of the primal sense of being viewed, followed, cared for, and judged by a transcendental being. Whatever lay beyond this crisis was just a desert of loss, disjunction, and inevitable shallowness. The modern Jewish writer, when he (and, rarely, also she) was sufficiently self-aware, knew he dwelt either in a spiritual vacuum or in a world infested by demons. At the same time, he knew there was no authentic "return" to the lost paradise, and every attempt at "regaining" it was illusory and bound to lead to an even deeper darkness of the soul. As for other upbeat illusionists—Zionists, socialists, even the individual groping for a self-realization through the illusion of erotic love—theirs were so many bubbles, which only the naive or devious would play with. All these illusions were bound to end in catastrophes—national, individual, political, military—Zionism from its inception was betrothed to death—and universal (at the time of the American odyssey to the moon, the critic demanded, in shrieking newspaper articles, the immediate deflection of the mission and the return of the astronauts to earth *before* they set foot on the other heavenly body). Tragic self-awareness could at least result in significant art. Thus, all the great Hebrew writers focused on the desolation resulting from the loss of religious faith—the critic forcefully and gracelessly superimposed this erroneous notion on the writing of writers, such as Gnessin,[48] in whose work the issue of faith and its loss had been secondary or marginal, a remembered but not re-experienced adolescent upheaval, which had been replaced with other social, intellectual, and emotional issues. These writers' sense of being, albeit often pessimistic or even tragic, stemmed from altogether different experiences and concerns, which the critic overlooked or discounted. Hence the narrowness of his interpretation of the works of writers such as Brenner, who grappled with the paradox of inevitability of suffering (as a quintessential dimension of the human condition) and the appropriate response to it, which at one and the same time subsisted of an acceptance of and of resistance to it through humanist activism.[49] And as for writers whose thematic circumference had no room in it for the crisis of faith or an equivalent crisis of disintegration due to loss of orientation and connection with origins—and such were the majority of the younger Israeli writers—Kurzweil relegated them to a place that was worse than a mere wasteland. Being in a vacuum, as painful as it was, could be a valuable experience, as long as vacuity was authentically acknowledged. However, being in a vacuum without authentically experiencing it could result only in intellectual flatness, emotional speciousness, and intellectual "levantinism." Kurzweil thus became the "scrooge" of Israeli writers, whom he damned systematically and almost automatically. He allowed for exceptions, but these, in most cases (but not in that of the poetess Daliah Ravikovitsh, whom he encouraged), were surprisingly off the mark, exposing the critic's rather pathetic lack of acumen, taste, and basic orientation in everything that belonged within the Israeli ambience. All in all, it was clear, that his "search for an Israeli literature"[50] was conducted in an imagined rather than a real literary territory, led nowhere, and was in essence inconsistent with the critic's basic assumptions, since according to these, there was no possibility for the existence of a worthwhile Israeli literature, as, indeed, for a culturally tenable "Israeliness."

In spite of all this, Kurzweil was an important and influential critic. Whereas his importance was based primarily on the brilliance and novelty of his interpretations of Agnon, consensually the major contemporary Hebrew master of prose fiction, it also was buttressed by his very serious, although deeply flawed, attempt to understand the new Hebrew literature as a whole and find a general criterion by which it could be judged. This elevated him to the status of a cultural critic of the kind known to English readers by models such as Matthew Arnold and T. S. Eliot, although he definitely lacked the generous mental equilibrium of the former and the superb literary taste and intuition of the latter. He managed, with insufficient knowledge of the facts (his acquaintance with Hebrew literature of both the Enlightenment and of the national renaissance was spotty at best) and with problematic conceptual tools, to do for the readers of his time what is now sometimes referred to as "problematizing" the literary corpus. His utter seriousness, as well as his unflagging vehemence had something attractive, even mesmerizing, about them, for they emanated from a genuine sense of crisis and fear of cultural degeneration. His view of the pre-Israeli and Israeli young intelligentsia was informed by suspicion and pedagogic mistrust, and there was quite enough in the cultural makeup of this intelligentsia to justify his worries. Unfortunately, his syntagmatic narrative of faith and its loss rendered him unable to differentiate between what was and what was not truly weak and justifiably blameworthy. In his historical overview, he was, in spite of his scathing sarcasm and seething acerbity, essentially a sentimentalist. His Judaism was supra-historical and totally projective. The Judaism he idealized was by far too harmonious, neat and orderly, and actually had never existed; for it was merely the Judaism of neo-orthodox propaganda. When the shallowness of that propaganda was exposed by those who like Scholem studied the antinomian and even nihilistic aspects of traditional Judaism, Kurzweil attacked them, vilified them as "Jewish demons," regarded them as the very personifications of the modern Jewish desolation. More pathetic than damaging, these attacks expressed sincere fears of a harassed intellectual; for Kurzweil felt threatened by his presumed victims not only as a scholar, but also, and perhaps mainly, as a person and a Jew, whose only area of inner tranquility—the imaginary area of the never-never land of a harmonious traditionalism and Jewish communality—was about to be shattered by the facts he did not wish to acknowledge.

Kurzweil's view of history was extremely linear and one-dimensional. To him historical reality could not be many things taking place at the same time, and historical development could not proceed both back and forth along many, sometimes parallel and sometimes intersecting roads. If historical reality was bewilderingly multifarious, he believed the duty of the intellectual was to simplify it and point to its "essence," which justified a highly selective and even more so exclusionary treatment of the facts. He therefore could not offer a convincing historical understanding of either the Jewish enlightenment or of its modern sequel. His view of the Hebrew literature of the Enlightenment had to be rejected even by his most loyal disciples. It simply did not dovetail with any reasonable reading of the texts, most of which he never mentioned. Whoever knows these texts cannot but see how he wanted to superimpose upon a full century of various literary developments some insights, which were borne out to an extent by some texts created immediately after it in the last decades of the nineteenth century, as the Enlightenment was being replaced by nationalism. The insights, which were partially cogent as far as the so-called transition generation of the 1880s and 1890s (late Lilienblum, Feierberg, young Bialik, a segment of Berditchevsky's work) was concerned—and not that there were not, even at that time, important writers who were not at all transitional in the accepted sense, and whose works called for altogether different and even contradictory insights—seemed to him relevant to *maskilim*, who had not anticipated the concerns of those who came after them.

The most basic mistake he made, however, inhered not in his misrepresentation of the Enlightenment, which was quite self-evident, and therefore of little consequence, but in his understanding of modern Jewish secularism in general and in that of modern Hebrew literature and Zionist culture in particular, and this mistake, not as self-evident, and therefore still lingering, was by far more fundamental. Kurzweil never realized that on a certain level, both Zionism and its literature never truly and fully cut itself off from Jewish religious transcendentalism. There were some exponents of Zionism, such as Herzl, Jabotinsky, and in an altogether different manner also Brenner, whose thinking was completely or almost completely detached from this transcendentalism. Others, however, such as A. D. Gordon and even staunch atheists such as Achad ha'am, were not as detached; and Zionism as a whole, the visionariness of D. Ben Gurion included, and the new Hebrew literature as a whole, went along with the transcendentalists, which made it so much easier for them to endow whatever ideal occupied the uppermost position in their thinking with a glowing halo of pseudo-religion: hence the many Zionist pseudo-religions, starting with Achad ha'am's concept of "national morality" (the legacy of the biblical prophets, which, presumably, had become the very essence of the Jewish "character," but was not that of a national dialogue with God, but rather a strict and consuming quest for justice) and with A. D. Gordon's "Religion of Labor" (it should, however, be remembered, that it was not Gordon himself who coined this popular and questionable appellation) and ending with Ben Gurion's ascribing to the Jewish state as such, a religious value and thus establishing an etatist religion of sorts. Ironically, it was Agnon, more than anybody else, who rejected this kind of covert religionism, claiming that A. D. Gordon's "Religion of Labor," that manual and particularly, agricultural labor, that many Zionists raised to the level of a cult, represented neither genuine religion nor honest-to-God labor, for labor was nothing less but also nothing more than what every honest person had to engage in so as not to become a burden to others, and the term *avoda* (labor) should have been left with its original meaning, which was that of the ritual at the Jerusalemite temple and consequently, prayer and study.[51] When it came to the Gordons, the protagonist of *A Guest for the Night* said to a group of A. D. Gordon's followers that he rejected the prophet of "the religion of labor" and rather stuck by *his* Gordon, who was none other than "our poet Y. L. Gordon,"[52] the great enemy of the Jewish rabbinical establishment, who could not approve of Zionism, because he suspected that an independent Jewish state would eventually be run by the Rabbinate.[53]

Whereas to Kurzweil secularism meant loss, reduction, and retraction, a concept fit to be discussed in terms of naught, or at least of paucity and shrinkage; in reality, Hebrew and Zionist secularism should be discussed in terms of ambivalence, ambiguity, and self-inflation or overextendedness. Secularizing Jewish culture, Hebraists and most Zionists were almost always moving along two parallel lines running in opposite directions. Every movement in the direction of reducing or nullifying the numinous charge inhering in a certain cultural value, of rendering this value, so to speak, less theologically "electric," was followed by a countermovement in the direction of recharging or re-electrifying the same or an adjacent object. The best illustration of this was the attitude of the new literature toward the Hebrew language. Hebrew, the writers of the nineteenth century bitterly complained, was reduced to skeletal holiness. It was buried in the synagogue and had to be "secularized," or as the *maskilim* liked to describe it, be taken by hand (by the new writer), led out of the synagogue, and be seen "on the high places of the city," where everybody, including non-Jews, would acknowledge its renewed vigor, its ability to be used as a language in which novels, love poems, textbooks of zoology, geography, and astrophysics, but also articles about hygiene and proper house maintenance, the realities of marriage and child bearing, the question whether corporal punishment should remain the prerogative of educators and whether the dead should be buried on the first or third days after their presumed demise (the issue of *Scheintod* was very "hot" in the early days of the Hebrew enlightenment) could be written. In short, Hebrew should become a living language (not to be confused with a spoken one), walking "in the lands of the living," mobile, protean, adaptable to almost any kind of communicational need. That was one aspect of the attitude toward the language. However, the same writers who thus emphasized the need for the secularization of the language also emphasized, with equal zeal, or actually with surpassing eloquence and by far more emotional emphasis, the need to sanctify the language and elevate it to a position that was perhaps less than divine but certainly more than angelic. It was not only the language of the Torah, "the only vestige" of ancient Jewish independence, as valuable as the temple and the land of Israel, but somehow also the guarantee for the continuity of Jewish national unity, and, of course, iridescent in its aesthetic perfection, of all languages the most beautiful and sublime. In the writings of nineteenth-century Hebraists, we often find the Hebrew language playing the role of a quasi-Masonic deity, whose acolytes gather secretly in the night to celebrate its resplendence.[54] Enormous importance was ascribed to "proper" Hebrew grammar (i.e., classical grammar, that of biblical Hebrew), as if abiding by it vouchsafed ritualistic "cleanliness," and reneging on it amounted to life in sin. The *maskilim* dwelt lovingly on each component of the grammar and never tired of warning their followers not ever to stop learning the latter's rather complex rules, even if they thought they have already mastered them. Studying Hebrew grammar was to them a virtuous and blessed activity in and of itself, independent of usage and application, even as the indefinite study of the Talmud was the highest ideal of traditional Jewish education, and they particularly fancied the difficult passages in the Bible, some of them rendered all but undecipherable by strange *hapax legomena* or sheer copiers' errors, which they kept tinkering with as if these were precious vessels of an immemorial ritual. In short, they could be said to have developed a grammatological theology of sorts. Abramovitsh, a sworn demystifier, ironically described in an early novel how his young protagonist, strolling in the woods on a fine summer day found there a group of young *maskilim* who were so absorbed in a heated discussion about the right meaning of an impossibly vitiated and unexplainable verse in the book of Ezekiel's prophecy, that they hardly paid attention to the verdure around them, or, indeed, remembered they were "in the lap of bountiful nature," rather than in a dark and airless house of study.[55] In fact, most of the *maskilim*, in their ecstatic adoration of Hebrew, could have joined Cabbalists (who ascribed to Hebrew, the words, and the sheer alphabet in its various possible combinations and permutations, supernatural powers, such as the power of creating something from nothing) and those medieval philosophers, like Yehuda Halevi, who believed Hebrew had existed before the creation of the world and was the language God used for parleying with the angels, as well as with Adam and Eve. At the same time, they ascribed to the language a national-political value and talked about it in military terms (well-chosen words were like carefully selected arrows that the warrior-poet would use in order to hit his target and pierce it). However, very few, if any, of them would have agreed with Eliezer Ben Yehuda, the so-called reviver of Hebrew, when in 1880 he opined, in an open letter to Smolenskin, that the language could be valuable to the non-scholar only when its study went together with the faith in and the work for the re-emergence of Jewish political independence in Eretz yisra'el and become there the spoken vernacular of a free people. "Had I not believed in the redemption of the Jewish people, I would have jettisoned the language as one discards an object of no value," he wrote.[56]

Most of his Zionist contemporaries recoiled from such a "cavalier" attitude even as most medieval thinkers had recoiled from Maimonides's dictum (in *Guide to the Perplexed*, third part, eighth chapter) stating that Hebrew was a "holy tongue" only and to the extent that it was used for imparting holy precepts, and that essentially there was no value-difference between Hebrew, Arabic, and other languages, since value depended on contents alone. Nor would most nationalist writers buy into Ben Yehuda's functionalist view of Hebrew and of the validity of its continued and enhanced usage as subservient to and dependent on the realization of the goals of political Zionism. Achad ha'am and the entire Odessa circle of Zionists and Hebraists vehemently rejected this view. In fact, they despised Ben Yehuda and derisively spurned his project of inventing (in their parlance, "fabricating") a new, flat, precise, and unencumbered Hebrew, unsentimentally made to cater to the needs of modern urbane communication. No, they said. Hebrew must richly resonate. It had to be suffused with associations of the sacrosanct sources, to re-orchestrate and synthesize in a new manner all its historical layers, elicit echoes from its hidden depths. The real guide to modern Hebrew should be not Ben Yehuda but Abramovitsh with his synthesis of biblical, Mishnaic, and Talmudic-Midrashic vocabularies. This led Hebrew writers throughout the first half of the twentieth century to conduct what Hazaz—himself one of the chief culprits—referred to as a dangerous "love affair" with the language,[57] which, in turn, rendered much of Hebrew writing of the period essentially untranslatable, since once the rich reverberation of the language was lost, nothing much, it seemed, remained. In the early fifties when Amichai defined himself as somebody who used only a small fraction of the words contained in the dictionary,[58] he stated one of the most significant and revolutionary principles that he thought should differentiate Israeli literature from the nationalist Hebrew one that had preceded it. But although Amichai had and still has many disciples in this respect, his advice was hardly followed by all and sundry. One has only to compare a novel by Amos Oz in its Hebrew original with its excellent translation by Nicholas de Lange, to see what inestimable service the translator tendered by wiping out a good deal of the writer's linguistic self-indulgence and narcissistic Hebraism, presenting the world with an Amos Oz who is by far more mature, restrained, and precise than the Hebrew writer actually was.

By and large, literary Hebrew, as secularized and as subjected to severe lexicological diets as it had been, has not altogether freed itself from self-adulation; an adulation, which sometimes found wonderful and at the same time quite horrific articulations as in the mammoth ode "Your Letters Are Carved" by the Hebrew American poet Regelson, published in 1948, the year in which Israeli independence was proclaimed. Here, in this sublime and monstrous poem about Hebrew as a supreme metaphysical entity, each segment of Hebrew grammar was expansively and beautifully transcendentalized.[59] Even the fact that Hebrew possessed no neutral gender, and therefore projected a universe in which everything was "sexualized," assuming either a feminine or a masculine guise, and engaging itself in intercourse between concepts of the opposite genders, released here a brilliant poetic overflow (the Israeli poetess Yona Wallach was to elaborate on this in her poem about the Hebrew language being "sex-maniacal"[60]). But what was all this adoration of language if not a replacement of one sort of transcendental charge by another? In fact, in Hebrew and Zionist culture, the secularization of the holy almost always had this flip side: the sanctification of the mundane. Scholem immediately sensed this when he arrived in Palestine in 1923 and encountered a Hebrew that was used by people buying groceries in the marketplace. The language, he wrote in the already mentioned open letter to Franz Rosenzweig (1926), was bursting with covert theological tensions, and thus was bound to blow in the faces of its naive speakers who never suspected that in their daily communication they were bartering conceptual explosives. And the covert *numen* inhering in the language was only one of many examples of the duality of the numinous secularized and the secular transcendentalized in modern Hebrew culture. Achad ha'am redefined prophecy for the Hebrew renaissance and rendered it a concept that Bialik and Tchernikhovsky could use in their grappling after the right articulation of their encounters with the "life force" they believed inhered in nature and the human psyche and had to be fanned and re-kindled from the ashes of the atrophied Jewish heart. His redefinition thoroughly secularized the concept, reducing the miraculous fire that burnt but did not consume the thorn bush Moses saw on Mount Horeb to a mere psychological élan, the overflow of the moralist's mental energy.[61] This earned for him severe strictures from Buber, Kaufman, and Kurzweil. However, what Buber (but not Kurzweil) also realized was the fact that as much as Achad ha'am secularized biblical prophecy, he also charged the national élan of his contemporaries with a prophetic sanctity.[62] The Zionist ideologue actually ascribed to modern Jewish nationalism the nature of a spiritual "essence," a Hegelian *Geist*. By doing that, he endowed specific psychic needs of the contemporary Hebraic community with the halo of an "absolute," and created the "religion" of Jewish nationhood.

Thus almost all experiences and emotions, including some negative and destructive ones (like war and death), could be absolutized. Even the heart-shattering fear and trembling Greenberg experienced when, as a soldier in World War I, he found himself the only person alive in an outpost of the Serbian enemy with all his Austro-Hungarian "soldiers brethren," who had participated in the attack, hanging faces down and boots up on the electrified barb wire that encircled the conquered outpost. When the moon appeared from behind the autumn clouds and shone over the worn cleats in the dead soldiers upturned boots, the poet had a negative epiphany:

> And this horrible splendor on those cleats in the boots of dead people
>   kicking against the skies.
> Electrified my life with dread shining unto death.
> I have seen with the eyes of the flesh a divinity with God's secret upon
>   a heap of cadavers."[63]

Every concept the poet used here (*zohar, elohut, sod eloha*) breathed with this reverse sanctity, the dreadful theologizing of tattered human flesh and the protest of young dead men whose right to live was stamped into the mire and crashed into the silence of death. Such a reverse sanctity could have hardly occurred in the war poetry of Greenberg's European contemporaries—Siegfried Sassoon, Wilfred Owen, Edmund

Blunden, and Georg Trakl—as phantasmagoric and apocalyptic as the English and the German poetry of "The Great War" was, it rarely, if ever, deified the massacre. When it mythologized war, the god that personified it was a demiurge, or a Satan, as in Ernst Stadler's famous "Der Krieg," not Job's God, to Whom the Hebrew poet directly referred (Job 29:2–4): "Oh that I were as in months past, as in the days . . . when the secret of God was upon my tent"; in Greenberg's poem, God's secret and proximity eerily permeated the bodies of the dead soldiers) but such deification was perfectly possible within the context of contemporary "secular" Hebrew poetry, and, to a lesser extent also Yiddish poetry (cf. Markish's "The Pile"[64]). Both Greenberg and Markish would refer to the heaps of Jewish cadavers as "cadaverous Sinai," "frightful Sinai," the Sinai from which the Torah may be given back to God by a people it could not protect.[65]

It was Kurzweil's failure in detecting this quintessential characteristic of modern Hebrew literature and culture that fatally impacted the entire structure of his meta-literary thinking. His factual and conceptual mistakes in reading Jewish history and literature of the nineteenth and twentieth centuries could perhaps be corrected, leaving his general schema in need of only partial restructuring. However, his simplistic understanding of Hebraic secularism, a concept so central to his thinking, could not be corrected without that schema being dismantled. In the final analysis, it was this insufficiency that relegated his concept of the new literature as the emblem of a new *khurban*, the downfall of Judaism, to the mere intellectual history of the era of the Holocaust and the birth of the Jewish state. Like that era, it is dramatic, almost operatic in its gestures of doom and gloom. It is, indeed, a riveting chapter in the history of the Hebrew meta-literary discourse; but it is definitely a closed chapter, a thing of the past, an episode in the history of Hebrew literature, rather than an entity that can come alive and contribute to an ongoing, future-oriented, theoretical dialogue.

Eight

Dov Sadan's Concept of *Sifrut Yisra'el*, and Why the "Old" Jewish Literary Discourse Became Irrelevant

Dov Sadan was the most intelligent, erudite, and mentally balanced among the Hebrew literary thinkers of his day. He too was driven by emotions and mental cravings; but with him, these cravings, of which he was aware and in control, had been successfully sublimated and thus expressed, if at all, in a careful and balanced manner that never disallowed contradiction. Sadan never exhibited what may be described as a critical "acting out." He seemed always relaxed and a bit amused. In fact, his charming sense of humor, reflecting a perfect mental equilibrium, his intricate and beautiful filigree style, and the meandering line of argument in his cleverly structured essays (he never wrote a book-length text, always essays and articles and mostly short ones) often hid from the untrained eye the fact that what he actually was saying was not only radical but also at times unreasonable, and, in rare moments, quite flabbergasting in its detachment from the reality he seemed so comfortably connected with. Reading an essay of his was very much like leisurely conversing with a wise and witty master, who seemed eager to entertain and inform rather than convince and control his listener. However, somehow the conversation, more often than not, led to places one did not know how one had gotten to and was not sure one wanted to stay in. Sadan, liked and admired by most, and very rarely at loggerheads with anybody, gave the impression of representing a consensus, while in reality nobody was as distant from the consensus, and, actually as subversive with regard to it, as he was.

Like Kurzweil he believed religion was and would always be the essence of the Jewish identity. In this, strangely enough, both agreed with the "Canaanites" whom Kurzweil attacked (wrongfully believing that they said openly what all Israeli young intellectuals thought or felt) and Sadan dismissed as irrelevant. Rattosh and his disciples defined Jews as a religious community or commonality (in contradistinction to the members of the Hebrew nation, the Jews had formed throughout the last two millennia not a nation but rather an *eda*, a religious-priestly concept of the community subservient to the ritual law as administered by the priest), thus pointing to religion as the core and essence of Jewish collectivity, even when individual members of the collective were already non-religious or even anti-religious. As long as one defined oneself as a Jew, one committed oneself, consciously or unwittingly, to a religious identity and at the same time removed oneself from history, since only "genuine" nations possessed a history. From this Rattosh "logically" (he had a Cartesian mind) deducted that only through the cutting off of the modern Jew's ties from that identity would that modern Jew be able to truly join national collectives; not only that of the young Hebrews in Palestine, but also, for instance, those of pluralist nations, such as the one evolving in the United States, where various ethnic minorities were melted and welded into new national groups. The fact that in other countries the assimilated Jew, who wanted nothing more than to be thus melted down and welded into the dominant national group, had to face anti-Semitism and social rejection, did not change the terms of the choice he had to make: either remain a member of a persecuted religious community or emigrate and eventually be absorbed into genuinely national bodies. Sadan and Kurzweil rejected this juxtaposition of Jewishness and nationhood; they believed Judaism had always conflated the two, since the revelation on Sinai was granted to a chosen nation rather than to select individuals, and the biblical covenant created a special relationship between God and a specific nation, rather than between God and his prophet or his emissary (this was originally Buber's position,[1] which he had poignantly formulated in his address to his Frankfurt *Lherhaus* community in 1934, already under the Nazi regime). However, they both agreed that the encounter with God, namely, the acceptance of national identity as defined by the religious norm, was the alpha and omega of Judaism. Kurzweil learned from this that Judaism as a civilization was irreparably moribund and that the Jewish love affair with secular nationalism was "demonic" and bound to end in a spiritual death. Sadan, however, firmly believed in the Jewish future. In Judaism, he said, the separation of nationhood from religion was temporary and bound to lead to a rapprochement and a new, yet uncharted, conflation of the two. His mental equilibrium was actually based on this faith in the eventual "homecoming" of modern Judaism. The lost son would find his way home as he did in the Christian parable; even if he did not at all want to go back to his father, in whose existence he did not believe anymore, he would somehow find himself at the father's ancestral door, ready to embrace and be embraced. History in its unfathomable dialectic would bring him there, willy-nilly. Nothing was irreparable, and no situation was final. Rattosh, Kurzweil, and Sadan reminded one of the three stages in the story of Oedipus. The first resembled victorious Oedipus, who, having killed his father (the Jewish ancestor) and solved the riddle of the sphinx (the problem of his identity), married his mother (Canaan, *Eretz yisra'el*), sired with her his children (the young Hebrews), and established his kingship. The second resembled the tragic Oedipus, aware of his fratricide (the death of the Jewish faith), of his incestuous relationship (Zionism) with his mother (*Eretz yisra'el*), and the unspeakable contamination of the children born out of this lethal wedlock (the young Israeli intelligentsia), then blinding himself (as Kurzweil metaphorically did) and preferring exile or death to life (Kurzweil committed suicide). Sadan was Oedipus in Colonus, blinded, but by far more perceptive and "seeing" into life and the future than he had been when his eyes still served him, and, above all else, wise and balanced, having transcended both the naiveté of gleeful possession and that of despair and psychotic acting out.

Sadan knew Jewish culture was in a deep crisis, but to him crisis presented not only dangers but also opportunities and new possibilities. What worried him most was not the presumed moribund condition of Judaism but its fragmentation (in this he resembled Achad ha'am, who had been worried not by assimilation, which he believed most Jews would avoid due their inherent penchant for competition through creative imitation, but by fragmentation due to acculturation into different host societies). Nowhere was this fragmentation more apparent than in the Jewish national literature, which had splintered into various mutually independent and also mutually competitive literatures, along the fault lines of languages and ideologies. There was the new Hebrew literature: secular, nationalist, rooted in the Enlightenment, and in the present, mostly Zionist; there was its twin and rival new Yiddish literature: also secular, mostly nationalist, and rooted in the Enlightenment, but in the present, mostly anti-Zionist or non-Zionist. There were the separate and inimical literatures of the Hasidic movement and its main rival, the rabbinical literature of the "opposers" (*mitnagdim*) to Hasidism; there were quite a few Jewish sub-literatures written in non-Jewish languages—but mainly for Jews, who albeit already cut off from their national languages, still were occupied by Jewish concerns and sentiments and not yet ready to become the avid consumers of the dominant non-Jewish culture that their sons and grandsons would certainly be. All these fragments reflected a fractured entity, which once had been whole and integral although never monolithic, since it harbored and balanced its inherent rival propensities. However, all these splinters were about to be reassembled and reunited. Sadan, of all theorists of the Jewish literary complex, was the one who most firmly believed in the continuity and integrality of a single, comprehensive Jewish culture and literature whose current fragmentation was temporary, or as he termed it, "episodic."

That does not mean that he did not acknowledge the severity of the current breakage. On the contrary, he was fully cognizant of the deep fissures the last two centuries (since the advent of Hasidism and Mendelssohnian enlightenment) opened in the very fundament of historical Jewish culture. He even schematized the net of these fissures by a diagram constituted (like the star of David) of two triangles, one superimposed upon the other. The first triangle was linguistic, its three heads—Hebrew, Jewish languages (Yiddish, Judesmo, etc.), non-Jewish languages—pointing in different directions. The second one, ideological, had for its three heads the rabbinical tradition, Hasidism, and modern, secular humanism. The two triangles were not identical and could not be subsumed by each other because each of the pointed heads of the ideological triangle splintered in different linguistic directions. Thus Hasidic literature was written in both Hebrew and Yiddish, and, in the twentieth century, also in non-Jewish languages (the Hasidic project of Buber); the rabbinical tradition resorted to Hebrew, Yiddish, and German (the literature of the neo-orthodoxy), and so on. When superimposed one upon the other, the two triangles exhibited the true complexity of the modern Jewish cultural condition, the permutational number of their opposing heads becoming so large as to call for calculation by algebraic equations. Thus Sadan schematized the complexity and discontinuity under discussion here. Essentially all these fragmentary Jewish literatures were new or even modern, in the sense that all of them had been jolted into being by the same crisis of modernism that had struck the European Jewish civilization in the seventeenth and eighteenth centuries. Hasidism was as much of a modern Jewish response to that crisis as the Jewish enlightenment, and the new orthodoxy, whether in Germany or in eastern Europe, triggered by the challenge of both the Enlightenment and Hasidism, was also new and different from the historical rabbinical or halakhic continuum. So were the Jewish literatures created since the nineteenth century in German and Russian as vehicles for enhancing the conflicting agendas of either the various enlightenments or of the orthodoxy. In fact, the splintering of Jewish Ashkenazic culture and literature was the staple characteristic of Jewish modernity, expressive of its quintessential nature.

Modernity, however, was by and large a historical, and therefore a surface phenomenon. Sadan believed that the national personality was multi-tiered or multilayered. Whether it was constructed according to the Freudian paradigm of id, ego, and super-ego, or it resembled in its structure other psychological paradigms of personality structure, it subsisted of a surface layer, which was historical and always in a state of flux, and deeper layers that were supra- or sub-historical and were largely immutable. Thus the modern condition, by separating the historical surface from the sub-historical infrastructure, created a cleavage that could not be permanent; for the national personality was not inherently schizoid; its current fragmentation did not reflect a congenital, structural lack of integrity. It amounted to a frenetic, imbalanced, but essentially adequate set of responses to an extrinsic, objective challenge; and the national core, still undivided, would eventually reassert its unity by gathering the fragmented responses and synthesizing them as a single, well-balanced response. The modern Jewish condition superficially resembled a schizo-affective pathology, but modern Jewish culture was not psychotic. It was only post-traumatic and was bound to regain its equilibrium.

Sadan believed that the sheer, sweeping centrifugal historical force, which had splintered Jewish culture, sending its fragments in all directions like so many smithereens, would necessarily, as if by the laws of physics, reach a point, at which it would wax centripetal, and with an equally accelerating movement, gather the smithereens and press them together into a single entity. This "inevitable" ingathering or "recapitulation" the theorist explained in terms that were intermittently Hegelian (and, within the Hebrew context, Krochmalian) and Freudian. According to Hegelian dialectical paradigms, the *Geist* of Judaic culture, evolving within the thesis/antithesis binarism, would inevitably reach the point of synthesis, and thus transcend binary oppositions (although the synthesis itself would eventually become a thesis that would trigger its antithesis, etc.). What's more, by the logic of this paradigm, the more "tension-full" and oppositional the relationship between the thesis and the antithesis, the stronger and more integral the synthesis it would eventually yield. If the modern condition, as an antithesis to the one that had preceded it, was characterized by radical fragmentation (versus relative unity), the future synthesis would be one of a more complex but also more solid integrality. The religious tradition, itself overcoming its inner dichotomies, would achieve a meaningful rapprochement with secular humanism; nationalism would be amalgamated with universalism; the secular nationalists would come back to religion, and religion, in its turn, would absorb much of the contents of both their humanism and nationalism; "the language of the fathers" (Hebrew) would make peace with the intimate "vernacular of the mothers" (Yiddish), with the latter receding back to its historical position as a secondary or ancillary language, peacefully cohabitating with its more dominant sister under the single roof of a harmonious diglossia; important Jewish texts written in non-Jewish languages would be returned to their home, *ligvulam*, to their territory, through adequate translations. A new, and to some extent unprecedented and at the moment unknowable, Jewish culture would emerge, in which every important component of the older cultures would be preserved but also metamorphosed; for this would not be an eclectic mixture, but rather a new compound: firm and chemically stable.

In Freudian terms (the reader may remember that in the 1930s, Sadan was the chief exponent of the psychoanalytical approach in Hebrew criticism; he was fully literate in the early Viennese psychoanalytic lingo), the adoption on the part of Jewish culture of rationalism and the notion that human life, individual and collective, must be rationally engineered (which are, philosophically, the gist of modernism) involved the repression of the non-rational components within the national psyche. That inevitably caused rifts and confrontations between the separated parts of the Jewish personality, whereas in the Middle Ages those parts, although in fierce rivalry already then, had nevertheless not been torn off from each other. Thus, modern Judaism suffered from psychic discrepancies between id, ego, and super-ego; between the conscious and the unconscious; between instinct and moral self-control and practical self-preservation. In that, it was not unlike modern Western civilization as a whole (cf. Freud's "Das Unbehagen in der Kultur" [the English rendering: "Civilization and its Discontents," is doubly inaccurate, for Freud spoke of culture and discomfort or uneasiness rather than of civilization and discontent) but only very much more radical in the tensions between its conflicting inner powers and therefore, so much more in a state of cultural "discomfort." The equilibrium of the future Jewish culture would resemble a psychic balance achieved through a successful therapy, with literature and literary criticism playing the roles of the analyst and analysand, provided that literary thinking underwent the *Lehr-Analyse* Sadan was providing. Already the greatest writers—Bialik, Agnon—were doing the work of both patient and therapist since their work brought to light internal conflicts, as well as offered means for transcending them through aesthetic sublimation. These writers were characterized by what Sadan called *kuliyut*, a neologism based on medieval Hebrew philosophical jargon. The medieval translators of the Jewish philosophical masterpieces of Saadia Gaon, Yehuda Halevi, and Maimonides (the so called Tibbonites, members of the family Ibn Tibbon who lived in Provence in the twelfth and thirteenth centuries) invented the substantive *kolut* (wholeness) and the adjectives *koliyi* or *koli*, by which they meant both general and all-inclusive. The soul could be *kolit* when it included and subsumed all the partial souls every human possessed (since humans consisted of matter, vegetative powers, life, and reason); or certain ideas or concepts could be regarded as *koliyim*, if they subsumed all the parts or components that were necessary for their being autonomous and independent of what they did not include. Sadan, whose coinage became prevalent in the Hebrew intellectual discourse, and can now be found in dictionaries, had in mind much more than mere subsumption. His concept indicated both inclusion and integration. What was characterized by it was at one and the same time autonomous because it contained all the different components, which together rendered it whole, integral, and continuous because all these components have been fused together. A writer whose work could be characterized by the term had achieved the highest degree of inclusion and integration; that is, all the different parts of the individual psyche and the national personality found their respective and mutually complementary voices in his or her work, but at the same time, their voices blended together and sounded as one voice with no discordance, just different registers being vocalized in harmony. Such a writer was not only a national therapist but also a precursor of the future Jewish culture, which, above all else, would be distinguished by its Jewish *kuliyut*.

As a matter of fact, Sadan's *kuliyut* could be rendered best as Jewish catholicism. This was so not only because the word catholicism combined the two Greek words—*cata* (entirely, absolutely) and *holon* (all, everything)—but also because it endowed this combination with a religious-mystical aura. It indicated a wholeness that had been achieved through the miracle of transubstantiation. Sadan's thinking was deeply rooted in religion and mysticism, and he could be safely described as the prophet of a future Jewish catholicism. At the core of his thinking, one found the concepts of epiphany and second coming, as well as the Freudian (essentially unrealizable) ideal of the perfectly orchestrated and balanced personality. If we do not ascribe to Sadan religiosity, we can never understand his optimistic eschatology, as well as never detect the well-hidden prophetic note, without which his cultural voice could not have been what it actually was. Sadan seemed never to be discouraged by the fact that none of his prophecies came true or even partially

and remotely could be seen as materializing. His prognoses never vindicated, he admitted that the current cultural condition did not show
much progress toward the future synthesis; or, rather that indications
of such progress could be detected only in the deepest layers of texts
written by the greatest contemporary writers. However, his faith braced
and upheld the critic. He was a perspicacious, well-balanced, wonder-
fully clever, and at the same time also a courageous, indeed, audacious,
believer. It is not easy to find in the world of modern literary criticism
and scholarship somebody who resembled him in this combination of
erudition, urbanity, wit, and faith, unless it was C. S. Lewis, perhaps
the most prominent modern literary scholar, who gracefully shouldered
the double burden of a vast textual erudition and total grounding in the
verifiable historical record, on the one hand, and the active search for
Christian grace on the other.

For Sadan's work as a literary critic, the best of his time, his elaborate
theoretical system together with his exquisite analytical intuitions and
his well-honed sensitivity to language and style worked wonders—up to
a point; a point at which the system failed him, and both the sensitivity
and the intuition seemed to have been quite suddenly abrogated. As
long as he had to deal with the complexities of writers such as Bialik,
Agnon, and Brenner, his system supplied him with the best theoretical
tools and conceptual insights that he needed to explore the totality of
the creative personality. Whether these writers actually incorporated in
their works the *kuliyut* he sought (Brenner obviously did not) or simply
brought together disparate memories and associations and incompatible insights and contradictory messages (as they certainly did in the
work of Agnon), the concept helped Sadan in never giving way to the
urge of achieving through arbitrary selection a two-dimensional, clear,
and simplistic mental image. No one was better equipped than he was
to account for ambiguities, which he saw as emanating from both the
multilayered individual personality and the stratified national-cultural
memory. In his already mentioned masterful analysis of the poetry of
Tchernikhovsky, he convincingly demonstrated how this poet's poetry
gushed forth from two separate and hardly interconnected psychic
sources, which were that of burgeoning Nietzschean individualism
and Hellenism of the European fin de siècle, and that of an intimate

memory of life within the traditional Jewish community. His more than one hundred studies of Bialik's poems and style added up to the most detailed, sensitive, and subtle critical analysis of the mythopoeia of this greatest of modern Hebrew poets. Guided by a psychoanalytic perception of Bialik as a person and a poet—who was so close to the primal origins of Jewish mythos and yet so scared of the uncontrolled energies they conveyed or rather radiated, that he flew in panic to the illusory refuge of Talmudic scholarship, the deductive rationalism of Achad ha'am, and the mimetic precision of Abramovitsh—he managed to discover every crevice and cranny in the poet's legacy, through which the primary powers could still be intuited and their thermal impact felt.[2] His Agnon criticism, although by far, less interpretative and detailed than that of Kurzweil, was, in the final analysis, more subtle and satisfactory, for Sadan never had to choose between one Agnon and the other, whose presence was as palpable as that of his "rival," between the Agnon who lamented the loss of the world of his childhood, and the one who subtly, but also quite ferociously, exposed its shortcomings, the Agnon who yearned for harmony and the one who, with evident pleasure, tore any semblance of harmony to shreds.[3] All the "Agnons" found a place in his scheme, and therefore, some of his Agnon studies are still challenging and energizing contemporary Agnon scholars. In a long series of very short and compact essays, which he wrote as the editor of the literary supplement of *Davar* when the need arose to celebrate a writer's anniversary or eulogize him after his death, he almost always pointed with amazing intuitive clarity to the very center of this writer's vision and personality.

And yet, as said before, Sadan could also disappoint as no other could. The disappointments were, of course, sharpened by justified great expectations. However, they pointed to a limitation that lay beyond mere temporary weakness and moments of non-focusing, which sometimes went together with excesses and dysfunctional erudition and anecdotage. It was not by sheer chance that he never had anything significant to say about some of the most momentous events in twentieth-century Hebrew literature, such as the publications of Gnessin's *Etsel* (*Alongside*, 1913), of Greenberg's *Eyma gedola veyare'akh* (*Great Dread and a Moon*, 1925) and *Anacreon al kotev ha'itsavon* (*Anacreon on the Pole of Sorrow*, 1928), Alterman's *Kokhavim bakhuts* (*Stars Outside*, 1938) and *Simkhat aniyim* (*The Joy of the Poor*, 1940), Rattosh's *Khupa shekhora* (*Black Canopy*, 1941), Yizhar's *Khirbet Khize* and *Hashavuy* (*The Prisoner*, 1949), let alone the publications of the early and seminal collections of poems by the new Israeli poets, such as Amichai and Zach. Something in his intellectual makeup, as well as in his system reined him in, stepped on the brakes where velocity and freedom of movement were called for. Some of Sadan's shortcomings and what they tell us about the inevitable sagging and sinking of the kind of theoretical discourse he was the master of will be discussed in the following.

After Sadan and Kurzweil, the meta-literary discourse we have been following petered out in both Hebrew and Yiddish. In Israel it ground to a halt in the mid-1950s, and where some critics tried to continue it further, their attempts, none of them on a grand scale, were met with indifference, and thus wilted without leaving much of a trace. In Yiddish, the blow inflicted upon both the language and its culture during World War II was of such magnitude that even though it could not, for a while, make poets and writers of prose fiction stop writing and publishing, serious literary criticism (as distinguished from historical literary scholarship), let alone literary theorizing, were soon extinct. The latter could hardly persist without a relatively sophisticated reading public and, even more importantly, without some prospects of a meaningful literary future. Theory, as we have seen, always included future projections. In fact, it was to guide and orientate literature in a hypothetical future that the past and the present were conceptualized and schematically theorized. With no meaningful future perspectives, meta-literary thinking lacks the oxygen it needs if it is to avoid asphyxiation. Thus, to the extent that such thinking persisted, its focus shifted from Hebrew and Yiddish to English, and its center—from Israel and Yiddish New York—to the English and Comparative Literature departments of American universities. I provide in the next endnote a far from exhaustive list of American publications—some book-length treatises or collections of articles; others, gatherings of papers read at conferences and symposia—which I regard as indicative that the discourse we focus on is still alive and valid in the largest and most culturally active contemporary Jewish diaspora; but I shall not try to tell the story of the survival of this discourse in the American academy, which should form a separate narrative in need of a special survey, and would project the Jewish concerns here mentioned onto the wide panorama of the vicissitudes of Anglo-American literary criticism and theory throughout the last three decades of the twentieth and the first years of the twenty-first centuries.[4]

We must dwell here, however, on the ramifications of the demise of the discourse in Israel. Its background and some of the reasons for it already have been discussed; but there were other reasons that should be mentioned here. To a large extent, the negative dynamics and the shortcomings of the discourse itself rendered its eventual drying up inevitable. It had reached its climax against the background of the Holocaust, the birth of Israel, and the brutal killing of prominent Yiddish writers and activists and the temporary abolition of Jewish cultural life in the Soviet Union during the last years of Stalin's reign of terror. This background, on the one hand, sharpened the Jewish sensibilities of the discourse and explained its dramatic and hyperbolic character. On the other hand, however, it left the theorists facing new realities, which they hardly understood, and clearly were unable to gauge their inherent creative potential. By the mid-1950s, the map of Jewish culture was thoroughly changed. Yiddish culture in North America entered an advanced phase of its decline. Although brilliant Yiddish poems and works of prose fiction were still being written by some of the old masters (such as Glatshteyn, Singer, and Grade), Yiddish readers were disappearing in ever larger numbers. With each subscriber of the *Forverts* (which once surpassed the *New York Times* in its circulation) who passed away, the number of Yiddish readers was reduced by more than one (since the newspaper would serve a household rather than a single reader). Commercial publication of Yiddish books—once a burgeoning industry—ground to a halt, which explains why the books being published were big, heavy, beautifully buckram-bound, and totally financed by philanthropists because they actually functioned as literary tombstones in the graveyard of a dying culture, never meant to be either sold or read. Yiddish newspapers folded one after another, and the once lively Yiddish theater of the lower East Side disappeared. The only master, a seasoned survivor, who managed to save himself and his work from sinking into this downward-spiraling vortex was I. B. Singer—for whom the writing of his stories and novels in Yiddish and their serialization (in the *Forverts*), now counted only as the first step toward their editing and rewriting (by various translator-editors in collaboration with the author) toward the publication of their official canonical versions in English. The success of other Yiddish writers who aspired to flourish through translations (such as Grade, who, energetically and quite vehemently, attempted to do this) was modest at best. In the Soviet Union, Yiddish culture was as good as executed together with its leaders: Bergelson and Markish. Its very limited and problematic revival after the "thaw" under the leadership of Khrushchev, wilted after a decade or so with most of the serious writers, (such as the novelist Elye Shekhtman), who endowed it with whatever substance it had, emigrating, mostly to Israel. Soon enough, the only relatively vital center of Yiddish creativity was the one headed by Sutskever in Tel Aviv, with some talented younger writers (such as Yosl Birshteyn and the poetess Rachel Fishman), forming for a short while the already mentioned *Yung yisro'el* group, helping him in maintaining the vitality and high level of the literary quarterly *Di goldene keyt*, which became the only significant Yiddish literary periodical whose publication was not disrupted until the end of the century when it too folded.

As for Hebrew writing, its existence outside of Israel had been undermined to the point of extinction by the Holocaust, Stalinism, and the acculturation of American Jewry. Whereas in the Soviet Union, Hebrew writers (such as the brilliant poet Chaim Lensky) perished either in the Gulag or as social outcasts, or kept their creativity as Hebraists well hidden (for instance, the interesting writer of prose fiction Tsvi Pregerezon, who managed to survive the Stalinist era as a respected mining engineer in Siberia, far from the toxic centers of the Communist state), Hebraists in the other eastern European republics perished during the years of Nazi occupation in the ghettos (like the scholar Ch. N. Shapira, the cultural leader of the Kaunas Ghetto) or in the Polish forests (like the outstanding expressionist poet Ber Pomerants), where they tried to find shelter with partisans. The few who survived emigrated to Israel as soon as World War II was over (like the young poet Abba Kovner, one of the leaders of the Vilnius anti-Nazi underground and the commander of a Jewish unit of partisans in the Rudniki forests). Hebrew writing in North America had wilted and all but disappeared long before the dotage of its Yiddish counterpart. Of all the important members of the New York Hebrew center, only the poet Preil remained in the city he loved and whose landscapes and rhythms informed his work; and he too conducted his literary life—by proxies and remote control—in Israel, where his poetry collections were published and cherished by the young Israeli intelligentsia. All the others either emigrated to Israel or sunk into inactivity and despondent marginality. These developments left only two branches of Jewish literary creativity that had not been lopped off by the terrible events of the 1940s and that now were filled with new creative sap: Israel, with its official, Zionist-Hebraic culture, and some Western countries, where Jewish writing in non-Jewish languages gradually acquired the density, richness, and high artistic level once characteristic of German-Jewish and Russian-Jewish writing. This happened and still happens primarily in the United States, where a robust American-Jewish literature now flourished, but also, if to a lesser extent, in France, Canada, Great Britain, and some Spanish-speaking countries in South America and Mesoamerica. There, in Mexico, Brazil, Argentina, and even Peru, new Jewish writers, most of them first or second generation children of eastern European immigrants, searched for means of articulating their sense of being post-Holocaust Jews, while at the same time tried, often successfully, to find their place within the American Spanish or Portuguese literary traditions of the countries where they had been born and raised. Using non-Jewish languages, their mother tongues and exclusive means of artistic self-expression, as well as the particular literary sound boards of their respective non-Jewish cultures, many Jewish writers outside of the United States and Israel came up with interesting results that still have not won the full recognition—as Jewish literary achievements—they deserve.

Under these circumstances, the value of any Jewish literary theory totally depended on its relevance to the prospects of a renewed Jewish creativity in Israel (in Hebrew) and the West (in English, French,

Spanish, and Portuguese). A literary theory, which could not project realistic future perspectives for writers living and working in these centers, thus helping them in shaping the literary rationale some of them were in sore need of, was doomed to irrelevance. And, unfortunately, the Jewish Hebrew and Yiddish literary theorists were singularly unable to offer young Jewish writers in either Israel or in Europe and the Americas as much as a grain of a worthwhile idea or concept these writers could put to use or apply. Little wonder, then, that the selfsame young writers soon enough lost interest in the theorists and their theories and pushed them out of their field of vision.

Kurzweil's view of Judaism as having descended into the limbo of secularism and alienation leading to the hell of "levantinism" was singularly non-conducive to any future-oriented progress. Whereas the critic incessantly warned against the impending sterility of Jewish cultural life, it was his own message that progressively became sterile and strident. We have already noted how unfruitful his dogged antagonism to Israeli writing was. Not that Israeli literature had no need of severe and demanding critics; however, the criticism should have differentiated between what was alive and potentially creative in the literature and what slowed down or hampered its growth. Thus, it could have energized its quest for stature and truth and enhanced its process of maturation. But Kurzweil was unable to gauge the depth and potential of the best Israeli literary achievements, such as Yizhar's great novel of the War of Independence, *Days of Ziklag*, in which he found nothing but the nihilism caused by the fear of death and the mental decomposition it triggered.[5] Whereas the novel certainly focused on existential fears (it subsisted of a series of interior monologues of a group of soldiers first conquering and then defending a distant and bare hill of some strategic importance in the Negev, constantly under a barrage of enemy fire and in mortal danger), it also contained an array of other topics and insights. Through the ruminations and associations of the protagonists, it offered an anatomy of the society and worldview of the Zionist pioneers as reflected in the consciousness of the children born and raised in their villages. It was informed by both humor and sarcasm through which the author conveyed his central message: the Ben Gurionist vision of a new Jewish state as a revival of ancient, biblical independence

(Ziklag had been the garrison village of the biblical David before he became the king of Judea and then of Israel as a whole, and thus represented an equivalent to the period in which the action of the novel took place; but the identification of the hill the protagonists conquered and desperately fought over as the archeological mound of ancient Ziklag—which presumably "justified" their struggle and endowed it with "meaning"—was a bogus one, based on amateurish and misguided archaeological detection—hence the significance of the Ziklag theme in the novel as representing the "visionary" but essentially unconvincing view of Zionism as a movement that drew its dynamics from ancient Judaic sources and revived an ancient Judaic hegemony). The critic saw none of these; nor was he appreciative of the novel's superb orchestration of the Hebrew language as a vehicle conveying the essence of the Palestinian landscape and ambience, the physical reality of its sands, horrendous sun, its blazing daytime azure skies, and the unspeakable beauty of its crystalline, dark blue, star-studded cold nights. Likewise he was immune to the power of Amos Oz's best novel *My Michael*,[6] where a riveting insight into the malaise of Israeli society at its anticlimax, the years directly following the excitement, euphoria, and tragedy of the 1948 War, was convincingly conveyed through the psychotic unraveling of the personality of the female protagonist. The publication in 1977 of the best Israeli novel yet, Ya'akov Shabtai's *Present Continuous*, left him indifferent, as did the publication of some of the best Israeli collections of poetry. Most of his rare recommendations were embarrassingly inadequate and gauche, indicative of both poor taste and limited understanding. In short, having written about Israeli literature for more than three decades, Kurzweil's contribution to its elucidation and guidance was almost solely that of imperceptive, albeit serious and dedicated, antagonism. Strangely, it would seem, he also contributed very little, if anything, to the understanding of the modern Jewish complex in its wider circumference. Strangely, because he himself was the direct product of the German-Jewish literary revival of the Weimar period, the reaction of some eminent German Jewish intellectuals to the cultural flatness produced by assimilation and the alarming untenability of the illusion of the Jewish-German "symbiosis." One could have expected that, being suffused with *Deutschtum* (his Hebrew, although heavily edited, never altogether shed the syntactic heavy-handedness of official discursive German), he would understand from within the creative potential of cultural hybridity such as that of the German Jewish writers he had read in his youth (some of whom, like Karl Kraus and, of course, Franz Kafka, he admired and emulated; Kurzweil experimented with Kafkaesque prose fiction, his initial dream having been to become a writer of modernist prose fiction rather than a literary critic; as a critic, however, he systematically imitated the expositional and satirical procedures initiated by Kraus in his *Die Fackel*). Presumably, he could apply the lessons of the inter-bellum German-Jewish literary model to the Jewish literature now being written in America. However, he had no interest in this literature and essentially showed no understanding of the problems and potential of a new Jewish literature created within a non-Jewish, post-Holocaust context. Even in his essays on Kafka and Kraus, he almost never focused on the Jewish aspects of their work, to which many non-Jewish critics and interpreters became progressively more sensitive. Of course, he never paid attention to the presence of novelists such as Henry Roth, Saul Bellow, and Bernard Malamud or to that of poets such as Charles Reznikoff and Delmore Schwartz. He never made it his business to seriously learn about American literature, which he believed was "naturalistic" and "flat" (his examples were questionable Hebrew translations from the works of Hemingway and Steinbeck, which enjoyed considerable popularity in the 1940s), and whose influence on Israeli writers (such as Yigal Mosenzon and Moshe Shamir), he believed was detrimental; for in addition to all his other flaws, he shared the snobbery of the European who despised *Amerika* and its presumed vulgarity, as well as the Western Jew's recoiling from Yiddish; for this critic, whose entire life work was based on the ideal of the pre-modern Jewish "organic" community defined by faith and social integration, never deigned to comment seriously on a single text by the greatest poet who had projected that ideal and recorded its dismantling—Sholem Aleichem.

Similarly disappointing was the inability of Halkin to contribute much to the understanding of whatever aspect of the modern, post-Holocaust Jewish literary complex. Again, superficially one would have expected from him a particularly sensitive appreciation of this complex.

A serious and talented Hebrew American poet and novelist, he had spent a few years in Israel in the 1930s, then went back to America, and finally returned to Jerusalem in 1949 as the heir of Klausner's position at the Hebrew University of Jerusalem as the institution's chief scholar in the field of the new Hebrew literature. The graduate of American colleges and universities, he had been fully exposed to modern Anglo-American literature. Whereas in his poetry he evinced, like most Hebrew American poets, a certain romantic conservatism (although he was the first Hebrew translator of a comprehensive selection from Whitman's *Leaves of Grass*, which, in his translation, projected a somewhat Mishnaic, scholarly, and less populist Whitman), his prose fiction, particularly his novel *Up to the Crisis*, was clearly influenced by current Anglo-American stream-of-consciousness fiction, as well as by the lyrical "oceanic" writing of Thomas Wolf. As a participant in the literary life of Hebraic New York (his aforementioned novel contained a brilliant lyrical essay on Jews' attachment to that city as the ultimate habitat for shtetl refugees, and on their contribution to its hectic intellectual and artistic life), he could have been expected to bring to the Hebrew literary discourse an understanding of Jewish-American writing, starting at the beginning of the twentieth century with the realist and naturalist novels of Cahan and Antin, then breaking into experimental modernism in the minimalist poetry of Reznikoff and the stream-of-consciousness fiction of Henry Roth, and then branching in different directions in the work of a host of younger writers. But he, too, did nothing of the sort. Indeed, he hardly mentioned the very existence of such a hybrid Jewish-American literature, or even the existence of the American-Yiddish poetry and fiction of the authors whom he knew personally. Whereas he focused on the canonical literature of the Hebrew renaissance (he spoke eloquently on Berditchevsky—in his introductory classes to modern Hebrew fiction at the Hebrew University—and wrote beautifully on Tchernikhovsky[7]), he would occasionally write on British and American writers such as D. H. Lawrence, G. B. Shaw, Aldous Huxley, and H. L. Mencken (besides an extensive scholarly essay on Walt Whitman), but never on Halpern, Glatshteyn, Opatoshu, Reznikoff, H. Roth, or Bellow. How could that be accounted for? Halkin's vision was probably severely limited by both his bitter experience as a Hebrew writer in a

Jewish society that had marginalized Hebrew and relegated it to mere preparation for participation in the synagogue ritual on one's bar mitzvah celebration and by a brand of strict and dire Zionism to which he gave poignant expression in his essay on Jews and Judaism in America.[8] The literary resentment and the ideological radicalism fed each other and shared a common denominator: a deep mistrust of American Jewry and a total lack of faith in its cultural future. Halkin painfully experienced the demise of the dream of a Hebraic intellectual life on American soil as he also witnessed the somewhat slower wilting of its Yiddish counterpart that had once made one envious of its temporary florescence. American Jewish life, it seemed, was being divested of all Jewish cultural values, quickly sinking into a vulgar hedonism and a cult of financial success, even as those in it who were truly interested in matters of the spirit were avidly investing themselves in American non-Jewish art, literature, politics, and intellectual academic activities. Thus Judaism as a civilization was about to be reduced to ritualistic vestiges devoid of real contents, which, for the time being, American-Jewish social life still needed for the purpose of covering, however partially, its crass materialistic nakedness and the schmaltz of its bourgeois bonhomie. Halkin carried in himself like a hard rock this bitter vision, accentuated by the corrosive humiliation of a talented writer, of whose work and achievements his native community neither could nor cared to be aware. It blinded him to the fact, that while all the negative developments he pointed to were obviously taking place, other ones were also gradually shaping up. Thus, the appearance of American English-writing novelists and essayists, who insisted on articulating clearly defined Jewish sensibilities, like Ozick or Arthur A. Cohen (the author of the novel *The Legend of the Last Jew on Earth* and brilliant books of Jewish philosophical and theological thought such as *The Natural and Supernatural Jew* and *The Myth of the Judeo-Christian Tradition*), meant little to him; or rather it came too late for him to fully register it, since he had already made up his mind, and he would doggedly and bitterly defend his gloom and doom positions. Thus for Halkin, only Israel held the promise of a vital Judaic future, including the future of a Hebrew literature, which was the only legitimate and enduring Jewish literature. However, it was exactly this attitude and the fervent expectations it entailed that all but ascertained the poet-scholar's disappointment with Israel as well. As a teacher at the Hebrew University who modernized the study of Hebrew literature there (by introducing both the analytical methods of the Anglo-American New Criticism and a broad cultural-sociological approach to the study of literary history), he met the best young writers and literary intellectuals of the nascent state who were eager to find in him a mentor. He himself was quite ready to don the mentor's cloak. However, one extended article he wrote on the poetry of the so-called *Palmakh* generation (the generation who came of age in the 1940s and whose defining experience was that of the 1948 War) sufficed as evidence of how out of synch with the Israeli poetic ambience its critic was. Not only did Halkin put on a par serious and complex poets such as Gilboa with mere rhymesters such as Michael Deshe, he also, and more importantly, remained quite deaf to the particular tonality of these poets, whose innermost concerns and intimate experiences he failed to intuit and understand. Instead of reaching for the core of their experience, attuning himself to the distress, sense of loss, and self pity of young people who had just now emerged from a war in which they had lost their best friends and regarding themselves as members of a sacrificed generation, and analyzing the stylistic and musical correlatives of this distress, he filled his essay with facile and self-evident sociological observations. In some of his comments (such as on Pinchas Sadeh's early quasi-Christological poems of a person then in a severe crisis of identity), he was not far from sheer obtuseness.[9] The disappointment of young readers was such, that all expectations of finding strength and guidance in a popular teacher's attention had to be abandoned. Halkin himself probably realized how off the mark his comments had been, for he refrained from publishing further comments on Israeli writing. Another literary historian and theorist was exposed, as far as the shaping of the Israeli literary rationale was concerned, as leading toward a dead end.

Sadan's scheme seemed more promising than that of others. Its "catholicism" seemed to mean all-inclusiveness (*Sifrut yisra'el* covers works written in Hebrew, other Jewish languages, and non-Jewish languages used by Jews) and to promise a dialectical comprehension of all ideological and linguistic cleavages as expressive of the tensions between the different parts of the national integral personality. However, the fruitful application of Sadan's scheme hit two obstacles that seriously subverted it. The first, and perhaps more important one, inhered in the theorist's definition of Jewish literature written in non-Jewish languages. Such a literature, the critic believed, had to be differentiated from non-Jewish literary texts written by Jews within the framework of the various national literatures which, since the beginning of the nineteenth century, they joined in ever larger numbers. His differentiation was articulated in a simple and compact formula: Jewish literature written in non-Jewish languages subsisted of literary texts created by Jews for Jews, that is, it was mainly targeted at a Jewish reading public. As soon as the intended reader of the text was the imagined and generalized German or Russian or American reader at large, the text did not belong anymore within *Sifrut yisra'el*. The differentiation was pat and clear; perhaps too clear. From the moment it was formulated (in 1950), it proved unhelpful. For one thing, it made Jewish literature written in non-Jewish languages the all-but-exclusive domain of third- and fourth-rate writers, for in modern times (unlike the high Middle Ages, for instance) no talented Jewish writer who resorted to a non-Jewish language targeted his work at a Jewish audience—solely, or even mainly. From Heine to Kafka, from Babel to Bruno Schultz, from Proust to George Perec, from Albert Cohen to Rosier, from Sassoon to Arnold Wesker, and from H. Roth to Ozick—all Jewish writers worth their salt—aimed high and insisted on carving a niche for themselves in the respective national German, French, Russian, English, and American literatures. What else could have been expected from a forceful and talented writer?! Who, then, were the writers Sadan had in mind? Groups of derivative and secondary writers who catered to the literary needs of Jewish communities in a state of transition. In Germany, for instance, Jewish national languages (Hebrew and western Yiddish) had become inaccessible to large parts of the semi-traditional Jewish community long before the process of acculturation enabled the members of those communities to join the German literary intelligentsia or consume its products. They still needed for entertainment and edification a literature, which while being written in proper, if often stilted, literary German, responded to their particularistic Jewish concerns and interests, paramount among them the apologetic urge to project a beautified, *Salonfähig* Judaism. This need was satisfied by writers such as Hermann Reckendorf (a mid-nineteenth century orientalist, a teacher of Hebrew and Arabic at Heidelberg, who translated the Koran and also penned a series of short Jewish-historical novels under the general title *The Mysteries of the Jews*); Markus Lehman (a rabbi at Mainz and the founder and editor of the Jewish Orthodox weekly *Der Israelit*, in which he also published historical novellas idealizing traditional Jewish life); Ludwig Philippson (a rabbi at Magdeburg who founded and edited the important weekly *Allgemeine Zeitung des Judentums*, where he published poems, prose fiction, and many articles. A consistent defender of the *Wissenschaft des Judentums*, he navigated between the Orthodox and the Reform movement and carried the banner of Jewish emancipation), et al. In Russia of the second half of the nineteenth century, a somewhat similar group of Jewish writers (such as Y. Y. Lerner, Lev Levanda, Grigory Bogrov) catered to Jewish communities that were already cut off from the Yiddish and the Hebrew of their parents but still unable or unwilling to participate in the burgeoning contemporary Russian literary culture. With no disrespect for the historical role these writers had played, one was allowed to ask whether their work was worthy of serious literary study, and whether the scholarly discipline, which should have focused on it, was not history (particularly the history of Jewish acculturation in the nineteenth century) rather than literary studies. Sadan's book, in which he commented also on some of the apologetic German Jewish writers of the kind we discussed,[10] was so much more readable, wise, and entertaining than any of the texts those writers had produced, as to raise the question whether the wasting of so much brilliance on such a mediocre literary corpus was "economically" justified. Who needed to read the writings of Lehman, Philippson, and Reckendorf when everything they had to say about Jewish life had been said so much better and more perceptively and compactly in the first chapter of Heine's *Rabbi of Bacherach*, while the second and third chapters of that brilliant unfinished historical novella problematized and enriched whatever had been said in the preceding one, injecting into this tale about a persecuted Jewish community, its leader the rabbi, and his beautiful wife, observations, questions, and projections that dramatized the problematic nature of Jewish modernity in its full complexity and richness, and raised issues and ideas that the relevance and actuality of would become clear only in the twentieth century? But Sadan wrote about Leopold Kompert rather than Heine.

If the *Rabbi of Bacherach* did not belong within the confines of a Jewish literature—because its author certainly targeted it at the general German and European public—who needed the literature from which it had been excluded?! These questions, as it turned out, had practical ramifications. In the early 1950s, Mosad Bialik, the public publishing house (maintained then by the World Zionist Organization), adopted, largely under Sadan's influence, a program called *Ligvulam*, the purpose of which was to bring back to the Israeli and Hebrew reader the works of those "straying" Jewish writers whose works, written in non-Jewish languages, would otherwise become unknown to Hebrew readers, and in some cases altogether forgotten. However, as soon as the publisher and his advisors set up priorities and commissioned translations, it became clear that Sadan's formula was unworkable. They felt they had to focus on Heine (whose entire non-fiction and prose-fiction was magnificently translated by Shmu'el Perlman), on the socialist Lassalle, on the Jewish Danish literary critic Georg Brandes, and on Georg Herman (also known as Jakob Borchardt, a German Jewish art historian who also wrote a Berlin Jewish-family saga), whereas Sadan directed them toward writers they did not believe could or should be of interest to readers. Clearly Sadan's formula allowed for the inclusion of a rearguard Jewish literature written in non-Jewish language in an interim phase in the development of modern Jewish cultural life when literary creativity was at a low ebb. This was an ephemeral, short-lived phenomenon that could interest the historian of ideas, tastes, and mores; however, as literature, its products were all but devoid of interest.

This lack of literary merit and interest, which rendered Sadan's program of literary "recapitulation" impracticable, pointed, however, to what, on the historical and theoretical levels, could be seen as the least of its problems. The program was unsound in many other ways. Historically, it was impossible to prove that the literature Sadan had in mind was really targeted at a Jewish reading public only, that it was not motivated by a wish to "improve" the image of Jewish historical life in the eyes of non-Jews. As Bialik had been quick to notice, the politics of the novels and poems the apologists had written were always pointed in the direction of the real or imagined non-Jewish reader (the writer always worked "under the surveillance of the masters, whose eyes watched and enslaved" him from behind his back). In the best case he produced "low-spirited defense, pleading for mercy."[11] Even if the texts under discussion were targeted at Jews and catered to their interests, their sheer accessibility to the non-Jewish reader diluted and weakened the compact "by Jews, for Jews" formula. One can enumerate the many "in between" cases (such as that of the Russian Jewish poet Frug) that corroborated this assertion. Sadan's formula begged other questions as well, such as whether the nature of a literary text could be exclusively decided by the extrinsic conditions of the readership it served and the "intentional fallacy" of the author's presumed intention, particularly when the intention and the historical readers the text was "aimed at," were the only criteria by which the particular text was differentiated from other texts focusing on similar topics. Thus, the works of the German Jewish apologists belonged within the theorist's *Sifrut yisra'el*, whereas the poems in Heine's *Hebräische Melodien* were excluded from it, although thematically and ideationally the latter were as "Jewish" as the former (if not more so), and only the fact that their author was so much more gifted and inspired than Philippson or Lehman and therefore his works (to the extent that the censors did not manage to confiscate them) were avidly read by all readers of German literature, that fact alone justified their exclusion. Could then the differentiation withstand a basic test of theoretical tenability, and was the exclusion based on it acceptable?

But, of course, these did not amount to the fatal flaw, which more than all others undermined Sadan's theory. That flaw inhered in the theory's evasion of the inherent hybridity and complexity of modern Jewish writing in non-Jewish languages; the complexity, which Franz Kafka so strikingly summed up in his much quoted letter to Max Brod (of June 1921), where he analyzed the "impossibilities" faced by Jews when trying to join the ranks of German writers: "The impossibility of not writing, the impossibility of writing German, the impossibility of writing differently"[12] or in his various comments on the strictures of intellectual anti-Semites, such as Hans Blüher, who insisted on the inability of German-Jewish writers to integrate their writing into the German literary fabric, and on the "enervation" these writers inflicted upon the "virility" of German culture—assessments Kafka seems to have been in basic agreement with (see the pleasure with which he quoted a particularly snide remark on the popular German-Jewish novelist Jakob Wasserman, in a letter written in 1922: "Even if Wasserman should rise at four in the morning day after day and his whole life long plow up the Nuremberg region from end to end, the land would still not respond to him and he would have to take pretty whisperings in the air for its response."[13]). As far as Kafka was concerned, the literature Jewish writers were producing for general German consumption, being quintessentially "Jewish," did not add much to German literature as such.[14] Sadan, however, refused to acknowledge the positive flip-side of Kafka's overtly negative remarks; the fact that they pointed to the existence of a Jewish literature, or a brand of Jewish writing, which albeit not targeted at a Jewish audience, nevertheless developed a distinct Jewish tonality (which Kafka designated as unintentional *mauscheln*—a verb indicating the Yiddishization of the German language; and what could mauscheln imply, when metaphorically applied to a literary text, if not the imbuing of this text with specific Jewish coloration?). Thus the critic's approach was by far too simple and reductive to even begin negotiating a cultural phenomenon that was extremely complex and fraught with ambiguities. Sadan sought taxonomic clarity and drew bold demarcating lines where no such clarity existed, and where boldly etched lines lead nowhere.

Whoever wished to do critical justice to the modern Jewish literary complex, particularly to its parts written in non-Jewish languages and within the contexts of non-Jewish national literatures (which are often the most interesting and vital parts of that complex) had to start by acknowledging the complexity, liquidity, and hybridity of the cultural and literary phenomenon he intended to examine. Jews became, in the beginning of the nineteenth century, and particularly in the twentieth century, a major driving force in three or four great Western literatures; and many of them, while being that, did not shed their Jewish concerns and sheer sense of being Jewish (because it was this sense with all its vagueness, the experience of *Judesein*, rather the abstract concept of identity, which most often lingered and would not be erased), but rather carried them with them right into the very core of the texts they produced. Proust carried it into the emotional and ideational cusp of his great novel, where it paralleled homosexuality as the sensibility of a rejected minority, which could enhance the creation and appreciation of art, the greatest of human achievements. Kafka identified it with the quintessential human weakness in the face of physical and metaphysical arbitrary, indifferent, or malicious "authorities." Were Proust and Kafka "Jewish" writers? Did *Swann's Way*, *Sodom and Gomorrah*, *The Trial*, and *The Castle* belong within whatever concept of a Jewish literary complex, as much as they definitely served as cornerstones in the edifices of modern French and German literature? The answers to these questions could not be a clear-cut yes or no. The truth here was to a large extent in the eye of the beholder. Buber, Rosenzweig, and Scholem firmly believed that Kafka was the quintessential modern Jewish writer. Others thought that Kafka's Jewishness was merely biographical and hardly pertained to the meaning of his fictions (the latter view has been almost consensually rejected by recent Kafka scholarship).[15] This confusing state of affairs could not be overcome by simplistic formulae predicated on the existence of self-evident continuities and discontinuities. One had to accept the reality that demonstrated how continuity and discontinuity were more often than not just two aspects of a single phenomenon. If the study of Jewish literatures taught one any worthwhile lesson, it was that in the realm of literature—of the spirit in general—causalities, "developments," continuities, and, of course, "progress," represented at best only one aspect of a multifaceted reality. As much as these concepts were applicable within a certain limited context of historical literary studies, they could never offer a comprehensive view of the literary phenomenon, particularly when it was worth studying, namely, when it approximated its full potential and complexity.

Also Sadan's fantastic dream of a Jewish spiritual continuity, which would eventually assert itself in a grand synthesis of faith and humanism, of normative spiritualism, and earthly etatism, rendered him insensible to the Israeli cultural ambience; and this constituted the second big obstacle against which his great critical project bumped. As much as his extremely narrow and exclusive definition of Jewish literature written in non-Jewish languages blinded him to the very vital developments in both pre-Holocaust and post-Holocaust Jewish writing in German, English, and French (the fact that he did not read the last two of these languages added, of course, a thick layer of insulation), his hoped for synthesis would not allow him to see what was taking place under his nose and in the language of which he was the consummate master. Strangely enough, he being primarily a Zionist, a Hebraist, and a student of Hebrew literature, what he had to say about Yiddish Israeli literature was by far more perceptive and helpful than what he had to say about canonical Hebrew Israeli literature. His one large-scale attempt in elucidating a central Hebrew Israeli literary text—Shamir's historical novel *King of Flesh and Blood*[16]—clearly illustrated his inability to shed light on what was really at the core of Israeli writing. Shamir's novel, written in the early 1950s, as the impact of the 1948 War was being internalized, and the significance of nascent statehood mulled over, used the parallelism between the present and the short-lived political supremacy of the *Hasmonean* dynasty in the third and second centuries B.C.E., as a means of examining the moral and political problems to which successful and forceful etatism inevitably gave rise. The writer, a seasoned Zionist-Marxist, thoroughly studied the historical record and interpreted it in terms of class struggle. Although he intended and largely succeeded in presenting each of the two contending forces, the Sadducee king and his Pharisee challengers, each through his own self-image and self-rationalization, his final verdict was clearly anti-etatist and anti-Ben Gurionist and amounted to a warning of Israeli literature against making itself serviceable to the state as such. Even old Klausner, a right-wing thinker, fully understood this meaning of the novel that he severely criticized both as a historian of the era of the Second Commonwealth and as a "political" Zionist who had joined forces with Jabotinsky.[17] Sadan, in his extensive study saw nothing in all these, or, if he saw what the novel was really about (as he must have), he chose to overlook what did not enhance his argument. The novel appealed to him as a first indication of the Jewish homecoming of young Israeli writers. The fact that the novel presumably sympathized with the Pharisees, the founding fathers of the Jewish halakhic tradition and was written in a style based on Mishnaic Hebrew (actually, the model Shamir followed was Bialik and Ravnitsky's Hebrew rendering of the Talmudic aggada) meant everything, whereas the fact that it truly empathized with the exploited peasants of Judea and Samaria (as represented by the folksy figure of the sage and miracle-worker Khoni) meant little. The critic made almost no effort to point to some correlations or connections between his neo-Jewish interpretation of the novel and the issues that ostensibly occupied the author's mind and clearly conditioned the plotting and structuring of the novel and the presentation of the conflict on which it focused. Shamir, according to Sadan, was unconsciously moving in the "right" direction—toward neo-Judaism. In fact, it was the critic who quite consciously moved in the wrong one.

Thus, we can conclude that the theoretical discourse here under consideration failed the two post-Holocaust outposts of Jewish literary creativity, Israeli literature and the new Jewish writing in the West, where they were most vulnerable. Both Israeli literature and that new post-Holocaust Jewish writing in non-Jewish languages, particularly the one evolving in the United States, were in need of a consistent rationale, of a theory that would have both articulated and examined the new cultural and literary dimensions of a meaningful Jewish self-expression after the industrial decimation of European Jewry and the rebirth of Jewish political independence, and the available theorists shortchanged those in whose hands the future of the Jewish literary complex was held. This was a failure of historical proportions, and it fully justified at the time the marginalization of the theoretical discourse and its eventual desertion. As it had been conducted, this discourse well deserved these wages of myopia and lack of realism. This brings us back to our initial suggestion that as deserved as these wages were, the self-punishment inflicted by the Israeli literary intelligentsia upon itself by altogether eliminating the Jewish literary theoretical discourse, was perhaps uncalled for. If the existing discourse became irrelevant, a new one could have been devised (as it was, to some extent, in the American academy). Much in the story of Israeli literature could have been different and perhaps better than it has been, had such a new discourse evolved. Hence a restatement of our opening questions: should this new discourse be started now, more than fifty years after the demise of the old one; and if it should, what can we take from the legacy of the old discourse, and what should we learn from its mistakes and failures?

Assuming that the answer to the first question is in the affirmative, we can dwell for a while on the possible answers to its sequel: what should we take with us from the failed old discourse and what should we learn from its mistakes? If we start with the second part of this double-headed question, then it seems by now, the answer should be clear enough. The basic, and indeed, fatal flaw in the old discourse inhered in its obsession with the issues of continuity and discontinuity. We can understand how this obsession with both horizontal and vertical continuities came about; what the emotional and cultural pressures were that triggered it, and how it was, in a way, a direct reflection of the revolutionary position the new Jewish literatures adopted and, at the same time, recoiled from, particularly under the impact of the Holocaust and the founding of Israel. Perhaps being locked between the horns of this dilemma—how to devise a Jewish culture that was both revolutionary and loyal to its antecedents—was inevitable at the time. That, however, is no reason for us to remain trapped there. We should be able to see this dilemma as essentially imaginary and refrain from being tempted by either the messianic dreams of those who believed in miraculous continuities or by the dramas of *Götterdämmerung* played by the romantic prophets of tragic discontinuity—not to speak of the totally irrelevant and naive élan of those who jubilantly celebrated new beginnings from scratch and demanded the total cleaning of the slate before anything new would be written on it. By now, all these are non-existent options, which have already done their share of damage. They deflected Kurzweil away from a balanced and realistic understanding of both Jewish traditionalism and Jewish secularist modernity and sent him right into a blind alley: the sentimentalist's fantasy world of a lost perfection and a demonic nihility that replaced it. They bridled Halkin with a pair of Zionist blinders so tight, with openings so small and narrow, that he could not see properly—not only the Israel that perhaps he could not truly observe and comprehend, his view of it being totally imbued with the tensions and concerns he had brought with him from his American past—but even his own America, in which he had been raised and that had endowed his romantic mysticism (as a poet) with the glitter of modernism. Above all else, they cut off Sadan, the cleverest and most knowledgeable of them all, from his formidable moorings—his unparalleled familiarity with the historical reality of Jewish literatures—that anchored him to the existential mundanity of writers as real people, who lived and worked in their respective here and now, and sent him up, like a Hegelian balloon chock full of Freudian hot air, into the skies of unrealizable and unhistorical syntheses, where realities as hard as rocks easily morphed, like so many figments of the scholastic imagination, into miasmatic clouds, floating, interpenetrating each other, merging, and transforming themselves into any fantastic formation the critic's wishful thinking favored. They rendered some of these fine and astute thinkers unnecessarily despondent, even despairing. Not that contemporary Jewish life was devoid of tragedy; but the respective tragedies they pointed to (the death of authentic Judaism; the inevitable spiritual and cultural demise of American Jewry) were not the real Jewish tragedies of the time. They made them hopeful where there was no room for realistic hope, or where the hope that perhaps could be reasonably entertained should have been of an altogether different kind. They blinded them, as well as so many others, to what was really taking place in Israel, as well as out of it—not just the social and political realities, but mainly the psychic and spiritual grappling.

It was not theory in and of itself that brought about these rather consistent series of failures; nor was it the fact that the theory in question shied away, by and large, from the formalist dissection of the literary text. It was rather the harnessing of theory to the problematic troika of newness, oldness, and continuity or alternatively, newness, oldness, and discontinuity. Of course, the historical reality contained all of these and much more; but the many components, which together made up this reality, had never frozen into either of these triangular formations. Moreover, these components kept changing, or at least assuming new forms due to changing circumstances. And if this was true for modern Jewish history as a whole, it was particularly true as far as modern Jewish intellectual and literary history was concerned.

On the whole, the modern Jewish literary complex was and is just that. A complex, a multifarious entity consisting of different connected, semi-connected, and unconnected particles, and as such complex, that is, complicated, difficult to understand and analyze. It was neither a system or a "poly-system," a "super-system" versus a "sub-system," or any other appellation the Tel Aviv structuralists gave it, replacing the old concepts of continuity with new ones, without any genuine change of significance, for all the concepts they used implied the same obsession with order and continuity; only the penchant for the neatness that their nomenclature smacked of was by far more compulsive than the yearnings of the old seekers of spatial and chronological continuities. Vast, disorderly, and somewhat diffuse, this complex was characterized by dualities, parallelisms, occasional intersections, marginal overlapping, hybrids, similarities within dissimilarities, mobility, changeability, occasional emergence of patterns and their eventual disappearance, randomness, and, when approximating a semblance of significant order, by contiguities. The latter concept, contiguity, I believe should replace that of continuity in our search for whatever moment of tangible contacts between the many players in the drama of the modern Jewish literary complex. It is a concept that a new theory of Jewish literatures must adopt, explore, and develop, and it will occupy the center of the concluding chapters of this essay. However, we are already allowed to say that the role played in this drama by contiguity was by far more significant than the one played by many of its secondary continuities. The latter characterized, if at all, some developments within each of the separate Jewish literatures. Of course, there, too, they were as imaginary as they were real; for most of these continuities to which the attention of literary historians was permanently attracted, were achieved through ongoing processes of canonization and de-canonization or divestments, which, as a matter of course, involved sturdy and sometimes brutal acts of exclusion and marginalization. Thus, influential critics formed their favorite "great traditions," which sometimes were as arbitrary and awkward as was F. R. Leavis's original "great tradition" with its exclusion of Fielding, Walter Scott, Dickens, Thackeray, Trollope, Meredith, Hardy, Joyce, E. M. Forster, and Virginia Woolf from the mainstream of the English novel. After these processes became transparent and were seen through, and the great traditions thus created were unraveled, the various literatures looked much less homogenous and continuous than they used to look.

As for contacts between the different Jewish literatures—even for those that had been historically and ideologically spawned together as twins, like the new Hebrew and the new Yiddish literatures—continuity appeared far less dominant than one used to think, and contiguity or tangency emerged as the main modality of what had been referred to as "literary evolution." This was true even—or perhaps particularly—in the famous cases of bilingual creativity, such as that of Abramovitsh and Peretz; those cases that seemed to justify Baal-makhshoves's slogan: two languages–one literature only. Since the view of modern Hebrew-Yiddish bilingualism thus captioned is still quite prevalent, we should, I believe, subject it to a more detailed and rigorous examination before we finally turn to the rather vague concept of literary contiguity.

Nine Jewish Diglossias—Differential and Integral

The Hebrew-Yiddish diglossia, or rather that of Yiddish and the holy tongue (*loshn-koydesh*, the term covering both Hebrew and Talmudic and Midrashic Aramaic), had prevailed among Ashkenazic Jews since the high Middle Ages—for almost a thousand years. This, of course, does not mean that its character remained the same at all times and places, or that it always served exactly the same cultural needs. Diglossias (situations in which two languages—or two varieties of one language, a "high" and a "low" one—are being used under different conditions or for different purposes in a community, often by the same people) and bilingualism (the ability to use—speak, read, write—two languages relatively fluently), like all other forms of linguistic usage are in constant flux, and often grouping them under one caption is confusing and misleading. They are therefore "untheorizable" if plucked out of historical contexts, and an attempt to describe them as if their functioning abided by constant rules or structural regulations, often leads to problematic results.[1] However, as fluctuating and changeable as the holy tongue–Yiddish diglossia had been throughout the Middle Ages, the Renaissance, and early modern times, it underwent drastic changes that gradually but thoroughly changed its character, starting in the second half of the eighteenth century. Two developments triggered the change: the gradual replacement of Yiddish by non-Jewish languages (German, French, Dutch, Italian) in western Europe (Germany, Alsace-Lorrain, North Italy, Holland, Switzerland) and the advent of the Hasidic movement in eastern Europe. Whereas the former gradually nullified the status of Yiddish as the spoken vernacular of western Ashkenazic Jewry, as well as that of its written language serving the religious-ritualistic needs of women and popular homiletic and entertainment literature, the latter toppled the equilibrium of the diglossia by assigning to Yiddish a role it had hardly played before—that of a "holy" Jewish language in its own right, in which sacred literature—hagiographic, allegorical, and narrative was written.

This elevation of Yiddish was dictated both by the egalitarian ideology and by the cultural politics of the Hasidic movement, which depended for its quick growth and spread over large sections of the eastern European Jewish continuum on the appeal of its propaganda to the Jewish masses, including women and the uneducated segments of the society. This rendered the resort to Yiddish as a culture language almost on a par with Hebrew absolutely necessary, and the Hasidic movement, in its dynamism and revolutionary élan, did not hesitate to "sanctify" the language and use it as the language for some of its most basic documents, such as the formative hagiographic collection of tales about, and sayings of, the founder of Hasidism, Rabbi Eliezer Baal-shem-tov, or the fascinating allegorical tales of Rabbi Nachman of Bratslav (the Baal-shem-tov's great-grandchild), which constituted the apogee of Hasidic narrative literature. Since these quintessential works were, of course, also translated into Hebrew (the language of Jewish males, particularly the better educated ones), a phenomenon, which had almost never been known before, emerged: a bilingual Jewish literature, whose essential character was non- or almost non-diglossic, namely, a literature in which the two Jewish languages functioned within a framework where the high-low sharply etched binarism became blurry and diffuse, and in which a single text would be produced almost simultaneously in both languages with both versions considered equally "holy" and normative.

In the history of earlier Jewish Ashkenazic literature, there were very few cases of such bilingually produced texts, and in each case the bilingualism was awkward and clearly fraught with difficulties due to the fact that it was not based upon a stable literary tradition. Thus, for instance, in the beginning of the seventeenth century, an anonymous epic poem, known as *Megiles Vints* (the scroll of Vints or the book of Vints; the title intended to call to mind that of the biblical book of Esther, which among Jews was known as *Megiles Esther* [the scroll of Esther] or the *megile*, the scroll), was written in both western Yiddish and German-Ashkenazic Hebrew.[2] The poem was commissioned by a certain community in Germany where a rebellion of the local artisans, lead by one Vints, was defeated by the "masters" of the town, the aristocracy and the clergy, who were aided by extrinsic powers. Vints, together with the other leaders of the uprising, were publicly executed, and the local Jewish community was jubilant; for the artisans' uprising had been informed by a strong anti-Semitic tendency and characterized by pogrom-like actions; so as long as it was not quelled, the local Jewish community feared for its life and property. Since the downfall of Vints resembled that of biblical Haman in the book of Esther (the text that supplied the model for all Jewish stories of great danger and a last-moment rescue), the leaders of the community decided to commemorate it in a special *megile* for the edification of future generations, who would learn from it that even when danger is imminent, one should not lose one's confidence in God, whose intervention can take place "within the blink of an eye." Clearly, the poem was written originally in literary, fluent Yiddish, by a writer or scribe who rhymed easily and knew how to handle the complicated stanzaic units of which the poem consisted. Why did those who commissioned the poem think a Hebrew version was also necessary? Probably because of the sanctity of Hebrew, the language in which the original *megile* was cast, and also, perhaps, because the poem was intended to remain readable for a long time to come, and the Hebrew language was associated with literary longevity. Written also in the holy tongue, the poem supposedly would withstand the test of time and bear witness to God's mercy and power in eras when Yiddish would be forgotten. The Hebrew version, however, was ridiculously inadequate. Ungrammatical, replete with strange neologisms (the legacy of the Ashkenazic *piyut*), and collapsing on its own strange syntax and unprofessional rhyming, it indicated something beyond the sheer limitations of an untalented adapter: the non-existence of a bilingual–bi-textualist tradition.

Hasidism changed all this. Although its Hebrew versions were as ungrammatical as *Megiles Vints*, if not more so, and were based both syntactically and vocabulary-wise on direct translations from the Yiddish (as a matter of course, all Yiddish idioms and many of its verb-conjugations were literally translated), the Hebrew of the Hasidic masterpiece certainly possessed a narrative flair of its own and is, ironically, by far more readable nowadays than the strictly grammatical, florid pseudo-biblical Hebrew of the *maskilim*, who poked fun at it and sometimes brilliantly imitated it. Indeed, the exponents of the Jewish enlightenment in eastern Europe, who (with a few exceptions) loathed Yiddish as a broken German and wished to see it obliterated and forgotten,[3] initiated their own Yiddish literature in response to the extraordinary success and wide circulation of its Hasidic Yiddish-Hebrew rival. Some of them, particularly the genial Perl, a Hebrew-Yiddish satirist of Swiftian caliber, created their own mirror-image version of a bilingual canon. Perl's superb parody-satire *Megale temirin* (the revealer of secrets, 1819), first cast in a Hebrew that mimicked and caricatured the Hebrew of Hasidic writing, presenting it as delightfully vitiated and corrupt, was translated by the author into fluent, colloquial Yiddish, which, lacking the brilliance and fun of the broken Hebrew version, rendered the epistolary story by far less delectable than it was in its original (in the special prologue to the Yiddish version, written in the form of a folksy dialogue, Perl indirectly but systematically referred to problems of translation and to the fact, that re-written in a different language, a text must undergo subtle changes of tonality, as well as of contents).[4] Then he went on to write a series of bilingual parodies of Nachman's tales, almost as brilliant as the stories of the Hasidic master himself.[5] However, throughout the first half of the nineteenth century, when almost all anti-Hasidic Yiddish writings were circulated in hand-written copies (most of them were to be published only in the twentieth century—the Yiddish version of *Megale temirin* in 1937)[6]—the Hebrew-Yiddish non-diglossic bi-textual bilingualism of the Enlightenment was an underground phenomenon; and, as such discontinuous and devoid of artistic rationale. It was only in the second half of the century, and particularly since the emergence of the new Jewish nationalism in the 1880s, when Yiddish secular writing found its "justification" and aesthetic raison d'être, that the bilingualism here under discussion was firmly established.

Nobody contributed to its florescence more than Abramovitsh (known by mistake as "Mendele the book peddler," for Mendele was Abramovitsh's chief fictional character and persona rather than his pen name), and that is why the Hebrew-Yiddish bilingualism of Abramovitsh is dealt with in this volume separately, and in considerable historical and literary detail. Its ups and downs, conundrums and solutions, creative agony and triumph, are both too complex and too important to be glossed over through a mere survey.[7] However, it is important for our purposes here to define as clearly as we can the character of this bilingualism at the most advanced stage of its crystallization; for it was this bilingualism that presumably justified the notion that Hebrew and Yiddish literatures formed a continuous, bilingual corpus of texts; and it is exactly this bilingualism, which when properly understood, showed how different and divergent the two literatures actually were. Indeed, it showed that the misguided slogan "Two languages—one literature" must be replaced by "One text (written in two languages)—two totally separate literatures." Hence the need to view Abramovitsh's bilingualism as a phenomenon, which for the lack of a more elegant gloss must be labeled bi-literaturalism; for as much as Abramovitsh was a writer who employed with the greatest mastery two languages and created in them parallel bilingual versions of his best works, he was also, and as importantly, a writer who learned to live and function separately in the very different frameworks of two divergent literary traditions. Indeed, more than anything else, he was a literary ambidextrous amphibian and the progenitor of a whole school of mostly less dexterous literary amphibians, who for a while could live in the water, as well as on dry land. That phase of "amphibianism" could not, however, continue for more than twenty to twenty-five years at the longest estimation. As soon as the very peculiar historical-cultural circumstances, which had made it possible, and, perhaps, also inevitable, changed, it became a thing of the past, with both literatures, the Hebrew and the Yiddish ones, asserting their divergent, and, in fact, oppositional and mutually exclusive, agendas.

These complex developments can be somewhat clarified if we define here two kinds of literary bilingualism. Using a mathematical metaphor, I shall label the first kind of bilingualism "integral," and the second one, "differential." The metaphor, one should remember, is merely a rhetorical means for enhancing the clear articulation of an argument and should not be carried beyond its rhetorical usefulness. Also both differential and integral bilingualism should not be regarded as monolithic and static. Within the two categories, changes regularly occur. Indeed, literary bilingualism in all its forms changes as it moves through time and space. Nevertheless the differentiation between the two categories is not only useful but actually essential in the context of our argument.

Differential literary bilingualism (or, for that matter, multilingualism) entails the use for literary purposes of two or more languages within a single cultural space, where each language is more or less systematically resorted to when certain, specific, literary tasks or projects are undertaken. The bilingualism or multilingualism is differential in the sense that it allots to each language its different and specific role or roles. It is characteristic of diglossic situations, but can often go far beyond the boundaries of the diglossic structure with its high-low duality and exhibit two or more high languages. As long as the role of each of these is clearly defined and more or less methodically adhered to by writers, who would not, in principle, use one language for the purpose of performing the task "belonging" to another one. In such cases, linguistic "differentialism" is dominant. A good example of such differentialism in the cultural and literary history of the Jews is supplied by the "Sephardic" (actually, Mediterranean) Jewish literature of the high Middle Ages, its so-called golden epoch (tenth to thirteenth centuries C.E.). Whereas contemporary Jews of Spain, Provence, North Africa, and parts of the Middle East, spoke in many languages and also started to evolve their own Spanish-Jewish language, the Judesmo, they wrote their multifaceted, rich, and extensive literature according to a system of linguistic differentiation as follows: Hebrew was used for canonical belles lettres, mainly poetry (both liturgical and secular) but also rhyming prose novellas (popular ballads and *romanzeros* would be written in Jewish-Spanish). The Hebrew canonical belles lettres contained macaronic poems, in which languages other than Hebrew—such as Arabic or medieval Spanish dialects—would be mingled with Hebrew. However, that in no way undermined the socio-literary norm: Hebrew was the language of poetry and most prose fiction, and it was a highly literary Hebrew, replete with sophisticated references to other texts (mainly the Bible), phonetic and semantic playfulness, and clever, sometimes off-color, double entendres. It was clearly aimed at an educated and rather limited literary audience, well-versed in the traditions of canonical Arabic poetry, the model for the Hebrew one; although the latter, in its liturgical part, which within the circumference of Jewish Sephardic literature was by far more communicative and less periphrastic than the Palestinian and Ashkenazic *piyut*, was meant to serve the community as a whole as part of the synagogue ritual. Hebrew non-fictional prose was used quite systematically by writers of halakhic and exegetical texts that were meant to serve a wide readership either within the context of standard Jewish education or for the practical purposes of studying and following the Jewish law. Possibly, these texts, or some of them, were meant to be used by Jews living outside the Jewish-Sephardic sphere, and with whom Hebrew was the only means of communication. Characteristically, such texts would be written in crystal clear, beautifully transparent, and straightforward Hebrew. Thus the Hebrew of Maimonides's masterpiece *Mishne tora*, his systematic summing up of the halakha in fourteen, logically differentiated and constructed parts, is perhaps the best and most exemplary in Jewish medieval writing, with only the Hebrew in the commentaries on the Bible and Talmud of Rashi (Rabbi Shlomo Yitskhaki), the great Ashkenazic exegete of the eleventh century, as a possible rival. But Sephardic commentaries on the sacred texts, such as Avraham Ibn Ezra's commentary on the Bible (twelfth century) and Nachmanides's commentary on the Pentateuch (thirteenth century), were also written in exemplary, simple Hebrew, which like that of Maimonides or Rashi can be easily understood today by educated Hebrew speakers and readers. Similarly, Hebrew would be the language used in treatises that were written in times of fierce anti-Jewish debates (initiated by the church), and whose purpose was to strengthen the Jewish community in its faith vis à vis its detractors, such as Nachmanides's *Sefer haviku'akh* (the book of debate or controversy).

True, Maimonides wrote his commentary on tractate *Avot* in the Mishna in Arabic rather than in Hebrew because the commentary and particularly its comprehensive introduction (known as "Eight Chapters of Maimonides") was informed by his philosophical understanding and formulation of Jewish ethics. Indeed, high literary and technical Arabic was the language of intellectual abstract or conceptual discourse. It was the language in which Saadia Gaon, Yehuda Halevi, and Maimonides wrote their major philosophical works (*The Book of Beliefs and Opinions* [10th century], *The Kuzari* [first half of the twelfth century], and

The Guide to the Perplexed [second half of the twelfth century], respectively) and in which treatises on grammar (such as Yona Ibn Janah's *Sefer hadikduk*, eleventh century), rhetoric and poetics (such as Moshe Ibn Ezra's *Shirat yisra'el*, twelfth century), or ethics (such as Bahya Ibn Paquda's *Khovot halevavot*, eleventh century) were written. This use of Arabic was necessitated not only by the fact that contemporary Hebrew was not in possession of the appropriate philosophical and technical terminology, but also by the wish of most writers to keep their circle of readers relatively small, containing only those who were well-versed in abstract and conceptual reasoning, seasoned and trustworthy Jewish intellectuals, who would not misunderstand or misuse the rationalist arguments of the learned authors.

In the thirteenth century, another language was invented for the purpose of blocking the reader's path to texts that were supposed to be perused only by the initiated—zoharic Aramaic. The language of Jewish mystical texts that had been written until that juncture was either Hebrew or Talmudic Aramaic. The Spanish cabbalist Moshe de Leon (also called Moshe ben Shem-tov), who wrote a series of cabbalist texts during the second half of the thirteenth century, used Hebrew in his early work. However, when he composed large parts of the cabbalist *Midrash*, which would eventually be known as *Sefer hazohar* (the book of splendor), and assume the status of the central and dominant cabbalist text, he invented a non-existent Aramaic. This, on the one hand, was aimed at buttressing the text's pseudoepigraphic claim. (It was supposed to have been written by the second century C.E. Mishnaic sage Shimon Bar Yohai and a group of his colleagues and disciples. In reality, however, the Zoharic language, was totally different from the Palestinian Aramaic of the era of Roman occupation.) On the other hand, it rendered the text accessible only to those who had been meticulously instructed, and thus constituted a code, which would be maintained in many cabbalist and Hasidic texts to our own day.

In the twelfth and thirteenth centuries, most of the philosophical and technical masterpieces of the Spanish era were translated into a very peculiar Hebrew—particularly by the well-known Provencal family of Ibn Tibbon: philosophers, physicians, scholars, and translators (Yehuda, Shmu'el, Moshe, and Ya'akov). Living in the Christian north, as well as on the borderline separating Sephardic from Ashkenazic Jews, the Ibn Tibbons were increasingly aware of the fact that, Arabic being unknown in those areas, they faced a sufficiently large Hebrew-reading public who was interested in the philosophical and scholarly books of their Spanish coreligionists, which, as long as they were not translated, remained inaccessible. The translators invented a philosophical and technical Hebrew that meticulously reconstructed the sophisticated Arabic texts with all their nomenclature and terminologies—that in spite of Maimonides's warning to Shmu'el, the translator of *The Guide to the Perplexed*, to avoid doing that, but rather attempt to re-articulate the argument without the philosophical jargon, and in as fluent and transparent Hebrew as was possible. The Tibbonites actually invented a new Hebrew, cumbersome, difficult, technical, and necessitating special training, which nevertheless eventually became one of the chief Hebrew styles for texts conveying abstract thinking and scholarly discourse. In this they paved the way for the eventual dismantling of Spanish-Jewish literary differentialism. In the fourteenth and fifteenth centuries, as the history of Jews in the Iberian peninsula drew closer to its termination by the exile in 1492 and 1497 of all unconverted Jews of Spain and Portugal, the differential linguistic system we have described was falling apart. With the entire peninsula being reconquered by Christians, Arabic became largely unknown, and major philosophical and theological texts, such as Gersonide's *God's Wars* (first half of the fourteenth century), Chasdai Kreskas's *God's Light* (second half of the same century), and Albo's philosophical magnum opus *The Book of Dogmas* (first half of the fifteenth century) were already written in Hebrew. The circumstances that had allowed for the protracted existence of a truly differential system had disappeared, and concurrently, Sephardic Jewry was writing the last chapter in its golden literary tradition. Not that its creativity was at an end. In the sixteenth and seventeenth centuries, its extensions in Palestine, Asia Minor, and Greece would become the main custodians of the mystical tradition (which would be refashioned by the Safed circle of cabbalists headed by Isaac Luria, and subsequently by his disciple Chaim Vital, and then by the Sabbatean messianic movement), while holding its own in the domain of the halakha (cf., the major Talmudist Yosef Karo, the author of the classical compendium of Jewish laws and mores *Shulkhan arukh* [a table set], which became the chief codex of Orthodox Jewry; upon being exiled from Spain, Karo settled down first in Turkey and then in Safed, where he was the head of a famous yeshiva). They also kept alive the tradition of Andalusian Hebrew poetry, both secular and liturgical. In the nineteenth and twentieth centuries, the Jews of Greece and parts of the Middle East experienced a brand of modern enlightenment of their own, quite different from the Italian-Dutch and German–eastern-European ones, which brought them in its own way to a close contact with modern European (particularly French) culture—hence the emergence in the twentieth century of literary luminaries such as the Corfu-born Albert Cohen (the author of the *Solal* novels and the magisterial *Belle du Seigneur*) and the Cairo-born Edmond Jabès (the author of *The Book of Questions* and *The Book of Resemblances*). The "Sephardic haskala" also triggered much writing in Hebrew and particularly in Judesmo (many dozens of novels and novellas, poetry, essays). Nevertheless, the classical Sephardic literary era ended with the downfall of its differential linguistic system.

Integral literary bilingualism or multilingualism is characterized by the resort, within a single cultural space (which is obviously in the processes of disintegration), to two or more different languages without allotting to each a distinct literary role and without avoiding constant literary "trespassing," that is, doing with one language what another one is presumed to be capable of doing; whereas such trespassing is relatively rare, but not altogether unknown, in the domain of differential bilingualism. Such bilingualism is integral in the sense that each of the languages used is perceived as an integer, a whole number, or a number that is not a fraction. Differential bilingualism does perceive the languages it employs as fractions, parts of a bigger and whole entity; that is why it insists on each language sticking to a prescribed communicative task or tasks. In contradistinction, literary integral bilingualism emerges where a cultural fragmentation of one kind or another, while it is not yet disruptive of the continuity of a given cultural space, nevertheless blurs the demarcation lines between the appropriate domains of each of the languages used and eventually prescribes the usage of each of the languages for the entire gamut of cultural-literary functions, including those parts of it that had been served by the other language.

Such integral multilingualism existed in Spain in the fourteenth and fifteenth centuries, as the reigning differential system collapsed. However, it seems that the best example of integral multilingualism in premodern Jewish cultural history can be found in the so-called Hellenistic era that had started after the conquest of Asia by Alexander the Great and the three dynasties that inherited his empire (fourth century B.C.E.) and continued for many centuries throughout the era of Roman supremacy. With the field of Hellenistic Judaism studies recently in a state of ferment (the cogency of the very concept of Jewish Hellenism or rather Hellenisms is being questioned),[8] a non-expert should not make hasty generalizations. However, it seems safe enough to assert that whereas the exposure to Greek, its culture, literature, and philosophy, was in one way or another a common denominator shared by almost all contemporary Jewish cultures (including that of rabbinic Judaism with its halakhic lore—their Mishnaic Hebrew, replete with Greek words, bore witness to that—and not only those of Egyptian Greek-speaking Jews and the priestly-Sadducee tradition of the so-called assimilators or Hellenizers in Palestine), the diversity of those cultures was paralleled only by the diversity of Jewish cultures in modern times.[9] Scholars have differentiated among at least three such cultures according to their respective understandings of the relationship between God and wisdom: (a) wisdom being a creation of God but inhering in the world, and as such accessible to human understanding through proper education and elucidation; (b) wisdom was transcendental and currently existed only out of the human world, which was essentially evil and devoid of understanding; as such it inhered in a messianic-metaphysical superhuman being, a divine "son of man," who would bring it to humankind at the end of time; (c) wisdom, being an aura or effulgence of God, could be identified with his "word" (logos), which had been transmitted to Moses and was incorporated in the Torah, which allowed for a philosophical rather than halakhic interpretation of the holy writ.[10] Without getting into the deep waters of this differentiation, we should turn our attention to the linguistic aspect of the cultural diversity. Three languages were resorted to by writers of the period: Hebrew (which fell into two separate idioms, indeed, two separate languages: that of the Mishna and of the rabbinical tradition, and that of the poetry and liturgy of the texts revealed in the caves near the Dead Sea, which is by far closer to the language of the Bible, but still distinctly different from it), Aramaic (which could be divided into spoken Aramaic and the Aramaic of the halakhic argument), and Greek (which was to be divided between the high literary Greek as used by writers such as Philo of Alexandria and Josephus Flavius and the popular post-classical Greek, the so-called *Koine*, in which the New Testament was written). It would seem that the issue of which language should be used for which purpose was rather fuzzy and confused. This was particularly the case of the Hebrew-Greek diglossia. Until half a century ago we had almost no Hebrew belle lettres of the period. Books of wisdom and history and so on, with the exception of parts of the *Ecclesiasticus* or *Wisdom of Ben Sira*, were preserved mainly in Greek, although many of these so-called apocryphal texts had been written originally in Hebrew. Had the library of the Dead Sea sect not been discovered, we would hardly have a notion of how poetic Hebrew of the period looked and sounded. The very fact that the Hebrew originals of those of the Apocrypha, which had been written in Hebrew, were not preserved indicated that at least some people of the period did not ascribe much importance to the difference between the languages and regarded them as interchangeable. Also, texts within the same traditions would be written in different languages. Thus, the first book of *Maccabees* was written in Hebrew and modeled after the historical books of the Bible, whereas the second *Maccabees* was written in Greek and based on Greek historiographical models. *The Wisdom of Solomon*, a book that pretended to be a direct continuation of biblical sapiential literature, was written originally in Greek. The first book of *Enoch*, a central document of the messianic "Enochite" tradition, a precursor of Christianity, was written in Aramaic, whereas the second one—in Hebrew. It would seem that for many Jews, the Torah itself, once it had been translated into Greek (the so-called translation of the seventy or the Septuagint), the Hebrew original ceased to enjoy an authoritative status. Moses' edicts could be studied and interpreted on the basis of the Greek version without any reference to it. Thus, Philo of Alexandria, the founding father of Jewish philosophy, based his vast project of reinterpreting philosophically and allegorically the Pentateuch on the Greek translation and probably did not know Hebrew at all. By the same token, the early Christians accepted the Septuagint as their official version of the Old Testament. This was perhaps why the rabbinical sages were so ambivalent in their evaluation of this translation. Whereas one Talmudic tradition regarded its production miraculous and indicative of divine intervention (presumably seventy or seventy-two sages, each working in seclusion and in ignorance of the work done by the others, produced exactly identical versions), another tradition lamented the production of this translation as a national disaster, saying that the day when the translation had been completed, was "as bitter to the people of Israel as the day when the golden calf had been fashioned."[11] The reason given to that view, namely, that the Torah in its divine uniqueness was untranslatable should be taken with a grain of salt because none of the sages had a quarrel with the second-century c.e. Jewish-Aramaic translation of the Pentateuch ascribed (wrongly) to Onkelus. On the contrary, this translation was praised and cherished and was for hundreds of years officially used in the synagogue as the weekly portion of the Torah was read on the Sabbath (the Aramaic version was read twice with the Hebrew original, which most members of the community did not understand, sandwiched between the two readings). Thus the Torah was not untranslatable as long as the translation followed the textual tradition of the Rabbis and was supervised by them, and as long as it did not replace the original Hebrew Bible (as later Greek translations done under rabbinical supervision, such as that of Aquila, were never allowed to do). The real issue was not the translatability of the holy writ, nor the imprecision and divergent glosses in parts of the Septuagint (this divergence is, of course, explainable by the translation being based on versions of the books of the Bible that were different from the ones upheld by the rabbis) but rather the threat of Hebrew being replaced by Greek, which shows that such replacing was at the time acceptable to many. What was feared was cultural usurpation rather than textual misprision.

This certainly invites comparisons between Hellenistic Jewish Alexandria and the Jewish Vienna of the turn of the nineteenth century and Jewish New York in the twentieth century. However, such comparisons, if they are not to yield facile and superficial insights, are better left to expert historians, whereas we should turn our attention here to the issues of Jewish literary multilingualism, and particularly to those of Hebrew-Yiddish literary bilingualism, in the nineteenth and twentieth centuries. Was the latter a differential or an integral bilingualism? The answer must be clear by now. Whereas the traditional, pre-modern Hebrew-Yiddish bilingualism can be, generally speaking, described as diglossic, and therefore differential (i.e., with each language allotted specific tasks and genres within the continuous space of traditional Jewish Ashkenazic culture), modern Hebrew-Yiddish bilingualism was in essence non-diglossic, and as such it progressively waxed integral. Not that the integral character of this bilingualism was clear to its practitioners from the very beginning. The early *maskilim* certainly conceived of their usage of Yiddish as ancillary and temporary, and as such, essentially diglossic. Even Abramovitsh in his first protracted phase of Hebrew-Yiddish bilingualism (from the second half of the 1860s through the 1870s) conceived of the relationship between his Hebrew writing of ideational, discursive, and scholarly texts and his Yiddish writing of prose fiction and also — alas! — poetry, in differential terms; and his way throughout the 1880s out of this differentiation and toward the integralism of his writing during the last twenty-five years of his life (he died in 1917) was fraught with grave difficulties (which are described and explained in the special chapter in this volume that focuses on Abramovitsh's bilingualism).[12] However, as soon as he started working on the creation of a double canon, in which most of his important texts would be presented in both Hebrew and Yiddish versions, he emphatically fashioned his own and his contemporaries' Hebrew-Yiddish literary bilingualism based on an integralist model.

The Hebrew-Yiddish bilingualism of Abramovitsh, his contemporaries, and disciples was integral because it was put at the service of two different literatures, each of which presumed to contain all the modalities and serve all the needs a national literature was expected to contain and serve. Thus, each of the two literatures conceived of itself as an integer, a whole number, rather than a fraction within a larger entity. In reality, the two literatures complemented each other, with each of them excelling in an area where the other one was lagging behind. Hebrew certainly had the advantage wherever either a high poetic diction or that of conceptual discourse were called for. With its long poetic tradition, going all the way back to the Middle Ages and from there to the Bible, it was the Jewish poetic language par excellence. Indeed, Hebrew poetry by far surpassed its Yiddish counterpart well into the twentieth century. Not before the flourishing of modernism in both literatures in the 1920s and 1930s was the gap between the two poetic traditions partially bridged. Pathos, inter-textual resonance, and the dexterous movement between the different layers of an ancient language, now modernized, came "naturally" to Hebrew poets, and thus their points of departure were in most cases ahead of those of the Yiddishists. Also, because it catered to better educated readers, Hebrew evolved an elastic and precise discursive style throughout the second half of the nineteenth century, as its non-fiction shed the floridity of pseudo-biblicism in the writing of masters such as Lilienblum, Y. L. Gordon, Abramovitsh, Frishman, Sokolov, and, more than all others, Achad ha'am. Thus Hebrew was more prepared to serve a literature of ideas, concepts, and criticism. It encountered, however, severe difficulties when it was faced with the tasks of creating realistic dialogue and description, in its attempts at writing prose fiction and realistic drama.[13] Here Yiddish certainly had the advantage, as indicated by Abramovitsh's decision, made as early as 1863, to write his stories, novels, and plays in Yiddish rather than in Hebrew—this, in spite of the severe cultural qualms he had had to suppress to take this step.[14] Yiddish offered him a welter of dialogical riches almost untapped by an artistic literature until then. This in itself created aesthetic difficulties, which he overcame by inventing the Mendele figure, as I have demonstrated in my book *A Traveler Disguised*.[15] However, once the Mendele persona—negotiating between dialogue, monologue, and description, between spoken dialects and a canonical literary Yiddish, and thus also between localism and Jewish generality—carried out the formidable artistic task with which it was burdened, and did it with unprecedented brilliance and excellence,[16] the trail toward the artistic Yiddish novel had been blazed. At the same time, a group of talented Hebrew novelists (Mapu, Smolenskin, Broydes) and writers of short stories (Y. L. Gordon, M. Brandshteter) were struggling with huge stylistic obstacles in their attempt at fashioning a realistic presentation of contemporary Jewish life with anything like a dialogical verisimilitude.

Thus the differences between the two literatures were real and acutely felt by the readers. Nevertheless, the dynamics of the literatures pushed their respective groups of leading writers toward overcoming these differences and gaining for "their" specific literature the advantages enjoyed by its concurrent Yiddish writers, while continuing to evolve and modernize the sturdy and workable models of prose fiction and drama they inherited from their *klassiker*, invested their best efforts in the creation of a modern Yiddish poetic tradition. With Peretz going before them, the American *Yunge* followed suit, preparing the language and creating the literary space in which the modernists, both in the United States and in eastern Europe, could act, achieve, and triumph. In Hebrew, a tremendous and highly successful effort to enhance, broaden, and deepen the realistic presentation of reality was undertaken by a host of very talented writers, both disciples and antagonists of Abramovitsh, such as Berditchevsky, Brenner, Shofman, Gnessin, Ben Tsiyon, young Agnon, A. Reuveni, A. Arieli-Orloff, Dvora Baron, and many others. The gap between Hebrew and Yiddish in this respect was all but closed long before Hebrew became the spoken language of Zionist Palestine, and the hurtle of creating a credible Hebrew dialogue had to be surmounted through any number of clever and creative stratagems.[17]

This mutual drive for integrality and wholeness in each of the two literatures represented the very essences of their parallel dynamisms. Of course, it emanated from ideological sources although not all writers impacted by it necessarily formulated a coherent ideological rationale or agreed with those who did (such as the purist Hebraists, best represented by Achad ha'am, or the committed Yiddishists as represented by Zhitlovsky or Birnbaum). Literary and cultural ideology can work and be articulated implicitly, as well as explicitly. It can inhere in the cultural and literary situation per se, and inform almost automatically those who find themselves in this situation as participants and activists. The ideologies here referred to were those of autonomous, self sustained, and auto-replenishing Hebraic versus Yiddishist secular Jewish cultures. The former would usually, albeit not always, project itself within Zionist perspectives and regard itself as the future cultural matrix of an independent, Hebrew-speaking community in Palestine, as well as those large or small communities in the Jewish Diaspora who would be guided and ethically sustained by such a community functioning as a "spiritual center." The latter would project itself within a perspective of Jewish cultural autonomy in the form of self-aware, self-educating, and to an extent, also politically self-controlling Yiddish speaking communities existing either in the midst of non-Jewish pluralist host societies or in a Jewish territory, independent or semi-independent, anywhere in the world but in Palestine. The projections were in essence mutually exclusive, and each of them insisted on the illusory nature of the other. Yiddishists rejected the Zionist dream as unrealizable and/or as reactionary or at best sustainable by small elite groups; Hebraists regarded Yiddish and its culture as ephemeral, a linguistic-cultural entity that was already being quickly eroded by the accelerating processes of Jewish acculturation both in the homelands of Ashkenazic Jews in Europe and in the immigration centers in Western countries. As mentioned previously, Achad-ha'am predicted as early as 1902 that Yiddish would be eliminated before the end of the twentieth century. Whereas many Hebrew writers disagreed with him, or at least were uneasy about the prospect of a Yiddish-less Jewish future, which he seemed to accept with perfect equanimity, the logic of his argument was that of their entire cultural-literary endeavor: Jewish "jargons" came and went; their eventual demise was unavoidable. Only Hebrew, the "eternal"-national Jewish language had, and will have, survived in the past, as well as in the future. With such parallel and contradictory ideological raisons d'être, both literatures were called upon to maximize their respective capacities to the point of total plenitude and thus, become fully able to take care of whatever cultural services the nation may require. For instance, they were called upon to harvest in their cultural granaries the best of all world literature in the form of up-to-date and adequate translations, whereas many of their historical readers at the time were proficient enough in at least one major European language in which an array of translations of the most valuable literary texts existed. The notion that Hebrew poets and writers should invest a considerable part of their creative energy in supplying their readers with a Hebrew Homer, Virgil, Shakespeare, Flaubert, Nietzsche, and even Tolstoy and Dostoevsky (the latter avidly read by many adherents of the Hebrew renaissance in the Russian originals), or that Yiddish writers should supply their readers with a Yiddish Heine, Ibsen, Hauptmann, Knut Hamsun, and Walt Whitman (scores of translations from the works of the latter appearing in the United States, where many readers were on the verge of reading Whitman in his original democratic English) made full sense only within the ideological parameters of linguistic and literary autonomy. Consciously and unconsciously it was based upon a mental image of the respective literatures as addressing monolinguistic, "normal" constituencies—imagined constituencies that would presumably materialize in the foreseeable future.

Within these ideological frameworks, each with its specific future predictions and expectations, the integral bilingualism of Abramovitsh and his followers made perfect sense—for a while. In fact, it was inevitable—as long as the public space, within which both Yiddishism and Hebraism fought over the soul of a relatively continuous community, was not torn asunder, as it would be after World War I. A writer like Abramovitsh, who had invested decades of literary toil in both Hebrew and Yiddish writing, was bound to come up with the idea of evolving a double Yiddish-Hebrew canon, which by its linguistic dualism would protect his investment whatever cultural scenario—the Yiddishist or the Hebraist—materialized in the near or distant future. To him the effort and time the realization of this monumental project demanded—a full two decades, a third of his creative career—was worthwhile, for he was a writer standing at the crossroads, refusing to give up on the road not taken, so he walked twice and traversed both roads. With endless patience and meticulous craftsmanship, he cast each of his major works in two versions, Yiddish and Hebrew, rewriting these works in the process and inventing an altogether new Hebrew Mendele persona, that of a witty and subversive scholar, rather than the cynical and loquacious folksy philosopher his Yiddish Mendele was. As one ponders from a historical distance, this backbreaking labor of love and ardor, one could not but see how, when assessed by our current criteria, it must be deemed strange, abstruse, indeed absurd. For whom, one asks, did the master prepare the Hebrew versions of his stories (for almost all his energy was invested in the adaptation of his Yiddish texts in Hebrew; translation in the opposite direction he usually left to others, even though the translators were not supposed to be acknowledged and called by name)? When Yosef Perl, seventy years earlier, undertook the translation of his Hebrew masterpiece into Yiddish, the project could have been justified in practical terms: both as an educator and as an artist, the author wished to reach the Yiddish-speaking masses to whom the Hebrew original was inaccessible, and whom he represented with flair—in the aforementioned dialogical prologue to the Yiddish version—by the figure of the *yishuvnik* (a Jew who lived in the countryside, away from the Jewish community, usually as a lessee of a farm; such people were "coarsened," being cut off from Jewish learning and ritual, and regarded as ignorant), whose appetite was wetted by the wonderful things he heard about the book he could not read. However, this definitely was not the reader Abramovitsh wished to serve. He wished to serve the turn-of-the-nineteenth-century Hebrew reader, who, as a matter of course, spoke and read Yiddish, and had already perused and enjoyed the texts, which were now served to him with a different sauce, in their Yiddish versions. This, I believe, is a quite unprecedented phenomenon in the history of translation: a text being worked upon for years with the purpose of offering it to those who have already read it with delectation. Why should a busy writer engage in such a redundancy? On top of the sheer senselessness of duplication, the writer, addressing a reading public whom he could not expect to be intrigued by the plot or characters of his tales (that reading public having become thoroughly familiar with them long before it approached the new versions), had to constantly surprise and excite his readers with stylistic fireworks since the attraction he was offering inhered in the language and the style of his narration rather than in the contents of the narrative. The overwhelming creative effort all this necessitated was, however, justified by the circumstances of the unique cultural situation, those of "biliteraturalism," that is, of two mutually competitive literatures and cultures evolving within a public space that had not yet splintered. Of course, once this space was splintered, a "Mendele project" of the kind undertaken by Abramovitsh quickly became unthinkable. But were such projects, as long as the cultural circumstances justified them, even evaluated them as supreme achievements, indicative of the continuity and integrality of a single Hebrew-Yiddish literature, as Baal-makhshoves, Niger, and Sadan believed? Of course, the very opposite was what the reality of the situation confirmed. Whoever heard about "one and only one" national literature in which an author writes the same text twice, with no practical necessity justifying the effort of duplication? It was only when the author believed he was working within the divergent contexts of two separate literatures, each with a trajectory of its own propelling it toward two totally different and mutually exclusive cultural futures, that such an anomaly could become for a time the norm. In a literature written in a cultural situation characterized by differential bilingualism or multilingualism, writers can and often do write in two or more languages and yet regard themselves as working within the confines of a single, continuous, multilinguistic literature. Yehuda Halevi's *Kuzari* belonged together with his poems within one single Jewish-Mediterranean literature. So were Ibn Gabirol's poetry and his neoplatonic philosophical treatise *Source of Life* (written in Arabic but preserved only in a Latin translation), Moshe Ibn Ezra's poetry and his Arabic treatise on Hebrew poetry, and Maimonides's Hebrew *Mishne tora* and Arabic *The Guide to the Perplexed*. All these authors conducted their writing practices by the differential rules of their literary culture. However, none of them would have dreamt of writing one text in two or more languages, for that would amount to an abrogation of the self-same rules. As Dante would not have written his Latin *Monarchia* and *De vulgari eloquentia* in the forceful and straightforward Italian of his *Vita nuova* and *Divina commedia*, and as Boccaccio would not have dreamt of writing his encyclopedic compendia (*De geneologia deorum*, *De claris mulieribus*, etc.) in the Italian of his *Decameron* or *Filostratro*, or Petrarch his *De vita solitaria* in the language of his famous sonnets; even so, the masters of the golden Spanish era of the Mediterranean-Jewish literature would not confuse and blur the linguistic boundaries set by the cultural-linguistic system that conditioned and channeled their literary production. They wrote their philosophical and scientific works in Arabic and left the translation of these works to those who wished to present them to readers who lived outside of the geographical and cultural boundaries of the aforementioned Jewish-Mediterranean sphere. Within the boundaries of the Ashkenazic diglossia of holy tongue, Yiddish writers like Levita could write scholarly texts in Hebrew and entertaining romances in Yiddish, but here too the production of any of these texts in two different linguistic versions was quite inconceivable. Literary differential bilingualism does not, as a rule, entail the fragmentation of an overall cultural-literary framework. As long as each of the languages is seen as a fraction rather than as a whole number, the unity of the entity consisting of these fractions can be maintained. As soon as literary integral bilingualism emerges, the fragmentation of the overall cultural-literary framework is already taking place. What rendered possible the kind of bilingualism or rather bi-literaturalism that Abramovitsh practiced was not the unity of a Hebrew-Yiddish literature—on the contrary, such a bilingualism, being thoroughly and purely integral, indicated the radical bifurcation of the literary progress—but the temporary continuity of a milieu, a public space, a cultural ambience, in which two contradictory powers clashed in their struggle over a hegemony, which would eventually allow for the exclusion of the rival. Such continuity was by necessity temporary, since the milieu or the ambience, being systematically polarized, would inevitably reach a point of splitting as soon as cultural conditions permitted, as they did when Hebraism became identified with the reification of the Zionist project in a Palestine that was Yiddish-repellent, and the initiation by the Soviet-Yiddish establishment of the systematic eradication of Hebrew culture and the persecution of its activists. However, the rift had become apparent long before these dramatic developments occurred. Whoever watched Y. L. Peretz closely during the last decade of his life (1905–1915) noticed how Hebrew and Hebrew writing progressively became a burden to the master, then the culture hero of the Yiddishists, which he privately wanted to be freed of (while publicly retaining the façade of bilingualism). Thus most of the Hebrew versions of his stories published during those years were actually based on translations done by others (such as the minor Hebrew novelist Y. Shaf) and slightly edited by the author. Sholem Aleichem, who wanted nothing better than to create his own Mendele-like double canon, could not realize this dream, and left the Hebrew translations of his works in the hands of his son-in-law, Y. D. Berkovits. Younger writers such as Asch, Nomberg, and Reizen, who had started bilingually, translating themselves from one language into the other, soon gave up on this ambidexterity. Thus even before World War I, the Mendele model lost one follower after another.

It became inimitable because it waxed culturally impracticable and ideologically untenable.

As noted earlier in this essay, that model gave rise to objections, with the chief objector, Berditchevsky, regarding it as culturally dangerous and aesthetically enervating. Berditchevsky, unlike Achad-ha'am and the other Hebraic purists, did not question the legitimacy of Jewish literary multilingualism. On the contrary, he believed that under existing cultural circumstances such multilingualism was not only legitimate but actually inevitable. He also did not object to writers resorting to more than one language and dividing their creative energy between them. In fact, although he was primarily a Hebrew writer, he himself left considerable Yiddish and German literary legacies. His objections—vociferous and cantankerous at times—were aimed at the Mendele model, which because of his respect for Abramovitsh's "genial" talents ("you don't quarrel with a genius"), he preferred to expose and attack in the works of other writers, particularly Y. L. Peretz.[18] In other words, he strongly rejected the notion that a single text could be written in more than one language, with each of its versions presumably of equal literary status as an independent "original," rather than as a unique and autonomous original versus its mere translation, namely, its dependent, diminished, and secondary reflection. Informed by the romantic principle of the integral unity of experience and its linguistic articulation, he could not accept the reality of a text existing in two original, linguistically differentiated versions. This, he thought, undermined the authenticity of the text in both its versions, and when such dualism became prevalent, as it was in the Hebrew and Yiddish literatures of his time, it blurred the specific "physiognomies" of both literatures and the integrity of the languages themselves whose unique "characters" were being compromised.

Berditchevsky's theories of language, translation, and the presumed uniqueness of the literary text—hardly in synch with current prevalent notions—cannot be discussed and criticized here. For the purposes of our argument, what should be somewhat elaborated on is his attitude toward the issue of differentialism versus integralism in literary multilingualism in general and in Jewish multilingualism in particular. Superficially, his campaign against the Mendele model could be seen as a call for a withdrawal from current integral bilingualism to the older Jewish differential multilingualism: what could be done in Hebrew should have been done only in Hebrew, and what could have been done in Yiddish should have been done only in Yiddish, and in an "authentic," that is, colloquial and un-Europeanized, one (Berditchevsky accused many of his Yiddish contemporaries of writing in Judaized modern German rather than in "real" Yiddish).[19] Linguistic division should thus presumably reflect a division of creative labor of the kind practiced by the great medieval masters. However, this was hardly what Berditchevsky had in mind. What he really demanded was the total separation of different Jewish literatures from one another. The various Jewish literatures, whether written in Jewish or non-Jewish languages, should insist on the preservation of the different personalities of each of them, which should not be adulterated or compromised by the proximity to, let alone the blending with, the specific personality of the others. The Mendele model was dangerous because it allowed for such approximations. When a writer resorted to more than one language—as he was perfectly allowed to do—he had to completely split himself in two or even three parts, for he was to abide by the linguistic and the mental idiom of each of the two or three different literatures he was contributing to, and be ever watchful of the boundaries between these literatures, which were never to be crossed or blurred. Abramovitsh's bi-literaturalism was therefore confusing and misguiding in its impurity. Berditchevsky insisted on the total "purity" of modern Jewish multi-litcraturalism—on uncompromised, "clean," and radical cleavages between the different Jewish literatures, separations that would clearly dissolve and annul any illusion about the existence of an *eyn-eyntsike* modern Jewish literature. Thus, as a central literary thinker of the Hebrew renaissance he was the ultimate integralist rather than a neo-differentialist. In this he was ready to follow his theoretical insights and differentiations to their bitterest and sometimes most absurd conclusions. For instance, in his German book *Vom östlichen Judentum: Religiöses, Literarisches, Politisches*, 1918 (on eastern Judaism: religion, literature, politics),[20] he never mentioned Abramovitsh as a Hebrew writer, focusing, in his discussion of the Hebrew nineteenth-century novel, on masters of "action-filled" Hebrew narrative such as Mapu, Smolenskin, and Broydes. Abramovitsh was relegated to the section dedicated in the book to Yiddish writing. Since the Hebrew versions of his major works were presumably mere translations and not original works, there was no need to mention them as contributions to the Hebrew novel. Berditchevsky discretely suppressed the fact that Abramovitsh was the most influential Hebrew writer of prose fiction at the turn of the nineteenth century because of its confusing theoretical implications.

In his own practice as a writer, Berditchevsky made every possible effort to abide by his own rules. His Hebrew writing was totally different from his Yiddish writing, and both were unlike his German writing. In each he developed an array of tonalities, which he kept strictly separate from those he used in the others. In Hebrew his articles and essays were written in a polemic, "disorderly," highly suggestive, and sometimes poetic manner, clearly influenced by that of Nietzsche's aphoristic works; whereas in his stories he either adopted the tone of an objective, old-fashioned chronicler or that of lyrical confession bordering on stream-of-consciousness narration. These tonalities were never employed in his Yiddish and German works. In the latter, non-fiction and scholarly texts would be written in the methodical manner characteristic of German conceptual discourse and replete with the terminology and jargon characteristic of that discourse. Short stories, no matter how close they were in content to some of the Hebrew stories, were written with an omniscient narrator setting their somewhat humoristic tonality and conveying the feeling of *Distanz* a German (or German Jewish) reader was supposed to experience when reading about the affairs of people in far-off eastern European villages. Berditchevsky tried to write in German an *Ich-Roman*, a confessional-lyrical novel with a first person narrator. Significantly, the project, although much work had been invested in it, never took off. What was eminently possible in Hebrew, was—for Berditchevsky—impossible in German—that, in spite of German literature offering any number of *Ich-Roman* models that Berditchevsky knew and admired. In Yiddish the writer adopted a totally new semi-folksy persona, whose somewhat ambivalent position was conveyed through its appellation: *a vayten korev* (a distant relative). Everything he wrote in this language smacked of intentional (and never really effortless) colloquialism and folksy intimacy. Even the literary criticism he wrote in this language assumed the form of a *shmus* (free, rambling conversation) and was never burdened by professional critical jargon or abstract aesthetic concepts. However, the fact that Berditchevsky insisted on writing literary criticism also in Yiddish amounted to a clear indication of his "integralist" intention to develop in each Jewish literature, in accordance with its specific personality or character, all the genres he was the master of. A decision to write literary criticism in Hebrew, pseudo folktales in Yiddish, and Jewish philological and literary scholarship in German would have been reminiscent of a differential approach. But Berditchevsky wrote—differently—literary criticism and pseudo-folktales in Hebrew, Yiddish, and German (in the latter, helped by his talented wife, Rachel Ramberg, in the form of adaptations of tales from the Midrash and Jewish medieval novellas). He wrote—differently—literary and social criticism and texts of Jewish scholarship in both German and Hebrew. In every way his legacy demonstrated how under modern conditions, each Jewish literature had to follow its own trajectory, even when written by a single writer and on matters and topics that were, by and large, identical. Thus he was, both as a theoretician and as a patrician, the prophet and exponent of modern Jewish multi-literaturalism.

Ten

Contiguity: Franz Kafka's Standing Within
the Modern Jewish Literary Complex

> Each of the two languages, Yiddish and Hebrew—although appar-
> ently developed by a single people—is a separate world unto itself.
> We can open windows from one to the other, but we cannot weld
> them into a single world.
>
> M. Y. Berditchevsky: "From Language to Language"[1]

Under the conditions we described, there could not exist a unified Jewish literature, and by the same token, there did not (and does not) exist one "modern Jewish canon." This is not the place to delve into the
complex issue of the aesthetic dynamics and politics of canonization
and canonicity; an issue that recently has attracted scores of scholars,
critics, and literary theorists engaged in the post-modernist dialogue in
general and in minority discourse theory in particular.[2] We know now
how canonization processes were always used—both consciously and
intentionally and also semi-consciously and naively—by elite groups
with vested interests in the promulgation and preservation of a certain
socio-cultural order for the purpose of super-imposing their preferences
on those who might have had different ones, thus inventing "great traditions" that legitimized their interests and marginalized those of the
others, and by and large working through appreciation and deprecia-
tion, through exclusion and inclusion, rewards and punishments, and
so on, projecting a value system favorable to their socio-cultural inclinations and commitments. The lesson we have been taught will not be
forgotten; nor will we avoid the historian's duty to examine accepted
canons critically, even distrustfully, and to unravel them where necessary. At the same time, however, we also must remember that canonization, being an unavoidable and indeed indispensable part of the process
of literary production and consumption, is in and of itself an aspect of   303
the objective historical reality of literature and the arts. As such, it calls
for meticulous and as-objective-as-possible examination on the part of
the literary scholar. As much as it is and must be an open-ended process

with the present and its concerns unavoidably impacting the view of the historical past, that past must also be given a say in deciding the direction in which this process and its scholarly rationalization can proceed. A new critic can (indeed, must) try to redefine tradition, but he cannot do this in a vacuum. He must inject his new insights and preferences into the concrete historical tissue, or the new serum would never be felt by the literary "body politic." Since each of the different modern Jewish literatures evolved its own canonization processes, propelled by the specific ideological undercurrents that flowed from the central rationale of the respective literature and informed by a dynamics that prescribed specific acts of inclusion and exclusion and centering and marginalization, no over-all Jewish canon can seriously be projected. In the literature of the Hebrew nationalist renaissance, the figures who counted more than others were Abramovitsh, Achad ha'am, Berditchevsky, Bialik, Tchernikhovsky, and Brenner. Of these three (Achad ha'am, Tchernikhovsky, and Brenner) had no place whatsoever in the contemporary Yiddish canon, two (Bialik and Berditchevsky) occupied in it very minor corners, and only one (Abramovitsh) was as central to the Yiddish canon as he was to the Hebrew one. By the same token, of the Yiddish contemporary "elect," Abramovitsh, Sholem Aleichem, Peretz, Asch, and Bergelson, only Abramovitsh was at the center of the rival canon, with Peretz lagging far behind as an important but by no means central writer of prose fiction. As we have seen, this had to do not only with the respective merits of each of the writers' contributions to their literatures, but also, and as importantly, with the ideological frames of reference within which these contributions were made. The same ideological context that elevated Peretz to the position of the culture-hero of Yiddishism barred him, in spite of his many excellent Hebrew short stories, from coming even close to the inner circles of the contemporary Hebrew canon. By the same token, and even more so, the qualities in Berditchevsky's personality and Hebrew work, which mesmerized his Hebraic followers, rendered his presence as a Yiddish writer quite unnoticeable (Peretz's strong disapproval all but sealed the fate of his Yiddish persona depriving it of substantial presence). These are facts that we can view and interpret in different ways; however, as facts they cannot be overlooked nor can their impact be minimized. A modern Jewish canon in which

Achad ha'am or Tchernikhovsky do not significantly figure is a travesty as far as the Hebrew reader aware of his literary tradition is concerned. By the same token, such a reader would never understand the total marginalization of Gnessin and the absence in the Jewish canon of Shteynberg. Not surprisingly, all attempts by modern scholars at projecting the existence of a general Jewish canon failed and were immediately seen through and exposed as unconvincing, as well as diffusing rather than focusing our critical thinking about the modern Jewish literary complex. Ruth R. Wisse's *The Modern Jewish Canon: A Journey Through Language and Culture* (2000), based on the strange (and unacceptable) decision to limit the canon almost exclusively to prose fiction failed to make a convincing case even for the proposition that there existed a modern Jewish narrative art that could be subsumed under whatever unifying concept, let it be labeled canon, tradition, or what have you. Of course, any critic is welcome to devise any anthology of modern Jewish writing he or she finds more attractive or edifying than its many possible alternatives, provided he or she cogently explains the rationale of the choice, and why the particular selection is significant and worthy of being shared with others. However, as intelligent and illuminating as the explanation may be, it can hardly enhance our thinking about the Jewish literary complex as a whole; for what can such anthologizing suggest if not another line of continuity, or yet another binary opposition of continuity versus discontinuity, superimposing an illusory order upon a vast cultural space where neither the concept of continuity nor that of discontinuity sheds much light. Indeed, as said before, a new Jewish literary thinking—a renewed theory of Jewish literatures, if you want—to be worth even a small part of the effort it would demand, must start by sloughing off those concepts, which in the past had imposed such severe limitations upon the old theory, and eventually doomed it to an untimely demise. The new thinking should leave continuities behind it (not that they do not exist, at least as helpful ancillary syntagms; but they are of secondary importance and have been overly studied and focused on) and focus instead on contiguities or tangentialities.

But what can be the concrete meaning of concepts such as contiguity (the state of being a borderline, of being in contact with something) or tangentiality (the position of a straight line or plane that touches a curvature at a point but if extended would not cross it at that point; which when used metaphorically points to a relatedness, a touching, which does not involve overlapping or penetration; a diminished form of relatedness), and how would they enhance our understanding of the Jewish literary complex? Of course, traditional and modern literary theory dealt with various modalities of literary contacts or touching. Old positivist theories offered causal explanations of literary phenomena in terms of influence and development, both conveying some sort of contact between one phenomenon and others, which the former engendered or endowed with a certain shape and direction. When modernist theory abandoned causal-positivist explanations of literary phenomena, the concept of "tradition" (particularly as developed by T. S. Eliot) replaced that of influence. Then the concept of influence, or rather of the *Anxiety of Influence*, was revived by Harold Bloom within a Freudian paradigm of literary history as a family romance where sons both mutilated and reinvented their fathers. Beyond such concepts implying some kind of "contact," lay other concepts, such as intertextuality, or the dialogue one writer conducts with the work of another through quotations, reference, subversion, defamiliarization (the Russian formalists famous *ostranenye*), parody, pastiche, and so on. Thus both literary continuity and innovation were explained by one or another brand of a dialectical thesis–anti-thesis–synthesis cycle: the dialectics of the son fending off the presence of the father with the help of the grandfather (the Russian formalists, who in their theory of "literary evolution" were every bit as Hegelian-oriented as were their Marxist enemies), or the dialectics of "misprision," based on the principle of the Oedipus complex, in itself a Hegelian paradigm with its thesis (father), anti-thesis (son), and synthesis (the balanced personality of the son who successfully worked through his Oedipus complex and overcame it, thus becoming ready to properly play the role of a father). To all these, sociological literary criticism added its important lessons, teaching us how to detect overt and covert contacts between members of the same literary "generation" or followers of the same literary trend or writers who were motivated or formed by a similar socio-political experience.

The problem with all these concepts, each of them helpful in its own way, is that all of them take us back with more or less emphasis to the matrix of continuity, from which we want and must break free. To be useful for us, contiguity must imply a kind of a light or diminished contact that would not throw us back into that trap; a contact that avoids all permanencies, is in flux, can be seen as random, and yet as indicative of mobility—free and unfettered—within a space that is vast and open, but then also, in the final analysis, not infinite, because it is circumscribed by a borderline, which can be very fine and barely noticed or deeply and clearly etched. In our case, this is the borderline of Jewishness; not of Judaism as a religious, civilizational, or national entity, "essence," or system, but of the perception of reality through (or also through) the screen of the experience of being "a Jew in the world," to use Buber's phrase[3]—an experience that can be as divergent and multifarious as that of being in love or of being sick. The German language aptly conveys our idea when it differentiates between *Jude*, *Judentum* or *Judaismus*, and *Judesein*—Jew, Judaism, and being a Jew. A Jew can be totally distanced from Judaism and yet share the experience of *Judesein*. One also can be oblivious of this experience or repress it; but when one does not do that, and one is a writer, one's writing would be—among many other things-"Jewish"; and this being experientially Jewish—no matter how the experience is perceived and evaluated, and also independently of its importance or centrality in the writer's overall perception of reality—is the only shibboleth that decides a writer's belonging or not belonging within the Jewish literary complex as much as it also supplies the only possible definition of the complex as a literary space. (This, provided that the term "belonging" itself is redefined or understood as non-exclusionary—a writer can simultaneously "belong" in many categories—his being a Jewish writer does not bar him from also being a German, a Russian, an American, or an Israeli one.) The concepts of contiguity and tangentiality should help us to understand the modalities of mobility within that space, the Jewish literary complex; a mobility, which often enough brings those or some of those who happen to share it—synchronically or diachronically—into some kind of contact, which can be strong and deeply experienced but also slight and non-penetrative. Thus, while these concepts can be seen as subsuming the more familiar ones such as influence, intertextuality, subversion, defamiliarization, and so on, they cannot be subsumed by any of them, for they must also convey other kinds of contacts—unintentional, unfocused, airy. As such, they must enable us to see contacts where they have not been detected yet. They must help us in reifying intuitions that have told us that within the space of literary *Judesein*, strange and wonderful encounters are discreetly and even unconsciously taking place, which the conventional critical imagination would never have dreamt were possible. It is only if they would do that, if they could take us to places vaguely surmised but never known, that they would help us in breaking through the barriers, which about half a century ago had more or less brought to a halt the critical quest whose greatest navigator was Sadan.

Clearly, to become really usable, the concepts must be pondered and then further developed within a full-scale theoretical-literary investigation, which this essay cannot presume to conduct. Nevertheless, in an attempt to render them somewhat less opaque they should be somewhat reified through at least one example of what seems to us a significant contact between two quintessentially modern Jewish writers whom no conventional wisdom would yoke together. One of these two is Franz Kafka, whom I believe any serious consideration of the modern Jewish literary complex must target as one of its most central figures of interest. Turning to Kafka, however, we should try, as much as possible, to superimpose upon our image (undoubtedly a justified one) of him as a bastion of German and European literary modernism of the twentieth century and a writer deeply rooted in German (Kleist) and other European (Flaubert,[4] Tolstoy, Dostoevsky) literary traditions, another image—the one entertained by the writer himself, who genuinely did not know to what literature he "belonged," and whether he belonged to any literary tradition at all. To Kafka, as we know, writing was both an obsession and an impossible venture, for while being mimetic, it "lacked the independence of the world." Unlike the maid who tended the fire or the cat who warmed itself by the stove, the writer had to either describe the maid and the cat or use them in a metaphorical context (the latter being necessarily fuzzy, and among the "things which make me despair of writing"). Thus the activities of the maid and the cat were "independent—ruled by their own laws," whereas "writing is helpless, cannot live in itself, is a joke and a despair."[5] In other words, whereas what literature referred to was "true," literature itself usually was devious, the written words being rarely "as distinct and frighteningly physical" as "this hand with which I write."[6] This, however, did not mean that literature and its words were devoid of potency of their own; only this could often be a demonic and self-destructive potency. For the more one writes, the more one realizes how "every word, twisted in the hands of the spirits—this twist of the hand is their characteristic gesture—becomes a spear turned against the speaker. Most especially a remark like this. And so ad infinitum."[7]

Not forgetting this overall context, it is nevertheless worthwhile to reexamine what Kafka said about Jewish writing; for the problematic nature of modern Jewish writing, and particularly of Jewish writing like his, which could not be done in any but the German language, and yet could never become truly German, intensely occupied his thoughts. In the already quoted letter that Kafka wrote to Brod in June 1921, he viscerally reacted to the issues contemporary Jewish German writers faced, to the ambience of "the small world of German-Jewish writing" in general, and to the brilliance of German-Jewish wit, which was best represented by the lethal irony and sarcasm characteristic of the satirical writings of Karl Kraus, which Kafka found delectable and repugnant at one and the same time.[8] This well-honed wit, which rendered Kraus the very impersonation of "the principle" informing German-Jewish writing as a whole, also relegated his writing, and therefore German-Jewish writing as a whole, to the category Kafka, as previously indicated, dubbed *mauscheln* (a verb derived from the Jewish name Moshe and describing the Yiddishized, ungrammatical German, as well as the body language of the itinerant Jewish peddler) "taken in the wider sense [i.e., metaphorically. D.M.], and that is the only way it should be taken." As elevated *mauscheln*, the writing under discussion here often amounted to nothing more than "self pitying appropriation of someone else's property."[9] That was why German-writing Jews did not really produce a German literature. Actually the issue of *mauscheln* was not used by Kafka as a one-way street. In his hands this term of abjection, with its unmistakable anti-Semitic overtones, became double-edged, cutting in both the negative and the positive directions. Overtly, it was used with the clear intention of belittling the contribution Jewish writers had made to German literature; whereas, covertly, it may have hinted that this contribution, whatever it was, had been made within a framework other than that of German literature. Kafka wrote:

> German literature existed before the emancipation of Jews and attained great glory. After all, that literature was, as far as I can see, in no way less varied than today—in fact, today there may be less variety. And there is a relationship between all this and Jewishness, or more precisely between young Jews and their Jewishness. . . . Psychoanalysis lays stress on the father-complex. . . . In this case I prefer another version, where the issue revolves not around the innocent father but around the father's Jewishness. Most young Jews who began to write German wanted to leave Jewishness behind them. . . . but with their posterior legs they were still glued to their fathers' Jewishness and with their waving anterior legs they found no new ground. Thus ensuing despair became their inspiration. . . . The product of their despair could not be German literature, though outwardly it seemed to be so. They existed among three impossibilities, which I just happen to call linguistic impossibilities:. . . . the impossibility of not writing, the impossibility of writing German, the impossibility of writing differently.[10]

This, by now, famous formulation, quoted and then discussed at length by Gilles Deleuze and Felix Guattari in their seminal essay *Kafka: Toward a Minor Literature*[11] should serve us in the present context for a purpose somewhat different from that of the French philosophers, although not necessarily contradicting it. Whereas Deleuze and Guattari found in Kafka's extraordinary formulations the essence of what they called "minor literature" (i.e., a literature written in a "de-territorialized" major language, refraining from artificially enriching the impoverished idiom, but, on the contrary, burrowing into it for the purpose of eliciting from it a heightened expressive tension, thus charging itself, directly and indirectly, with collective-political significance),[12] we may find in them one of the most sensitive and cogent descriptions of what we call the Jewish literary complex; for what was the upshot of Kafka's list of three mutually contradicting impossibilities if not an implicit acknowledgement of the sheer existence of that complex and the delicate demarcation of its outer boundaries along the fault line separating the "impossible to write" (which was what literature as a whole was; only Jewish literary writing was "more so") from the "impossible not to write," (which was the only justification of literature, including its various Jewish brands). Since Jews, or at least some Jews, wished to write and be accepted as German writers, and often were accepted as such, but for both intrinsic and extrinsic reasons (the former by far outweighing the latter in importance) found their work not entirely belonging within the German matrix, this work of theirs also belonged within another, rather diffuse, literary entity that was related to the fact that their "failure" as German writers had to do with their being Jewish. As German writers, Kafka said, they produced "a gypsy literature which had stolen the German child out of its cradle and in great haste put it through some kind of training, for someone has to dance on the tightrope. But it wasn't even a German child, it was nothing; people only said that somebody was dancing . . ."[13]

However, Kafka himself acknowledged the untenability of this devastating verdict. Hemmed in by their "three impossibilities," German-Jewish writers were left with despair (*Verzweiflung*) as their only source of inspiration, he said; but then, he had to ask himself what was wrong with that; for as much as drawing inspiration from despair might have barred those writers from being truly "German" ("The product of their despair could not be German literature"), in and of itself it did not diminish the value of their writing, since despair was "an inspiration as honorable as any other"[14] (who could attest to the veracity of this dictum with more authority than Kafka?). Thus the cradle could not have been truly empty, whether the child in it was German or not. Of course, the works of Heine, Kraus, Kafka, Walter Benjamin, Paul Célan and so many others amounted to so much more than a "nothing." Somebody *was* dancing on the tightrope, and what an extraordinary dancer he was. Could all those who "merely said that somebody was dancing" have been hallucinating or fantasizing? Did they actually see a dancer of sorts? And since no one could know "the dancer from the dance," there must have been there, somewhere, not only worthwhile writers but also a worthwhile literature. The entire "spectacle" was the dynamic embodiment of a kind of a liminal Jewish literary phenomenon, which flourished on both sides of the borderline that separated the various non-Jewish national literatures from whatever did not "belong" in them. Indeed, Kafka's brilliant metaphor shed light on the outer reaches

of a Jewish literary complex, the fuzzy end of a galaxy. The farther from
that borderline one moved inward, away from the specific non-Jewish
national literature under discussion (in this case, German literature),
the deeper one penetrated the galaxy, and the more chances one stood
of seeing how disparate bodies roaming within that complex came in
touch, whether gently or collisionally, intentionally or randomly, directly or obliquely; for the complex was awash with a variety of literary
entities, some of which achieved, temporarily rather than permanently,
contiguity with one or some of the others. Were Kafka's metaphors
and the rationale one could elicit from them not superior as historical models to Sadan's simplistic and untenable "by Jews for Jews" formula? Sadan's mistake emanated, of course, from his very projection of
a unified or continuous single Jewish literature, a catholic *sifrut yisra'el*.
Since no such literature existed, none of its descriptions or definitions
proved pertinent. But that did not necessarily mean that "nothing" existed. Something, which was neither a ghost nor a figment of anybody's
imagination, did in fact exist; but it was not "a Jewish literature," a
sifrut yisra'el. Rather it was a conglomerate of literary entities of different kinds, sizes, and extents of longevity. Not all of them amounted to
literatures, fully equipped with all the habitual literary accoutrements.
Some—the Hebrew and the Yiddish ones, for example, did, while others did not. Thus, the Jewish literary complex did not necessarily fall
into either the category of a minor literature (in the sense imputed to
the term by Deleuze and Guattari) or that of a major one, whatever the
definition of literary majority. As a matter of fact, the differentiation between the two kinds of literature is not conducive to the understanding
of the dynamics of the complex. Whereas Yiddish literature was mostly
"minor" in the Deleuzian sense (particularly in America, where Yiddish existed as a "de-territorialized" language), Hebrew literature, particularly since the language had been re-territorialized, but even before
then, was marked by some of the characteristics of a major literature
(which, of course, did not at all mean that it also was a better one). It
would be rather difficult to conceive of writers such as Bruno Schulz,
Babel, and Bellow as contributors to a minor literature. However, once
we make the Jewish literary complex as a whole our subject of study,
we can safely put aside the major/minor, as well as many other binary

oppositions; for what really counts is the dynamics of the complex as dictated by the movement of diverse entities within it, the brands of contiguity these entities formed when coming in touch with each other, and their mutual "sympathies" and rejections. It is through the example of Kafka that we illustrate some of the latter, starting with his reaction to contemporary Yiddish and Hebrew literatures; a reaction that the extensive Kafka scholarship has only half understood because it focused exclusively on Kafka's attachment to Yiddish, and by overlooking the Hebrew component of the equation, partly misunderstood the Yiddish one as well. True, the so-called Hebrew component found only rare and muted articulations in Kafka's diaries, letters, and so on, and as such, was hardly noticeable to whomever was not fully sensible of the role Hebrew and its culture played in the mind of people, who like Kafka, were deeply intrigued by the rebirth of a modern, secular Jewish culture in the era of its nationalist renaissance. Our purpose here is to fill this gap and, thus, shed some light on the dynamism of the Jewish literary complex during that era.

✳

Kafka, as is well known, knew Judaism in his childhood and early youth only through the ritual of the synagogue or rather "temple" (for the synagogue he knew was that of the assimilated, Germanized, middle-class Jewish society), from which he recoiled since it struck him as hollow, formalistic, and devoid of any experiential content. This recoiling had much to do with his ambivalent relationship with his father—to him, the representative of this ossified Judaism and the one who demanded loyalty to it.[15] In his late twenties, however, he was brought back to adult awareness of his Jewishness as a person and artist by the Zionism of the circle of Prague Jewish German writers and intellectuals to which he became attached, particularly by that of his closest friends, Brod and Felix Weltsch, and at the same time by his encounter with the Yiddish theater and through it, also with Yiddish and its literature. Whereas the first of these two developments occurred when he launched his career as a writer in the second half of the first decade of the twentieth century, the second took place as he stood on the verge of finding his true literary voice, just before the superbly creative year (1912), in which he wrote "The Judgment," *The Metamorphosis*, and most of the existing segments of the unfinished novel *The Man Who Went Missing* (incorrectly labeled by Brod *America*). It has become almost a truism to connect this portentous awakening to literary greatness with this double and inherently conflictive encounter (Zionism/Yiddish), as well as with the author's seriously established love relationship with his Jewish fiancée-to-become, Felice Bauer (Kafka's earlier love affairs had been short summer dalliances). Felice was a Hebrew-learner and a Zionist (with Kafka supporting and even prodding her onward in her activities as a Zionist), and both made a decision—in the first evening of their acquaintance (in the apartment of Brod's parents)—to travel together to Palestine, for a visit, and perhaps also as preparation for a future aliya (immigration in the laudatory Zionist parlance; the word actually means elevation, upward movement). At the same time, Kafka immersed himself—for a few months—in his fascination with the Yiddish theater and the Yiddish language. As mentioned previously, there was a discrepancy, in fact, a real contradiction, between these two forms of Jewish self-awareness— Zionism, Hebrew, and Palestine on the one hand, and Yiddish theater and literature, on the other hand; a contradiction Kafka seemed—but only seemed—unaware of.

His love affair with Yiddish started quite abruptly in early autumn 1911 when a traveling troupe of Yiddish actors came from the provincial Galician capital of Lemberg (nowadays Lviv)and settled in Prague for the autumn and part of the winter of 1912. It was an infatuation, and nothing less than bizarre, although Kafka's biographers, particularly the German ones (Wagenbach, Stach, André Peter Alt) would hardly call it that (for fear of sounding anti-Semitic?). This particular Yiddish-Galician ensemble was not the first one to court the interest of Prague Jews. A year earlier another ensemble had appeared, most probably as non-professional as the current one. But then, for whatever reason, Kafka did not catch the bug. Although he had attended some of the shows the ensemble had staged, he did not deign as much as to mention them in his diary. Now he did not let an evening go without frequenting the Savoy, a second-rate hotel-restaurant, on the tiny stage of which the troupe performed its repertoire, which was the stock-in-trade of such wandering Yiddish troupes (who called themselves Jewish-German and spoke, on stage, a quasi-Germanized Yiddish):[16] operettas by Goldfaden; "shocking" melodramas of betrayal, villainy, murder, and, of course, of ill-starred pure-hearted lovers; which were either slipshod adaptations of European and American boulevard dramas or original concoctions by three-penny "dramaturges" (such as Yosef Latayner, Khaykl Hurwitz, Zigmunt Faynman, Moyshe Richter, and their ilk), who supplied the Yiddish theaters of Manhattan's Lower East Side and London's Whitechapel or wandering Yiddish troupes in Poland with grist for their mills. Or they would put on the somewhat better fare penned by Goldfaden, the so-called father of the Yiddish theater, the author and composer of Yiddish operettas such as *Shulamith* and *The Witch*, and Ya'akov Gordin, the chief literary playwright of the New York Yiddish stage at the turn of the nineteenth century and the author of serious melodramas, among them domesticated "Jewish" versions of *King Lear* and *Faust*. The elegant (he was always a meticulous and brisk dresser; indeed as the American Kafka expert Mark Anderson has shown, a veritable "dandy" in his own way[17]) and highly critical Kafka, who never missed a premiere of an Arthur Schnitzler play, but systematically found the products of the acclaimed Viennese playwright flat and unsatisfactory, was spell bound. He watched again and again the rather inane dramas played in the Savoy by semi-professional actors in a language he only half understood. Late at night, not before he had spent some time with the actors, particularly with Manya Tshizhik (to whom he played the role of a theatrical admirer and a prospective lover), and more importantly, with the young male "star" Yitskhak Levy, he would go home and spend hours recording in his diary with his habitual attention to the slightest detail and in dreadful seriousness the plots of the nondescript dramas, which he learned by heart. He twice watched Goldfaden's "historical" operetta *Shulamith* (it was actually "a real opera and not a mere operetta," he indignantly insisted),[18] and no doubt hummed to himself the "hit" lyric of the play, "*In beys hamikdesh in a vinkele kheyder*" ["In the Jerusalemite temple, in a far off chamber"], known better by its mellifluous refrain as "*rozhikalekh un mandlen*" [little raisins and almonds]), which Manya Tshizhik, playing the role of a girl who went crazy because she was deserted by her lover who had married somebody else, responding to protracted applause, sang three or four times as an encore. He would remember at least the refrain so well, that when writing *The Metamorphosis* about ten months later, he would make Gregor Samsa's sister offer her brother, a young travel agent who had morphed into a "monstrous vermin," a dinner fit for an insect, consisting of half-rotten vegetables, a piece of moldy cheese, some left-over sauce, but also *"ein paar Rosinen und Mandeln"*[19] (a few raisins and almonds). Why were the raisins and almonds, quite unnecessarily, thrown into the unappealing menu (of course, Gregor pushed them aside, so that their smell would not interfere with his real enjoyment of the rancid leftovers)? Probably because the author wanted to send a secret message to his Jewish friends, who had watched *Shulamith* with him, and were the only ones who could understand the Jewish hint or joke.

Kafka was clearly fascinated with the Jewish—or rather Yiddish—body he saw displayed on the little stage: ugly, funny, attractive in its repulsiveness. He was both attracted and repelled by the charms of frumpy Jewish bohemianism. On the one hand, he "courted" Manya Tshizhik and perhaps was also drawn to Levy in a manner that was all but homoerotic. On the other hand, he was afraid of catching lice from his new friends and was disgusted with Levy's gonorrhea. In any case, he meticulously described in his diary the exaggerated movements and gestures of the actors; how they danced Hasidic dances holding in their hands the clapped on side locks that were about to drop; how the actresses, equipped with wide backsides, kept bumping them against the men actors—either because the stage was so tiny or because they wanted to elicit laughter from the public; how the prima donna, Ms. Tshizhik, spread her hair so that it would cover the strange protrusions on the skin of her face; and how her "manly mouth" was surprisingly devoid of the slight moustache, which usually went together with such mouths. He particularly liked the posture, gestures, and voice inflexions of Levy, a Warsaw yeshiva student, who had fled his Hasidic home, worked as a laborer in a Parisian factory, then opted for the life—from hand-to-mouth—of a wandering actor and bohemian. Dr. Kafka became both a "groupie" and a patron of Levy. As the "Representative of the government" (Kafka's own, sardonic self description; was he not an im-

portant employee of the governmental insurance company, responsible
for checking industrial accidents throughout a large part of Bohemia,
and then paying injured workers their compensations, which, nobody
knew better than he, were fraudulently reduced to a minimum?!), he
protected him. When Levy once, in a scuffle with other actors, tore the
curtain of the Savoy's stage and was collared by a waiter and thrown out
to the rainy autumnal street, Kafka hastened to his rescue.[20] Otherwise,
he would spend with him countless afternoons, guiding him through
the quaint romantic alleys of old Prague, visit him in his hotel room
for the purpose of learning from him about Yiddish literature and the
Talmud—all these to the mounting chagrin and exasperation of his parents, Hermann and Julie Kafka, who regarded Levy as something the
cat dragged in, absolutely not *Salonfähig*, and their son as someone who
quite criminally wasted the precious time he should have dedicated to
the asbestos factory he half-owned (together with his fresh brother-in-
law, Karl Hermann; both partners were financed by Hermann Kafka—
Karl's money was his wife's dowry; Franz's was given in the hope that
he would eventually give up his position as a *Concipist* (junior official)
and become an independent entrepreneur. In the meantime, he was
supposed to take care of the family's investment and see that its hard-
earned capital was not being squandered, which he consistently failed to
do. The project went bankrupt within a short time.[21] Hermann did not
mince words, telling his son that his protégé was "vermin," a dirty vagabond, and reminding him that whoever went to bed with a lousy dog
should expect to wake up with lice.[22] Franz, deeply offended, never forgot this and would bring it up in the long list of complaints contained
in his rather narcissistic *Brief an den Vater*,[23] in spite of the fact that his
own attitude toward the Yiddish troupe in general and Levy in particular was deeply ambivalent, certainly not free of prejudices and stereo-
typical images, informed by strong, not fully conscious affect triggered
by what was to him the personification of the Jewish "body." Attracted
and at the same time repelled by Levy, he was nevertheless fascinated by
him in a particularly muddled manner, regarding him as having become
"indispensable" to him. To him, Levy was the representative *Ostjude*,
an authentic exponent of an old religious civilization replete with old-
world intimacy and emotionalism, weak and deformed, and yet also

strong and alluring. He totally disregarded the fact that the actor was a secularist, who fled his yeshiva and whatever it stood for, regarded himself as a modernist and as an inspiring artist, who was fully aware of the inadequacy of his own stagecraft and aspired to nothing better than the elevation of the contemporary Yiddish theater to the level of the famous Viennese Burgtheater. In this respect, as in many others, he was very much like Leo Rafalesko (originally Leyb Rafalovitsh), the protagonist of Sholem Aleichem's comic-tragic theater novel *Wandering Stars*, which was being published in weekly sequels in the same days and months Kafka was struck with the magic of Levy and Tshizhik. As a matter of fact, it is through this novel and its satirical exposé of the life and "art" of theatrical troupes such as those of Shtchupak and Muravsky; Getsl, the son of Getsl; and Holtsman and Shvalb; that we can get a full and realistic picture of the troupe that caught the attention of Kafka and some of the other Prague Jewish intellectuals, understand why they functioned the way they did—why, for instance they would speak Germanized Yiddish when they could have used their Galician or Bessarabian Yiddish, and so on.

The actor, of course, saw through his patron's misunderstanding or unwillingness to see in him the real person he was, and although he took from him everything he could get and demanded more (he would go on writing to him, asking for money), he could hardly have had a high opinion of his admirer's perception. Twenty years later, in an article he published in the Warsaw literary weekly *Literarishe bleter* on the occasion of Max Brod's fiftieth anniversary, he referred to his patron in passing as "the strange writer" and made much of his connections with the respectable and well-known Dr. Brod, a writer of wide European reputation. Nevertheless, he allowed himself a light and ironic tone even with regard to him and the entire circle of Prague's Jewish intellectuals, who, he said, were "excited and attracted" by the "religious and exotic qualities of Eastern Jewry," and no doubt made fools of themselves by taking for good money the "classics" they played: "Latayner, Hurwitz, and Company." To the readers of the Yiddish weekly in 1934, the latter were charlatans and hacks, and the pleasure their plays gave to those highly educated but presumably not-too-clever half-*Yekkes* of Prague must have been a subject for jokes and derisive comments, as they certainly were for Levy himself. One can almost hear his groan of impatience and the barely repressed tittering as after each show he would be sent—his heavy "Hasidic" make-up barely washed off—by the manager of the ensemble to his "admirers," Dr. Brod, Dr. Kafka, Dr. Hugo Bergman, and the other Drs. whom he was supposed to engage in learned conversations about Talmud, Cabbala, Zohar, Hasidism, Hebrew and Yiddish litera-ture, and so on; he, Levy himself, being a half-educated youngster, who knew about most of these matters only the little he had brought with him from home and the yeshiva. Once, he remembered, he had been unable to countenance these intellectuals' smug adoration of the exotic traditional Jewish fur hats (the *shtraymlekh*) and silken *kapotas*, as well as of all those other things young eastern European Jews like himself were only too glad to have shed and gotten rid of, and he told them to their faces: "the fanatic eastern European Jewry can impress you mod-ern, cultivated Jews, but we are happy that we pulled ourselves out and freed ourselves from this world." Brod "only smiled good naturedly."[24] Kafka, it would seem, never heard what he did not want to hear, for he would have otherwise recorded Levy's civilized rebuke in his diaries (as he recorded almost everything the actors said: for instance, an alterca-tion between Levy and Manya; the latter, being a fiery socialist, admired the poetry of the anarchist poet David Edelshtat, whereas Levy preferred that of Morris Rosenfeld, a socialist, too, but tarnished by his Zionist inclinations).[25] In the reaction of those Prague intellectuals to the Yid-dish theater there was more than a modicum of willed stupidity and self-serving smugness. The Yiddish actors were to them just figments of their own imagination, not real people. Kafka's ambivalent identification with Levy was thoroughly theatrical, in the sense that it was the identification of an observer, a member of an audience, with a make-believe person, an image, which fed his cherished fantasies.

Be that as it may, Kafka enjoyed not only the Yiddish shows but also "recitals" (solo-readings) given by Levy, in which the actor would be given free range for exhibiting his various talents (he was also a re-citer of poetry and a reader of humoresques, which, unlike the stuff he had to play on the stage, was of a canonical level) and also make some much needed money. The better known of these occasions (which he meticulously recorded in his diary, dwelling on voice inflections and body language, as well as on contents) took place just before Levy's leave-taking of Prague and his patrons there, on February 18, 1912. It was Kafka himself who arranged for this recital to take place and who also introduced the evening. In vain he sought to enlist the help of others in the preparation of the event. He tried, unsuccessfully, to harness the young members of the Bar Kochba Zionist students club (the same club in which, a few years earlier, Buber had read his famous "Three Lectures on Judaism" that Kafka attended). But the young activists, all ardent Hebraists—whether they knew or yet did not know Hebrew—and believers in the return to the ancient sources, were uninterested in enhancing a Yiddishist agenda. So he drafted his friend, the blind writer Oskar Baum, demanding from the poor man to be the moderator of the evening, introduce the actor, and open his recital with a short description of Yiddish and its charms—a language the prospective audience, respectable and well-off members of the city's Jewish middle class, despised and disassociated themselves from. However, Baum, albeit a timid man of good will, bolted at the last moment, so Kafka, in addition to renting a hall, writing the invitations, printing the announcements, and defraying all costs, reconciled himself to the delivering of the introductory keynote speech, the only public speech he ever gave—with the exception of professional papers on work-related accidents that he delivered in factories and various conferences as the representative of the state-run insurance agency he worked for[26]—his *Einleitungsvortrag über Jargon* (Introductory Lecture about Yiddish).[27] For the purpose of doing that, he carefully read M. Pines's *L'Histoire de la littérature Judéo-Allemande*, a dissertation submitted at the Sorbonne only a short time before (1911). We shall come back to the contents of this lecture or speech to which the Zionist Prague weekly *Selbstwher* (edited by Felix Weltsch) referred in a rather light vein as Dr. Kafka's "lovely, charming speech," whereas to Levy's acting and reciting it referred as a performance of "gay profusion," in which "what was lacking in artistry was gained by a degree of historical documentary value." "It was so interesting," the writer of the short review added, to hear eastern Jewish poems and songs, recited and sung, by someone who "was not only an Eastern Jew . . . but also without western schooling."[28] In short, the evening was a success, but also not taken very seriously. Levy left, and at 36 Nicklasstrasse—the home of the Kafkas—a family, whose patience had been tried to the point of distraction, uttered a sigh of relief.

The entire affair has of course been regurgitated ad nauseam by a host of Kafka experts (starting almost forty years ago with Evelyn Torton Beck in her *Kafka and the Yiddish Theater: Its Impact on his* Work) and his biographers, from Brod to Reiner Stach.[29] Many not particularly wise things have been said about the affair, not only by those who made absurd claims (such as Evelyn T. Beck, who maintained that the impact of his exposure to the Yiddish theater changed Kafka's "style"), but even by some of the very intelligent commentators (such as Stach), who never understood, or never dared to say, that Kafka, propelled by emotions, attractions, and repulsions of which he was not fully conscious or in control, had, to some extent, made a fool of himself. Motivated by concerns about his own body, and, by inference, his Jewishness as a physical condition and identity,[30] his "crush" on Levy (whose surname was identical to that of Kafka's mother) certainly had something puerile about it. Of course, as Kafka was probably one of the most intelligent people alive at the time, his foolishness is of interest to us as only few sages' wisdom can be. This blocking of intelligence and repressing of clear-sightedness, on the part of a person whose perspicacity and intuitive understanding of people and situations were nothing less than phenomenal, are in themselves pregnant with meaning. Particularly since they would be from time to time "lifted," leaving Kafka himself perplexed and overwhelmed, asking himself what he was doing in the company of people (the Yiddish actors) with whom, presumably he had nothing in common?! A good part of the particular rancor, with which he mentioned the Levy affair in his letter to his father, had to do with the fact that he himself had partly shared his father's abjection and outrage. When Kafka would resume the attitudes prescribed by his infatuation, he would "will" himself to do that; when he wrote those lengthy and indescribably boring summaries of the plots of eminently forgettable melodramas he must have intentionally rendered himself obtuse and a bad writer to boot. This was for him a mental exercise of sorts; for teaching oneself to think stupidly can be, for a superbly clever person, a difficult and effort-consuming task. As such, and when properly understood, Kafka's temporary "craziness" about the Lemberg Yiddish troupe who had caught his attention just a few months before he discovered his full literary potential can tell us much about himself and his attitude toward the new Jewish cultural project, particularly as it manifested itself in his "takes" (misguided and misinformed as they were) on both the Hebrew and Yiddish new literatures, as we see in the following.

In one of his recitals (taking place on October 20, 1911), Levy read Morris Rosenfeld's "Di likht ferkoyferin" ("The Candles Vendor")—a tearjerker not devoid of melodramatic impact (it tells the story of a penurious street vendor, who, with a baby in her arms, desperately tried to eke out a living by pleading with the indifferent passers-by to buy from her a penny's worth of Sabbath candles; she is eventually found frozen to death still holding on to the corpse of the baby)—a Sholem Aleichem humoresque, and a short story by Peretz. To bring the evening to its moment of climax, he added to these Bialik's own Yiddish version of "In the City of Slaughter," his famous Hebrew prophetic "burden," written originally in the wake of the Kishinev pogrom of Easter 1903. This was the most important public poem written at the time in either Hebrew or Yiddish, which through its brilliant (but also flat and reductive) Russian translation by Jabotinsky had electrified the young Russian Jewish intelligentsia, triggering the organization of Jewish self-defense militias. Never before, perhaps since biblical days, had a Jewish poem achieved the horrific rhetorical level of this text, in which an outraged and humiliated God, talking to his prophet, blasted Jewish cowardice and lack of manly dignity in rumbling, withering, long, and slow verses of imprecations and condemnations. One can easily evoke the mental image of the Yiddish actor hurling Bialik's deadly verses at an audience who hardly understood them, but seeing the actor's expression and body language and hearing his voice pendulating between shouts and terrible whispers, it certainly understood that the matter thus touted was of the utmost seriousness, as indeed it was. Kafka, understandably, was interested in Levy's gestures and voice inflections more than in the contents of the texts he read. In the diary entry he wrote later that evening, he did not bother to mention the titles of the texts the actor read (with the exception of that of Rosenfeld's poem). However, when he came to Bialik's famous poem, he saw fit to enter in parentheses a short comment, which was, in the context of our argument, of the outmost importance, and should be quoted here first in the original German and then in Joseph Kresh's English translation. Originally Kafka's characterization or "definition" of the poem ran as follows: *"nur hier hat sich der Dichter, um sein den Kischinewer Pogrom für die jüdische Zukunft ausbeutendes Gedicht zu popularisieren, aus dem Hebräischen in der Jargon herabgelassen und sein ursprünglich hebräisches Gedicht selbst in Jargon übersstzt."*[31] The English translation opens up the tight, if not cramped, syntax of the one long German sentence and thus, somewhat flattens its suppressed but lethal ironic tone. What, in the German original, Kafka seems to be saying with an expressionless poker face, the English version reduces to the wry expression of open sarcasm: "the one instance, where the poet stooped from Hebrew to Yiddish, himself translating his original Hebrew poem into Yiddish, in order to popularize this poem, which, by making capital of the Kishinev pogrom, sought to further the Jewish cause."[32] The translation conveys the contents rather than the "music" of Kafka's comment, and it completely misses the point by replacing the pejorative appellation "Jargon" with the objective and normative "Yiddish." Yiddish is the language of Jews, whereas Jargon is the linguistic hotchpotch to which Jews, presumably, had reduced the beautiful German language. The difference between the two should not be overlooked.

Kafka's comment sports two well-honed points, and both are so deeply and dexterously stuck into the very core of the object at which they are aimed that they would have drawn blood, could a dismissive, actually disdainful, critical comment on a poem have done that. The sarcasm in which one of these points had been dipped is rather of a simple nature. Kafka is certainly ridiculing the presumed snobbism of the Hebrew national poet who allegedly stayed perpetually up in his Hebraic heights, allowing himself to "stoop" to the lowly and disfigured language Jews spoke and understood (and thus "Jargon," and not "Yiddish") only once, and for the very practical purpose of popularizing a poem that had to have as wide a circulation as was possible. The word "Jargon" is repeated twice—rather unnecessarily content-wise, for Kafka wants to ironically emphasize the "sacrifice" the poet had made. The poem was "originally written in Hebrew"—of course, how else?—and, lo and behold, the poet "himself" translated it into Jargon. He certainly stooped to conquer. The second point, however, is immeasurably sharper and deadlier. The poet, Kafka said, wrote his poem to "capitalize" on, profit from (the German verb *ausbeuten* is usually used in the context of financial gain deriving from the substantive *Ausbeute*, which means profit, proceeds) the Kishinev disaster, in which about fifty people were murdered, hundreds were beaten and maimed, scores of younger and older women were gang-raped, Jewish houses and stores were broken into, robbed, and destroyed, synagogues were being used as outhouses and stank with the hooligans' feces and urine, and Torah scrolls were pulled out of the arks, then torn and desecrated with human excrement. True, the poet did not wring personal profit from the pogrom. He rather used it politically to enhance a Jewish agenda. He did it for "the Jewish Future"—a trite expression here used as a euphemism for Zionism, of which Kafka might have approved as a political movement, but not, it seems, as an agenda that could be enhanced by capitalizing on the murder and raping of Jews, and particularly not through literature. Kafka's entire comment is informed by the implicit questions: Did the enhancement of any political cause, as acceptable and even approvable as it may be in itself, justify the making of a poetic capital out of the terrible suffering of thousands of people? Was a poet (*Dichter*), no matter how positive his public intentions, allowed to do this? Could a poet who did that still be considered a poet true to the genuine call of literature, or did he, by doing this, turn a deaf ear to that call, thus becoming a mere "poet"? Above all else, was a poet allowed to denigrate, indeed, vilify, the victims of an atrocity, present the men among them as cowardly eunuchs, voyeurs, who, never lifting a finger, were fascinated by the sight of their own women being raped, and the living women who had undergone rape as "unsullied corpses,"—was he allowed to thus spiritually brutalize those who had already been physically brutalized for the sake of whatever ideological "future"? Did he not, by doing that, align himself with the victimizer, as traumatized people often do? Had he not bought into the latter's inhumanity?

In large part, Kafka's bitter comment was based on misinformation (which only goes to show how credible Levy's information as an "expert" in Jewish literary matters was). For one thing "In shkhite shtot," Bialik's own Yiddish version of his famous "Be'ir haharega," was neither the poet's only nor his first poem written "by himself" in Yiddish. It had been preceded by no less than ten other poems written "originally" in Yiddish, including some very well-known ones, such as "Oyf dem hoykhn barg" ("On the High Mountain"), a romantic poem of yearning for the naiveté and happiness of childhood; the dark prophetic "Letste vort" ("Final Word" or "Last Utterance"); and, in between them, the lovely "Unter di grinike beymelekh" ("Under the Green Bushes"), an exquisitely musical and poignant declaration of the poet's love for Jewish children, the tiny "*Moyshelekh, Shleymelekh,*" whose bodies consisted of "straw, smoke, and little feathers," but their large eyes "glowed and sparkled."[33] The latter poem became immediately a favorite, and, set to music, achieved the status of a folksong, which Levy could have sung or recited, were he not ignorant of the poem's existence or of the fact that Bialik was its author. After the publication of "In shkhite shtot" in 1906 (together with "Dos letste vort" in a little book under the title *Fun tsar un tsorn,* [*Of Sorrow and Outrage*]) and before Kafka wrote his comment, Bialik published five more Yiddish poems (Yiddish adaptations of Heine's "Prinzessin Sabbath" and of some of Yehuda Halevi's poems). In 1913 he would collect his Yiddish poems in a book, a first edition (with an introductory essay by Baal-makhshoves), which would be enlarged and complemented (by translations from the Hebrew done by others) during Bialik's lifetime in two subsequent editions (1918, 1922). So much for the accuracy of "*nur hier hat sich der Dichter—in den Jargon herabgelassen.*" As for the sarcastic "*herabgelassen*" (stooped) itself, it was even more misguided and nonsensical than the notion of "In shkhite shtot"'s being the single case of the poet's "stooping" to the debased Jargon. Being primarily a Hebrew poet, Bialik nevertheless loved Yiddish and thought very highly of its great literary masters, Abramovitsh, Sholem Aleichem, and Peretz, with all of whom he was on the closest terms of friendship and mutual admiration. He beautifully adapted into Hebrew a series of Yiddish folksongs and wrote other original ones featuring folk motifs. He was trusted by the strict and pedantic Abramovitsh with the translation into Hebrew of his *Fishke the Lame* (re-titled in Hebrew *The Book of Paupers*). Both as an editor and as a publisher, Bialik systematically published the works of Yiddish writers and did his best to coax them into adapting their works into Hebrew themselves. In 1927, already in Palestine, he got himself into a stormy public controversy and was harshly castigated by Hebraic purists for warmly welcoming to the country well-known Yiddish writers (Sholem Asch and Peretz Hirsbeyn) and insisting on that occasion on the need for amity between Hebrew and Yiddish writers, the two languages being like the biblical Naomi and Ruth, the old, bereaved Judean woman and her supportive Moabite daughter-in-law, who, having joined the people of Judea, became the founding mother of the Davidic dynasty.[34] In short, Kafka was utterly wrong in accusing the Hebrew poet of a disdainful and snobbish attitude toward Yiddish and Yiddish writing. As for "Be'ir haharega" or "In shkhite shtot" itself, Kafka somewhat misunderstood this horrific and nihilistic poem, in which the idea of capitalizing on the Kishinev pogrom for enhancing whatever political cause was far from the poet's mind. Dark, complex, and incredibly cruel and demeaning, this poem debunked both Judaism and the Jewish people and declared the moral bankruptcy of Jews and their God alike. Nor was there any truth in the notion that the poet translated his own poem into Yiddish for the purpose of popularizing it. If popularity was what he was seeking, the poem had already garnered as much of it as it possibly could through the Russian translation of Jabotinsky and the already existing Yiddish translation or adaptation done by no less than the Yiddishists' culture hero, Peretz himself. Bialik said that his own adaptation was the result of his artistic dissatisfaction with that of Peretz. This was called in question by scholars (since Bialik, as translator of his own work, borrowed much from his predecessor, with the latter's full permission).[35] In any case, Bialik hardly needed any additional popularity for his Hebrew poem (originally published in 1904), which by 1906 had already become known throughout the Jewish world. In short, Kafka's comment contained as many mistakes and misconceptions as one could possibly squeeze into one sentence.

Nevertheless, and irrespective of all the necessary corrections, his snide remark is an eye-opener. It is the most glaring and important of quite a few pieces of evidence that are clearly indicative of how distasteful Kafka found the entire project of a nationalist, "heroic," Jewish (particularly Hebrew) culture, of which Bialik's poem was indeed the best and most characteristic example. As much as he approved (not without ambivalence) of Zionism as a movement of Jewish revitalization through re-territorialization and manual labor, pulling Jews out of the modernist urban labyrinth, and inhabiting the open spaces of an unencumbered agricultural community, he equally hated its political show as a pseudo-government and its cultural and literary protest against Jewish weakness and lack of virility—of which "Be'ir haharega" was the most visceral and poisonous articulation. Characteristically, Kafka expressed his disapproval through omission and silence rather than through open condemnation. Never again, in any of the many documents he left behind him (diaries; letters; conversations, jotted down and preserved by admirers, such as Brod, Gustav Janouch, and Dora Diamant; and a host of observations, aphorisms, and unfinished fragments) would he as much as mention Bialik's name. This itself calls for our attention, for Kafka was undoubtedly fully aware of Bialik's wide reputation and the national spiritual significance ascribed to his poetry by people he knew, whether intimately (like Brod and Weltsch) or from a respectful distance(such as Buber and Rosenzweig). In the Zionist Prague weekly *Selbstwher* (the title itself, *Self-Defense* was reverberating "Bialikly"), which Kafka religiously read until a very short time before his death, and in which he published some of his own work (such as the quintessential "Before the Law" parable), as well as in Buber's prestigious *Der Jude* (where he published his "Report to the Academy" and "Jackals and Arabs"; Buber even offered him the editorship of this major Jewish-German monthly, which he, of course, refused) Bialik was mentioned and praised on a constant basis. Kafka also most probably read young Scholem's translation into German of Bialik's essay "Halakha ve'aggada," which has been discussed in these pages. Not once would he as much as mention Bialik's name—not even in one of those unmercifully long letters to Felice Bauer, where Zionism and Zionist activities were so often dwelt upon. Nor would he dream of meeting with Bialik or attending some event in which the Hebrew poet was present or spoke, although somehow the two writers' trajectories seemed more than once to have intersected each other. For example, in late summer 1913, after a crisis—one of many—in his relationship with Felice, Kafka, on his way to a much needed vacation in Italy (Venice, Riva), stopped for a while in Vienna as a participant in an international conference focusing on work-related accidents but also for the purpose of attending the eleventh Zionist Congress—for which he protracted his stay in town, adding to it an entire week, which had to be subtracted from his vacation. He found the experience devastating and wrote to Brod, a fully committed Zionist, how "it was hard to imagine anything more useless than such a congress," and how alienated, "cramped and distracted" he felt, sitting in one of the hall's galleries and wishing he could "throw spitballs at the delegates" as did a certain girl (actually, Lisa Weltsch, who had come with him from Prague), sitting in an opposite gallery.[36] He did not deign to dedicate as much as one word to the cultural aspects of the congress, mention Chaim Weizmann's speech about the purchase of land and the plans for establishing a Hebrew university on Mount Scopus, or about the showing of the first documentary film featuring the Zionist pioneers and their travails in Palestine (done by the Russian-Jewish filmmaker Noah Sokolovsky). As for the many "literary people" who were gathered there, he said that he knew almost none and nothing of them. The literary people he had in mind were probably German-writing Zionists. However, among the literary luminaries whose presence added to the glitter of the event were many Hebrew ones, with Bialik at their head. Bialik, as mentioned in a former chapter, arrived as the keynote speaker of the Conference on Hebrew Language and Culture that took place conjointly with the Zionist Congress. In this conference, he crossed swords with Frishman, whose speech (on the second day of the conference) was understood as a statement diametrically opposed to the one made by Bialik. The event, which was already mentioned in this essay, was regarded as a sensation and was widely covered by the press, including the German Zionist press, which Kafka certainly read. Not a word did Kafka utter about it, as if it never happened. Nor would we have known, with Kafka as our witness, that at the very same time, the first professionally played and directed Hebrew theater event was taking place in Vienna—a play staged in Hebrew in a respectable Viennese theater by Nahum Zemach, the future founding father of the Habima ensemble in Moscow. The ardent fan of the tattered Galician Yiddish troupes did not deign to attend the show or bother to mention its very existence, although we may assume that his impressions of a drama conducted in biblical Hebrew would have rather interested his Prague friends, such as Brod, Weltsch, and Hugo Bergman.

There was certainly a "system" in Kafka's unrelenting *zum Tode schweigen* (kill through silence), for it encompassed the entire space of the Hebrew renaissance. Whereas, as already mentioned, he read assiduously Pines's Sorbonne dissertation about the history of Yiddish literature (and, like the good student he had been, took notes), he never read, as far as we know, Slouschz's parallel Sorbonne dissertation about the history of the new Hebrew literature (1903). He constantly queried Levy and others (such as the Prague Hebrew poet Langer)[37] about the Talmud, the *Zohar*, and about modern Yiddish writers. The latter he mentioned in his diaries often enough—both the canonized ones (Abramovitsh, Sholem Aleichem, Spektor, Peretz, Rosenfeld et al.) and a host of peripheral ones—as if he did not know, or did not acknowledge, the difference between the two groups. He mentioned with respect Jacob Adler, "the great eagle," the foremost Yiddish actor and theater manager of Manhattan's Lower East Side, and even recorded the rumors that he had by then become a millionaire.[38] In contradistinction, he almost never asked about Hebrew writing, although he was surrounded by people who were at least as knowledgeable about it as Levy was about Yiddish literature. In any case, he dedicated not one word to the Hebrew writers and intellectuals, whose work had been translated into German—for instance, Achad ha'am, about whom he heard Buber talking with much respect (albeit also with some reservations) when he attended the latter's lectures on Judaism at the Bar Kochba club (Kafka, by the way, was not impressed by these lectures, which had electrified the German-speaking young Zionist intelligentsia; he thought they were philosophically eclectic, conflating ideas that did not dovetail).[39] Nor did he pay the slightest attention to Achad ha'am's rival, Berditchevsky, who published articles and short stories in German, the already mentioned survey of eastern European Jewish culture and politics, and the two comprehensive anthologies of Midrashic and medieval tales, which, presumably should have interested Kafka as an unadulterated expression of "authentic" Judaism. In vain would we look in Kafka's letters and diaries for a reference to this Jewish writer and scholar who lived in Germany, was suffused with its literature and philosophy, and was, like himself, deeply interested in Nietzsche. The same goes for Agnon's tales that started to appear in German translations (among the translators: Scholem) after World War I. This, then, was more than mere indifference or ignorance. Kafka could not have been ignorant of the existence and reputations of these writers, since all of them were mentioned and (to some extent) discussed in the Zionist periodicals he systematically read. Rather, this looks like a discrete boycotting. Kafka, it would seem, did not want to know of, or have anything to do with, the new Hebrew literature, which, at the time, was advocating "für die jüdische Zukunft," as he said in his comment on Bialik.

There was one well-known Hebrew writer Kafka did mention several times: Brenner. Kafka was eager to learn Hebrew from a relatively early date and was struck (and made jealous) by Felice Bauer, upon their first meeting in the apartment of Brod's parents, declaring that she had been devoting a lot of time to the learning of the Hebrew language (he immediately produced an issue of the monthly *Palaestina*, which he "happened to have" with him, flaunting his less impressive Zionist credentials).[40] Although he had quite a few able teachers, his progress was painfully slow, which exasperated him and made him stop his studies; thereafter he would resume them after intervals of varying lengths. When in 1922 he decided once again to resume Hebrew lessons, his teacher, Pu'ah Ben-tovim, a likeable Palestinian young woman who arrived in Prague as a student, had an idea that seemed bright enough: an intelligent and sophisticated person like Kafka should learn Hebrew not from the simplistic and boring textbooks and grammar manuals fit for schoolboys, but rather by delving headlong into a serious and engaging literary work that would attract the student by its literary merit and facilitate the process of acquiring the language. She chose Brenner's Palestinian novel *Shekhol vekishalon* (*Bereavement and Breakdown*), which had appeared in an attractive, clearly printed, little volume two years earlier. Brenner was regarded then not only as the modern Hebrew novelist par excellence, but also as a martyr and a Zionist "saint," having been murdered less than a year earlier (May 1921) and his body mutilated by Arab rioters near Jaffa. Ben-tovim probably also believed Brenner would interest Kafka because he was known as a "pessimist" who had conducted in his works of prose fiction an unrelenting exploration of suffering, humiliation, existential malaise, and fear of death, as well as for his ethical sensibility. She thought she made a good choice and eventually would tell of Kafka having "identified" with the suffering and humiliation of the novel's protagonist, Yehezkel Khefets.[41] Ben-tovim was, however, wrong. The reading of the novel proved to be extremely difficult and unattractive, not only because of the level of the language, for which the student was not prepared, but also because Kafka did not at all care for it, or, for that matter, for pessimism as such. Being the well-mannered and sensitive person he was, he probably refrained from telling his enthusiastic young teacher (whom he liked) what he reported to his friends in his letters written from Berlin (where he lived with his Jewish lover, Dora Diamant, from September 1923 to March 1924, when, having entered the terminal phase of his illness, he was transferred to Austrian sanatoria). Ben-tovim, who could not follow him to Berlin, nevertheless managed to visit him and Dora in their rented apartment at Steglitz, checked Dora's Hebrew proficiency (the latter, a daughter of a devout Hasid who had fled her home, was a Zionist and a lover of both Hebrew and Yiddish writing), and declared her fit to continue guiding the ailing student in the reading of Brenner's novel. Since Franz and Dora were then "planning" their emigration to Palestine and the learning of Hebrew became part of the ritual that supported their fantasy of sharing a future there as a married couple, the reading of the novel wearily went on. Kafka wrote, however (October 1923), to Robert Klopstock (a Jewish-Hungarian medical student whom he had befriended, and who would take care of him during the last months of his life and also inject him with the lethal dosage of morphine that would put an end to his suffering) that the reading was becoming intolerably irksome (he managed to read only thirty pages) because the novel was "not very good," its "chemical formula" of bereavement *and* breakdown was unappealing, and in general he found it "difficult for me in every respect." He also said he did not understand the two concepts Brenner had conjoined in his title, although he got the idea that the two presented "an attempt to set down the quintessence of misfortune" (the slight irony in Kafka's tone could not be mistaken).[42] To Brod he wrote: "I am not enjoying the book very much as a novel." He had always been, he said, a little "in awe" of Brenner, he did not know why; "probably there has always been talk of his sadness. And 'Sadness in Palestine?' . . ."[43] There are quite a few Hebrew and Jewish critics who like to couple Kafka's and Brenner's names as close figures in "the Modern Jewish Canon."[44] Reading these comments on *Shekhol vekishalon*, which many regard as Brenner's best work of fiction, might have helped in disabusing them of such an erroneous view. Kafka, who never really cared for sadness per se,[45] and whose view of life was informed by a dark but often quite irascible sense of humor (as Weltsch demonstrated in a brilliant essay)[46] and did not share most of Brenner's ethical and aesthetic preferences, could not have approved of this writer. It was only a vulgarized, "Kafkaesque" Kafka who could be deemed mentally and artistically close to a writer like Brenner. In any case, it is clear that the only contemporary Hebrew writer Kafka made an effort to get to know did not appeal to him at all. Thus, he would not waste on him even a casual remark in his diary entries of 1922 (the last year of his diary writing; in 1923 he jotted down a few lines only). Nor do we find any mention of Brenner in Dora Diamant's memoirs.[47] In spite of the fact that she had to read his novel with Kafka, the novel presumably did not leave a scratch on her memory. Had the adored Kafka said something interesting about or even against *Bereavement and Breakdown*, she would have certainly remembered and recorded it. Most probably the reading was a boring chore to her as it was to him; something their pathetic dream of a happy life in a Hebrew-speaking Palestine needed as a support, a straw to hold on to; but at the same time, something on which there was no need to waste conversation.

The complex issues and perhaps unanswerable questions that are raised by Kafka's attitude toward Zionism as a nationalist ideology and a political and social movement cannot be discussed here (they are now being discussed by a host of Kafka scholars, and the most recent Kafka encyclopedias and *Handbücher* contain many articles dedicated to this topic; a particularly perspicacious presentation of the issues involved and the recent literature on them was written by Mark H. Gelber).[48] It seems that both those who relegate to Zionism a central role in the author's life and work and those who altogether deny its importance are off the mark. The slippery truth is to be found somewhere between these two simplistic attitudes. There can be no doubt, that as an option of Jewish rejuvenation, it interested—even stirred and attracted— Kafka, who, in spite of his total disapproval of the Zionist establishment was curious enough to spend a whole week of insomnia and headaches listening to the deliberations of the eleventh Zionist Congress. His dreams of visiting Palestine, and then emigrating to it, were never given up, and at some points also seemed to assume a semi-practical character (as, for instance, in his acceptance of the Bergmans' generous proposal that when he came, their Jerusalem apartment would be at his disposal). These dreams were not unlike his ties with women—necessary and wished for but also bound to end in failure and withdrawal. Of course, he did nothing (with the exception of his ineffective study of Hebrew) to bring them to realization. They were part of his fantasy of escaping "that old crone," Prague; but they also presaged—as his dreams of marriage did—the elimination of his functioning as a writer, which rendered their eventual cancellation absolutely necessary. Some of Kafka's stories are definitely amenable to "Zionist" interpretations; but then the same stories are also, and as legitimately, open to an interpretation as anti-Zionist satires or as stories without any message pertaining to Zionism. For example, "A Report to the Academy" can be read (as it has been) as a blistering satire on Jewish assimilation. The monkey "Red Peter," captured and carried away from his African jungle, who found no "way out" of his cage but that of becoming half-human, drinking the liquor he loathed, and exchanging coarse jokes with his captors, might have represented the assimilated, "Europeanized" Jew, who had broken away from his ghetto-cage by losing his true identity. However, by the same token, Peter could have represented the Herzlian Zionist, who could find no "way out" of the cage of anti-Semitism (as so poignantly described in the opening chapters of Herzl's *Altneuland*) but that of shedding his Jewish identity and becoming "like all the nations," as Herzl's Zionist dream actually projected him. The same goes for the puzzling "agricultural motif" in "Investigations of a Dog," where the Talmudic or scholastic canine desperately explores the riddle of the growing of food out of the earth. Jewish agriculture and the movement "back to the land" and to nature were, of the various aspects of Zionism, perhaps those Kafka found most attractive (himself wishing to become an agricultural laborer and often dabbling with gardening), and he read everything he could lay his hands on about the new Jewish agricultural settlements in Palestine. So the motif might have represented a

Zionist yearning with which the author sympathized. At the same time, the convoluted discursive treatment of this motif in Kafka's story also could be interpreted as a hilarious take on the Zionist making the wish of reassuming the simple life of the agricultural laborer the basis of a complex philosophical system (that of A. D. Gordon, for instance, of whom Kafka might have heard from Gordon's admirer Bergman. Gordon, by the way, was in Prague in 1920, attending a unification conference of two labor Zionist parties: *Hapo'el hatsa'ir* and *Tse'irey tsiyon*) or of a sophisticated allegorical reading of literature (see Brenner's clever allegorization of the witch's kitchen scene from the first part of Goethe's *Faust* in his novel *Mikan umikan* (From One Side and from the Other Side).[49] The dog's talmudism and pseudo-theologizing of agriculture could be as much the butt of the author's satire as the articulation of a desperate yearning. Perhaps they were both.

We cannot, however, keep the same balanced or open-ended view of Kafka's response to the modern Jewish nationalist cultural project. Here, it would seem, his verdict was systematically negative. Whatever his attitude toward Zionism, clearly a literature that he regarded as militating for the Zionist agenda by making use of Jewish suffering was to him unacceptable. Whether he articulated his rejection of such a literature and the cultural project it stood for through occasional snide remarks, or, more systematically, through ear-splitting silence, the rejection was firm and unrelenting. Kafka, one can say, was "rubbed the wrong way" by a cultural project that found its radical articulation either in Bialik's condemnation of Jewish cowardice and sexual timidity, in Brenner's horrific vilification of Jews as parasites and sheer "vermin,"[50] or in Berditchevsky's call for total revolution and the "transvaluation of all [Jewish] values": "We are either the last Jews or the members of a new nation."[51] Kafka could accept—with criticism but also with sympathy—Zionist novels such as Brod's *Jüdinnen* (1911) and *Arnold Beer: Das Schicksal eines Juden* (1912) because they were not informed by a similar anti-Jewish resentment.[52] The Zionist Hebrew literature must have repulsed him, and he more than once made known his lack of interest in it, whereas the Talmudic aggada and the Hasidic tales, sayings, and hagiographies (to which he must have gained access, like most German-Jewish readers, mainly through

Martin Buber's famous adaptations) elicited from him admiration and keen interest. Of course, one can justifiably ask, how could he be favorably impressed by an ideology and a political movement that called for a revolutionary change in the Jewish mode of existence, and at the same time reject the cultural and literary project that militated for the selfsame change by exposing the vitiating inadequacy of existing Jewish life patterns? This question, if unanswerable, would not present the only insoluble conundrum with which Kafka's work and personality present us. However, perhaps the question could have been answered through a differentiation between a legitimate socio-political discourse and literature. Whereas the former was expected to point to ways and means of effecting social and political changes, the latter's existence was justified only if, through a desperate but at the same time also consistent and unflagging search for truth, it could affect spiritual transformation. A literary text the reading of which did not trigger a spiritual change of heart should not have been written, Kafka believed, and that change of heart could happen only when literature freed itself from all ulterior motives, as positive in and of themselves as they possibly were, and without a commitment to anything but an ultimate truth and total unconcern with anything to which the verb *ausbeuten* (making use of, capitalizing on) could be applied. Otherwise it would play directly into the hands of the ever-lurking falsehood. Literature should exist when it could do what Kleist did in *Michael Kohlhaas* or in "Die Marquise von O" or what Flaubert did in *L'Éducation sentimentale* and *Bouvard et Pecuchet*; but, as far as Kafka was concerned, not what it did in Bialik's "In shkhite shtot."

The comment on this poem is interesting in the way it seems to contradict itself. Whereas the expression *"jüdische Zukunft"* (Jewish future) seems, at least at surface level, to be pregnant with positive connotations, the verb *ausbeuten* conveys, within the context of the comment, a totally negative message. This dichotomy may indicate that Kafka was facing a genuine paradox. We can, but we do not have to, read the "Jewish future" ironically. Maybe the comment said that Zionism was genuinely working for a better Jewish future. As such it represented a positive force with which one could sympathize and perhaps also identify. At the same time, one could not accept a literature that manipulated, for an acceptable political cause, the suffering and victimizing of human beings. After all, Kafka was not the only one who rejected Bialik's poem on this ground. Abramovitsh, himself a visceral satirist, whose commitment to the amelioration of the Jewish condition through a scathing critique could not be questioned, loathed this poem, saying: "listen to this and be flabbergasted! Villains, preying animals, the scum of the earth, attacked me, my wife, and my children, killed, murdered, and perpetrated every possible abomination—then *he* [Bialik] comes, stands over me as an unctuous preacher, moralizes, spreads salt on my wounds—I wallow in the dirt—and he stands over me, whip in hand, and whips, whips. . . ."[53]

As for Kafka's protection of Yiddish from Bialik's assumed (quite wrongly) disdain, as well as his generally positive attitude toward the language, its culture, and its literature, they too should be seen for what they really were. There is no doubt that Yiddish elicited from Kafka sympathy, indeed, real warmth. True, he never tried to master or learn it. Nevertheless, it certainly was closer to his heart than the modern Hebrew he did try to learn with scanty, if any, results. It is an interesting question in itself: how is it that a person as intelligent and stubborn as Kafka could not master, although he certainly invested efforts in doing so, the elements of a language every average school child could master if properly guided and if made to do the hard work that the learning of a foreign language required. When Kafka *wanted* to learn a language, he certainly could do that. For instance, once he made up his mind that he needed and wanted to become proficient in Czech, a language most of his German-Jewish comrades had no use for, he mastered the language and was able to read and speak it (and suggest changes to be made in Milena Jesenska's Czech translations of his stories). Thus his inability to master Hebrew begs a psychological explanation (although Kafka warned us against psychology, labeling it "sheer impatience," like all "human errors"; and comparing its interpretation of human behavior to "the reading of mirror writing," a "laborious" process that reveals nothing but the self evident and thus amounts to an exercise in futility).[54] Certainly the language presented him, on top of its grammatical complexity, with certain mental blocks; and we are allowed to assume that coming in contact with its literature, as represented by Bialik's poem, was not conducive to the removal of these mental impediments.

He certainly wanted to gain access to the Bible and the other ancient sources. During the time he spent in Berlin, shortly before his death, he methodically frequented—as long as his health permitted—the academic institute for Jewish Studies founded by Leo Beck, where he relished N. H. Torczyner's lectures on the Bible (Torczyner, one of the foremost Hebrew philologists, would later teach Hebrew at the Hebrew University of Jerusalem, under a Hebraized name: Naphtali H. Tur-Sinai), as well as lectures on the Talmud. However, modern Hebrew, it would seem, miffed him. In any case, neither in his diaries nor in his letters would he ever express himself about it with even a smattering of the intimate and loving tone he would assume when talking about Yiddish, whose inflections and rhythms he identified with the very essence of the "Jewish temperament." For instance, within the context of an evening dedicated to Yiddish folksongs, he also attended a Yiddish lecture given by the Yiddishist activist Birnbaum (mentioned earlier several times); he first recoiled from the gauche sentimentality of the speaker, who would in almost every sentence address his audience as *mayne tayere* (my dear ones) ad nauseam, and, as Kafka said, to the point of being ridiculous. But then, as he recorded his impressions in his diary, he thought better of the matter. In Yiddish, he wrote that repeating expressions such as *vey iz mir* (alas, poor me) or *s'iz fil tsu reden* (there is much to be said about it) was "not intended to cover up embarrassment but [were] rather intended, like ever-fresh springs, to stir up the sluggish stream that is never fluent enough for the Jewish temperament."[55]

Did all this mean that, while rejecting the nationalist ardor of contemporary Hebraists, Kafka embraced the more folksy brand of Yiddishist nationalism? This was at the time a prevalent attitude that went far beyond the circle of committed Yiddishists such as Dr. Birnbaum and the other organizers of the Czernowitz conference. It was shared, as noted earlier, by some Zionists as well. Herzl believed that in the Jewish state, the elite would speak German while the common people would remain loyal to their Yiddish (in his *Altneuland*, as Achad ha'am bitterly remarked, Hebrew was the language of ritual and nationalist school songs, while its serious study was relegated to the academy). Socialist Zionists such as Borokhov and Ya'akov Zerubavel, were ardent

Yiddish lovers. However, Kafka's attitude toward Yiddish was totally unlike theirs, and naive Yiddishists should take care not to embrace him too tight to their hearts. Kafka's Yiddishism calls for clarification and demystification. He never shared the Yiddishist ideology of Yiddish as the basis of a new secularist-humanist Jewish culture—an ideology with political implications he would never have acceded to. His thoughts about Yiddish, as well as his public activities on its behalf, were based on a historical error, which the aforementioned treatise by Meir Pines had not helped in correcting, perhaps because Kafka himself was quite adamant in his decision to deflect any fact that could have clashed with his Yiddish fantasy.

To start with, his appreciation of the language was never truly free from an ambivalence similar to that which characterized his fascination with the Yiddish actors. Nothing highlights this ambivalence better than the aforementioned "introductory lecture" with which he launched Levy's recital. Kafka started by chiding his audience, acculturated German-speaking Jews, who looked down upon the Jewish "Jargon," telling them that they understood Yiddish more than they thought or admitted. Acculturated as they were, they were not that distant from the ghetto Jew who remained ensconced in their consciousness speaking there his language. If they could only relax and suppress their Yiddish-phobia (*Angst vor dem Jargon*), they would certainly enjoy the evening. But then Kafka went on to describe what Yiddish presumably really was, and it became immediately clear that the audience's "Angst" was not only "understandable" but, as he hastened to say, also quite justifiable. Yiddish was a young, underdeveloped language—still chaotic, devoid of normative grammar, imprecise, and with articulation that tended to be "short and hasty" (*kurz und rasch*). It was replete with foreign words whose arbitrary usage created a commotion and nervous volition. It conveyed meaning through its separate words rather than through syntax and other unifying semantic means, as truly cultivated languages did. It was a neglected language held in contempt; hence its arbitrariness in spite of its closeness to German. Whereas the latter had undergone through regulative processes that gradually released the new High German out of the primitive medieval Mid-German, Yiddish—residing in the ghetto—stuck to its primitive beginnings, for "once you are in the ghetto, you do not bestir yourself so quickly" (*Was einmal ins Ghetto kam, rührte sich nicht so schnell*). At the same time Kafka never hinted at the need of modernizing Yiddish, extending its boundaries, regularizing its grammar, and enriching its vocabulary. Clearly a call for such a linguistic upgrading, which would become part of every Yiddishist cultural agenda, rubbed him the wrong way; because to him Yiddish, being the language of the ghetto, was charming and attractive exactly because it was what he believed it was: an emblem of whatever was static, old fashioned, primitive, and medieval in Jewish traditional communal existence. It was the language of a sequestered, handicapped, despised community that compensated for its essential paralysis by a superficial haste, clamor, imprecision, and volatility. Kafka wished his Prague middle-class audience (and by inference, all westernized Jews) would acknowledge the whispering Yiddish voice which—forgotten and repressed—went on prattling inside their minds. This was necessary not because this voice could offer his listeners access to hidden cultural treasures, but because it made possible a confrontation with their continued existence as frightened and vulnerable Jews, as well as a realization of how brittle and unreliable was the thin ice of Europeanism upon which they stood. Such confrontation and realization were existentially and morally valuable, because they pointed to the "truth," and as such facilitated authenticity in one's self perception, the avoidance of bad faith. Thus Yiddish, understood as the symbol of Jewish weakness, did not call for revolutionary fiats (Zionist, communist, Bundists, etc.) of self-empowerment, but rather an acceptance of minority and marginality. Jews should stop living in a wishful fantasy world and accept the truth of their stunted existence.

As in the case of his critique of Bialik's poem, it matters little that Kafka was quite wrong—from the objective philological viewpoint—in what he said about Yiddish and its alleged characteristics. In his justification, one might note that Yiddish scholarly philology and linguistics were at their infancy at the time he made his pronouncement and that the view he conveyed was banal and shared by many (it was nothing but the residue of the rejection of Yiddish by the Jewish enlightenment). What matters are not the false notes but rather the music that breathes through them and makes them come alive; and this music emanated from the very core of Kafka's self consciousness as a Jew and as a person. Little wonder that within such a context Yiddish literature could be seen and appreciated only as he saw and appreciated it. When shown by Janouch a German anthology of so-called new "ghetto" tales by Yiddish writers, Kafka told his interlocutor: "Peretz, Asch, and all the other eastern European Jewish writers always write stories which are in fact folk-stories. And that is quite right," and as it should have been.[56] The fact is that these stories, even when they disguised themselves as folktales (as Peretz did in his *Folkstimlekhe geshikhten* [Stories in the Manner of the Folk]), opposite of what Kafka believed them to be: modern tales carrying humanistic, often revolutionary messages and packaged in a diaphanous folkloristic cellophane. What Peretz and his followers set out to do was nothing less than reprocessing the tradition, retelling its myths and fables and redefining their meaning in current European terms, so as to fashion out of them a bridge over the chasm separating the Jew from contemporary culture. But Kafka refused to see them as such and insured himself against the shattering of his illusions by refraining from really examining them, reading the stories through his habitually critical eyes. An interesting incident can shed light on this baffling issue. During World War I, with Berlin full of Jewish refugees, including unsupervised children, Felice Bauer—prodded and encouraged by her on-again off-again fiancé—volunteered as a part-time teacher in a charitable institution for Jewish children. She requested that Kafka recommend to her age-appropriate Jewish reading material (in German) and after consulting Brod, he suggested a German translation of a collection of Sholem Aleichem stories. But then, having for once truly *read* the stuff he had recommended, he realized how far, in fact, the tales of the Jewish humorist were from the folktales he had deemed them to be. Quickly rescinding his recommendation he explained that the stories were *zu ironisch und kompliciert*.[57] I quote the original German because the English translation—"too sarcastic and complicated"[58]—is misleading. Kafka talked here not about sarcasm, but about irony, of the many brands of which sarcasm is the crudest and most obvious. For once he did justice to the texts he commented on, seeing that irony, the subtle contradiction between surface and depth, the telling and what actually was told, was their dominant trope (indeed, it was the trope informing much of contemporary Yiddish writing), and that therefore they were not "complicated" but rather complex, as they certainly were. However, such insights were rare in his comments about Yiddish writing—not because he could not but rather because he would not see through its surface.

In general, he systematically refused to acknowledge current Yiddish culture and literature for what they were: a clear and forceful call—one of many—to secularize and "humanize" the Jewish masses; to cut off current Jewish life and culture from their moorings in the world of Jewish religious tradition; to effect a cultural revolution that would "modernize" Judaism, freeing it from the old way of life and from the halakhic norm. In this there was no substantial difference between Yiddishism and Zionism. Kafka did not want to know all this. He insisted on seeing current Yiddish culture as a direct continuation of the traditional ghetto culture. He never truly internalized the fact that the new Yiddish literature that Levy was supposed to be an expert in was founded, together with its new Hebrew counterpart, in Germany of the late eighteenth century as part of the Jewish "Enlightenment Revolution," and that for a long time its main raison d'être was its ability to fight Hasidism on its own ground and fend off its widespread literary influence. With a person as intelligent as Kafka was, we can be sure that this refusal to face up to the historical realities must have been at least partly conscious and willed. It was based not on ignorance but rather on a conscious refusal to accept the Yiddishist claim to modernity at face value; a decision that was not devoid of cunning and a patronizing attitude. Of course, he knew that Levy did not come to Prague from his Warsaw yeshiva but rather from Paris, Zurich, and Vienna; but he discretely pooh-poohed his touted modernism, as well as his wish to elevate Yiddish theater to the level of the Burgtheater. Levy *thought* he had been to Paris and Vienna and "saw the world," but Kafka *knew* he was still in his Warsaw yeshiva, not having mentally distanced himself from his Hasidic home at all. We remember the "good natured" I-know-better smile with which Brod reacted to Levy's protest. Of course, those Prague sophisticates knew what the paltry actor *really* was or represented: a fantasy consisting of exotic fur hats, silk kaftans, Cabbala, *Zohar*, Talmud, and what not. Kafka was too insightful not to see the difference between the pseudo-Hasidic Peretz stories Levy recited and the authentic tales and sayings he heard from Dora Diamant (who saw herself as having saved her soul by turning her back on the Hasidic world of her father, a follower of the Rebbe of Gur) and from his Prague acquaintance, the already mentioned Hebrew poet Langer (as a youth Langer had left his assimilated family to become a follower of the Tsadik of Belz; then, back in Prague, wrote on Jewish cultural topics and composed his exquisite poems in the manner of the medieval Spanish masters). But he chose to overlook these differences, both because he wanted to believe in the existence of a Jewish cultural continuum and because he laughed off the European pretensions of the Yiddish writers and playwrights. The modern Yiddishists were in his eyes not much different from the assimilated Prague Jews who were afraid of the Yiddish-speaking ghetto Jew who lingered inside them; only their fear focused on the ghetto Jew rather than on his Yiddish parlance.

That was at the root of his refusal (undoubtedly conscious and willed) to differentiate between canonical Yiddish literature and the cheapest boulevard productions of hacks. The strange, all but comic, serious attention he paid to the plays of Latayner, Hurwitz, and Faynman; the unbelievable patience and precision with which he recorded their idiotic plots, surprises, and "recognitions" were all part of a consistent exercise in an intentional desensitization, for the purpose of supporting an imagined world, which would have otherwise collapsed. He could not care less about the fact that by 1911, there already existed a modern Yiddish dramaturgy that garnered successes on respectable European and American stages (like the sensational success of Asch's *God of Vengeance*, when staged in Berlin a few years earlier by Reinhardt with the role of the protagonist played by the German stage star Rudolf Schildkraut, a Rumanian Jew);[59] for what could the popular success of Asch's unsophisticated social melodrama mean to a person who sniffed disgustedly at Schnitzler's psychological plays? What could be the literary weight of a modern Yiddish literature when measured by a person who had almost no good word to say on contemporary German and Austrian writing (Kafka pointedly preferred "marginal" figures such as Robert Walser to the "great" names of contemporary German writing—with the exception of Thomas Mann, whose *Tonio Kröger* he loved; he loathed most of the current expressionist poetry by luminaries such as Else Lasker-Schüler, although he had good things to say about the by-far less so-phisticated expressionist poetry of Franz Werfel, which, he said, almost reminded him of the Yiddish of the actors he loved. . . .)?[60] When litera-ture had to be measured by the achievements of Kleist, Flaubert, Dos-toevsky, and Tolstoy, the difference between Peretz and Rosenfeld could be seen as negligible. Thus the division of Yiddish writing into canon and sub-canon made no sense to Kafka. Yiddish had to represent one, monolithic tradition, which could not be judged by modern European criteria: the tradition of the eastern European Jewish ghetto.

The intriguing, in fact, crucially important, question was what exactly Kafka identified as the essence of this tradition. Here, unfortunately, I have to place myself on the side of the opposition to the great Jewish hermeneutists—Buber, Rosenzweig, and Scholem. I find their theologi-cal reading of Kafka unconvincing, and its demolishing critique by Wal-ter Benjamin (as well as Benjamin's devastating critique of Brod's Kafka monograph), Hannah Arendt, and, perhaps, more rigorously than both, Theodore Adorno (in his superb "Notes on Kafka") very convincing. The Jewishness of Kafka was neither theological nor mystical. He did not write, as all three luminaries contended, a twentieth-century version of the book of Job, in which God's answer from the whirlwind was muffled and obfuscated by "miraculous transmission failure" (Buber),[61] and yet, he, the stubborn Jew that he was, stripped bare, exposed, and desperate as he was, refused to believe in a world controlled by a malevolent demi-urge, or accept a "Pauline" view of existence as ruled by evil forces, which only the direct and unexplainable intervention of Jesus could vanquish. Rather he [Kafka] represented the Jew who believed, and therefore could expect no miracle "as much as in daytime one does not see any stars" (Buber, quoting an aphorism from Kafka's "Blue Octavo Notebooks").[62] What seems to me a cogent reading of the novels and the short stories does not dovetail with such harmonious, albeit dialectical, messages. In fact, I believe *The Castle*, to the extent that it deals with religion at all (that is, if the institution of the castle in any way represents a religious order), is one of the fiercest anti-religious literary texts ever written. Nor can I follow in the wake of Scholem's reading of *The Trial* as a secular projection of the lore of the Cabbala, and the argument following the reading of the "Before the Law" parable (in the Cathedral scene) as a bona fide "summing up of Jewish theology" through a reconstruction of the dialectics of Talmudic argument.[63] I think Benjamin was right when he warned his friend not to be carried away, for to the extent that Kafka referred to traditional religious symbols and to Talmudic cogitation he presented them in a state of total decay and decrepitude.[64] Thus, it is very doubtful that the writer really established a living connection with the mystical lore of either the Cabbala or Hasidism. In any case, I have still to read a convincing and thorough study, which would textually and clearly prove the existence of such a connection.[65] Indeed, I think the opposite can be proven. What hypnotized Kafka when he was sitting in the small hall of the Savoy, following the inane plots of Latayner's and Richter's plays, had nothing to do with either the Cabbala or the Talmud, but had everything to do with the poignant, pathetic, and grotesque wretchedness of both the actors and the plays. One could sense this clearly as one reads both the lines and between the lines of the long and far-from-attractive entries in Kafka's diary and fully gauges the depth of their ambiguities, their attraction-repulsion duality. In the actors and their "Jewish" bodies, in their movements, singing, and dancing, which he watched with what the actors themselves undoubtedly called *kelberne hispales* (calf-like admiration), he saw the personification of Jewish helplessness and weakness: the helplessness and the funny wretchedness of Herod's army—three little unimpressive men with carton helmets falling over their faces, stepping each on the feet of the other because the stage was so small and also for the purpose of making the audience laugh—why not? The actors tittering on the stage during the scene of the chief actor's operatic death and his wife (with the strange protrusions on the skin of her face and the disheveled hair that hid them) tearing the heavens with her shrieks! The dapper Kafka embraced this wretchedness. He "loved" it, believed in it, "accepted" it—while asking himself from time to time what on earth he was doing in the company of these lice-infested miscreants. It was exactly this wretchedness and misery that kindled Bialik's horrific rage; for the poet identified—*malgré lui*—with the miscreants, far more than Kafka ever did, and felt himself contaminated and humiliated by their wretchedness. Bialik's identification was transformed into the demonic energy that informed his whiplash-like verses—indeed, if words could kill, he would have whipped the poor Jews of Kishinev to death. Kafka's ambivalent identification was transformed into the movement of a hesitant caress. There was no way for him to restrain his rejection of the great pogrom poem, as much as there was no way for Bialik to accept the storyteller's embracing of the weak and the deformed. For Kafka, the actors and their pitiful theater represented not Judaism as such—a religion, a civilization, an aggregate of sacred texts—but rather *Judesein*, the experience of being a Jew; the experience of being what he felt he had been, puny and (in his own eyes) ungainly, as he watched his father's "strength, health, appetite, loudness of voice, eloquence, self-satisfaction, worldly dominance, endurance, presence of mind—vigor, noise, and hot temper";[66] or as he experienced a bodily shrinkage when gawking at his naked father (in a changing cell of a local swimming pool) towering above him "strong, tall, broad."[67] That was the real gist of his "charming" public lecture of February 18, 1912.

Elias Canetti unfolded in his work *Kafka's Other Trial,* on the Kafka-Felice Bauer-Grete Bloch triangle (I intentionally sidestep Canetti's interpretation of *The Trial* itself as a direct reflection of this triangle, the only part of this essay in which it is not one of the best and most brilliant ever written on Kafka), an amazingly penetrating and precise picture of Kafka's self-image as it was reflected in the letters to Felice and the ethos it was informed by. Among other insights, here is how Canetti ties Kafka's bodily self-image with his recoiling from marriage:

> Of all writers, Kafka is the greatest expert on power. He experienced it in all its aspects, and he gave shape to his experience. . . . [68]

Confronted as he was with power on all sides, his obduracy sometimes offered him a reprieve. But if it was insufficient, or it failed him, he trained himself to disappear; here the helpful aspect of his physical thinness is revealed, though often, as we know, he despised it. By means of physical diminution, he withdrew power *from himself,* and thus had less part in it. Most astounding of all is another method he practices, with sovereign skill—since he abominated violence, but did not credit himself with the strength to combat it, he enlarged the distance between the stronger entity and himself by becoming smaller and smaller in relation to it. Through this shrinkage, he gained two advantages: he evaded the threat by becoming too diminutive for it, and he freed himself from the exceptionable means of violence; the small animals into which he liked to transform himself were harmless ones.[69]

And in another place:

> Fear of a superior power is central to Kafka, and his mode of resistance of such a power is transformation into something small. [...] But no situation is less favorable to this withdrawal than marriage. One must always be there, whether one wants it or not, for part of the day and part of the night—one's own magnitude corresponding to one's partner, a magnitude which may not change; otherwise it would be no marriage at all. But the place of smallness, which exists even in marriage, is usurped by the children. Thus it is really envy that Kafka feels in the presence of children, but envy of a kind different than that which might be expected: an envy coupled with disapproval. "At first children seem to be usurpers of smallness, the smallness into which he would like to slip. But it turns out that they are not actually small beings who want to disappear as he wants to. They are the false smallness, exposed to the noise and unpleasant influences of the adults—smallness goaded into becoming bigger, and also wanting just that, the very opposite of his deepest natural tendency, which is to become smaller, quieter, lighter, until one disappears."[70]

These brilliant observations belong, of course, within their context, which is that of Kafka's impossible relationship with Felice; but as Canetti clearly shows (and his corpus of proofs can be easily tripled and quadrupled), they shed light on the author's work as a whole—even on "The Metamorphosis," where Samsa is doomed to a terrible death not by becoming an insect (the German text never uses the term), but by becoming a monstrously big creature, totally out of all proportions, or as the German text puts it, *einem ungeheueren Ungeziefer*[71] (monstrously big vermin; the adjective *ungeheuer* conveys both hugeness and monstrosity). Gregor's metamorphosis was incomplete. He lost the form of man but retained his size and mentality. In other words, he lost his power, or ability to control his family, but not his wish to do so. Rather than withdrawing from power, Kafka's saving strategy, he became the personification (or rather animation) of its vacuous and deceptive nature (he seems frightening, but he is actually harmless and very vulnerable). Would he have morphed into a real cockroach, he would have been saved from a life of slavery to his own grandiosity and denial of sexuality or to his family's irksome dependence, which he willed and fostered. Our purpose here, however, is not to use Canetti's insights for the purpose of offering new interpretations to some of Kafka's most complex creations, but rather to show how apt and enlightening they can be when applied to the issues and topic which concern us here, namely, Kafka's attitude toward the various options of a Jewish literature.

Smallness, diminution, was what Kafka both identified with and was repelled by. "Nothing frightens like small things," he once wrote to Brod. Yet, as Canetti observed, it also indicated his "deepest natural tendency," the tendency to become smaller, which was concomitant with the tendency of "a man who was lacking in power to withdraw from power in whatever form it might appear."[72] This "tendency," wish ("to become smaller, quieter, lighter, until one disappears"), and therefore frightening "more than anything else," also contained a deeply humanistic critique of power; a critique, which could be and was applied to cultural power—an entity Kafka rejected with vehemence perhaps greater than that of his rejection of physical, political, legal, and financial power. Thus, for instance, in his stories, Kafka was suspicious and often viscerally critical of the power of words, which, as we have seen, he identified as the power of the evil spirits who "twisted every word" one said, turning it as a spear against the speaker. Thus words with their "characteristic" twist of hand were not that different from the knife wielded by K.'s executioners, who in the final scene of *The Trial*, was thrust into K.'s heart and then "turned . . . there twice."[73] It was the violence perpetrated by words that rendered them in their turn deserving of reciprocal violence; their role as executioners, twisting their spears into the heart of their victim—that invited their own execution by burning (however, Kafka himself could not carry out this draconian sentence and relegated the execution of his own words to Brod, who fortunately rejected this role, and to Dora Diamant, who foolishly followed her lover's orders). By the same token, Kafka was suspicious of the power of information and learnedness, which he ridiculed in many of his stories (such as "The Village Schoolmaster," "A Report to an Academy," "Investigations of a Dog"); the power of codices, the law (which could be nothing more than the infernal machine of the penal colony, which wrote its "sacred" edicts not on vellum but on "leather," perforating the skin of living people and making them bleed to death, as in "In the Penal Colony"; or it could be utterly arbitrary as in "The Problem with Our Laws," *The Trial*, and *The Castle*); the power of advocacy and argument (as in the many figures of attorneys in Kafka's stories, one of them being Bucephalus himself, the mythological horse of Alexander the Great; also the pernicious casuistry of the priest in the cathedral scene of *The Trial*, where he attempted to prove, by using "Talmudic" logic, that the man in the fable "Before the Law," and by inference, K. himself, had not been maliciously misled and cheated by the powers that were); and the last but not least—the ambiguous power of "talent" (see the painter Titorelli in *The Trial*; the dogs' choir in "Investigations of a Dog," the preposterous "talent" of the "Hunger Artist," and the childishly narcissistic demands of adoration and special treatment on the part of Josephine the Singer, who actually had no real talent).

In culture as in life, smallness was desirable as it was also frightening; and in Jewish culture, Yiddish (as Kafka understood it) represented smallness or minority, not necessarily or not only in the sense ascribed to this concept by Deleuze and Guattari. It was a vernacular (and as such stood on the lowest rung in Henri Gobard's tetralinguistic ladder (consisting of language as vernacular, vehicular, referential, and mythic);[74] it was maternal (*mame-loshn*) and feminine, and therefore unable to shoulder the burden of "big" cultural messages, which were necessarily paternal and masculine; it was a language without specific territory—that of emigrants, wanderers; and it was the language of the weak, the monopolized, the exploited. Hebrew was the exact opposite of Yiddish. True, it had been de-territorialized and thus weakened, but it once had had a firm territorial basis and was about to be re-territorialized (if the Zionist dream became a reality); it was masculine, "the language of the fathers," the male ancestors (traditional Jewish women could not speak or read it); it was, of course, not only "informational" (i.e., "the language of sense and culture entailing a cultural re-territorialization,")[75] but also, above all else, mythic or anagogic: the language of prophecy, poetry, ritual, everything hieratic and theurgical. Although it did not yet possess real power (with which the realization of Zionism would endow it, rendering it the language of government and the military), it *pretended* to possess it (otherwise Bialik would not have written "Be'ir haharega" the way he did), or at least it hoped to possess it. In other words, at least in the present, it amounted to either Krilov's huffing and puffing frog, whose wish was to inflate itself to the size of an ox, or, in the best case, it was the weak child, who, "exposed to the noise and unpleasant influences" of its ideologues and poets, was "goaded into becoming bigger; and also wanting just that"(Canetti). The ideologues and the poets were "goading" the Hebrew cultural experiment, weak and underdeveloped as it still was, into being (or pretending to be) what Bialik wanted the victims of the Kishinev pogrom to have been: heroes. Instead of behaving like cowards, hiding, peeping like mice from their holes, they should have attacked the enemy, or committed suicide, or at least gone crazy, or gouged (like Oedipus) their eyes that observed the rape of their women (the poet actually said that, condemning those who "didn't gouge their eyes or lose their minds");[76] or do something similar, as long as it was on a sufficiently grand scale. But Kafka was on the side of the mice or the moles and shared their instinctual flight to the hole or the burrow. Thus, the national Jewish cultural project, particularly in its Hebraic part, rubbed him the wrong way and won his (mostly) silent rejection. Hebrew literature in particular seems to have set his hair on end, because he felt that it had committed itself to the preposition of power or to a quest for self empowerment, and literature could not achieve its goal if it did not adopt the "politics" of withdrawal from power. Kafka, "of all writers—the greatest expert on power," having experienced it "in all its aspects" and given a shape to his experience, could not but have recoiled from the most prominent exponents of the Hebrew literary project: Bialik, Tchernikhovsky, Berditchevsky, Brenner. Had he known the work of a poet such as David Fogel or the prose fiction of Dvora Baron, or some parts of Agnon's oeuvre (such as *A Simple Story* or "Ovadia the Cripple" or "The Doctor and his Divorcee" and "Fernheim"), his judgment would, perhaps, have been less harsh. He knew, of course, that literature itself must have its power, which rendered even the best of it of ambiguous value and perhaps deserving the auto-da-fé he said should eliminate his own writings. Nevertheless, for him a literary work was of some import only if it could change its reader, "break" something inside him, deeply penetrate him. For works that did this, he had the highest respect, and to some of the authors who wrote them (Kleist, Flaubert, Grillparzer, and Dostoevsky) he referred as the four writers *die Ich . . . als meine eigentlichen Blutsverwandten fühle* ("I consider to be my true blood-relations"). [77] Literature needed the power to "break open" things. Yet it could perform this forceful act of penetration only if it gave up on power. This was one of the central paradoxes of which literature was made, and it informed everything Kafka wrote and did as a writer and was the source of his magic, the overwhelming attraction we experience as we enter his sphere of influence. "There is something most profoundly exciting about this tenacious attempt, on the part of a man who was lacking in power, to withdraw from power in whatever form it might appear," commented Canetti in an already quoted paragraph in his essay. It was a withdrawal that went far beyond ethical considerations and became a temperament, a mental language, as well as a body language. How could this man be impressed by a "national poet" who roared like a wounded lion when a genuine Jewish national poet should presumably have squeaked like Josephine, a regular mouse who was chosen by the "mouse folk" as its representative exactly because she was nothing more than a regular mouse, piping and squeaking feebly as all mice did? Or he should have been like the small marten-like animal with the bluish-green fur who inhabited the synagogue in the distant village in the mountainous region in Kafka's "In Our Synagogue," a quintessential Jewish statement, where the frightened, small rodent represented the essence of *Judesein* as distinguished from Jewish religion, ritual, civilization.[78] At most it could be like a cunning old jackal who wailed through the nights of the desert, tore the flesh of cadavers while fantasizing about tearing open the jugular of Arabs. Why should he be a Bialik when he could have been a Latayner or an Goldfaden, writing tuneful, melancholy lyrics about *"ein paar Rosinen un Mandeln"*?

Eleven

Contiguity: How Kafka and Sholem
Aleichem Are Contiguous

Given this understanding of Kafka's antithetical position (one of "negative contiguity") within the modern Jewish literary complex, particularly vis à vis its Yiddish and Hebrew components, we should ask now
whether he can be seen as positively contiguous to any Hebrew or Yiddish writer, and if he can, how this positive contiguity can be defined and
demonstrated. Of course, many Hebrew and Yiddish writers have been
referred to as Kafkaesque since the term became popular (in the 1940s
and 1950s) as a frequently—much too frequently—used adjective. It is a
debased and unhelpful term, not only because the way it is being used
it has little, if anything, to do with the staple characteristics of Kafka's
fictional "world," but mainly because it is imprecise and sloppy in and of
itself.[1] Anything that has to do with alienation, is vaguely nightmarish,
oppressive, bureaucratically exasperating, or even slightly strange and
ominous is referred to as Kafkaesque, with the adjective retaining not as
much as a trace of the writer's commitment to clarity, meticulous precision (in both style and narrative presentation), logical causality (in the
developing of plot and character), and, yes, to his particular sense of humor, without which Kafka would not have been the Kafka we know and
would not have attracted to his work even a fraction of the insatiable
interest and curiosity it most definitely commands. Kafkaesque writers
can be found for a penny a dozen, whereas there is only one Kafka.

Much of what has been said about Kafka's influence on Hebrew literature is contaminated by such lack of critical rigor. The Hebrew master,
who more than all others was said to have been under Kafka's influence,
is Agnon, whose contacts with Kafka's legacy are supposed to have informed his relatively late "meta-realistic" stories such as the dream-like,

351

nightmarish tales he wrote beginning in the early 1930s (most, but not all, of them were collected in the cycle whose title was wrongly translated as *The Book of Deeds*, when it actually meant simply *The Book of Tales*)[2] and the large sections in the novel *Temol shilshom* (*Yesteryear*), where the narrative focus shifts from the human protagonist, Yitskhak Kummer, to his animal counterpart, the "philosophical" dog Balak, who eventually brings about Kummer's death (by rabies). The latter was supposed to be embossed with the indelible imprint of "Investigations of a Dog."[3] Whether these parts of Agnon's oeuvre were actually influenced by Kafka, or, as the writer himself consistently maintained, were utterly free from such influence, is a matter of slight significance. The essential point is that even if influenced by Kafka, Agnon had never internalized any of his quintessential narrative procedures, which clearly articulated Kafka's narrative worldview, as well as conditioned his narrative technique. Thus, Kafka's way of initiating a nightmarish or fantastic situation only to further develop it—in almost all of his stories—in total accordance with the rules of mundane reality and logical causality, without adding to it as much as a smattering of fantasy (Samsa having one morning awoken from "uneasy dreams" to find himself morphed into a "monstrous vermin"; Blumfeld returning one day from his office work to find in his old bachelor's apartment two little balls which, constantly jumping, kept following him, etc.) was never adopted by Agnon. In the latter's nightmarish tales, time (particularly "Jewish" holy time, such as the first day of the new year or the Day of Atonement) and space (particularly the dual "Jewish" space; that of the destroyed Polish shtetl and of the yet unredeemed Jerusalem) were constantly being unrealistically warped, with the protagonist falling through the cracks pried opened by endless disruptions in the surfaces of a disintegrating chronotope. The only Kafka stories that these tales call to mind are "A Country Doctor," "The Bucket Rider," "A Common Confusion," and temporarily, also the first chapter of *The Castle* (temporarily, because all the oddities of time and space Joseph K. encounters in this chapter are eventually revealed as mundane and utterly "logical," when judged by the criteria of the quasi-feudal society K. encounters in the village he had reached, and whose "logic" he failed to internalize). However, while "A Country Doctor," The Bucket Rider," and "A Common Confusion" are certainly vintage Kafka, their technique, particularly that of the first two, follows in the wake of the common expressionistic fantasy or dream tale, whose format Agnon had absorbed in his early youth, even before Kafka wrote "The Judgment" and "The Metamorphosis." Besides, the fantastic treatment of time and space in "A Country Doctor" is informed by Hasidic motifs of "Kefitsat haderekh" ("A Miraculous Shortcut"),[4] which Agnon had absorbed as a child, and for which he certainly was in no need of Kafka's mediation.

Another staple Kafka narrative procedure that Agnon rarely had use for was that of the discursive and argumentative disquisition, mingled with narrative elements. Benjamin compared this amalgam to that of the Talmudic aggada, where the homiletic narrative illustrates, deconstructs, and is mingled with the rabbinical argument.[5] The two basic characteristics of stories of this kind are, therefore, their narrative performative (and thus, their essentially dramatic, theatrical ambience) and their all but ritualistic use of the procedures of a fully articulated logical syllogism. They are to be read as if said aloud (the Hebrew verb h-g-d), as learned monologues, in which a certain point or hypothesis is defined and then debated at length, intermingling with the logical and rather orderly presentation of the various aspects of the debated hypothesis whatever narrative contents the story was meant to possess (see stories such as "A Report to the Academy," "The Great Wall of China," "Investigations of a Dog," "The Burrow," "Josephine the Singer," "Jackals and Arabs," "The Cares of a Family Man," "The Problems of Our Laws," and, of course, the argumentative dialogue that follows "Before the Law" in *The Trial*). That is why the Balak chapters in *Yesteryear* are so unlike Kafka's stories of this kind, including "Investigations of a Dog." Whereas the latter are almost always written in the form of a logical address, a formal or semi-formal "presentation" (aimed at an "academy," a journalist, a traveler, an unidentified group that is nevertheless characterized by its erudition, pedantry, and interest in rather arcane topics, or at us, the readers, projected as such a group), Balak's painful musings are systematically conveyed by an omniscient narrator, who reproduces them as he would have reproduced the thoughts of human characters: chaotic, flowing, unsystematized. Kafka's monologists are always out to make a point, correct a mistake, present an idea, which at surface level seems farfetched, as corresponding to the truth, differentiate, qualify, refute, and so on; in short their rhetoric is based on the logic of demonstration, proof, and persuasion; Balak's ideas are often erratic, fantastic, "canine." The very tonality of the Balak chapters in Agnon's novel is different from that of Kafka's animal parables.

The truth is, that where Agnon is sometimes really "touching" Kafka, always unintentionally and not through the mediation of any influence, direct or indirect, it is in those stories and novels of his where he focuses on weak and limited protagonists, who seem to accept their limitations and try to live with them. Such are Hershl Hurwitz and Yitskhak Kummer, the protagonists of two of the author's five full-fledged novels (*A Simple Story* and *Yesteryear*, respectively), as well as those of many of his short stories and novellas. Agnon was an expert on human weakness and limitations. He was, among the chief Hebrew masters, perhaps the only one who knew how to bring to narrative life protagonists who were non-intellectual, inarticulate, and humble; and it was in this that he perhaps came closer than many to the other great Jewish writer, his contemporary. Thus, if *Yesteryear* was in any way contiguous to a Kafka story, it was not so in its fantastic and grotesque sections but rather in its straightforwardly realistic ones, where the horrible fate of an *homme moyen sensuel*, a regular and rather unimpressive person, was unfolded. That this man, for "sins" that were in no way graver than those of his fellow men, was sentenced to die truly "*wie ein Hund*" (like a dog; K.'s final words in *The Trial*) invites a comparison with Kafka, which can be more convincing and fruitful than any comparisons between Balak and the protagonist of "Investigations of a Dog." It also invites an exploration of the two masters' ties with Flaubert and a juxtaposition of their idiosyncratic readings of his masterpieces. However, what can be of real importance is not the existence or non-existence of a demonstrable influence of one of the two writers on the other one; but rather the two writers' treatment of issues of power, weakness, intentional or unintentional withdrawal from power, the aspiration of becoming powerful and so on, issues that were absolutely central to any modern Jewish self-awareness and self-evaluation (to use once again Brenner's coinage). The comparison is particularly intriguing and worthwhile because Agnon sometimes seemed to approximate Kafka's positions with regard to these issues although he had been from the very vantage point of his creative trajectory a committed (and even radical) Zionist, and in the second half of his career also a practicing religious Jew. As such, he could "understand" (if not accept) Jewish weakness—even the weakness of a Zionist pioneer like Kummer, who made aliya, and then, once in Palestine and losing his bearings, was swept back to the barren world of orthodox *Me'a she'arim* (Hundredfold; the name of the neighborhood in "new" Jerusalem, where the fanatically orthodox lived and still live)—because Agnon viewed the modern Jewish condition as tragically schizophrenic, and therefore as deeply flawed in all its manifestations, Zionism included. Those who truly wanted to be "redeemed" (the Zionists) had lost touch with the only redeemer (God, the religious tradition), and those who had not lost touch with the redeemer lost their will to be redeemed (orthodox Jewry). Both camps were ferociously active, and the agricultural and colonizing activity of the Zionists was by far more creative and future-oriented than that of the orthodoxy, which limited itself to fending off modernity. Nevertheless, Zionist activity, too, took place in a spiritual vacuum, and therefore the weakness of Kummer, who was torn apart because he needed to belong in both worlds, the Zionist and the religious-orthodox ones, was not only understandable but actually symbolic of Jewish modernity as a whole. Having said that, we should nevertheless be always on our guard with regard to Agnon's acceptance of Jewish weakness; for more often than not, it is conveyed in subtle ironic terms, which imply a pervasive albeit discrete rejection. Thus, for instance, Hershl Hurwitz's acquiescence of the loss of his lover, his withdrawal back into normalcy from the mental breakdown that this loss had triggered, and his settling down to a questionable conjugal happiness can (and perhaps should) be read with the taste of the narrator's muted but corrosive irony in the reader's mouth. If the narrator does, the "implied author" does not approve of Hershl's defeatism. The same goes for Raphael from "The Tale of the Scribe," Agnon's *Hungerkünstler* (hunger-artist), who, dedicating himself to his "art" (the writing of Torah scrolls), forgot about all physical needs and instinctual drives—only to find himself polluting the scroll he wrote in memory of his departed wife (with whom he had no sexual intercourse, although both had been praying for pregnancy and progeny) when in a moment of aberration, and having clad it in his wife's wedding gown, he mistook it for the woman he still loved. The seemingly innocent story, written in the form of the hagiographic biography, treats the theme of self-abnegation with muted but fierce irony, which is essentially different from the tone of the hunger-artist's confession in Kafka's story.

Irony had functioned in both the Yiddish and Hebrew new literatures as one of the tools of exposing and ridiculing Jewish impotence. The best example of its functioning as a satirical tool was given by Peretz in his famous short story "Bontshe shvayg," where a passive and terribly exploited and cheated simpleton, who had never protested or complained (hence the appellation *shvayg*, the one who keeps his mouth shut), was presented as a saint only to be made bitter fun of at the end of the story, where Bontshe, already in heaven, when offered by the heavenly court the opportunity to choose whatever compensation he wanted for his ruined earthly existence, chose a buttered roll. Although Agnon's irony was more sophisticated by far, the distance between it and that of "Bontshe shvayg" was perhaps shorter than we think. By and large, it was very difficult for both Hebrew and Yiddish modern writers to approve of passivity and "accept" not Jewish weakness per se (which was a given under the circumstances), but the acquiescence of it, the viewing of smallness, and the relinquishment of self-assertion as positive (or maybe positive, since we remember that Kafka was also frightened by small things) characteristics or attitudes. That is why it makes little, if any, sense, to couple Kafka with Brenner, and not necessarily because the former disapproved of the latter's novel and pessimism, but because Brenner demanded from his protagonists, from himself, and from his reader, the heroic efforts that were needed to overturn the Jewish condition and stand it on its head, making agricultural laborers out of petty merchants, rootless intellectuals, and members of the liberal professions. Ironically, it was in his last novel, *Shekhol vekishalon*, the one Kafka disapproved of, together with some other stories written relatively late in the author's truncated career that Brenner, perhaps, somewhat narrowed the gap separating his attitudes from those of Kafka; for in these late works, he mitigated his heroic humanist ethos and not only acknowledged weakness and shortcomings as inalienable parts of the human condition (this, in his fierce demand for total veracity and realism, he had done in all of his works), but also conveyed the notion that under certain circumstances, the acceptance of one's weakness and shortcomings was morally acceptable. However, even in these works, and particularly in *Breakdown and Bereavement*, Brenner was not focusing on themes that could hardly appeal to Kafka, by which I refer to the fact that the protagonist of Brenner's novel possessed a psychotic personality and periodically sank into madness (psychosis also played an important role in the author's early novel *Misaviv lanekuda* [*Circling the Dot*]). Much of the novel's psychological interest emanated from the author's exploration of sexual psychosis (symbolized by the protagonist's physical condition as a person suffering from a hernia). Kafka might have been turned off by this. As a person who knew everything one could know about the neuroses, despair, guilt, fear, and the sense of inner emptiness, he was not particularly interested in psychosis; that, in spite of his referring to himself (and to his uncle Rudolf) as both living "on the verge of madness."[6] The number of references to insanity or psychosis in his diaries, letters, aphorisms, and non-fictional writings is surprisingly small, whereas in his stories and novels, such references are hardly to be found. Significantly, in almost all those references, Kafka explained either to himself or to an addressee how he managed to avoid insanity by accepting his limitations and weakness or by practicing his art as a writer. To Felice Bauer, he told how he, by not rebelling against his parents, managed to hold onto sanity because "I cannot rebel against the laws of nature without going mad."[7] To Milena Jesenska he wrote about his acceptance of impotence as a Jew facing an anti-Semitic rabble: "Any attempt to get through this on my own is madness and is rewarded by madness."[8] In his letters to Brod, he pointed to writing and literature, tortuous and difficult as they were, as shielding him from insanity: "Writing sustains me. [...] My life [...] when I don't write is [...] unbearable [...] and has to end in madness; [...] a non-writing writer is a monster inviting madness."[9] He was fully aware of his "fragile" existence hovering "over a darkness from which the dark power emerges when it wills, and heedless of my stammering, destroys my life;"[10] but succumbing to madness seemed to him the easy way out, involving a questionable "contentment" that he rejected ("the way a faintly burbling madness which one takes for the melody of life leads to contentment").[11] He was, of course, cognizant of Freud's theories and aware of their applicability to some of his stories, but had little respect for them, and "considered them always as a very rough and ready explanation, which didn't do justice to detail, or rather to the real heartbeat of the conflict."[12] In any case, he never really focused on a person's total loss of the sense of reality. To him, mental suffering was amenable to description and endless analysis as long as the sufferer was aware of reality and of his place in it. Felice could perhaps see him as a "madman," but he knew he was anything but crazy, and in his letters to her, he rationally and analytically explained the difference between madness and his neuroses; for once a person's ties with reality and rationality snapped, that is, psychosis kicked in, mental suffering became dull, uninteresting, and perhaps also hardly imaginable to him. This, by the way, also points to the differences between him and Agnon, who was also interested in madness, and wrote in *A Simple Story* the best Hebrew work of fiction focusing on a psychotic breakdown (much of Agnon's writing in the 1930s was based on Freudian insights, particularly those contained in his *Traumdeutung*). Above all else, however, Brenner and Agnon, too, but particularly the former, should not be coupled with Kafka because their writing could not be understood out of the context of a Zionist revolution, which to each of them, separately and quite differently, was the only possible Jewish revolution. As for Brenner, his critique of Judaism as a whole, and of the Jewish exilic tradition in particular, was so scathing and fierce as to be justifiably pointed to as an illustration of Zionist-Jewish self-hatred, would have been totally at loggerheads with Kafka's notion of authentic *Judesein*. The little frightened animal from Kafka's "In Our Synagogue" would have been acceptable to Brenner (as symbolizing Jewishness) only within a context of self-lacerating condemnation, but not as an acceptable symbol of authentic Jewishness, with which Kafka could identify (in contradistinction to the synagogue itself and its vacuous ritual).

If we are therefore unable to see either Brenner or Agnon as positively contiguous to Kafka, then who, in the modern Hebrew and Yiddish—quite-separate—canons, can be seen as approximating a closer and more comfortable contact with this greatest of Jewish writers in modern times? Perhaps the modern national Jewish literatures were in their very essence anti-"Kafkaesque"? The truth is that they were.

Nevertheless, within these literatures there were moments of sudden clear-sighted stepping out of the power and empowerment ethos, to which the literatures as a whole were by and large committed. Such a moment arrived, for instance, when I. B. Singer, a sworn Schopenhauerian pessimist, a believer in the merits of passivity, and a writer who consistently pointed to the illusionary nature of activism (which was nothing more than a self-extradition into the hands of the evil powers) emerged as the last master of a literary tradition about to peter out. I. B. Singer became famous for "Gimpel the Fool," his parody on Peretz's "Bontshe shvayg." There, the exploited and betrayed protagonist, perfectly aware of being sinned against and cheated, too, knowingly chose passivity and a quietist humane ethos as the wisest tactic of deflecting violence and was therefore rewarded with the talent of telling tales—of becoming a writer through withdrawal from power. I. B. Singer was to a considerable extent a Kafka follower, as he himself would have certainly asserted.

However, the sweetest and most luminous of these moments of detoxification, the self-cleansing from the heady elixir of empowerment had occurred many decades before the arrival of Gimpel and in the work of Sholem Aleichem; to be exact, in 1895, when the Yiddish humorist made the greatest discovery of his career: the character of Tevye the dairyman and the uses of the monologue form as employed in Tevye's tales (let us once again remember how important the monologue form was to Kafka; a good part of his best shorter works were written as monologues—often in a vividly imagined or clearly referred to performative context. What are "Report to the Academy," "A Hunger Artist," "The Burrow," "The Bucket Rider," or "Josephine the Singer" if not dramatic monologues waiting for performative realization? Benjamin believed all Kafka tales, the novels included, constituted "a code of gestures" for which the theater was "the logical place." Whatever the specified tale's other components, "the gesture remained the decisive thing, the center of the event."[13] This can certainly be said, with equal, if not more, justification of each and every work of Sholem Aleichem. Of course, a positive contiguity between the two Jewish writers would not depend on one common characteristic only; nor would it necessarily involve a direct exposure of each or one of the two to the work of the other. Sholem Aleichem, who died in 1916, did not know of the existence of Kafka; the latter, of course, knew of that of Sholem Aleichem. He heard about him from Levy, listened to the actor's recitation of some of the Yiddish writer's "humoresques," and read some of his stories that were translated into German (Ritchie Robertson's suggestion that he might have read a book by Sholem Aleichem in its Yiddish original is patently wrong).[14] The episode of his recommending (to Felice Bauer) Sholem Aleichem's stories as age-appropriate reading material for children and then immediately rescinding his recommendation has already been mentioned and commented on. It indicated a sudden understanding on his part of the complexity and ironic quality ("ironisch und kompliciert"[15]) of the tales he had earlier deemed harmless folktales. It was a moment of some importance; however, it is not that kind of contact we have in mind.

In her *The Modern Jewish Canon: A Journey through Language and Culture*, Ruth R. Wisse seems to be on the verge of a really important breakthrough when she makes the connection between Sholem Aleichem and Kafka, saying: "Kafka's *The Trial* begins just where *Tevye the Dairyman* leaves off."[16] The two Jewish writers, the scholar-critic observes, were actually reacting to a similar Jewish situation of persecution and weakness: the pogroms of 1903 and 1905 and the Beilis blood libel accusation and trial (1911–1913), which Sholem Aleichem avidly followed from the various Italian, Swiss, and German sanatoria where he was convalescing from his collapse from open pulmonary tuberculosis in 1908 (Kafka will be diagnosed with the same sickness in 1917), Kafka was following with the same interest through the weekly reports in the *Selbstwher*. Sholem Aleichem worked his impressions of the Beilis case into his novel *The Bloody Hoax*, while Kafka probably used it for the bringing to life of the "Russian" chaotic background in "The Judgment" (where the protagonist, Georg Bendemann, reads about the riots in Kiev, Beilis's hometown, in the letters he receives from his friend in Russia). Dora Diamant also told about a play based on the Beilis case that Kafka either wrote and destroyed or planned to write.[17] In Tevye's last tale, "Lekh lekha" ("Get Thee Out"), Tevye, who constantly mentions Beilis and his unspeakable accusation and suffering, had been presented with an official decree, arbitrary and cruel (for no transgression of his is mentioned), giving him three days for selling his property and leaving the village in which he had been born and lived his life, and in the opening episode of *The Trial* (both texts being written in the same year: 1914) K. is being notified, also officially and as arbitrarily and cruelly, of his being accused (and under interrogation) of an unspecified crime. The "Jewish" resemblances Wisse points to are real enough and whet the appetite for more insights on her part, until she comes to her point of reversal: what is of importance to her are not the background resemblances but rather the difference of the respective writers' attitudes. "The surprise lies rather in the contrast of treatment,"[18] she writes, and the letdown is immediate and painful. Everyone knows that there are differences between Sholem Aleichem and Kafka; they are self-evident and as such, of slight interest. One hardly needs the perception of a thoughtful and well-trained critic to see them. However, what about the deeper, running resemblances that bring Kafka and Sholem Aleichem close to each other; resemblances that depend not on mere background but on similarity in attitudes, of ethical positions, if not in narrative treatment (although such similarities can also be detected)? About them, Wisse has nothing to say. Frankly, having just read through her interpretation of *Tevye* (which occupies the first chapter of her monograph) and particularly her comments on the "Lekh lekha" tale, one should not have entertained high expectations, for Wisse misunderstood and misinterpreted Sholem Aleichem's masterpiece, which is, perhaps, the prime text in the modern Jewish literary complex that is most contiguous to Kafka's stories and novels. As dissimilar to *The Trial* and the Kafka short stories as it is, it is also their close relative, as we shall see; and it is when one discovers that unexpected but very real, albeit completely unintentional, relatedness that one realizes how reading the modern Jewish complex with the principle of contiguity or tangentiality in mind could help fathoming it, grappling for the unexpected realities that are still hidden in its depths. Demonstrating this hypothesis would necessitate a relatively detailed, although by no means exhaustive, analysis of *Tevye*, which would therefore be the only text subjected to such an analysis in the framework of this essay. As much as this is not an essay in interpretative criticism, this analysis is necessary, because on it hinges the concept of positive contiguity that this essay purports to recommend as a replacement or at least a corrective of the prevalent concept of Jewish literary continuity.

❄

> I will speak, that I may find relief;
> I will open my lips and answer.

—Job 32:20

For more than a century *Tevye der milkhiker* (*Tevye the Dairyman*) has been universally acknowledged as Sholem Aleichem's consummate masterpiece. Endowed with a depth of humanity, a delicate equilibrium between tragedy and comedy, and an overwhelmingly vivacious comic narration, the interrelated Tevye tales soared above the author's other achievements, brilliant as many of them were. Their vitality was such that they have survived a score of translations of uneven quality and questionable fidelity, various stage adaptations (including one prepared by the author himself), which for ideological or commercial considerations wrenched the heart of the tales out of its original ribcage, crudely transmuting and obfuscating the meaning of the work as a whole, and even a successful stage version as one of Broadway's schmaltziest musicals, which superimposed upon the popular imagination a Tevye figure—a diluted, semi-Judaized Zorba—who tenuously, if not accidentally—resembled Sholem Aleichem's original creation no more than a beautified postcard resembled the reality of a foreign city. To withstand all this treatment, a work of art had to possess a formidable inner strength. Our task here is to point to the source or sources of this strength.

This is by no means an easy task, in spite of the fact, that throughout the last century, the *Tevye* tales have been constantly commented on and reinterpreted by some of the best critics and literary scholars, whose field of study was the new or modern Yiddish literature. Much of what these commentators and scholars said and wrote is of lasting critical value and should certainly be consulted by serious readers. However, to the best of my knowledge, no one yet has put a finger on the very core of the work, the source from which its extraordinary brilliance directly emanates. Whereas literary scholars invested efforts in worthwhile but ancillary positivistic projects such as the study of the protracted genesis of the *Tevye* cycle[19] (the eight or nine[20] units of which were created in a rather desultory fashion throughout the last two decades of the author's life) and the gradual formation of its canonical version, literary critics dwelt mainly on either the social and cultural implications of the various tales or on the character of Tevye and its symbolic or archetypal significance. Both topics were, of course, of considerable importance, but the study of neither could yield a full understanding of the work's unique qualities.

The social and cultural insights the stories directly and indirectly offered were indeed significant and absorbing. A historical panorama, the unfolding of which would have normally necessitated the writing of a large cycle of voluminous novels, was squeezed here into eight short novellas, in which the affairs of a provincial dairyman and the fortunes of his daughters became the prisms through which much of what was essential in the history of the Jews in the Czarist empire during the last two turbulent decades of its existence was refracted. Because the tales were written intermittently during these decades, the author was in a position to look in each of them at a different or a new aspect of a progressively endangered existence of Jews within a hostile non-Jewish population and under a hostile autocratic regime. Starting with the rustic mock-idyll that told the story of Tevye's "miraculous" deliverance from penury, and of how he came to possess the few milking cows that enabled him to make ends meet as a dairyman, the tales gradually shed light on wider historical arenas, pointing to issues and realities that loomed far beyond the provincial circumference of the protagonist's activities and interests: the revolutionary mood that swept the Czarist empire in the first years of the twentieth century; underground revolutionary activities and the regime's attempts at squashing them through exiling or hanging the activists; the failed 1905 revolution and the Czar's reneged-on promise of a liberal constitution, which triggered widespread anti-Jewish pogroms of unprecedented ferocity; the egotistic and hedonistic culture that emerged in the wake of the stillborn revolution, with its emphases on unbridled sexual gratification and the liberation of women from bourgeois, as well as other traditional restrictions, on the one hand, and its epidemic of suicides, on the other (by focusing on these topics the Tevye tales written in the years 1906–1909 clearly displayed the author's exposure to the "Silver Age" Russian literature that became prominent at the time); the rise of a new Jewish plutocracy through shady construction and supplying deals during the Russo-Japanese war; and finally the waves of vicious anti-Semitism, both popular and official, which engulfed the Jewish population of the Empire in the years preceding the outbreak of World War I, finding expression in the famous Beilis blood-libel trial (1911–1913) and the expulsion of Jews (as fraudulent exploiters of the naive Slavic peasant) from the countryside. Thus the cycle, from its quasi-pastoral beginning to the pandemonium of its ending, where Tevye, once a rooted villager, emerged as a homeless refugee randomly roaming by foot, cart, and train throughout the Ukraine, dreaming of emigration to a destination not yet decided upon, was chock-full of historical vistas and socio-cultural insights, which certainly were and still are of great interest. However, the greatness of the *Tevye* tales did not inhere in this historical panorama; nor even in its peculiar, somewhat skewed, reflection in Tevye's mind. The narrative art of Sholem Aleichem here (as in the author's other chief creations), while making full use of a given socio-cultural milieu, completely transcended its sheer mimetic presentation. It was not as a historical pseudo-novel that the *Tevye* cycle carried this art to the ultimate realization of its aesthetic potential.

Nor did this realization occur through a presentation of Tevye himself as an archetypal hero, a folksy philosopher, a symbol of Jewish endurance, fortitude, tenacity, ability to hold on to life—against terrible odds—through a well-balanced personality, a benevolent humanity, and an unbreakable *bitokhn* (confidence) in a divine providence. Here many critics, from the beginning of the twentieth century to the very recent past, following various brands of nationalistic ideology, were actually led astray, reading into the text their ideological preferences rather than paying close attention to what the text itself conveyed. In their defense, one may say that more than once the author himself, in his comments and conversations, joined them in artificially enlarging the dimensions of his own protagonist, inflating his significance beyond the stretchable limits of its actual bulk, as, for instance, in his attempts to endow Tevye with a biblical aura by comparing his miseries to Job's tragic travails.[21]

However, by doing that Sholem Aleichem showed—as he often did on similar occasions—that as soon as he switched from narration to commentary, to talking at the conceptual level and in the capacity of an "intellectual," he was neither cleverer nor more perceptive than his lesser critics. There was a world of difference between his Tevye narcissistically comparing himself to the great biblical sufferer, which he often did, and the author grandiloquently reiterating Tevye's claim to a Job-like tragic elevation.

The real Tevye, as he was reflected in his own monologues (all his tales being written in the form of dramatic monologues recited by himself for the benefit of the literary persona "Sholem Aleichem," a silent but solidly present interlocutor), had nothing exemplary (in the moral sense) about him. He was certainly a kind and benevolent person who loved his family and worked hard to put bread on its table, but he was neither a good husband nor truly a good father, and in general he exhibited various patterns of narcissistic behavior and was not an easy person to live and communicate with. In fact, in all aspects of his personality but one—his extraordinary talent as a raconteur—he was a deeply conventional, limited, and flawed person of his time and class, locked within the narrow cage of his social consciousness and personal, rather inflated, imagined identity as "the quintessential Jew." This was amply illustrated by his vast respect for money and social status, as well as by his disrespect for women and his nagging need to assert his male superiority over them (born out by his mantras: "Tevye is not a woman," and "a woman remains no more than a woman," as well as by his parading, in the most inappropriate situations, his Jewish "erudition," book learning being in traditional Jewish society the exclusive prerogative of males. In Sholem Aleichem's best works, protagonists who constantly parade their Jewish learning by quoting existing, as well as non-existent, sources are not only poor learners, with a very limited and spotty erudition, but, more importantly, men who are thoroughly insecure about their virility and their role as patriarchs and leaders of their families. Their constant and irksome exhibiting of their "knowledge," is a kind of a male exhibitionism, a textual "flashing," through which they repeatedly expose their "spiritual" genitals).[22] Both values, a virile self-confidence and social and financial security, were beyond his reach, since he was passive and devoid of self-confidence to the point of paralysis. Hard working as he was, he totally lacked faith in his ability to bring about the changes that he desired: those of becoming affluent and of leaving the village and his hard productive labor there as a dairyman, and joining the traditional shtetl society, where he would be respected as a learned and generous philanthropist. Such goals, if they were to be achieved at all, should have been reached either through sheer luck (also understood as God's good will) or through the efforts or the attractiveness of others, such as his beautiful daughters, who, through lucrative marriages, would be in a position to free their father from hard work and exile from the normative Jewish community, or a millionaire son-in-law, who would have trusted him, Tevye, with the well-paid job of supervising laborers performing the menial tasks, the burden of which he and the members of his family now shouldered; not that Tevye could, for the life of him, understand how these successful others had achieved the power and riches he coveted. Mentioning such a person he would characteristically add a comment such as "he was a total nobody, but managed to find his way there [to financial success]—nobody knows how and wherefrom,"[23] as if acumen, effort, and business sense constituted a mystery he could not gauge and also was definitely uninterested in. These people, presumably, had *mazel* (luck). If they also worked hard and made sacrifices ("true, in the first few years he tore himself to shreds, almost died of hunger, but now . . ."),[24] these had nothing to do with their success. In Tevye's philosophy, human self-improvement and human will were totally divorced from each other. Enterprise, courage, and practical cleverness never counted with him as means of achieving a goal, which only luck or the unfathomable will of God were able to miraculously provide. Thus if success is *bashert* (decreed), it would come of itself right to one's home without any effort on one's part. If, God forbid, one is doomed to misfortune, one "can talk until blue in the face, which would help one like yesteryear's snows."[25] What is the connection between self-protection and talking "until blue in the face"? Talking is the only reality Tevye really knows, and talking much, to the point of splitting one's sides (*tsezerterheyt*) is his only survival tactic.

From the very beginning of his first tale, Tevye stuck to the formula: man could not improve his lot by his own volition or *seykhel* (cleverness). This constituted the very essence of his religion, for Tevye, for all his piety and purported intimacy with God, actually conceived of God in terms that were not that different from those he would use when speaking of luck or sheer chance. His religious *bitokhn* (confidence), when closely examined, rarely amounted to more than a passive acquiescence with "things as they were"; for if things were the way they were, it must have been God who had wanted them to be so; otherwise they would have been different. He repeatedly proffered sayings such as "Praise God for He is good—for whatever He does, is good; that is, it should have been good, for try to be clever and improve on Him! . . . you'll have to acknowledge that you are a fool, and that you'll not change the world."[26] Or, "God himself hates a beggar; for would He have loved him, the beggar would not have been a beggar."[27] God was thus identified with "reality" in the crudest sense of the term; an essentially static and unchangeable reality, made up of "things" or circumstances, which usually were devastating and monstrously unjust, although they could sometimes, by a fluke, also be unexpectedly and unexplainably overturned—why and how no one could know or should ask since no answer would be forthcoming. That was why comparing Tevye with Job was so misleading, the point made by the book of Job being that questioning God's ways was not only necessary but indeed inevitable if one was to retain active faith in Him. Tevye's narcissistic need to view himself as a later-day Job, who was, as the ancient one had been, utterly free from responsibility for the disasters inflicted upon him, was completely understandable (exactly because Tevye knew in his heart that he *was* responsible for much of the harm he and the other members of his family had sustained). But that self-serving comparison completely bypassed the biblical Job's moral courage and the readiness for a confrontational (and therefore vital) I-Thou dialogue with God that the Bible ascribed to moral paragons such as Abraham, Moses, Jeremiah, and Job. Indeed, it amounted to the very opposite of this courage and risk-taking. Thus, far from being the faith of a biblical Jew, Tevye's faith was anti-biblical and un-prophetic, the faith of a fatalist rather than that of a fervent believer in God as the just "judge of all earth," and as such, accountable for the inherent injustices of the world and bound to be challenged by an Abraham: "Shall not the judge of all the earth do right?!" (Genesis 18:25).

The only domain where Tevye could be seen as "great" was the place where narrative performance counted. What Tevye inadvertently told about himself as a husband and a father was far from appealing or morally acceptable. However, the telling itself, as much as it was self-serving and inherently apologetic, was delectable. In other words, Tevye's greatness belonged in the realm of the aesthetic rather than in those of moral sensibility or intellectual acuity. Tevye's narration was nothing less than intoxicating and seductive, and the best proof of this was the critics' (and readers') love for Tevye, which blinded them to his many failings and shortcomings. The theories about his heroism and exemplary self-conduct amounted to little more than the effusions of the myopic infatuated. Tevye, one may say, managed to dupe many of his readers. The artistic brilliance of his tales emanated, therefore, neither from the protagonist's ethical character nor from the social background the tales unfolded, but rather from the telling itself; from the narrative and rhetorical situation that repeated itself from one tale to another, and presented the loquacious Tevye as endlessly talking to his ubiquitous interlocutor, "Sholem Aleichem." For *Tevye der milkhiker*, like many other top-notch creations of Sholem Aleichem, was before all else a story about talking and listening and their mutually complementary dynamics; of telling propelled by a nagging need for self-exposure, and of the absorption of what was told, which emanated from the need to reflect the naked image, to serve it as a mirror. Thus the verbal interaction that took place in each of the tales, rather than the tales' contents, defined and prescribed the very essence of the reality conveyed by Tevye; a rhetorical rather than a mimetic reality. Whatever mimetic reality Tevye's narrative contained was, of course, significant and interesting—indeed, it was riveting; however, it was not half as real or fascinating as the talking itself, its rhetoric, meandering line of progression, and changing rhythms.

This was so for quite a few reasons. For a starter, Tevye, as said before, was a highly accomplished raconteur, a person who not only knew how to make the best of a good story, but also took great pleasure in doing so. No matter how tragic the contents of his stories, or even how personally humiliating the events they unfolded were, we could count on Tevye to tell them as effectively as he possibly could. There was never a dull moment with Tevye. He never suffered the dejection and pain he talked about to be lugubriously narrated. Like in the Greek epics, the darkest scenes (content-wise) were brilliantly illumined by the light of the telling; and as in the biblical narrative, no matter what the content was, a lively narrative pace was never allowed to flag. Whether indulging in cogitation, moralizing, describing people and events, or meticulously quoting dialogues, Tevye always remained in control of a narrative system, which could be happy in its rhythms and devastating in its content. His sense of impotence in the face of life's vicissitudes never contaminated its dexterous and clever narrative articulation. In short, Tevye impacted his audience, the persona Sholem Aleichem, and through it—us, the readers—first by the how of his telling and only then, by the what.

Then, as raconteurs committed to effective telling often do, he told the truth, but not necessarily the whole truth or anything but the truth; for a genuine storyteller would not allow the facts to spoil the story and undermine its dramatic effect. We have to remind ourselves that Tevye, being the sole source of the information contained in his tales, which could not therefore be either corroborated of refuted through any other source, presented us with narrated facts, the veracity of which could not, by definition, be firmly established. Thus, he was one of those storytellers, who when listened to, one had to keep in the back of one's mind a certain reservation, a shadow of suspicion. If one permitted oneself to forget this and easily succumbed to the charm and warmth of the narration or accepted its confessional tonality at face value, the little discrepancies strewn all over the stories should have helped one in maintaining one's vigilance. Tevye skillfully manipulated the rhetoric of sincerity, but he was not always in full control of it, and when he momentarily slipped, we had our chance of glimpsing through the cracks in his various masks.

The discrepancies referred to here were not necessarily those that scholars pointed to and accounted for as the inevitable results of the long and tortuous process of the composition of the tales at different times and places, and under changing circumstances of health, residence, fluctuations of income, and commitment to various publishers or editors. These circumstances were supposed to account, for instance, for the inconsistency concerning the actual number of Tevye's daughters; for although he constantly presented himself as the father of seven daughters, Tevye actually told only about five of them, barely mentioning a sixth, and altogether forgetting about the seventh.[28] This might or might not have been the result of hectic and changing working conditions. Although the author might have "reserved" the two missing daughters for further *Tevye* tales that he did not live long enough to write, the references to the "seven daughters" also could have been a sheer rhetorical ploy on Tevye's part, a little fiction invented for the purpose of projecting himself as a "biblical" patriarch, albeit with a comic twist: did not Job sire seven sons? Tevye, being a comic or a parodied Job, was blessed with daughters instead of sons; and as everybody knew, being the father of so many females was by no means a laughing matter: "*az men hot tekhter fargeyt der gelekhter*," (having daughters, one's smile was wiped off one's face).[29] Claiming parenthood to seven daughters, Tevye could have been quoting a magic number in a bathetic rather than pathetic context. It might have been a mock-dramatic gesture too good to be missed, even if the facts had to be tinkered with a little.

Be that as it may, the tales, however, displayed other, more significant discrepancies, which certainly could not be dismissed as technical oversights on the part of the author. A good example of these pitted one against the other of Tevye's two assessments of the marriage of his youngest daughter Beylke (her name clearly highlights her sellable asset: beauty) to the millionaire Pedatsur. Much of Tevye's penultimate tale, "Tevye fort keyn erets yisroel" ("Tevye Leaves for the Land of Israel"), was dedicated to the negative portrayal of the rich son-in-law, whom Tevye seemed to abhor not only morally but also physically, frequently mentioning his rotundity, glistening baldness, or his thin and high laughter, a feminine trait. Tevye also ridiculed the nouveau riche décor of Pedatsur's palatial town house, which was full of mirrors and clocks of all styles and blocked by heavy, ostentatious furniture. He went so far as to castigate his daughter for marrying a man she could not love (so he assumed) and being kept in his home like a captive "princess among the hundreds of mirrors and thousands of watches."[30] Hodl, her older sister, who had married a penniless revolutionary for love and then went to Siberia to share with him his fate as a political exile, he said, had fared much better than she, and so on and so forth. Tevye, in other words, rode the high moral horse as a modernist, asserting that love, genuine attraction, and idealism rather than wealth and comfort should have decided the choice of a spouse—that, in spite of the fact that until now he had systematically urged his daughters to marry for money and convenience. This moral conversion of Tevye who suddenly waxed a "modern" humanist as the boldest among his daughters, would have sounded more convincing if it would not have occurred within the context of his bitter personal disappointment with his millionaire son-in-law; for when he had been invited by Pedatsur to visit the young couple, he dreamt of being offered a lucrative job as an overseer in his son-in-law's burgeoning construction business. We are allowed to assume that had any of these wishes been realized, Tevye would have hardly mentioned Pedatsur's baldness and thin laughter, and perhaps he would have been impressed with the garish décor of his home. It was only when he realized that Pedatsur viewed him, the rustic father-in-law, as a social embarrassment to be stashed away as far and as quickly as possible (by sending him to the far away Holy Land for the rest of his life), that his aesthetic and humanistic sensibilities were awakened. In any case, these presumed sensibilities dominated the entire presentation of his daughter's fate, as it was dramatized in this tale. Tevye was so "disgusted" with his son-in-law that, while conveying his negative impressions to "Sholem Aleichem," he failed to pay tribute even to the fact that Pedatsur, with not a little effort and much bribery, managed to whisk away Hodl and her incarcerated husband out of Siberia and beyond the boundaries of the Czarist empire.

In his ultimate "Lekh lekha" tale, however, Tevye looked at the Pedatsur "misalliance" from an altogether different angle. In the meantime, the millionaire-constructor had lost all his assets and emigrated together with his wife to America, where both worked hard and "made a living," clinging to each other as if their bond was based on a much firmer ground than Tevye had allowed. Suddenly Tevye bewailed here his own and his daughter's bad luck. He particularly regretted the deterioration of his daughter's fortunes. Here she had been living in the lap of comfort and luxury, and now she was doomed to hard work—like her father. Nor did he despise now the Pedatsurs' pretentious town house, which he had ridiculed in the earlier story. On the contrary, the loss of the house, he said, could and should have been prevented, if only the young couple had followed his, Tevye's, practical advice; for had he not urged his Beylke—indeed he had "begged" of her—that she would coax her husband into purchasing "outright" the rented mansion and register it "in her name,"[31] so as to protect this income-generating equity from creditors?! Tevye forgets now the image of Beylke as a captivated bird in a golden cage, replacing it by that of the irresponsible, pampered young woman who would not take her father's practical advice. Who was then the "true" Tevye—the practical man of the tale "Lekh lekha," who wished his daughter would have retained and protected her property, or the "idealist" of "Tevye fort keyn erets yisroel," who all but urged her to leave her bald, effeminate, and crass husband? The answer to this question must be: both or neither; for the truth of Tevye's tales was not his own but rather that of the particular story he happened to tell. As much as the earlier tale had been informed by anger and disgust, and, therefore, considerations other then moral and aesthetic ones could not be permitted to mar its unified effect; the later one, reflecting the mood of a refugee who was trying to come to terms with losses and deprivations, consoling himself with the thought that at least his fate was not different from that of a vast number of other Jews, had no room in it for moral indignation and aesthetic recoiling. Would Tevye have revealed in the earlier story, that no matter how disgusted he had been with Pedatsur's baldness and thin laughter, he nevertheless wanted him to purchase his home and register it in his wife's name, he would have destroyed the specific tonality of that tale and blunted the edge of its stormy emotionalism. By the same token, his dwelling on matters of physical attractiveness and ostentatious behavior would have seemed out of place in a story that told about how the roof came falling down on Tevye's head and those of many other Jews, whereas the "practicality," husbandry, and protecting one's property (*fun a bisl un a bisl . . . vert a fule shisl*[32] [something and another something add up to a full dish]) seemed to naturally belong here. So Tevye had eliminated from the first story some very important details, which he then "remembered" in the following one, and "forgot" in the second story the details that had seemed so important in the preceding one. In other words, when he told a story, Tevye followed the story's inner (or aesthetic) logic rather than the "naked," factual truth.

Another example: In "Shprintse" (the name of this daughter of Tevye is bitterly ironic because it indicates hope; *esperanza*), the sixth and most tragic of Tevye's tales, the protagonist told "Sholem Aleichem" of his daughter's suicide by drowning after being seduced by a rich city boy (to whom she had been introduced by Tevye himself). Starting the woeful tale with the description of how the strapping young man and his friends, invited by Tevye to his cottage as guests for the Pentecost's traditional dairy dinner, made their first appearance on the stage of the impending tragedy, Tevye strangely waxed lyrical about the beauty of the village at springtime and the pleasures of living in the "lap" of bountiful nature. This, after having told "Sholem Aleichem" often enough how distasteful to him was life in the countryside (*in a dorf, mishteyns gezogt, me vert fargrebt,* [in a village, woe to me, one becomes coarsened];[33] or "What's the use of beautiful daughters if you are stuck with them in a godforsaken corner, where one's eyes never rest on a living person?"),[34] and how fervently he wished to move to a proper Jewish shtetl, where the values of Judaism were appreciated (particularly when they went together with some wealth). Suddenly Tevye, in a poetic mood hardly appropriate for a bereaved father, fell here into a reverie about the lushness of the surrounding greenery and the beauty of the magnificent canopy of blue sky. "No," he concluded, refuting an imaginary objection, "say what you will, tempt me to leave the village for the best job in town, I would not for the world swap places with you!"[35] This, of course, did not hinder him from reverting a few pages later to his original pro-urban position. Once he started fantasizing about his daughter marrying her lover-boy (who also happened to be the scion of a very rich family), he saw himself again in town, affluent, an important member of the community, a philanthropist, and an acknowledged scholar.

What could explain this blatant discrepancy? The inherent needs of the story itself—Tevye was about to tell a very painful tale, which he felt he had to aesthetically and morally organize around the binary oppositions of: nature/civilization, innocence/moral corruption, naiveté/cunning, village/city. His daughter (and by inference himself as well) would be representing the virtues of nature, innocence, naiveté, and the village, whereas the seducing young man, and even more so his rich relatives, would stand for the corrupt civilization of city, money, and moral irresponsibility. Tevye and his daughter would become thus the blameless rustic victims of heartless city predators; innocence and beauty were to be vitiated by the ugliness and immorality of idle high-middle-class people who disdained to accept in their midst the daughter of a poor but honest man who earned a living by the sweat of his brow. They even attempted bribing this paragon of honesty, offering monetary compensation for the young man's "indiscretion" (which, of course, he rejected), and also in other ways represented the ugliness and corruption of urban life. What would suit better the launching of such a moral parable than an encomium to the beauty of the countryside (which is not "a godforsaken corner where one's eyes did not rest on a living person" anymore) and a diatribe against the town, where one could not see the sky, only roofs and smokestacks?! Tevye, as the expert storyteller he was, knew that his neat (too neat) presentation of the fateful romance had to be buttressed by such a village/town contradiction if it was to make its full impact. Everything in the tale was tailored with this in the narrator's mind. Even his initial hearty welcome after a long separation from his "Pani Sholem Aleichem" was aesthetically conditioned by the drama of the destruction of the life of an innocent village girl through the reference to the long time that had elapsed since the last meeting of the two by the idiomatic expression: *Vey-vey, vifil vasern es zenen opgelofn*[36] (Oh-me, how much water has flowed under the bridge), thus preparing the scene of Shprintse's throwing herself from the bridge into the running water of the river at the end of the story. Clearly, the stage had to be set for a melodrama that would start as an eclogue and end as a tragedy. Such a melodrama would also minimize, if not obliterate, Tevye's own role in it in any guise other than that of the innocent victim. Thus, instead of demanding from himself an account for his own share in arranging for the disastrous meeting of the youngsters (he was justifiably asked by the boy's uncle what, as a reasonable man, he could have thought when he had brought the two together) he "forgot" momentarily his true feelings about living in the village and swore by his love for it. Tevye, obviously, sacrificed a part (an important part) of the truth for the sake of heightening the moral coloring of the drama he was about to unfold, while minimizing his own ambivalent role in it. It was hard to tell which carried more weight with him when structuring the story as a clash between irreconcilable oppositions—the aesthetic considerations, which demanded that the Shprintse tale would emerge as "strong" and affect-full as it could possibly be, or his personal need for excuses and justifications. Since, however, both needs complemented rather than negated each other, the issue could be left undecided.

Yet another, and perhaps even more edifying, instance of a narrative discrepancy occurs in "Lekh Lekha," the story about the expulsion from the village. Tevye's oldest daughter, Tseytl (by now a widow and living with her children in her father's house, which must now be summarily vacated), is trying to make peace between her father and his "lost" daughter Khave, who had converted to Christianity. Khave now wants to leave her gentile husband and join her father in exile. Tevye refuses even to contemplate such a possibility. Tseytl's interceding touches a raw nerve, and their altercation waxes very emotional. When she finally appeals to his compassion and begs that he take pity on his erring daughter, he, in uncontrollable rage, blurts: "You talk to me about pity? Where was her pity when I stretched myself like a dog before the priest, cursed be his name, kissing his feet, with her, perhaps, hiding in the adjacent room, overhearing, perhaps, every word I said?"[37] In his fifth story, "Khave," Tevye described in full detail his meeting with the priest, presumably reproducing verbatim every word that had been exchanged as the latter adamantly refused to allow for a meeting of Tevye and his daughter. Nowhere did Tevye say anything about kissing the priest's feet—literally or metaphorically. On the contrary, he told about his poor wife's request that he would do just that, fall to the priest's feet, appeal to his compassion and pity, and about his own proud and angry retort: he would never do that, and his wife must be out of her mind to have suggested such a crazy idea. And indeed his role in the dialogue with the priest, as it was recorded in the story, was that of a proud Jew, behaving in a way that was worthy of Shakespeare's Shylock. He told the priest exactly what he thought of him as a seducer and a thief of souls and left his house banging the door. Who then was the real Tevye, the one who kissed the priest's feet or the one who cursed him? Clearly, one of the two versions of the story was not true; and it looks like it was the one in which Tevye behaved like the exemplary Jew he was not. Also, the entire tonality of the "Khave" tale would have been undermined by a truthful account of the encounter with the priest, since the account, in all its details, was geared toward a self-presentation of Tevye as the strictly normative Jew who would not deign even to exchange a word with his daughter after her conversion, which to him signified a spiritual death, worse by far than a physical one.

Tevye, then, is what the theorists of the "rhetoric of fiction" used to call an "unreliable narrator,"[38] and the fact that his unreliability was conveyed by very subtle means (and therefore escaped the eyes of untrained readers) does not in any way diminish the justification of such a characterization of him. The question of why he needed to manipulate the truth has been partly answered: he needed to charm his listener and buy his sympathy both because he wanted to tell a good story and because he needed to avert, or at least soften, the rather harsh judgment that this listener would have otherwise passed on him. Tevye, we must realize, had much to account for. He knew that in spite of his hard work as a breadwinner and his love for his wife and daughters, he had never taken good care of his family. When it came to forestall trouble or effectively confront it when it had already happened, he had always chosen the easy way out; allowed trouble, when it came, to run its full course without doing anything to stop or abate it. He also knew that more often than not, he had brought trouble home by his own volition, displaying a strange self-defeating pattern of passive-aggressive behavior the origins of which he could not fully gauge. This leitmotif of bringing home the source of trouble, which culminated in the Shprintse tale, had been sounded early on already in Tevye's second tale "A boydem" (the literal meaning of the word is an attic; however, in an idiomatic context, it indicates a nil result of what looked like a big to do; something along the line of a big deal resulting in nothing). Here Tevye brought home a distant relative Menakhem Mendl (the protagonist of Sholem Aleichem's other *chef d'oeuvre*), whom he encountered in a very sorry condition in the streets of Yehupets (Kiev). Menakhem Mendl was a young provincial, who, having arrived by sheer chance in Odessa, had been sucked there into the dream of quickly achieving fabulous riches through stock-exchange speculations. He had lost there all the money he had on him (the remnants of his dowry) but instead of going back home to his wife and children, he moved to Yehupets, where he once again frequented the stock exchange and where he once again lost whatever additional sums his wife had sent him. Tevye decided to bring the hungry and bedraggled man home to the village so as to feed him a nourishing meal and offer him a good night's rest. There, at Tevye's table, however, Menakhem Mendl, managed to squeeze out of his host his meager savings, promising to make his money grow by leaps and bounds. Of course, the money was as good as lost the moment it left Tevye's cottage. Tevye himself wondered how he could have made such a fool of himself, ascribing his silly behavior, as always, to God's will (in this case: God's ill will): "If God wants to punish a person, he deprives him of his good sense."[39]

By the beginning of the fourth tale, "Hodl," Tevye knew for sure that something was fundamentally wrong with him; otherwise he would have refrained from bringing home the young revolutionary Feferl, who separated him from the daughter he loved best (her name, Hodl, deriving from the verb *hodevn*, to cultivate, raise, and in that sense also feed and pamper, indicated her position as her parents' favorite), who eventually followed him to Siberia. What rendered him, he asked, the magnet to which all troubles clung? "What was at the root of this? Perhaps my innate gullibility, which makes me trust everybody? . . . But what am I to do, I ask you, if, in spite of everything, such is my nature?"[40] Of course, this behavior, which would become progressively more self-destructive, was caused by more than sheer gullibility. Tevye was not a simpleton as much as he was able and, indeed, forced, on certain occasions, to suspend his good sense and act stupidly. What made him do that he never fully understood nor acknowledged. He never faced the fact that each of his "mistakes," as represented by the fatal guests he brought home, corresponded in his fantasy to a need or a desire of his: the craving for riches, the need for self-importance, the yearning for male-issue, young men who either intellectually or even physically and erotically attracted him, allowing him to fantasize about playing the role of a father figure or an educator to them; unconsciously or semi-consciously transmitting to his daughters, who were very much attuned to their father's secret wishes, his interest in these men, savoring through the connection established between the desired young men and his daughters a closeness he craved for himself. Tevye could not know much about the workings of this underground motivation of his; but he also could not but feel that somehow, by following his desires and fantasies, he had let down those who were closest and dearest to him. In fact, his was a very common case where those who depended on narcissistic people (particularly parents) paid the price of the latter's self-centered behavior.

By the same token, Tevye could not but be aware of the fact, that he had systematically evaded people, particularly the members of his family, when they urgently needed his attention and help. He did that either by talking too much, but never to the point, or by altogether refraining from talking where a supportive dialogue was sorely needed (as was the case when Shprintse, realizing that she was about to bring shame on the heads of her parents, started her downward sliding toward the lethal depression that ended in the psychotic moment of her self-destruction; through refraining from talking to her, Tevye certainly reinforced her own view of her out-of-wedlock pregnancy as unacceptable, an unspeakable sin, and a scandal, which had to be avoided or eradicated by self-elimination). Tevye rarely spoke up when talking could perhaps do some good. His famous loquacity, for instance, totally left him when he had to advocate for himself and his daughter vis à vis the relatives of Shprintse's seducer who intimated that her being seduced was nothing but a trap set up by Tevye with her consent. His more obvious fault, however, was that of pushing away people by talking to them in a manner that was both irrelevant and offensive.

Much, perhaps too much, has been written about Tevye's wit, his playful game of quoting and mistranslating the sacred texts, of flaunting his rather limited Jewish erudition.[41] Whether what he wanted to convey through his "learned" references was pertinent or utterly beside the point, it always served psychological needs that have been overlooked by the commentators. What has rarely been noticed is how much of a defense mechanism this "clever" pseudo-scholarly discourse of his was, and how much aggression was released through it. On the one hand,

Tevye intentionally talked "above the heads" of a certain kind of inter-locutor (particularly those who had a social and financial advantage over him), just in order to humiliate them, making them feel stupid and ig-norant (or at least believing that such would be the effect of his remarks, for Tevye could not at all conceive of the possibility that people with little or no respect for Jewish traditional learning would not be offended by the exposure of their unfamiliarity with the Jewish sources). With such "customers" he often invented non-existing sources, quoted un-real Talmudic sayings cast in bogus Aramaic, imagining that by shoving those false quotations down the throats of people who were not in a position to question or refute them, he triumphantly demonstrated his imagined superiority. On the other hand, he quickly hid behind his quo-tations and references as soon as a serious issue needed to be contem-plated and a difficult decision made. When his wife, Golde, reminded him that they urgently needed to arrange for the marrying off of their older daughters, he responded by referring her to God's providence, an idea he was ready to buttress by a series of midrashim, upon which, Golde, fully aware of his subterfuges, cut him short, maintaining that "grown daughters were a good enough midrash in their own right." [42] After his daughter Khave's elopement with her gentile lover (which he could have seen coming, if he would have cared to do something about it before it was too late), he pounced on poor Golde: how could she, a mother, not have seen what was going on under her nose and in her own house and courtyard! And why she did not alert him in time by telling him about the unholy courtship. Once again, Golde's answer was cutting: how and why could she tell him anything? "When one tells you something, you immediately respond with a biblical quotation. You buzz my head off with quotations and think you have done your share!" [43] Although for a moment he seemed to be struck with the bitter truth contained in his wife's rebuke, Tevye immediately sought shelter behind his habitual disrespect for women: "She has a point," he said; he should not have blamed her, for she was only a woman, and "what could a woman understand?"!

The most blatant example of this strategy of shutting off reality with clever words is to be found in the opening section of the seventh tale, where Tevye tells "Sholem Aleichem" about Golde's last days. The woman, having lost her wish to live, became desperately sick. With one of her daughters exiled to Siberia, another converted to Christianity, and yet another having taken her own life, Golde's grip on life was quickly loosening, and she knew she was dying. Whatever her deteriorating physical condition was, Tevye never thought of seeking help for it in time (when he finally brought in a physician, she was already dead). Himself bitter and sarcastic, he was more interested in settling accounts with God than in looking after his wife; and with her, sinking right in front of his eyes, all he could offer her was some argument concerning God's handling of the world's affairs. Again Golde stopped him short, and in a whispering voice put to him a simple question, which amounted to her ultimate response to his intentional obtuseness. "I am dying, Tevye," she quietly said. "Who will cook your dinner?"[44] Never had our protagonist been floored by such a direct, authentic, and devastating existential statement. Never was the hollowness of his wit and "learning" so sweepingly exposed. However, Tevye held on for dear life to his quibbling, his only defense. As much as he was touched by Golde's words and the poignant eye contact that went with them, his response consisted of a proverb, a biblical quotation, a midrash and yet another midrash. What else was left for him to say under the circumstances? Throughout his life he wrapped himself with this insulating stuff, and it was too late to tear open his cocoon. Indeed, by doing that he would have probably exposed himself to the same withering radiation that had killed Golde.

That was one of his reasons for telling his stories to "Sholem Aleichem." Tevye had to go on talking, narrating, being clever and funny, quoting, and playfully mistranslating. This was his hold on life, for what was he if not a Jewish Scheherazade whose head would be cut off the morning after he lost his ability to charm and please through narrating (which calls to mind Benjamin's comment: "In the stories which Kafka left us, narrative art regains the significance it had in the mouth of Scheherazade: its ability to postpone the future."[45] By the way, Sholem Aleichem wrote in 1915 a veritable Jewish "Thousand and One Nights," where a "Scheherazade" in the form of a Polish shtetl Jew told about the horrors he had experienced during the early days of the German occupation of Poland in World War I. This audaciously experimental text, an

attempt at portraying disasters and atrocities in a humorous tone, was—
on the one hand, a continuation of the *Tevye* tales and on the other—a
precursor of Holocaust literature).[46]

Talking, however, did not altogether assuage his guilt feelings, of
which he must have been more than semi-conscious. Of course, he was
not ready to fully expose these feelings, even to himself. He halfheartedly divulged them only where the "sin" involved was deemed to be
sheer naiveté and gullibility, and its results were not catastrophic. Thus,
he admitted the stupidity of his succumbing to Menakhem Mendl's
outlandish promises and the naiveté he evinced by bringing home the
revolutionary Feferl and allowing him to stay there almost as a member
of his family. He also rather grandiosely took upon himself the "heavy"
responsibility for Beylke's marriage to her millionaire, which he narcissistically interpreted as an act of self-sacrifice on her part for his, Tevye's,
benefit (never realizing that the notion of marrying for money as a
means for ensuring one's security and happiness had been systematically transmitted by him to his daughters. Beylke might have internalized this message and acquiesced in the match with a millionaire for her
own selfish sake, as she more than once asserted). All these, of course,
did not add up to an insupportable burden of guilt. Other sins, both
of commission and of omission, for which mental and moral collapse
could (and perhaps should) have been the price, such as his share in the
undoing of his daughter Shprintse, or his refraining from seeking help
for his dying wife, Golde, he could not afford to admit. However, his
guilt feelings in these more severe cases seeped through the cracks in his
mask of innocence. For example, toward the end of the Shprintse tale,
he suddenly put to "Sholem Aleichem" an uncharacteristic and unexpected question. It was a question, he said, he had intended for some
time to ask his learned and worldly friend: why the eyes of people who
died by drowning were always open, whereas usually dead people's eyes
were shut? He would have "Sholem Aleichem" explain the *seykhel* (reason, logic) of this phenomenon.[47] However, Tevye did not wait for an
answer to his question. Instead, he suddenly cut the conversation short
and bolted, excusing himself by mentioning his being pressed for time.
One had to think of the next ruble and where it could be found, he said;
and therefore one had to let the dead bury the dead and put the past

behind one's back. Both the unexpected question and the sudden haste (that, after having taken as much time as was necessary for the telling of the Shprintse tale at great length) hinted at what Tevye was about to divulge, had he not caught himself in the nick of time. Haunted by the widely open, fixed and staring eyes of his dead daughter as he saw her for the last time, he was on the verge of acknowledging his devastating guilt feelings, for he clearly ascribed to this stare an accusatory expression, projecting onto it his self-accusation. He recoiled from doing that only after he had already spilled half of the beans. His question was, of course, as clumsy as it was uninformed and disingenuous. Tevye probably knew that "most people" did not die with their eyes shut; rather their eyes were shut by those who attended to them so as to produce the semblance of sleep—for the benefit of the mourners. But Tevye had seen his daughter before this calming semblance could have been effected, and the horrible stare was indelibly embossed onto his memory. Indeed, throughout the story the image of his drowned daughter being fished out of the river haunted him, triggering, as we have noted, quite a few Freudian slips, such as the idiomatic "water under the bridge" at the beginning of the story, which conveyed the gnawing but well dissembled self-accusation that informed it as an undercurrent. However, as in the question about the open eyes of those who died by drowning, Tevye recoiled in panic not only from self-exposure, but also from full self-awareness. Unconsciously, he attempted to shut off his daughter's wide open eyes, if not by his own hand, then by the clods that now covered them: "those covered by the sods must be forgotten," he said as he was taking his leave.[48]

Realizing that Tevye, for all his lighthearted prattling, was gnawed by guilt explains an important nuance in his narration that has not been sufficiently noticed (and that Wisse's comment on Tevye's final monologue, "Lekh lekha," proved how misleading such a failure could be). As a rule, when talking about blows inflicted on the national collective, on Jews as a harassed ethnic minority living in an avowedly anti-Semitic environment, Tevye's mood immediately improved, indeed it soared; and that in spite, or, paradoxically, because, of himself being one of the afflicted. No matter how many conventional expressions of sorrow he piled one upon the other ("What times we live in! What a miserable time to be a Jew!", etc.),[49] and how many times he mentioned the urgent need for the coming of the Messiah and the desperation of the people, which nothing but divine redemption could assuage, he himself was in high spirits—by far higher than those he had exhibited in his first tale, where he told about his unbelievable good luck. Enigmatically, it was particularly on such unhappy occasions that his "dialogue" with God, usually replete with both bitterness and self-effacement, was for once spirited and upbeat, refreshingly free of sarcasm, as well as servility. This changed tonality, which cropped up, for instance, in the references to the 1905 pogroms in the opening section of the Shprintse tale, totally dominated "Lekh lekha," Tevye's last tale (or couple of tales, since most Yiddish editions contained besides this final eighth tale also a truncated ninth, "Vekhalaklakes," which was actually a variant of an episode included in the eighth), the main topics of which were pogroms, the Beilis blood libel, and the expulsion of Jews from the villages. Here Tevye was more than self-controlled; he was actually relaxed and almost happy (in the "Vekhalaklakes" fragment he was positively exuberant). This good mood was not at all the result of the self-delusion Tevye had exercised on other occasions. The protagonist was fully aware of the fact, that objectively his situation had never been worse, and that within a short time he might be reduced to beggary and vagrancy. Nevertheless, his mood was one of genuine equanimity. Expelled from his cottage, where he had spent his entire life, got married, and raised children, he was not nearly as dejected and elegiac as he had been (in his former tale) when selling his old horse in preparation for the voyage to the Holy Land that never took place. The wailings of his daughter, Tseytl (now, as mentioned before, a widow living with him together with her children—another burden he was supposed to support in his old age) positively disgusted him as a hysterical reaction worthy of a mere "female." Her emotional outburst confirmed the low opinion of women he had always had. She unnecessarily emitted *tishe bov* noises,[50] he said (the ninth of the month of Av was a day of national mourning; according to tradition, both Jerusalemite temples had been reduced to ashes on that day). In another place, he superciliously commented: *Mayn tokhter hot zikh vider tseyalet vi a yidene tsu venesayne toykef.*[51] Tevye referred to the portion of Yom Kippur liturgy called *ya'alot*, a suppliant liturgical poem, with each stanza starting with the Hebrew verb *ya'ale*, (let it rise), as well as to the famous *piyut* "Unetane tokef" (and we shall express the awesome sanctity of the day). These liturgical poems, written in the neologistic and very difficult Hebrew of the medieval Ashkenazic *paytanim*, could not be understood by women (and most men as well); however as soon as the first words were recited by the cantor, a hysterical wailing would burst in the women's section of the synagogue. Tevye's reference was thus informed by a well-honed male sarcasm: his daughter's uncontrollable crying was not only presumably unjustified by the occasion (since it was neither Yom Kippur nor the ninth of Av), but, triggered by something she supposedly could not understand. It also expressed the inherent female dumbness: "These women, do you hear me, are not pulling your leg. As soon as something happens, immediately there is weeping. Tears are cheap with them."[52] In contradistinction, he, Tevye not only flaunted his sangfroid ("Tevye is not a woman"), but also patronizingly spoke of "our old Jewish God," as if He were a familiar, elderly, but still well-liked, poor relative.

How is all that to be understood? Ruth Wisse explained this as "turning history into humor," a characteristic Tevye stratagem through which he maintained his mental fortitude and asserted his will to endure.[53] Nothing can be further from the subtle truth of this closing link in the *Tevye* chain. The particular humor that informs this story is derived not from transcending through laughter a catastrophic historical event, but rather from finding in such an event a refuge from the torments of personal responsibility, since history is impersonal and collective. Tevye is elated because the collective catastrophe relieves him, if only temporarily, of responsibility for his fate, and thus from his guilt feelings. Surely, being expelled from one's home and cut off from one's source of income was a disaster; however, for once, it was a disaster one had not brought upon oneself and one's family. Tevye's conscience was as clean as that of an innocent child; for was he responsible for the state of Jewry?! Taking care of the nation's fate was God's business, and the onus was on Him. Being a victim rather than a culprit felt good; and besides, when hundreds of thousands were afflicted, one's personal losses, even the loss of a suicidal daughter and that of a good and loyal wife, whom had not been properly taken care of in her moment of need, were somehow

minimized and marginalized. *"Tsores rabim khatsi nekhome!"*[54] (the tribulation of the many is half consolation), Tevye said with obvious satisfaction when he learned that he was not the only local Jew to be expelled
and that the rich and powerful householders of the neighboring shtetl
Anatevke would soon follow since the authorities in their unfathomable
wisdom were about to redefine small provincial towns as villages, and
thus apply to them the decree of expulsion to their Jewish inhabitants.
"What am I, all of a sudden: God's only child?"[55] he rhetorically asked
his daughter, inviting her to compare her fate as a mere roofless refugee
with that of Mendl Beilis, incarcerated and tried for the preposterous
crime of having allegedly murdered a Christian boy and used his blood
for baking his Passover *matsot*. By comparing herself to that sacrificial
lamb who was "atoning for all our sins by going through torments of
hell," she should have learnt to count her blessings.[56] In short, for once
Tevye was truly happy because he could with easy conscience shift all
responsibility for his and his family's undoing to something bigger than
himself: *"vos se vet zayn mit klal yisroel, dos vet zayn mit reb yisroel"* (what
befalls the Jewish collective would also befall the individual Jew).[57]

The tale "Lekh lekha" could bring the Tevye cycle to something like
a genuine closure because of this immense relief it conveyed. National
tragedy signaled a personal release from responsibility. In terms of extrinsic plot, the cycle as a whole, its ultimate tale included, did not lead
to a full denouement. Conceivably, the cycle could have been continued, as the author most probably intended it to be (after all, he had
two more daughters to account for). Tevye, a refugee, might have met
his "Sholem Aleichem" again—anywhere: in Kiev, Odessa, Warsaw, or
New York (unless in the meantime the good Lord would see fit to surprise his "children of Israel" by sending to them the long awaited redeemer)[58] and tell him of his further adventures. Intrinsically, however,
the cycle did come to an end because its essential plot was not that of
Tevye's social and familial life, but rather that of his guilt and search
for absolution through narration, and once the onus of guilt had been
shifted from his shoulders to whoever was responsible for national disasters, Tevye's tragedy arrived at its moment of catharsis. In fact, if the
Tevye-Job analogy was at all valid, it was not because Tevye resembled
Job, which he did not, but because God "answered" his complaints as

he had answered Job's—"out of the whirlwind" (Job 38:1), the whirlwind or storm being a Jewish holocaust. It was only through holo-
causts that God now "spoke" to his chosen people and silenced their
complaints. Hence, Tevye's obsessive references to him in the two last
tales as a "strong" God, whereas in the earlier tales he referred to him—
mostly ironically—as a "good" and "merciful" God. In any case, Tevye,
the obsessive talker, could be silenced, as Job had been ("I . . . repent
in dust and ashes," Job 42:6) because God asserted himself through a
disaster and thus "purged" all human beings of moral responsibility.
"You don't argue with God, and you don't offer him advice how to
handle the world. When he says 'the heavens are mine and the earth is
mine'—you know that he is the boss whom you must obey."⁵⁹ Obeying
the "boss," however, even when his decrees are cruel and indeed devastating, promised internal harmony and freedom from guilt, for through
it one regained an all but childish state of innocence. This is what Tevye
learned from national tragedy.

If silencing Tevye signaled the end of his story, then his talking constituted the center, the very axis, of the world that had been created in this
story as long as it was propelled onward. Tevye's loquacity informed this
world and lent it whatever significance it possessed. The narrative dynamism that made *Tevye der milkhiker,* as a whole, tick was that of obsessive
verbalizing as the result of a progressively growing pressure exerted by
a burden of guilt, which, in its turn, lead to a progressively accelerating
search for absolution. What really determined the scope and nature of
this dynamism was the constant revving up of the telling engine rather
than the specific contents of what was told. As much as the act of confession per se, rather than the specific confessed sins or the specific acts of
atonement, demanded from the sinner constituted the theological essence of the ecclesiastic ritual that reopened the gate to a state of grace,
to the same extent Tevye's incessant verbalizing, his roundabout and perhaps not entirely conscious inching toward a confession, constituted the
aesthetic, as well as psychological essence of Sholem Aleichem's masterpiece. Otherwise Tevye would not have sought the company of his "Pani
Sholem Aleichem" in the wake of each disastrous event in his life.

From one tale to the next, his need for and dependence on this chosen interlocutor became more pressing and also more openly declared.

Already in the first tale he said that although the event of his "striking it rich" had taken place nine or ten years earlier, "Sholem Aleichem" was "almost the first" to hear of it.[60] Somehow this ebullient raconteur, if he was to be taken at his word, had reined himself in until then, refraining from touting his story of "miraculous" deliverance, and waiting for the meeting with "Sholem Aleichem" to open up and release the until then silenced news about the reversal of his fate. Telling "Sholem Aleichem" about the disappointment of having married his eldest daughter to a penniless and ignorant tailor (rather than the rich and powerful widower Leyzer Volf), Tevye held on to his interlocutor for such a long time that he had to end his tale with an apology: "I'm afraid I've bothered off your head today even more than on all other occasions."[61] When he came to the shameful story of Khave's elopement and conversion, Tevye swore that no ear but that of "Sholem Aleichem" would catch as much as the slightest noise of it. He explained his need to make his interlocutor aware of what had happened by quoting God's famous rhetorical question regarding His decision of telling Abraham of His intention to soon annihilate the sinful cities of the plain: "Do I hide it from Abraham?! (Genesis 18:17).[62] Thus Tevye compared the relationship of trust and closeness between himself and the writer with the supreme biblical model of trust and closeness between God and a human being. From a friend such as "Sholem Aleichem," Tevye said, he could not hide even his most shameful of secrets; he could only hope "Sholem Aleichem" would not reveal it to anyone else. As for the horrendous Shprintse tale, Tevye, a bereaved father, strangely launched it with an incongruous burst of mirth, as well as with a jolly pun: "You, Pani Sholem Aleichem, deserves a large, hearty 'sholem aleichem' [welcome]!"[63] It seemed that Tevye's need to tell his "friend" this particularly unsettling tale was so pressing, that at seeing him and foretasting the relief he would soon experience (once the story would have been off his chest), he could not control a short outburst of happiness. In "Tevye fort keyn erets yisroel," the tale started with Tevye's panicky questions pertaining to Sholem Aleichem's health. The story being written in 1909, a rumor of the writer's severe health crisis in the summer of 1908 must have reached the protagonist (for the persona "Sholem Aleichem," while being an autonomous and fictional entity, was anchored in and

nourished by the historical reality of Sholem Aleichem's biography).
He was already wondering whether his ubiquitous interlocutor had not
"given up the few rubles and betook himself to a place where one did
not eat anymore radish with chicken fat,"[64] that is, had given up the
spirit. Tevye had tried to reassure himself by contending that an intelligent person like his "Sholem Aleichem" could not have done such
a dumb thing. "Lekh lekha" was launched with Tevye proclaiming: "I
have already been looking for you for a long time, seeing that plenty of
fresh merchandise had been accumulated with me for you. I kept asking myself: where were you? How come one didn't see you?"[65] Tevye,
expressed here his growing dependence on his interlocutor in terms
of the dairy industry. The quality of the perishable dairy products depended primarily on freshness, and therefore the timely selling of these
products was of critical importance, and a good dairyman would not
let too much "merchandise" accumulate in his pantry; rather he would
urgently seek customers who would relieve him of the surplus. Thus,
Tevye's mercantile metaphor clearly conveyed his sense of being heavily burdened by the story he had to tell while it was still "fresh." By
quoting, in this context, God's anguished question "*ayeko*" (where are
you?) aimed at Adam, hiding, ashamed of his nakedness, in the biblical story about the expulsion from paradise (Genesis 3:9), he endowed
his need to see Sholem Aleichem and talk to him with a metaphysical
significance; and, in fact, his need for and dependence on his chosen interlocutor did emanate from a metaphysical source—from an awareness
of being shamefully "naked" and guilty in the sense imparted to shame
and nakedness by the first story about guilt in the history of the world.

Therefore, the critical questions we have to answer are: Why Tevye
chose "Sholem Aleichem" as his father-confessor, and why or how did
"Sholem Aleichem" acquiesce in playing the role of such a confessor,
taking upon himself the responsibility of "purging" Tevye's guilt and
"absolving" him? The answer to both questions must be: "Sholem
Aleichem" was chosen for the role and also agreed to play it primarily
because he was a writer, a virtuoso storyteller, a man of words, a manip-
ulator of real life events for the purpose of sublimating them into exuberant and "funny" works of art. In other words, "Sholem Aleichem"
was chosen because he resembled Tevye, duplicating his behavior at

a "higher" and more symbolic level. Thus he could become his alter and higher ego, or, in fact, his super ego, and as such, the authority who could judge and absolve—the latter function activated particularly through the employment of humor, since humor was the strategy (Freud said: the narcissistic strategy) the super ego employed for the purpose of shrinking or minimizing the ego's painful feelings of hurt and guilt.[66] The symbiosis Tevye-Sholem Aleichem was based, therefore, upon the literary status or elevation of the "Sholem Aleichem" persona, endowing it with the high position that rendered its functioning as a super ego possible. This, by the way, was exactly the use the historical Sholem Aleichem got out of his artistic persona in the wake of the humiliating crisis he underwent in 1890, when he lost all his own assets and those of his wife's rich family through disastrous stock-exchange speculations; fled his creditors and wandered for many months in various European cities while abandoning his family in Odessa high and dry, and leaving it to his mother-in-law-to cut a deal with his creditors and pay part of his debts by selling her jewelry. Once back in Odessa, and eking a miserable living as a broker and a Russian-Hebrew writer (during the 1890s there was still no European Yiddish press and publishing industry that could financially support even the most popular of Yiddish writers), he overcame shame and assuaged his guilt feelings through artistic sublimation, calling "Sholem Aleichem" to the rescue of Sholem Aleichem. Indeed, he could be said to have outgrown his rather mediocre literary beginnings of the 1880s, and emerged as the great writer he became in the 1890s, through internalizing the lessons of the 1890 debacle and making good literary use of them. His two chief works of fiction were started immediately after and as a direct result of his downfall. In 1892 he worked his self-destructive stock exchange obsession into the epistolary masterpiece *Menakhem Mendl*; and in 1895, he worked into his first Tevye tale his despair as a penniless provider, responsible for a large family, and doomed for life to the backbreaking labor of quickly and unceasingly producing new ("fresh") literary "merchandise" (his "dairy products"—short stories, humorescues, feuilletons, and eventually novels and dramas). Like his Tevye, from now on he would have to withstand the pressure and swallow the occasional humiliation that were the lot of a producer who had to quickly sell his products to customers upon whose satisfaction and clamoring for more he would perennially depend. The parable of *Tevye der milkhiker* was the artistic result of the author's acceptance of the producer's toil and short-range dependence and of his ability to blunt the edge of whatever pain this acceptance involved by humor and comic narration.

Having said that, we nevertheless still must succinctly delineate the maturation chart of the Tevye-Sholem Aleichem symbiosis. The foundations of this symbiosis were laid bare at the very beginning of the narrator-writer interaction, namely, in Tevye's first tale, and even more so in Tevye's letter that in the original 1895 version of the story served as its epilogue or as an appendix to it (in the canonical editions, it functioned as a prologue to the entire cycle under the biblical title "Katonti," [I Am Unworthy], a reference to Jacob's humble acknowledgement of the mercies and good will shown to him by the angels in Genesis 32:10). Purportedly the purpose of the letter was to thank "Sholem Aleichem" for his intention of putting Tevye "in a book," an honor he was unworthy of and so on. The letter contained, however, implicit background information, as well as explicit statements that did not exactly dovetail with its language of humility and self-effacement. The most interesting piece of the latter was Tevye's reference to the fact that his acquaintance with "Sholem Aleichem" had been started quite a few years before the meeting that became the occasion of the telling of his story. To be more exact, Tevye well remembered his earlier contacts with the writer, although he was not sure that the writer, on his part, also remembered them; since the writer had been in those "good years" a rich entrepreneur, who could afford a summer house of his own in Boyberik (the suburb of Yehupets-Kiev where most of Tevye's customers resided and where the recent meeting between the dairyman and the writer had taken place), and Tevye could hardly expect a rich person, as "Sholem Aleichem" had been, to remember his supplier of dairy products. Thus, Tevye had known his future interlocutor for a long time. This begs the question why he waited for all these years (nine or ten) before telling him his "wonderful" story. The answer was obvious: Tevye waited because before Sholem Aleichem's fortunes took a nose dive, approaching him with the life story of a mere pauper would have amounted to an insufferable presumption. Tevye would not have dreamt of sharing his personal history with an esteemed and well-paying customer. He could sell him a cow (which he had done) but never a story of the kind he now unfolded.

Circumstances had changed, however, and with them the telling of Tevye's story had become less presumptuous. Tevye's "rising" from the low position of a day laborer to that of an independent (albeit hard-working) merchant, a producer cum supplier of sought-after goods, and Sholem Aleichem's downfall, which reduced him from the high position of a gentleman of independent means to the low one of a mere writer, who now eked out a living by scribbling books—to that of a producer cum supplier of goods of another kind, had put the two on a par, so to speak. Not that Tevye forgot the difference between a published author, who was by definition a learned person, and a rustic dairyman. He never failed to acknowledge this difference, defer to his interlocutor in all matters pertaining to learning and erudition, and also find other ways of giving him the ego-massage at which he, who had practiced for years the art of keeping disgruntled customers pleased, was an expert. Nevertheless, he did not refrain from discreetly reminding "Sholem Aleichem" of the lamentable shrinkage of the social gap between them. He did that, for instance, at the end of the first tale, where he urged both himself and his interlocutor to go back to work and attend to their respective "businesses," since both were not in a position to indulge in pleasant conversation for its own sake. Each had to go back to his means of production: *Ir tsu ayere bikhlekh, ikh tsu mayne teplekh un tsu mayne kriglekh* . . . (You to your little books, I to my little pots and to my little jugs).[67] The list of three diminutive ("*bikhlekh . . . teplekh . . . kriglekh . . .*") conveyed not only Tevye's understanding of books as mere containers (like pots and jugs) into which one poured one's verbal merchandise, but also his sense of the existence of a certain parity between himself and his interlocutor as small fry, people who, far from playing an important role in the world, offered the public items to which the language of diminution was applicable. Whereas this equalization rendered the telling of Tevye's story socially acceptable, the question remains of why should the dairyman tell "Sholem Aleichem" his story even now; what, under the changing circumstances, could be the purpose of the telling? The purpose could be quasi-commercial. Under the new circumstances, Tevye had something valuable to "sell" to "Sholem Aleichem," or as he delicately put it: "It's worth your while, I swear, to listen to the entire story, from start to finish."[68] That was why he emphasized that he had not told this story to "almost" anyone else; in other words, that it was "fresh," untouched merchandise. The story, therefore, was told with the clear intention of it being made use of as literary raw material. That, in spite of the fact that here, too, as he would in the Khave tale, Tevye requests that the author would change the name of his protagonist, and thus protect him, from exposure.[69] Even that request was halfheartedly made, since Tevye expected not only to share the author's honorarium, but actually use his being "described" as commercial advertisement. Thus, he said, he counted on Sholem Aleichem's "noble character" with regard to remuneration but also expected from him to work on his, Tevye's, public relations "so that your little book may do some good to my business."[70] Tevye even added in a post scriptum the address to which the money should be sent and mentioned his need for money for the purpose of marrying off his oldest daughter.

Thus *Tevye der milkhiker* was based on a literary deal, and its commercial beginnings were not altogether forgotten even as their initial practical presuppositions were transcended. Tevye would continue referring to his stories as "fresh merchandise" and offer them to "Sholem Aleichem" as literary raw material. Gradually he would become even more aware of their value as such material and consequently, grow more sure of himself (at the beginning, he occasionally apologized for taking the writer's time and "chewing his ears off"). He would urge "Sholem Aleichem" to pay close attention, since the given story "may yet prove useful to you," or supply him with "something to write about."[71] Even as he pleaded for the writer's discretion with regard to the Khave tale, he knew that his initial request that "Sholem Aleichem" would altogether refrain from making use of it could not have been followed, since it went against the grain of the unwritten agreement between them, and the writer would use it anyhow. So he reformulated his request, proposing a change of names and the elimination of all hints that would point in his direction ("as if it's not me. Forget about Tevye!").[72] Oblivion was, however, the last thing Tevye really wanted, for he wished and needed to be written about. Otherwise he would not have approached a writer in the first place, let alone a writer who was known for using real life events of "simple" Jews like Tevye as one of the sources of his inspiration. In the early days of the Yiddish press, people were afraid of being "described," namely, publicly exposed through literary ridiculing. Tevye knew he was being described and cooperated with the author who inflicted this *bashraybung* (description) upon him: "take nor a bashraybung mit mir," (indeed, I am fit for a description), he proclaimed.[73] This need for self-exposure, as well as self-advertisement had been inherent in Tevye's offer of a literary deal from its very inception.

But the deal and the self-exposure it involved quickly assumed emotional dimensions, which they had not originally encompassed; dimensions that found expression in the gradual heightening of pathos in both the narration and the contents of Tevye's tales. The bonding of protagonist and literary persona progressively became more emotionally charged, stronger, and more complex. The sheer literary "agreement" between the two evolved into a symbiosis leading to mutual interpenetration. Tevye identified with his writer and gradually shared with him typical authorial concerns of structuring, plotting, digressing, and reverting to the main plot line. Referring to these concerns at the beginning in traditional formulaic terms such as "Let us leave now, as they say in your little books, the prince and turn to the princess,"[74] he eventually replaced them by current literary terminology such as the Hebrew expression *nakhzor le'inyanenu harishon* (let's come back to our initial topic);[75] or use other non-traditional, current literary phraseology, such as the expression *lo arkhu hayamim* (and it did not take much time before . . .),[76] which contemporary Hebrew writers of prose fiction used when skipping a lacuna of dead time in their plots. If the "little books" in which the segmentation of the plot was indicated through the prince-princess formula were traditional, characteristic of folksy chapbooks, the ones that referred to the initial topic or the quick passage of eventless time, were modern. In fact, we realize that Tevye started following the writing career of his "Sholem Aleichem" and that he now read and internalized his stories. Thus, for instance, in "Vekhalaklakes," where Tevye, in the jubilant mood we already mentioned (the story dealt with the 1905 pogroms), celebrated the cleverness of Jews, who unlike the ignorant and slow-witted gentiles, were knowledgeable "in the little black letters," he reminded "Sholem Aleichem" of what he had recently said in one of his books: "How can a Gentile be compared with a Jew? A Gentile is a Gentile, and a Jew is after all a Jew, and as you yourself say in one of your stories: to be a Jew one must be born one."[77] Undoubtedly Tevye referred here, in a text written in 1914 or shortly after, to Sholem Aleichem's novel *The Bloody Hoax*, published only two years earlier, in which the same idea was developed as an elaborate tragic-comedy about a Jew and a Gentile unsuccessfully swapping identities only to become aware of the fact that in matters pertaining to Jew-Gentile differences, no disguising can hide the truth for more than a very short time. Thus, Tevye presumably had read this very long and intricate novel, written against the backdrop of the Beilis affair.

"Sholem Aleichem," on his part, allowed his protagonist to occupy and use his sensibilities. By the third tale, at the latest, he stopped presenting Tevye as a "type," a jolly "character," one of the many he made fun of and regaled his readers with. He stepped, so to speak, into his protagonist's shoes and moved ever larger parts of his mental being into a convergence, or at least a position of overlapping, with Tevye's interiority. As Brenner aptly put it, "Sholem Aleichem" became "Tevye's bard," even his "stenographer *de gracia dei*,"[78] taking dictation and adding to his protagonist's flow of speech the amenities of felicitous *écriture*. In other words, some merger must have taken place, bringing together the literary persona and the fictional character.

This symbiosis between two such different entities—a traditional, half-educated, provincial dairyman and the literary persona of a modern writer—became possible because it satisfied urgent needs, both conscious and unconscious, of both parties. Tevye, as mentioned before, achieved through it a catharsis of sorts, a relief from his pent-up guilt feelings, which only a "Sholem Aleichem," an artist and a storyteller, could deliver. The protagonist instinctively understood that without the mediation of artistic perception, his confessions could not yield the absolution he craved. He intuited the existence of a spiritual kinship between himself and the writer, and this made him turn to him rather than to the traditional sage, a learned rabbi or the Hasidic saint, to whom his traditional upbringing and intellectual frame of reference should have directed him. He knew he had to be viewed by somebody who perceived reality as raconteurs do: as an aesthetic continuum, and judged by aesthetic criteria, the only ones Tevye could live up to. Everybody else would have judged him as too flawed or sinful for forgiveness, and as richly deserving his tragic fate. A rabbi would have found the way Tevye had brought up his daughters and supervised their behavior too scandalous for words; for it absolutely contradicted the basic tenets of both the halakha and the tradition. How could a God-fearing Jew have permitted his unmarried daughters to become friendly with young men of questionable morals and spend time with them without chaperoning? How could he have accepted, no matter how grudgingly, the friendship he saw evolving between a daughter of his and a non-Jew? How could he have brought home a handsome young man he himself characterized as a "charlatan" and a "hollow nut" and let him involve a daughter of his in a love affair that included sexual intimacy? What could a man who had done all these have expected? Tragedy was inevitable, and a severe punishment was sure to come. By the same token, blaming God for the results of one's own behavior amounted to the worst kind of blasphemy, as much as comparing oneself to the saintly Job, no less, the man who was "perfect and upright, and one that feared God and eschewed evil" (Job 1:1), was the height of chutzpa! How could Tevye have deluded himself into the crazed notion that God had inflicted upon him undeserved calamities and into the temerity of questioning God's justice and indulging in sarcastic remarks at His expense. No, judged by conventional religious norms, Tevye was a "bad" Jew, who should have prostrated himself before God and dedicated the rest of his life to repentance, ascetic self-denial, even self-imposed exile! Such would probably have been the reaction of a rabbi or a *tsadik* (a Hasidic leader), would Tevye have told them the stories he told "Sholem Aleichem." At the same time he could not have expected a judgment less harsh from the rabbis' opponents, the secularists and humanists; for they would have damned him for being passive, unable to fend for himself and protect his family, for evading his moral responsibilities, for shifting the burden of his failings onto an irrelevant God, for being deeply prejudiced against women, and altogether spiritually swaddled and mummified within an irrelevant textual cocoon, and so on. (Thus in an early perceptive comment on the character of

Tevye, written in 1908 by Baal-makhshoves, which unfortunately had been buried under the mountain of Tevye's praises as sung by the sentimentalists of an entire century, the protagonist was described, rather pejoratively, as the epitome of Jewish conservatism, a person who exists in a state of "frozen stasis," is "a feminine type rather than a masculine one"; is thoroughly limited, "does not see what goes on around him, and is altogether lacking in intuition with regard to people who are not of his generation and life style," and as a person, who together with his extreme opposite, Menakhem Mendl, personified the downfall of the Jewish people, who, if they cling to such models would be doomed to total destruction, and remain "like a handful of sand on the shore of universal human existence.")[79] True humanists, whose vision was not marred by apologetics and Jewish self-pity, could hardly regard Tevye as a "good" and upright man. Moralists would have pointed with derision to his craving for riches achieved through no effort of his own; socialists would have decried his respect for money, power, and social status. Feminists would have fulminated against his treatment of his wife; existentialists would have regarded him as the quintessential practitioner of bad faith, a person who was not honest and authentic enough to look reality in its face; Jewish scholars would have laughed at his scholarly pretensions and pronounced him a fake, a pseudo-scholar—Tevye controlled no more than the rather short list of texts an average Jew was automatically acquainted with, if he regularly said his daily prayer, occasionally attended the synagogue on the Sabbath, and added to the accumulation of texts he absorbed in this way the book of Psalms (which many Jews repeated verbatim, barely understanding the text) and the tractate *Avot* in the Mishna (which traditional Jews were supposed to read on Sabbath); and these he freely mangled, distorted, and mistranslated. At the same time, those without Jewish learning, like his wife, would have accused him of obfuscating important issues by deflecting whatever point was being made or serious question asked through irrelevant quotations, references, and questionable analogies. In short, everybody but a "Sholem Aleichem" would have regarded him as blameworthy, deeply flawed, indeed, quite impossible. Only a writer could "accept" him, even look up to him as towering above nondescript humanity through his inspired loquacity and riveting telling.

In fact, nobody but a "Sholem Aleichem" would want to listen to Tevye, lend him an ear. Strangely enough, it has never been noticed, that the people who surrounded Tevye—almost with no exceptions—were sick and tired of him, abhorred his incessant talking, and stopped listening to it as soon as the first biblical verse or Midrashic example would embellish it. In other words, to those who had to live with him, Tevye had become an irking nuisance. This applied not only to the members of his family (and particularly to his poor wife), but also to his customers and to other people who had to communicate with him for whatever practical purpose such as Ephraim the matchmaker, Leyzer Volf the butcher, and Pedatsur, the millionaire son-in-law. That was the reason for his headlong falling in love with whomever did not immediately recoil from his discourse, and, for a while, was willing to enter his game of witty repartees, altercation, and quotations, such as the young revolutionary Feferl. Tevye brought Feferl home and actu-ally coaxed him into living there at his expense simply because he was starved for the company of responsive conversationalists who would not reject him. In fact, he had fallen in love with Feferl even before his daughter Hodl did (upon their first meeting, Tevye had to confess: "As I converse with him I feel that my heart is drawn toward this chap"),[80] as much as he fell in love with the "charlatan" Aronchik, who would eventually seduce his daughter, not only because he was overwhelmed by his exuberant virility, but also because the young man was willing to listen to him, put questions to him, and treated him, so Tevye naively believed, like the sage he wanted to be taken for. He would do almost anything for whomever would listen to him. So much more so for a "Sholem Aleichem," who savored every word he uttered, understood the indirect relevance of his quotations, and appreciated the subversive wit of his mistranslations (of course, all, or at least most, of Tevye's "mistakes" were intentional and subversive, undermining, for the fun of it, the sacred sources to which he professed loyalty). Such a listener was to him a heaven-sent boon, an inestimable trove. He possessed "golden" ears, "worth a million," and in need of being immediately in-sured for a large sum of money, as a character in another Yiddish classic (Glatshteyn's *Ven yash iz geforn* [*When Yash Traveled*]) said about an-other literary persona who knew how to listen.[81] In fact, Tevye treated his "Sholem Aleichem" like a lover in a spiritualized erotic sense of the term: somebody who was willing both to penetrate Tevye's mind and be penetrated by his tale.

But what was Tevye to "Sholem Aleichem"? Why would the writer permit his protagonist to cease being an object of comic description and become a subject whose interiority defined the boundaries of the narrative world, occupied its entire expanse, and left almost no lebensraum for the "implied author" as an autonomous entity? In other words, why did the literary persona bond so tightly with the protagonist? For one thing, Sholem Aleichem did what every writer who was worth his salt would have done: he stuck by his "informant," the one who delivered first-rate stories; and Tevye certainly offered Sholem Aleichem the best stories he would ever lay hands on. No authentic writer would have rejected the love and trust of a raconteur of Tevye's stature. Then, as said before, Sholem Aleichem, himself representing a flawed person who sought redemption through art, shared the protagonist's predicament and identified with his pain and needs. Thirdly, and most importantly, Sholem Aleichem, as an artist and a thinker (who cogitated through narration, characters, situations, and above all else "gestures," as Benjamin said with regard to Kafka)[82] accepted, as he did in most of the author's best works, the impotence of his protagonists, their passivity and ability to hold on to life through sheer endurance, inertia, and garrulity. These were to him the people who experienced the human condition authentically. His acceptance of them, while not characteristic of all his works, and particularly not of those sections in his writings in which he discursively commented on the current national Jewish situation, became the staple characteristic of whatever part of his oeuvre in which his brilliance as a writer of stellar quality was displayed. Suspending extrinsic judgment, eschewing ideological fiats, and allowing his protagonists to advocate for themselves, Sholem Aleichem embraced the kind of people other writers satirized. Even when prevaricating and self-servingly obfuscating reality, they were his people. He was never offended by either their lies to others or by their self-delusions and *mauvaise foi*, which to him were as precious as any truth, being, under the circumstances, the only truths these people could afford. Never demanding from them heroics of any kind, he suffered them to bombard their own consciousness and that of everybody around them with words. He accepted their bavardage as their hold on life and sole means of avoiding mental breakdown, and he made brilliant artistic use of it—nowhere more brilliant than in *Tevye der milkhiker*, where he first discovered this winning formula; for all the meticulously and artistically conceived characters he created were veritable Scheherazades, living from day to day thanks to their ability to externalize their suffering in the form of an enticing and "happy" prattling.

And what about us, the readers? We also are invested in the Tevye-Sholem Aleichem symbiosis; that is, we become part of it, of course, only in our capacity as readers, that is, as people who, for a while, are ready to suspend judgment and abide by aesthetic criteria. Were we to have lived with a Tevye-like person, we would have rejected him as impossible and irrelevant. Would he have tried, as he must to impress us with his stories and clever quibbling, we would have fled him as a nuisance and a pest. Who would want to listen to a Tevye? Fortunately, we did not have to endure Tevye in real life. That was why we could love and look up to him as long as he was safely ensconced in a book. The same loquacity, which would have turned us off, acquired in the book, the enticing quality of flowing honey of which we could not have enough. As readers we definitely wanted to listen, regretted the relative shortness of the cycle of Tevye's tales, and wished there were more of them, as there probably would have been, were the untimely deceased author given more years of productive life. We were even willing to be hoodwinked by Tevye and say and write rather unwise things about the admirable qualities he never possessed; for most of us still refuse to see where the greatness of Sholem Aleichem's chief creation rests.

In *Tevye der milkhiker*, Sholem Aleichem wrote the most audacious critique of the "heroic" humanist ethos that dominated modern, secular, and particularly nationalist, Jewish culture—which he himself, as a run-of-the-mill Jewish intellectual of the turn of the nineteenth century, swore by in his many moments of mediocrity. However, once he emerged as the genial artist who blazed new trails into a new kind of Jewish culture, he started undermining this ethos, burrowing underneath it. Whereas modern, secular Jewish culture reprimanded "traditional" Jews, criticized them for being weak, passive, unrealistic, and tardy, and urged them by both positive exhortation and biting satirical jabs to grab history by its horns, replace texts and words by deeds and actions, inertia by revolution, weakness by self-empowerment, minority by majority, Sholem Aleichem, in his moments of true greatness, embraced passivity, weakness, wordiness, inertia, and minority—everything almost everybody else rejected: nationalists as much as assimilationists, Zionists as much as diasporites (such as the Bundists and the folkists), socialists as much as capitalists, Marxists as much as utopianists. Whatever all these "guides of the Jewish perplexed" derided and despised, he accepted, or rather, found a way of presenting without judging. Not in vain he was rejected as a mere *badkhen* (wedding jester) by almost all nationalist critics and intellectuals (the prominent exceptions were Berditchevsky, Bialik, and Brenner) until the Russian literary intelligentsia, upon the publication of his selected works in Russian translation (1911–1913), started to sing his praises, alerting the Jewish intellectuals to the fact that a great writer was living and working in their midst. Sholem Aleichem simply undermined their projects of national self-empowerment, social radicalism, and the artistic quest for literary "majority."

This is exactly why and where Sholem Aleichem stands as close to Kafka as anybody in the Jewish literary complex. Kafka, as much as he too positioned his characters not only "before the law," and subservient to its brutal force, but also outside its domain; for if the law was ancient, mythical, the legacy of prophets and sages, of forefathers and progenitors, it was in a way decayed and decadent to the point of a charade; not only because it became unintelligible throughout the ages, but also because, as Benjamin observed, the experience of those who were subjected to it was even more ancient than the law itself; it was pre-mythic and "autochthonous," that is, it emanated from the very earth from which Kafka's characters, in the form of beetles, cockroaches, mice, and moles, emerged and to which they ran for shelter.[83] Thus, the law could be revered and discounted at the same time (Benjamin on Kafka's perception of the law: "The law which is studied but no longer practiced is the gate to justice"). This is exactly the position of the law in *Tevye the Dairyman*: it is studied; it is quoted and misquoted; it is verbally played with and humorously referred to; but it is also irrelevant because real life cannot anymore be measured by it. Or if it were to be measured by it, then the measuring was false, arbitrary, and morally irrelevant (compare Sholem Aleichem's stories focusing on the law, whether that of the Torah or that of the state, such as "Dos tepl" ["The Little Pot"] or "A nisref" ["Burnt Out"] with Kafka's stories focusing on the same topic, such as "The Refusal" and "The Problem of Our Laws," in addition, of course, to *The Trial*).

Systems of ethical norms were perhaps sacrosanct, but they could not be applied to real life, which both predated and submerged them. This was, in essence, Sholem Aleichem's immensely important discovery as he hit upon his Tevye character. In a culture rooted in the rabbinical halakha and transcending it only in order to replace it as a normative system by other systems—as demanding and as alien to existence per se as it was (Zionism, socialism, humanism, etc.)—he had the necessary geniality (for what he had was not conscious ideational courage, but rather a kind of genius, which he could articulate only through a *gestus*, a story about an event, a deed, a gesture; never in conceptual terms) without which he never could have stepped out of the power game of norms—of judgmental representation of reality. However, in his best works he did step out of this game, refusing to play by its rules, presenting existential reality, with all its blemishes and shortcomings, as in some way transcending these rules. After he established this formula of transcendence in the first *Tevye* tales, he went on to further develop it in an array of short stories, which in depth, originality, and authenticity approximate the supreme achievement of Kafka, the very apex of modern Jewish writing: a loquacious market vendor approaches a rabbi, presumably with a ritual-dietary halakhic question, but actually for the purpose of attacking him as a man (men having reneged on her by letting her do the hard work of life and then dying and leaving her emotionally shortchanged) and as a scholar representing a system that by definition is just and impervious to criticism. A young man who lives as a parasite with his in-laws, as the husband of their mentally unbalanced daughter who does not love him, approaches a popular writer. Presumably he seeks his advice, whether he should or should not get a divorce; but when the expected advice comes ("divorce her!"), he attacks the writer in an attempt to prove to him that he, the writer himself, under the circumstances would not have done "the right thing," had it meant, as it does in the case of the seeker of the advice, penury, loneliness, and total insecurity. An old cantankerous bachelor, a dormant homosexual, who has established a symbiosis of sorts with three women, all of whom he "loves" and presumably wants to marry (but in the meantime helps in marrying off to other men) approaches a famous writer seeking a solution for the "riddle" of his sexual and emotional life, but suspecting beforehand what his "psychological" solution must be, attacks him and through him "psychology" as a science and as an ethical system. An arsonist who set his store on fire for the purpose of collecting an exaggerated insurance compensation attacks the people of his hometown for disapproving of a deed that caused them no personal harm and infringed only on something as remote from and indifferent to the maelstrom that is life as the criminal law. In the stories of these and many other injured people, all allowed to advocate for themselves without any judgmental intervention on the part of the implied author, existence is pitted against norm, human smallness against the vacuous greatness of moral and social systems, life against law, trouble against trial. All of them are left with no moral conclusions but point through their entire narrative fabric to the bitter conclusion with which the discussion and the deconstruction of the "Before the Law" parable in *The Trial* is concluded by the priest with the brutal assertion: "You don't have to consider everything true, you just have to consider it necessary," as well as with K.'s response to it: "A depressing opinion; lies are made into a universal system."[84] Where Sholem Aleichem approximated the depth of Kafka's parables, there the modern Jewish literary imagination celebrated, by exercising a "negative capability," its greatest triumphs.

Twelve Conclusion: Toward a New
Jewish Literary Thinking

Reverting to our general argument, we can now conclude it with some final remarks. The modern Jewish cultural condition resembles a heap of metal chips strewn over a wide plane on which different and often contradictory magnetic forces exercise contradictory influences. Most probably these chips never constituted a single, solid object. Those who maintain that the term "Jewish culture" should be replaced by the plural Jewish cultures[1] seem to be closer to the historical truth. Also the "Jewishness" of these cultures cannot be defined by extrinsic and fixed criteria, for they are Jewish because Jewish communities, as well as individuals at different times and places defined them as such. Non-Jewish host-societies contributed their share to the fluctuating process of Jewish self-definition by superimposing upon Jews their own projections of them as "the other," and they, as we know, did not differentiate between Jews who abided by the strictures of the rabbinical halakha and Jews who turned their back on them. Whereas Judaism (the very term is problematic and actually forced upon Jews from the outside—by Hellenistic defenders of paganism in ancient times and Protestant-German essentialist culture taxonomists in modern times) had probably never formed a single coherent cultural entity; its staple characteristic in modern times (since the second half of the eighteenth century) has been centrifugal splintering. True, this outward movement was from time to time slowed down and to some extent, even reversed—by events such as the emergence of modern (romantic), racial rather than religious anti-Semitism and its ever growing influence throughout the second half of the nineteenth century and the entire twentieth century; the advent of Jewish nationalism in the last decades of the nineteenth century;

403

the revving up of the Zionist project due to the geo-political changes brought about by World War I; the destruction of European Jewry during World War II and the cohesive dynamics it triggered around the Jewish world and particularly in North America; the establishment of the State of Israel and its successive and unresolved conflicts with the Palestinians and its neighboring Arab states; and the reemergence of both popular and ideological (left-wing) anti-Semitism in the last decades of the twentieth century. However, the essential and pervasive mobility of historical Jewish life remained throughout centrifugal, and the distances between various Jewish communities, trends, and experiential modi vivendi keep growing. If Israel was supposed to become "a spiritual center," counterbalancing the process that Achad ha'am described as "fragmentation" (rather than assimilation), its success in playing this role has been at best partial, and, at least for the time being, its centripetal-attraction power seems to have progressively diminished. At this juncture, its role as a polarizing factor is almost on a par with that of a unifying one. That the cultural Jewish situation evolving under such circumstances is complex and multifaceted goes without saying. No attempt to streamline it can succeed, and sheer intellectual honesty demands the acknowledgement of this. Even Israeli culture today is an aggregate of different Jewish and non-Jewish cultures, with common denominators that tend to disappear under close scrutiny. The only solid common denominator that at one and the same time both shrinks and pries open cultural gaps in Israel is the Hebrew language, which is now spoken as fluently by young orthodox Jews as by secularists, by Israeli Arabs, as well as by Jewish Russian immigrants. To a very large extent, this victory of Hebrew widens the gap between Israeli culture and Jewish culture outside of Israel because in Israel, traditional Jewish multilingualism is on the wane (although far from disappearing altogether) and would probably peter out or be replaced by Hebrew-Arabic bilingualism.

Whereas no single Jewish literature can exist under these circumstances — and probably no single Jewish literature had ever existed after biblical times — a freely floating, imprecisely defined, and widely inclusive Jewish literary complex does exist; and it exists because many (albeit by no means all) Jewish writers and readers feel and behave as if it did.

A Jewish writer (who can, as a matter of course, be also an American or a French or a German writer) is a writer whose work evinces an interest in or is in whatever way and to whatever extent conditioned by a sense of *Judesein*, being Jewish, or is being read by readers who experience it as if it showed interest and were conditioned by the writer's being Jewish. That this gives rise to any number of literary hybrids, and excludes in advance any essentialist notion of a Jewish literary "purity," is simply a fact of our cultural life, which must be faced, for the price of avoiding it is literary and cultural myopia or speciousness. The question that this essay posed to itself and its reader was whether under such circumstances, the Jewish literary complex as such can be profitably studied; and the answer that has been given to the question was that it could, provided one started thinking in terms of positive and negative contiguity rather than those of continuity and discontinuity. These terms, when further developed, can be used as a basis for a literary thinking that need not be chaotic, opportunistic, and even unsystematic. A new Jewish literary theory, which would inherit from the old one only its basis of erudition, as well as its ardent interest in and commitment to whatever is Jewish in literature, is possible. At least it is a possibility that is worth looking into or rather working on, for the theorist cannot be a mere impressionist. He must not only observe, but also fashion the tools that would improve perception and perhaps bring things that have been overlooked into sharp visibility.

The multifariousness of the modern Jewish literary complex, not to mention its somewhat chaotic nature, should not discourage but rather should encourage a systematic and methodologically coherent thinking about it. It was not the coherence of the subject that actually goaded Hebrew and Yiddish literary criticism in the first half of the twentieth century into devising their respective syntagmatic-theoretical overviews. Rather the severances, the disconnects, the dissonances, and the contradictions in the subject and the need to conceptually "surmount" them did it. The same disconnects and contradictions could trigger a new theoretical thinking, informed, not by such a need and the futile (if heroic) spiritual quests it lead to, but by an altogether different need and one as urgent: to get far enough into mental and conceptual space where a point can be established from which the entire Jewish literary galaxy can be observed and studied; a point from which both the tragedy of the presumed demise of Judaism and the consequent petering out of an authentically Jewish literature, and the divine comedy of a Jewish culture and literature, which going through the hell of separation and schizoid fragmentation, were somehow bound to undergo therapeutic purgation, and eventually find their way to a paradise of a harmonious reunification—both would be seen for what they were: understandable but unnecessary over-dramatized reactions to a condition that must be accepted as a given if it is ever to be observed by calmer and clearer eyes, unclouded by the pathetic fallacy. The news about the imminent death of Jewish literature was premature; so were the predictions about the imminent demise of the Jewish spirit—through vulgarization more than through sheer acculturation—outside of Israel and particularly in North America. The promises of a "re-Judaization" of Jewish culture through a new synthesis of faith and modernism failed, and could not but fail, to materialize. Although Jewish religious orthodoxism became in the second half of the twentieth century unexpectedly stronger and more fashionable than it had been in the century that had preceded it, its re-invigoration, rather than leading in the direction of synthesis, has, and still is, driving in the opposite direction, that of further and ever more radicalized polarization—cultural, social, and political. The crisis of Jewish identity, which rendered possible the birth of the new Jewish orthodoxy, is a chronic one. Whatever other phenomena it may bring to the surface of Jewish cultural life, it is not about to disappear. The modern Jewish condition is one of a permanent identity crisis. In fact, the most stable characteristic of the modern Jewish identity is its permanently being in a state of crisis. Whether the very concept of crisis is semantically serviceable as a definition of a condition, which has now been prevalent for almost three centuries, and, which all indications points to its interminable continuation in the future, is a question that deserves a separate deliberation.

In the meantime we have not only an Israeli Jewish (as well as non-Jewish) aggregate of literatures written, at least for the time being, in no less than six languages (Hebrew, Arabic, Yiddish, Russian, English, French)—some of them (particularly the Hebrew and the Russian ones) vibrant enough—experiencing the ups and downs most other literatures undergo in our times, but also new Jewish literatures evolving in non-Jewish languages in both the Americas, as well as in western Europe and post-Soviet Russia; literatures of considerable volume and merit that are being created both within the literary traditions of their respective languages and countries and through the wider and less clearly defined modalities of the Jewish literary complex. In the United States in particular, this new American Jewish literature steadily grows in strength and public appeal. It encompasses at this point a large community of writers and culture agents and approximates in productivity and cultural contribution the Hebrew literature of Israel. Some of the participants in this community even regard themselves as more "Jewish" than most Israeli writers, whose work a stellar novelist and literary thinker such as Cynthia Ozick may regard as Jewishly "pagan," as she believes most of the American Jewish writing is and has been since it joined the modernist project of maximizing aesthetic potential rather than following clearly defined moral tenets (hence the "pagan" nature of this project). Jewish writing, Ozick believes, should be conditioned by the tenets of "classical" Judaism (i.e., Judaism based not on emotional and mental quests but rather on a prescribed way of life, codex of behavior)—another essentialist trend that can play an important role but would never "overcome" the historical reality of Judaism, that being simply whatever Jews experience as the core of their collective ethnic being. Thus Jewish writing cannot and will not be identified with either a normative "Jewish" way of life (halakha) or a romantic or mystical yearning (aggada); although it can encompass both halakha and aggada and much more besides as a cluster of experiential modalities. Open-ended and yet never devoid of an experiential core (the contents of which is not to be extrinsically dictated), Judaism, or rather Jewishness, being Jewish, thus understood, supplies us with the only viable definition of Jewish writing. In consequence, the new literary thinking must be as open-ended, never tie itself to any specific Jewish canon, and be ever ready to apply itself to whatever literary corpus experienced as "Jewish" in the most inclusive sense of the term, even and particularly, when such corpus seems totally alien, in language, form, and content, to anything beforehand identified as "Jewish." As such it must develop concepts that would at one and the same time be elastic and "stretchable," as well as precise and analytical.

If it can live up to these standards, this new Jewish literary thinking should be of importance not only to those who are interested in
Jewish literatures per se. Much of what motivated the old Jewish literary thinking, particularly its Hebraic-Zionist exponents, was a search
for Jewish cultural normalcy. As much as the goal of Herzlian political
Zionism had been the establishment of a "normal" (i.e., nineteenth-
century western, liberal) Jewish nation state, the goal of many cultural
Zionists was the normalization of Jewish culture and the establishment
of a normal national Hebrew literature created by native speakers and
under conditions of cultural freedom and self-reliance. Both goals have
been only partially met. The problems of Israel as an "incomplete"
democratic nation-state, both in the present and in the future (when
its Jewish majority may be eliminated by the growth of its non-Jewish
population; particularly if the Israeli occupation of the so-called West
Bank lingers) call for a separate discussion. However, it can be safely
asserted here that Israeli Hebrew literature is *not* a normal national literature since it is not even the literature of the "Israeli nation" (if such
a thing exists) and is certainly not *the* literature of the Jewish nation.
Rather it consists, as various and inherently discontinuous Hebrew literatures have since the end of the biblical era, of some among many
Jewish literatures as much as it also belongs within other, non-Jewish,
contexts (Mediterranean, Middle-Eastern, and, in its part written in
Arabic, also Arabic, and so on). In this sense, the position of Israeli
Hebrew literature within the general Jewish literary complex, important and vibrant as it is, can be said to be "traditional" and continual
rather than revolutionary and altogether new. This may be a cause for
chagrin in certain circles and give rise to imaginary scenarios of change
or to whatever new definitions of literary normalcy; the real question
that must be addressed, however, is not whether and how this situation
can be changed, but rather how and when the Israeli literary rationale
would finally be freed from the normalcy obsession. If it can and will,
then this rationale may really become of real significance—not only for
Israelis and the upholders of Israeli culture who live outside of Israel.

Current understanding of the processes of literary production in the
various western languages tells us how and at what price the enviable
normalcy of most western literatures was achieved. What these litera-

tures have evolved since the concept of national literature was absorbed by their official ideologies was not normalcy in the medical sense of the term but rather in its political or legal sense—as control and governance through the application of a set of norms, which proved serviceable to a ruling elite, and eventually were regarded by it as expressive and protective of "universal" values—aesthetic, ethical, and rational ones. Of course, this universalism was illusionary as much as it was useful. Thus western literatures, all of which started as aggregates, written in many different dialects and articulating diverse sensibilities, were eventually streamlined and "unified" into normative traditions. The upside of this was the invention through literature of a national ethical identity and the buttressing of this identity through an intra-literary relatedness that enhanced the evolving of continuities through various kinds of dialectical mechanisms (such as the one Harold Bloom pointed to in his *The Anxiety of Influence*). Wherever these continuities could be based on models of truly exceptional excellence (Dante, Shakespeare, Goethe) their claim to ethical universality elicited a wider and quicker consensual acknowledgement. However, the process also had its dark flipside, which was that of repressive exclusion or marginalization of whatever was seen as unresponsive to the "universal" norm, or, in other words, whatever directly or indirectly challenged its claim to universalism and unmasked the particularism and the particularist interests this presumed universalism camouflaged and hid (often also from the eyes of its naive enforcers). The toll was heavy, and it could be mitigated only if and where the ruling elite was so well entrenched as to leave some margin or breathing space for whatever was not in total accordance with its norms (thus in English literature, the existence of some Scottish, Welsh, and Irish residual literary cultures became permissible as long as their inhabitants remained under the tutelage of the official ideologues, critics, and culture leaders such as Samuel Johnson or Mathew Arnold). This happened in the various western literatures at various times in accordance with the political evolvement of the respective nation states, as well as other contributing factors. Thus French literature was perhaps the first to become a "national" literature. English literature came next, but not before the full assertion of English dominance throughout the British Isles. In Russia, the absolutism of the Romanovs rendered a similar development possible during the second half of the eighteenth century, and the emergence of the Russian classics (Pushkin, Lermontov, and Gogol) during the first half of the nineteenth century lent it a universalist aura (although it involved both the intentional and unintentional marginalization of writing in non-Russian languages, such as Ukrainian; Gogol was a Ukrainian by origin but functioned as one of the founding fathers of the Russian literary tradition). In Germany, the process of inventing a German national literature was started only in the nineteenth century and was totally conscious and politically motivated[2] although here, too, the presence of the classics (Lessing, Herder, Goethe, Schiller, Kant) made possible the conflation of its blatant nationalism and etatism with ethical universalism.

In modern Jewish literature, similar processes were arrested or slowed down due to the fact that even among Ashkenazic Jews, no dominant elite emerged that could support and enforce the "nationalization" of literature. As in other cultures, the concept of a national literature was a product of cultural modernity and had hardly existed before its advent. However, in Jewish history, modernity spelled the diffusion of social and cultural dominance. Western European, Ashkenazic Judaism was separated from its eastern European wing. Within eastern Europe, the social and cultural developments that were triggered by the dissolution of the Polish state and the consequent dissolution of its Jewish pre-modern power structures left early modern Jewish society with fiercely competitive elites, which fought each other tooth and nail throughout the second half of the eighteenth and the entire nineteenth centuries. We saw how the founding fathers of the Hebrew literature of the Enlightenment defined the literature they were creating as a national or rather *the* national Jewish one and themselves as the "watchmen unto the house of Israel"; but how could they assert their dominance as long as they occupied the tiny public space of a few thousands readers, and, even more importantly, as long as they did not win the support of at least a large enough part of the rising Jewish middle class? Such support was not forthcoming before the relative Hebraization of the lower middle class toward the end of the nineteenth century, when also the necessary classics (the Hebrew Abramovitsh, Achad ha'am, and particularly Bialik) emerged, adding their respective contributions to the nascent

Hebraic universalism. However, by that time the Jewish upper middle class had been Russianized and the Jewish masses found their voice through Yiddish literature, with its own masters who endowed it with the ethical universalism it craved (the Yiddish Abramovitsh, Sholem Aleichem, and particularly Peretz). Altogether, the historical situation was such that no one Jewish literature could convincingly claim national dominance, which was one of the reasons why the concept of *eyn-eyn-tsike* Hebrew-Yiddish literature was invented in the first place.

This angered the respective literary ideologues no end and explained the political motivation of their craving for literary normalcy; Achad ha'am gleefully predicted the death of Yiddish and the survival of only one, sempiternal Jewish literature, the Hebrew one, and thus kindled the ire and the enthusiasm of the participants in the Czernowitz Conference, who pronounced Yiddish literature the natural literature of the folk, denigrating the cultural value of the nation-state as such, and so on. In spite of this tradition of venomous polemics, if we honestly ask ourselves whether this total abnormalcy of the Jewish literary complex impoverished or enriched it, our answer must be, that although it did both, its advantages by far outweighed its disadvantages. Whereas political Jewish abnormalcy had its severe downside (although without it, the creation of the great Jewish community in North America, which actually vouchsafed the survival of the Jewish people in the terrible vicissitudes of the twentieth century, would not have been possible), culturally this abnormalcy was, in the final analysis, tremendously invigorating and worth maintaining. It released, particularly in the first half of the twentieth century, unprecedented Jewish creativity; and even after the Holocaust and the gradual disappearance of modern Yiddish culture (an immense loss), it seems to reassert this creativity through the fruitful counterpoint of Israel versus the Jewish Diaspora. In certain respects, it pays to be somewhat abnormal.

This Jewish cultural abnormalcy has become of considerable interest to non-Jews as well, since certain western cultures developed, throughout the second, postcolonial half of the twentieth century, symptoms of similar abnormal conditions. The Nazis and the cultural anti-Semites that had preceded them charged German Jewry with the unpardonable crime of having "Judaized" German culture and undermined its racial purity. The truth was, of course, that pre-Nazi German Jewry had made such a huge contribution to modern German culture, that in the post-Nazi era, German culture had had to struggle for decades with the absence of its Jews before it regained equilibrium. Be that as it may, some European cultures and literatures are now being "Judaized" with or without Jews, in the sense that their established cultural norms, based on the dominance of a relatively stable ruling elite, are now being challenged and "eroded" by "hordes" of repressed minorities, until now discriminated against by gender, ethnic origin, language, and so on. Even French, first and foremost among European national literatures and traditionally extremely loyal to its Cartesian traditions of clarity, intellectuality, and formal poise, had to gradually learn, throughout the twentieth century (from the 1930s) to listen to altogether different "French" voices, among them those of the French African colonies;[3] and then, in the last decades of the century, to accommodate a growing community of francophone writers, most of whom live and work in France but refrain from sloughing off their native African or Asian legacy and abide by the aesthetic and intellectual norms of the particular French brand of ethical universalism. Has this development enriched or "bastardized" French culture? One can quote diametrically opposed answers to this question. Of course, chauvinist and racist prophets decry from the rooftops this hybridization of what had presumably been pure; but as far as the future of French society and culture can be foreseen at this point, their outrage would be of no avail. Perhaps soon enough French theorists would have to assume the burden of developing theories of literary contiguity. Don't we see everywhere the concept of literary evolution being wrenched out of linear-chronological paradigms and replaced by more diffuse spatial ones? Even the concept of innovation through defamiliarization with its grandfather-grandson connection (the grandson, rebelling against his father utilizes the model of the grandfather, which had been rejected by the father), which served the Russian formalists rather as the Oedipus complex served the followers of Freud, has been proclaimed too linear and causal to serve as a useful developmental model, as much as the Oedipus complex itself was dethroned by Deleuze and Guattari as a viable developmental psychological model. In any case, the understanding of Jewish literatures in their mutual attractions, repulsions, and sheer indifference, cannot be sustained by a model that predicates the "murder" of the father as the only or the main paradigm of change. Perhaps it can be better served by psychological models based on the vicissitudes of siblinghood (both the belonging to and the competing over the parents and their love, as well as the many other modalities of positive and negative relatedness through which the dynamics of siblinghood are acted out) — a field relatively and problematically neglected by psychoanalysis.

We need new theoretical models that would allow not only for causality and development but also for a certain randomness and various forms of non-developmental co-existence. We need them not only for the purpose of better understanding the Jewish literary complex, but also for being more honest and perceptive with regard to the reality (or rather realities) of the Israeli cultural situation and its essential Jewish and Israeli "legitimacy." As noted before, Israeli culture is at this juncture so heterogeneous and fragmented as to be viewed as an aggregate of various, mutually non-complementary cultural dialects. It certainly possesses a "canonical" core that is secular, Hebraic, Ashkenazic, or informed by modern "Ashkenazic" mentality, and Zionist (although it also harbors a critique of Zionism of an essentially "corrective" rather than dismissive kind). However, the centrality and dominance of this canonical core has been systematically challenged and weakened throughout the last three decades. Whereas during the first twenty-five years of the existence of Israel, a very solid Israeli ruling elite, whose values and ideals this canonical culture articulated, vouchsafed its dominance, this elite has been progressively eroded, and with it, at different velocities and in different ways, a good part (although not all) of the position of power formerly held by the old cultural order underwent a process of deterioration and is now in the condition of relative decay. The truth about Israeli culture shows its face in its burgeoning popular segment, where all semblances and symbols of a coherent "Israeliness" have been relegated to the domain of a kitschy nostalgia, and whatever is alive and authentic is partial, fragmentary, and devoid of all pretensions to universal representativity. What a cultural thinking guided by the principle of contiguity (rather than continuity and integrality) can contribute to this fragmentary Israeli culture is not only better and more honest self-awareness, but also a recognition that the current situation, which is conventionally believed to be a cause for worry and a temporary phase in the development of a nascent society, also possesses assets and positive potential. Whereas the heterogeneity of Israeli culture might diminish with time, one wonders whether one should hold one's breath in expectation of such a development. One wonders if one truly wishes to see the "Russian" influence on current Israeli culture (due to the very distinct cultural physiognomy of more than a million Russian immigrants) quickly dissolving within an indistinct general Israeli *tarbut*. One rather wishes to see this process of streamlining being slowed down and even resisted, allowing the "Russians" to do for Israeli culture—in the arts, the sciences, and education—what the German immigrants of the 1930s, who were very slow and unwilling to part with their language and their cultural legacy, had done for the eastern European Zionist culture they found in mandatory Palestine. The same can be said for the intellectuals who brought with them the energies and cultural perspectives of Middle Eastern cultures from centers such as Baghdad, Alexandria, and Cairo.

Israeli literature can by no means regard and present itself as *the* contemporary Jewish literature, as it used to do in its days of adolescent self-confidence. It must learn to accept the presence of other Jewish literatures without self-effacement but with the respect that would indicate self-confidence and true coming of age. There is no one single dominant Jewish literature; there is not even a "choir" of various Jewish literatures, because the basic harmony that sustains a polyphony is simply not there. There is rather a "complex," a wide, not always clearly defined, Jewish literary space, in which all sorts of literary phenomena, contiguous and non-contiguous, move, meet, separate, and put more and more distance among themselves. This recognition, on the part of Israeli writers, is important not only because an acknowledgement of reality is conducive to truthfulness and mental equilibrium, but also because it amounts to a pre-condition for a genuine interest in the "other" literatures, from which Israeli writers can perhaps learn as much as non-Israeli Jewish writers can learn from the Israelis. An acknowledgement of cultural contiguity can lead not only to mutual respect but also, and more importantly, to mutual acquaintance. At the same time, Israeli literature can and should be loyal to itself, to its particular ways of perception, to its myths and symbolism; for if it is not *the* Jewish literature with capital J and L, it is as legitimately Jewish as any of its counterparts. Thus, a critique of Israeli literature as not "Jewish" enough (as leveled, for instance, by the novelist Aharon Applefeld) is unjustified and misleading. Upon the recent death of S. Yizhar, the Israeli literary culture hero, Applefeld had the honesty but also the shortsightedness to severely criticize Yizhar's prose fiction for being obsessively preoccupied with landscape, flora, fauna, geography, even geology, rather than with people, books, ideas, history, spirituality.[4]

The critique demanded courage because Yizhar's sensibilities formed the very core of what may be termed an "Israeli ethical universalism"; at the same time, however, it was shortsighted not only because Yizhar's overwhelmingly rich and complex evocation of the Palestinian space and landscape projected, as can be easily demonstrated, the perception and thinking of the people who encountered this landscape, and the narrators' language (which was that of these fictional protagonists, since most of Yizhar's works were written in the format of interior monologues) was replete with direct and indirect references to literary sources (particularly the Bible), thus interlacing the fabric of narration with "bookish" motifs and reminiscences; it was even more fundamentally wrongheaded because of the writer's failure to recognize the essential "Jewish" significance of Yizhar's preoccupation with space and spatial modalities of perception. For Yizhar's "world," the quintessential literary product of the culture of the Zionist pioneers, gave full and magnificently orchestrated expression to that great yearning of Jewish modernity: its quest for locus, for place, for re-territoriality, for having earth under one's feet in the measure of the sky over one's head (to use Bialik's dictum: a people had skies over its head in the measure of the earth under its feet). Labor Zionism in particular embroidered this yearning onto its banner, in its call for a Jewish reunion with the "cosmos" and the elements (A. D. Gordon) through physical labor in the open spaces of Palestine. However, this quest for space was not limited to the exponents of Zionism. It was shared by almost all modern Jewish ideologies and informed the aesthetics of both Hebrew and Yiddish literature. It rendered the realistic or metaphorical, impressionist or expressionist "conquest" of concrete space one of the chief desiderata of the new literatures and marked the achievements in this respect of some of their greatest masters (not only Abramovitsh, Bialik, Tchernikhovsky, Gnessin, Shlonsky, Lensky, Alterman et al. but also Yiddish masters, such as Bergelson, Markish, Mani Leyb, the great Yiddish New York poets, Sutskever, Elye Shekhtman) as constituting building blocks for a new Jewish perception of reality. When Yizhar brought this general *drang nach Raum* to its moment of total realization, sacrificing to a large extent memory and history to accentuate the new sense of the spatial here and now, he was therefore not less "Jewish" than any of these masters. Applefeld is, of course, within his rights as a critic and a reader when he distances himself from this kind of "spatial" Jewishness; clearly it does not dovetail with his particular Jewish experience, which is that of a Holocaust survivor who had evaded death by hiding, or by disappearing into a darkness that erased the distinctiveness of place and rendered locus as ambivalent and liminal as existence itself, hanging between being and non-being. This, however, does not justify the Jewish delegitimization of Yizhar's spatial consciousness. Nobody, not even Applefeld, possesses a monopoly over Jewishness.

A separate issue of considerable importance is that of the possibility or impossibility of Jewish-Palestinian literary Israeliness and the chances of a Jewish-Arab Israeli culture. Here the semblance of a possible, albeit problematic, symbiosis, which was created during the first decades of Israel's existence, has been, at least for the time being, shattered by more recent events. The Israeli Palestinian poetry of these decades, as well as the works of the most important Palestinian novelist of the time, Emil Habibi (the author of the brilliant *The Opsimist*), certainly created the impression that Palestinian writers (writing, of course, in Arabic, but being more or less systematically translated into Hebrew and widely read) could articulate their protest and criticism of the ruling Jewish society in an idiom that was distinctly Israeli, and thus become part of a coalescing Israeli literary culture. The fact that the ideological infrastructure of their writing was communist (Habibi was for many years a member of the Israeli Knesset representing the Israeli Communist party), informed by a universalist ideology that transcended both

Jewish and Arabic nationalisms, greatly contributed to the survival of the fragile symbiosis. The symbiosis reached its fullest realization with the appearance in the late 1960s and early 1970s of the highly talented Anton Shammas, a bilingual poet and novelist, whose *Arabesques*, written originally in Hebrew and then also in Arabic was one of the best Israeli novels of the 1980s. However, the literary trajectory of Shammas is indicative of the falling apart of the symbiosis. In spite of wide recognition on the part of the Israeli reading public and its critical establishment (or perhaps because of this recognition, among other things), the writer felt he could not maintain his position as a Hebrew-Arabic Israeli-Palestinian writer. The tensions and dichotomies inherent in this position must have become, since the 1980s, unbearable. Shammas cut short the very vital, albeit strident and harsh, dialogue with Israeli literature he had conducted both in *Arabesques* and in a series of important articles, left Israel, and stopped publishing belles lettres. *Arabesques* has yet to be followed by a second novel, which goes to show how the victims of the lingering Israeli-Palestinian conflict are to be found not only among those impacted by suicide bombers, as well as the horrors of the Israeli occupation of the West Bank. Clearly this situation cannot be changed unless the conflict achieves resolution. Thus, the reappearance of a strong Palestinian voice in Israeli literature is something to be ardently wished for not only for the purpose of regaining a cultural equilibrium, but also as an indication of a general rapprochement between Jews and Arabs in Israel; for the continuation of the occupation and the conflict threatens Israel's cultural health as much as it undermines its political, social, and ethical viability.

Abramovitsh and His Mendele
Between Hebrew and Yiddish

Breathing Through Both Nostrils?
Shalom Ya'akov Abramovitsh Between Hebrew and Yiddish

I

When the topic of Hebrew-Yiddish bilingualism is mentioned, the first name to come to mind is that of Shalom Ya'akov Abramovitsh to whom we fondly, albeit erroneously, refer as *Mendele Moykher Seforim*, Mendele the Book Peddler (Mendele being the protagonist of some of Abramovitsh's tales and the "persona" addressing the readers in most of them). This immediate associating of Abramovitsh and Jewish bilingualism is, of course, well deserved and only to be expected. Whereas Hebrew-Yiddish bilingualism was practiced by many nineteenth- and early twentieth-century Jewish writers—from Yosef Perl to Peretz and his disciples—some of them resorting to it occasionally and others on a constant basis—it was Abramovitsh who not only invested unprecedented creative effort in its maintenance, but also, more than anybody else, systematized it both as a literary-artistic modality and as a national-cultural option.

Getting into print while still in his early twenties (1857) as a budding educator and essayist, Abramovitsh's literary, stylistic, and ideological frame of reference was that of the Hebrew enlightenment movement and its literature. In 1860 he left his imprint as one of the pioneers of professional Hebrew literary criticism, then still in its birth throes. In 1862 the scope of his work was widened, as he published the first parts of a comprehensive Hebrew zoology textbook and of a Hebrew didactic novel (the second Hebrew novel to focus on current Jewish life in eastern Europe; it had been preceded only by the first parts of Mapu's *Ayit tsavu'a* [*The Hypocrite*]). Thus, functioning for seven years as solely

421

a Hebrew writer, Abramovitsh made a place for himself as an active and upcoming member of the new Hebrew literary generation, who in the 1850s and 1860s infused the sagging corpus of the Hebrew literature of the Enlightenment with new vitality, bringing to it new ideas and concepts, and replacing old and by now dysfunctional genres by new ones (the didactic biblical epic—by the elliptical, shorter, and more dramatic narrative poems of Y. L. Gordon; Lucan satire—by the novel of intrigue and high romance; the rhetorical manual—by combative literary criticism).

However, in 1864 he made a decision of far-reaching consequences, publishing a satirical novella, *Dos kleyne mentshele* (*The Little Man*, *The Parasite*) in Yiddish. From that point on, throughout more than fifty years of literary activity until his death in 1917, Hebrew-Yiddish bilingualism was the staple characteristic of his literary production. Moreover, he dedicated more than twenty years, a third of his career, to a project—unique in its scope and aesthetic underpinnings—that entailed two separate but mutually complementary activities: the rewriting of his major works in much enlarged and stylistically more polished versions, and, at the same time, the recasting of these works in Hebrew and Yiddish parallel versions. This was done with the intention of creating a double, bilingual canon. The toil this tinkering with his own texts absorbed was revved up to a breakneck intensity as the author's seventy-fifth anniversary drew near. This event was to be marked by the publication of two parallel sets of Abramovitsh's works; and, indeed, two such sets did appear: the Hebrew *Mahadurat hayovel* (Jubilee edition, 1909–1912), in three hefty volumes, and the Yiddish *Yubileum oysgabe* (1911–1912), in seventeen slimmer ones. The difference of size between the two sets was considerable and indicative of the fact that the two were not fully commensurate, mirroring each other. The Yiddish one was by far more comprehensive than the Hebrew one, both because the author had written quite a few Yiddish tales that had no Hebrew equivalents, and because the Hebrew edition (for reasons to be indicated later) was a selection rather than an exhaustive, collected works edition, containing about half of the author's Hebrew output. Nevertheless, with Abramovitsh's five major extended works of fiction, or short novels, forming the core of both sets, the two Jubilee editions

were viewed as proof of the essential bilingual nature of Jewish literature and became the mainstay of the theoretical notion summed up by
the critic Baal-makhshoves (Isidor Elyashiv) in his well-known essay
about the inherent unity of contemporary Hebrew and Yiddish literatures, "Tsvey shprakhen—eyn eyntsike literatur" ("Two Languages—
One Literature Only," 1918).[1] As such they also set up a norm or a model
many contemporary writers aspired to incorporate in their own work,
namely, the model prescribing the crafting of major literary texts (particularly texts of prose fiction, but also, quite often, poetic texts) in two
"original" parallel versions: Hebrew and Yiddish ones.

The influence of this model was, for some time, so prevalent and
strong that writers wished to be seen as living up to it even when this
entailed literary deception. For example, Sholem Aleichem, a trilingual
writer (Yiddish-Hebrew-Russian), whose contribution to Yiddish literature utterly dwarfed, in quantity and quality, his not altogether successful forays into Hebrew and Russian writing, nevertheless wished
to be seen as following in the wake of his mentor Abramovitsh as a
Yiddish-Hebrew bilingualist. In 1911, as the first comprehensive edition
of his Yiddish works was being published (the so-called Progress edition, 1909–1914), he went through the motions of launching a parallel Hebrew one with the publication of a Hebrew version of *Tevye der
milkhiker* (*Tevye the Dairyman*; in Hebrew *Tovya hakholev*) as its first volume. In a special introduction, which was supposed to serve as an entry
to the edition as a whole, the author referred in a humoristic manner to
the current tug of war between Hebraists and Yiddishists (the days being
those of the aftermath of the so-called Czernowicz Language Conference of 1908, in which Yiddish had been proclaimed a Jewish national
language), comparing it to the struggle of those biblical twins Esau and
Jacob in the womb of their mother Rebecca, and presenting himself
as having transcended it, fully reconciling the "festive" Hebrew to the
lively and mundane Yiddish.[2] Actually, neither the Hebrew version
of Tevye nor the introduction to it were written by Sholem Aleichem
himself. Both had been penned by his son-in-law, the Hebrew-Yiddish
writer Y. D. Berkovits.[3] This rather unsavory episode is pointed to not
with the intention of questioning Sholem Aleichem's integrity—the sin
he committed was not at all rare in its day, and luminaries such as Peretz

and Abramovitsh himself did their share of similar resorting to shadow-translators—but rather as an illustration of the almost hypnotic influence of the bilingual-parallelistic model, which we may refer to as "the Mendele model." Would Sholem Aleichem have not aspired to live up to it, beyond his linguistic means, so to speak, he might have spared himself this blemish on his record, which he deeply regretted.[4]

The influence of the Mendele model, having peaked, in the last years before World War I, faded rather quickly after the War was over. In the 1920s it was marginalized, and in the 1930s it all but disappeared. Most of the writers who had resorted to it before the war had to make a choice and channel their creative efforts into one of the two linguistic venues. The choice of Hebrew eventually was followed in most cases by an emigration to Palestine (Ya'akov Shteynberg, Berkovits). The choice of Yiddish often went together with self-immersion in non- or anti-Zionist public activity (see the case of Nomberg, the sensitive Hebrew-Yiddish portraitist of the young and "uprooted" Jewish intellectual, who became after World War I one of the spokesmen of the Jewish Folkist party in Poland). Of the generation who had made their literary debuts in the first decade of the twentieth century, basically only Shneur maintained throughout his career a bilingual activity, producing prose fiction mainly in Yiddish and poetry mainly in Hebrew. Among the writers who emerged in the inter-bellum period, the number of genuine bilingualists was very limited. In Europe one can think only of Aaron Zeitlin, and, for a time, Greenberg, whose breaking away from Yiddish in 1923, coming together with his Zionist conversion and aliya, caused a scandal and triggered charges by Yiddishist detractors of cultural betrayal.[5] In the United States, Hebrew writers in financial difficulties would write for the Yiddish press. However, genuine Hebrew-Yiddish bilingualism was to be found perhaps only in the early work of the poet Preil, who was, for a time, torn between his loyalty to the Yiddish Introspektivist group, whose modernist urban poetics he had internalized, and his Hebraic legacy as a scion of a family of Lithuanian Hebraists.

Clearly, the socio-cultural background of Jewish literary production in this period was not conducive to the maintenance of bilingual activity, and the different ideological and artistic directions followed now by the two literatures, the Hebrew and the Yiddish ones, rendered such activity all but impossible. However, for a considerable time, namely, the twenty or twenty-five years of the so-called Jewish nationalist renaissance, from the beginning of the 1890s to the outbreak of World War I, the Mendele model was not only functional and, as said before, influential, but also emblematic. It represented an integral dimension of this renaissance and responded to a real cultural need. Whereas the impression this created in the minds of some influential critics, such as the already mentioned Baal-makhshoves and later also Niger and Sadan,[6] that the new Hebrew and Yiddish literatures actually formed one, single and integral, bilingual literature, was false and untenable, the cultural need that gave rise to the phenomenon was felt as real, and, indeed, potent. So much so, that the strong opposition to the Mendele model, triggered in some quarters even as it exerted its great influence, was of no avail and as pertinent as the arguments articulated by the opposing faction might be, it was generally discounted, not even eliciting a counterargument.

Thus, for example, the thinker-scholar and writer of prose fiction, Berditchevsky waged for more than a decade bitter cultural-aesthetic warfare, denouncing the Mendele model as detrimental to genuine creativity in either Hebrew or Yiddish. His opposition to the model was not that of the Hebraist purist (as was that of the chief Zionist philosopher of the time, Achad ha'am). Himself a trilingual writer (Hebrew-Yiddish-German), Berditchevsky did not object to bilingualism or even multilingualism in Jewish writing. Rather, as an existentialist thinker, who believed in the strong ties between authentic culture and the realities of individual and social life as they were, he regarded a Jewish literary bi/multilingualism as inevitable under the cultural-historical circumstances of the time and even recommended it when and where it could be construed as an authentic response to these circumstances. However, the production of one, specific literary work in two linguistically differentiated versions, both aspiring to the status of an original, was anathema to him because it undermined the essential aesthetic norm predicating the total and indivisible unity of contents and expression in a truly integrated literary text, the unique continuity that erased the border between what the text conveyed and its stylistic articulation. If one and the same message, he argued, could be articulated twice, in

two different linguistic guises, each assuming the authority of independent articulation (rather than one of the second playing the subservient
role, dependent on the other, namely, the role of a mere translation),
then something must have gone very wrong with either the ideational
formation of the message or its linguistic articulation or both.[7]

Within the sphere of the aesthetic and poetic presuppositions then
current in Hebrew and Yiddish literatures and their concomitant literary-critical rationale, this presented a very strong, perhaps irrefutable,
argument. Nevertheless it made no impression whatever on the leaders
of both literatures, the Hebrew and the Yiddish, of the time, such as
Bialik and Peretz. The former cast his most powerful and influential
public utterance, the poem "In the City of Slaughter" in two clearly
independent and quite divergent versions, a Hebrew one ("Be'ir haharega") and a Yiddish one ("In shkhite shtot"). The latter published most
of his best short stories in parallel Yiddish-Hebrew versions. None of
the young writers of the time (Shteynberg, Shneur, Nomberg, Berkovits, Asch et al.) paid much attention to Berditchevsky's diatribes. Even
those Hebrew writers who regarded themselves as Berditchevsky's followers and internalized much of his cultural thinking (such as Brenner
and Gnessin) disregarded his dictum in this particular matter. The former, as an influential literary critic, never mentioned the older writer's
crusade; and the latter, an artist of supreme aesthetic sensibility, went
on and did exactly what Berditchevsky forbade—he wrote the same
short story, "In the Vegetable Fields" in both Hebrew ("Baganim") and
Yiddish ("Tsvishn gertener") versions. All these underline the existence
of an objective need for the Mendele parallelist model; a need that emanated from the sheer aesthetic, cultural, and social substrata from which
the two literatures sprang at the time, and as such was, as far as most
contemporaries were concerned, self-evidently valid and above being
questioned. Thus by exploring this need and detecting its sources one
can arrive at a better understanding of the conceptual underpinnings of
the Jewish literary renaissance. In the following chapters I shall attempt
such exploration and detection through historically tracing the evolving
of the model in Abramovitsh's career of six decades and elicit from that
process the explanation that would shed some light on the period under
discussion, that of the last third of the author's long trajectory.

II

For a clear understanding of Abramovitsh's Hebrew-Yiddish bilingualism, some preliminary remarks on the nature of literary bilingualism are necessary. The concept of literary bilingualism is a fuzzy one. It is rather like a large umbrella under which several, quite divergent, bilingual options found shelter. Literary bilingualism changes as it moves through time and space. The Hebrew/Aramaic bilingualism of the time of the Mishna and Barayta was quite different in cultural content and function from the Hebrew/Greek bilingualism of the same time. Both instances of bilingualism were fundamentally different from the Hebrew/Arabic one of Yehuda Halevi in Spain of the twelfth century and from that of Maimonides in Cairo half a century later. In Palestine of the centuries preceding and following the fall of the Second Commonwealth, Hebrew was the language of scripture, the liturgy, the codified law, and the mystical lore and poetry that was preserved in the Dead Sea scrolls, while Aramaic served as the spoken mundane language but also as that of the halakhic disquisition that preceded codification. The boundaries separating Hebrew from Greek were less clearly demarcated, with some of the apocrypha written originally in Hebrew and others in Greek, with no clearly defined system allotting to each of the two languages a specific function. In medieval Spain and North Africa, Hebrew would be either the language of halakhic codices and biblical exegesis or the virtuosic language of a poetry rooted in liturgy and sacred sources but perfectly usable within a secular, even profane, context of, for instance, sensual love. Arabic—abstract and radically conceptualized—was used in philosophical and scientific texts.

One can mention many other historical examples of bilingualism, essentially different from each other in both background and purpose. However, for a start, some order can be imposed upon this bewilderingly protean phenomenon by grouping the various bilingual systems into two large groups or categories, which elsewhere I dubbed "differential" and "integral."[8] Since Abramovitsh in different periods of his long career practiced both differential and integral literary bilingualism, we don't have to waste time here on abstract definitions of the terms. Rather we can arrive at such definitions by following the writer's changing bilingual tactics, which is what we shall do. However, let us keep in mind, even as we are about to start our fact-finding procedure that since Abramovitsh resorted at different times and under different circumstances to both kinds of literary bilingualism, as well as to some borderline hybrids between the two, there can be no use for or justification of any sweeping generalization that supposedly covers his bilingual practice as a whole. Rather we must see each of the bilingual systems he adopted within its separate and specific context and try to understand the dynamics that brought about the shifts from one system to another; for the bilingualism manifested in the Mendele model was not only different from the one that had informed the author's practice before the late 1880s, but actually amounted to its opposite—a new literary tactic born out of the crisis of insufficiency that rendered a former one unusable. For our purposes, the understanding of the nature of that crisis and the historical situation that triggered it, is as important as the understanding of each of the different bilingual systems to which the author resorted.

For almost thirty years, from the beginning of his literary activity in the late 1850s and up to its temporary, but quite prolonged, cessation in the early 1880s, Abramovitsh constantly produced texts first only in Hebrew (1857–1863) and then in both Hebrew and Yiddish (starting in 1864) within a systematic overall framework that coalesced in the 1860s and then became stable and fully functional in the 1870s. In the latter decade, the author, moving to and fro between the two languages, wrote some of his most important works in each of the two languages: in Yiddish—fictional masterpieces such as *Di klyatshe* (*The Nag*, 1873) and *Kitser maso'es Binyomin hashlishi* (*The Abridged Travels of Benjamin the Third*, 1878); and in Hebrew—some crucially important non-fictional monographs and essays such as "Ma anu?" ("What Are We?" 1875, a historiosophical disquisition on the formation of the Jewish essence or "character" throughout the ages) or "Ahava le'umit vetoldoteha" ("National Self-Love and Its Consequences," a monograph on nationalism and chauvinism that was published, like *Maso'es Binyomin hashlishi*, in 1878, and contained perhaps the best guide for a real understanding of the assessment of the Jewish condition vis à vis European nationalism and colonialism, which formed the conceptual core of the brilliant Yiddish satire). We must inquire what was the bilingual system or framework that controlled and channeled the author's production during this more-or-less first half of his career.

It was through this system that young Abramovitsh imposed some order and consistency on his writing activity. His early years of literary apprenticeship were characterized by a certain confusion and lack of focus. The young writer knew he wanted to write, but he did not yet know what exactly he wanted to write about; or rather he seemed to want to write on all the topics and to practice almost all the literary genres that innovative, contemporary Hebrew writers favored. Still resorting in the very beginning of his literary apprenticeship to some of the old, and by that time, quite decrepit literary genres and themes, such as heavy-handed neoclassical poetry (the results—highly forgettable), biblical commentary, and the ubiquitous disquisition about the importance of education (that being the major concern of the exponents of the early Hebrew enlightenment since Vayzel's "Divrey shalom ve'emet," the 1782 brochure in which the educational and cultural agenda of the Hebrew enlightenment had been spelled out for the first time), he quickly turned his back on them, preferring novelty and experimentation. However, he seemed unable to decide which of the new options that contemporary Hebrew writing offered would form the focus of his work: literary criticism, popular scientific compendia, non-fiction dealing with current collective issues (known in eastern Europe as *publitsistika*), or prose fiction focusing on current social issues? He dabbled in all of these, publishing within less than three years an extensive critical polemic ("Mishpat shalom," 1860), the first part of a didactic Hebrew novel (*Limdu hetev*, 1862) a zoological compendium (*Toldot hateva*, 1862), and quite a few articles on topical issues. Unfriendly critics were quick to detect the disorientation underlying this hectic and unfocused productivity. "Shining upon us at first from the world of criticism, poetry, and exegesis, Mr. Abramovitsh immediately reappeared as a zoologist, and then peeked at us from the domain of fiction (only a small part of which we have been shown with the rest remaining unveiled)," one of them sarcastically commented.[9]

The turn to Yiddish in 1864, while seemingly adding to all these the heterogeneity and complexity of bilingualism, actually lead to the relative simplification and rationalization of the author's activity. As Abramovitsh himself described it in an autobiographical sketch he wrote in 1889, this was an extremely difficult shift, fraught with consternation and fears of loss of cultural and literary status. However, the shift actually was triggered by a process of maturation, of a literary coming of age, and of authorial stock-taking, which, simplifying and streamlining the writer's creative production, resulted in the crystallization of two totally differentiated literary personae, each with a clearly delineated physiognomy and function of its own: the Yiddish Mendele the book peddler, a subtle fictional creation of a Janus-faced folksy raconteur and commentator, and the Hebrew Abramovitsh, a modern, well-educated intellectual, polemicist, and cultural activist. The former—a loquacious provincial, a born story-teller, a master of the meandering ironic causerie, who belonged within the traditional Jewish community, but also, as an itinerant bookseller of the old kind, who spent most of his time not inside the Jewish villages of the Ukraine but, with horse and wagon, in the sandy or boggy roads between them, lived on the margins of this community, and therefore was able to critically observe it from a certain distance. The latter—a disciplined and erudite thinker, interested in history, science, and current intellectual and political affairs, a master of the straightforward and well-organized conceptual discourse, and clearly a person who lived socially and intellectually in the world of Jewish modernity. Mendele gradually became the sole custodian of Abramovitsh's works of belles lettres—prose fiction and also, problematically enough, poetry; Abramovitsh retained control over everything that belonged within the category of non-fiction and discursive prose. Both were productive and diligent, committed and hard working literary producers—each in his way.

Whereas the importance of the Mendele persona is self-evident to any student of the modern Jewish literatures, that of Abramovitsh, its Hebrew counterpart, should be emphasized and somewhat clarified because the development of the Mendele model around the turn of the nineteenth century involved the intentional suppression of the Abramovitsh side of the equation and the relegating of its literary achievements to oblivion. This led to the previously mentioned fact that about half of the Hebrew output of the author—exactly that part for which the Abramovitsh persona was responsible—was never collected in any edition of the writer's works; an omission, that in its turn, resulted in further encouraging the indifference toward and eventually ignorance of this part of his legacy—to the point that even among the so-called Abramovitsh scholars, not more than two or three evinced interest in and knowledge of it.[10] It is therefore important that we remind ourselves of the fact that from the perspective of those who had viewed the literary scene before the late 1880s, the Abramovitsh figure loomed at least as large as the Mendele one. The former occupied a very central position in an arena that formed in its day, the decades immediately preceding and following the advent of Zionism in the early 1880s, the very center of contemporary Hebrew writing. Whereas both prose fiction (the novels of Mapu, Smolenskin, Broydes, as well as shorter works of fiction written by Y. L. Gordon, Brandshteter, and others) and narrative poetry (where the centrality of Gordon was unchallenged) were robust and vital more than they had ever been since the inception of the "new" Hebrew literature in the late eighteenth century, it can be argued that the main business of contemporary Hebrew writing, or at least a very large part of it, was done within the boundaries of the already mentioned genre of *publitsistika*.

This genre, based on the model of its contemporary Russian counterpart, although focusing on current "burning" issues, covered at the time the sum total of intellectual discourse in Hebrew writing. It encompassed a wide range of topics that were pertinent to a comprehensive and often incisive examination of the Jewish collective condition viewed within the widest possible social, cultural, and historical contexts. For many years, well into the twentieth century, writers who practiced solely or mainly this non-belletristic genre (such as Lilienblum and Achad ha'am) were regarded as the mainstays or leaders of contemporary Hebrew writing. Other writers, who also made important contributions as poets or writers of prose fiction (such as Y. L. Gordon, Smolenskin, Peretz, Berditchevsky, and Brenner) nevertheless invested in their non-belletristic *publitsistika* as much energy and talent as they invested in their poetry or prose fiction. Their readers often were attracted to their non-belletristic articles not less, and perhaps even more than to their poems, novels, and short stories. This must be emphasized since conditions of literary production have thoroughly changed so that the genre of *publitsistika*, often reduced to mere journalism, has been drastically marginalized in current Israeli literature. However, in the 1860s and 1870s, when this genre, which had been present in one or another form since the inception of the new Hebrew literature sixty or seventy years earlier, came of age and peaked to its full ideational and rhetorical sweep, it was the *forme maîtresse* of Hebrew writing. At this point, it served as the crucible in which a new kind of a national soul-searching (what Brenner would dub: *ha'arakhat atsmenu*, self-evaluation or self-criticism), an assessment of the national historical trajectory and its future direction, of current weaknesses and future prospects, took place, resulting in a newly fashioned concept of national identity. This concept certainly also informed the novels and the narrative poetry of the period. But not in vain did the foremost poet (Gordon) and the foremost novelist (Smolenskin) of the 1870s channel about half of their creative energy into the burgeoning arena of contemporary *publitsistika*, where they joined forces with writers who dedicated almost all their efforts to the enhancement of the ongoing, discursive dialogue that was taking place there. They did that because it was primarily in this arena that the process of taking stock of the national social and cultural assets and needs was evolving. Consequently, even the poetry and prose fiction these writers wrote was chock-full of discursive-essayistic passages and dialogues, in which the thrust of *publitsistik* deliberation reached full swing.

The Hebrew Abramovitsh was one of the prominent figures among these paragons of non-belletristic writing, quite or almost on a par with Gordon, Smolenskin, and Lilienblum, fully participating in the evolving reassessment of the national character, past and present, both agreeing and disagreeing with his fellow chief publitsists (see, e.g., his fierce polemic with Lilienblum in his "Et ledaber," ["A Time to Speak Out," 1871]), charting his own path in the ongoing examination of contemporary Jewish society from a proto-socialist viewpoint (the foundations of Jewish socialism being laid then by publitsists such as Lilienblum, A. S. Liberman, and "Ben Nets," the latter soon to be known as the Yiddish socialist poet and agitator Morris Vintshevsky). Thus to many readers of the time, certainly to most Hebrew ones, the Abramovitsh persona overshadowed the Mendele one, which only from the late 1880s on, and particularly during the 1890s and the first decade of the twentieth century managed to altogether push its rival away from the literary limelight.

Thus, during the 1860s and 1870s, Abramovitsh organized his literary production within the framework of a balanced, differential bilingualism; differential in the sense that each of the languages employed by the writer was not only connected with one of his two different literary voices or personae, but also was meant to serve different needs and was targeted at a different reading public. It took the writer several years to achieve this clear-cut differentiation and pursue its inherent dynamics to their final logical conclusions. During the second half of the 1860s, as the linguistic barrier between the two personae and the two genres (Yiddish, fiction; Hebrew, non-fiction) was gradually being buttressed and heightened, the author still half-heartedly went on producing in each of the languages what he was supposed to produce only in the other one. Thus he finished writing the Hebrew novel that he had launched in 1862, publishing it in 1868 under the title *Ha'avot vehabanim* (*The Fathers and the Sons*).[11] On the other side of the equation, he seemed in 1865 to be on the verge of writing in Yiddish a popular survey of the natural sciences, to which a novella published through the agency of Mendele under the title *Dos vintshfingerl* (*The Magic Ring*) was supposed to serve as a narrative introduction (the purported author of the scientific compendium, himself born in an eastern European Jewish village, was telling the Yiddish readers how he had been made to shake off his childish superstitious belief in magic rings and embrace the only "real" magic ring, which was science).[12] Later in that decade he even published what might have been a chapter of a Yiddish book of zoology (dealing with the whale) and together with his friend Y. L. Binshtok, he adapted Jules Verne's *Cinq semaines en ballon* in the belief that a science-fiction romance was a better tool for introducing the simple Yiddish reading public to scientific thinking than a regular scientific textbook like his Hebrew *Toldot hateva*.

By 1869, however, this talking from both sides of his linguistic mouth was stopped. No new Hebrew work of fiction was to appear until 1886, and clearly, during the 1870s Abramovitsh had no intention of writing any such work. Everything that fell within the rubric of belles lettres was to be written in Yiddish and stamped with the Mendele imprint: stories and novels (*Fishke der krumer* [*Fishke the Lame*, 1869], *Maso'es Binyomin hashlishi*, 1878, and an expanded version of *Dos kleyne mentshele*, 1879), dramas (*Di takse* [*The Tax*, 1869]), allegory (*Di klyatshe*, 1873), even narrative poetry (*Yudl*, 1875). On the other hand, all nonfiction, such as the second and third volumes of *Toldot hateva* (1872, 1876) and all articles and monographs, was written in Hebrew and through the Abramovitsh persona. The author also wrote his personal diary in Hebrew. In his diary, he jotted down new ideas for stories and articles, such as his understanding of Hasidism not as a rival of the Enlightenment, but rather as a transitional phase between the rabbinical tradition and Jewish modernity—one of the many original ideas and concepts the author proposed in this decade (the 1870s) when he was thinking long and hard about Jewish history and the ways in which it had formed the Jewish character.[13]

If this total differentiation between the author's two personae and two corpora of writings separated from each other along the linguistic and generic fault lines seems, when taken out of its historical context, rather schizoid and strange, it actually amounted to an adequate and, indeed, ingenious response to a revolutionary historical-cultural situation. Abramovitsh himself explained[14] his decision, arrived at in 1864, to write his works of fiction in Yiddish and through the persona of Mendele the book peddler, as resulting, on the one hand, from his wish to render his work "useful" to the "people," to whom Hebrew was inaccessible, and, on the other hand, from his need to protect his personality and literary reputation from the stigma of dabbling with a vernacular supposedly devoid of cultural status and literary tradition. Thus he wrote his Yiddish stories, which became fairly popular (particularly *Dos kleyne mentshele* and *Di klyatshe*) hiding behind the Mendele persona and hinting at the real author behind it by clever acronyms such as AYSh (Abramovitsh, Ya'akov Shalom), which the simple reader, if he paid attention to them at all, understood as the Hebrew word "ish" (man). There is no need to doubt the sincerity of these explanations, although the fact that they were made in Hebrew and in the late 1880s, when the author was investing much effort in reinventing himself also as a Hebrew writer of prose fiction through the creation of a Hebraic Mendele, nonexistent until this point, should warn us against accepting them at face value. Clearly, they served Abramovitsh's apologetic purposes at this juncture, with the influence of early sentimentalist Zi-

onism cresting toward a heady peak, and the author attempting to re-
furbish and modernize his Hebrew persona in a way that would enable
him to move into the new public arena that the advent of Zionism
had opened up. Also the argument that Yiddish must be resorted to
if Jewish literature was to be useful to the "people" was as trite as it
was true. Almost all nineteenth-century Yiddish writers ubiquitously
evoked it, using its self-evident pragmatic validity as their cultural fig
leaf. Abramovitsh himself strangely contradicted the sheer pragmatism
of this argument, even as he was asserting it (in his 1889 biographical sketch), by unabashedly pointing to his "penchant" for Yiddish in
stark sexual metaphors, confessing that as much as his connection with
the language had started as an illicit extra-marital affair, which had to
be covered up, it gave him so much pleasure, that eventually he had
to confer upon this linguistic concubine the decent status of an official common-law wife, cohabit, and successfully sire with her a line
of healthy progeny. However, even if we are to accept Abramovitsh's
explanations as valid, we still must integrate them within a wider historical context in order to understand the fully-fledged and rather strict
differential bilingualism they purported to justify.

III

In the late 1850s and the early 1860s, the years of Abramovitsh's literary apprenticeship, a revolutionary development changed the nature
and scope of both the Hebrew and the Yiddish literatures of the
Enlightenment. This change was rendered possible not only by the
emergence of a new generation of writers, some of whom have already
been mentioned, but also, and perhaps more importantly, by the creation of a new Jewish literary public space, or rather public spaces. It was
this new public space that enabled the new writers to assert themselves
and gain public presence, as, of course, it also shaped, to a large extent,
their literary messages and means of articulating them. The creation of
this public space, which manifested itself during the years under discussion here by the appearance, one after another, of Hebrew weeklies
(*Hamagid*, *Hakarmel*, and then mainly *Hamelits* and *Hatsefira*), was

made possible by the termination in the mid-1850s of the repressive regime of Nicholas I with its inherently inimical attitude toward public debate and freedom of speech, no matter how limited, and the onset of the liberalization of public life in the Czarist empire under the regime of Alexander II. As this extrinsic, political development intersected with an intrinsic emergence of a new Jewish intelligentsia, inspired by current models of Russian civic and critical writing (the influence of contemporary Russian literary criticism was paramount), a new and relatively free and busy Jewish literary "republic" was established. Once instated, this new republic rendered its predecessor, the old and extremely confined and cramped *Brudeschaft* of the earlier Hebrew enlightenment, totally passé, much to the chagrin of some of the older writers who shuddered to see the windows of their stuffy and cozily undusted rooms thrown widely open with cold winds of harsh criticism and lively debate sweeping away the pages of their outdated manuscripts. The literary critic A. U. Kovner, himself the enfant terrible of this new era, justifiably pointed to the emergence of the new weeklies, which relegated to the past the old-style periodicals of the Hebrew enlightenment—sedate, usually devoid of incisive inter-maskilic debate and self-criticism, and also appearing irregularly and infrequently—as the event that heralded the advent of a new kind of literature, different and cut off from the older literature of the "Mendelssohnian" enlightenment.[15] It was this new public space, with the new brands of *publitsistika* and literary criticism it engendered, which also supplied the new fiction and poetry with the resonance and feedback that they required for their development as vital literary venues.

Abramovitsh, like most of his contemporaries, was the natural inhabitant of this new Hebrew public space. Throughout his career, he would systematically conceive of writing as a public activity and would always navigate his literary practice in accordance with what he believed to be the needs of the literary "republic"; indeed, his entire authorial sensorium would be attuned to these needs and hence his ability to reorganize his writing and more than once change its direction. In this as in many other things, he remained the true child of the revolution in Hebrew letters of the 1850s and the 1860s, formed and shaped by the new literary ambience in which it took place. In 1863, however, with the appearance of the first Yiddish weekly *Kol mevaser* (as a supplement to the Hebrew *Hamelits*) and its quite astounding warm reception by a relatively large reading public, the existence of which had been until this point unsuspected, and, of course, untapped, he realized that in fact two parallel but also very different Jewish literary public spaces were being formed. The success of his first Yiddish story (*Dos kleyne mentshele*), which was widely read when first serialized in *Kol mevaser* and then sold well in book form, convinced him of the potential and vitality of this other, still very new and malleable public space that he was determined to inhabit even as he stuck to most of the positions he had already occupied in its more entrenched Hebrew counterpart.

He carefully studied the differences between the two spaces. The first, the Hebrew one, possessed the respectability and seriousness that went together with the "sublimity" of the Hebrew language and its long literary traditions going all the way back to the Bible, as well as by the stern and principled teachings of the thinkers of the Hebrew enlightenment such as Krochmal (known as RANAK) and Levinson (known as RIVAL). True, even this "august" literary venue started to open up in the 1850s and 1860s and attract a wider and more popular reading public than the one it had addressed in the first half of the century. Mapu's historical romances engaged readers that were interested in the complications of their plots of love and intrigue more than in the ideas about the duality (the corporeal and libidinous versus the spiritual and the religious) of the Jewish psyche and history the author absorbed from Krochmal's philosophical analysis of the dynamics of Jewish history. Kalman Shulman's adaptation of Eugène Sue's *Mystères de Paris* scored a sensational success with these readers. However, Abramovitsh correctly understood that the Yiddish language would be by far more conducive, and the expectations of its new readers would be far more receptive, to writing of the kind of satirical and topical (rather than romance-like and historical) fiction he wanted to write than Hebrew and its readers. If he needed proof of that, it was amply supplied by the writing and lukewarm public reception of his own first Hebrew novel, *Limdu hetev*, in which the creation of dialogue and the description of the physical realities of current Jewish life had entailed severe difficulties (of those he bitterly complained in the introduction to the story)[16] and often involved the literal translation of idiomatic expressions that had to be referred to their Yiddish originals in cumbersome notes.

Understanding that discursive writing on both topical and historical issues, both included in the aforementioned *publitsistika*, was to form the very center of the new Hebrew public space, he decided to address his Hebrew readers only as a writer of nonfiction, a serious thinker, and a methodical scientific educator. The Yiddish reading public, the rudiments of which had to some extent already coalesced by the success of earlier popular writers, such as Dik, was by far larger, but, by the same token, less educated than the Hebrew one and less interested in ideas and conceptualized issues. Whereas the latter was comprised almost entirely of readers who were not only equipped with the necessary linguistic proficiency but also already committed to the Enlightenment and its agenda, the former contained a large contingent of readers that were not averse to reading the stuff the new writers turned out, provided it was entertaining enough, but by no means could be regarded as adherents of the Enlightenment. Many of Dik's readers regarded his stories as quasi-traditional didactic-moralistic chapbooks. Linetski's *Dos poylishe yingl* (*The Polish Lad*, 1867), which, like *Dos kleyne mentshele*, was also serialized with resounding success in *Kol mevaser*, was relished by many Hasidic readers who enjoyed its jabs at their leaders, the *tsadikim*, while dismissing its maskilic and anti-hasidic message.[17]

Abramovitsh believed in approaching these readers in a roundabout, ironic way through a persona that to some extent would look like them, speak their language, articulate ideas and insights that were not alien to their mental world, and at the same time evolve a satirical and critical discourse that would subtly undermine their traditional thinking and beliefs. Under the given cultural circumstances, the invention of such a persona was inevitable if this new, heterogeneous, Yiddish-speaking public space was to be successfully manipulated; and, indeed, as soon as Abramovitsh invented his Mendele and rendered him a familiar public presence in his *Dos kleyne mentshele*, similar personae appeared everywhere in contemporary Yiddish writing (to mention only two: Linetski's "Eli kotsin hatskhakueli" and S. Bernshteyn's "Shilshom bar-yente"), none of them–at least until the appearance of the Sholem Aleichem persona in the 1880s—as subtle, nuanced, and potentially useful as Mendele, but all of them funny, entertaining, and of a satirical bent. As a matter of fact, the Mendele persona and its gradual development, better than anything else, defined the new Yiddish public space, its scope, limitations, and modalities at least for a decade and a half. It fully responded to the needs and proclivities of its inhabitants until the late 1870s and early 1880s when the Yiddish reading public not only was growing by leaps and bounds,[18] but also, due to new historical circumstances, was changing in character—and waxing responsive to the emotional manipulation of the melodramatic romances of J. Dinezon; and particularly those of N. M. Shaykevitsh and his imitators—much more than it had ever been attuned to the ironies and satirical reduction to the absurd of writers of the Mendele school. Thus Abramovitsh's turning to Yiddish and his invention of Mendele in the mid-1860s indicated more than anything else the writer's acute sensibilities as a public figure equipped with antennae able to register potential trends before they were decoded by others, as well as with the talent and energy needed for creatively navigating and being carried forward by them.

Throughout the 1870s, and particularly toward the end of the decade, Abramovitsh achieved full control of the differential bilingual system that allowed him to employ both his personae in an orderly and effective manner. This found full expression not only in the proportional investment of energy in the Yiddish fictional masterpieces (*Di klyatshe* and *Maso'es Binyomin hashlishi*) and the major Hebrew non-fictional monographs, but also in the enhanced crystallization of the Mendele persona itself, which loomed larger and more prominent as the author reached, in the late 1870s, a decision to publish the first "collected" edition of Mendele's Yiddish works. In the early 1870s, for some time, he entertained the idea of adding to his Mendele another Yiddish persona, that of *Yisroel der meshugener* (crazy Yisroel), whose life story was told by himself in *Di klyatshe*. As much as this brilliant allegory was still presented as based on a manuscript edited, improved, and published by Mendele, who also introduced it with one of his by now famous *Omar Mendele* (Thus spake Mendele) introductions, the author also wanted to develop its protagonist, Yisroel, as a conversationalist and a commentator in his own right, who would evolve a causerie of his own independently of Mendele and his ministrations.[19] As an intellectual and a committed public activist, Yisroel could presumably offer a discourse that would aim at "higher" and more conceptual topics or aspire to moments of higher lyrical and pathetic expressiveness than those within the range of the Mendele discourse. If Abramovitsh would have persisted in this idea and created on top of the set of his Mendele texts another set of *ksovim* (writings) presided over by his Yisrolik, the gap between his Yiddish and Hebrew personae would have been considerably narrowed; for Yisrolik was at least as close to the Abramovitsh persona as he was to the Mendele one, and indeed, could have served as a connecting link between the two. Thus, the writer's differential bilingualism would lose much of its precision and clarity. However, significantly, Abramovitsh decided to abort the Yisrolik project and stick by Mendele as his unchallenged and sole Yiddish spokesman.

A similarly futile attempt made by Abramovitsh in the 1870s to barge beyond the boundaries of the Mendele narration led him to the domain of poetry for which he had neither talent nor much of a self-critical discerning. Clearly what he produced in this domain was, by far, of a lesser literary and historical import than his eventually abandoned plan of exchanging or complementing the services rendered by the folksy and cynical Mendele with those of the madman, intellectual Yisrolik with his idealism, sentimentalism, and lyrical outbursts. The latter could not be successfully continued after the publication of *Di klyatshe*, but at least they fueled and elevated one masterpiece, a complex and multilayered story that amounted to the author's most original statement as an imaginative thinker and also exhilarated and educated a huge reading public. As such it broadened the scope of Yiddish prose fiction and laid the foundation for its further evolvement (for instance, in many of Peretz's psychological and ideational tales; *Di Klyatshe* being the first modern Yiddish text by which Peretz was impacted—through a Polish translation—and impressed[20]). In contradistinction, Abramovitsh's work as a poet and a poetic translator and adaptor made no discernible contribution to contemporary Yiddish poetry, of all literary genres practiced at the time in Yiddish the most awkward and underdeveloped. As a matter of fact, his poetic products were distinctly inferior to those of some of his contemporaries, such as the poet Mikhl Gordon, a relative of Y. L. Gordon, the Hebrew master, let alone the few Yiddish poems

Y. L. Gordon himself wrote, in which some of the stylistic élan and wit of his Hebrew works was approximated.[21] Not that Abramovitsh refrained from investing hard work and good intentions in his rather ambitious poetic project. His *Yudl*, a long narrative allegory in which the fate of the protagonist incorporated a view of Jewish history not much different from the one that had informed *Di klyatshe*, was laboriously written in two different versions.[22] However, with the complex protagonist-narrator Yisrolik the "madman" gone, and his interactions with his mother on the one hand and the hallucinatory nag on the other not adding to the historicist ideation their psychological depth and fantastic visionariness, the ideas wilted right in front of the reader's eye like water plants removed from their element. What was left of them was further devastated by a particularly long-winded diction characterized by redundancy, mechanical scanning and uninteresting, hackneyed rhyming. The garrulous, idiomatic Yiddish that was so dexterously employed by the Mendele persona in its causerie turned upon itself in the serious and pathos-filled poem and was revealed as essentially nonpoetic and strangely devoid of grace and nuance. The same can be said about the ambitious poetic task with which Abramovitsh went on to burden himself as a translator of Psalms and of two extensive units of Jewish liturgy, the hymn "Perek shira," an ode to God's creation and the glory of nature rooted in the Jewish mystical tradition and based on biblical and some post-biblical sources, and the *zemirot*, the songs sung around the Sabbath table. An old-fashioned literary Yiddish translation of all these texts being habitually appended to the *korben minkhe* siddur, the Yiddish daily prayer manual prepared for women, Abramovitsh's idea was to replace this translation by a new one, written in current idiomatic Yiddish, and perhaps also to corner the burgeoning book market of women's prayer books.[23] In retranslating Hebrew sacrosanct texts into modern, idiomatic Yiddish, he followed in the wake of the maskilic tradition that had been initiated at the beginning of the nineteenth century by Mendl Lefin in his translations of Proverbs and Ecclesiastes; (in fact, Lefin's translation of Ecclesiastes, having appeared only in 1873, the time when Abramovitsh launched his project, it might have served as the trigger). However, whereas Lefin had succeeded in conveying epigrammatic biblical wisdom in a lively modern Yiddish style that was as witty, although not as elevated, as the ancient Hebrew originals, and perhaps added to them the piquant salinity of a daily-used and far from ceremonious vernacular, Abramovitsh drowned the Hebrew texts he adapted and belabored in sugary, paraphrastic repetitions and in cliché-ridden rhymes. His translation of Psalms was never published (although he has been said to have kept tinkering at it throughout his life) and was eventually lost; but by the few examples that survived,[24] we can gauge the depth of the translator's bad taste and infelicity as a writer of wordy, stanzaic, rhyming verse. The same can be said, even with more justification, about the translation of "Perek shira" (which did appear in 1875), where each succinct, dense, and forceful biblical quotation was developed through overextension, dilution, repetition, and pathetic interjections into a longish, verbose poem. The attempt of some recent scholarship to "upgrade" Abramovitsh's poetry and discover in it all sorts of historical interests notwithstanding,[25] the real historical significance of both *Yudl* and the translations from the liturgy transpires when they are examined and understood as proof of how impossible it was for Abramovitsh as a consummate Yiddish artist, and perhaps for nineteenth-century Yiddish literature as a whole, to successfully break away from prose-fiction written in the Mendele style, that is, as a loquacious meandering monologue suffused with folksy wit and naive cunning. The fact that the author's forays into poetry were discontinued after 1875 and that the Psalms translation was not included in the *Yubileum oysgabe* of his collected Yiddish works should be regarded as an indication of Abramovitsh's fully internalized realization of the artistic impasse he had driven himself into and of his courage in cutting his losses and avoiding in the future similar expensive and wasteful detours.

Clearly, this decision was reached also after a careful assessment of the wishes and the capabilities of the contemporary Yiddish reading public. The writer realized that in spite of the success of *Di klyatshe* (which could have been ascribed to the lively pathetic and comic allegorical tale rather than to the interest aroused by its historiosophical and moralistic significance), he could not rely on a Yisrolik-type persona to successfully maintain a lively rapport with the Yiddish readers; so he let Yisrolik remain the protagonist of just one story, which was now to form a mere link in a chain of stories controlled and unified by Mendele. At the same time he must have realized that the translations from the liturgy, in which Mendele had no role at all (they were published under Abramovitsh's own name and thus presented the only instances in which the Abramovitsh imprimatur was borrowed from the Hebrew publications and used in Yiddish ones) failed to elicit enthusiasm from the reading public. He therefore understood that his hold on that public totally depended on the popularity of the Mendele fiction. As a result, he raised the status of the latter from that of a mere publisher of other people's manuscripts to that of an authoritative literary factotum. Already in *Di klyatshe*, Mendele featured as the creative editor of Yisrolik's supposedly confused and incomplete manuscript; in *Maso'es Binyomin*, he presented himself as a co-author, a skillful adapter who knew how to abridge and entertainingly rewrite the protagonist's various travelogues. His presence was to become ever more pervasive.[26]

Preparing enlarged versions of *Dos kleyne mentshele* and *Fishke der krumer*, Abramovitsh launched in 1879 the publication of *Mendele's Collected Works*, opening the first volume (*Dos kleyne mentshele*; the publication of the second one was deferred to 1889) with a brilliant general introduction entitled "Mendele the Book Peddler's Introduction as He Appeared Before the Public with his Works." Here Mendele offered "his readers" a detailed physical portrait of himself, told about his hometown Tsviashits (town of hypocrites), about the history of his business as a book peddler and a publisher since his comfortable years of bed and board with his in-laws had come to an end, and even coyly revealed the name of his spouse (Yente), "since as everyone knows, our Jewish writers have a habit of inserting their pious wives into their books, calling them by their proper names." At the same time, he cleverly managed to avoid burdening his persona with too many specific and identifiable features. The more Mendele talked about himself, the more of a Jewish everyman he seemed. In any case, the introduction, a minor masterpiece in its own right now regrettably missing from most collected editions of the author's Yiddish works,[27] clearly intended to present the "Works of Mendele" as a closed, autonomous, and self-sufficient system; "a Mendele world," radically independent of the same author's Hebrew works of non-fiction. Indeed, Abramovitsh conceived now of his works as existing in two separate spheres, which presumably, never intersected, and roaming as they were within one authorial space, they nevertheless were "unaware" of each other's existence.

IV

The publication of Mendele's works was meant to be continued. A second volume (containing a new and enlarged version of *Fishke der krumer*) was all but ready for the printer. However, at this point a devastating personal tragedy (the writer's son—joining a revolutionary group, was exiled, converted to Christianity, and married a non-Jew) triggered a hiatus in Abramovitsh's literary career. Then during 1881–1882, in the wake of the assassination of Alexander II, came the backlash of widespread pogroms throughout the southern provinces of the Czarist empire. Those, unabated (if not actively encouraged) by the authorities, overwhelmed the Russian-Jewish adherents of the Enlightenment and gave rise to the Russian Zionist movement known as *Khibat tsiyon* (The Love of Zion). Then Abramovitsh and his family moved from Zhitomir, where they resided the 1870s, to Odessa, the new capital of Jewish modernity in Czarist Russia and the hub of the recently organized Zionist movement. Pioneering new approaches to Jewish education, the leaders of the Odessa community decided to establish in their town a semi-modern yeshiva high school, which would serve mainly youngsters with some Talmudic learning who came to Odessa from the small hamlets of the Czarist Jewish pale. They searched for a principal who would put together, pedagogically and organizationally, their new institution of Jewish learning, and the candidacy of Abramovitsh won their approval. The writer, in dire financial straits and in urgent need for a change, accepted their offer. All these blows, upheavals, and changes, as well as the hard work he had to invest in the yeshiva, sapped his creative energies for four years. From 1884 to 1885, he gradually emerged from his authorial paralysis and found himself in a social and intellectual milieu that was very different from the one he had been exposed to in the Volhynian provincial centers, Berditchev and Zhitomir, where he had spent the first two decades of his career as a writer. He quickly realized that the public space into which he must now reinsert himself was very different from the one that had defined the parameters of his literary activity in his earlier career and that he was facing challenges for which he had no ready answers.

These challenges emanated from the fact that the reading public, or rather publics, that he must engage not only had changed, but also had become structurally stratified and complex in a manner quite bewildering and paradoxical. The Yiddish reading public was split in two unequal parts each of which pulled the writer in a different direction. As said before, the mass of Yiddish readers grew now at a dizzying pace, while their literary interests and expectations plummeted to the *Schund* level of Shaykevitsh and his many followers. Under the tutelage of these popular writers, the Yiddish literary market was monopolized by melodramatic novels of intrigue, "sinful" love, and high adventure that, written in a Germanized, stilted Yiddish, were being produced on a quasi-industrial basis. A writer who wished to reach a wide-reading public had to somehow cater to the interests and preferences of this naive and barely literate audience. On the other hand, a small but very significant and influential Russian-Jewish intelligentsia emerged in the 1880s, which, under the influence of the nascent Jewish nationalism and "back to the people" *narodnik* trend, became attuned to and appreciative of Yiddish writing, expecting it to rise to a canonical level as prescribed by current Russian literary norms, and actively encouraging whatever development seemed to lead toward such elevation. As much as these people understood Yiddish writing as "a people's literature" (*folksliteratur*) rather than a normative national literature, they still expected it to be both mimetically reflective (and if necessary, also satirically critical) of the simple people's life and to artistically reveal the moral value and humane beauty that were supposedly "hidden" underneath the uncouth manners and the vulgarity of the "common people"—rather in the way Russian writers of the period treated peasants and manual laborers in their stories. Abramovitsh lived now at the very hub of this new intelligentsia, many members of which huddled together in the new Jewish center of Odessa. He could not remain indifferent to the judgment of people such as Dubnov, the historian who also wrote influential literary criticism under the pen name Criticus, or the culture activist Menashe

Margolis, who became his personal friend. At the same time, he was wary of being cut off from his popular moorings and forfeiting the sympathy of the wider reading public. Thus, finding himself in the position of the servant of two masters, he had to find a way of pleasing both. Carefully navigating his literary vessel between the dangerous shoals of *Schund* popularity and the boulders of nationalistic elitist "populism," he was searching for a literary voice or manner that would address different reading publics.

As for the Hebrew reading public, it too underwent far-reaching structural changes. For one thing, it too grew immensely in numbers. Sokolov, the famous Hebrew journalist (who was to become a Zionist diplomat and, toward the end of his life, also the president of the World Zionist Organization), said that in the 1880s modern Hebrew writing was, in a sense, reborn, because, quite suddenly, the meager audience of the haskala literature (which, he said, had never numbered more than a few thousand) exploded into a burgeoning reading public of more than one hundred thousand.[28] It is doubtful that the shift was as dramatic as Sokolov maintained; and we have already suggested that the sudden growth in the 1860s of the number of readers of Hebrew novels, whether original or adapted, had indicated the addition already at that time of a more popular audience to that of the traditional adherents of the Hebrew enlightenment and old-time readers of its publications. However, there can be no doubt, that the explosion Sokolov identified was real and that Hebrew writing in the 1880s acquired an altogether new social base. The fact that in the second half of the decade the two main weeklies of the Haskala, *Hamelits* and *Hatsefira*, started to appear as dailies with a fairly wide circulation speaks for itself; that on top of about a dozen new literary almanacs and periodicals—some of them fat volumes of many hundreds of pages—that were published and apparently found buyers and readers, a brisk activity of both private and public publishing houses (such as *Akhiasaf*, *Sifre agora*, and eventually *Tushiya*) never flagged until well into the first decade of the twentieth century.

This dramatic growth was caused by two or three quite separate, but also mutually complementary developments. The pogroms of 1881–1882 and the new assessment of the prospects of Russian Jewry it triggered politicized to a considerable extent the traditional Jewish middle class of the Czarist empire. Whereas the mental horizons and the curiosity of this middle class had been limited to local matters, the concerns of small, provincial communities and their immediate vicinities, or to particular Jewish concerns caused by regulations and ukases (regarding, clothing, education, army service, taxation) of the authorities that were regarded as oppressive, now these horizons were greatly expanded and globalized. Matters such as Russian and European international politics, the fortunes of European colonialism and particularly those pertaining to the Middle East and Palestine, the accelerated pauperization of the population throughout the Jewish pale in the Czarist empire now entering into a relatively advanced and dynamic phase of capitalist socio-economic development, Jewish mass emigration out of the empire, and the social and economic circumstances prevailing in the western countries where Jewish proletarianized immigrants had to survive—all these became of vital interest to many dozens of thousands of new readers—topics they would read about, discuss, and eagerly follow the debates that they triggered among the pundits of the Hebrew press. This awakened interest turned whoever had sufficient proficiency to the Hebrew weeklies and dailies, where a lively political discourse quickly developed. For those who knew no Russian or whose Russian (or rather Ukrainian) was colloquial and minimal, this was the only source that could quench their journalistic thirst, and under these circumstances it was little wonder that Hebrew dailies cropped up one after the other starting in 1886.

A parallel but quite independent development was the gradual semi-secularization of traditional Jewish society; a secularization that was social and "practical" rather than ideological. Traditional Jews who would by no means view themselves as secular or as followers of the Enlightenment were now taking for granted that a certain exposure to the non-traditional and also the non-Jewish spheres was practically unavoidable. They saw to it that their children would be taught Hebrew and Russian and a growing number of them would seek for their children a Russian secondary school education, which supposedly would enhance their professional or commercial careers and chances in the Jewish matrimonial market.

Both developments, as much as they broadened the boundaries of the Hebrew reading public, also changed its taste and expectations.

This was by far a more popular and less erudite audience than the one Abramovitsh had addressed in his earlier Hebrew monographs, published in the periodicals of the 1870s in many sequels and over relatively long periods of time. Abramovitsh himself described this new Hebrew public in one of the short stories he wrote in the 1880s as impatient and unable or unwilling to follow a long and conceptualized historical disquisition ("Master of the world! . . . you know the character of your people, whose souls are very very thirsty for the news and rumors floating in your world; however, their wish is to know everything without frequent intellectual effort or loss of time or money. Rather they wish to absorb everything effortlessly, in a single glance").[29] Book-length essays such as Smolenskin's "Et lata'at," Lilienblum's "Orkhot hatalmud," or Abramovitsh's "Ma anu?" could not hold the interest of these readers, to whom now a new slew of journalists with lighter feathers, such as the above-mentioned Sokolov or Y. L. Kantor (the editor of *Hayom*, the first Hebrew daily), Epshteyn, Ravnitsky, E. L. Levinsky, and many others, catered.

Also these readers became avid consumers of historical novels on topics such as the expulsion of Spanish Jews, the horrors faced by the Marranos at the courts of the inquisition, blood libels and persecutions of Jews in the medieval cities of Germany, the sanctification of the holy name in the days of the Crusades, and so on. These novels, produced mainly by traditionalist and apologetic German Jewish writers (who wrote for internal Jewish consumption) in the middle of the nineteenth century, were now adapted into Hebrew with or without an additional Zionist flavor, and soon enough, Hebrew writers (among them the ubiquitous Shaykevitsh, who attempted to corner this new market, as well as that of the popular Yiddish romance) added their original contributions. Thus, for instance, the most popular sequence of Hebrew novels to appear in the 1890s, *Zikhronot leveyt David* (*The Annals of the Davidic Dynasty*), consisted of an amalgam of an adaptation of Hermann Reckendorf's novelistic sequel *Die Geheimnisse der Juden* (1856–1857) and original additions penned by the Hebrew adapter, Avraham Shalom Fridberg.

For Abramovitsh this was an entirely new Hebrew literary milieu, a milieu that was not particularly attuned to his ironic and satirical manner, and which clearly undermined the strict division that had made possible his earlier differential bilingualism (Hebrew—serious non-fiction; Yiddish—satirical Mendele-type fiction). It contradicted the logic that had informed this bilingualism and rendered its basic social and aesthetic assumptions obsolete. The writer had to ask himself whether he should or could now reassert himself in Hebrew as a writer of nonfiction. Wasn't the kind of nonfiction he had written passé? Would he be able to compete as a writer of nonfiction with the Sokolovs, Frishmans, Kantors, Epshteyns, and Levinskys, let alone with Achad ha'am, who since his emergence as a Hebrew essayist and publitsist in 1889 completely changed the aesthetics, style, and structure of Hebrew nonfictional writing, creating for Hebrew *publitsistika* a shining new model? And was his earlier decision to write fiction only in Yiddish still viable? Wouldn't he be better equipped for the purpose of making a place for himself, and a central one at that, in the new Hebrew literary arena by now turning back to the writing of fiction in Hebrew? To all these questions, Abramovitsh had no immediate and clear-cut answers.

On top of all that, it became quite clear, that for reasserting his position either as a Hebrew or as a Yiddish writer, Abramovitsh would have to change his thematics. The pogroms of 1881–1882 as a historical watershed and the advent of Jewish nationalism and its main political expression, Zionism, relegated the topics of his earlier stories to the quite irrelevant past. The social and cultural issues these stories had focused on were historically anchored in the 1840s and 1850s and reflected contemporary concerns of the Russian Jewish community, or those of the Russian Jewish enlightenment movement, particularly those pertaining to desired changes in Jewish education and the depravity and brutality of the *kahal*, the local Jewish communal leadership, which in the days of Nicholas I exploited and terrorized the weaker sections of the community by its ability to arbitrarily raise the special Jewish communal taxes (particularly the tax on kosher meat) and to dispose of its critics by having them drafted into the Russian army for a service of twenty-five years. In the 1880s, these once-burning issues lost their relevance (which was regained in the 1890s as the plight of the *kantonistn*, the Jewish conscripts to the army of Nicolas I, suddenly regained its hold over the popular imagination). Abramovitsh, when rewriting his earlier works, would have to "update" them thematically in one way or another. Thus he would update *Fishke der krumer* both through adding to the story a substantial section that took place in modern Odessa and satirically reflected on Russian Jewish modernity, and by interpreting (in a new introduction written in the form of an open letter to his friend Margolis) the novel's tale of the wandering of itinerant Jewish beggars as a parable emblematic of Jewish wandering in general (the "eternal Jewish knapsack"), and, thus, also of the contemporaneous Jewish mass migration out of the Czarist empire. *Dos vintshfingerl,* that early story propagating the replacing through scientific education of a superstitious, irrational, and passive approach to reality by a rational, informed, practical, and active one, would be rewritten as a comprehensive historical novel covering the miserable Jewish life in Russia from the 1840s to the present, starting and ending with the description of the habitual Mendele towns and hamlets in their current, namely, post-pogroms situation and probably also pointing toward some "solution" of the Jewish problem in the spirit of Leon Pinsker's famous *Autoemancipation* brochure,[30] which Abramovitsh now adapted in Yiddish under the title "A Sgule far yidishe tsores" ("A Remedy for Jewish Troubles").

Abramovitsh was now surrounded by thinkers and public activists, whose point of departure was that of the new ardent Jewish nationalism, that he himself had already examined, with serious reservations and doubts in the 1870s. Almost all his new Odessa acquaintances were Zionists, for some of whom (such as Pinsker in the 1880s and Achad ha'am in the 1890s), he had great respect (the former was all but idealized in one of his short stories), while he was critical of others and ambivalent with regard to the movement itself and its prospects. Nevertheless, if he was to be accepted and respected by this nationalist intelligentsia, he could not afford to remain indifferent to the issues that troubled and excited it: the pogroms, the future prospects of the Jewish contingent in Czarist Russia, emigration, the Zionist project. His relevance as a writer clearly depended on his ability to meaningfully react to those issues; and having nothing but disrespect for both the unfounded Zionist optimism and the strident wailing of contemporary sentimentalist Jewish writing, he experienced great difficulties in finding the proper artistic voice through which he could comment on the current Jewish situation in a manner both in accordance with his own skeptical outlook and approved by the enthusiastically nationalist readers he now wanted to address. Indeed, his reappearance as a Jewish writer in the 1880s entailed something of a renewed self-invention and the throes of a second literary birth.

V

The first move Abramovitsh made in the process of his comeback was not propitious and indicative of a clear sense of self-orientation. He published in 1884 a second drama (second to *The Tax* of 1869), *Der priziv* (*The Draft*), a title which replaced the earlier *Keminheg yid* (*According to Jewish Custom*) in an attempt to focus attention on the crux of its dramatic plot, the havoc wreaked on the life of a Jewish middle-class family by the drafting of a young man into the Russian army. Whereas *The Tax* had been first and foremost a satire and a protest boiling with rage, a document of scathing social criticism (of the Jewish communal leadership), and, as a matter of fact, one of the seminal early texts of the Jewish proto-socialist literature, this second play of Abramovitsh was more of a genuine bourgeois melodrama written with an improved dramatic skill but with greatly diminished élan (which is why it is, by far, less readable than *The Tax*), a stage-worthy family *Trauerspiel* replete with moments of comic relief, as well as with folksongs.[31] However, *Der priziv* could hardly touch the public's nerve, which the writer had to get his finger on. Whereas the issue of the drafting of young Jewish men into the Russian army (already under regulations that were very different from the draconic ones that had prevailed in the days of Nicholas I) was still of considerable social and familial significance and would be dealt with later by many Yiddish and Hebrew writers, and particularly by Sholem Aleichem, it certainly lacked the topical intensity that it once had had. Against the backdrop of pogroms and mass emigration, its importance shrunk. It was certainly a wrong step on the part of Abramovitsh to pick it as the first social issue to focus on. Then, as a truly dramatic text, it lacked the biting irony and subversive cleverness of the Mendele causerie, the charmingly complex and meandering plot line of the Mendele tales.

All in all, *Der priziv* was a mistake and a flop. It was not widely read or commented on when it appeared, which the author, after the successes he had scored with *Di klyatshe* and *Maso'es Binyomin*, must have experienced as a humiliating failure. It also has been all but avoided by Abramovitsh scholars throughout a century of commentary, literary analysis, and historical research.[32]

The writer had therefore no choice but to fall back on his plan from the late 1870s of republishing his collected earlier Yiddish works in enlarged, improved, and, as indicated, updated, versions. *Fishke*, which in the meantime assumed (primarily through the efforts of young Sholem Aleichem as a literary critic) the status of a classic, an authentic Jewish love story (in contradistinction to the inauthentic romances of the Shaykevitsh school), was to launch the new collected edition. It was once again rewritten, as was, to a lesser degree, *Di klyatshe*, both texts appearing (in 1889) as the first two volumes of a new set of *Ale verk fun Mendele Moykher Seforim*, with the original Mendele introduction of 1879 and the new open letter to Margolis serving as an overture to the planned sequel of volumes. At the same time, Abramovitsh also started rewriting *Dos vintshfingerl*, which was to become his most ambitious and expansive novel (the first two parts were published in the 1888 and 1889 volumes of Sholem Aleichem's *Folksbiblyotek*). All these creative efforts contributed to the buttressing of his status as a classic author, an exemplary Yiddish stylist, and the great Yiddish master of mimetic description; a status that was also enhanced at the time by the publication of his two masterpieces of the 1870s, *Di Klyatshe* and *Maso'es Binyomin*, in Polish translations, rendering him the first Yiddish writer to win the attention of a non-Jewish reading public.

However, as much as this elevation was welcome and encouraged, it had its negative flip side as well, mainly the wrapping of the writer's public image with a certain aura of old-fashioned respectability and slow-paced seniority. This certainly did not sit well with a writer who had set out in the 1860s to infuse Jewish literature with topicality, update its social relevance, and energize it through lively wit and the sense of the comic. In 1888, Sholem Aleichem (in his introduction to his novel *Stempenyu*) "crowned" the fifty-three-year-old Abramovitsh as the "grandfather" of the new Yiddish literature, and the title, like many of Sholem Aleichem's creations, appealed to the popular imagination and stuck. It would follow its bearer throughout his lifetime, as well as for many decades beyond it. Whereas this "coronation" served very well the literary interests of its initiator, pointing to himself as to a representative of a new and by far more dynamic literary generation, it is doubtful that it gladdened the heart of the "grandfather" himself; for piling compliments on the supposedly hoary head of this ancient literary paragon, Sholem Aleichem subtly (and also not so subtly) pointed to all the characteristics of the older writer's narrative art that endowed it with a baroque and heavy-handed quality and underlined its indirectness and structural complexity.[33] Abramovitsh's reaction to this coronation must have been deeply ambivalent and probably contained more than a smattering of anger, which at that juncture could not be given vent to openly, since the presumptuous and self-appointed "grandson" also happened to be the munificent editor and publisher who paid "grandpa" an extraordinarily generous honorarium and royally wined and dined him in upper-crust Odessa hotels. As flattered as he must have been, Abramovitsh hardly wished to be regarded as the old and sublimely remote master the younger writer made him appear. The elevated but somewhat soporific image only rendered that much more urgent the need to relate to the burning issues of the hour, to impact the literary intelligentsia as living in the present, experiencing its tensions and sharing its pains, rather than resting on one's laurels. Indeed, this need became now pressing.

The difficult question, however, was how this need could be satisfied. Of course, the difficulty did not inhere in the issue of choosing topics of immediate relevance, but of discovering an adequate artistic approach to such topics, which practically meant the fashioning of the appropriate tools with which the topics could be effectively treated without undermining the infrastructure of the author's style and manner; and it seemed, that at least for the moment, the writer could not find or fashion the tools he needed. He was faced by questions such as: Would the habitual Mendele causerie still be useful as an adequate narrative method? Have the new historical circumstances not rendered its slow epic pace, meandering progression, and endemic irony out of date? What could be the role of a Mendele, the cynical old-style book peddler, who along his way also collected among small, backwater, Ukrainian villages the manuscripts he eventually edited and published, in a situation defined by pogroms, urbanization, and mass emigration? Would not his creaking wagon and old horse be ridiculously out of place in a world of quick railway transportation, ocean liners carrying thousands of emigrants, and noisy modern cities? Were not these proverbial emblems of Abramovitsh's art—the horse, the wagon, the sandy or boggy Volhynian roads, the occasional meetings *unterwegs* ("while traveling") with other travelers making their way by foot or wagons, the rural, dirty, bedbug-infested inns with their drunk Ukrainian peasants and cunning Jewish innkeepers, the occasional frightening gendarme, the sparse little forests, and the fields of wheat and maize under the blazing summer sun—were not all these in themselves as much as pointing to the Mendele world as inherently belonging in a past that was now both irrelevant and tediously familiar? In other words: Had not Abramovitsh already used his Mendele *nusekh* (manner) to death? But did he have any alternative *nusekh* that would fit a changing reality? And what about Mendele's irony, the chief trope and the rhetorical mainstay of Abramovitsh's Yiddish writing; how would it withstand a new reality that now called for pathos rather than irony, for tears rather than sardonic smiles? Not in vain was current writing in both Yiddish (Dinezon; Spektor in a popular novel such as *Aniyim ve'evyoynim*, the Yiddish *Les Misérables;* even Sholem Aleichem in his early novels) and in Hebrew (the sentimentalist *Khibat tsiyon* poetry, Smolenskin's Zionist novel, the tragic posture of the historical novels about the Marranos and the martyrs in the days of the Crusades or the Chmielnitsky Rebellion, the somber descriptions of current mundane Jewish life in the writings of younger Hebrew writers of prose fiction such as A. Z. Rabinovitsh or Ben Avigdor and his school of primitive naturalists) informed primarily by pathos, the patronizing and often ironic attitude of the *maskil* toward the traditional Jew, his satirical butt, having been replaced by emotional empathy and pretended nationalist bonding. But could Abramovitsh shed the satirical mode? Would his narrative art survive such a denudation?

Nowhere were the difficulties the writer now faced more clearly present than in a story he started writing toward the end of the first half of the 1880s—when exactly this happened (1883? 1884?) is unknown. It was a story focusing on the aftermath of the pogroms in a Ukrainian shtetl, and as much as the author tried to get it going, it would not take off. The untitled large fragment, published in 1940 by the curators of the "Mendele Museum" in Odessa, under the title "Di milkhomes fun habose komande" ("The Battles of the Riffraff"),[34] clearly indicates what the main difficulty was. Abramovitsh decided to cast this story in the epistolary mode. It was to be written in the form of an exchange of letters between Mendele and a friend. For that form to be employed, Mendele's lifestyle had to be changed, or, at least, temporarily suspended; for the habitual Mendelean life of an itinerary book peddler, always on the move, would not, under the primitive conditions of the Ukrainian countryside, allow for an ongoing correspondence. As a letter writer, Mendele had to be rendered stationary; so Abramovitsh stranded him in the hamlet of Kabtsansk, from which he could correspond and describe the ravages and disorientation caused by the pogroms. This entailed a radical shift from Abramovitsh's earlier rhetoric of fiction. Although he had used the occasional letter in two or three of his stories, and once (in the enlarged *Fishke der krumer*) even made Mendele himself write a letter, the epistolary mode, already successfully employed in the early writings of Sholem Aleichem, was totally alien to him and indeed conflicted with his essentially epic manner, as well as with the employment of his main rhetorical tool, the ongoing and as if desultory monologue of Mendele. Moreover, the premises of the epistolary narrative mode were bound to blur the characteristics of Mendele not only as an epic narrator and an ironic persona but also as a fictional character. Stranding Mendele in his Kabtsansk home (where we never see him in any of the author's other Mendele tales; he is always away from home), his character could not remain what it consistently had been. Among other things, he had clearly been a person with no significant family ties, which went together with his essential solitude, as well as with his somewhat arid and bitter irony. He was married, of course, and had sired children, but he gave them very little thought. When occasionally he would refer to them—almost never by name— the reference would be abstract and devoid of any vestige of familial closeness. We are not even told how many children he had. Clearly, in his emotional life, his family played a role infinitely smaller than the one played by his constant friend and interlocutor, his horse. Now, stranded in Kabtsansk, and living for the nonce in the midst of a large family that had just undergone the harrowing trauma of the pogrom, Mendele, if he was to strike us as a three-dimensional fictional character, had either to develop emotional family interactions or acknowledge the reality of his alienation and relative asexuality. But the writer could not flesh him out as such a "round" character without destroying his useful "flatness," which was essential if he was to retain his function as raconteur and commentator. In short, Mendele could hardly function in a story written in the epistolary manner; and Abramovitsh, being the perceptive and self-critical artist he was, could not but have realized the fact that his story was a flop. So he temporarily gave up on it, leaving it as a fragment that he never intended to publish.

VI

At this point, in 1885 or in early 1886, Abramovitsh made an astounding discovery: the Yiddish pogrom story, which had evaded his grasp, needed to be written in Hebrew rather than in Yiddish. In other words, for the story to be successfully written, the rules of differential bilingualism, by which the writer had until now meticulously abided, had to be abandoned, thrown to the winds. Why was that? The author could have arrived at this conclusion from three or four different directions. First, as already noted, he realized that his days as a Hebrew nonfiction writer, a publitsist and an essayist, were over. If he was to be active as a writer in this new arena of nationalist, largely Zionist, Hebrew literature, it was only through prose fiction; for only prose fiction, with its potential of polyphony and imaginative freedom, would allow for ideational and emotive ambivalence and for treating important public issues with the discretely subversive irony that would never be acceptable in a straightforward, univocal nonfictional statement.

Secondly, and more importantly, he knew that the topics he wanted to focus on now were the selfsame topics that were endlessly debated by the new publitsists, whose articles were consumed by the tens of thousands of readers of the Hebrew dailies and periodicals.[35] Abramovitsh had to reassert his position as an important Hebrew writer by writing for those dailies and periodicals on the same contemporary and topical issues; however, he had to approach them from a unique vantage point, different from that of the publitsists, more entertaining and at the same time more open-ended or ideologically ambivalent. The format of the newspaper and the literary periodical prescribed the turning away from the novel (as much as the enlarging of shorter fiction into fully fledged novels was now the writer's main project in his Yiddish writing) toward the short story and the short novella. Moreover, addressing a politicized reading public, these new short stories had to contain commentary and discussion as much as description and action. In short, Abramovitsh could renew himself as a writer by becoming the author of reflective and deliberative short stories with current public topics.

Thirdly, all these called for a new kind of narrator-commentator; in other words, a new Mendele, worldly and knowledgeable enough for the tasks this new narrator-commentator was to face. The cynicism of the old Mendele, who saw through the pious pretensions of the petty inhabitants of Kabtsansk and Glupsk, would not suffice for a thorough critique of the Zionist project or for a serious discussion of the nature of modern anti-Semitism. And yet, the new Mendele should not wax verbose and too serious. His causerie, like that of his former self, had to remain light, funny, and relaxed, and his jabs—biting but cleverly and gracefully delivered. He would have to be able to handle moments of high pathos, which current circumstances often justified; however, that only meant that his antidotes of satire and irony had to become more concentrated, expressive of a higher comic inventiveness. Such a new Mendele should be able to see every issue from conflicting directions; he should be able to acknowledge the seriousness and importance of the issues that led people like Pinsker, Lilienblum, and Achad ha'am to Zionist conclusions, but also to satirize the praxis of the Zionist organization they created and express doubts with regard to the chances of the Zionist ideology ever being practically implemented. He should at one and the same time mercilessly satirize the current nationalist sentimentalism but also adopt, with moderation, some of its pathos. He should, as the author himself was to phrase it, oscillate "between laughter and tears," offensiveness and vulnerability. In short, Abramovitsh had to invent a much more nuanced and flexible Mendele, and he had to do it in Hebrew—cut off from the suppleness and almost limitless flexibility of idiomatic Yiddish. Was he up to such a task?

Fourthly, the Hebraization and upgrading of Mendele could be successfully effected, if Mendele could add to the already existing dimensions of his character as a folksy, Jewish, cynical philosopher the dimension of a Hebrew scholar, namely, of an erudite *loshn koydesh* (a linguistic concept that traditionally covered both biblical and Mishnaic Hebrew and the Aramaic of the Talmud and the midrashim) student, a *lamden* (a scholar), with a trove of biblical and Talmudic associations and quotations at his disposal. This could never be done in Yiddish, since the Yiddish-reading public did not possess even a fraction of the erudition that was necessary for a learned Mendele to poke fun by standing the sacred sources on their heads by quoting them out of context or rather within new and cleverly inappropriate contexts. To understand the humor of a scholar manqué, one had to be sufficiently familiar with both the contents and the rhetoric of his scholarship, even as the pointed wit of a defrocked priest would be completely dulled and flattened by the ignorance of a listener unacquainted with church lore and patristic phraseology. Thus, the Yiddish Mendele could have been allowed to use only those meager rudiments of Jewish textual erudition that were at the disposal of the common, relatively uneducated eastern European Jew, a character such as Sholem Aleichem's Tevye the dairyman, who, for all his pretensions, really controlled little beyond the daily prayer, the Torah as read in weekly portions on Sabbath, the book of Psalms, the tractate *Avot* (the only part of the Mishna with which non-scholars were acquainted), and a smattering of Rashi's commentary on the Pentateuch (rather than Rashi's commentary on the Talmud, which constituted the traditional scholar's bread and butter). The Yiddish Mendele could use all these, not too often though, and in well-measured, small quantities, as a Jewish "condiment," with which he could have spiced his narrative. Much more than that would be demanded if Mendele was to perform now as the witty scholar he was becoming.

Fortunately, this was exactly what the new Hebrew reading public allowed Mendele to offer. It can be safely maintained, that the new

Mendele was created as a result of the propitious meeting between the old Hebraic Abramovitsh and the new Hebrew readers. These new readers had to be themselves somewhat scholarly, or at least they displayed enough of a textual memory to make scholarly "resonance" possible. As a matter of fact, it was in the 1880s and 1890s that the prototypical Hebrew reader of the era preceding the modernization of Hebrew as a spoken language appeared in numbers sufficiently large to render the so-called renaissance of Hebrew literature possible; the reader who could be counted on to be able to respond to his writers' inherently Jewish intertextuality. As noted before, the reading public of the Hebrew dailies was enlisted from the large reservoir of the traditional or the semi-traditional Jewish middle class, which insisted on exposing its youngsters to a prolonged Jewish education. Thus almost all contemporary Hebrew readers were graduates of the *bes-medresh* (house of study) or the yeshiva, and as much as they could be naive and uninformed in all non-Jewish matters or in matters pertaining to social, cultural, and economic life under the circumstances of modernity, nobody could be as attuned as they were to the clever conversation of a *talmid-khokhem* (Jewish scholar) commenting half-seriously, half-jokingly on current Jewish affairs and concerns.

Not in vain the 1880s was the decade in which the genre of the feuilleton became immensely popular in Hebrew literature and was practiced by masters such as Y. L. Gordon (who Hebraized its French appellation, dubbing it, in the wake of a Talmudic expression, "*tslokhit shel pleyton*," i.e., a bottle of rosewater), Sokolov, and Frishman. This Parisian-Viennese mixed genre, which demanded finesse, cleverness, a light touch, and a lively wit rather than systematic, inductive ratiocination, incisive argumentation, and a pedantic bent, was very welcome by the new Hebrew readers, who would not read Gordon's magisterial "Bina leto'ey ruakh" ("A Lesson to Those of Aberrant Spirit"), a devastating attack on the enemies of the Enlightenment and a brilliantly argued polemic in which the agenda of the Enlightenment was redefined, justified, and substantiated, but consume his feuilletons, peppered with Talmudic wit and acumen, as literary delicacies. A Hebrew feuilletonist flair could not be achieved without Talmudic erudition. It was based on the tonality of light conversation of scholars who could make a point or a joke by a mere reference to a commonly shared knowledge of a large corpus of traditional Jewish texts.

Abramovitsh, a graduate of the Lithuanian yeshivas, a Talmudic scholar, as well as a *maskil* who had totally internalized the love of the adherents of the Hebrew enlightenment for the Bible as a whole and for its more difficult poetic sections in particular, and a born wit, found himself now in an ideal position from which he could engage the new Hebrew readers, entertain them, play semantic games of hide-and-seek with them, and at the same time convey to them his serious messages as an astute observer of the collective welfare and the vicissitudes of contemporary Jewish existence. Of course, to do that he had to greatly upgrade his Mendele's Jewish erudition, as well as streamline it through the new feuilletonist channel. Mendele had to become not only more learned and witty, but also more sensitive, and, where necessary, empathic, even pathetic. Biblical Hebrew, being so inherently prone to be pathetic and reach for the sublime, would help him in this; however, it also had to be carefully curbed both through parody and through mixture with post-biblical Hebrew and Aramaic, if the pathos was not to overwhelm the irony and the wit of Mendele's conversation. So Abramovitsh set out to evolve a new and contemporary *nusekh Mendele*, through which he would appear not only as the representative of the old Glupsk (in Hebrew: Kesalon) and Kabtsansk (in Hebrew Kabtsiel), but also as a contemporary observer and commentator who is fully cognizant of the fact that most of his readers were themselves by now already far away from the old Ukrainian villages from which they had moved to the bigger urban centers of the Czarist empire—Odessa, Warsaw, St. Petersburg—or emigrated out of the country to London's Whitechapel or New York's Lower East Side. He was also aware of the emergence of the Jewish nostalgic yearning for the shtetl, supposedly intimate and utterly devoid of the chilling urban alienation the immigrants had to become accustomed to (the shtetl's depressing provincialism and stultifying atmosphere now being gradually forgotten). Thus, when the new Mendele would now tell about Glupsk and Kabtsansk, he would do it as the modern amateur anthropologist, the expert who would discuss with his readers the peculiarities of "the old home," and also, half-jokingly, would show them how much of its legacy was still part and parcel of their current "modern" being, that is, how deeply and indelibly the imprint of the shtetl civilization was embossed onto the very grain and fabric of their social and individual lives.

The new Hebrew story he began writing in 1886 started with the following declaration:

> Thus spoke Mendl: This town of Kesalon, with which I shall start my tale, is very important, since it stands for the entire Jewish [Russian] pale, and not in vain was it elevated to the status of a city and a mother in Israel; for there is not one among our local Jews who is not, to a lesser or larger extent, related to Kesalon, and who is not imprinted with at least a tiny fraction of its unique characteristics. If you yourselves, dear Sirs, were not born in Kesalon, I trust your parents had been; and if Kesaloni blood does not trickle through all your arteries and members, at least it has found its place in one of the nooks of your brain. I had been a boy and now I am old, but I've yet to see one of our brethren through whose actions and behavior, whether in worldly or in spiritual matters, some Kesaloni characteristics do not peek and show. Whether they are ignorant or learned, poor or rich, some of the impressions of Kesalon are stuck in them "as goads and as nails fastened." A pleasant smile hovers over my lips now as I remind you of Kesalon; a smile of one who brings good tidings and regards from a mother to her children, or from grandmother to her grandchildren, or to relatives from their aunt; of one whose stories intend to cause good spirits, and who seeing his readers happy makes him too happy.[36]

This was Mendele's new self-introduction in his new role. It launched a story that was published—not at all by sheer accident—in the first Hebrew daily *Hayom*, under the somewhat cumbersome biblical title "Beseter ra'am," ("In the Secret Place of Thunder"; compare: Psalms 81:8). The title clearly indicated that the story would eventually deal with the pogroms, since the pogroms had by now been consistently referred to in the Hebrew press (for the purpose of circumventing the Russian censor) by the biblical euphemism *sufot banegev*, tempests or whirlwinds in the South (compare: Isaiah 21:1), and tempests, particularly the famous Russian summer tempests, went together with crashing thunder. Thus, the title raised readers' expectations and promised them a story about how Mendele found shelter and was spared when his town was hit by the "tempests" (this was implied by God's intervention as evidenced by the psalmist: "Thou didst call in trouble, and I rescued you; I answered thee in the secret place of thunder"). However, Abramovitsh was in no haste to arrive at the story's main topic. Before doing that he had to give his Mendele an ample opportunity to parade his newly acquired mastery as a *talmid-khokhem manqué*. He did it, first, by systematically Hebraizing or rather biblicizing the topography and toponymy of his stories. The biblical titles, such as "Beseter ra'am" or "Bymey hara'ash" ("In the Days of the Earthquake") or "Lo nakhat beya'akov" ("There Is No Good in Jacob"), all based on biblical references, went together with the fact that the stories were now taking place not in the Slavic-Yiddish Glupsk, Kabtsansk, and Tuneyadevke, but rather in the Hebraic Kesalon, Kabtsiel, and Betalon.

This was by far more than a mere nominal transformation; for the new names, while retaining the satirical generalization intended by the original Ukrainian-Yiddish ones (Glupsk—city of fools; Kabtsansk—pauperville; Tuneyadevke—town of idlers or bums; the Hebrew names have similar meanings), also sent the readers to far-off biblical landscapes. Kesalon, for example, although on some level it served as the proper name for a town of *kesilim* (fools), was in fact not a real equivalent of Glupsk. Abramovitsh's erudite readers knew that it was the name of a biblical city or citadel located within the domain of the tribe of Judah (cf., Joshua 15:10), and because it perched on the borderline separating that domain from the land of the enemies of Judah, the Edomites, was strategically situated on the top of a high hill and was also well fortified; hence its name; for the Hebrew word *kesel* originally referred to the strong muscle of the hip, which also protected the kidneys, and thus, metonymically, also to the kidney itself. Indeed, this was also the metaphorical origin of the word *kesil*, which indicated a fool of a special kind. Whereas its opposite, the word *peti*, deriving from the root *p.t.h.* (to open) designated a fool of the naive and trusting kind, a person "open" to manipulation, bereft of protective critical intelligence; the word *kesil* pointed to the strong-headed and stubborn kind of fool, who, albeit not devoid of intelligence, is so wrapped up in himself and mistrustful of others as to be unable to learn from experience, to correct his own errors, to change. Thus the Hebrew Kesalon was not characterized as the seat of foolishness per se, as much as it was designated as the town of people who could not learn from experience and change their ways, which was the reason for their repetitive commercial blundering, leading time after time to bankruptcy and destitution. Of course, the fact that the place of such commercial blundering was called by a biblical name indicating strength and fortification added a subtle comic dimension to the descriptions of its inhabitants—cunningly foolish or cleverly thickheaded.

The discrepancy between the name and the reality it stood for was developed into a system as the new Mendele went on presenting Kesalon to his readers.[37] The city, he said, was "thoroughly Jewish," and this was brought forth by its houses and streets. For "the wisdom of masons is despised in it [in Kesalon], and it does not follow in their practices [or ordinances]." The houses were low and neglected. They were not "standing upright," confronting heaven with their "chutzpa" (i.e., evincing irreverence for God). Outwardly they were discolored and devoid of all ornament, for "favor is deceitful and beauty is in vain," and in any case, a graceful young woman is in no need of cosmetics. The Jewish home, however, was "all glorious within," so the outside could be left covered with filth. The intrinsic glory of the Jewish house was projected through a picture of the crowded interior of a characteristic one-room apartment where the kitchenware, the washing pails, the brooms, and other cleaning utensils covered the walls. The roofs of Kesalon, Mendele had to confess, were rather unsafe; for they were built without parapets. For some reason the rules prescribing the erecting of parapets didn't apply here, and so on, and so forth.

Not a single word in this satirical description escaped the dense net of quotations and allusions that was programmed to arrest the reader's attention and titillate his textual memory. Thus it regaled him with funny discrepancies between the sacrosanct texts and the lowly sights of the squalid Jewish quarter Mendele described. Starting by comparing the indelible impressions of Kesalon to goads and the nails the steadfastness of which was compared by Ecclesiastes to that of the wise precepts of the sages (12:11: "the words of the wise are as goads and as nails fastened by the master of assemblies"), Mendele proceeded to evoke another verse from Ecclesiastes—"the poor man's wisdom is despised" (9:16) through which he conveyed the disrespect in which the people of Kesalon held the wisdom of masons. Moses' warning not to follow the ways, practices, and ordinances of the Egyptians (Leviticus 18:3) was referred to and compared to the stubborn decision of the inhabitants of Kesalon not to follow the practices and ordinances of proper masonry (after all, they were *kesilim*, i.e., stubborn and contrary, unable to learn and change). Their refusal to build their houses straight and high was "justified" through a reference to the Talmudic pejorative comment of the young women of Jerusalem (in the times of the prophet Isaiah) who used to walk erect (*Yoma* 9b), or as the prophet put it: they walked "with stretched forth necks" (Isaiah 3:16). It was further explained as complying with the Talmudic rebuke to scholars who walked briskly (or with wide steps) and held themselves erect, for "whoever walks erect," no matter how short is the distance he covers, is like "pushing away the feet of the *shekhina*," the divine immanence (*Berakhot* 43b). This was connected by Mendele with Rav Nachman's comment on *chutzpa klape shmaya* ("irreverence for heaven," i.e., for God), which sometimes was acceptable to and even enjoyed by God Himself (Sanhedrin 105a). Then Mendele fully reminded his readers of the scholarly debate between the schools of Shammai and Hillel, the famous rival Mishnaic sages, with regard to proper adornment of a bride on her wedding day, and whether she should be allowed to wear cosmetics. While doing that, he did not forget to quote Rav Dimi's (*Ketubot* 17a) mentioning of the wedding singers who would praise the bride: "without mascara and rouge and cosmetics, and nevertheless a graceful gazelle." Then, he switched to the ode to the enterprising and virtuous woman (in the book of Proverbs) whose virtues rendered external beauty unnecessary, since "favor is deceitful and beauty is in vain"(31:30). Then, quite naturally, he was reminded of the psalmist's praise for the royal bride as she was being brought to the king's palace with all her dowry: "the king's daughter is all glorious within" (Psalms 45:13). That led him, when talking about the utensils in a Jewish kitchen, to the psalmist's furious deprecation aimed at the historical enemies of Israel ("Moab is my washpot; upon Edom do I cast my shoe"; 60:10) and to Isaiah's promise that King Elyakim would be a mainstay of and would bring much honor to the Davidic dynasty ("And I will fasten him as a nail in a sure place . . . and they shall hang upon him all the glory of his father's house, the offspring and the issue, all vessels of small quantity, from the vessels of cups, even to all the vessels of flagons"; 22:23–24). Then he arrived at *din ma'ake*, Moses' prescription pertaining to the erecting of a parapet on the roof of one's new house: "When you build a new house you should erect a parapet to your roof" (Deuteronomy 22:8), and indulged in a pseudo-Mishnaic explanation of why this prescription did not apply in the town of Kesalon, and so on. This entire trove of references was squeezed into a few descriptive sentences.

One has to reconstruct the mindset and the associative cogitation of a late nineteenth-century Hebrew reader to realize how funny, entertaining, and scandalous such a discourse must have struck him. It certainly was "above the heads" of most contemporary Yiddish readers, even as it is totally incomprehensible to most Hebrew readers of our own day. A reader, however, with whom the erudite references would resonate, could not fail to see how biting was the "justification" of Kesalon's squalor in terms of sublime scripture and Talmudic acumen; how wittily subversive, for example, was the equation of the Jewish kitchen with the glory of the biblical king, who was so entrenched in his seat of power that the entire dynasty, down to least important members of the extended royal family, could safely depend on his protection and favor. Gradually, as Mendele's new presentation of the old Jewish habitat in the heart of the Ukraine unfolded, the reader also realized how through the scholastic witticisms, now an integral part of the book peddler's discourse, an important dimension had been added to the projected portrait of the Jewish shtetl: a mock-heroic one. The mundane Yiddish Glupsk, its name and the style of its description changed, was now constantly measured against a heavenly city, and thus presented as its earthly vitiated reflection.

This presentation, like most mock-heroic equations of the sublime and the bathetic, formed a rhetorical two-way street and paradoxically sent the readers in two contradictory directions: on the one hand, the equation underlined the vitiation of the sublime model, namely, the squalor and the provincialism of the shtetl; on the other hand, however, it pointed to the fact, that albeit degraded and corrupt, the shtetl, as the current Jewish polis or body politique, was not only of a high origin but also had a high destiny. Thus, for instance, the description of a summer Sabbath afternoon in Kesalon[38] endowed the town and its relaxed inhabitants with a quasi-biblical aura. It was the hour of the "evening offering," as if the sacrificial ritual of the Jerusalemite temple was still maintained in Kesalon (Mendele applied here the language of King Ahaz's directives: "And King Ahaz commanded Urijah the priest, saying: Upon the great altar burn the morning burnt offering, and the evening meat offering" and so on; [2 Kings 16:15]); however, the sun was still blazing, for God pulled the sun out of its sheath (compare *Gitin* 76a) for the purpose of drying the town's bogs and "lakes of dung" (*agmey refesh*—a playful correction of Isaiah's *agmey nefesh* [19:10], which probably meant *agumey nefesh*—dispirited, crestfallen). Thus in many places, dry highways emerged for God's chosen people, his "peculiar treasure" (compare with the psalmist's assertion of God's special relationship with Jacob and Israel, "His peculiar treasure"; 135:4), to safely take their afternoon medicinal, even as Deutero-Isaiah promised that those who would return from Babylonia to Jerusalem would find their way back as smooth as "highways . . . exalted" (49:11), and "the way of the Lord" in the desert "would be made straight," high and dry (40:3–4). The town was humming with the buzz of Jews, who having woken up from their afternoon nap, now thronged the streets; the younger ones walking—for health and pleasure—while the older ones were sitting on the porches, sneezing and yawning to their hearts' content. Children, boys and girls, were playing: two boys holding on to the *talit* of a third one who gleefully galloped like a frisking colt. It was all an elaborate take on Zechariah's vision of Jerusalem redeemed: "Thus saith the Lord: I am returned unto Zion [...] There shall yet old men and women dwell in the streets of Jerusalem [...] and the streets of the city shall be full of boys and girls playing in the streets thereof" and so on(8:3–4). That the author saw fit to throw into his pastiche of redemptory prophecy also the rather mundane and business-like "two who hold on to a *talit*—one says all of its is mine, the other says all of it is mine" from tractate *Nezikin*, did not diminish either the irony of the comparison of Kesalon with *Jerusalem liberata* nor its hidden glory, but simply added textual depth and sheen to the glittering brocade he weaved.

VII

"Beseter ra'am" was a strangely constructed story, which reflected the inherent difficulties the author faced when reinventing himself as a Hebrew raconteur.[39] The strangeness of the structure inheres in the fact that the treatment of the story's main topic, the one indicated by its title—the thundering tempests of the pogroms and their aftermath— was not as much as mentioned in the first chapter and completely relegated to the second one. This can by no means be explained "intrinsically," in terms of the artistic organization of the narrative materials within the autonomous boundaries of the text as separate and self-contained, and attempts at offering such an "integrated" view of the story have not been productive. The dichotomy within the story cannot be accounted for without the realization that the writer felt obliged to do two different things and that this obligation directly followed from his deviating for the first time from the principles of his differential bilingualism. On the one hand, he felt that the treatment of the pogrom theme, as well as other current themes and issues, had to be conducted in Hebrew as part of a new dialogue with the new Hebrew reading public. On the other hand, he had to become an established and familiar Hebrew literary persona who would do the processing of his narrative and ideational materials. Thus his new persona had to be presented to the Hebrew readers and its special Hebraic competence needed to be exhibited, even flaunted, and that was exactly the task that kept the author busy in the first chapter of his first new Hebrew story. One can read this chapter as an almost autonomous general introduction to the Hebraic Mendele "world." Once the new Mendele had been paraded before the readers, he could start functioning as the raconteur and commentator he was supposed to be as he actually did in the second chapter of the story, where the narrative materials that had already been processed, albeit unsatisfactorily, in the Yiddish epistolary fragment "The Battles of the Riffraff," were reconceptualized and recast as part of a new deliberative Mendele tale. Hence, the unbalanced and not really unified structure of the Hebrew story, where the great overture to the Hebrew Mendele cycle of tales and the specific story of Mendele's travails during and after the pogrom were yoked together.

This explains many of the oddities of "Beseter ra'am," for instance, the quite drastic difference in tonality and style between the two chapters. Clearly, the second and more narrative and emotive one could not sustain the parodist virtuosity of the first; for as much as the new Mendele was to remain from now on the erudite and pseudo-scholastic *talmid-khokhem*, the level of his scholastic extravaganza had to be lowered and its density had to be considerably diluted if he was to be useful in conveying a narrative sequence of events, to sketch a character, and evolve a modicum of emotive lyrical self-expression. Thus the brocade fabric of the first chapter had to be thinned and rendered more pliable in the second one. This involved the acquiring and exercising of new skills, and "Beseter ra'am" was more than anything else the laboratory where this was accomplished.

This is the reason for the long gestation period the writing and publication of this rather short story demanded. Its first chapter, published in Y. L. Kantor's *Hayom*, was not immediately followed by the second one. As a matter of fact, a full year elapsed before the second chapter together with an improved version of the first appeared in Kantor's periodical *Ben ami* (the daily *Hayom* having folded in the meantime) with the editor's apology and explanation of how "the continuation of the story could not see the light before these days."[40] Clearly the author faced considerable difficulties in making the transition from Mendele's self-presentation to his recasting the pogrom narrative in the terms of his new *nusekh*. Then there was another—marginal, but quite curious and telling—indication of the author's disorientation at this juncture. Whereas the first chapter had been presented in its *Hayom* 1886 version as having been originally written in Yiddish, then translated into Hebrew by me, "*hakotn Mendele Moykher Seforim*" (modest Mendele the book peddler), in its *Ben ami* 1887 version, the entire story was offered as Mendele's Hebrew work, with no mention of the existence of a Yiddish version. Since no Yiddish version of the first chapter of "Beseter ra'am" was ever found or published (the entire story as published in the various Yiddish editions of Abramovitsh's works is a translation from the Hebrew original done by M. Olgin), we can safely assume that the reference to a Yiddish original was fictional and indicative of the author's inability or unwillingness at this point (1886) to altogether part with the modalities of his earlier Yiddish-Hebrew bilingualism, that is, with the notion that all his Mendele-related works of fiction originated in Yiddish. It was exactly this notion that Abramovitsh would firmly put behind him with the re-publication of the entire "Beseter ra'am" in 1887, as well as in the other Hebrew short stories and novellas he would publish in the balance of the 1880s and throughout the 1890s. *Hakotn Mendele* would shed here the modesty of a mere translator and unabashedly present himself as the Hebrew author of the stories.

Taking apart the mainstays of differential bilingualism was fraught with artistic dangers. Even after the publication of "Bester ra'am" in its entirety, Abramovitsh's bilingualism showed signs of disorientation and confusion. The differential system had clearly run its course and waxed dysfunctional under the new circumstances. Its forked roots, once firmly struck in two separated public domains, were weakened and exposed to the blistering air of a new era. Yet Abramovitsh still held on, for almost a decade, to some of its components. If in the earlier part of his career, the linguistic difference meticulously conflated with the generic one—Yiddish for belles lettres; Hebrew for nonfiction—now this clear-cut differentiation could not be upheld; fiction, from now on the sole genre practiced by the writer, had to be written in both languages. However, a differentiation of sorts could still be precariously maintained by associating each of the two languages with a certain *kind* of fictional writing.

Hebrew was employed in short stories focusing mainly on the topical issues that attracted the new politicized Hebrew reading public. At the same time Yiddish was the language in which the author's older stories were now fleshed out, achieving the dimensions and complexity of the novel form. In Hebrew, Mendele now traveled by trains to Odessa (Hebraized as *Shikhor* because of its position as a port open to the Black [in Hebrew: *shakhor*] Sea and also as a place analogous to the biblical *Shikhor*, a poetic name of Egypt) and Warsaw (Hebraized by mere rearrangement of the consonants contained in its name as the biblical *Be'er sheva*); while in Yiddish he still made his rounds with his wagon and old horse between Glupsk, Kabtsansk, and Tuneyadevke. Thus, during the years 1887–1890, "Beseter ra'am" and "Shem vayefet ba'agala" ("Shem and Japheth in the Train Compartment") appeared in Hebrew; the latter story focused on modern anti-Semitism. In the same years, the enlarged and reworked versions of *Fishke, Di klyatshe,* and *Dos vintshfingerl* (the first two parts) appeared in Yiddish. In the first half of the 1890s, Abramovitsh dedicated almost all his energies to his Hebrew writing—publishing "Lo nakhat beya'akov" ("There Is No Good in Jacob"), the brilliant "Bymey hara'ash" ("In the Days of the Earthquake," the author's subtle and perceptive critique of the Zionist project), and the longer novella *Byshiva shel ma'ala uvyshiva shel mata* (*In the Heavenly Assembly and in the Earthly One*, a story focusing on the behavior of people during a pogrom) in 1892, 1894, and 1894–1895, respectively. Of these, only the first one was also adapted and published in Yiddish under the title "Di alte mayse" ("The Old Story," 1895).

The paucity of Abramovitsh's Yiddish publications in these years was at least partly caused by the sudden disappearance of Yiddish literary periodicals, in general, and of those periodicals the author felt comfortable working for, in particular. We can assume, that had Sholem Aleichem been able to maintain the publication of his *Folksbiblyotek* after the financial fiasco that eliminated his capital and assets in 1890, Abramovitsh would have continued working on and publishing parts of the extended *Dos vintshfingerl* there and possibly other Yiddish works as well. With the demand for new Yiddish material at a low ebb, and, in contradistinction, the flowering of Hebrew literature and the proliferation of its periodicals on the rise, the writer quite understandably responded to the requests of Hebrew editors (most of whom were his friends and acquaintances as members of the Odessa Zionist circle) and wrote mainly for them. Admittedly such extrinsic circumstances always influence literary production; and yet, they do not fully explain this phenomenon that the Abramovitsh scholarship has yet to elucidate: the all but total absorption, for about a decade, of an established and highly regarded writer of Yiddish fiction in the writing of fiction in Hebrew and almost only in Hebrew. This unexplained submergence had also to do with factors other than the availability of publication outlets. Chief among these was the writer's wish or need to develop and explore the new Hebrew discourse he had created in the 1880s; to realize its rich and yet unexhausted artistic and polemic potential. Also the political atmosphere of these years immediately preceding the emergence of political Zionism and the founding by Theodore Herzl of the World Zionist Organization, strongly attracted Abramovitsh and pushed him in the direction of playing his role as a Hebrew public figure.

Significantly, he would never translate or adapt in Yiddish most of the stories he wrote and published during these years. The only exception to this, the already mentioned adaptation of "Lo nakhat" as "Di alte mayse," is in itself indicative and revealing; for "Lo nakhat" was the only Hebrew text produced at the time that focused on an "old" or traditional topic, the tyrannical behavior of an upstart who assumed a position of power within a traditional, old-style Lithuanian Jewish community. Played against the historical backdrop of the 1840s, this story purported to teach a relevant lesson in the 1890s. Whether or not it succeeded in doing that, it nevertheless inhabited a world apart from that of the truly contemporary (and by far more accomplished artistically) political stories such as "Shem and Japheth in the Train Compartment" and "In the Days of the Earthquake." The fact that when invited by the Yiddish novelist and editor Spektor to contribute to his *Hoyzfraynt*, the only "older" or conservative Yiddish literary publication that was still appearing from time to time, Abramovitsh chose to adapt this lesser story speaks for itself. It could belong within the cycle of his Yiddish stories because it was "old," as the title itself indicated, and because it did not presume to project an up-to-date social milieu. As for the other Hebrew stories written at this juncture, they would not be adapted in Yiddish before the publication of the 1911–1912 *Yubileum oysgabe* would render such adaptation obligatory; and then the Yiddish versions would be supplied by others (such as the already mentioned Olgin), with or without the addition of the author's slight editing.[41] Clearly, to him the "modern" stories were inherently and essentially Hebraic. Thus, the new kind of bilingualism, which would prescribe the existence of parallel Hebrew-Yiddish versions of the author's important works, did not emerge before well into the second half of the 1890s.

VIII

The transition was gradual, progressing as if unconsciously or semiconsciously from one publication event to the other. The earliest of these events took place in 1894 when Abramovitsh published another Hebrew story with the Aramaic title "Petikhta,"—which means an introduction or a prologue—together with his Hebrew short story "In the Days of the Earthquake." Brilliant and deliberative, it resembled very much the other Hebrew works of those years. Whoever reads it together with "In the Days of the Earthquake" cannot fail to see the thematic and stylistic common denominators: in both stories, Mendele arrives (by train) in the city of Shikhor, experiences alienation and solitude, eventually meets with the local Zionist activists (in "In the Days of the Earthquake") or with a group of Hebrew writers and cultural activists (in "Petikhta"), and with their leaders, the "Karlini" (Leon Pinsker—Karlin being a town adjacent to Pinsk—the readers could be trusted to understand the name as referring to that of the *Khibat tsiyon* leader) in the former, and the writer and educator Rabbi Shlomo of Kesalon (Shalom Jacob Abramovitsh himself), in the latter. Both stories start with Mendele crestfallen and quite disgusted with his profession of selling and publishing Jewish books. However in both he undergoes a change of mood, and, as the stories reach their respective closures, he rededicates himself to his mission of proliferating Jewish literature. He is about to return to his Ukrainian *shtetlekh* and to his activities as a disseminator of culture and literature—reinvigorated, with a renewed sense of purpose. In "Days of the Earthquake," he abandons his naive dream of becoming a comfortable farmer in Palestine, understanding that he is unfit for the difficult role of a Zionist pioneer, and that by continuing to play his important cultural role, he would contribute to the collective good more than he would in any other walk of life. In "Petikhta," he leaves Rabbi Shlomo, having committed himself to be the publisher of the extended autobiographical narrative Shlomo has been convinced he should write. In both stories, current political, cultural, and literary issues are discussed and the new Jewish nationalist discourse is amply illustrated. Indeed, "Petikhta" was in every way a sequel to the author's other Hebrew stories and when Abramovitsh collected these stories and published them in a book (1900), he included in it "Petikhta" as an autonomous, self-contained Hebrew narrative.

However, "Petikhta," as its title proclaimed, was meant to serve as an introduction or an overture to a larger work of fiction, which as the story's contents clearly indicated was to be Abramovitsh's own somewhat fictionalized autobiography written as a novel—the novel Mendele was supposed to publish as soon as it was written. And, as a matter of fact, "Petikhta" eventually was incorporated into Abramovitsh's auto-biographical *Shloyme reb Khayims* (*Shlomo the Son of Reb Khayim*), as its Yiddish version was called, or *Bayamim hahem* (*In Bygone Days*) and occasionally *Khayey Shlomo* (*Shlomo's Life Story*), as the Hebrew version would be intermittently titled. There can be little doubt that when in the mid-1890s, the author planned this last extended work of fiction of his, he intended to write it in Hebrew. Otherwise, what was the sense in writing its extensive introductory chapter in that language? However, it would seem, that as he started writing the story itself, focusing on his childhood in the small Belorussian town of Kapulye of the 1830s and 1840s, Yiddish became his language of choice. In any case, the first part of the novel (the second part of which would be left unfinished at the writer's death in 1917) was ready for publication in Yiddish rather than in Hebrew toward the end of the 1890s and was serialized in 1899 in *Der yud*, the Yiddish Zionist weekly. The Hebrew version was to follow later with clear indications of its being based on the already existing Yiddish text. We are faced with the question that Abramovitsh himself certainly pondered: why would he write his autobiographical novel in Yiddish after he had started it in Hebrew? The answer to this must be that a story about familial and communal life in a shtetl of the first half of the nineteenth century "begged" to be told in Yiddish. Whereas "Petikhta," with its modern urban ambience and the current cultural and literary is-sues it focused on, lent itself quite "naturally" to be told by the Hebraic Mendele. The chapters that followed it, firmly anchored in the world of Jewish old-style provincial life in the era of Nicholas I and replete with ethnographic details (the preservation of a detailed picture of Jewish traditional life in "Those Bygone Days" being the declared goal of the writing of the novel) were the stuff the writer knew how best to deal with in Yiddish and through his Yiddish Mendele. Thus, the new novel he was writing made Abramovitsh realize that the semi-differential bi-lingualism he still was holding on to was not working anymore. As we saw, as a linguistic regulative system, this semi-differential bilingualism allowed the writer to write fiction of a certain kind (shtetl life in "by-gone days")—in Yiddish and fiction of a different kind (modern, urban, political, intellectual)—in Hebrew. Now, writing a novel in which both kinds of fiction were conflated, the author, absurdly, followed the system's regulations by starting it in Hebrew and then switching to Yiddish. Thus, he faced a paradox or an aporia that could be surmounted only through a final abolition of the differential and semi-differential bilingualisms and by replacing them with a new system that would make possible the writing of the entire novel in either of the two languages or in both of them.

The next publication event that led in a similar direction occurred in 1896 when Abramovitsh decided to create a Hebrew version of his *Maso'es Binyomin hashlishi*. Whereas until now, none of his Hebrew stories had been based on an existing Yiddish text, here, for the first time, the writer faced the task of producing a Hebrew equivalent of one of his best-known Yiddish fictions. This did not necessarily mean that at this point he decided to produce equivalent versions of all his important Yiddish works. The creation of the Hebrew *Mas'ot Binyamin hashlishi* still could have been conceived of as a limited enterprise, the author's response to a particularly propitious set of circumstances, rather than the beginning of the realization of the comprehensive project of producing a parallel Yiddish-Hebrew canon. Of all his Yiddish fiction, *Maso'es* was the most political and "international" one. Written in 1878, the year of the Berlin Congress, in which a major European statesman—the (converted) Jew Benjamin Disraeli—together with the German *Kanzler* Bismarck negotiated the various European interests in the Middle East, the novel offered a comprehensive, satirical view of the Jewish political condition (of passivity and total lack of political clout) against the backdrop of contemporary European imperialism and colonialism. Choosing to locate his plot chronologically in the years of the Crimean War of 1855–1856, the first "all-European" war after the Napoleonic era, which also was triggered by conflict of interests among the European powers with regard to the Middle East, the author could present his protagonist's dreams of reinstating a Jewish independent state in Palestine as pathetically vacuous by juxtaposing them with the real political struggle (between Great Britain and France on one side and the Czarist empire with its mid-European allies on the other) for control over the same strategic territory.[42] This was as close as the writer would ever come in his Yiddish work to the writing of political fiction, a subgenre that in the 1880s and 1890s would dominate his Hebrew stories. What then was more self-evidently "logical" than rewriting *Maso'es* in Hebrew in 1896?! This was the year in which Theodore Herzl (whose Jewish name was Benjamin Ze'ev), the Viennese journalist about to emerge as the founding father of political Zionism and a European Jewish diplomat in his own right, published his *Judenstadt*, arguing the case for reinstating an independent Jewish commonwealth. Rumors, about the convening in the near future of a Jewish congress in which a Zionist shadow government would be elected for the purpose of negotiating with the Ottoman authorities and the European powers the establishing of a Jewish state in Palestine, reached every Zionist group in eastern Europe and were endlessly discussed in Odessa, the hub of the Russian Zionist organization. Abramovitsh, always skeptical, could not but see his Benjamin reincarnated in the figure of Binyamin Herzl. His satire, having acquired a new topical relevance, begged to be integrated into the writer's ongoing dialogue with his Hebrew readers, whose avid interest in the prospects of Zionism under the leadership of the new "Benjamin" could be taken for granted. Thus, the creation of the Hebrew version of *Maso'es Binyomin* might still have been triggered by current conjuncture rather than by a literary plan with far-reaching implications.

However, even if that was what triggered the author's decision to adapt this particular work of his (with interesting additions and deletions) in Hebrew, the success and warm reception of his Hebrew Benjamin mock-epic changed the course of his bilingual writing. Clearly it was in 1896 that his grand project of reorganizing his oeuvre within a double, self-mirroring Hebrew-Yiddish canon not only became fully conscious, but also was crystallized and spelled out as a regulative principle, which from now on would channel much of Abramovitsh's authorial activity. In that year Achad ha'am, about to launch the publication of his prestigious literary Hebrew monthly *Hashilo'akh*, approached him, wishing to secure his participation in this new venture. The writer responded positively, indicating his wish of serializing in *Hashilo'akh* a Hebrew version of the already existing parts of his comprehensive historical novel *Dos vintshfingerl* (the 1888–1889 version) now to be given the biblical Hebrew title *Be'emek habakha* (*In the Vale of Tears*, a prevalent, albeit incorrect, interpretation of Psalms 84:7), also famous as the title of Yosef hacohen's seventeenth-century chronicle of the expulsion of Spanish Jewry from the Iberian peninsula and familiar to all readers with a traditional background from Shlomo Alkavets's *piyut* "Lekha dodi," ubiquitously recited or sung as part of the reception of the Sabbath. This decision to adapt in Hebrew his most extensive and ambitious Yiddish fiction was not made in response to any particular political or social set of circumstances. True, Abramovitsh, who wanted his contribution to *Hashilo'akh* to conform as precisely as possible to the revered philosopher's editorial intentions and peculiar literary taste, knew Achad ha'am would approve of this serious panoramic novel more than of a satire such as *Maso'es Binyomin* or a story of the Jewish criminal underworld such as *Fishke der krumer*. Achad ha'am, he well knew, was not favorably impressed by current Hebrew belles lettres. As far as he was concerned, they were by far too self-centered and relied too much on current non-Jewish romantic models. In his new monthly, which was to be dedicated to a serious discussion of the Jewish condition, past and present, he would make room, he said, "for good stories about our people's life in the past or the present, which would faithfully portray our condition in different times and places, or shed some light on this or the other unexplored corner of our internal world."[43] *Dos vintshfingerl*, its ironic Yiddish title replaced by a pathetic Hebrew one (pointing to recent Jewish history as "a vale of tears," comparable to the national tragedy of the expulsion of Spanish Jewry), was exactly what Achad ha'am's literary project could use. As a "history" of Jewish life in nineteenth-century Czarist Russia, it focused on the collective rather than the individual, on history rather than on romance, on a critique of the national response to crisis rather than on the articulation of the writer's own internal conflicts. So Abramovitsh's choice of the text to be serialized in *Hashilo'akh* (during the first two years of the monthly's existence) was intentional and calculated. Nevertheless, together with the adaptation in Hebrew of *Maso'es Binyomin*, the Hebraization of *Dos vintshfingerl* must have formed a part of a coalescing plan of producing Hebrew versions for all of the writer's major Yiddish works. There was no sense in doing for *Dos vintshfingerl* what was not to be eventually done for *Fishke* and *Di klyatshe*. With those three works, with the addition of the already adapted *Binyomin,* existing in both Yiddish and Hebrew versions, the core of the Mendele world would become bilingual in an altogether new sense. Thus, Abramovitsh set out in 1896 on the long way toward the realization of the grand project that would be accomplished throughout a decade and a half, culminating in the publication of the two jubilee editions of 1909–1912.

It should be immediately added that this project, was conceived of from the very start within a flexible framework. It was never meant to be driven toward a total commensurateness of parallelism between the two parts of the double canon. Abramovitsh probably decided at quite an early stage that his two earliest works of fiction, still very much imbued with the ideas and concerns of the Enlightenment literature in its naive and openly didactic phase, would not be included in the parallel project. Thus the early Hebrew *Ha'avot vehabanim* (in a new version) was to be included only in the Hebrew jubilee edition (a Yiddish translation by B. Epelboym would be posthumously added to the writer's collected Yiddish works in 1923), while the early Yiddish *Dos kleyne mentshele,* which as a matter of course found its place in all Yiddish editions of the author's collected works, was never meant by the author to be translated into Hebrew (a much belated Hebrew translation by S. Luria appeared in 1984). Similarly the two dramas, *The Tax* and *The Draft,* were not to be translated into Hebrew—an extraordinarily difficult, if not impossible, task under contemporary linguistic circumstances; and, of course, the Yiddish poetic works, written in the 1870s, were never regarded as part of the project. The Hebrew short stories of 1886–1895 were, of course, conceived of as part of the project; they were too important to be left out of the Yiddish canon. However, as we noted, Abramovitsh never brought himself to invest the necessary effort in their translation into Yiddish, and their Yiddish versions would be prepared by shadow-translators. On the other side of the equation, the writer made the effort of rewriting in Hebrew only some (the best) of the Yiddish short stories he wrote throughout the first decade of the twentieth century, when the existence of a burgeoning daily Yiddish press justified—financially and artistically—the production in Yiddish of short stories. Thus, the stories that added up to the cycle called *Sefer habeheymes* (*A Bestiary*), among them the masterpiece "Dos kelbl" ("The Calf"), were recreated in Hebrew (the title of "The Calf" being replaced by the funny "Eglato shel tosfot yomtov" ("The Heifer of Yomtov, the Master of Talmudic Novelle"). The story explains how the poor animal came to be associated with the famous rabbi and Talmudic exegete Yom Tov ben Avraham Ishbily, better known as RITBA, whereas quite a few lesser stories (such as "The Discovery of Volhynia," "Because of a Seat at Eastern Wall," "The Book of Metamorphoses," etc.) were left without Hebrew equivalents and are still unknown to the Hebrew reader. At the same time, the Hebrew cycle of stories focusing on the Jewish holidays (called, when published for the first time in *Hashilo'akh* of 1912, *From Israel's Hidden Treasure*) and the two earlier Hebrew "addenda" to *Maso'es Binyomin*, brilliant parodies on contemporary Hebrew scholarly writings done by amateur philologists who slavishly imitated the worst models of the heavy-handed German scholarly discourse, as well as an acerbic political critique of Herzl's futile shuttling between Sultan and Kaiser in his voyages in Europe and to the Middle East, were not translated by the author into Yiddish.

All these notwithstanding, the parallel project was essentially carried out and its goals achieved. Abramovitsh was willing to pay the stiff price the realization of this ambitious project demanded, which was that of investing the better part of his creative energies throughout the last two decades of his life in the production of the highly polished parallel versions of his old works rather than in creating new ones. He insisted on the parallel set, including his own original bilingual renderings of at least his five major works: *Dos vintshfingerl*, *Fishke der krumer*, *Di klyatshe*, *Maso'es Binyomin*, and *Shloyme reb Khayims*. For instance, as brilliant as was the Hebrew version of *Fishke der krumer*, prepared in 1901 by no lesser a translator than Bialik, the chief Hebrew poet of the era, for serialization (under the title *Sefer hakabtsanim*, *The Book of Paupers*) in Frishman's weekly *Hador*, it would not be allowed to serve as the final Hebrew version to be included in *Mahadurat hayovel*. The novel had to be readapted in Hebrew—an immensely time- and effort-consuming task—by Abramovitsh himself. In addition to the five novels, the two parallel sets included other important works (such as the above mentioned *Sefer habeheymes*), which the author himself composed in both Hebrew and Yiddish at a very high creative cost.

Both sets were presented as the collected works of Mendele Moykher Seforim (although in both, the name Sh. Y. Abramovitsh appeared in parenthesis under Mendele's name, as if the latter was a mere nom de plume). Thus both excluded almost any work that did not dovetail in one way or another with the Mendele schema or could not be located in one section or another of the Mendele world. The only item in the Hebrew jubilee edition that was not altogether "Mendelean" was the new version of the early novel *Ha'avot vehabanim* (no more a genuine intrigue and romance novel of the Enlightenment as much as a clever parody on the Enlightenment novel and its conventions). All the articles and monographs were suppressed to the extent that they were virtually forgotten. In any case, no posthumous edition of the author's Hebrew works included significant additions to what was contained in the 1909–1912 jubilee edition. This, in its turn, lead to the considerable shrinkage of the intellectual and informational validity of almost the entire critical tradition, which exclusively focused on the Mendele sphere as if it encompassed the entire textual and ideational expanse of Abramovitsh's works. Also, and as importantly, this was how the writer's bilingualism became to be perceived and understood only from its integral aspect or as it crystallized during the last phase of his career. The long history of bilingual production that had preceded that phase was forgotten, and the many changes, as well as moments of disorientation, crisis, and self-contradiction that had characterized this earlier history were lost sight of. What was actually a path full of bumps and sharp turns was straightened into a plumb-line street.

IX

In what sense was Abramovitsh's integral bilingualism integral? With the mathematical terms used in a metaphorical sense, they also can be applied with a certain degree of specificity and clarity to matters linguistic. Bilingualism becomes integral when both of the languages it involves are treated as integers, whole numbers as distinguished from fractions. In the socio-linguistic sense, a language amounts to an integer when it is perceived as potentially covering all the communicational needs of the group that speaks and writes it, or all levels of expression, as differentiated by the tetralingual model set by Henri Gobard: the vernacular, the vehicular, the referential, and the mythological, namely, the languages of mundane speech, of officialdom, of cultural communication (including literature, particularly the part of it written in prose, both fiction and nonfiction), and that of hieratic (and, by inference, also prophetic and poetic) and oneiric signification.[44] A language is fractional when it is perceived as covering only a part of the communicational needs of the group that uses it, or only one or some levels within a multi-tiered expressional system. For instance, a language can be seen as a vehicle fit to serve mundane speech and elevated belles lettres but unfit to serve philosophical, scientific, and religious communication (as was Italian in Dante's Italy). Differential bilingualism, such as that of vernacular versus Latin or Hebrew versus the Arabic in medieval Europe, is therefore historically more prevalent than integral bilingualism, since it existed for long periods of time when universally accepted civilizational norms prescribed the use of more than one language for different communicational purposes. Western medieval and renaissance civilizations were inherently bilingual (Latin/vernacular) and differential, since each of the two languages they used had its more-or-less specific functions and satisfied specific communicational needs within a more-or-less stable and unified culture system. Most (but not all) post-biblical Jewish civilizations were similarly inherently bilingual or multilingual, as well as differential, since in most of them, Hebrew played a role clearly differentiated from the ones played by other Jewish or by non-Jewish languages.

Integral bilingualism seems at first sight to entail a contradiction in terms: if a language is perceived as an integer, how can it be yoked with another language, which is also perceived as integral, within the diglossic framework of bilingual usage? However, a certain kind of historical-cultural dynamism does lead to integral bilingualism, and it is the dynamism of cultural disintegration or fragmentation. When under certain conditions, the integrity of a given civilization is compromised, its core splitting into two or more rival cultural-linguistic cores or foci, the phenomenon of integral bilingualism or multilingualism is almost bound to emerge. Thus, for example, the Hebrew/Greek bilingualism of the second half of the era of the Second Commonwealth seems to have been of the integral type. Whereas in Egypt of the last centuries before the Common Era, a monolingual Jewish culture was established, which in spite of its strong ties with the Jerusalemite temple, not only spoke, read, and wrote in Greek, but also used this language for prayer and the study of the Torah,[45] in Palestine of the same time, the so-called apocrypha were written in either Hebrew or Greek with no clear definition of the cultural and literary-specific roles of each of the two languages. Thus, two historical books on the rebellion of the Maccabees were written, one in Hebrew (and based on the model of the historical books of the Bible), and the other in Greek (and based on the model of Greek classical historiography). Those books that were originally written in Hebrew survived in most cases only in their Greek translations because the notion that the difference between the two languages was significant and that therefore the original version of a given text should be preserved, became vague and infirm in the circles in which these books were produced and read. Clearly, this was a situation of cultural fragmentation that was to reemerge (in a different form, of course) in modern times when divergent and relatively non-interdependent, post-traditional, Jewish cultures flourished in Hebrew, Yiddish, German, Russian, and eventually also English and French. As long as this process of cultural and linguistic fragmentation was in its early phases, an integral bilingualism of sorts (like the Hebrew-German one in Germany at the turn of the eighteenth century, or the Russian-Hebrew one in the Czarist empire throughout the second half of the nineteenth century) emerged. Once the processes of emancipation, emigration, acculturation, modernization, and Zionist repatriation in Palestine reached advanced levels of realization and ideological self-consciousness, this bilingualism would be replaced by monolingualism.

The integral bilingualism of Abramovitsh was the most significant literary-cultural indication of such a fragmentation process having, around the turn of the nineteenth century, taken place and reached a fairly advanced level of self-consciousness within the modern, secular, and nationalist Jewish intelligentsia in eastern Europe. Whereas the Hebrew-Yiddish bilingualism of the Jewish enlightenment era can be regarded as essentially differential, with each of the two languages serving different needs and goals of a more or less unified cultural agenda, the advent of modern Jewish nationalism undermined this differentialism. The enlightenment movement viewed Yiddish as a necessary evil, a communicational tool that had to be resorted to if the ideals and concepts of the haskala were to impact the Yiddish-speaking masses. But nationalism, imbued with romantic Weltanschauung, brought to Jewish culture an altogether new concept of language as not only binding the national group into an integrated, and therefore functional, communicational unit, but also as representing the quintessence of the group's collective psyche, its mental and imaginative core—all widely circulating romantic notions initiated by the cultural philosophy of Johann Gottfried Herder. The Enlightenment measured and assessed language mainly by its mimetic or referential functions, as a proper and clearly organized system of signs representing both the extrinsic world, "things," and differentiable concepts and ideas. Romantic nationalism measured and assessed language by its expressive and non-referential function—not as a system of representation through precise signification but rather as an all important expressive "being" unto itself, a primarily independent entity rather than a set of signs signifying entities extrinsic to it. Language was supposed to comprise the very locus of mental and emotional existence, the hub of the inner life of the individual and the integrated community. Thus, once modern Jewish culture became imbued with nationalist-romantic notions and concepts, the view of Yiddish as a mere tool could not be retained. It had to be replaced—sooner rather than later—by a view of Yiddish as "essence," as the ideational and emotional core of the Yiddish-speaking group. Without this change taking place, first semi-consciously, and then with full and clearly articulated ideological self-consciousness, modern, that is, romantic, Yiddish literature, could not have flourished as it did around the turn of the century.

As this literature flourished, becoming at one and the same time more dynamic and ideologically self-conscious, it could not perceive either itself or the Yiddish language as culturally "fractional." Mounting tensions inevitably pushed its exponents toward a perception of both the language and its literature as integers, cultural-aesthetic wholes, and this perception had to be openly declared, as it was in the already mentioned Czernowitz Language Conference of 1908, as well as developed into a self-conscious, modern, nationalist Jewish ideology, the one that was to be referred to as Yiddishism. A similar process, of course, also took place in modern Hebrew culture, as it prepared itself for its role as the culture of a Hebrew-speaking community in Palestine. Thus, while a process of ideological and organizational differentiation and fragmentation was splitting the new Jewish nationalism into various and rival segments (Zionist, territorialist, Bundist, autonomist, etc.), the Hebrew-Yiddish duality was bound to evolve from a differential into an integral duality, which would eventually lead to a total separation between two nationalist, modern Jewish cultures, a Hebraic and a Yiddishist one. This separation was preceded by a transition phase in which the integral duality did not yet realize its full pulverizing and fragmentizing potential. No cultural entity represented this transitional era better than the Mendele model.

What this model represented was not only, or even mainly, integral bilingualism per se. Such a bilingualism was only the fertile ground out of which sprouted a phenomenon which, for lack of a less awkward appellation, we shall call bi-literaturalism. This rather monstrous coinage should signify a concept predicating the need, created under special and always temporary cultural circumstances, for the production of two separate and mutually independent literatures that exist within a still unified public space—public space held together by its historical roots, existing within one circumference, but at the same time being progressively destabilized, torn from within by its own centrifugal dynamism, and about to split amoeba-like into two independent spaces. Such bi-literaturalism should be clearly differentiated from the duality of two different literatures sharing one language, such as that of Hebrew rabbinic literature versus modern, secular, nationalist Hebrew literature. These two kinds of Hebrew writing clearly do not belong within one literature, no matter how ardently nationalist apologists like Sadan, in their yearning for a national cultural unity or catholicity, would like them to conflate and merge. However, not sharing a unified cultural habitat, these two Hebrew literatures present us with a "static" duality that is altogether different from the dynamic and highly volatile Hebrew-Yiddish duality inherent in the double Mendele canon, since the latter evolved as it did exactly because it emerged and reached full stature within such a habitat. Perhaps in the first half of the eighteenth century, when Moshe Luzzatto wrote both his brilliant allegorical dramas based on the dramatic models of the late Italian renaissance and his pietistic moralist manual *Mesilat yesharim* (*The Path of the Righteous*), not to speak of his unpublished Cabbalist treatises, a dynamic bi-literaturalism of the kind here under discussion, still existed in Hebrew writing. Possibly, somewhat similar bi-literaturalist dynamics were at work (in both Hebrew and Yiddish writing) in the first decades of the nineteenth century as the two rivals, the Hasidic movement and the Enlightenment, fought over the soul of one community. It was perhaps within this context that texts created both by the Hasidic masters, such as Reb Nachman of Bratslav, and by their bitter maskilic opponents, such as Yosef Perl, had to be produced in parallel Hebrew-Yiddish versions. However, essentially the most developed and clearly articulated modern Jewish bi-literaturalism emerged toward the end of the century as modern Jewish nationalism was gradually split into its two main cultural-political parts: the Hebraic-Zionist one, and its rival, that of Yiddishism informed by various brands of anti-Zionist or non-Zionist diaspora and territorialist nationalism. As stated previously, Abramovitsh and his Mendele model stand out as the chief emblem of this fully fledged bi-literaturalism.

It is of some interest to compare this concept of cultural-literary dualism with the one developed by Gilles Deleuze and Felix Guattari as they redefined the concept of minor literature.[46] As is well known, to them, minor literature was not a literature of an inferior artistic merit, but rather a literature developed under the conditions of deterritorialization of language and culture, namely, a literature written beyond the boundaries of the territory where native speakers of its language lived, like the literature written in German in Prague or the literature written in French in the erstwhile Francophone colonies or by immigrants from such colonies now living and writing in France itself. The linguistic impoverishment such deterritorialization causes can, of course, be artificially compensated for by "thickening" and deepening of expression through the use of intentionally "enriched" vocabulary and symbolic or oneiric gestures. It can, however, be acknowledged, "accepted," and made use of—the starkness and thinness of expression being not only insisted upon but also intensified and rendered more visible and accentuated. It is then that authentic "minor" literature is produced (Deleuze and Guattari's chief example of such a literature is the lifework of Franz Kafka). Facing its major counterpart (i.e., the literature written in the same language where this language is fully alive), this minor literature offers an insight into the human condition that is different from, and sometimes more piercing and far-reaching, than the insights offered by writers who work under the conditions of a cultural-linguistic majority.

This division of literature into major and minor can be usefully applied to various phenomena of difference and relationship characterized by cultural inequality in modern Jewish literatures, such as the general dependence of modern Jewish literatures on models imported from non-Jewish ones, the tension between Hebrew and Yiddish writing until the beginning of the twentieth century, the tenuous relationship around the turn of the nineteenth century between eastern European Yiddish literature and its American (deterritorialized) counterpart, the Peretz-Sholem Aleichem rivalry, and so on. However, it is not conducive to the understanding of the Hebrew-Yiddish bi-literaturalism here under discussion unless one uses it as a contrasting foil, a diametrically opposed model, which can enhance our perception through difference. The bi-literaturalism represented by the Mendele model emanated not from the acceptance of the condition of minority and its use as an aesthetic and cultural weapon, but rather from a rejection of that condition and the avid reaching for its opposite—the condition of majority. If during most of the nineteenth century, the Hebrew-Yiddish diglossic dyad was marked by some of the characteristics of the major/minor complex, the bi-literaturalism that flourished toward the end of the century, entailed an elimination of the unequal dyadic relationship and its replacement by one of equality.

What happened can be well expressed by the currently fashionable metaphor of decolonization. Yiddish and its secular literature were "colonized" during the nineteenth century in the sense that that they were perceived as merely instrumental or ancillary, a tool fit to do the hard, "coarse" labor Hebrew or Russian could not do because they were inaccessible to the masses. As such, it was subservient to those other languages and their literary and cultural agendas. Moreover, it was a vernacular and the language of the "natives" (native speakers), devoid of vehicular, referential, and mythological capabilities, to use once again Gobard's model. Toward the end of the century, a cultural-political shift occurred. As much as Hebrew, now under the influence of Zionism, aspired to enlarge its capacity beyond the boundaries of the mythological and referential—its traditional seat of power—and become also a vernacular (a spoken language) and a "native" (both in the sense of a native language and in that of a language spoken by natives: farmers, peasants, laborers, people firmly ensconced in their native habitat and engaged in the primary processes of production), Yiddish, now informed by the ideology of Yiddishism, aspired to transcend the vernacular-native level and reach for the referential and mythological heights. The Mendele model graphically and emblematically delineated this shift. In it, a horizontal duality entailing an above/below or an upperdog/underdog relationship was turned around the pivotal figure of Mendele to the point of verticality, where the above-below duality was replaced by a side-by-side one. For what did this model prove if not the possibility of producing literary twins, a Yiddish-Hebrew Gemini, each as healthy and robust as its sibling?

Thus the model, rather than validating the notion predicating the existence of one, continuous Hebrew-Yiddish literature, suggested the opposite notion of bi-literaturalism. According to the latter, Baal-makhshoves's slogan: "Two languages–only one literature," should be replaced by slogans such as: One and only one story or poem—two separate and mutually independent literatures; or one community of readers—gradually being torn apart by the polarizing dynamics of two cultures with their respective and mutually exclusive literatures.

X

If we ask why Abramovitsh so inexorably, as it seems, moved toward bi-literaturalism, we must first insist on the fact that is not often mentioned and that is rarely understood: from the mid-1890s on, he was writing in both languages within one public space, that is, for more or less the same reading public. This is particularly true with regard to his Hebrew Mendele corpus. Whereas in the 1870s, "Ma anu?" was targeted at a reading public altogether different from the one that read *Di klyatshe*, and, what's more, a reading public that hardly knew the author's Yiddish works and, in any case, was not interested in them, all the Hebrew readers, who read *Sefer hakabtsanim* or *Be'emek habakha* a decade and a half later, had already read and enjoyed *Fishke der krumer* and *Dos vintshfingerl*. To a lesser degree, many of those who had read the Yiddish texts were able and eager to savor also their Hebrew counterparts. It is important to remember that the writer not only wrote his works within a still functional diglossic situation, but actually counted on it for the artistic efficacy of his texts, particularly the Hebrew ones. Indeed, the final dissolving of the diglossia had, as far as this efficacy was concerned, quite catastrophic results, as we shall see. In any case, Abramovitsh did not write for Hebrew readers who were not Yiddish speakers and readers. Thus, no understanding at any level of his integral bilingualism is possible without taking into account the continuity and relative integrity of his reading public, at least when viewed from the Hebrew perspective. In other words, one cannot understand the relationship between the two Mendele sets without assuming that both were aimed at more or less the same imaginary reader. Therefore, the pertinent question one must ask is why would Abramovitsh take the trouble to produce texts in one language for readers who had already absorbed them in another language?

We can think of at least three different motives for Abramovitsh burdening himself with the extremely difficult realization of the double Mendele plan. One is the elevation of Yiddish literature around the turn of the century to the status of a national institution, its value being acknowledged and advertised not only by Yiddishists but also by the Russian and eventually part of the German-Jewish intelligentsia. As we saw, Abramovitsh was caught unaware by this development when he was crowned in the 1880s by Sholem Aleichem as the grandfather of the new Yiddish literature, its founding father and greatest *klasiker*. That, as we noted, had its negative, as well as positive aspects. However, throughout the 1890s and particularly during the first decade of the twentieth century, the writer not only grew accustomed to his unexpected role as cultural royalty, but also expected homage and held a literary court. Here was Yiddish literature, which had been totally devoid of status and public recognition when, as one of its pioneers in the 1860s and 1870s, he wrote some of its first masterpieces, growing at a dizzying pace, assuming the role of a national arbiter, both in eastern Europe and North America, being translated into Russian, German, and English, praised not only by Jewish intellectuals such as Dubnov and Buber, but also by Russian critics and writers, such as Gorky and Alexander Amfiteatrov; why and how could Abramovitsh distance himself, under such circumstances, from this great national project in which he had invested so much effort when the public acknowledgement of that effort was nil. Thus, when the Czernowitz Yiddishist conference of August 1908 saw fit to send him a congratulatory telegram, rather like a burgeoning national assembly sending its felicitations to a monarch too old and elevated to actually take part in its deliberations, he accepted this accolade as his due, in spite of the fact that the anti-Hebraist thrust of that conference, which caused outrage in the Odessa Hebrew enclave, could not have appealed to him. The oscillation toward Hebrew, which he had experienced in the early 1890s, had to be arrested or counterbalanced once Yiddish journals and literary periodicals, as well as commercially active publishing houses, appearing one after the other during the first years of the twentieth century, offered reasonable outlets and publication opportunities. Abramovitsh had to keep and buttress his position as a major Yiddish writer. This was only to be expected.

But then Hebrew literature was also experiencing a renaissance of its own and assuming not only the role of a flourishing national literature, but also that of a prophetic "watchman unto the house of Israel." The presence in it of brilliant new talents such as those of Bialik and Achad ha'am, as well as those of their many disciples and followers, endowed it with unprecedented national respectability. Abramovitsh was regarded as one of the bastions of this Hebrew renaissance. Together with Achad ha'am and Bialik, he co-founded the so-called *Nusakh Odessa* (the Odessa manner or the Odessa style) in contemporary Hebrew culture and writing: a style that comprised the components of clarity (of vision, description, structure, argumentation, style), Jewish originality (in terms of style, theme, and mood; roots struck deeply in the Jewish sources), critical self-awareness (expressed in national self-criticism and a general dislike for enthusiasm and overstatement), and national responsibility and restrained pathos. In the august triad of the founding fathers of this "classical" cultural option, he represented the supreme mimetic and satirical observer of Jewish reality, while the philosopher represented clarity of argument and incisive self-analysis, and the poet incorporated the new Jewish subjectivity and gave expression to the historical national pain and sense of deprivation. Could he have removed himself from this prestigious edifice, one of whose main pillars he was?

On top of this, he also could not remain altogether indifferent to the predictions made by his Odessa friends concerning the impending demise of modern Yiddish culture or rather the inevitably short duration of its current vitality. This prognosis—the second among the three motives discussed here—was shared by most of the members of the Odessa circle, including some, who, like Bialik and Ravnitsky, evinced—in sharp contradistinction to their mentor and ideologue, Achad ha'am—very positive and supportive attitudes toward Yiddish and its literature. Even they could not but agree with their mentor's chilling analysis offered in 1902 in his famous lecture-essay "Tekhiyat haru'akh" ("The Renaissance of the Spirit"). Here Achad ha'am incisively diagnosed Yiddish culture as moribund, in spite of its temporary effervescence. Jews always invented or adapted useful jargons that served some of their needs for longer or shorter periods, and then, invariably, discarded them. The fate of Yiddish could not be different from that of those other jargons. Already the language was in a process of quick demographic regression; a process, the pace and geographical expansion of which totally depended on the pace and depth of the modernization various Ashkenazi-Jewish contingents were undergoing in different places. Wherever acculturation and modern education struck roots, Yiddish was in a state of decay. That was true for eastern Europe, where Yiddish was still the spoken language of the bulk of the less modernized Jews; and it was so much more true in the western centers of immigration, such as the United States, where the language was kept alive only by new waves of Yiddish-speaking immigrants. Since this ongoing massive immigration would inevitably slow down and eventually peter out, while the harsh demands of melting-pot acculturation were bound to persist, the children of the first-generation immigrants would inevitably slough off their mother tongue. Thus, even the near future of Yiddish in places such as Great

Britain and the United States was dim. In two generations, within the life span of a single person, the Jews in these places were about to have on their hands two "dead" Jewish languages, Hebrew and Yiddish. The historical record of two and a half millennia showed, however, that they would discard their jargon and stay morally and culturally committed to the preservation of their national language, which was also the language of their religion and the sacred texts that formed the core of their identity. Thus Hebrew was bound to survive Yiddish. Important texts written in the about-to-be-abandoned jargon, be they as significant and influential as Maimonides's *Guide to the Perplexed*, would keep their place in the national memory only if, and as, translated into Hebrew; that is, they would be remembered only in their Hebrew translations and not in their original versions, even if these translations would be as awkward and as unpalatable as was Shmu'el Ibn Tibbon's Hebrew version of Maimonides's philosophical masterpiece. As for the current situation, "the best of the Jargon writers are themselves conscious that the Jargon and its literature are doomed to oblivion, and that only Hebrew literature can survive among Jews forever; and it is for this reason that they have their works translated into Hebrew, in order to gain admittance into our national literature and secure their survival."[47]

The last remark was certainly a direct reference to Abramovitsh, who was Achad ha'am's favorite author of prose fiction (as much as Abramovitsh was in awe of Achad ha'am's intellectual prowess and respected his views and ideas). This is not the place to criticize Achad ha'am and point to the weakness of his argument (weakest among the points he made was the naive belief that modern acculturated Jews would necessarily remain loyal to Hebrew and its literature "forever"). However, we can safely assume, that this argument left its deep imprint on Abramovitsh's mind. If the forecast of the cultural future of Russian Jewry was to be based on what he, Abramovitsh, saw around himself in Odessa, where the acculturated Jewish middle class was thoroughly Russianized, and the Yiddish brought by its parents from the shtetl had been unappreciated, abandoned, and forgotten, then Achad ha'am's prognosis was frighteningly accurate. Thus, Abramovitsh could not but share at least some doubts concerning the prospects of Yiddish, and these certainly played a part in his bi-literaturalism. His logic was that of avoiding risks, of cultural and literary long-term health insurance. He was following the recommendation of the biblical sage, who urged: "It is good that thou shouldest take hold of the one; yea, also from the other withdraw not thy hand; for he that feareth God shall discharge himself of them all" (Ecclesiastes 7:18). Hebrew and Yiddish literatures amounted to different projects with divergent historical trajectories, and he, Abramovitsh, would participate in both of them, bequeathing to each a legacy that would be treasured in the hulls of those two sea-worthy vessels that were sailing in different directions and were to face different sea dangers. At the root of his bi-literaturalism, hope and fear, faith and doubt, played opposite but mutually complementary roles.

The third motive was undoubtedly the most important one: Yiddish and Hebrew offered two totally different artistic options that were equally dear to the writer's heart and within his grasp. The two languages activated in him two different and only partially complementary powers. Whereas Yiddish energized his mimetic and expressive capabilities, Hebrew fuelled his wit, parody, and ideational brilliance. In Yiddish, his Mendele achieved maximal efficiency when he described, created dialogue, and articulated emotions. The Hebrew Mendele reached his acme when he wittingly commented, parodically quoted and misquoted, and ironically cogitated. The writer could by no means give up any of these felicities. Thus, when Abramovitsh made his reinvented Hebrew Mendele retell the tales that had already been told in Yiddish, the task he burdened himself with was not that of translation in the accepted sense of the term, or, at least, not only that of translation in that sense. Since such a translation was essentially superfluous, and the Hebrew readers could not be expected to read the Hebrew versions of the stories for the plot, the characters, the descriptions of nature and society, these versions contained as mere translations from the Yiddish, additional ingredients that were not to be found in the Yiddish originals but had to be added to them. But what could these new ingredients be? They could hardly be subsumed by sheer linguistic difference. Whereas a few writers, literary scholars, and linguists might have been intrigued by the question of whether and to what extent the writer was successful in translating a text originally written in idiomatic Yiddish into a highly literary Hebrew, the wider reading public could not have been expected to read with pleasure the Hebrew texts with only this professional and technical literary concern in mind. If the Hebrew texts were to attract and please, something transcending mere translation, successful and even brilliant as it might be, had to endow the story with a new flavor. Thus, a new poetics of translation had to be devised, the poetics of translation plus x. The question was, of course, of what did the added x actually consist?

Berditchevsky was right on target in his article "Milashon lelashon" ("From One Language to Another")[48] when he challenged the common notion that the success of Abramovitsh's Hebrew versions of his Yiddish tales inhered in the author's ability, due to his encyclopedic control of biblical and post-biblical Hebrew, as well as of the Aramaic of the Talmud and the Midrash, to find for his idiomatic Yiddish appropriate Hebrew equivalents, and through a synthesis of the various layers of the language create a semblance of a lively, all-but-colloquial, Hebrew discourse. Quoting Ravnitsky's description of Abramovitsh's tireless search for Hebrew equivalents ("Reb Mendele would not find rest before he discovers everything he needs in the treasures of the Bible, the Talmud and the Midrashim, the doors of which stand wide open before him and nothing in them escapes his eye"),[49] he suggested that it was not erudition in the service of precision that explained Abramovitsh's stylistic virtuosity, for what the writer offered were not Hebrew replicas of Yiddish texts, but rather new Hebrew texts imbued with an altogether different "spirit" or effluvium. Serving in the Yiddish and the Hebrew versions of his stories essentially the same narrative "meat," Abramovitsh had to garnish each of the dishes with distinctly different sauces (Abramovitsh, by the way, loved such culinary metaphors and often used them, referring to himself as a chef, knowledgeable about all "spices" and "condiments," whose role was to supply his Jewish brethren with generously spiced "delicacies," set them before them and enjoy their evident pleasure in consuming this "tasteful repast"[50]). What the writer was looking for in the various sources were not equivalents but rather the non- or anti-equivalents—possible witty additions to the Yiddish originals that would render them different from the new Hebrew versions. Those often were found through quotation and allusion that allowed for combinations of opposites, intentionally "wrong" contextualizations,

ironies (pointing to one meaning while seemingly insisting on its opposite), literalizations of metaphors, metaphorizations of literal expressions, and so on. These were the tropes that formed the systematic base
of Abramovitsh's Hebrew stylistics. Through them, he constantly titil-
lated the Hebrew reader of the day, whose *girseta deyankuse* (learning
done in one's young days) was thus re-activated by the most delectable
stylistic comedy of errors. Abramovitsh never forgot for more than a
few paragraphs the "bonus" he owed that kind of reader, and as he was
performing the task of the translator, his supply of additional "pepper"
and other special "condiments" was always within reach.

Thus, for example, as he launched the Hebrew *Be'emek habakha* with
the same description of the dire poverty of the inhabitants of Kabtsiel[51]
with which he had started the enlarged version of *Dos vintshfingerl*
(where the hamlet was called Kabtsansk), he systematically added the x
to the translation, rendering it a translation plus x. Where the Yiddish
version said that Kabtsansk was totally devoid of sources of income,
and therefore its inhabitants went begging from one another, he added
in the Hebrew version that in this way they were "living off each other,"
reminding the reader of the Talmudic story about King David, who
would spend his nights studying the Torah, and when once approached
by the sages who tried to divert his attention to the mundane fact that
the people of Israel needed *parnose* (income to live on) because "the
meager quantity cannot satisfy the hunger of the lion," he impatiently
sent them away by saying "go and live off each other" (*Berakhot* 3b). Inserting into the description of Kabtsiel's pauperism the rather non-em-
pathic vocabulary of the scholar-king who could not be bothered with
earthly concerns, Abramovitsh sharpened the ironic edge of a contrast;
for in Kabtsiel people did not help each other, as King David suggested,
but rather competed to death with each other. In the Yiddish version,
Mendele highlighted this irony by a joke based on Tevye-like mistranslation of an expression from the liturgy: *vekabtsenu yakhad* (which refers
to the "gathering together" of all the Jews, exiled and dispersed as they
were, by God in the days of the messianic redemption), applying it to
the inhabitants of Kabtsansk, who, by huddling together and dispos-
sessing each other, became "all of them *kabtsonim*" (paupers). In the
Hebrew version, the irony of this funny mistranslation (rendered there

as: they became "one company of sheer paupers") was largely expanded through an additional Aramaic misquotation: *vehai khavruta lahem mituta* ("and that companionship is [like] death to them"). The erudite reader was reminded of the story about the embarrassment and agony of the Mishnaic sage Khoni (the Jewish Rip van Winkle), who slept for seventy years, and when he woke up could not find a friend or an acquaintance or anybody who would acknowledge his learning. When he was treated with disrespect in the house of study, he prayed to God to finish him off and would not let go until God relented and killed him. To this story the Talmudic master Rava added the rhyming proverbial saying: "That's what people say: o khavruta o mituta" ("either companionship or death; without companionship life is not worth having"; *Ta'anit* 23a). The popular saying Rava quoted was stood on its head cleverly by Abramovitsh. Whereas it represented companionship and death as irreconcilable opposites, Mendele presented them as mutually complementary entities, one leading to the other: the companionship of beggars spells death to all of them. Hence Kabtsiel, a hamlet of sheer paupers, is a place of death.

Quite often the Hebrew Mendele allowed himself to digress far and wide beyond the reach of the Yiddish text, by which digressions he could regale the Hebrew reader with scholarly spoofs that could not be replicated in Yiddish. For instance, in the fourth book of *Dos vintshfingerl*, the wild speculative nature of commercial transactions as they were being effected in the town of Glupsk was conveyed through a dialogue between the sedate and careful commercial agent Rafael and the impatient broker Reb Asher Lublinsky, the latter incorporating the "spirit" of Glupsk's hazardous commercialism. In the Hebrew version, this dialogue was cut short and partly replaced by a paragraph in which Rafael's observations and thoughts about Glupsk and its "crazy" merchants were summed up by Mendele in a delicious pseudo-midrash.[52] Everything in this tongue-in-cheek midrash appealed to the Hebrew reader's erudition and sense of the textual grotesque. Kesalon (the Hebrew version of the Yiddish Glupsk) as a whole was nothing but a slip, an error, an unintended miscarriage on the part of the creator; it was "like an error which had proceedeth from the ruler." As such, that is, as a mere mistake, it had an appropriate myth of origin, being created by the pagan god Mercury in an hour of unholy mirth. This god of merchants, bums, and thieves, known as a cheat, a prankster, and above all else as a master of the practical joke, took a cane and planted it in the muddy bottom of river Sirkhon (stink), now a mere brackish brook, but once a mighty watery thoroughfare. As flotsam accumulated around the cane and formed a shallow shoal, Jews—lost and scattered, hurt and hasty—pounced on this piece of questionable land, inhabited it in a disorderly manner, procreated, grew and multiplied exceedingly, built many big and small stores, and started to conduct business, buy, and sell. Thus the unsafe commercialism of the town was prefigured by its mythological origin as a city built on mere flotsam, devoid of firm foundation. The reader was reminded of various biblical precedents, starting with Ecclesiastes's rather ominous pronouncement: "There is an evil which I have seen under the sun, like an error which proceedeth from the ruler," (10:5) and ending with the description in the book of Genesis of the colonization of the land of Goshen by the Hebrews—with its ominous consequences of this land becoming their house of bondage ("And Israel dwelt in the land of Egypt, in the country of Goshen; and they had possessions therein, and grew and multiplied exceedingly," 47:27). On top of that, the reader was offered a mock-epic analogy, comparing Kesalon with the mighty city of Rome; for as the Midrash (*Sifrey*, portion "Ekev") told: when King Solomon, the builder of the Temple, wedded the daughter of Pharaoh—which, it seems, amounted to a grave sin on his part—the angel Gabriel went down and planted a cane in the sea, creating a shoal on which the city of Rome was founded (the city that would eventually destroy Jerusalem and the Temple). And since the Jewish Kesalon was compared to the city of Rome, the pagan gods must have participated in its foundation. As a city of devious and speculating merchants, its godfather therefore had to be Mercury, the cheat and the prankster, who under the name of Merkulis was often mentioned in the Talmud, tractate *Avoda zara* (pagan ritual). The passage as a whole projected the image of Kesalon as both comic and ominous. In the manner of the mock-epic, it comically mythologized it. We have already noted that with Abramovitsh, the Hebraization of the Jewish reality of the Ukrainian *shtetlekh* inevitably lead to their mythologization and bathetic "elevation"; only this time

the mock-epic analogy projected the Jewish town not as a downgraded
Jerusalem with prospects of messianic redemption, but as a grotesque
Rome—facing decline and fall. Thus the Hebrew versions treated the
shtetl not in terms that were commensurate with those of its description in Yiddish, but rather in diametrically opposed ones, not through
equivalents but rather through anti-equivalents.

XI

Often in the extensive memoirist literature written by people who
knew Abramovitsh in his days as royalty residing in his Odessa court,
an anecdote—whether historically authentic or apocryphal—is told
about the answer the master would give to those who asked him how
he could write his tales in two languages. The writer, twitching his
delicate but quite sharply formed nose would say: there are many Jews
whose noses are constantly blocked because of a chronic cold; they can
hardly breathe through one nostril. But as for me, blessed be God, I
am healthy, and I breathe freely through both my nostrils. The answer,
as one would expect from a professional wit, was apt, well-honed,
and funny. However, if the impression it gave was that Abramovitsh's
bilingualism came naturally and almost unconsciously as the metaphor
of breathing through both nostrils implied, then the master was intentionally misleading his interlocutors. As we have seen, bilingualism,
from 1864 on, was to Abramovitsh both necessary and problematic. As
historical conditions changed, it demanded from him constant reorganization of his authorial practice and reformulation of his poetics.
Starting with Hebraic monolingualism, then establishing, with much
effort, an effective and workable differential Hebrew-Yiddish bilingualism, he had eventually to renounce that bilingualism and replace
it by another, a shift that was not achieved without a prolonged period
of disorientation and confusion. Finally, with tremendous effort,
and after a temporary regression to a new Hebraic monolingualism,
Abramovitsh found his way to fully integral bilingualism, on which
he based his exemplary bi-literaturalism. There was nothing easy or
natural about all this. Rather, the entire process was fraught with diffi-

culties, always entailing both trial and error. It also involved pondering choices, surmounting aporias, making conscious decisions, and taking considerable risks.

As said at the beginning, the bi-literaturalism Abramovitsh reached during the last phase of his development, as great as its impact had been, could not be maintained for more than a short period. With the cultural physiognomy of Ashkenazic Jewry drastically changing after World War I as a result of the war itself, the Russian Revolution that came in its wake, the establishment of the Soviet Union, the quick progress of the Zionist project in mandatory Palestine, the acculturation and Americanization of the immigrant community in the United States as mass immigration from eastern Europe was brought to a halt in 1924, and the many other significant social and political developments of the inter-bellum period, the relative continuity of the public space that rendered bi-literaturalism possible, was shattered. With Hebrew and Yiddish serving totally separated and differentiated communities, the trajectories of their literatures increasingly pointed in opposite directions. However, by the same token, we can now clearly see that as long as this unified public space was more or less intact, integral bilingualism and the resulting bi-literaturalism were historically inevitable, and no theoretical challenges of the kind attempted by Berditchevsky could undermine their normative status. In fact, Berditchevsky himself vaguely understood that when in the midst of his bitter campaign against anybody who wrote the same work in two linguistically differentiated versions, he said: "I am not talking of Mendele; for the genius everything is permissible."[53]

One cannot, however, refrain from taking note of the pathos and irony with which the historical fate of Abramovitsh's bi-literaturalism reverberates. Both long-term insurance policies that the master purchased with the sweat of his brow fell through. Superficially viewed, his careful calculation seems to have been vindicated. The flowering of Yiddish literature was cut short both by the processes Achad ha'am had pointed to, but also, and infinitely more tragically, by the catastrophic fate of eastern European Jewry—physically destroyed by Hitlerism and spiritually and culturally by Stalinism. Hebrew literature survived and even struck deeper roots as Hebrew became the spoken language of a growing Jewish community in Palestine and eventually the official language of the independent Jewish state. Thus, it seems, at least one of the two horses Abramovitsh had bet on won. However, this is only superficially true. Essentially, Abramovitsh suffered a double loss. As the wide Yiddish-reading public tragically shrunk and all but disappeared, the growing Hebrew-reading public lost its ties with the sources, the familiarity with which was essential for the Hebrew Mendele to make sense. It was exactly the success of the Zionist revolution and the reinstatement of Hebrew as a spoken language that undermined the complex parodist construction the writer had erected in an effort to add to the Hebrew versions of his tales the particularly tangy flavor that rendered them so palatable to a certain kind of reader. But this kind of reader all but disappeared. Almost nobody in Israel or among Hebrew speakers outside of Israel nowadays can read and truly enjoy the Hebrew versions of the Mendele tales. With the exception of a handful of scholars and a few secularized yeshiva students who also happened to know the Bible by heart (which most yeshiva students don't), nobody can even understand what the Hebrew Mendele said when he was trying to be witty. Instead of offering the Hebrew readers translations plus x, the Hebrew tales now bewilder and repel them by a translation minus x, the x standing for the rich Jewish intertextuality the contemporary reader cannot understand and appreciate and therefore experiences as so much ballast and obsolete verbiage. The ultimate irony of our story inheres in the fact that Abramovitsh's stories, in order to stand a chance of becoming readable again, must be re-translated into Hebrew from their original Yiddish versions; for as different in every possible way as the contemporary Hebrew reading public is from the Yiddish reading public of a century ago, it is still much closer to that reading public than to its Hebrew historical counterpart. With no new Jewish diglossia on the cultural horizon (unless it is the Hebrew/English one now being created in the streets of New York and Los Angeles), the Hebrew of today is a continuation of Yiddish much more than of the Hebrew of yesteryear.

Notes

Notes to Chapter One

1. Eisig Silberschlag. *From Renaissance to Renaissance*, vol. 1 and 2, New York 1973 and 1977.

2. Baruch Kurzweil, *Sifrutenu hakhadasha: Hemsekh o mahapekha?* Jerusalem and Tel Aviv 1959, p. 4.

3. Yitskhak Erter, *Hatsofe leveyt yisra'el*, ed. Y. Fridlender, Jerusalem 1996, p. 62.

4. In his essay "Tsvey shprakhen--eyn eyntsike literatur," Baal-makhshoves, *Geklibene verk*, New York 1953, pp. 112–123.

5. Achad ha'am said this in his essay "Tekhiyat haru'akh," *Kol kitvey Achad ha'am*, Jerusalem and Tel Aviv 1947, p. 176. Achad ha'am wrote about Jewish artists and writers working in non-Jewish contexts: "Indeed, these very men, with their great gifts, are themselves a proof that we still have within us, as a people, a perennial spring of creative power. For try as they will to conceal their Jewish characteristics, and to embody in their work the national spirit of the people whose livery they have adopted, the light of literary and artistic criticism reveals quite clearly their almost universal failure. Despite themselves, the spirit of Judaism comes to the surface in all they attempt, and gives their work a special and distinctive character, which is not found in the work of non-Jewish laborers in the same field." (Achad ha'am, *Selected Essays*, trans. Leon Simon, Philadelphia 1912, p. 265).

6. Gershom Scholem, *Od davar*, ed. A. Shapira, Tel Aviv 1989, p. 337.

7. See the letter of Rosenzweig to Gertrud Oppenheim (May 25, 1927) as quoted in Martin Buber's essay "The How and the Why of Our Bible Translation," M. Buber and F. Rosenzweig, *Scripture and Translation*, trans. Lawrence Rosenwald and Everett Fox, Bloomington, IN 1994, p. 219.

8. Dov Sadan, "Al sifrutenu—Masat mavo," Jerusalem 1949. See also *Avney bedek*, Tel Aviv 1962, pp. 9–93.

9. "Al sifrutenu," pp. 59–60.

10. See S. N. Eisenstadt, *Jewish Civilization: The Jewish Historical Experience in a Comparative Perspective*, Albany, NY 1992.

11. See David Biale ed., *Cultures of the Jews*, New York 2002.

12. In his essay "Mendele ushloshet hakerakhim," H. N. Bialik, *Divrey sifrut*, Tel Aviv 1965, p. 127.

Notes to Chapter Two

1. Leo Wiener, *The History of Yiddish Literature in the Nineteenth Century*, New York 1899.

2. Cf. Reuven Braynin, *Peretz ben Moshe Smolenskin: Khayav usfarav*, Warsaw 1896; and *Avraham Mapu: Khayav usfarav*, Pietrikov 1900.

3. Nahum Slouschz, *La renaissance de la literature hebraique (1743–1885): Essai d'histoire litteraire*, Paris 1903. Slouschz adapted and enlarged his French dissertation as the Hebrew *Korot hasifrut ha'ivrit hakhadasha*, 1–3, Warsaw 1905. An English translation (done from the French by Henrietta Szold) appeared as *The Renaissance of Hebrew Literature*, Philadelphia 1909.

4. Meir Pines, *L'histoire de la Litterature Judeo-Allemande*, Paris 1911.

5. Israel Davidson, *Parody in Jewish Literature*, New York 1907.

6. Yosef Klausner, *Historya shel hasifrut ha'ivrit hakhadasha*, 1–6, Jerusalem 1930–1950.

7. Zalman Reyzen, *Leksikon fun der yidisher literatur, prese un filologye*, 1–4, Vilnius 1928–1930.

8. *Ale ksovim fun Shloyme Etinger* 1–2, ed. Max Weinreich, Vilnius 1925.

9. Max Weinreich, *Shtaplen: Fir etyuden tsu der yidishe shprakhvisenshaft un literaturgeshikhte*, Berlin 1923; *Bilder-geshikhte fun der yidisher literatur*, Vilnius 1928.

10. Fishl Lakhover, *Toldot hasifrut ha'ivrit hakhadasha*, 1–4, Tel Aviv 1930–1948.

11. Ch. N. Shapira, *Toldot hasifrut ha'ivrit hakhadasha*. Kaunas and Tel Aviv 1939.

12. To a large extent, Shapira based his views on the insights contained in Scholem's seminal study "Mitsva haba'a ba'avera" (1936). Cf. G. Scholem, *Mekhkarim letoldot hashabta'ut vegilguleha*, Jerusalem 1974, pp. 9–67. See also its English version ("Redemption through Sin") in G. Scholem, *The Messianic Idea in Judaism*, New York 1971, pp. 78–141.

13. M. E. Waxman, *History of Jewish Literature* 1–5, New York 1941–1960.

14. Israel Zinberg, *Di geshikhte fun der literatur bay yidn*, 1–8, Vilnius 1929–1937; the unfinished ninth volume appeared posthumously in New York, 1965. Both the English (*Jewish Literature*) and the Hebrew (*sifrut yisra'el*) renderings of the author's title obfuscated the significance of the carefully formulated Yiddish original.

15. Baruch Rivkin, *Grunt tendentsn fun der yidisher literatur in Amerike*, New York 1948.

16. Max Erik, *Konstruktsye shtudyen*, Warsaw 1924.

17. Max Erik, *Vegn altyidishn roman un novele*, Warsaw 1926; *Geshikhte fun der yidisher literatur fun di eltste tsaytn biz der haskole tkufe*, Warsaw 1928.

18. Meir Viner (together with A. Gurshteyn), *Problemes fun kritik*. Moscow 1933.

19. Tsvi Vislavsky, *Haroman vehanovela besifrut hame'a hatesha-esre*, Jerusalem 1961.

20. Cf. "He'arot sotsyologiyot le-'hamatmid," in Tsvi Vislavsky, *Eruvey rashuyot*, Tel Aviv 1944, pp. 1–22.

21. Cf. his essay "El hashitin," Dov Sadan, *Beyn din lekheshbon*, Tel Aviv 1963, pp. 3–13.

22. Ibid., pp. 14–34

23. David Kena'ani, *Lenoga ets rakav: Livkhinat shirato shel Uri Tsvi Greenberg*, Merkhavya 1950.

24. Strauss's lectures and articles were posthumously collected by T. Ruebner and published as *Bedarkhey hasifrut*, Jerusalem 1959.

25. Kurzweil's articles on Agnon were collected in *Masot al sipurav shel Sh. Y. Agnon*, Jerusalem and Tel Aviv 1963.

26. Yehezkel Kaufmann, *Gola venekhar*, 1–4, Tel Aviv 1929–1930.

27. S. Zemach, *Al hayafe*, Tel Aviv 1939; and *Hasekhok*, Jerusalem 1948.

28. Bialik's chief statement on matters pertaining to poetic language, his essay "Giluy vekhisuy balashon" (cf. *Divrey sifrut*, pp. 19–24) has been shown to be deeply influenced by Potbnja's posthumously published *Lectures on the Theory of Literature* (1907).

29. Frishman defined and enhanced his lyrical agenda in many essays, reviews, and articles, and particularly in his series of essays written as "letters" (to an imaginary female correspondent) on literature. See his *Mikhtavim al devar hasifrut: Kol kitvey David Frishman*, vol. 2, Warsaw 1914.

30. Cf. David Fogel, "Lashon vesignon besifrutenu hatse'ira," *Siman keri'a* 3–4 (1974): pp. 388–391.

31. See Frishman's essay "Mendele mokher sefarim: Erko ve'erekh sefarav," in *Kol Kitvey David Frishman*, vol. 3 *(Partsufim)*, Warsaw 1914, pp. 151–195.

32. M. Mezheritsky, "Fishke der krumer: Stil un kompozitsye," *Di royte velt* 12 (1927): pp. 104–128.

33. Cf. his collected Hebrew poems, *Sha'ot vador*, Jerusalem 1951.

34. In many of these cases, the presumed marginality was imaginary and based on the poet-critic's unfamiliarity with the traditions of Hebrew literary criticism and the processes of canonization in Hebrew literature. Thus A. Ben Yitskhak had been the "toast" of the Hebrew so-called Moderna of the 1930s (A. Shlonsky and his disciples) and had been celebrated by Leah Goldberg in her *An Encounter with a Poet* (1952). About the cases of Fogel and Preil, see Dan Miron "Ahava hatluya badavar: Toledot hitkabluta shel yetsirat Fogel," in Ziva Ben-Porat, ed., *Aderet levinyamin: Sefer hayovel levinyamin Harshav*, vol. 1. Tel Aviv 1999, pp. 29–98; and Dan Miron "Beyn haner lakokvavim: Al shirat Gavriel Preil," in Gavriel Preil, *Asfan Setavim*, Jerusalem 1993, pp. 275–381.

35. See Nathan Zach's essay, "Hakol hamakharish," which appeared as an introduction to Y. Shteynberg, *Mivkhar: Lirika ureshimot*, Tel Aviv 1963.

36. Zach's many articles in which his project was carried out remain uncollected. See his *Zeman veritmus etsel Bergson uvashira hamodernit,* Tel Aviv 1966. His essay on Fogel, "Be'ikvot meshorer shenishkakh," was published in *Masa* (September 23, 1954); his famous attack on Alterman, "Hirhurim al shirat N. Alterman," appeared in *Akhshav* 3–4 (1959): pp. 109–122; his essay on Y. Shteynberg, "Hakol hamakharish," served, as mentioned before, as an introduction to a selection from Shteynberg's poetry and essays, Tel Aviv 1963; his essays on G. Preil, "Aklim perati," appeared in *Al hamishmar* (January 2, 1954)and in "Mivkhano shel hashir," *Masa* (October 4, 1959) and "Besiman hasha'a hamefuyeset" in *Molad* 153–154 (1961): pp.181–189.

37. See Kafka's letter to Max Brod from Matliary, June 1921. Franz Kafka, *Letters to Friends, Family, and Editors*, trans. Richard and Clara Winston, New York 1977, p. 289; and see below, chapter 10 of this book, pp. 309–312.

38. Peretz often repeated this demand. See, e.g., his article "Vos felt undzer literatur," *Ale verk fun Y. L. Peretz*, vol. 7, New York 1947, pp. 270–279.

39. Yehoash's translation of the Bible, which became the standard Yiddish version, was crafted during the years 1909–1927.

40. The translation appeared in Montreal in the years 1945–1949.

41. Cf. Y. Y. Shvarts's *Undzer lid fun Shpanye*, New York 1932, as well as his translations of Bialik's complete poetry (New York 1935) and a selection from that of Tchernikhovsky's (New York 1957).

42. Cf. Avrom Vevyorke, *Revizye*, Kharkov-Kiev 1931.

43. Cf. the already mentioned campaign of M. Viner and A. Gurshteyn in their *Problemes fun kritik,* n. 27.

44. Cf., e.g., Max Erik's *Fashizirter yidishizm un zayn visenshaft*, Minsk 1930.

45. Cf. Miriam Segal, *A New Sound in Hebrew Poetry: Poetics, Politics, Accent*, Bloomington, IN 2010.

46. See Ze'ev Jabotinsky, *Autobiografya*, Jerusalem 1947, p. 25.

47. See his "Khazon akhad haligyonot," "Kelev bayit," and particularly "Sefer hakitrug veha'emuna," in vols. 2 and 3 of *Kol kitvey U. Z. Greenberg*, ed. Dan Miron, Jeruslaem 1991.

48. Cf. Michael Gluzman, *The Politics of Canonicity: Lines of Resistance in Modernist Hebrew Poetry*, Stanford, CA, 2003, pp. 117–126.

49. Cf. his articles posthumously collected in the volume *Sifrut yehudit balashon ha'ivrit*, ed. Sh. Shifra, Tel Aviv 1982. See particularly the articles "Sifrut yehudit balashon ha'ivrit," pp. 37–42 and "Sifrut yisra'elit o klal-yehudit," pp. 43–50.

50. The title of Shmuel Niger's collection of reviews and literary articles, New York 1922.

51. See the author's introduction to Vayzel's *Shirey tif'eret*, vol. 1, Berlin 1789, pp. 2–13.

52. Cf. Gordon's introduction to his *Mishley Yehuda* (1860) in Y. L. Gordon, *Shirim*, Tel Aviv 1964, pp. 175–179.

53. *Kol kitvey A. Y. Paperna*, ed. Yisrael Zemora, Tel Aviv 1952, pp. 91–130.

54. Cf. his article on that novel. Ibid., pp. 147–166.

55. Sh. L. Gordon, *Torat hasifrut* 1–2, Warsaw 1902; see also A. Barash, *Torat hasifrut* 1–2, Tel Aviv 1931.

Notes to Chapter Three

1. Cf. "Tekhunat hatsofe," Erter's introduction to his sequel of satires in *Hatsofe leveyt yisra'el* (chap. 1, n. 4), pp. 61–63.

2. See in N. H. Vayzel's introduction to his epic *Shirey tiferet*, vol. 1, Berlin 1789, pp. 3–5; and see also "Hamelitsa medaberet," S. Levisohn's introductory ode opening his rhetorical-poetic manual *Melitsat yeshurun* (1816), in Levisohn, *Melitsat yeshurun*, Tel Aviv 1945, pp. 7–15.

3. Cf. his poem "Khalom erev," in Adam Hakohen Lebenzon, *Shirey sefat kodesh*, pt. 1 in *Kol shirey Adam umikhal*, vol. 1, Vilnius 1895, pp. 201–205.

4. See this letter as incorporated in their "Nakhal habesor," a programmatic brochure announcing the appearance of the periodical and also reprinted in its first issue, *Hame'asef*, vol. 1 (1883): pp .3–5.

5. Cf. *Kol Kitvey A. U. Kovner*, Tel Aviv 1947, pp. 32–45.

6. Cf., e.g., Morris Neiman, *A Century of Modern Hebrew Literary Criticism: 1784–1884*, New York 1983.

7. I could not find in English an extensive treatment of the genre of *publitsistika*. The best critical comments can be found in German and Russian. See, e.g., Harry Pross, *Publizistik: Thesen zu einem Grund colloquium*, Berlin 1970. See also Wilmot Haacke, *Publizistik und Gesellschaft*, Stuttgart 1970.

8. See Brenner's appraisal: "Avi hapublitsistika shelanu: Al khayey M. L. Lilienblum" in Brenner, *Ketavim*, vol. 3, Tel Aviv 1978–1985, pp. 1214–1222.

9. See Adam Hakohen Lebenzon's introduction to his collection of exegetical glosses on the Bible *Be'urim khadashim o torat ha'adam* (Vilnius, 1858).

10. See a summing up of such attempts in Dov Taylor's introduction to his translation of Perl's satire: *Joseph Perl's Revealer of Secrets: The First Hebrew Novel*, Boulder, CO 1997, pp. xxxv–li. Perl who translated Fielding's *Tom Jones* (from German into Yiddish) and who himself wrote a Yiddish historical novel under the title *Antignos* (which remained unpublished and has not survived) knew perfectly well what a novel was, and he never referred to his popular Hebrew satire as one.

11. See a historical analysis of the "*romanen*-polemic" (the polemic concerning novels) in Dan Miron, *Beyn khazon le'emet*, Jerusalem 1979, pp. 231–256.

12. Cf., e.g., the chapter "Barukh haba" in Abramovitsh's first Hebrew novel, *Limdu hetev*, Warsaw 1862, pp. 22–32.

13. Mapu asserted this dictum in many of his letters. See *Mikhtevy Mapu,* ed. Ben-Tsiyon Dinur, Jerusalem 1970. See there pp. 77, 220, 231, and 284, among many others.

14. Gottlober actually started a new periodical, *Haboker or*, for the purpose of combating Smolenskin's "heresies" and fending off the influence of his popular monthly *Hashakhar*. The issues of the two first years of *Haboker or* (1876–1877) were replete with anti-Smolenskin diatribes.

15. Fin's historical overview formed part of his extended review of Adam Hakohen's poems; it is often referred to as the first modern Hebrew critical essay "proper." It was published as "Bikoret shirey sefat kodesh" in the almanac *Pirkhey tsafon*, vol. 2 (1842), pp. 91–117.

16. See his introductory note ("Davar el adat kor'ay") to the third part of the novel *Ayit tsavu'a* (1863), Kol *Kitvey A. Mapu*, Tel Aviv 1939, p. 312.

17. "Hale'umiyim harishonim bame'a hakodemet," *Kol kitvey M. L. Lilienblum*, vol. 3, Odessa 1912, pp. 93–99.

18. "Bikoret lekhol shirey Gordon," *Kol kitvey M. L. Lilienblum*, vol. 2, pp. 26–78.

19. N. Sokolov, *Sin'at olam le'am olam*, Warsaw 1882.

20. See Sokolov's essay "Khen ivry" in P. Shifman, ed. *Bikurim*, Vilnius 1910, pp. 641–644.

21. See above chap. 2, n. 31.

22. See in his essay "David Frishman," *Ishim*, vol. 2, Tel Aviv 1935, pp. 27–30. See also my study "Lefesher hamevukha basifrut ha'ivrit bitkufat ha'tekhiya' shela," Dan Miron, *Bodedim bemo'adam*, Tel Aviv 1987, pp. 21–111.

23. See Achad ha'am's essays "Priest and Prophet" and "Moses" in his *Selected Essays*, pp. 125–138 and 306–330, respectively; *Kol kitvey Achad ha'am*, pp. 90–92, 342–347. See also his " Hamusar hale'umi," *Kol kitvey*, pp. 159–164.

24. See the essay "Past and Future," *Selected Essays*, pp. 80–90; *Kol kitvey*, pp. 81–83.

25. See the essay "The Spiritual Revival," *Selected Essays*, pp.253–305; *Kol kitvey*, pp. 173–186.

26. See "Halashon vesifruta" *Kol kitvey*, pp. 93–97.

27. See "Shilton hasekhel," *Kol kitvey*, pp.355–369.

28. See in "Halashon vesifruta," *Kol kitvey*, pp. 94–95.

29. See "Te'udat Hashilo'akh," *Kol kitvey*, pp. 126–128.

30. A detailed description of the polemic can be found in A. A. Rivlin, *Pulmos bashira*, Tel Aviv 1966.

31. Yisroel Aksenfeld, *Dos shterntikhl*, ed. M. Viner, Moscow 1938, p. 117.

32. See the chapter "Language as Caliban" in Dan Miron, *A Traveler Disguised: The Rise of Yiddish Fiction in the Nineteenth Century*, New York 1973, pp. 34–66.

33. See Abramovitsh's biblio-autobiographical article "Reshimot letoldotay," *Kol kitvey Mendele mokher sefarim*, Tel Aviv 1947, pp .1–6.

34. See Ya'akov Dinezon, "Di yidishe shprakhe un ire shrayber," *Hoyzfraynd*, vol. 1 (1888), pp. 1–20.

35. Eliezer Shulman, "Di geshikhte fun der zhargon literatur," in *Dos yidishe folksbiblyotek*, vol. 2 (1889), pp. 115–134.

36. Sholem Aleichem, "Tsu mayn biyografye," an appendix to the second volume of the author's autobiographical novel *Funm yarid*, *Ale verk fun Sholem Aleichem*, New York 1917–1923, vol. 37 (*Funm yarid* 2), pp. 273–281.

37. See the dedicatory open letter that served as introduction to his novel *Stempenyu*, *Ale verk fun Sholem Aleichem*, vol. 11 (*Yidishe romanen*), pp. 123–126.

38. See his article "A brif tsu a guten fraynt," *Dos yidishe folksbiblyiotek*, vol. 2 (1889), pp. 304–308.

39. See his keynote speech at the Czernowitz conference, *Briv un redes fun Y. L. Peretz*, ed. N. Mayzel, New York 1944, pp. 371–374.

40. See Peretz's article "Bildung," *Ale verk fun Y. L. Peretz*, vol. 8, pp. 3–17.

41. See the already mentioned article "Vos felt undzer literatur," in chap. 2, n. 37 above.

42. See his undated letter to Bialik, *Ale verk fun Y. L. Peretz*, vol. 10, p. 252.

43. See B. Y. Bialostotsky, *Yidisher humor un yidishe leytsim*, New York 1963, pp. 119–120.

Notes to Chapter Four

1. See Bialik's letter to Achad ha'am, *Igrot Bialik*, ed. F. Lakhover, Tel Aviv 1938, vol. 1, pp. 84–86.

2. See Peretz's already mentioned undated letter to Bialik, chap. 3, n. 42 above.

3. In "Hameshulash," the concluding chapter of his essay "El hashitin," *Beyn din lekheshbon*, pp. 10–13.

4. See in Bialik's essay, "Shiratenu hatse'ira," *Divery sifrut*, p. 117.

5. See in Bialik's essay "Khevley lashon," *Divery sifrut*, p. 9.

6. See Berditchevsky's series of articles "Leharkhavat hasifrut," M. Y. Bin Goryon (Berditchevsky), *Ma'amarim*, Tel Aviv 1960, pp.153–158.

7. See Achad ha'am's article "Tsorekh vykholet," *Kol kitvey Achad ha'am*, pp. 128–132.

8. See Berditchevsky's articles "Shelosha devarim," "Mezamrim bastav," "Divrey shira," *Ma'amarim*, pp. 173–177.

9. See Berditchevsky's articles "Shira ivrit," "Bikhtav uva'alpe" and "Davar midavar", *Ma'amarim*, pp. 174, 177, 180–181, respectively.

10. See Berditchevsky's article "Ivrit ve'aramit," *Ma'amarim*, 178–179.

11. See also the articles "Ba'am uvasefer," and "Yehudit ve'ivrit," *Ma'amarim*, 184–190.

12. See" Yipuy hasafa hayehudit," *Ma'amarim*, pp. 190–191.

13. See Berditchevsky's Yiddish essays "Sholem Aleichem" and "Vider Sholem Aleichem," M. Y. Bin Goryon (Berditchevsky), *Yidishe ksovim fun a vaytn korev*, Berlin 1924, vol. 5, pp. 117–120.

14. See "Tishtush hagevulim," *Ma'amarim*, pp. 191–192.

15. Cf. the chapter on Abramovitsh's bilingualism, below, pp. 412–498.

16. See Achad ha'am's letter to Y. Klausner of January 9, 1903, *Igrot Achad ha'am*, vol. 3, Jerusalem and Berlin 1924, pp. 93–94.

17. See Buber's early Zionist writings in Gilya G. Schmidt, ed. and trans., *The First Buber: Youthful Zionist Writings of Martin Buber*, Syracuse, NY, 1999. See there particularly Buber's report on the fifth Zionist Congress (pp. 94–100) and his article "A Spiritual Center" (pp. 118–128).

18. See his article "Altneuland," *Kol kitvey Achad ha'am*, pp 313–320.

19. See Ernprayz's article "Hasifrut ha'ilemet," *Hashilo'akh* 17 (1907): pp.387–396.

20. See in "Khevley lashon," Bialik, *Divrey sifrut*, p. 8.

21. See in "Shiratenu hatse'ira," *Divrey sifrut,* p. 108.

22. Ibid., pp. 117–118.

23. Bialik's speech was worked into an article, "Hasefer ha'ivri," *Divrey sifrut,* pp. 25–42.

24. Ibid., pp. 45–70.

25. Ibid., pp. 19–24; the essay was translated into English by Jacob Sloan. See Robert Alter, ed., *Modern Hebrew Literature*, New York 1975, pp. 130–137.

26. See *Divery sifrut*, pp. 23–24.

27. "Khalfa al panay," *Shirim*, pp. 228–229.

28. "Ekhad ekhad uv'eyn ro'e," *Shirim*, pp. 221–224.

29. "Yehi khelki imakhem," *Shiri*m, 119–120.

30. See "Letoldot hashira ha'ivrit hakhadasha," *Devarim sheba'al pe*, vol. 2, pp. 9–18.

31. See "Od letoldot Shabetai Tsvi," S. I. Ish-Hurwits, *Me'ayin ule'ayin,* Berlin 1914, pp. 259–285. The quotations are from pages 284–285.

32. See Bialik's public lecture "Al shiratenu ukevutsat meshorerim," *Devarim sheba'al pe*, vol. 2. pp. 214–221.

33. See Brenner's article "Ba'itonut uvasifrut (al khezyon hashmad)" in Y. Ch. Brenner, *Ketavim*, vol. 3, pp. 476–487. The article caused a huge scandal and triggered a stormy controversy, and the affair became known as "The Brenner event." See Anita Shapira, *Brenner: Sipur khayim*, Tel Aviv 2008, pp. 192–207.

34. See his "Azkara leyalag," *Ketavim*, vol. 3, pp. 887–966.

35. See "Ha'arakhat atsmenu bishloshet hakerakhim," *Ketavim,* vol. 4, pp. 1223–1296.

36. See the conclusion of the addenda ("Milu'im") to "Ha'arakht atsmenu," *Ketavim,* p. 1296; and in Brenner's novel *Mikan umikan, Ketavim*, vol. 2, pp. 1273–1282, 1321.

37. See Frishman's thirteenth "Letter about Literature," *Kol kitvey David Frishman*, vol. 2, pp. 180–189.

38. See Klausner's article "Shira unevu'a" and particularly his direct assault on Frishman in his "Yefey haru'akh." The former was collected in Yosef Klausner,

Ch. N. Bialik: Veshirat khayav, Tel Aviv 1951, pp. 30–59; the latter was published in *Hashilo'akh* 23 (1910): pp. 289–297.

39. See his article "Shira unevi'ut," in Y. L. Baruch, *Besa'art hayamim*, Tel Aviv 1960, pp. 297–305.

40. See Bialik's "Be'ir haharega," *Shirim*, pp. 350–360, particularly verses 138–167 there.

41. See Frishman's sarcastic article "Hatekhiya," published in the daily *Hatsefira*, and later, retitled "Al hasifrut hayafa," collected in *Kol kitvey David Frishman*, vol. 5 (*Arukot uketsarot*), pp.107–117. For Bialik's response "Tse'irut o yaldut?" see his *Divrey sifrut*, pp. 43–47.

42. See his letters to Y. H. Ravnitsky (1895), *Igrot*, vol. 1, pp. 70, 82.

43. See the unfolding of this development in Bialik's poetry in Uzi Shavit's monograph, *Khevley nigun*, Tel Aviv 1988.

44. See Shats's article "Galut shiratenu haklasit," *Al gevul hademama*, Tel Aviv 1929, pp. 99–107. The article was translated into English by Barbara Harshav and appended to Benjamin Harshav's *Language in Time of Revolution*, Berkeley, CA 1993, pp. 216–221.

45. See Shaul Tchernikhovsky, "Lishe'elot hamivta vehanegina," *Hasafa* 1 (May 1912): pp. 27–31.

46. For an analysis of Jabotnisky's poetic politics, see my study "Terumato shel Ze'ev Jabotinsky lashira ha'ivrit hamodernit," in Z. Jabotinsky, *Ilan metsal bagay*, Tel Aviv 2005, pp. 13–128.

47. For a discussion of the accentuation issue in its wide context, see the two first chapters in the already mentioned monograph (see chap. 2, n. 44 above) by Miriam Segal, *A New Sound in Hebrew Poetry*, pp. 20–73.

48. See Khone Shmeruk, *Peretz's yi'esh vizye: Interpretatsye fun Y. L. Peretzes 'Bay nakht oyfn altn mark'*, New York 1971.

49. See M. L. Halpern, *In New York: A Selection*, trans. and ed. Katheryn Hallerstein, Philadelphia 1982, p. 103.

50. The information about this polemic I owe to Gabriella Safran's seminal study "'Reverse Marranism,' Translateability, and the Theory and Practice of Secular Jewish Culture in Russian," where all the sources for the references and quotations can be found. Cf. Anita Norich and Yaron Z. Eliav, eds., *Jewish Literatures: Context and Intertext*, Providence, RI 2008, pp. 177–200.

51. See a draft for an article under the title "Sifrut yisre'elit belashon lo'azit," Ch. N. Bialik, *Ketavim genuzim*, Tel Aviv, pp. 337–342.

52. See in Shmu'el Kats, *Jabo: biyografya shel Ze'ev Jabotinsky*, vol. 2, Tel Aviv 1993, pp. 691–692.

53. See Kafka's already quoted letter to Max Brod of June 1921, Franz Kafka, *Letters to Friends, Family and Editors*, pp. 286–289; and see also further on in this volume, pp. 309–312.

54. See Gabriella Safran's above-mentioned study (n. 88), p.180.

Notes to Chapter Five

1. Shtibl, an oil magnate and a large-scale entrepreneur, was to become not only the chief Hebrew publisher of the post-war years, but also the ideal publisher, the one whose loyalty and fervor as a culture activist were legendary. See his biography by Dania Amikhai-Mikhlin, *Ahavat A. Y. Sh.*, Jerusalem 2001.

2. See Frishman's essay "Uri Nissan Gnessin," *Kol kitvey David Frishman*, vol. 3, (*Partsufim*), pp. 71–75.

3. See "Igeret ketana mi-New York," G. Preil, *Asfan setavim*, Jerusalem 1993, p. 75.

4. See Hillel Bavli's well-known American idyll, "Mrs. Woods," in H. Bavli, *Shirim*, Tel Aviv 1938, vol. 1, pp. 136–145.

5. See his essays "Amerika shelanu" and "Amerikaniyut vesifrutenu," S. Halkin, *Aray vakeva: Iyunim basifrut*, New York 1942, pp. 64–69, 70–75. See also S. Halkin, *Derakhim vetsidy derakhim basifrut*, Jerusalem 1969, vol.1, pp. 70–74.

6. See his essay "Tekhumey shiratenu," in *Aray vakeva*, pp.35–43 and *Derakhim vetsidey derakhim*, vol. 1, pp. 35–42.

7. See *Hedim* 1, no. 3, pp. 46–49, and an improved version in A. Shlonsky and L. Goldberg, eds., *Shirat Russia*, Tel Aviv 1942, pp. 148–150.

8. See A. Shlonsky's miniature essay "Godrim ufortsim," *Hedim* 1, no. 3, pp. 61–62.

9. This was Gordon's long established doctrine. See his articles "Mitokh keri'a" and "Me'inyan le'inyan be'oto inyan," A. D. Gordon, *Ha'uma veha'avoda*, Haifa 1956, pp. 273–300; and see "Hasofrim veha'ovdim," the keynote speech here referred to, ibid., pp. 301–323.

10. See Shlonsky's poem in *Shisha sidrey shira*, Tel Aviv 2002, vol. 1, p. 49; and Uzi Shavit's article "Hashir haparu'a: Kavim lesignona ule'aklima hasifruti shel hashira ha'eretz-yisre'elit bishnot ha'esrim," *Te'uda* 5 (1986): pp.165–183.

11. See Uzi Shavit's study of Fogel's prosody, "David Fogel and Hebrew Free Verse: Is There a Fogelian Nusah in Hebrew Poetry?" *Prooftexts* 13, no. 1, pp. 65–86.

12. Greenberg's protest against the norm of condensation or brevity found expression in many of the literary articles he wrote throughout the 1920s. See, particularly his essay "Klapey tish'im vetish'a," *Kol kitvey U. Ts. Greenberg*, ed. Dan Miron, Jerusalem 1991–2004, vol. 16, pp. 195–217.

13. See his "Tosefet ha'elementim utemurat hamusagim beda'at ha'adam," *Kol kitvey U. Ts. Greenberg*, pp. 218–224.

14. For Greenberg's prediction that Christian Europe would eventually murder its Jews, see his Yiddish poem (written in 1923) "In malkhes fun tselem," *Gezamlte verk*, ed. Kh. Shmeruk, Jerusalem 1979, vol. 2, pp. 457–472; and his Hebrew poem (written in 1931) "Ba'ey bamakhteret," *Kol kitvey*, vol. 5, pp. 11–15.

15. All these were spelled out in various parts of Greenberg's vast corpus, particularly in the aforementioned "Klapey tish'im vetish'a," but also in many other articles, as well as in poems such as the apostrophe to E. A. Poe in the Yiddish

cycle "Mefisto," *Gezamlte verk*, vol. 2, pp. 362–364; or the Hebrew poem "Masa el Eyropa," *Kol kitvey*, vol. 1, pp. .98–102; or the poem "Kehilot hakodesh bagola," *Kol kitvey*, vol. 3, pp.82–85.

16. See his essays "Al hasipur ha'ivri" and "Megamat haharkhava shel hasipur ha'ivri," Y. Rabinovitsh, *Masluley sifrut*, Tel Aviv 1971, vol. 1. pp. 63–76, 77–89.

17. See his essay "Al hahashva'a," S. Zemach, *Masa uvikoret*, Tel Aviv 1954, pp. 140–144.

18. See "Al shirat ha'avoda," Ya'akov Shteynberg, *Reshimot*, Tel Aviv 1928, pp. 142–152.

19. See "Shloshet hasefarim hana'alim," *Kitvey Y. Shteynberg*, Tel Aviv 1937, vol. 3, pp. 36–39. See also "Ba'avotot hatanakh" and "Ishim min hakhumash," ibid., pp. 61–68.

20. See the magisterial essay "Ivrit," *Kitvey Y. Shteynberg*, pp. 40–53.

21. See "Hashura," the essay containing the gist of Shteynberg's poetics, *Kitvey Y. Shteynberg,* pp. 216–237.

22. See, among other articulations of Shteynberg's anti-Talmudic sentiments, his conclusions in "Moreshet hagalut," *Kitvey Y. Shteynberg*, pp. 345–357.

23. See "Epope'a ivrit" and "Sefer shirat yisra'el," *Kitvey Y. Shteynberg*, pp. 271–277.

24. See "Anshey ru'akh," *Kitvey Y. Shteynberg*, pp. 318–320.

25. *Reshimot*, 1928, pp. 147–148.

26. N. Zach, in his already mentioned "Hakol hamakharish," (chap. 2, n. 35) thoroughly misunderstood the ramifications of Shteynberg's Zionist action-oriented poetics. There can be little doubt about how vehemently Shteynberg would have rejected Zach's poetry and poetics, which were, in fact, diametrically opposed to those of the old poet.

27. See, for instance, Shlonsky's use of the model as justifying the modernists' rebellion against poetic tradition in general and the dominance of Bialik in particular in his poem "Hitgalut," *Shisha sidrey shira*, vol. 1, pp. 9–10.

28. See G. Talpir, *Ra'av*, Tel Aviv 1927, p. 21.

29. See in his article "Aley kaspit zo," *Kol ketavav shel U. Ts. Greenberg*, vol. 15, p. 163.

30. See descriptions of this development in Hannan Hever, *Paytanim uviryonim: Tsmikhat hashir hapoliti ha'ivri be'ertz yisra'el*, Jerusalem 1994; and Dan Miron, *Akdamut le U. Ts. G.*, Jerusalem 2002, pp. 89–114.

31. "Re'itikhem shuv bekotser yedkhem," *Shirim,* pp. 238–239.

32. Z. Jabotinsky, "Hameshorer lishe'avar," in *Al sifrut ve'omanut*, Jerusalem 1948, pp. 345–351.

33. A. Shlonsky, "Re'inukhem shuv bekotser yedkhem" and "Khevley shir" in *Ketuvim* 6 (1931–1932), the issues of Nov. 4 and 26, 1931.

34. See his article "Bama'agal," N. Alterman, *Bama'agal*, Tel Aviv 1971, pp. 7–10.

35. See his essay "Al habilti muvan bashira," *Bama'agal*, pp. 11–17.

36. See his "Hashir hazar," in *Shirim mishekvar*, Tel Aviv 1970, pp. 46–48.

37. See a survey of this trend in early Hebrew Palestinian writing in Gila Ramras-Rauch, *The Arab in Israeli Literature*, Bloomington, IN 1989, pp. 3–44.

38. Idelsohn, a pioneer of Jewish musicology, expressed his views and gathered many non-Ashkenazic melodies and synagogal music in books such as *Otsar neginot yisra'el* in ten volumes (various places of publication, 1914–1932); *Toldot hanegina ha'ivrit*, Berlin 1924; *Shirey teyman*, Cincinnati 1931.

39. See Y. Karni's essays "Ha'omanim bamoledet" and "Ha'am hazamar" in *Hedim* 1, no. 2, pp. 36–38, and Y. Rabinovitsh's detailed rebuattal under the ironic title "Neshikat hagamal," *Hedim* 1, no. 4, pp. 39–51.

40. See David Ben Gurion's perspicacious assessment of the ramifications of the 1929 riots in his speech-article "Darkenu hamedinit le'akhar me'oraot av," D. Ben Gurion, *Anakhnu ushkheneynu*, Tel Aviv 1931, pp. 212–233.

41. See A. Shlonsky, "Piku'akh nefesh," *Hashomer hatsa'ir* 41–42, November, 3, 1939.

42. A. Shlonsky, *Sisha sidrey shira*, vol. 4, p. 90.

43. Ibid., pp. 75–78.

44. Leah Goldberg, "Al oto hanose atsmo," *Hashomer hatsa'ir* 34–35, August 9, 1939.

45. N. Alterman, "Mikhtav al oto hanose," *Hashomer Hatsa'ir* 38–39, September 22, 1939.

46. See N. Alterman, "Olam vehipukho" in *Bama'agal*, Tel Aviv 1971, pp. 32–38.

47. For a detailed synopsis of this debate (in which Shlonsky, Goldberg, and Alterman were joined by others), see Uzi Shavit, *Lo hakol havalim vahevel: Hakhayim al kav hakets al pi Alterman*, Tel Aviv 2007, pp. 10–25.

Notes to Chapter Six

1. Cf. "Misifri 'El takhlit hapashtut,'" *Kol kitvey U. Ts. Greenberg*, vol. 15, pp. 167–171.

2. See "Introspektivizm" in *In zikh: A zamlung introspektive lider*, New York 1920, pp. 5–27.

3. For the chief Inzikhists' view of Yeho'ash, see Y. Glatshteyn, "Yeho'ash," in *In tokh genumen*, New York 1956, pp. 64–69; A. Glants-Leyeles, "Mayne bagegenishn mit Yeho'ash," *Velt un vort*, New York 1958, pp. 26–45.

4. This—in a public lecture Glatshteyn gave at a YIVO occasion a few days before his death in 1971. The anti-Rosenfeld campaign of the *Yunge* was waged primarily by the poet M. L. Halpern. See his articles: "An ofener briv tsu Moris Rozenfeld," *Der kibitzer*, New York, Dec. 2, 1910, pp. 10–15. and "Der alter un der nayer Moris Rozenfeld," *Literatur un leben*, Warsaw 1915, pp. 100–112.

5. A. Glants-Leyeles, *Fabyus lind*, New York 1937, p. ix.

6. Judd L. Teller, "Yiddish Literature and American Jews: Have They Come to a Parting of the Ways? *Commentary*, vol. 17 (1954): pp. 31–40.

7. B. Rivkin, *Grunt-tendentsn,* (see ch. 2, n. 15 above), p. 16.

8. This was a title of a manuscript of his, which was, like the *Grunt-tendentsn,* posthumously published; B. Rivkin, *A gloybn far umgloybike,* New York 1947.

9. Kh. Shmeruk, *Peretses yi'esh vizye,* p. 318.

10. Ibid., pp. 54–56.

11. See Cynthia Ozick's "Envy: Or, Yiddish in America," *The Pagan Rabbi and Other Stories,* New York 1976, pp. 39–100.

12. See I. B. Singer's articles "Problemen fun der yidisher proze in Amerike," *Svive,* no. 2 (March–April 1943): pp.2–13; and "Arum der yidisher literatur in Poyln," *Tsukunft* (August 1943): pp. 468–475. In the former, the author maintained that no Yiddish novel or short story with background other than the eastern European one could be truly successful. The fact that he himself went on to write many such novels and short stories, some of which were of considerable artistic merit, presented, of course, a self-contradiction. However, at the same time it also reflected the shift in the author's literary identity, his sense of having become an American Jewish writer whose language was Yiddish rather than a Yiddish writer in the traditional sense of the term, which implied a conscious choice, an embracing of Yiddish and its modern secular culture, rather than a sheer and self-explanatory resorting to the language one could best express oneself in.

13. See the short story "Mase Tishevits," I. B. Singer, *Der shpigl un andere dertseylungen,* Jerusalem 1975, pp. 12–22. The English version of this story, under the title "The Last Demon," is included in I. B. Singer, *Collected Stories,* New York 2004, vol. 1, pp. 429–438.

14. See David Bergelson, "Dray tsentern," *In shpan,* no. 1 (1926): pp. 84–96.

15. See Greenberg's poem XI in the cycle "Beyn damim ledamim," *Kol kitvey U. Ts. Greenberg,* vol. 3, pp. 53–54.

16. See Mikhail Krutikov's article "Soviet Literary Theory in the Search for a Yiddish Canon: The Case of Moshe Litvakov," in *Yiddish and the Left,* ed. G. Estraykh and M. Krutikov, Oxford 2001, pp. 226–241.

17. See *Mishpat hadybbuk,* Tel Aviv 1926. The full text of this public "trial" has been recently reprinted in *Al na tegarshuni: Iyunim khadashim be 'Hadybbuk,'* ed. D. Yerushalmi and S. Levy, Tel Aviv 2009, pp. 315–356.

18. See Brenner's essay "Ha'arakhat atsmenu bishloshet hakerakhim" (ch. 4, n. 35) and Gordon's rebuttal, also titled "Ha'arakhat atsmenu," A. D. Gordon, *Ha'adam vehateva.* Haifa 1957, pp. 211–268.

19. David Bergelson, the master of Yiddish prose, said that when writing his stories in Hebrew as a young beginner, the intertextuality of the language oppressed him to the point that he felt that even if he as much as sneezed, biblical and Midrashic quotations would burst out of his nose. See David Bergelson, *Bam Dnyeper,* vol. 2, Moscow 1940, pp. 118–119.

20. As G. Scholem pointed out in his open letter to F. Rosenzweig (under the title "Hatsharat emunim lasafa shelanu"), *Od davar,* pp. 59–60.

21. See particularly *Die Sagen der Juden*, Frankfurt am Main 1913–1927; *Der Born Judas*, Frankfurt am Main 1916–1922, and *Tsefunot va'agadot*, Tel Aviv 1960.

22. For this, see Rapoport's learned and lengthy footnotes to his adaptation of Racine's *Esther*, *She'erit yehuda*, published in *Bikurey ha'itim*, 1828, pp. 171–254. See esp. pp. 178–184. See also Yosef Klausner, *Historiya shel hasifrut ha'ivrit hakhadasha*, vol. 2, pp. 229–230.

23. See his poem "El ha'agada," *Shirim*, p. 25–27.

24. See in Achad ha'am's article: "Halashon vesifruta," *Kol kitvey Achad ha'am*, p. 96.

25. See Nachman Ben-Yehuda's monograph *The Massada Myth: Collective Memory and Mythmaking in Israel*, Madison, Wisconsin 1995.

26. See his article "Hamusar hale'umi," *Ma'amarim*, pp 106–107.

27. See his early poem "Belyel khanuka" (1896), S. Tchernikhovsky, *Shirim*, Jerusalem and Tel Aviv 1943, pp. 32–34.

28. See in his narrative poem "Brit mila," ibid., pp. 151–152.

29. Ya'akov Kahan, *Shirim*, Odessa 1914, pp. 241–246.

30. See Tchernikhovsky's poems "A Song to Astarate and Bel" (*Shirim*, pp. 248–251), "The Death of the Tammuz" (ibid., pp. 252–255), "I Am Pleased When I See" (ibid., pp. 288–289), "My Astarate, Will You Tell Me" (ibid., pp. 289–290). And particularly the sonnets "And This to Judea" and "Hannibal" (ibid., pp. 315–316).

31. *Kol kitvey U. Ts. Greenberg*, vol. 2, pp 7–31.

32. See in his "Kefitsat haderekh," ibid., vol. 1, pp. 69–74.

33. See his poem "Al hasena," *Shisha sidrey shira*, vol. 3, pp. 34–35.

34. See David Roskies, *The Jewish Search for a Usable Past*, Bloomington, IN 1999.

35. See his public lecture "Vegn der yidisher literatur" in *Briv un redes fun Y. L. Peretz*, pp. 377–381.

36. In "Reshimot letoldotay," *Kol kitvey Mendele mokher sefarim*, p. 4.

37. See Sholem Aleichem's series of articles under the title "Der yidisher dales in di beste verke fun undzere folks-shrayber" published in *Dos Folksblat* in 1889.

Notes to Chapter Seven

1. See Rattosh's previously mentioned essay "Sifrut yehudit balashon ha'ivrit," above, chap. 2, n. 48.

2. See S. Halkin, *Zeramim vetsurot basifrut ha'ivrit*, ed. Ts. Kagan, Jerusalem 1984.

3. See Hannan Hever, *Producing the Modern Hebrew Canon*, New York 2002; Michael Gluzman, *The Politics of Canonicity*, Stanford, CA 2005.

4. See Chana Kronfeld, *On the Margins of Modernity: Decentering Literary Dynamics*, Berkeley, CA 1993.

5. Among Sadan's many articles, which deserve to be mentioned here, see

"Neginat levay: Lederekh hakhariza hapenimit beshirat Bialik," *Knesset* 1 (1936): pp. 111–115; "Te'omim babituy," *Knesset* 2 (1937): pp. 150–161; "Al haner hadaluk," *Knesset* 3 (1938): pp. 79–87.

6. See B. Kurzweil's anti-Scholem polemic in his article "He'arot le'Shabtai Tsvi shel Gershom Shalom," in *Bema'avak al erkhey hayahadut*, Jerusalem and Tel Aviv 1969, pp. 99–134.

7. See his critique of Lakhover in his extended essay "Hanakhot yesod shel sifrutenu hakhadasha," in *Hasifrut ha'ivrit: Hemshekh o mahapekha?* pp 13–19.

8. The title of his essay on Luzzatto; *Divrey sifrut*, pp. 103–106.

9. See Bialik's comments on Vayzel in "Shiratenu hatse'ira," *Divrey sifrut*, p.109, and in a lecture collected in *Ketavim genuzim*, pp. 326–329; and his lecture on Luzzatto, ibid., pp. 322–326.

10. F. Lakhover, *Toldot hasifrut ha'ivrit hakhadasha*, Tel Aviv 1928, pp. 9–44.

11. Y. Klausner, *Historiya shel hasifrut ha'ivrit hakhadasha*, vol. 1, pp. 9–19.

12. See C. N. Shapira, *Toldot hasifrut ha'ivrit hakhadasha*, Kaunas 1939, pp. 47–58.

13. See his poem "Bedimdumey mashi'akh," *Shisha sidrey shira*, vol. 2, pp. 116–117.

14. Eliezer Shteynman, *Bemizre hazeman*, Tel Aviv 1931.

15. See his book *Bema'agal hadorot*, Tel Aviv 1944.

16. Collected in his book *Al gevul hayashan vehakhadash*, published posthumously, Jerusalem 1951.

17. See Chaim Shirman, *Letoldot hashira vehadrama ha'ivrit*, Jerusalem 1979, vol. 2.

18. See Shirman's studies "Hadrama ha'ivrit bame'a hasheva-esre" and "Hamakhazot shel Moshe Chayim Luzzatto," ibid, pp. 125–138, 161–175.

19. See Devora Bregman's monograph *Shevil hazahav: Hasonet ha'ivri bitkufat harenesans vehabarok*, Jerusalem 1995, and her extensive annotated anthology *Tseror hazehuvim: Sonetim ivri'yim mitekufat harenesans vehabarok*, Jerusalem 1997.

20. In his series of articles "Divrey shalom ve'emet," which were written in response to the Habsburg emperor Josef II's "Edict of Tolerance" of 1781.

21. See, e.g., his studies of Frankism in G. Scholem, *Mekhkarim umekorot letoldot hashabeta'ut vegilguleha*, Jerusalem 1974, pp. 9–216.

22. See Shmu'el Verses, *Haskala veshabeta'ut: Toldotav shel ma'avak*, Jerusalem 1988.

23. See Sh. Y. Agnon, *A Guest for the Night*, trans. Misha Louvish, New York 1968.

24. See Z. Reizen, *Fun Mendlson biz Mendele*, Warsaw 1923.

25. See in *Arkhiv far der geshikhte fun yidishn teater un drama*, vol. 1 (*Filologishe shriftn* 4), Vilnius 1930, pp. 94–146.

26. *Ale verk fun Yisro'el Aksenfeld*, vol. 1, ed. M. Viner, Kharkov-Kiev 1931, and *Dos shterntikhl*, ed. M. Viner, Moscow 1938.

27. Max Weinreich, *Geshikhte fun der yidisher shprakh*, vols. 1–4, New York 1973; see also a condensed one-volume English translation, M. Weinreich, *History of the Yiddish Language*, trans. Shlomo Nobel, Chicago 1973.

28. See above, chap. 1, n. 4.

29. See his article "Sholem Aleichem" in *Geklibene verk*, pp 191–203.

30. Ibid., pp.221–238.

31. See Elyashiv's Hebrew articles "Sekira ureshamim," *Hazman* (the daily), 2 Adar, 5, 5665 (1905), and "Mikhuts lamakhane," *Ha'olam*, February 25, 1908.

32. The Yiddish original was published in Detroit in 1941. An English translation is available: Sh. Niger, *Bilingualism in the History of Jewish Literature*, trans. Joshua A. Fogel, Lanham, MD 1999.

33. See *Akhisefer: Ma'asef ledivrey sifrut, kheker haleshonot beyisra'el vetirgumim min hashira hayidit*, ed. Sh. Niger and M. Ribolov, New York 1943.

34. Dov Sadan, *Al sifrutenu: Masat mavo*, Jerusalem 1950; see also in Sadan's book *Avney bedek*, Tel Aviv 1962, pp. 9–93.

35. See about this in Yehoshua Porat's intellectual and political biography of Rattosh, *Shelakh ve'et beyado*, Tel Aviv 1989, pp. 197–199; and also see Liat Shtayer-Livni and Ya'akov Shavit's article "Yonatan Rattosh, ha'kena'anim veyakhasam lasho'a," in *Sho'a mimerkhak tavo: Ishim bayeshuv ha'eretz-yisra'eli veyakhasam lanatsim velasho'a*, ed. Dina Porat, Jerusalem 2009, pp. 85–99.

36. See Y. Rattosh's article "Mineged la'aretz," in *Sifrut yehudit balashon ha'avrit*, (chap. 2, n. 48 above), pp. 75–82.

37. See Rattosh's comments on S. Yizhar's early novellas in his article "Haberikha el hametsi'ut: Layla beli yeriyot le-S. Yizhar," ibid. pp. 53–58.

38. Chaim Gouri candidly reported his short-lived "love affair" with Canaanism in his "Hasha'a hakena'anit," *Im hashira vehazeman*, vol. 1, Jerusalem 2006, pp. 237–265.

39. See, e.g., Gouri's series of reportages about the Eichmann trial in his *Mul ta hazekhukhit*, Tel Aviv 1962, or Hanoch Bartov's novel *Pits'ey bagrut*, Tel Aviv 1988.

40. See his review of *Kokhavim bakhuts* in A. Kariv, *Iyunim*, Tel Aviv 1950, pp. 232–236.

41. See his articles "Olam vetilo" and "Kelalot ufratot," A. Kariv, *Atara leyoshna*, Tel Aviv 1956, pp. 30–115.

42. In his article "Ba'avotot hahavay" (first published in 1919), S. Zemach, *Masot ureshimot*, Ramat Gan 1968, pp. 39–61.

43. Y. A. Lubetsky, "Lidmuto harukhanit shel rav Mendele," *Kol kitvey Mendele*, vol. 7, Berlin and Jerusalem 1922, pp. 136–142.

44. Y. Glatshteyn, "Fishke der krumer," *In tokh genumen*, New York 1947, pp. 453–469.

45. See Kariv's essay on Frishman in *Atara leyoshna*, pp. 133–236; and his essays on Tchernikhovsky in his *Mishilshom ad hena*, Tel Aviv 1973, pp. 165–203. His essay on Brenner was collected in his *Neratka et hashalshelet*, Tel Aviv 1965, pp. 117–165.

46. See his beautifully written, bilingual (Hebrew-Yiddish), pseudo-historical essay-idyll *Lita mekhorati*, Tel Aviv 1962.

47. See B. Kurzweil, *Masot al sipurav shel Sh. Y. Agnon*, Jerusalem and Tel Aviv 1964.

48. See Kurzweil's essays on Gnessin in his *Beyn khazon leveyn ha'absurdi*, Jerusalem and Tel Aviv 1966, pp. 293–318.

49. See Kurzweil's understanding of Brenner's response to human suffering, ibid., pp. 261–292.

50. *Khipus hasifrut hayisra'elit*, Ramat Gan 1982, the title given posthumously to B. Kurzweil's collection of articles that contains his attacks on Israeli writers. See there his articles on Israeli fiction, pp. 22–60.

51. See in Agnon's *Temol shilshom: Kol sipurav shel Shmuel Yosef Agnon*, vol. 5, Tel Aviv and Jerusalem 1960, pp. 176–177, 539–542.

52. See ibid., vol. 4, pp. 99–100.

53. For this prediction of Y. L. Gordon, see his "Hashmata," a chapter from an extended article published in the weekly *Hamelits*, which had to be excised due to the objections of the Russian censor, and therefore had to be published outside of the Czarist Empire, in the Viennese monthly *Hashakhar*, vol. 2 (1871): pp.154–156; and see also Gordon's article "Ge'ulatenu ufedut nafshenu," *Hamelits* 17, no. 12 (1882).

54. See, e.g., Adam hakohen Lebenzon's "Dedication" to the queen of languages, the inimitable Hebrew, of the first volume of his collected poems (1842)in his *Shirey sefat kodesh, Kol shirey Adam uMikhal*, vol. 1, Vilnius 1895, pp. 7–9.

55. See in his *Ha'avot vehabanim, Kol kitvey Mendele*, p. 16.

56. See "Mikhtav leven-yehuda," Eliezer Ben Yehuda, *Hakhalom veshivro*, ed. R. Sivan, Jerusalem 1978, pp. 49–54.

57. See Chayim Hazaz's essays and speeches on the Hebrew language as a literary vehicle in his *Mishpat hage'ula*, Tel Aviv 1977, pp. 13–48.

58. See his poem "El male rakhamim," *Shirey Y. Amichai*, vol. 1, Tel Aviv and Jerusalem 2002, p. 86, and see also Yehuda Amichai, *A Life in Poetry: 1948–1994*, trans. Benjamin and Barbara Harshav, New York 1994, p. 31.

59. See "Khakukot otiyotayikh," in A. Regelson, *Khakukot otiyotayikh*, Tel Aviv 1964, pp. 7–26.

60. See the poem "Ivrit," Yona Wallach, *Tat hakara niftakhat kemo menifa*, Tel Aviv 1992, pp. 180–182, and see its English translation (by Lisa Katz) in *Hebrew Feminist Poems*, ed. Shirley Kaufman et al., New York 1999, pp. 189–191.

61. See in Achad ha'am's essay "Moshc," *Kol kitvey Achad ha'am*, p. 344. See also in Achad Ha-am, *Selected Essays*, p. 316.

62. See, e.g., Buber's comments on Achad ha'am in his monograph *On Zion: The History of an Idea*, New York, trans. Stanley Godman, New York 1973, pp. 143–147.

63. See the poem "Hazkarat neshamot," *Kol kitvey U. Ts.* Greenberg, vol. 1, p. 138.

64. Peretz Markish, Di kupe, Warsaw 1922.

65. In Greenberg's *Streets of the River*, the comparison of Auschwitz to Mount Sinai features as one of the connecting metaphorical motifs that unify the extensive poetic statement. See in poems such as "Keter kina lekhol beyt yisra'el" (*Kol kitvey U. Ts. Greenberg*, vol. 5, p. 47); "Al da'at le'an" (ibid., p. 106); "Shir al har makhpela" (ibid., vol. 6, p. 10); "Omar le'elohim" (ibid., p.33).

Notes to Chapter Eight

1. See "The Jew in the World," Martin Buber, *The Jew and the World*, trans. Olga Marx, New York 1948, pp. 167–172.

2. See, e.g., his seminal article "Al haner hadaluk," *Knesset*, 3 (1938): pp. 79–87.

3. See, e.g., his articles "Im arba'at kerakhav," "Konsept lemikhtav berakha," "Even hakhakhamim ugelilata," in Dov Sadan, *Al Sh. Y. Agnon*, Tel Aviv 1978, pp. 9–27, 41–48, 68–76.

4. Alter, Robert, *Hebrew and Modernity*, Bloomington, IN 1994.

Alter, Robert, *The Invention of Hebrew Prose: Modern Fiction and the Language of Realism*, Seattle 1988.

Dauber, Jeremy, *Antonio's Devils: Writers of the Jewish Enlightenment and the Birth of Modern Hebrew and Yiddish Literature*, Stanford, CA 2004.

Gluzman, Michael, *The Politics of Canonicity: Lines of Resistance in Modernist Hebrew Poetry*, Stanford, CA 2003.

Harshav, Benjamin, *The Meaning of Yiddish*, Berkeley and Los Angeles 1990. (Reprinted 1990, Stanford University Press, Stanford, CA.)

Harshav, Benjamin, *Language in Time of Revolution*, Berkeley and Los Angeles 1993. (Reprinted 1993, Stanford University Press, Stanford, CA.)

Harshav, Benjamin, *The Polyphony of Jewish Culture*, Stanford, CA 2007.

Hever, Hannan, *Producing the Modern Hebrew Canon: Nation Building and Minority Discourse*, New York 2002.

Kronfeld, Chana, *On the Margins of Modernism: Decentering Literary Dynamics*, Berkeley and Los Angeles 1995.

Miron, Dan. *A Traveler Disguised: A Study in the Rise of Modern Yiddish Fiction in the Nineteenth Century*, New York 1973.

Miron, Dan, "Modern Hebrew Literature: Zionist Perspectives and Israeli Realities," *Prooftexts* 4 (1984): pp. 46–69.

Miron, Dan, *The Image of the Shtetl and Other Studies of Modern Jewish Literary Imagination*, Syracuse, NY 2000.

Miron Dan, *The Prophetic Mode in Modern Hebrew Poetry*, New Milford, CT 2010.

Moseley, Marcus, *Being For Myself Alone: Origins of Jewish Autobiography*, Stanford, CA 2005.

Norich, Anita and Eliav Yaron, eds. *Jewish Literatures and Cultures: Context and Intertext*, Providence, RI 2008.

Ozick, Cynthia, *Art and Ardor*, New York, 1983.

Ozick, Cynthia, *Metaphor and Memory*, New York 1991.

Ozick, Cynthia, *Fame and Folly*, New York 1996.

Ozick, Cynthia, *Quarrel and Quandary*, New York 2000.

Ozick, Cynthia, *The Din in the Head*, New York 2006.

Rosen, Norma, *Accidents of Influence*, Albany 1992.

Roskies, David G., *A Bridge of Longing: The Lost Art of Yiddish Storytelling*, Cambridge, MA 1995.

Roskies, David G., *The Jewish Search for a Usable Past*, Bloomington, IN 1999.

Tucker, Irene, *A Probable State: The Novel, the Contract, and the Jews*, Chicago 2000.

Wirth-Nesher, Hana ed., *What is Jewish Literature?* Philadelphia 1994.

Wisse, Ruth R., *The Modern Jewish Canon: A Journey through Language and Culture*, New York 2000.

5. See his article "He'arot leferek meroman khadash le-S. Yizhar," *Khipus hasifrut hayisra'elit*, pp. 124–133.

6. See his "Hasusa ha'apokaliptit tsohelet betraklin hasipur hayisra'eli," ibid., pp. 298–306.

7. See his beautifully crafted essay "Sha'ul Tshernikhovsky: Tevel ve'adam," in *Derakhim vetsidey derakhim basifrut*, vol. 2, Jerusalem 1969, pp. 18–32.

8. S. Halkin, *Yehudim veyahadut be'amerika*, Jerusalem and Tel Aviv 1947; see also S. Halkin, *Tsiyonut shelo al tenay*, Jerusalem 1985, pp. 44–91; and see there other comments on the national and cultural prospects of American Jewry, pp. 118–203.

9. See his article "Kirkhey shira tse'ira bashanim ha'akharonot," *Bekhinot* 1 (April 1952): pp. 6–25, and *Derakhim vetsidy derakhim*, vol. 1, pp. 101–137.

10. See Dov Shtok, *Hanamer vydido hamenamnem*, Tel Aviv 1951.

11. Bialik, *Ketavim genuzim*, pp. 341–342.

12. Franz Kafka, *Letters to Friends, Family, and Editors*, New York 1977, p. 289.

13. Ibid., p. 347.

14. Ibid. p. 288. See also below, chap. 10, pp. 309–312.

15. See, e.g., Ritchie Robertson, *Kafka: Judaism, Politics, and Literature*, New York 1985; or recent biographies such as Reiner Stach, *Kafka: The Decisive Years*, trans. Shelley Frisch, New York 2005; and Nicholas Murray, *Kafka*, New Haven 2004.

16. See his article "Derekh merkhav: Al Moshe Shamir," *Beyn din lekheshbon*, pp. 283–300.

17. See his article "Beyt khashmonay be'aspaklarya akuma," in Yosef Klausner, *Be'ayot shel sifrut umada*, Tel Aviv 1956, pp. 171–184.

Notes to Chapter Nine

1. See Itamar Even Zohar, "Leverur mahuta vetifkuda shel leshon hasifrut hayafa bediglosiya," *Hasifrut*, 2, no. 2 (January 1970): pp. 286–302.

2. See the poem in both its versions and its historical-literary analysis in Max Weinreich, *Shtaplen: Fir etyuden tsu der yidisher shprakhvisenshaft un literaturegeshikhte*, Berlin 1923, pp. 140–192.

3. See Dan Miron, "A Language as Caliban," *A Traveler Disguised*, pp. 34–66.

4. See the text of the Prologue (ed. Simkha Katz) in YIVO-Bleter, vol. 12 (1938), pp. 566–575; and see its English translation in Dov Taylor's translated and annotated edition of *Megale temirin*, pp. 265–273 (see above, chap. 3, n. 10).

5. See *Ma'asiyot ve'igrot mitsadikim amityim ume'anshey shelomenu*, ed. Kh. Shmeruk and Sh. Verses, Jerusalem 1970.

6. *Perl's Yidishe ksovim*, ed. Y. Vaynelez, Vilnius 1937.

7. See below, pp.421–498.

8. See Gabrielle Boccaccini, "Hellenistic Judaism: Myth or Reality?" in *Jewish Literatures and Cultures: Context and Intertexts*, ed. A. Norich and Y. Z. Eliav, Providence, RI 2008, pp. 55–76.

9. See, among other recent assessments of the culture or cultures of Jewish Hellenism, Erich S. Gruen's *Heritage and Hellenism: The Reinvention of Jewish Tradition*, Berkeley and Los Angeles 1998.

10. See Boccaccini's article (n. 8 above).

11. For the positive view of the Septuagint, see *Megila* 9b; for the negative one, *Sofrim* 1.7.

12. See below, pp.421–498.

13. See Robert Alter's *The Invention of Hebrew Prose: Modern Fiction and the Language of Realism*, Seattle 1988.

14. See in his "Reshimot letoldotay," *Kol kitvey Mendele*, pp. 4–5.

15. Dan Miron, *A Traveler Disguised*.

16. See in my article "Sh. Y. Abramovitsh and his 'Mendele,'" Dan Miron, *The Image of the Shtetl and Other Studies of Modern Jewish Literary Imagination*, Syracuse, NY 2000, pp. 81–127.

17. See Itamar Even Zohar, "Ma bishla Gitl uma akhal Tshitshikov—le'ma'amad hadenotatsya bileshon hasifrut ha'ivrit badorot ha'akharonim," *Hasifrut*, 6, no. 23 (October 1976): pp. 1–6.

18. See, among other articles pertaining to this, "Tishtush hagevulim," *Ma'amarim*, pp. 191–192.

19. See his article "Ba'am uvasefer," ibid., 184–187.

20. See its Hebrew version, M. Y. Bin Goryon (Berditchevsky), *Al admat nekhar*, trans. A. Barash and Sh. Herberg, Tel Aviv 1936.

Notes to Chapter Ten

1. *Ma'amarim*, p. 184.

2. See, among others, Robert von Halberg, ed., *Canons* (Chicago 1984); Karen R. Lawrence ed., *Decolonizing Tradition: New Views of Twentieth-Century "British"*

Literary Canons (Urbana. IL. 1992). Canonization in modern Hebrew literature has been discussed by Hannan Hever, *Producing the Modern Hebrew Canon*, New York 2002; and by Michael Gluzman, *The Politics of Canonicity in Modern Hebrew Poetry*, Stanford, CA 2005. See a "conservative" position in the debate over canonicity in Frank Kermode, *Pleasure and Change: the Aesthetics of Canon*, New York 2004.

3. See Buber's already mentioned seminal essay in *The Jew and the World*, pp. 167–172.

4. See Charles Bernheimer's excellent *Flaubert and Kafka: Studies in Psychopoetic Structures*, New Haven 1982. The Kafka-Tolstoy connection has yet to be studied in depth, as I believe, it should. The one European masterpiece on which both *The Metamorphosis* and *The Trial* drew was, after Kleist's *Michael Kholhaas*, Tolstoy's *Death of Ivan Ilych*, which Kafka repeatedly read (See F. Kafka, *Diaries*, trans. Joseph Kresh and Martin Greenberg, New York 1975, p.398, n. 121).

5. *Diaries*, p. 398.

6. *Letters to Friends, Family, and Editors*, p. 288.

7. *Diaries*, p. 423.

8. Kafka used to compare his enjoyment of Kraus's satirical monthly with "enervating orgies"; see his letter to his young friend Robert Klopstock of February 29, 1924, *Letters to Friends, Family, and Editors*, p. 409.

9. Ibid., p. 288.

10. Ibid., pp. 288–289.

11. Gilles Deleuze and Felix Guattari, *Kafka: Toward a Minor Literature*, trans. Dana Polan, Minneapolis 1986.

12. See the chapter "What is a Minor Literature," ibid., pp. 16–27.

13. *Letters to Friends, Family, and Editors*, p. 289.

14. Ibid.

15. The main, though not single, document that richly illustrates this is Kafka's famous *Letter to his Father*, trans. Ernst Kaiser and Eithne Wilkins, New York 1953. See also Max Brod's description of Kafka's negative childhood "Jewishness" in his *Franz Kafka: A Biography*, trans. G. Humphreys Roberts and Richard Winston, New York 1963, pp.25–30. Most Kafka biographies follow in this in the wake of Brod's pioneering one (published originally in 1937).

16. The historical origin of this "Yiddish-Deutsch" phenomenon is of some interest. The modern "professional" Yiddish theater had been established by A. Goldfaden in Rumania during the Russian-Turkish War of the 1870s, when and where it catered to the Jewish contractors (and their many helpers) who supplied the fighting Czarist army with food and clothing. Having won an astounding success, Goldfaden then toured the entire Jewish-Russian pale to standing ovations, which triggered the emergence of other theatrical troupes as well. In 1881–1883, however, the successful new Yiddish theater bumped into a formidable obstacle. In the wake of the assassination by Russian revolutionaries of Alexander II, the authorities progressively tightened their grip on all public gatherings in

the Empire, looking particularly askance at those conducted in languages, Yiddish among them, which the representatives of the authorities could not understand. Thus, in 1883, a special ukase prohibited the staging of plays in Yiddish anywhere within the boundaries of the Czarist Empire. Goldfaden's group fell apart, with most of its "stars" emigrating to the United States and London. However, some of the lesser "directors" found a way around the ukase. They dubbed their troupes "Jewish-German" and advertised their plays as being staged in German (a language which was not prohibited). Actually they resorted to a heavily Germanized non-idiomatic Yiddish, which rendered utterly impossible the staging of serious realistic dramas with a credible dialogue. This was a numbing setback for the nascent Yiddish theater, which was doomed to abide for two decades by a repertoire of trash, gory melodramas, tearjerkers, and operettas. Almost no serious Yiddish writer (with the exception of Goldfaden and later Ya'akov Gordin) contributed to this repertoire, although many first-class Yiddish writers wrote plays, which were staged in the twentieth century by the Jewish art theaters of the inter-bellum period. Although in 1911 the ukase of 1883 had already become largely inapplicable, and furthermore, the ukase as such never pertained to Galicia and Bohemia, which formed parts of the Habsburg Empire, the trashy theater Kafka was exposed to retained the "tradition" of the "Yiddish German" theater, its language, its repertoire, and its melodramatic style of acting.

17. See Mark Anderson, *Kafka's Clothes: Ornament and Aestheticism in Habsburg Fin de Siècle,* Oxford 1995.

18. *Diaries*, p.76.

19. Franz Kafka, *Ein Landarzt und andere Drucke zu Lebzeiten*, Frankfurt 1994, p. 117.

20. Ibid., pp. 77–78.

21. See the entire "asbestos" episode in R. Stach, *Kafka: The Decisive Years,* trans. Shelley Frisch, Orlando FL 2005, pp. 35–39, 125–129.

22. *Diaries*, pp. 137–138.

23. Franz Kafka, *Letter to his Father/Brief an den Vater*, a bilingual edition, p. 25.

24. Levy's article was published in issue 34 of the 1934 run of the Warsaw Yiddish weekly (pp. 557–558) under the title "Tsvey prager dikhter" ("Two Prague Poets"). See its English translation in Evelyn Torton Beck's *Kafka and the Yiddish Theater: Its Impact on his Work*, Madison, WI 1971, pp. 220–223.

25. *Diaries*, p. 86.

26. See Franz Kafka, *The Office Writings*, ed. Stanley Corngold, Jack Greenberg, and Benno Wagner, trans. Eric Patton and Ruth Hein, Princeton 2009.

27. See Franz Kafka, *Beschreibung eines Kampfes und andere Schriften aus dem Nachlass*, Frankfurt 1993, pp. 149–153.

28. The review, in an English translation, was appended to Evelyn Torton Beck's *Kafka and the Yiddish Theater*, Madison, WI 1971, p. 227.

29. See, for instance, Reiner Stach, *Kafka: The Decisive Years*, pp. 54–70.

30. See Sander Gilman's *Franz Kafka, The Jewish Patient*, New York and London 1995.

31. Franz Kafka, *Tagebücher 1909–1912*, Frankfurt 1990, pp. 71–72.

32. *Diaries,* p .81.

33. See these poems in the variorum edition of Bialik's poetry, vol. 3, Tel Aviv 2000, pp. 33–35, 44–49, and 42, respectively.

34. See *Devarim sheba'al pe*, vol. 2, pp. 211–213.

35. See the introduction to the Yiddish version of the poem in the aforementioned variorum edition of Bialik's poems, vol. 3, pp. 69–72.

36. See *Letters to Friends, Family, and Editors*, p .100.

37. See *Diaries*, pp. 341, 348–349, 355, 394.

38. Ibid., p. 87.

39. See R. Stach, *Kafka: The Decisive Years*, p. 62.

40. Ibid., pp. 98–99.

41. See Yoram Bar David, *Kafka udemuyotav: Beyn yahadut nisteret lisgida lelo ya'ad*, Tel Aviv 1998, p. 88. Bar David bases his assertions on the evidence of a letter Pu'ah Ben-tovim wrote to Max Brod in June 1921.

42. See *Letters to Friends, Family, and Editors*, pp. 390, 395.

43. Ibid., p. 388.

44. See, e.g., the chapter focusing conjointly on both writers in Ruth Wisse's *The Modern Jewish Canon*, pp.65–98.

45. See Brod's memories of his friend's habitual joviality and wit in *Kafka: A Biography*, pp. 39–40.

46. Felix Weltsch, *Religion und Humor im Leben und Werke Franz Kafkas*, Berlin 1957.

47. See Kathi Diamant, *Kafka's Last Love: The Mystery of Dora Diamant*, New York 2003.

48. See the article "Zionism" in Richard T. Gray, Ruth V. Gross, Rolf J. Goebel, and Clayton Koelb eds. *A Franz Kafka Encyclopedia*, Westport, CT 2005, pp.303–304. See also Mark H. Gelber, "Kafka und Zionistische Deutungen," in *Kafka-Handbuch: Leben-Werk-Wirkung*, ed. Bettina von Jagow and Oliver Jahrhaus, Göttingen 2008, pp. 293–303.

49. *Ketavim*, vol. 2, p. 1276.

50. See his critique of Jewish life in "Ha'arakhat atsmenu bishloshet hakerakhim," and the acrimonious "Milu'im" (addenda) to this essay, Brenner, *Ketavim*, vol. 3, pp. 1225–1278, 1279–1296.

51. See his article "Setira uvinyan," *Ma'amarim*, pp. 29–30.

52. See Galili Shahar and Michal Ben-Horin, "Franz Kafka und Max Brod," *Kafka-Handbuch*, pp. 85–96.

53. See in Y. D. Berkovits, *Harishonim kivney adam*, Tel Aviv 1953, vol. 2, p. 118.

54. See Franz Kafka, *The Blue Octavo Notebooks*, trans. Ernst Kaiser and Eithne Wilkins, Cambridge, MA 1991, pp. 15, 53.

55. *Diaries*, p. 173.

56. Gustav Janouch. *Conversations with Kafka*, trans. Goronwy Rees, New York 1971, p. 109.

57. Franz Kafka, *Briefe an Felice*, Frankfurt 2003, p. 711.

58. Franz Kafka, *Letters to Felice*, trans. James Stern and Elizabeth Duckworth, New York 1973, p. 511.

59. When Rudolf Schildkraut visited Prague in his sensational role as a Jewish owner of a brothel in Max Reinhardt's production of Sholem Asch's *God of Vengeance*, Kafka's Boswell, the young Czech writer Gustav Janouch, brought up this "Jewish" theatrical event in his conversations with his mentor. Kafka seems to have expected this. For some time, Schildkraut, who had been catapulted to fame by his acting in the role of Shylock in Shakespeare's *Merchant of Venice* and also by impersonating many other Jewish characters, was referred to by some of the influential theater critics of the day as a "Jewish" actor, and much was said about his Jewish acting-style. Kafka disagreed with this notion. He said to Janouch: "Rudolf Schildkraut is recognized as a great actor, but is he a great Jewish actor? In my opinion this is doubtful. Schildkraut acts Jewish parts in Jewish plays. But since he does not act exclusively in Jewish [i.e., Yiddish. D. M.] for Jews, he is not an expressly Jewish actor. He is a borderline case, an intermediary, who gives people an insight into the intimacy of Jewish life. He enlarges the horizons of non-Jews, without illuminating the existence of the Jews themselves. This is only done by the poor Jewish actors who act for Jews in Jewish." Gustav Janouch, *Conversations With Kafka*, p. 69.

60. See his thrashing of Lasker-Schüler in Franz Kafka, *Letters to Felice*, pp. 190–191. For the many good things he said about Werfel's poetry and dramas (but not about his novels), see *Diaries*, pp. 145, 208, 267, 318 (here the association of a Werfel drama with the Yiddish theater), etc.

61. See in his article "The How and Why of our Bible Translation" in Martin Buber and Franz Rosenzweig, *Scripture and Translation*, p. 219.

62. See Martin Buber, "Kafka and Judaism," in *Kafka: A Collection of Critical Essays*, ed. Ronald Gray, Englewood Cliffs, NJ 1962, pp. 157–162.

63. See Scholem's comments on *The Trial* in *Od davar*, p. 337.

64. Benjamin and Scholem discussed Kafka in a series of fascinating letters. Gradually, Benjamin distanced himself from Scholem's "theological" positions, with which, at the beginning, he had partly agreed. Finally, he clearly articulated his own position in a letter from August 11, 1934. See *The Correspondence of Walter Benjamin*, ed. G. Scholem and T. W. Adorno, trans. Manfred R. Jacobson and Evelyn M. Jacobson, Chicago 1994, pp. 452–454.

65. See a worthy, but, to my mind, not entirely convincing attempt in Karl Erich Grözinger's *Kafka and Kabbalah*, trans. Susan H. Ray, New York 1994.

66. See in *Letter to his Father*, pp. 13, 17.

67. Ibid., pp. 19–21.

68. Elias Canetti, *Kafka's Other Trial: The Letters to Felice*, trans. Christopher Middleton, New York 1974, p .80.

69. Ibid., pp. 88–90.

70. Ibid., pp. 35–36.

71. *Ein Landarzt und andere Drucke zu Lebzeiten*, p. 93.

72. *Kafka's Other Trial*, p. 80.

73. Franz Kafka, *The Trial*, trans. Breon Mitchell, New York 1998, p. 231.

74. Deleuze and Guattari, *Kafka: Toward a Minor Literature*, p. 23.

75. Ibid.

76. Bialik, *Shirim*, p. 352.

77. See his letter to Felice Bauer of September 2, 1913, *Briefe an Felice*, p. 460; *Letters to Felice*, p. 315.

78.See Franz Kafka, *Das Ehepaar und andere Schriften aus dem Nachlass*, 1994, pp. 34–38 and "The Animal in the Synagogue" in Franz Kafka, *Parables and Paradoxes*, ed. N. Glatzer, New York 1961, pp. 49–59.

Notes to Chapter Eleven

1. *The Kafka Encyclopedia*, p. 156 (see chap. 10, n. 48 above) sums up its definition of the term "Kafkaesque" by branding it "much too broad and imprecise to be useful as a serious category of literary criticism."

2. For an argument, to my mind unconvincing, concerning the plausibility of the notion that the stories collected in Agnon's *Sefer hama'asim* were historically, ideationally, and technically related to Kafka's stories, see Arnold J. Band, "The Author, His Code, and His Reader: The Kafka-Agnon Polarities," in *Studies in Modern Jewish Literature*, Philadelphia 2003, pp. 227–240.

3. See, e.g., Hillel Barzel, *Beyn agnon lekafka: mekhkar mashve*, Ramat Gan 1972, pp. 264–281.

4. See Nicholas Murray, *Kafka: A Biography*, p. 285; and Ritchie Robertson, *Kafka: Judaism, Politics, and Literature*, New York 1985, p. 118.

5. See in his essay "Franz Kafka: On the Anniversary of his Death," *Walter Benjamin: Selected Writings*, vol. 2, ed. Michael W. Jennings, Howard Eiland, and Gary Smith, trans. Harry Zohn, Cambridge, MA, 1996–2003, pp. 802–803.

6. Franz Kafka, *I Am a Memory Come Alive: Autobiographical Writings*, ed. N. Glatzer, New York 1974, p. 1.

7. Franz Kafka, *Letters to Felice*, p. 525.

8. Franz Kafka, *Letters to Milena*, trans. Tania and James Stern, New York 1965, p. 225.

9. *Lettres to Friends, Family, and Editors*, p. 333.

10. Ibid.

11. Ibid., p. 140.

12. See Brod's biography, p. 20.

13. See in *Walter Benjamin: Selected Writings*, vol. 2, pp. 801–802.

14. *Kafka: Judaism, Politics, and Literature*, p. 18.

15. See chap. 10, n. 58.

16. *The Modern Jewish Canon*, p. 66.

17. See also Arnold Band's articles: "The Beilis Trial in Literature: Notes on History and Fiction," *Studies in Modern Jewish Literature*, pp. 33–50; and "Franz Kafka umishpat Beylis," *Hasifrut*, 6, no. 22 (April 1976): pp. 38–45.

18. *The Modern Jewish Canon*, p. 67.

19. See, e.g., Khone Shmeruk's "*Tevye der milkhiker:* Letoldoteha shel yetsira" in *Ayarot ukherakim: Perakim bytsirato shel Shalom aleykhem*, Jerusalem 2000, pp. 9–32.

20. The ninth Tevye story, "Vekhlaklakes," is only a variant of a part of the eighth, "Lekh lekha," which brings the cycle to a full closure. First published in 1914 under the title "Mir hobn a shtarken got," this truncated Tevye tale was rewritten and republished in 1916 under its current title and as Tevye's "last tale." Whether it forms an integral part of the cycle the author dubbed *Gants Tevye der milkhiker* (*The Complete Tevye the Dairyman*) remains an open question, for the author did not live to publish an edition of *Tevye* that included the chapters written in 1914.

21. See the introductory address to "my friend" the reader in the first Hebrew edition of *Tovya hakholev*, Warsaw 1911, pp. i–iv; and see also in *Shalom aleykhem: Mivkhar sipurim*, ed. David Roskies, Tel Aviv 2008, pp. 27–28. The introduction, however, was not written by Sholem Aleichem himself, although it was signed by him. The actual writer was the real translator (whose name was not mentioned, as if the Hebrew version had been prepared by the author), Sholem Aleichem's son-in-law, the Hebrew-Yiddish writer Y. D. Berkovits (see Berkovits, *Harishonim kivney adam*, vol. 4, pp. 179–182). Nevertheless, the introduction certainly reflected the author's own rather banal reading of his own masterpiece.

22. The best example of such a "flasher," besides Tevye, is Shimon Eli, the protagonist of one of Sholem Aleichem's most subtle short stories, "Der ferkishefter shnayder" ("The Bewitched Tailor"), known also as "A mase on an ek" ("A Story without an End"). See *Ale verk fun Sholem aleykhem*, New York 1917–1923, vol. 16 (*Oreme un freylekhe* 1), pp. 9–68.

23. See *Gants Tevye der milkhiker, Ale verk*, vol. 5, p. 28. All English translations from *Tevye* are mine [DM].

24. Ibid.

25. Ibid., p. 15.

26. Ibid., p. 121.

27. Ibid., p. 104.

28. See in the above-mentioned article of Khone Shmeruk, "*Tevye der milkhiker:* Letoldoteha shel hayetsira" (above, n. 19).

29. *Gants Tevye*, p. 31.

30. Ibid., p. 184.

31. Ibid., p. 203.

32. Ibid., p. 214.

33. Ibid., p. 9.

34. Ibid., p. 123.

35. Ibid., p. 149.

36. Ibid., p. 143.

37. Ibid., p. 217.

38. See Wayne C. Booth, *The Rhetoric of Fiction*, Chicago 1961. The concept of reliable and unreliable narrators is central to Booth's entire argument and appears in various sections of the book. An "unreliable narrator" is defined in pp. 158–159 and applied in pp. 174–175, 239–240, 300–308, 339–374.

39. *Gants Tevye*, p. 43.

40. Ibid., p. 95.

41. See, e.g., Michael Stern, "Tevye's Art of Quotation," *Prooftexts* 6 (1986): pp. 79–96.

42. *Gants Tevye*, p. 96.

43. Ibid., p. 131.

44. Ibid., p. 169.

45. *Walter Benjamin: Selected Writings*, vol. 2, p. 807.

46. See "Mayses fun toyzend eyn nakht," *Ale verk fun Sholem aleykhem*, vol. 3 (*Mayses un fantazyes*), pp. 135–232.

47. Ibid., p. 162.

48. Ibid., p. 163.

49. Ibid., p. 199.

50. Ibid., p. 213.

51. Ibid., p. 216.

52. Ibid.

53. *The Modern Jewish Canon*, pp. 57–60.

54. *Gants Tevye*, p. 210.

55. Ibid., p. 213.

56. Ibid., pp. 208, 214.

57. Ibid., p. 213.

58. Ibid., pp.229–230.

59. Ibid., p. 212.

60. Ibid., p. 39.

61. Ibid., p. 91.

62. Ibid., p. 122.

63. Ibid., p. 143.

64. Ibid., p. 167.

65. Ibid., p. 199.

66. Sigmund Freud, "Humour," *The Complete Psychological Works of Sigmund Freud*, vol. 21, trans. James Strachey, London 1961, pp. 159–166.

67. Ibid., p. 40.

68. Ibid., p. 16.

69. Ibid., p. 40.

70. Ibid., pp. 10–11.

71. Ibid., p. 220.

72. Ibid., p. 140.

73. Ibid., p. 95.

74. Tevye repeats this formula several times; see, e.g., p. 126.

75. *Gants Tevye*, pp. 182, 204.

76. Ibid., p. 174.

77. Ibid., p. 229.

78. See his article "Leshalom aleykhem," Brenner, *Ketavim*, vol. 4, p. 1422–1428.

79. See Baal-makhshoves's article "Sholem aleykhem" in *Geklibene verk*, pp. 172–190. See particularly pp. 179–183.

80. *Gants Tevye*, p. 100.

81. Ya'akov Glatshteyn, *Ven Yash iz geforn*, New York 1938, p. 172.

82. *Walter Benjamin: Selected Writings*, vol. 2, pp. 801–802.

83. Ibid., pp. 795–797.

84. *The Trial*, p. 223.

Notes to Chapter Twelve

1. See David Biale ed., *Cultures of the Jews*, New York 2002; see esp. the editor's Preface (pp. vii–xxxiii) and Conclusion (1147–1150).

2. See Peter Uwe Hohendahl, *Building a National Literature: The Case of Germany: 1830–1870*, trans. Renate Baron Franciscono, Ithaca, NY 1989.

3. See Lylian Kesteloot, *Black Writers in French: A Literary History of Negritude*, trans. Ellen Conroy Kennedy, Washington, DC 1991.

4. See "Al pi tehom," Aharon Applefeld interviewed by Amira Lam, *Shiv'a ya-mim*, suppl. to *Yedi'ot akharonot*, November 24, 2006, pp. 17–22.

Notes to Abramovitsh and His Mendele Between Hebrew and Yiddish

1. Baal-makhshoves, *Geklibene verk*, New York 1953, pp. 112–123.

2. See "El yedidi hakore" ("To My Friend, the Reader"), in *Tovya hakholev*, Warsaw 1911, pp. i–iv.

3. See Y. D. Berkovits, *Harishonim kivney adam*, vol. 4, Tel Aviv 1953, pp. 96–101.

4. Ibid., pp. 179–182.

5. These triggered stormy polemics particularly between Greenberg and I. J. Singer. The latter's article "Der dikhter onem ayin un di shprakh fun di nalevkes" was published in the Warsaw Yiddish weekly *Literarishe bleter* in the

issue of April 24, 1925. For Greenberg's responses, see his articles "Pina leyidish o makhteret" and "Literarishe bleter, varsha," in *Kol kitvey U. Ts. Greenberg*, vol. 15, Jerusalem 2001, pp. 85–87; and vol. 16, Jerusalem 2004, pp. 73–75, respectively.

6. See Shmu'el Niger, *Di tsveyshprakhikeyt fun undzer literatur*, Detroit 1941; and Dov Sadan, *Al sifrutenu: Masat mavo*, Jerusalem 1950.

7. See Berditchevsky's articles gathered in the section "Inyaney lashon" ("Matters Pertaining to Language") in his collected essays and articles, *Kitvey M. Y. Bin-Goryon (Berditchevsky), Ma'amarim*, Tel Aviv 1964, pp. 178–192; see particularly "Milashon el lashon," "Akhat ushetayim," and "Tishtush hagevulim," ibid. pp. 183–184, 191–192.

8. See Dan Miron, *Harpaya letsorekh negi'ah: Likrat khashiva khadasha al sifruyot hayehudim*, Tel Aviv, 2005. See above in this volume, pp. 123–135.

9. See Neta Galov's article "Etsa tova" ("Good Advice") in *Hamelits*, fifth year, 46 (1865): p. 695.

10. It was, paradoxically, a Yiddish-Soviet critic and scholar that more than anybody else showed interest in Abramovitsh's Hebrew articles and monographs in his attempt to trace the development of the writer's literary and social thinking throughout the 1860s and 1870s. See M. Viner's comprehensive study "Mendele in di zekhtsiker un zibitsiker yorn" ("Mendele in the 1860s and 1870s") in M. Viner, *Tsu der geshikhte fun der yidisher literatur in 19-en yorhundert*, vol. 2, New York 1946, pp. 74–221. Hebrew summaries of the aforementioned articles and monographs can be found in Y. Klausner's history of the Hebrew literature of the enlightenment period, Y. Klausner, *Historiya shel hasifrut ha'ivrit hakhadasha*, vol. 6, Jerusalem 1958, pp. 361–368, 397–407.

11. This would not, perhaps, have taken place, had the second part of *Limdu hetev* been published in 1864 or 1865. But the manuscript of this second part was lost, and the author rewrote the entire novel, which was also translated from the Hebrew manuscript (by Abramovitsh's close friend Y. L. Binshtok) into Russian and published (1867) even before the publication of the full Hebrew version.

12. I. Y. Sh. (acronym of Sh. Y. Abramovitsh), *Dos vintshfingerl*, Warsaw 1865.

13. See excerpts from this diary (in Yiddish translation, which clearly reflects the Hebrew original) in A. Vorobeytshik, ed., *Mendele un zayn tsayt-materyaln tsu der geshikhte fun der yidisher literatur in 19-ten yorhundert*, Moscow 1940, pp. 41–49.

14. In his article "Reshimot letoldotay," which he wrote in 1889 for inclusion in a lexicon of currently active Hebrew writers by *Hamelits* celebrating the publication of its one-thousandth issue. See *Kol kitvey Mendele mokher sefarim*, Tel Aviv 1947, pp. 1–6.

15. See his article "Zeman haliteratur hayoter khadasha" in *Kheker davar*, Warsaw 1865, pp. 41–45.

16. See S. Y. Abramovitsh, *Limdu hetev*, Warsaw 1862, pp. 1–4.

17. See A. Tsederboym's introduction to the first edition of *Dos poylishe yingl* in book form, Odessa 1869; and see M. Spektor, *Mayn lebn*, Warsaw 1927, vol. 2, pp. 14–15.

18. About the quick growth of the Yiddish reading public at the time, see Shmu'el Niger, *Dertseylers un romanistn*, New York 1946, vol. 1, pp. 84–98.

19. On this possible development and the reasons for its abandonment, see my study "Pirkey mavo l'susati," *Hado'ar*, 51, nos. 35, 38, 39 (1972).

20. Peretz read *Di klyatshe* in its Polish translation (published in 1886) and mistook its author for Sholem Aleichem. He used it, however, as a vantage point from which he set out to define his own identity as a Yiddish writer. See his letters to Sholem Aleichem of June 17 and July 4, 1888 in *Kol kitvey Y. L. Peretz*, vol. 10, ed. Sh. Meltzer, Tel Aviv 1960, pp. 211–218.

21. See Y. L. Gordon, *Sikhes khulin*, Warsaw 1886.

22. See Kh. Shmeruk, "Der tsveyter nusekh fun Mendele Moykher Seforims po'eme *Yidl*," in *Shloyme Bikl yoyvel bukh*, New York 1968, pp. 318–333.

23. See Y. Klausner, *Historya shel hasifrut ha'ivrit hakhadasha*, vol. 6, p. 360.

24. See Kh. Shmeruk, "Tirgumey tehilim leyidish bydey Mendele Mokher Sefarim," *Hasifrut* 1 (1968): pp. 337–342.

25. See Shmeruk's above mentioned articles, as well as Shalom Luria's introduction to his edition of Abramovitsh's "Perek Shira," Haifa and Tel Aviv 2000, pp. 11–28. Luria went so far as to retranslate Abramovitsh's infelicitous Yiddish text into an even more awkward and trite Hebrew one, thus endowing the original with a modicum of grace and fluency, which the comparison with its translation highlighted.

26. About this progress of the Mendele persona, see Dan Miron, *A Traveler Disguised*, New York 1973, pp. 130–248.

27. See this introduction in *Gezamelte verk fun Mendele Moykher Seforim*, vol. 3, ed. M. Viner, Moscow 1935, pp. 199–204; and see my comments on it in Dan Miron, *A Traveler Disguised*, pp. 165–168.

28. See N. Sokolov, "David Frishman," *Ishim*, vol. 2, Tel Aviv 1935, p. 27. See also the discussion of this development in Dan Miron, *Bodedim bemo'adam: Lidyokna shel harepublika hasifrutit ha'ivrit bereshit hame'a ha'esrim*, Tel Aviv 1987, pp. 56–85.

29. *Kol kitvey Mendele Mokher Sefarim*, Tel Aviv 1947, p. 379.

30. Abramovitsh hinted at this ideological direction of his novel by making its protagonist, Hirsch Ratman, promise (in what was originally the prologue but eventually became the epilogue to the novel) that in a treatise that would follow the novel, he would point to "that thing that is now emerging from the chaos we face, appearing on the horizon of our world, and is, for the time being, blurred by the twilight of a dawning era." Ibid. p. 250.

31. The presence of the folksongs, as well as the melodramatic quality of *Der priziv* remind us of the fact that the play was planned and written at the heyday of

the recently established professional Yiddish theater, when the success of Gold-faden's troupe, founded in Rumania during the Russian-Ottoman War of 1876–1877, triggered the forming of similar troupes throughout the Ukraine, as well as in Abramovitsh's new hometown Odessa. Goldfaden's favorite comedies, melodramas, and operettas were known for their catchy lyrics, which the author himself set to music. These songs, now sung everywhere, assuming the status of pseudo-folksongs, might have prompted Abramovitsh's decision to stud his melodrama with authentic folksongs. Clearly he aimed at having his drama performed and sung. He might have thought for a while that the theater rather than published prose fiction would offer a proper venue for a rapprochement with his Yiddish public, appealing through a melodrama vacillating between tears and laughter to the new sensibilities of the time. If that was his intention, he was particularly unlucky, for in 1883 the authorities, in the wake of the assassination of Alexander II, came out with a ukase strictly forbidding all public performances conducted in Yiddish; Goldfaden's troupe disbanded; its leaders and some of its "stars" emigrated to the United States. Thus when *Der priziv* appeared, it could only be read. However, as a text aimed at readers rather than a theater audience, with songs unsung and a dialogue that was in need of an actor's pathetic and comic gestures to achieve full efficacy, its potential was severely limited.

32. Ruth Wisse wrote on the Ur-version of the drama, basing her description on archival materials. See R. R. Wisse, "'Keminheg yid': An unbakanter ksav-yad fun Mendele Moykher Seforim," in *For Max Weinreich, on his Seventieth Birthday*, The Hague 1964, pp. 337–344.

33. See the introduction (written in the form of an elaborate dedication) to *Stempenyu*, *Ale verk fun Sholem aleykhem*, vol. 9, New York 1917–1923, *Yidishe romanen*, pp. 123–126.

34. See "Fun Mendeles literarisher yerushe" in *Mendele un zayn tsayt*, pp. 11–17.

35. There was no such Yiddish press in eastern Europe of the late 1880s and the 1890s; it would emerge only in the first decade of the twentieth century, or, to be exact, in 1899, with the launching of the Zionist Yiddish weekly *Der yud*, and then in 1903, with the appearance of the first Yiddish daily, *Der fraynd*.

36. *Kol kitvey Mendele Mokher Sefarim*, p. 377.

37. Ibid.

38. Ibid., p. 378.

39. See another reading of the story in Anat Vaysman's "Mendele khozer likhsalon, Abramovitsh khozer la'ivrit: Keri'a baytsira 'Beseter ra'am,'" *Rega shel huledet: Mekhkarim besifrut ivrit uvsifrut yidish likhvod Dan Miron*, Jerusalem 2007, pp. 78–89.

40. *Ben ami*, April–May (1887): p. 1.

41. This is a most complex and bewildering chapter in Abramovitsh's literary biography. To a very large extent, we owe its clarification to the bio-bibliographical

exploration done by Yekhiel Sheyntukh; see his study: "Sipurav haketsarim shel Mendele Mokher Sefarim al nuskha'oteyhem," *Hasifrut* 1 (1968): pp. 391–409.

42. See Dan Miron and Anita Norich, "The Politics of Benjamin III: Intellectual Significance and Its Formal Correlatives in Sh. Y. Abramovitsh's *Maso'es Binyomin hashlishi*," *The Field of Yiddish: Studies in Language, Folklore, and Literature*, Fourth Collection (1980), pp. 1–115.

43. Achad ha'am, *Al parashat derakhim*, vol. 2, Berlin 1930, p. 5.

44. See Gilles Deleuze and Felix Guattari, *Kafka: Toward a Minor Literature*, trans. Dana Polan, Minneapolis 1997, p. 23.

45. The Jewish-Egyptian philosopher, Philo of Alexandria, whose work was written mainly in the form of philosophical, moralistic, and allegorical commentaries on the Pentateuch, did not know Hebrew, never read the five books of Moses in the original, never doubted the validity of his hermeneutic glosses in spite of them being based on a translation (the Septuagint), and was uninterested in and probably unaware of biblical exegesis as it was evolving in the lore of his contemporaries, the sages of the Mishna.

46. Gilles Deleuze and Felix Guattari, *Kafka: Pur une literature mineure*, Paris 1975.

47. *Al parashat derakhim*, vol. 2, p. 128. See also Achad ha'am, *Selected Essays*, trans. Leon Simon, Philadelphia 1912, p. 284–285.

48. *Kol kitvey Micah Yosef Bin Goryon (Berditchevsky): Ma'amarim*, p.184.

49. See the section "Bakhayim uvasifrut," Y. H. Ravnitsky, "Al signono ha'ivry shel Mendele Mokher Sefarim," *Ha'omer* 1 (1907): pp. 23–31.

50. See the conclusion of Mendele's introduction to *Maso'es Binyomin hashlishi*, the Yiddish version in *Geklibene verk fun Mendele Moykher Seforim*, New York 1946–1949, pp. 162–163; the Hebrew version in *Kol kitvey Mendele Mokher Sefarim*, p. 57.

51. *Kol kitvey Mendele Mokher Sefarim*, p. 145.

52. Ibid., p. 190.

53. *Kol kitvey Micha Yosef Bin Goryon (Berditchevsky): Ma'amarim*, p. 184.

Index

531